Steps to Writing an Argument

The cover of this book makes a visual argument about genetically modified food. Use these steps to develop your own arguments about food or other topics in the book.

Step 1 Find a Topic

Read your assignment and determine what type of argument is called for (see pages 25–26).

Find a topic that interests you by reading, talking, and exploring (see pages 23–34).

Step 2 Make a Claim and Support It with Good Reasons

Make a claim designed to change readers' views or persuade them to take action.

List your main points and think about the order of those points.

Step 3 Think About What's at Stake

What exactly is the problem or issue, what causes it, and who is most affected?

Has anyone tried to do anything about it? If so, why haven't they succeeded?

Step 4 Analyze Your Potential Readers

Who are your readers?

How familiar will they be with what you are arguing?

Which claims are they most likely to accept and which will they disagree with?

Step 5 Write a Draft

Introduction

Set out the issue or problem, and give some background if necessary.

Argue for the seriousness of the issue or problem.

Give your thesis in one sentence.

Body

Present and interpret your evidence and its significance.

Keep your focus narrow and make your structure clear to your readers.

If you are proposing a solution to a problem, state your solution and its benefits.

Take a few minutes to think about other views on your issue or problem.

Conclusion

Leave your readers with something interesting and provocative.

Issue a call to action—if your readers agree with you, they will want to take action.

Step 6 Revise, Edit, Proofread

For detailed instructions, see Chapter 4.

For a checklist to use to evaluate your draft, see pa

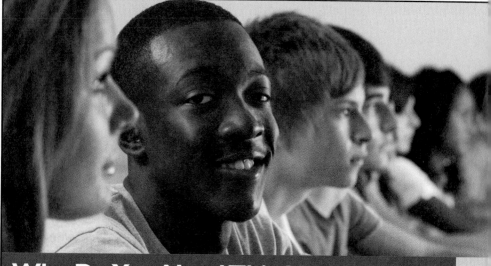

Why Do You Need This New Edition?

If you're wondering why you should buy this new edition of *Good Reasons with Contemporary Arguments*, here are seven great reasons!

1. Do you like to keep up with current debates and controversies? See the **nearly 100 readings throughout the book, half of them new to this edition,** on topics ranging from video games to sustainable food, from immigration to globalization.

2. Would you like a head start on researching topics for argument papers? See the new **"Issue in Focus" sections** in Chapters 22–28 for groups of readings that explore multiple perspectives on a specific topic such as climate change or biometrics.

3. Looking for help with **critical reading** and analyzing arguments? Chapters 2 and 5 have great new material on "mapping" an argument as a way to understand it, on exploring multiple points of view, and on writing an analysis paper.

4. Would you like a clear and simple overview of the steps you should follow when writing an argument? See the revised, at-a-glance design of the **step-by-step writing guides** in Chapters 8–13.

5. Do you like to look at model papers to see how other students tackle an assignment? See the new, updated, and **fully annotated sample papers** in Chapters 2, 5, 6, 7, 8, 9, 10, 12, 13, and 20.

6. Want some help coming up with good ideas for argument papers? New and updated **"Finding Good Reasons"** assignments in Parts 1 and 3 provide topics and short writing tasks that will help kick-start your thinking about your own assignments.

7. Are you being asked to develop visual and multimedia texts in your course? Chapters 14 and 15, on designing and presenting your work, have been completely revised and include **new help with multimedia assignments** and advice for how to best communicate with words, images and graphics.

Good Reasons with Contemporary Arguments gets even better when used with **Pearson's MyCompLab**—the gateway to a world of online resources and to an **interactive eText version of *Good Reasons with Contemporary Arguments*** developed specifically for you!

Good Reasons with Contemporary Arguments

FIFTH EDITION

Lester Faigley
University of Texas at Austin

Jack Selzer
The Pennsylvania State University

Longman

Boston   Columbus   Indianapolis   New York   San Francisco   Upper Saddle River
Amsterdam   Cape Town   Dubai   London   Madrid   Milan   Munich   Paris   Montreal   Toronto
Delhi   Mexico City   Sao Paulo   Sydney   Hong Kong   Seoul   Singapore   Taipei   Tokyo

In memory of our teacher and friend, James L. Kinneavy (1920–1999)

Executive Editor: Lynn M. Huddon
Senior Development Editor: Michael Greer
Senior Supplements Editor: Donna Campion
Senior Marketing Manager: Sandra McGuire
Production Manager: Eric Jorgensen
Project Coordination, Text Design, and Electronic Page Makeup: PreMediaGlobal
Cover Design Manager: John Callahan
Cover Designer: Kay Petronio
Cover Illustration/Photo: Ryman Ryman/Photolibrary
Photo Researcher: Poyee Oster
Senior Manufacturing Buyer: Dennis J. Para
Printer and Binder: RR Donnelley & Sons, Inc./Crawfordsville
Cover Printer: Lehigh-Phoenix Color/Hagerstown

For permission to use copyrighted material, grateful acknowledgment is made to the copyright holders on pp. 604–606, which are hereby made part of this copyright page.

Library of Congress Cataloging-in-Publication Data

Faigley, Lester, 1947–
  Good reasons with contemporary arguments / Lester Faigley,
Jack Selzer. — 5th ed.
    p. cm.
  Includes index.
  ISBN 978-0-205-00093-7
  1. English language—Rhetoric. 2. Persuasion (Rhetoric) 3. Report writing.
I. Selzer, Jack. II. Title.
PE1431.F35 2010
808'.042—dc22

                                        2010046879

1 2 3 4 5 6 7 8 9 10—DOC—13 12 11 10

Longman
is an imprint of

www.pearsonhighered.com

ISBN-13: 978-0-205-00093-7
ISBN-10:   0-205-00093-2

Detailed Contents

Analyzing Arguments

Writing Arguments

PART 4

Designing and Presenting Arguments

PART 5

Researching Arguments

PART **6**

Contemporary Arguments

Alternate Contents: Types of Arguments

Proposal Arguments

Visual Arguments

Irony and Satire in Arguments

Arguments That Cite Sources

Preface

Nothing students learn in college will prove to be more important to them than the ability to write an effective argument.

Students are aware that campus life is itself filled with arguments. There are hot-button public issues that engage the academic community—binge drinking, for example, or making the university more environmentally sustainable, or how to improve campus housing or study abroad opportunities. Meanwhile, in the classroom and in research programs, you and your academic peers present arguments on current controversies such as climate change and economic policy as well as on scholarly topics such as the workings of evolution, the cultural achievements of ancient Egypt, or the means of determining the material composition of the planet Mercury.

After college, students will particularly need to communicate their ideas and point of view effectively. Their livelihood and their engagement in the community will depend on it. Sometimes as citizens students will be moved to register views on the local school system or local downtown development; or as members of a neighborhood group or a civic organization, they will be suggesting ways of making a positive difference. And certainly in the workplace they will often be making arguments to propose ideas.

Good Reasons with Contemporary Arguments gives students a set of rules of thumb that can be used in college and after in order to mount effective arguments. For a number of years we have studied arguments, taught students how to argue, and listened to others talk and write about the art of persuasion. What we have found is that while there is no simple recipe for effective arguments, there are strategies and tactics that writers can rely on in almost any situation to ensure that their ideas are considered seriously.

New to This Edition

- **Fifty new professional readings**, including essays by Michael Pollan, Anne Lemott, Thomas Friedman, Clay Shirky, Bernadine Healy, Andrew Sullivan, and many others.

- **Redesigned "Steps to Writing" guides** provide a concise, visual overview of the process for drafting, developing, and revising each type of argument covered in *Good Reasons with Contemporary Arguments,* helping students to review and apply the concepts and strategies presented in each chapter.

■ **New mini-arguments**, including many visual and multimodal examples, represent every type of argument with an accessible, contemporary example to help students recognize and grasp how different kinds of arguments work today.

■ **Four new sample student papers and new annotations on all sample student papers** in the book provide working models students can use to help revise and develop their own work on every type of argument covered in *Good Reasons with Contemporary Arguments*.

■ **New coverage on designing and presenting multimodal arguments:** Chapter 6 has a new title, "Analyzing Visual and Multimedia Arguments," to reflect its new, broader focus on new media and online texts; Chapter 14 has been similarly updated, expanded, and re-titled to include new coverage of designing multimedia arguments; many of the new examples in the book focus on ways writers are using new forms of digital and multimodal rhetoric to create and deliver arguments to their audiences.

■ Students will find **learning objectives** in the **Quick Take preview** at the beginning of each chapter in Parts 1–5, reflecting the content that appears in that chapter, and instructions at the end of every chapter for finding supporting resources and assessment activities in MyCompLab.

Resources for Teachers and Students

Instructor's Manual

The **Instructor's Manual** that accompanies this text was revised by Brian Neff, of The Pennsylvania State University, and is designed to be useful for new and experienced instructors alike. The Instructor's Manual briefly discusses the ins and outs of teaching the material in each chapter. Also provided are in-class exercises, homework assignments, discussion questions for each reading selection, model paper assignments and syllabi, and strategies for integrating the resources in MyCompLab into your course. This revised Instructor's Manual will make your work as a teacher a bit easier. Teaching argumentation and composition becomes a process that has genuine—and often surprising—rewards.

An Interactive Pearson eText in MyCompLab

An e-book version of *Good Reasons with Contemporary Arguments* is available in MyCompLab. This dynamic, online version of the text is integrated throughout MyCompLab to create an enriched, interactive learning experience for students.

MyCompLab is an eminently flexible application that empowers student writers and teachers by integrating a composing space and assessment tools with multimedia tutorials, services (such as online tutoring) and exercises for writing, grammar, and research.

A CourseSmart eTextbook

Good Reasons with Contemporary Arguments is also available as a CourseSmart etextbook. This is an exciting new choice for students, who can subscribe to the same content online and search the text, make notes online, print out reading assignments that incorporate lecture notes, and bookmark important passages for later review. For more information, or to subscribe to the CourseSmart etextbook, visit www.coursesmart.com.

Social Media Resources

Join us to create an online community around your course. For additional teaching tips and other resources and announcements, visit Pearson's Facebook fan page for this book (www.facebook.com/faigleyseries).

Acknowledgments

We are much indebted to the work of many outstanding scholars of argument and to our colleagues who teach argument at Texas and at Penn State. In particular, we thank the following reviewers for sharing their expertise: Debra Breckheimer, El Camino College; Jo Ann Dadisman, West Virginia University; Gwyn Enright, San Diego City College; Africa Fine, Palm Beach Community College; Robert Pontious, Brunswick Community College; Katherine B. Rigsby, University of South Alabama; Simone Scott, Academy of Art University; and Sarah Jane Sloane, Colorado State University. We are also grateful to the many students we've taught in our own classes, who have given us opportunities to test these materials in class and who have taught us a great deal about the nature of argument. Special thanks go the students whose work is included in this edition.

We have greatly benefited from working with Lynn Huddon, executive editor, and Michael Greer, development editor, whose talent and creativity continue to impress us and who contribute much to both the vision and the details of *Good Reasons with Contemporary Arguments*. They are the best, and we much enjoy working with them on this and other books. Susan "George" Shorn was also a member of the team for this edition and helped us in many ways. Laura Newcomer provided excellent, expert assistance in locating potential selections for Part 6. Special thanks go to Brian Neff for an outstanding revision of the Instructor's Manual. Lindsay Bethoney at PreMediaGlobal and Jacqueline Martin and Eric Jorgensen at Pearson Longman did splendid work in preparing our book for publication. We were quite fortunate to again have Elsa van Bergen as our copyeditor, who has no peer in our experience. Finally, we thank our families, who make it all possible.

Lester Faigley

Jack Selzer

Reading and Discovering Arguments

1 | Making an Effective Argument

QUICK TAKE

In this chapter, you will learn that

1. Arguments in college writing are different from arguments in casual conversation (see below)
2. People who argue responsibly give evidence for their claims and cite their sources (see page 6)
3. Written arguments are like turns in an ongoing conversation (see page 7)
4. Your readers will take you seriously if you convince them that you are concerned, well informed, fair, and ethical (see page 10)

MadV's *The Message* consists of a series of extremely short videos from YouTube members of words written on hands.

What Exactly Is an Argument?

One of the best-known celebrities on YouTube is an anonymous video director who wears a Guy Fawkes mask and uses the name MadV. In November 2006 he posted a short video in which he held up his hand with the words "One World" written on his palm and invited viewers to take a stand by uploading a video to YouTube. They responded by the thousands, writing short messages written on their palms. MadV then compiled many of the responses in a 4-minute video titled *The Message* and posted it on YouTube.

MadV's project has been praised as a celebration of the values of the YouTube community. The common theme that we all should try to love and better understand other people is one that few oppose. Yet the video also raises the question of how any of the goals might be achieved. One hand reads "Stop Bigotry." We see a great deal of hatred in written responses to many YouTube videos. Slogans like "Open Mind," "Be Colorblind," "Love Is Stronger," "No more racism," and "Yup One World" seem inadequate for the scope of the problem.

Like the ink-on-hand messages, bumper stickers usually consist of unilateral statements ("Be Green," "Save the Whales," or "Share the Road") but provide no supporting evidence or reasons for why anyone should do what they say. People committed to a particular cause or belief often assume that their reasons are self-evident, and that everyone thinks the same way. These writers know they can count on certain words and phrases to produce predictable responses.

In college courses, in public life, and in professional careers, however, written arguments cannot be reduced to signs or slogans. Writers of effective arguments do not assume that everyone thinks the same way or holds the same beliefs. They attempt to change people's minds by convincing them of the validity of new ideas or the superiority of a particular course of action. Writers of such arguments not only offer evidence and reasons to support their position but also examine the assumptions on which an argument is based, address opposing arguments, and anticipate their readers' objections.

Extended written arguments make more demands on their readers than most other kinds of writing. Like bumper stickers, these arguments often appeal to our emotions. But they typically do much more.

- They expand our knowledge with the depth of their analysis.
- They lead us through a complex set of claims by providing networks of logical relationships and appropriate evidence.
- They build on what has been written previously by providing trails of sources.

Finally, they cause us to reflect on what we read, in a process that we will shortly describe as critical reading.

Finding Good Reasons

Who's using up Earth's resources?

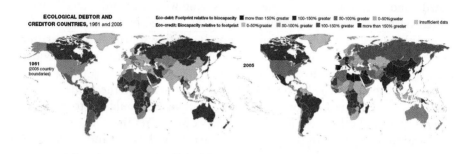

ECOLOGICAL DEBTOR AND CREDITOR COUNTRIES, 1961 and 2005

Eco-debt: Footprint relative to biocapacity ■ more than 150% greater ■ 100-150% greater ■ 50-100% greater ▦ 0-50%greater
Eco-credit: Biocapacity relative to footprint ▦ 0-50%greater ■ 50-100% greater ■ 100-150% greater ■ more than 150% greater ▩ Insufficient data

1961 (2005 country boundaries)   2005

In the *Living Planet Report* for 2008, the World Wildlife Fund compared the ecological footprints from 1961 and 2005 for each country on Earth. The ecological footprint of a country is determined by its population, the amount of food, timber, and other resources consumed by its average citizen, the area required to produce food, fishing grounds, and the area required to absorb CO_2 emissions minus the amount absorbed by oceans.

Countries fall into four categories: ecological debtor nations (which consume more resources than they can produce), ecological creditor nations (which produce more than they consume), and two categories of ecologically balanced nations, where production and consumption are relatively balanced. In this map you can see that the United States, Mexico, Western Europe, China, India, Pakistan, Japan, and the nations of the Middle East have become ecological debtors with footprints more than 50 percent of their biocapacity—what they are able to produce. Nations such as Canada, Russia, Australia, New Zealand, and most nations in South America are ecological creditors, with footprints less than 50 percent of their biocapacity. In its entirety, the *Living Planet Report* makes the argument that nations should live in balance with what their land, rivers, lakes, and seas can support.

Write about it

1. What might be some of the causes of the differences among the ecological footprints of nations?
2. What is likely to happen in the future when some nations have enough resources (such as clean water and food) and others lack them?
3. Does the map succeed as an argument on its own? Does it contain any of the features of written arguments listed on pages 5–6?

Writing Arguments in College

Writing in college varies considerably from course to course. A lab report for a biology course looks quite different from a paper in your English class, just as a classroom observation in an education course differs from a case study report in an accounting class.

Nevertheless, much of the writing you will do in college will consist of arguments. Some common expectations about arguments in college writing extend across disciplines. For example, you could be assigned to write a proposal for a downtown light-rail system in a number of different classes—civil engineering, urban planning, government, or management. The emphasis of such a proposal would change depending on the course. In all cases, however, the proposal would require a complex argument in which you describe the problem that the light-rail system would improve, make a specific proposal that addresses the problem, explain the benefits of the system, estimate the cost, identify funding sources, assess alternatives to your plan, and anticipate possible opposition. It's a lot to think about.

Setting out a specific proposal or claim supported by reasons and evidence is at the heart of most college writing, no matter what the course. Some expectations of arguments (such as including a thesis statement) may be familiar to you, but others (such as the emphasis on finding alternative ways of thinking about a subject and finding facts that might run counter to your conclusions) may be unfamiliar.

WRITTEN ARGUMENTS . . .	WRITERS ARE EXPECTED TO . . .
State explicit claims	Make a claim that isn't obvious. The main claim is often called a **thesis.** (see pages 40–41)
Support claims with reasons	Express reasons in a **because clause** after the claim (We should do something *because* _____). (see pages 25–26)
Base reasons on evidence	Provide evidence for reasons in the form of facts, statistics, testimony from reliable sources, and direct observations. (see pages 37–38)
Consider opposing positions	Help readers understand why there are disagreements about issues by accurately representing differing views. (see pages 29–31)
Analyze with insight	Provide in-depth analysis of what they read and view. (see Chapters 5 and 6)

(continued)

WRITTEN ARGUMENTS . . .	WRITERS ARE EXPECTED TO . . .
Investigate complexity	Explore the complexity of a subject by asking "Have you thought about this?" or "What if you discard the usual way of thinking about a subject and take the opposite point of view?" (see pages 34–36)
Organize information clearly	Make the main ideas evident to readers and to indicate which parts are subordinate to others. (see pages 44–45)
Signal relationships of parts	Indicate logical relationships clearly so that readers can follow an argument without getting lost. (see page 51)
Document sources carefully	Provide the sources of information so that readers can consult the same sources the writer used. (see Chapters 20 and 21)

How can you argue responsibly?

In Washington, D.C., cars with diplomatic license plates are often parked illegally. Their drivers know they will not be towed or ticketed. People who abuse the diplomatic privilege are announcing, "I'm not playing by the rules."

When you begin an argument by saying "in my opinion," you are making a similar announcement. First, the phrase is redundant. A reader assumes that if you make a claim in writing, you believe that claim. More important, a claim is rarely *only* your opinion. Most beliefs and assumptions are shared by many people. If a claim truly is only your opinion, it can be easily dismissed. If your position is likely to be held by at least a few other people, however, then a responsible reader must consider your position seriously. You argue responsibly when you set out the reasons for making a claim and offer facts to support those reasons. You argue responsibly when you allow readers to examine your evidence by documenting the sources you have consulted. Finally, you argue responsibly when you acknowledge that other people may have positions different from yours.

How can you argue respectfully?

Our culture is competitive, and our goal often is to win. Professional athletes, top trial lawyers, or candidates for president of the United States either win big or lose. But most of us live in a world in which our opponents don't go away when the game is over.

Most of us have to deal with people who disagree with us at times but continue to work and live in our communities. The idea of winning in such situations can only be temporary. Soon enough, we will need the support of those who were on the other side of the most recent issue. You can probably think of times when a friendly argument resulted in a better understanding of all peoples' views. And probably you can think of a time when an argument created hard feelings that lasted for years.

Usually, listeners and readers are more willing to consider your argument seriously if you cast yourself as a respectful partner rather than as a competitor. Put forth your arguments in the spirit of mutual support and negotiation—in the interest of finding the *best* way, not "my way." How can you be the person that your reader will want to join rather than resist? Here are a few suggestions for both your written arguments and for discussing controversial issues.

- **Try to think of yourself as engaged not so much in winning over your audience as in courting your audience's cooperation.** Argue vigorously, but not so vigorously that opposing views are vanquished or silenced. Remember that your goal is to invite a response that creates a dialogue.

- **Show that you understand and genuinely respect your listener's or reader's position even if you think the position is ultimately wrong.** Remember to argue against opponents' positions, not against the opponents themselves. Arguing respectfully often means representing an opponent's position in terms that he or she would accept. Look for ground that you already share with your opponent, and search for even more. See yourself as a mediator. Consider that neither you nor the other person has arrived at a best solution. Then carry on in the hope that dialogue will lead to an even better course of action than the one you now recommend. Expect and assume the best of your listener or reader, and deliver your best.

- **Cultivate a sense of humor and a distinctive voice.** Many textbooks about argument emphasize using a reasonable voice. But a reasonable voice doesn't have to be a dull one. Humor is a legitimate tool of argument. Although playing an issue strictly for laughs risks not being taken seriously, nothing creates a sense of goodwill quite as much as tasteful humor. A sense of humor can be especially welcome when the stakes are high, the sides have been chosen, and tempers are flaring.

Arguments as Turns in a Conversation

Consider your argument as just one move in a larger process that might end up helping you. Most times we argue because we think we have something to offer. In the process of researching what has been said and written on a particular issue, however, often your own view is expanded and you find an opportunity to add your voice to the ongoing conversation.

A Case Study: The Microcredit Debate

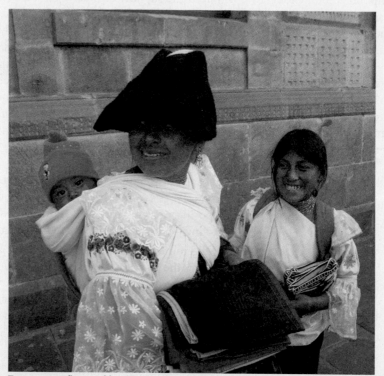

Two women financed by microcredit sell scarves in Quito, Ecuador.

World Bank researchers reported in 2009 that 1.4 billion people—over 20 percent of the 6.7 billion people on earth—live below the extreme poverty line of $1.25 a day, with 6 million children starving to death every year. One cause of continuing extreme poverty is the inability of poor people to borrow money because they have no cash income or assets. Banks have seldom made loans to very poor people, who have had to turn to moneylenders that charge high interest rates sometimes exceeding 100 percent a month.

In 1976, Muhammad Yunus observed that poor women in Bangladesh who made bamboo furniture could not profit from their labor because they had to borrow money at high interest rates to buy bamboo. Yunus loaned $27 to forty-two women out of his pocket. They repaid him at an interest rate of two cents per loan. The success of the experiment eventually led to Yunus securing a loan from the government to create a bank to make loans to poor people. The Grameen Bank (Village Bank) became a model for other microfinancing projects in Bangladesh, serving 7 million people, 94 percent of whom are women. For his work with the Grameen initiative, Yunus received the Nobel Peace Prize in 2006.

Microcredit now has many supporters, including Hollywood stars like Natalie Portman and Michael Douglas, companies like Benetton and Sam's Club, and former

President Bill Clinton. But the success in Bangladesh has not been replicated in many other poor countries. Many critics point to the shortcomings of microcredit. This debate can be better understood if you consider the different points of view on microcredit to be different voices in a conversation.

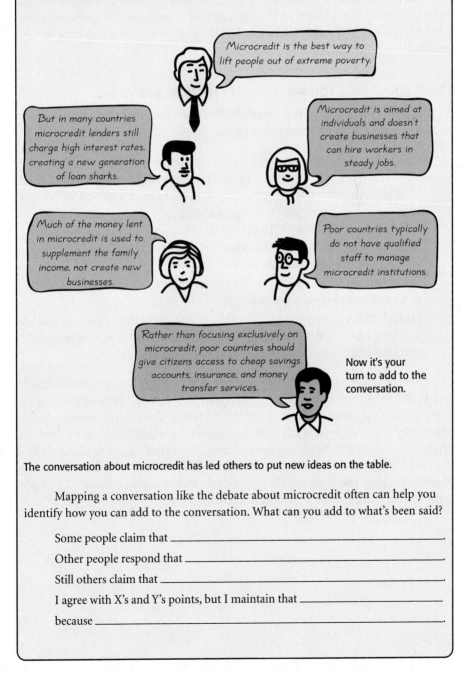

The conversation about microcredit has led others to put new ideas on the table.

Mapping a conversation like the debate about microcredit often can help you identify how you can add to the conversation. What can you add to what's been said?

Some people claim that _____.

Other people respond that _____.

Still others claim that _____.

I agree with X's and Y's points, but I maintain that _____

because _____.

Think About Your Credibility

A few writers begin with instant credibility because of what they have accomplished. If you're a tennis player, likely you will pay attention to advice from Serena Williams. If you're interested in future trends in computers and entertainment, you'll listen to the forecasts of Steve Jobs, the cofounder and CEO of Apple. But if you are like most of the rest of us, you don't have instant credibility.

Think about how you want your readers to see you

To get your readers to take you seriously, you must convince them that they can trust you. You need to get them to see you as

Concerned. Readers want you to be committed to what you are writing about. They also expect you to be concerned with them as readers. After all, if you don't care about them, why should they read what you write?

Well informed. Many people ramble on about any subject without knowing anything about it. If they are family members, you have to suffer their opinions, but it is not enjoyable. College writing requires that you do your homework on a subject.

Fair. Many writers look at only one side of an issue. Readers respect objectivity and an unbiased approach.

Ethical. Many writers use only the facts that support their positions and often distort facts and sources. Critical readers often notice what is being left out. Don't try to conceal what doesn't support your position.

The cover of this book, for example, makes a visual reference to genetically modified (GM) food, which is highly controversial in Japan and Europe and has become increasingly controversial in the United States. The central issue is whether genetically modified food is safe, but the effects on ecosystems, the gene flow into crops that are not genetically engineered, and the control of our food supply by a handful of corporations are also major issues. Because most people in the United States know little about genetically modified food, you will gain credibility by presenting a balanced overview of each of these issues.

Build your credibility

Know what's at stake. What you are writing about should matter to your readers. If its importance is not evident, it's your job to explain why your readers should consider it important.

LESS EFFECTIVE:

We should be concerned about two-thirds of Central and South America's 110 brightly colored harlequin frog species becoming extinct in the last twenty years. (*The loss of any species is unfortunate, but the writer gives us no other reason for concern.*)

MORE EFFECTIVE:

The rapid decline of amphibians worldwide due to global warming may be the advance warning of the loss of cold-weather species such as polar bears, penguins, and reindeer.

Have your readers in mind. If you are writing about a specialized subject that your readers don't know much about, take the time to explain key concepts.

LESS EFFECTIVE:

Reduction in the value of a debt security, especially a bond, results from a rise in interest rates. Conversely, a decline in interest rates results in an increase in the value of a debt security, especially bonds. (*The basic idea is here, but it is not expressed clearly, especially if the reader is not familiar with investing.*)

MORE EFFECTIVE:

Bond prices move inversely to interest rates. When interest rates go up, bond prices go down, and when interest rates go down, bond prices go up.

Think about alternative solutions and points of view. Readers appreciate a writer's ability to see a subject from multiple perspectives.

LESS EFFECTIVE:

We will reduce greenhouse gas and global warming only if we greatly increase wind-generated electricity. (*Wind power is an alternative energy source, but it is expensive and many people don't want windmills in scenic areas. The writer also doesn't mention using energy more efficiently.*)

MORE EFFECTIVE:

If the world is serious about limiting carbon emissions to reduce global warming, then along with increasing efficient energy use, all non-carbon-emitting energy sources must be considered, including nuclear power. Nuclear power now produces about 20 percent of U.S. electricity with no emissions—the equivalent of taking 58 million passenger cars off the road.

Be honest. Readers also appreciate writers who admit what they aren't sure about. Leaving readers with unanswered questions can lead them to think further about your subject.

LESS EFFECTIVE:

The decline in violent crime during the 1990s was due to putting more people in jail with longer sentences.

MORE EFFECTIVE:

Exactly what caused the decline in violent crime during the 1990s remains uncertain. Politicians point to longer sentences for criminals, but the decrease in the population most likely to commit crimes—the 16-to-35 age group—may have been a contributing factor.

Write well. Nothing impresses readers more than graceful, fluent writing that is clear, direct, and forceful. Even if readers don't agree with you in the end, they still will appreciate your writing ability.

LESS EFFECTIVE:

Nobody can live today without taking some risks, even very rich people. After all, we don't know what we're breathing in the air. A lot of food has chemicals and hormones in it. There's a big hole in the ozone, so more people will get skin cancer. And a lot of people have sexually transmitted diseases these days. (The impact of the point is lost with unfocused writing.)

MORE EFFECTIVE:

We live in a world of risks beyond our control to the extent that it difficult to think of anything that is risk free down to the most basic human acts—sex in an era of AIDS, eating in an era of genetically altered food, walking outside in an ozone-depleted atmosphere, drinking water and breathing air laden with chemicals whose effects we do not understand.

For support in learning this chapter's content, follow this path in MyCompLab:
> Resources > Writing > Writing Purposes > Writing to Argue or Persuade.
Review the Instruction and Multimedia resources, then complete the Exercises and click on Gradebook to measure your progress.

2 | Reading Arguments

QUICK TAKE

In this chapter, you will learn that

1. Controversies that are represented in the media as having two sides often involve many nuanced positions (see below)
2. Reading an argument critically involves asking questions before you start reading and rereading it several times (see page 14)
3. Mapping an argument is a good way to understand its structure (see page 17)

Explore Controversies

People in general agree on broad goals for their society: clean water, abundant healthy food, efficient transportation, good schools, full employment, affordable health care, safe cities and neighborhoods, and peace with others near and far. People in general, however, often disagree on how to define and achieve these goals. Controversies surround major issues and causes.

Often controversies are portrayed in the media as pro and con or even take on political labels. But if you read and listen carefully to what people have to say about a particular issue, you usually find a range of different positions on the issue, and you often discover nuances and complexities in the reasons people offer for their positions.

Find controversies

Online subject directories can help you identify the differing views on a large, general topic. Try the subject index of your library's online catalog. You'll likely find subtopics listed under large topics. Also, your library's Web site may have a link to the *Opposing Viewpoints* database.

One of the best Web subject directories for finding arguments is Yahoo's Issues and Causes directory. This directory provides subtopics for major issues and provides links to the Web sites of organizations interested in particular issues.

Yahoo! Issues and Causes directory (dir.yahoo.com/Society_and_Culture/Issues_and_Causes/)

Read Critically

After you survey the landscape of a particular issue, turn to careful reading of individual arguments, one at a time.

Before you begin reading, ask these questions

- ■ Where did the argument first appear? Was it published in a book, newspaper, magazine, or electronic source? Many items in library databases and on the Web were published somewhere else first.
- ■ Who wrote this argument? What do you know about the author?
- ■ What does the title suggest argument be about?

Read the argument once without making notes to gain a sense of the content

- ■ When you finish, write one sentence that sums up the argument.

Finding Good Reasons

Has the Internet made everyone writers?

Video blogs, known as vlogs, became a popular genre on YouTube.

Before the Internet was invented, readers had to make some effort to respond to writers by writing to them directly, sending a letter to the editor, or even scribbling or spray-painting a response. The Internet has changed the interaction between writers and readers by allowing readers to respond easily to writers and, in turn, turning readers into writers. Look, for example, at Amazon.com. An incredible amount of writing surrounds any best-selling book—often an author's Web site and blog, newspaper reviews, and over a hundred readers' reviews. Or read a political, sports, culture, fashion, or parenting blog and the comments by readers of those blogs. Think about how the Internet has changed the relationship between readers and writers.

To find a blog that interests you, use a blog search engine such as Bloglines (www. bloglines. com), Google Blog Search (blogsearch.google.com), IceRocket (blogs.icerocket.com), or Technorati (www. technorati. com).

Write about it

1. Using a blog search engine or an online newspaper, find a blog by an author, politician, or news columnist. Answer as many of the questions for critical reading on page 16 as you can.
2. Write a summary of the blog entry.
3. What kinds of reasons do blog writers give for their responses to what they read?
4. How are blogs and online book reviews like or unlike traditional book reviews in print?

Read the argument a second and third time and make notes

- Go back through the text and underline the author's thesis.
- Does your sentence and the author's thesis match? If not, look at the text again and either adjust your sentence or check if you underlined the correct sentence.
- How is the argument organized? How are the major points arranged?
- What reasons or evidence does the writer offer in support of the thesis?
- How does the writer conclude the argument? Does the conclusion follow from the evidence presented?
- Who is the intended audience? What does the writer assume the readers know and believe?
- Do you detect a bias in the writer's position?
- Where do the writer's facts come from? Does the writer give the sources? Are the sources reliable?
- Does the writer acknowledge other views and unfavorable evidence? Does the writer deal fairly with the views of others?
- If there are images or graphics, are they well integrated and clearly labeled?

Annotate what you read

- **Mark major points and key concepts.** Sometimes major points are indicated by headings, but often you will need to locate them.
- **Connect with your experience.** Think about your own experiences and how they match up or don't match up with what you are reading.
- **Connect passages.** Notice how ideas connect to each other. Draw lines and arrows. If an idea connects to something from a few pages earlier, write a note in the margin with the page number.
- **Ask questions.** Note anything that puzzles you, including words you don't know and need to look up.

Map a controversy

Read broadly about an issue and identify three or more sources that offer different points of view on that issue. The sources may approach the issue from different angles or raise different questions instead of simply stating differing positions on the issue. Draw a map that represents the different views. The map on the next page shows some of the different positions on sustainable agriculture.

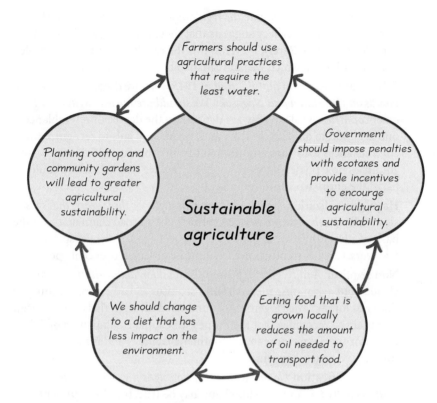

Map of different issues about sustainable agriculture

Recognize Fallacies

Recognizing where good reasons go off track is one of the most important aspects of critical reading. What passes as political discourse is often filled with claims that lack evidence or substitute emotions for evidence. Such faulty reasoning often contains one or more **logical fallacies**. For example, politicians know that the public is outraged when the price of gasoline goes up, and they try to score political points by accusing oil companies of price gouging. It sounds good to angry voters—and it may well be true—but unless the politician defines what *price gouging* means and provides evidence that oil companies are guilty, the argument has no more validity than children calling each other bad names on the playground.

Following are some of the more common fallacies.

Fallacies of logic

- **Begging the question** Politicians *are inherently dishonest because no honest person would run for public office.* The fallacy of begging the question occurs when the claim is restated and passed off as evidence.

■ **Either-or** *Either we eliminate the regulation of businesses or else profits will suffer.* The either-or fallacy suggests that there are only two choices in a complex situation. Rarely, if ever, is this the case. Consider, for example, the case of Enron, which was unregulated but went bankrupt.

■ **False analogies** *Japan quit fighting in 1945 when we dropped nuclear bombs on Hiroshima and Nagasaki. We should use nuclear weapons against other countries.* Analogies always depend on the degree of resemblance of one situation to another. In this case, the analogy fails to recognize that circumstances today are very different from those in 1945. Many countries now possess nuclear weapons, and we know their use could harm the entire world.

■ **Hasty generalization** *We have been in a drought for three years; that's a sure sign of climate change.* A hasty generalization is a broad claim made on the basis of a few occurrences. Climate cycles occur regularly over spans of a few years. Climate trends, however, must be observed over centuries.

■ **Non sequitur** *A university that can raise a billion dollars from alumni should not have to raise tuition.* A non sequitur (a Latin term meaning "it does not follow") ties together two unrelated ideas. In this case, the argument fails to recognize that the money for capital campaigns is often donated for special purposes such as athletic facilities and is not part of a university's general revenue.

■ **Oversimplification** *No one would run stop signs if we had a mandatory death penalty for doing it.* This claim may be true, but the argument would be unacceptable to most citizens. More complex, if less definitive, solutions are called for.

■ ***Post hoc* fallacy** *The stock market goes down when the AFC wins the Super Bowl in even years.* The *post hoc* fallacy (from the Latin *post hoc, ergo propter hoc,* which means "after this, therefore because of this") assumes that events that follow in time have a causal relationship.

■ **Rationalization** *I could have finished my paper on time if my printer had been working.* People frequently come up with excuses and weak explanations for their own and others' behavior. These excuses often avoid actual causes.

■ **Slippery slope** We shouldn't grant citizenship to illegal immigrants now living in the United States because no one will want to obey our laws. The slippery slope fallacy maintains that one thing inevitably will cause something else to happen.

Fallacies of emotion and language

■ **Bandwagon appeals** *It doesn't matter if I copy a paper off the Web because everyone else does.* This argument suggests that everyone is doing it, so why shouldn't you? But on close examination, it may be that everyone really isn't doing it—and in any case, it may not be the right thing to do.

- **Name calling** Name calling is frequent in politics and among competing groups. People level accusations using names such as radical, tax-and-spend liberal, racist, fascist, right-wing ideologue. Unless these terms are carefully defined, they are meaningless.
- **Polarization** *Feminists are all man haters.* Like name calling, polarization exaggerates positions and groups by representing them as extreme and divisive.
- **Straw man** *Environmentalists won't be satisfied until not a single human being is allowed to enter a national park.* A straw man argument is a diversionary tactic that sets up another's position in a way that can be easily rejected. In fact, only a small percentage of environmentalists would make an argument even close to this one.

Note fallacies while you read

Marta Ramos noted a fallacy in James McWilliams's argument against locavorism. You can read her rebuttal argument on pages 180–183.

Consider fruit and vegetable production in New York. The Empire State is naturally equipped to grow a wide variety of fruits, including pears, cherries, strawberries, and some peaches. But none of these compare to its ability to grow apples and grapes, which dominate production (accounting for 94 percent of all fruit grown).

At current levels of fruit production, apples are the only crop that could currently feed New Yorkers at a level that meets the U.S. Recommended Dietary Allowances. Every other fruit that the state produces is not being harvested at a level to provide all New Yorkers with an adequate supply. Other fruits such as bananas and oranges are not produced at all because conditions are unfavorable for growing them.

What does this situation mean in terms of feeding the state with the state's own produce?

In a nutshell, <u>it means citizens would have to give up tropical fruits altogether</u>; rarely indulge in a pear, peach, or basket of strawberries; and gorge on grapes and apples—most of them in processed form (either as juice, in a can, or as concentrate).

McWilliams makes a straw man argument. Locavores prioritize locally produced food but don't argue that it's only what people should eat.

McWilliams, James. "On Locavorism." *New York Times.* New York Times, 26 Aug. 2008. Web. 8 Apr. 2010.

Map and Summarize Arguments

When you finish annotating a reading, you might want to map it.

Draw a map

Marta Ramos drew a map of James McWilliams's argument.

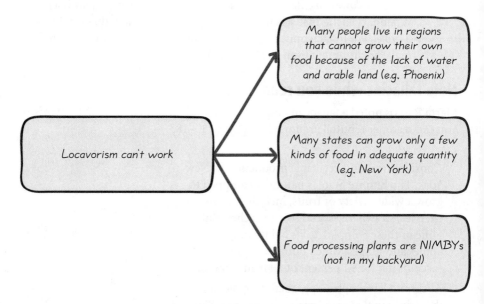

Map of the argument in James McWilliams's "On Locavorism"

Write a summary

A summary should be concise but thorough representation of the source.

- Begin your summary with the writer's name, the title of the argument, and the main point.
- Then report the key ideas. Represent the author's argument in condensed form as accurately as you can, quoting exact words for key points (see pages 253–254 for how to quote and integrate an author's words into your summary).
- Your aim is to give your readers an understanding of what the author is arguing for. Withhold judgment even if you think the author is dead wrong. Do not insert your opinions and comments. Stick to what the author is saying and what position the author is advocating.
- Usually summaries are no longer than 150 words. If your summary is longer than 150 words, delete excess words without eliminating key ideas.

McWilliams, James. "On Locavorism." *New York Times*. New York Times, 26 Aug. 2008. Web. 8 Apr. 2010.

Summary

In "On Locavorism," James McWilliams argues that locavorism—the develop of local food-supply systems—is an impractical goal. He offers three reasons why locavorism is not achievable. First, many people live in regions where they cannot grow their own food because of lack of water and arable land (for example, Phoenix). Second many states can grow only a few kinds of food in adequate quantity (for example, New York), thus restricting food choices and limiting consumption to processed fruits and vegetables for much of the year. Third, many people will not like food processing plants near their homes.

PEARSON
mycomplab

For support in learning this chapter's content, follow this path in MyCompLab:
 ▷ Resources ▷ Media Index ▷ Visual Analysis and Rhetoric.
Review the Instruction and Multimedia resources, then complete the Exercises and click on Gradebook to measure your progress.

3 | Finding Arguments

In this chapter, you will learn that

1. Everyday conversations with friends can be rich sources of ideas for written arguments (see page 23)
2. Writing assignments often contain key words that you can use to determine the type of argument you need to write (see page 25)
3. Reading widely about a topic will help you become familiar with the points of view already being debated on an issue (see page 31)
4. Reasons need to be supported with good evidence (see page 37)

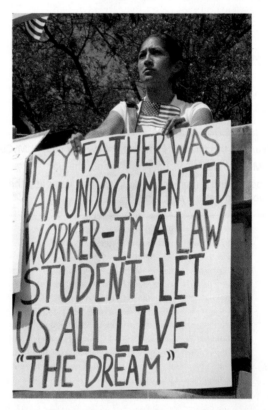

Slogans are meant to persuade, but technically they are not arguments because they lack reasons. Nevertheless, you can often supply a reason for a claim made on a sign. What reason might the demonstrator give to support her claim LET US ALL LIVE "THE DREAM"?

Find Arguments in Everyday Conversations

Let's look at an example of a conversation. When the pain in his abdomen didn't go away, Jeff knew he had torn something while carrying his friend's heavy speakers up a flight of stairs. He went to the student health center and called his friend Maria when he returned home.

JEFF: I have good news and bad news. The pain is a minor hernia that can be repaired with day surgery. The bad news is that the fee we pay for the health center doesn't cover hospital visits. We should have health coverage.

MARIA: Jeff, you didn't buy the extra insurance. Why should you get it for nothing?

JEFF: Because health coverage is a right.

MARIA: No it's not. Everyone doesn't have health insurance.

JEFF: Well, in some other countries like Canada, Germany, and Britain, they do.

MARIA: Yes, and people who live in those countries pay a bundle in taxes for the government-provided insurance.

JEFF: It's not fair in this country because some people have health insurance and others don't.

MARIA: Jeff, face the facts. You could have bought the extra insurance. Instead you chose to buy a new car.

JEFF: It would be better if the university provided health insurance because students could graduate in four years. I'm going to have to get a second job and drop out for a semester to pay for the surgery.

MARIA: Neat idea, but who's going to pay for it?

JEFF: OK, all students should be required to pay for health insurance as part of their general fee. Most students are healthy, and it wouldn't cost that much more.

In this discussion, Jeff starts out by making a **claim** that students should have health coverage. Maria immediately asks him why students should not have to pay for health insurance. She wants a **reason** to accept his claim.

Distinguishing arguments from other kinds of persuasion

Scholars who study argument maintain that an argument must have a claim and one or more reasons to support that claim. Something less might be persuasive, but it isn't an argument.

A bumper sticker that says NO TOLL ROADS is a claim, but it is not an argument because the statement lacks a reason. Many reasons support an argument against building toll roads.

- We don't need new roads but should build light-rail instead.
- We should raise the gas tax to pay for new roads.
- We should use gas tax revenue only for roads rather than using it for other purposes.

When a claim has a reason attached, then it becomes an argument.

The basics of arguments

A reason is typically offered in a **because clause**, a statement that begins with the word *because* and that provides a supporting reason for the claim. Jeff's first attempt is to argue that students should have health insurance *because* health insurance is a right.

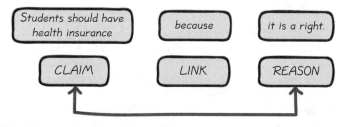

The word *because* signals a link between the reason and the claim. Every argument that is more than a shouting match or a simple assertion has to have one or more reasons. Just having a reason for a claim, however, doesn't mean that the audience will be convinced. When Jeff tells Maria that students have a right to health insurance, Maria replies that students don't have that right. Maria will accept Jeff's claim only if she accepts that his reason supports his claim. Maria challenges Jeff's links and keeps asking "So what?" For her, Jeff's reasons are not good reasons.

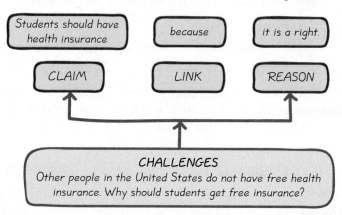

By the end of this short discussion, Jeff has begun to build an argument. He has had to come up with another claim to support his main claim: All students should be required to pay for health insurance as part of their general fee. If he is to convince Maria, he will probably have to provide a series of claims that she will accept as linked to his primary claim. He will also need to find evidence to support these claims.

Benjamin Franklin observed, "So convenient a thing it is to be a rational creature, since it enables us to find or make a reason for every thing one has a mind to do." It is not hard to think of reasons. What *is* difficult is to convince your audience that your reasons are good reasons. In a conversation, you get immediate feedback that tells you whether your listener agrees or disagrees. When you are writing, you usually don't have someone you can question immediately. Consequently, you have to (1) be more specific about what you are claiming, (2) connect with the values you hold in common with your readers, and (3) anticipate what questions and objections your readers might have, if you are going to convince someone who doesn't agree with you or know what you know already.

When you write an argument, imagine a reader like Maria who is going to listen carefully to what you have to say but who is not going to agree with you automatically. Readers like Maria will expect the following.

- A **claim** that is interesting and makes them want to find out more about what you have to say
- At least one **good reason** that makes your claim worth taking seriously
- Some **evidence** that the good reason or reasons are valid
- Some acknowledgment of the **opposing views** and **limitations** of the claim

The remainder of this chapter will guide you through the process of finding a topic, making a claim, finding good reasons and evidence, and anticipating objections to your claim.

Find a Topic

When your instructor gives you a writing assignment, look closely at what you are asked to do. Assignments typically contain a great deal of information, and you have to sort through that information. First, circle all the instructions about the length, the due date, the format, the grading criteria, and anything else about the production and conventions of the assignment. This information is important to you, but it doesn't tell you what the paper is supposed to be about.

Read your assignment carefully

Often your assignment will contain key words such as *analyze, define, evaluate,* or *propose* that will assist you in determining what direction to take. *Analyze* can mean several things. Your instructor might want you to analyze a piece of writing (see Chapter 5), an image (see Chapter 6), or the causes of something (see Chapter 9). *Define* usually means writing a **definition argument**, in which you argue for a definition based on the criteria you set out (see Chapter 8). *Evaluate* indicates an **evaluation argument**, in which you argue that something is good, bad, the best, or the worst in its class according to criteria that you set out (see Chapter 10). An assignment that contains the instructions *Write about an issue using your personal experience* indicates a **narrative argument** (see Chapter 11), while one that says *Take a position in regard to a reading* might lead you to write a **rebuttal argument** (see Chapter 12). *Propose* means that you should identify a particular problem and explain why your solution is the best one in a **proposal argument** (see Chapter 13).

What Is Not Arguable

- **Statements of fact.** Most facts can be verified by doing research. But even simple facts can sometimes be argued. For example, Mount Everest is usually acknowledged to be the highest mountain in the world at 29,028 feet above sea level. But if the total height of a mountain from base to summit is the measure, then the volcano Mauna Loa in Hawaii is the highest mountain in the world. Although the top of Mauna Loa is 13,667 feet above sea level, the summit is 31,784 above the ocean floor. Thus the "fact" that Mount Everest is the highest mountain on the earth depends on a definition of *highest*. You could argue for this definition.

- **Claims of personal taste.** Your favorite food and your favorite color are examples of personal taste. If you hate fresh tomatoes, no one can convince you that you actually like them. But many claims of personal taste turn out to be value judgments using arguable criteria. For example, if you think that *Alien* is the best science-fiction movie ever made, you can argue that claim using evaluative criteria that other people can consider as good reasons (see Chapter 10). Indeed, you might not even like science fiction and still argue that *Alien* is the best science-fiction movie ever.

- **Statements of belief or faith.** If someone accepts a claim as a matter of religious belief, then for that person, the claim is true and cannot be refuted. Of course, people still make arguments about the existence of God and which religion reflects the will of God. Whenever an audience will not consider an idea, it's possible but very difficult to construct an argument. Many people claim to have evidence that UFOs exist, but most people refuse to acknowledge that evidence as even being possibly factual.

If you remain unclear about the purpose of the assignment after reading it carefully, talk with your instructor.

Thinking about what interests you

Your assignment may specify the topic you are to write about. If your assignment gives you a wide range of options and you don't know what to write about, look first at the materials for your course: the readings, your lecture notes, and discussion boards. Think about what subjects came up in class discussion.

If you need to look outside class for a topic, think about what interests you. Subjects we argue about often find us. There are enough of them in daily life. We're late for work or class because the traffic is heavy or the bus doesn't run on time. We can't find a place to park when we get to school or work. We have to negotiate through various bureaucracies for almost anything we do—making an

Finding Good Reasons

Are traffic enforcement cameras invading your privacy?

Picture Proof

Automated red-light enforcement systems vary in their approach, but they combine two main elements: sensors that detect potential violations, and cameras that substantiate them.

CAMERA

❶ Sensors in the pavement detect cars crossing the stop line after the signal turns red, prompting a camera to take an initial photo from the rear as the car crosses the line.

❷ A second photo is taken after the vehicle enters the intersection. In some systems, it is a head-on view shot by a second camera, providing a picture of the driver as well as of the car and license plate.

CAMERA

Sources: City of San Diego; District of Columbia Metropolitan Police

Frank O'Connell/The New York Times

Cameras that photograph the license plates and drivers of vehicles who run red lights, speed, or ride illegally in high-occupancy-vehicle (HOV) and bus lanes are currently in use in many U.S. cities and states. Cameras aimed at catching speeders, already common in Europe, are beginning to be installed in U.S. cities as well. Traffic cameras have become money machines for some communities, but they also have provoked intense public opposition and even vandalism—people have spray painted and shot cameras in attempts to disable them.

Write about it

1. How do you feel about using cameras to catch red-light runners? Speeders? Illegal drivers in HOV and bus lanes? People who don't pay parking tickets? Make a list of as many possible topics as you can think of about the use of cameras to scan license plates.

2. Select one of the possible topics. Write it at the top of a sheet of paper, and then write nonstop for five minutes. Don't worry about correctness. If you get stuck, write the same sentence again.

3. When you finish, read what you have written and circle key ideas.

4. Put each key idea on a sticky note. If you think of other ideas, write them on separate sticky notes. Then look at your sticky notes. Put a star on the central idea. Put the ideas that are related next to each other. You now have the beginning of an idea map.

appointment to see a doctor, getting a course added or dropped, or correcting a mistake on a bill. Most of the time we grumble and let it go at that. But sometimes we stick with a subject. Neighborhood groups in cities and towns have been especially effective in getting something done by writing about it—for example, stopping a new road from being built, getting better police and fire protection, and getting a vacant lot turned into a park.

Listing and analyzing issues

A good way to get started is to list possible issues to write about. Make a list of questions that can be answered "YES, because . . ." or "NO, because . . ." Think about issues that affect your campus, your community, the nation, and the world. Which issues interest you? About which issues could you make a contribution to the larger discussion?

Campus

- Should students be required to pay fees for access to computers on campus?
- Should smoking be banned on campus?
- Should varsity athletes get paid for playing sports that bring in revenue?
- Should admissions decisions be based exclusively on academic achievement?
- Should knowledge of a foreign language be required for all degree plans?
- Should your college or university have a computer literacy requirement?
- Is there any way to curb the dangerous drinking habits of many students on your campus?

Community

- Should people who ride bicycles and motorcycles be required to wear helmets?
- Should high schools be allowed to search students for drugs at any time?
- Should high schools distribute condoms?
- Should bilingual education programs be eliminated?
- Should bike lanes be built throughout your community to encourage more people to ride bicycles?
- Should more tax dollars be shifted from building highways to funding public transportation?

Nation/World

- Should driving while talking on a cell phone be banned?
- Should capital punishment be abolished?
- Should the Internet be censored?
- Should the government be allowed to monitor all phone calls and all e-mail to combat terrorism?
- Should handguns be outlawed?
- Should beef and poultry be free of growth hormones?
- Should a law be passed requiring that the parents of teenagers who have abortions be informed?
- Should people who are terminally ill be allowed to end their lives?
- Should the United States punish nations with poor human rights records?

Narrowing a list

1. Put a check beside the issues that look most interesting to write about or the ones that mean the most to you.
2. Put a question mark beside the issues that you don't know very much about. If you choose one of these issues, you will probably have to do in-depth research—by talking to people, by using the Internet, or by going to the library.
3. Select the two or three issues that look most promising. For each issue, make another list:
   - Who is most interested in this issue?
   - Whom or what does this issue affect?
   - What are the pros and cons of this issue? Make two columns. At the top of the left one, write "YES, because." At the top of the right one, write "NO, because."
   - What has been written about this issue? How can you find out what has been written?

Explore Your Topic

When you identify a potential topic, make a quick exploration of that topic, much as you would walk through a house or an apartment you are thinking about renting for a quick look. One way of exploring is to visualize the topic by making a map.

If you live in a state on the coast that has a high potential for wind energy, you might argue that your state should provide financial incentives for generating more electricity from the wind. Perhaps it seems like a no-brainer to you because wind power consumes no fuel and causes no air pollution. The only energy required is for the manufacture and transportation of the wind turbines and transmission lines. But your state and other coastal states have not exploited potential wind energy for three reasons:

1. **Aesthetics.** Some people think wind turbines are ugly.
2. **Hazard to wildlife.** A few poorly located wind turbines have killed birds and bats.
3. **Cost.** Wind power costs differ, but wind energy is generally more expensive than electricity produced by burning coal.

To convince other people that your proposal is a good one, you will have to answer these objections.

Possible objections to wind energy

ugly

hazard to wildlife

higher cost $$$

The first two objections are relatively easy to address. Locating wind farms 10 kilometers offshore keeps them out of sight of land and away from most migrating birds and all bats. The third objection, higher cost, is more difficult. One strategy is to argue that the overall costs of wind energy and energy produced by burning coal are comparable if environmental costs are included. You can analyze the advantages and disadvantages of each by drawing maps.

Advantages/disadvantages of coal-fired power plants

PLUS
Lower retail cost

MINUS
Coal mining destroys forests

MINUS
Hot water kills fish

MINUS
Solid wastes

MINUS
Air emissions include
• carbon dioxide
• sulpher dioxide
• mercury
• arsenic
• carbon monoxide

MINUS
Fuel costs because coal must be transported

Advantages/disadvantages of wind energy

These maps can help you organize an argument for providing financial incentives for wind energy.

Read About Your Topic

Much college writing draws on and responds to sources—books, articles, reports, and other material written by other people. Every significant issue discussed in today's world has an extensive history of discussion involving many people and various points of view. Before you formulate a claim about a significant issue, you need to become familiar with the conversation that's already happening by reading widely about it.

One of the most controversial and talked-about subjects in recent years is the outsourcing of white-collar and manufacturing jobs to low-wage nations. Since 2000 an estimated 400,000 to 500,000 American jobs each year have gone to cheap overseas labor markets. The Internet has made this migration of jobs possible, allowing companies to outsource not only low-skilled jobs but highly skilled jobs in fields such as software development, data storage, and even examining X-rays and MRI scans.

You may have read about this or another complex and controversial topic in one of your courses. Just as in a conversation with several people who hold different views, you may agree with some people, disagree with some, and with others agree with some of their ideas up to a point but then disagree.

CNN commentator Lou Dobbs has been sharply critical of outsourcing. In *Exporting America: Why Corporate Greed Is Shipping American Jobs Overseas* (2006), Dobbs blames large corporations for putting profits ahead of the good of the nation. He accuses both Republicans and Democrats of ignoring the effects of a massive trade deficit and the largest national debt in American history, which Dobbs claims will eventually destroy the American way of life.

Thomas Friedman, columnist for the *New York Times*, takes a different viewpoint on outsourcing in *The World Is Flat: A Brief History of the Twenty-first Century* (2006). By *flat*, Friedman means that the nations of the world are connected like never before through the Internet and the lowering of trade barriers, putting every nation in direct competition with all the others. Friedman believes that outsourcing is not only unstoppable, but also desirable. He argues that Americans need to adapt to the new reality and rethink our system of education, or else we will be left hopelessly behind.

If you decide to write an argument about the issue of outsourcing, you might use either Dobbs's or Friedman's book as your starting point in making a claim. You could begin by taking on the role of **skeptic,** disagreeing with the author; the role of **contributor,** agreeing with the author and adding another point; or the role of the **analyst,** finding some points to agree with while disagreeing with others.

The skeptic: Disagreeing with a source

It's easy to disagree by simply saying an idea is dumb, but readers expect you to be persuasive about why you disagree and to offer reasons to support your views.

X claims that ——————————, but this view is mistaken because ——————.

Example claim: Arguing against outsourcing resulting from free trade policies

Thomas Friedman claims that the world is "flat," giving a sense of a level playing field for all, but it is absurd to think that the millions of starving children in the world have opportunities similar to those in affluent countries who pay $100 for basketball shoes made by the starving children.

Example claim: Arguing in favor of outsourcing resulting from free trade policies

Lou Dobbs is a patriotic American who recognizes the suffering of manufacturing workers in industries like steel and automobiles, but he neglects that the major cause of the loss of manufacturing jobs in the United States and China alike is increased productivity—the 40 hours of labor necessary to produce a car just a few years ago has now been reduced to 15.

The contributor: Agreeing with a source with an additional point

Sources should not make your argument for you. With sources that support your position, indicate exactly how they fit into your argument with an additional point.

I agree with _____ and will make the additional point that

_____.

Example claim: Arguing against outsourcing resulting from free trade policies

Lou Dobbs's outcry against the outsourcing of American jobs also has a related argument: We are dependent not only on foreign oil, but also on foreign clothing, foreign electronics, foreign tools, foreign toys, foreign cars and trucks—indeed, just about everything—which is quickly eroding the world leadership of the United States.

Example claim: Arguing in favor of outsourcing resulting from free trade policies

Thomas Friedman's claim that the Internet enables everyone to become an entrepreneur is demonstrated by thousands of Americans, including my aunt, who could retire early because she developed an income stream by buying jeans and children's clothes at garage sales and selling them to people around the world on eBay.

The analyst: Agreeing and disagreeing simultaneously with a source

Incorporating sources is not a matter of simply agreeing or disagreeing with them. Often you will agree with a source up to a point, but you will come to a different conclusion. Or you may agree with the conclusions, but not agree with the reasons put forth.

I agree with _____ up to a point, but I disagree with the conclusion _____ because _____.

Example claim: Qualifying the argument against outsourcing resulting from free-trade policies

Lou Dobbs accurately blames our government for giving multinational corporations tax breaks for exporting jobs rather than regulating the loss of millions of jobs, but the real problem lies in the enormous appetite of Americans for inexpensive consumer products like HD televisions that is supported by borrowing money from overseas to the point that our dollar has plummeted in value.

> **Example claim: Qualifying the argument in favor of outsourcing resulting from free-trade policies**
>
> Thomas Friedman's central claim that the world is being "flattened" by globalization and there is not much we can do to stop it is essentially correct, but he neglects the social costs of globalization around the world, where the banner of free trade has been the justification for devastating the environment, destroying workers' rights and the rights of indigenous peoples, and ignoring laws passed by representative governments.

Find Good Reasons

Get in the habit of asking these questions every time you are asked to write an argument.

Can you argue by definition?

Probably the most powerful kind of good reason is an argument from definition. You can think of a definition as a simple statement: _____ *is a* _____. You use these statements all the time. When you need a course to fulfill your social-science requirement, you look at the list of courses that are defined as social-science courses. You find out that the anthropology class you want to take is one of them. It's just as important when _____ *is not a* _____. Suppose you are taking College Algebra, which is a math course taught by the math department, yet it doesn't count for the math requirement. The reason it doesn't count is because College Algebra is not defined as a college-level math class. So you have to enroll next semester in Calculus I.

Many definitions are not nearly as clear-cut as the math requirement. If you want to argue that figure skaters are athletes, you will need to define what an athlete is. You start thinking. An athlete competes in an activity, but that definition alone is too broad, since many competitions do not require physical activity. Thus, an athlete must participate in a competitive physical activity and must train for it. But that definition is still not quite narrow enough, because soldiers also train for competitive physical activity. You decide to add that the activity must be a sport and that it must require special competence and precision. Your because clause turns out as follows: *Figure skaters are athletes because true athletes train for and compete in physical sporting competitions that require special competence and precision.*

If you can get your audience to accept your definitions, you've gone a long way toward convincing them of the validity of your claim. That is why the most controversial issues in our culture—abortion, affirmative action, gay rights, pornography, women's rights, privacy rights, gun control, the death penalty—are argued from definition. Is abortion a crime or a medical procedure? Is pornography protected by the First Amendment, or is it a violation of women's rights? Is the death penalty just or cruel and inhuman? You can see from these examples that definitions often rely on deeply held beliefs.

Because people have strong beliefs about controversial issues, they often don't care about the practical consequences. Arguing that it is much cheaper to execute prisoners who have been convicted of first-degree murder than to keep them in prison for life does not convince those who believe that it is morally wrong to kill. (See Chapter 8.)

Can you argue from value?

A special kind of argument from definition, one that often implies consequences, is the argument from value. You can support your claim with a "because clause" (or several of them) that includes a sense of evaluation. Arguments from value follow from claims like _____ *is a good* _____, or _____ *is not a good* _____.

Evaluation arguments usually proceed from the presentation of certain criteria. These criteria come from the definitions of good and bad, of poor and not so poor, that prevail in a given case. A great burger fulfills certain criteria; so does an outstanding movie, an excellent class, or the best laptop in your price range. Sometimes the criteria are straightforward, as in the burger example. A great burger has to have tasty meat—tender and without gristle, fresh, never frozen—a fresh bun that is the right size, and your favorite condiments.

But if you are buying a laptop computer and want to play the latest games along with your school tasks, you need to do some homework. For realistic graphics the best laptop will have a fast chip, preferably a dual core system. It will be equipped with a wireless modem, so you have access to the Internet at wireless hot spots. The battery life should be at least two hours, the hard drive should be large enough for your needs, the construction should be sturdy, and the warranty should cover the computer for at least three years. The keys for evaluation arguments are finding the appropriate criteria and convincing your readers that those criteria are the right criteria (see Chapter 10).

Can you argue from consequence?

Another powerful source of good reasons comes from considering the possible consequences of your position: Can you sketch out the good things that will follow from your position? Can you establish that certain bad things will be avoided if your position is adopted? If so, you will have other good reasons to use.

Causal arguments take the basic form of _____ *causes* _____ (or _____ *does not cause* _____). Very often, causal arguments are more complicated, taking the form _____ *causes* _____ *which, in turn, causes* _____ and so on. In one famous example, environmentalist Rachel Carson in *Silent Spring* makes powerful arguments from consequence. Rachel Carson's primary claim is that *DDT should not be sprayed on a massive scale because it will poison animals and people.* The key to her argument is the causal chain that explains how animals and people are poisoned. Carson describes how nothing exists alone in nature. When a potato field is sprayed with DDT, some of that poison is absorbed by the skin of the potatoes and some washes into the groundwater, where it contaminates drinking water. Other poisonous residue is absorbed into streams, where it is ingested by insect larvae, which in turn are eaten by fish. Fish are eaten by other fish, which are then eaten by waterfowl and people. At each stage, the poisons become more concentrated. (See Chapter 9 for additional examples of causal arguments.)

Proposal arguments are future-oriented arguments from consequence. In a proposal argument, you cannot stop with naming good reasons; you also have to show that these consequences would follow from the idea or course of action that you are arguing. For example, if you are proposing designated lanes for bicycles on the streets of your city, you must argue that they will encourage more people to ride bicycles to work and school, reducing air pollution and traffic congestion for everyone. (See Chapter 13.)

Can you counter objections to your position?

Another good way to find convincing good reasons is to think about possible objections to your position. If you can imagine how your audience might counter or respond to your argument, you will probably include in your argument precisely the points that will address your readers' particular needs and objections. If you are successful, your readers will be convinced that you are right. You've no doubt had the experience of mentally saying to a writer in the course of your reading, "Yeah, but what about this other idea?"—only to have the writer address precisely this objection.

You can impress your readers if you've thought about why anyone would oppose your position and exactly how that opposition would be expressed. If you are writing a proposal argument for a computer literacy requirement for all high school graduates, you might think about why anyone would object, since computers are critical for our jobs and lives. What will the practical objections be? What about philosophical ones? Why hasn't such a requirement been put in place already? By asking such questions in your own arguments, you are likely to develop robust because clauses.

Sometimes, writers pose rhetorical questions. You might say, "But won't paying for computers for all students make my taxes go up?" Stating objections explicitly can be effective if you make the objections as those of a reasonable person with an alternative point of view. But if the objections you state are ridiculous ones, then you risk being accused of setting up a **straw man**—that is, making the position opposing your own so simplistic that no one would likely identify with it. (See Chapter 12.)

Find Evidence to Support Good Reasons

Good reasons are essential ingredients of good arguments, but they don't do the job alone. You must support or verify good reasons with evidence. Evidence consists of hard data, examples, personal experiences, episodes, or tabulations of episodes (known as statistics) that are seen as relevant to the good reasons you are putting forward. Thus, a writer of arguments puts forward not only claims and good reasons but also evidence that those good reasons are true.

How much supporting evidence should you supply? How much evidence is enough? As is usual in the case of rhetoric, the best answer is, "It depends." If a reader is likely to find one of your good reasons hard to believe, then you should be aggressive in offering support. You should present detailed evidence in a patient and painstaking way. As one presenting an argument you have a responsibility not just to *state* a case but to *make* a case with evidence. Arguments that are unsuccessful tend to fail not because of a shortage of good reasons; more often, they fail because the reader doesn't agree that there is enough evidence to support the good reason that is being presented.

If your good reason isn't especially controversial, you probably should not belabor it. Think of your own experiences as a reader. How often do you recall saying to yourself, as you read a passage or listened to a speaker, "OK! OK! I get the point! Don't keep piling up all of this evidence for me because I don't want it or need it." However, such a reaction is rare, isn't it? By contrast, how often do you recall muttering under your breath, "How can you say that? What evidence do you have to back it up?" When in doubt, err on the side of offering too much evidence. It's an error that is seldom made and not often criticized.

When a writer doesn't provide satisfactory evidence to support a because clause, readers might feel that there has been a failure in the reasoning process. In fact, in your previous courses in writing and speaking, you may have learned about various fallacies associated with faulty arguments (pages 17–19).

Strictly speaking, there is nothing false about these so-called logical fallacies. The fallacies most often refer to failures in providing evidence; when you don't provide enough good evidence to convince your audience, you might be accused of committing a fallacy in reasoning. You will usually avoid such accusations if the evidence that you cite is both *relevant* and *sufficient*.

Relevance refers to the appropriateness of the evidence to the case at hand. Some kinds of evidence are seen as more relevant than others for particular audiences. On the one hand, in science and industry, personal testimony is seen as having limited relevance, while experimental procedures and controlled observations have far more credibility. Compare someone who defends the use of a particular piece of computer software because "it worked for me" with someone who defends it because "according to a journal article published last month, 84 percent of the users of the software were satisfied or very satisfied with it." On the other hand, in writing to the general public on controversial issues such as gun control, personal experience is often considered more relevant than other kinds of data.

Sufficiency refers to the amount of evidence cited. Sometimes a single piece of evidence or a single instance will carry the day if it is especially compelling in some way—if it represents the situation well or makes a point that isn't particularly controversial. More often, people expect more than one piece of evidence if they are to be convinced of something. Convincing readers that they should approve a statewide computer literacy requirement for all high school graduates will require much more evidence than the story of a single graduate who succeeded with her computer skills. You will likely need statistical evidence for such a broad proposal.

If you anticipate that your audience might not accept your evidence, face the situation squarely. First, think carefully about the argument you are presenting. If you cannot cite adequate evidence for your assertions, perhaps those assertions must be modified or qualified in some way. If you remain convinced of your assertions, then think about doing more research to come up with additional evidence.

PEARSON
mycomplab

For support in learning this chapter's content, follow this path in MyCompLab:
> Resources > Writing > The Writing Process > Planning.
Review the Instruction and Multimedia resources, then complete the Exercises and click on Gradebook to measure your progress.

4 | Drafting and Revising Arguments

QUICK TAKE

In this chapter, you will learn that

1. Focusing and evaluating your thesis is critical to writing a successful argument (see below)

2. Keeping your readers in mind will help you write your argument (see page 43)

3. Writing an engaging title and introduction will draw your readers into your argument (see page 46)

4. Evaluating your draft using specific strategies will help you identify your goals for revision (see pages 48–49)

People frequently revise things that they own. What objects have you revised?

State and Evaluate Your Thesis

Once you have identified a topic and have a good sense of how to develop it, the next critical step is to write a **working thesis**. Your **thesis** states your main claim. Much writing that you will do in college and later in your career will require an explicit thesis, usually placed near the beginning.

Focusing your thesis

The thesis can make or break your paper. If the thesis is too broad, you cannot do justice to the argument. Who wouldn't wish for fewer traffic accidents, better medical care, more effective schools, or a cleaner environment? Simple solutions for these complex problems are unlikely.

Stating something that is obvious to everyone isn't an arguable thesis. Don't settle for easy answers. When a topic is too broad, a predictable thesis often results. Narrow your focus and concentrate on the areas where you have the most questions. Those are likely the areas where your readers will have the most questions too.

The opposite problem is less common: a thesis that is too narrow. If your thesis simply states a commonly known fact, then it is too narrow. For example, the growth rate of the population in the United States has doubled since 1970 because of increased immigration. The U.S. Census Bureau provides reasonably accurate statistical information, so this claim is not arguable. But the policies that allow increased immigration and the effects of a larger population—more crowding and higher costs of health care, education, and transportation—are arguable.

> **Not arguable:** The population of the United States grew faster in the 1990s than in any previous decade because Congress increased the rate of legal immigration and the government stopped enforcing most laws against illegal immigration in the interior of the country.
>
> **Arguable:** Allowing a high rate of immigration helps the United States deal with the problems of an increasingly aging society and helps provide funding for millions of Social Security recipients.
>
> **Arguable:** The increase in the number of visas to foreign workers in technology industries is the major cause of unemployment in those industries.

Evaluating your thesis

Once you have a working thesis, ask these questions.

- ■ Is it arguable?
- ■ Is it specific?
- ■ Is it manageable given your length and time requirements?
- ■ Is it interesting to your intended readers?

Example 1
Sample thesis

> We should take action to resolve the serious traffic problem in our city.

Is it arguable? The thesis is arguable, but it lacks a focus.

Is it specific? The thesis is too broad.

Is it manageable? Transportation is a complex issue. New highways and rail systems are expensive and take many years to build. Furthermore, citizens don't want new roads running through their neighborhoods.

Is it interesting? The topic has the potential to be interesting if the writer can propose a specific solution to a problem that everyone in the city recognizes.

When a thesis is too broad, it needs to be revised to address a specific aspect of an issue. Make the big topic smaller.

Revised thesis

> The existing freight railway that runs through the center of the city should be converted to a passenger railway because this is the cheapest and quickest way to decrease traffic congestion downtown.

Example 2
Sample thesis

> Over 60 percent of Americans play computer games on a regular basis.

Is it arguable? The thesis states a commonly acknowledged fact. It is not arguable.

Is it specific? The thesis is too narrow.

Is it manageable? A known fact is stated in the thesis, so there is little to research. Several surveys report this finding.

Is it interesting? The popularity of video games is well established. Nearly everyone is aware of the trend.

There's nothing original or interesting about stating that Americans love computer games. Think about what is controversial. One debatable topic is how computer games affect children.

Revised thesis

> Computer games are valuable because they improve children's visual attention skills, literacy skills, and computer literacy skills.

Finding Good Reasons

Should driving while talking be banned?

In a movement to improve driving safety, California, Connecticut, the District of Columbia, New Jersey, New York, Oregon, Utah, and Washington have passed laws banning the use of handheld cell phones while driving except for emergency workers and people making 911 calls. Several other states have banned cell phones while driving for drivers aged 18 and younger.

Proponents of the ban point to a National Highway Traffic Safety Administration study, reporting that approximately 25 to 30 percent of motor vehicle crashes—about 1.2 million accidents each year—are caused by driver distraction. Opponents of the ban argue that anything that distracts the driver—eating potato chips, talking with passengers, spilled coffee—can cause an accident. The answer, they say, is driver education.

Write about it

1. Write a thesis arguing in support of a ban on cell phones while driving, against a ban, or in support of a more limited position such as banning cell-phone use for drivers 18 and under.

2. Think about the audience that would likely oppose your position. For example, if you support a ban on talking while driving, think about the likely responses of high school students, salespeople who spend much of their workdays driving from place to place, and workers who receive assignments by phone. What good reasons would convince readers who hold an opposing view?

3. What reasons would people who oppose your position likely offer in response? What counterarguments could you give to answer these objections?

Think About Your Readers

Thinking about your readers doesn't mean telling them what they might want to hear. Instead, imagine yourself in a dialogue with your readers. What questions will they likely have? How might you address any potential objections?

Understanding what your readers know—and do not know

Your readers' knowledge of your subject is critical to the success of your argument. If they are not familiar with the background information, they probably won't understand your argument fully. If you know that your readers will be unfamiliar with your subject, you have to supply background information before attempting to convince them of your position. A good tactic is to tie your new information to what your readers already know. Comparisons and analogies can be very helpful in linking old and new information.

Understanding your readers' attitudes toward you

To get your readers to take you seriously, you must convince them that they can trust you. You need to get them to see you as

- **Concerned:** Readers want you to be committed to your subject. They also expect you to be concerned about them. After all, if you don't care about them, why should they read what you write?
- **Well informed:** Many people ramble on about any subject without knowing anything about it. College writing requires that you do your homework on a subject.
- **Fair:** Many writers look at only one side of an issue. Readers respect objectivity and an unbiased approach.
- **Ethical:** Many writers use only the facts that support their positions and often distort facts and sources. Critical readers often notice what is being left out. Don't try to conceal what doesn't support your position.

Understanding your readers' attitudes toward your subject

People have prior attitudes about controversial issues. You must take these attitudes into consideration as you write or speak. Imagine, for instance, that you are preparing an argument for a guest editorial in your college newspaper. You are advocating that your state government should provide parents with choices between public and private schools. You plan to argue that the tax dollars that now automatically go to public schools should go to private schools if parents so choose. You have evidence that the sophomore-to-senior dropout rate in private schools is less than half the rate in public schools. Furthermore, students from private schools attend college at nearly twice the rate of public-school graduates. You intend to argue that one of the reasons private schools are more successful is that they spend more money on instruction and less on administration. And you believe that school choice speaks to the American desire for personal freedom.

Not everyone on your campus will agree with your position. How might the faculty at your college or university feel about this issue? How about the administrators, the staff, other students, and interested community members who read the student newspaper? What are their attitudes toward public funding of private schools? How are you going to deal with the objection that many students in private schools do better in school because they come from more affluent families?

Even when you write about a much less controversial subject, you must think carefully about your audience's attitudes toward what you have to say or to write. Sometimes your audience may share your attitudes; other times, your audience may be neutral. At still other times, your audience will have attitudes that differ sharply from your own. Anticipate these various attitudes and act accordingly. If these attitudes are different from yours, you will have to work hard to counter them without insulting your audience.

Organize Your Argument

Asking a series of questions can generate a list of good reasons, but even if you have plenty, you still have to decide which ones to use and in what order to present them. Thinking about your readers' knowledge, attitudes, and values will help you to decide which reasons to present to your audience.

Writing plans often take the form of outlines, either formal outlines or working outlines. A **formal outline** typically begins with the thesis statement, which anchors the entire outline

---

Managing the Risks of Nanotechnology While Reaping the Rewards

THESIS: The revolutionary potential of nanotechnology has arrived in an explosion of consumer products, yet our federal government has yet to recognize the potential risks or to fund research to reduce those risks.

I.   Nanotechnology now is in many consumer products.

   A.   The promise of nanotechnology to revolutionize medicine, energy production, and communication is years in the future, but consumer products are here now.

   B.   Nanotechnology is now in clothing, food, sports equipment, medicines, electronics, and cars.

C. Experts predict that 15 percent of manufactured products worldwide will contain nanotechnology in 2014.

D. The question that hasn't been asked: Is nanotechnology safe?

II. Americans have little awareness of nanotechnology.

A. Companies have stopped mentioning and advertising nanotechnology.

B. Companies and the insurance industry paid $250 billion in asbestos claims in the United States alone.

C. Companies fear exposure to lawsuits if nanotechnology is found to be toxic.

A **working outline** is a sketch of how you will arrange the major sections.

Managing the Risks of Nanotechnology While Reaping the Rewards

SECTION 1: Begin by defining nanotechnology—manipulating particles between 1 and 100 nanometers (nanometer is a billionth of a meter). Describe the rapid spread of nanotechnology in consumer products including clothing, food, sports equipment, medicines, electronics, and cars. State projection of 15 percent of global manufactured goods containing nanotechnology in 2014.

SECTION 2: Most Americans know nothing about nanotechnology. Companies have stopped advertising that their products contain nanotechnology because of fear of potential lawsuits. Asbestos, once thought safe, now is known to be toxic and has cost companies $250 billion in lawsuits in the United States alone.

SECTION 3: Relatively little research has been done on the safety of nanotechnology. No testing is required for new products because the materials are common, but materials behave differently at nano-scale (example—aluminum normally inert but combustible at nano-scale).

SECTION 4: Nanoparticles are highly mobile and can cross the blood-brain barrier and through the placenta. They are toxic in brains of fish and may collect in lungs.

SECTION 5: Urge that the federal government develop a master plan for identifying and reducing potential risks of nanotechnology and provide sufficient funding to carry out the plan.

Write an Engaging Title and Introduction

Many writers don't think much about titles, but they are very important. A good title makes the reader want to see what you have to say. Be specific as you can in your title, and if possible, suggest your stance.

Get off to a fast start in your introduction. Convince your reader to keep reading. Cut to the chase. Think about how you can get your readers interested. Consider using one of the following.

- State your thesis concisely.
- Provide a hard-hitting fact.
- Ask a question.
- Give a vivid description of a problem.
- Discuss a contradiction or paradox.
- Describe a scenario.

Managing the Risks of Nanotechnology While Reaping the Rewards

The revolutionary potential of nanotechnology for medicine, energy production, and communication is now at the research and development stage, but the future has arrived in consumer products. Nanotechnology has given us products we hardly could have imagined just a few years ago: socks that never stink; pants that repel water yet keep you cool; eyeglasses that won't scratch; "smart" foods that add nutrition and reduce cholesterol; DVDs that are incredibly lifelike; bandages that speed healing; tennis balls that last longer; golf balls that fly straighter; pharmaceuticals that selectively deliver drugs; various digital devices like palm pilots, digital cameras, and cell phones that have longer battery lives and more vivid displays; and cars that are lighter, stronger, and more fuel efficient. These miracle products are now possible because scientists have learned how to manipulate nano-scale particles from 1 to 100 nanometers (a nanometer is a billionth of a meter; a human hair is about 100,000 nanometers in width). Experts estimate that 15 percent of all consumer products will contain nanotechnology by 2014. In the rush to create new consumer products, however, one question has not been asked: Is nanotechnology safe for those who use the products and the workers who are exposed to nanoparticles daily?

Write a Strong Conclusion

Restating your thesis usually isn't the best way to finish a paper. Conclusions that offer only a summary bore readers. The worst endings say something like "in my paper I've said this." Effective conclusions are interesting and provocative, leaving readers with something to think about. Give your readers something to take away besides a straight summary. Try one of these approaches.

- Issue a call to action.
- Discuss the implications.
- Make recommendations.
- Project into the future.
- Tell an anecdote that illustrates a key point.

The potential risks of nanotechnology are reasonably well known. Among the more obvious research questions are the following:

- How hazardous are nanoparticles for workers who have daily exposure?
- What happens to nanoparticles when they are poured down the drain and eventually enter streams, lakes, and oceans?
- How readily do nanoparticles penetrate the skin?
- What happens when nanoparticles enter the brain?
- What effect do airborne nanoparticles have on the lungs?

Nanotechnology promises untold benefits beyond consumer goods in the fields of medicine, energy production, and communication, but these benefits can be realized only if nanotechnology is safe. The federal National Nanotechnology Initiative spent over $1.7 billion in 2009 on nanotechnology science and engineering research, but it budgeted only $74 million on environmental, health, and safety research in 2009. The federal government needs to create a master plan for risk research and to increase spending at least tenfold to ensure sufficient funding to carry out the plan.

When you finish your conclusion, read your introduction again. The main claim in your conclusion should be closely related to the main subject, question, or claim in your introduction. If they do not match, revise the subject, question, or claim in the introduction to match the conclusion. Your thinking evolves and develops as you write, and often your introduction needs some adjusting if you wrote it first.

Evaluate Your Draft

To review and evaluate your draft, pretend you are someone who is either uninformed about your subject or informed but likely to disagree with you. If possible, think of an actual person and imagine yourself as that person.

Read your draft aloud all the way through. When you read aloud, you often hear clunky phrases and catch errors, but just put checks in the margins so you can return to them later. You don't want to get bogged down with the little stuff. What you are after in this stage is an overall sense of how well you accomplished what you set out to do.

Use the questions in the box on the next two pages to evaluate your draft. Note any places where you might make improvements. When you finish, make a list of your goals for the revision. You may have to write another draft before you move to the next stage.

Checklist for evaluating your draft

Does your paper or project meet the assignment?

- Look again at your assignment, especially at key words such as *define, analyze causes, evaluate,* and *propose.* Does your paper or project do what the assignment requires? If not, how can you change it?

- Look again at the assignment for specific guidelines including length, format, and amount of research. Does your work meet these guidelines?

Can you better focus your thesis and your supporting reasons?

- You may have started out with a large topic and ended up writing about one aspect of it. Can you make your thesis even more precise?

- Can you find the exact location where you link each reason to your thesis?

Are your main points adequately developed?

- Can you explain your reasons in more detail?

- Can you add evidence to better support your main points?

- Do you provide enough background on your topic?

Is your organization effective?

- Is the order of your main points clear? (You may want to make a quick outline of your draft if you have not done so already.)

- Are there any abrupt shifts or gaps?
- Are there sections or paragraphs that should be rearranged?

Are your key terms adequately defined?

- What are your key terms?
- Can you define these terms more precisely?

Do you consider other points of view?

- Where do you acknowledge views besides your own? If you don't acknowledge other views, where can you add them?
- How can you make your discussion of opposing views more acceptable to readers who hold those views?

Do you represent yourself effectively?

- Forget for the moment that you wrote what you are reading. What is your impression of the writer?
- Is the tone of the writing appropriate for the subject?

Can you improve your title and introduction?

- Can you make your title more specific and indicate your stance?
- Can you think of a way to start faster and to get your readers interested in what you have to say?

Can you improve your conclusion?

- Can you think of an example that sums up your position?
- Can you discuss an implication of your argument that will make your readers think more about the subject?
- If you are writing a proposal, can you end with a call for action?

Can you improve your visual presentation?

- Is the type style easy to read and consistent?
- Would headings and subheadings help to mark the major sections of your argument?
- If you have statistical data, do you use charts?
- Would illustrations, maps, or other graphics help to explain your main points?

Respond to the Writing of Others

Your instructor may ask you to respond to the drafts of your classmates. Responding to other people's writing requires the same careful attention you give to your own draft. To write a helpful response, you should go through the draft more than once.

First reading

Read at your normal rate the first time through without stopping. When you finish you should have a clear sense of what the writer is trying to accomplish. Try writing the following:

- **Main idea and purpose:** Write a sentence that summarizes what you think is the writer's main idea in the draft.
- **Purpose:** Write a sentence that states what you think the writer is trying to accomplish in the draft.

Second reading

In your second reading, you should be most concerned with the content, organization, and completeness of the draft. Make notes in pencil as you read.

- **Introduction:** Does the writer's first paragraph effectively introduce the topic and engage your interest?
- **Thesis:** What exactly is the writer's thesis? Is it clear? Note in the margin where you think the thesis is located.
- **Focus:** Does the writer maintain focus on the thesis? Note any places where the writer seems to wander off to another topic.
- **Organization:** Are the sections and paragraphs arranged effectively? Do any paragraphs seem to be out of place? Can you suggest a better order for the paragraphs?
- **Completeness:** Are there sections or paragraphs that lack key information or adequate development? Where do you want to know more?
- **Sources:** Are outside sources cited accurately? Are quotations used correctly and worked into the fabric of the draft?

Third reading

In your third reading, turn your attention to matters of audience, style, and tone.

- **Audience:** Who are the writer's intended readers? What does the writer assume the audience knows and believes?

- **Style:** Is the writer's style engaging? How would you describe the writer's voice?
- **Tone:** Is the tone appropriate for the writer's purpose and audience? Is the tone consistent throughout the draft? Are there places where another word or phrase might work better?

When you have finished the third reading, write a short paragraph on each bulleted item above. Refer to specific paragraphs in the draft by number. Then end by answering these two questions:

- What does the writer do especially well in the draft?
- What one or two things would most improve the draft in a revision?

Edit and Proofread Carefully

When you finish revising, you are ready for one final careful reading with the goals of improving your style and eliminating errors.

Edit for style

- **Check connections between sentences and paragraphs.** Notice how your sentences flow within each paragraph and from paragraph to paragraph. If you need to signal the relationship from one sentence or paragraph to the next, use a transitional word or phrase (e.g., *in addition, moreover, similarly, however, nevertheless*).
- **Check your sentences.** Often you will pick up problems with individual sentences by reading aloud. If you notice that a sentence doesn't sound right, think about how you might rephrase it. If a sentence seems too long, consider breaking it into two or more sentences. If you notice a string of short sentences that sound choppy, consider combining them.
- **Eliminate wordiness.** Look for wordy expressions such as *because of the fact that* and *at this point in time*, which can easily be shortened to *because* and *now*. Reduce unnecessary repetition such as *attractive in appearance* or *visible to the eye* to *attractive* and *visible*. Remove unnecessary words like *very, really,* and *totally*. See how many words you can remove without losing the meaning.
- **Use active verbs.** Make your style more lively by replacing forms of *be* (*is, are, was, were*) or verbs ending in *–ing* with active verbs. Sentences that begin with *There is (are)* and *It is* can often be rewritten with active verbs.

Proofread carefully

In your final pass through your text, eliminate as many errors as you can. To become
an effective proofreader, you have to learn
to slow down. Some writers find that moving from word to word with a pencil slows
them down enough to find errors. Others
read backwards to force them to concentrate on each word.

- **Know what your spelling
  checker can and can't do.**
  Spelling checkers are the greatest
  invention since peanut butter.
  They turn up many typos and
  misspellings that are hard to
  catch. But spelling checkers do
  not catch wrong words (*to much*
  for *too much*), missing endings
  (*three dog*), and other similar errors.

You can get one-on-one help in developing your ideas, focusing your topic, and
revising your paper or project at your
writing center.

- **Check for grammar and punctu-
  ation.** Nothing hurts your credibility more than leaving errors in what
  you write. Many job application letters get tossed in the reject pile because of a single, glaring error. Readers probably shouldn't make such
  harsh judgments when they find errors, but often they do. Keep a grammar handbook beside your computer, and use it when you are uncertain
  about what is correct.

For support in learning this chapter's content, follow this path in MyCompLab:
> Resources > Writing > The Writing Process > Drafting and > Revising.
Review the Instruction and Multimedia resources, then complete the Exercises and
click on Gradebook to measure your progress.

Analyzing Arguments

PART

2

5 | Analyzing Written Arguments

QUICK TAKE

In this chapter, you will learn that

1. A rhetorical analysis aims to understand how people attempt to persuade through language and other actions (see below)

2. A rhetorical analysis examines how a text is structured, including choices of language, subject matter, organization, and appeals to the audience (see pages 55–59)

3. A rhetorical analysis considers the broader context, including how a particular text takes part in a larger conversation going on at the time (see pages 59–63)

What Is Rhetorical Analysis?

To many people, the term *rhetoric* means speech or writing that is highly ornamental or deceptive or manipulative. You might hear someone say, "That politician is just using a bunch of rhetoric" or "The rhetoric of that advertisement is very deceptive." But the term *rhetoric* is also used in a positive or neutral sense to describe human communication; for instance, *Silent Spring* is one of the most influential pieces of environmental rhetoric ever written. As a subject of study, rhetoric is usually associated with effective communication, following Aristotle's classic definition of rhetoric as "the art of finding in any given case the available means of persuasion."

Rhetoric is not just a means of *producing* effective communication but also a way of *understanding* communication. The two aspects mutually support one another: becoming a better writer makes you a better interpreter, and becoming a better interpreter makes you a better writer.

Rhetorical analysis can be defined as an effort to understand how people attempt to influence others through language and more broadly every kind of important symbolic action—not only speeches, articles, and books, but also architecture, movies, television shows, memorials, Web sites, advertisements, photos and other images, dance, and popular songs. It might be helpful to think of rhetorical analysis as the kind of critical reading discussed in Chapter 2. Critical reading—rhetorical analysis, that is—involves studying carefully any kind of persuasive action in order to understand it better and to appreciate the tactics involved.

Build a Rhetorical Analysis

Rhetorical analysis examines how an idea is shaped and presented to an audience in a particular form for a specific purpose. There are many approaches to rhetorical analysis and there is no one "correct" way to do it. Generally, though, approaches to rhetorical analysis can be placed between two broad extremes—not mutually exclusive categories but extremes at the ends of a continuum.

At one end of the continuum are analyses that concentrate more on texts than on contexts. They typically use rhetorical concepts to analyze the features of texts. Let's call this approach **textual analysis.** At the other extreme are approaches that emphasize **context** over text. These focus on reconstructing the cultural environment, or context, that existed when a particular rhetorical event took place. That reconstruction provides clues about the persuasive tactics and appeals. Those who undertake **contextual analysis**—as we'll call this second approach—regard particular rhetorical acts as parts of larger communicative chains, or "conversations."

Now let's examine these two approaches in detail.

Analyze the Rhetorical Features

Just as expert teachers in every field of endeavor—from baseball to biology—devise vocabularies to facilitate specialized study, rhetoricians too have developed a set of key concepts to describe rhetorical activities. A fundamental concept in rhetoric is audience. But there are many others. Classical rhetoricians in the tradition of Aristotle, Quintilian, and Cicero developed a range of terms around what they called the canons of rhetoric in order to describe some of the actions of communicators: *inventio* (invention—the finding or creation of information for persuasive acts, and the planning of strategies), *dispostio* (arrangement), *elocutio* (style), *memoria* (the recollection of rhetorical resources that one might call upon, as well as the memorization of what has been invented and arranged), and *pronuntiatio* (delivery). These five canons generally describe the actions of any persuader, from preliminary planning to final delivery.

Over the years, as written discourse gained in prestige against oral discourse, four canons (excepting *memoria*) led to the development of concepts and terms useful for rhetorical analysis. Terms like *ethos, pathos,* and *logos,* all associated with invention, account for features of texts related to the trustworthiness and credibility of the writer or speaker (ethos), for the persuasive good reasons in an argument that derive from a community's mostly deeply held values (pathos), and for the good reasons that emerge from intellectual reasoning (logos). Fundamental to the classical approach to rhetoric is the concept of *decorum,* or "appropriateness": Everything within a persuasive act can be understood as reflecting a central rhetorical goal that governs consistent choices according to occasion and audience.

An example will make textual rhetorical analysis clearer. If you have not done so already, read "The Border Patrol State" by Leslie Marmon Silko in Chapter 11 (pp. 160–166). In the pages that follow, we use the concepts of classical rhetoric to better understand this essay.

Silko's purpose and argument

What is the purpose of Silko's essay? She wrote the essay well over a decade ago, but you probably find it to be interesting and readable still because it concerns the perennial American issue of civil rights. Silko's essay is especially relevant in light of recent debates concerning the Arizona immigration bill and surrounding controversies about the enforcement of state and federal immigration laws. In this case, Silko takes issue with practices associated with the Border Patrol of the Immigration and Naturalization Service (INS). She feels they are reenacting

The statue of Castor stands at the entrance of the Piazza del Campidoglio in Rome. A textual analysis focuses on the statue itself. The size and realism of the statue makes it a masterpiece of classical Roman sculpture.

the long subjugation of native peoples by the white majority. Silko proposes that the power of the Border Patrol be sharply reduced so that the exploitation of her people might be curtailed, and she supports that thesis with an essay that describes and condemns the Border Patrol's tactics.

Essentially Silko's argument comes down to two good reasons: the Border Patrol must be reformed because "the Immigration and Naturalization Service and Border Patrol have implemented policies that interfere with the rights of U.S. citizens to travel freely within our borders" (para. 8), and because efforts to restrict immigration are ineffective and doomed to fail ("It is no use; borders haven't worked, and they won't work," para. 16). Silko's essay amounts to an evaluation of the Border Patrol's activities, an evaluation that finds those activities lacking on ethical and practical grounds.

Silko's use of logos, pathos, and ethos

Logos

When Silko condemns the unethical actions of the Border Patrol early in the essay, she combines ample evidence with other appeals, including our sense of what is legal, constitutional, fair, and honorable. When she explains the futility of trying to

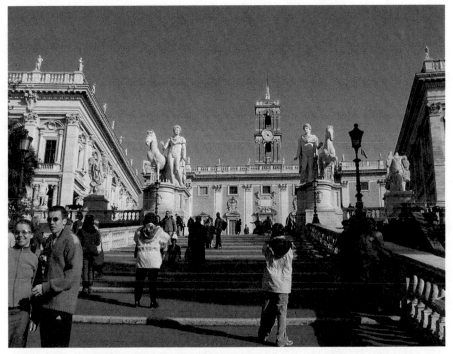

A contextual analysis focuses on the surroundings and history of the statue. According to legend, Castor (left of staircase) and his twin brother Pollux (right of staircase), the mythical sons of Leda, assisted Romans in an early battle. Romans built a large temple in the Forum to honor them. The statues were discovered in the sixteenth century and in 1583 were brought to stand at the top of the Cordonata, a staircase designed by Michelangelo as part of a renovation of the Piazza del Campidoglio commissioned by Pope Paul III Farnese in 1536.

stop immigration, she appeals again to her readers' reasonableness: Constructing walls across the border with Mexico is foolish because "border entrepreneurs have already used blowtorches to cut passageways through the fence" (para. 15), because "a mass migration is already under way" (para. 16), and because "The Americas are Indian country, and the 'Indian problem' is not about to go away" (para. 17).

The bulk of "The Border Patrol State" amounts to an argument by example. The single case—Silko's personal experience, as a Native American, with the border police—stands for many such cases. This case study persuades as other case studies and narratives do—by serving as a representative example that stands for the treatment of many Native Americans.

Pathos

The logical appeals in Silko's essay are reinforced by her emotional appeals.

- The Border Patrol is constructing an "Iron Curtain" that is as destructive of human rights as the Iron Curtain that the Soviet Union constructed around Eastern Europe after World War II (para. 15).

- "Proud" and "patriotic" Native Americans are being harassed: "old Bill Pratt used to ride his horse 300 miles overland . . . every summer to work as a fire lookout" (para. 1).
- Border police terrify American citizens in a way that is chillingly reminiscent of "the report of Argentine police and military officers who became addicted to interrogation, torture, and murder" (paras. 3–5).

The essay's most emotional moment may be when Silko describes how the Border Patrol dog, trained to find illegal drugs and other contraband, including human contraband, seems to sympathize with her and those she is championing: "I saw immediately from the expression in her eyes that the dog hated them" (para. 6); "The dog refused to accuse us: She had an innate dignity that did not permit her to serve the murderous impulses of those men" (para. 7). Clearly the good reasons in "The Border Patrol State" appeal in a mutually supportive way to both the reason and the emotions of Silko's audience. She appeals to the whole person.

Ethos

Why do we take Silko's word about the stories she tells? It is because she establishes her *ethos*, or trustworthiness, early in the essay. Silko reminds her readers that she is a respected, published author who has been on a book tour to publicize her novel *Almanac of the Dead* (para. 3). She buttresses her trustworthiness in other ways too:

- She quotes widely, if unobtrusively, from books and reports to establish that she has studied the issues thoroughly. Note how much she displays her knowledge of INS policies in paragraph 9, for instance.
- She tells not only of her own encounters with the border police (experiences that are a source of great credibility), but also of the encounters of others whom she lists, name after careful name, in order that we might trust her account.
- She demonstrates knowledge of history and geography.
- She connects herself to America generally by linking herself to traditional American values such as freedom (para. 1), ethnic pride, tolerance, and even a love of dogs.

This essay, because of its anti-authoritarian strain, might seem to display politically progressive attitudes at times, but overall, Silko comes off as hard-working, honest, educated, even patriotic. And definitely credible.

Silko's arrangement

Silko arranges her essay appropriately as well. In general the essay follows a traditional pattern. She begins with a long concrete introductory story that hooks the reader and leads to her thesis in paragraph 8. Next, in the body of her essay, she supports her thesis by evaluating the unethical nature of INS policies. She cites their violation of constitutional protections, their similarity to tactics used in nations that are notorious for violating the rights of citizens, and their fundamental immorality. She also emphasizes how those policies are racist in nature (paras. 11–13).

After completing her moral evaluation of INS policy, she turns to the practical difficulties of halting immigration in paragraph 14. The North American Free Trade Agreement (NAFTA) permits the free flow of goods, and even drugs are impossible to stop, so how can people be stopped from crossing borders? Efforts to seal borders are "pathetic" in their ineffectiveness (para. 15). These points lay the groundwork for Silko's surprising and stirring conclusions: "The great human migration within the Americas cannot be stopped; human beings are natural forces of the earth, just as rivers and winds are natural forces" (para. 16); "the Americas are Indian country, and the 'Indian problem' is not about to go away" (para. 17). The mythic "return of the Aztlan" is on display in the box cars that go by as the essay closes. In short, this essay unfolds in a conventional way: it has a standard beginning, middle, and end.

Silko's style

What about Silko's style? How is it appropriate to her purposes? Take a look at paragraphs 3 and 4. You will notice that nearly all of the fourteen sentences in these paragraphs are simple in structure. There are only five sentences that use any form of subordination (clauses that begin with *when, that,* or *if*). Many of the sentences consist either of one clause or of two clauses joined by simple coordination (connection with conjunctions such as *and* or *but* or a semicolon). Several of the sentences and clauses are unusually short. Furthermore, in these paragraphs Silko never uses metaphors or other sorts of poetic language. Her choice of words is as simple as her sentences. It all reminds you of the daily newspaper, doesn't it? Silko chooses a style similar to one used in newspaper reporting—simple, straightforward, unadorned—because she wants her readers to accept her narrative as credible and trustworthy. Her tone and voice reinforce her ethos.

There is more to say about the rhetorical choices that Silko made in crafting "The Border Patrol State," but this analysis is enough to illustrate our main point. Textual rhetorical analysis employs rhetorical terminology—in this case, terms borrowed from classical rhetoric such as ethos, pathos, logos, arrangement, style, and tone—as a way of helping us to understand how a writer makes choices to achieve certain effects. And textual analysis cooperates with contextual analysis.

Analyze the Rhetorical Context

Communication as conversation

Notice that in the previous discussion the fact that Leslie Marmon Silko's "The Border Patrol State" was originally published in the magazine *The Nation* did not matter too much. Nor did it matter when the essay was published (October 17, 1994), who exactly read it, what their reaction was, or what other people were saying at the time. Textual analysis can proceed as if the item under consideration "speaks for all time," as if it is a museum piece unaffected by time and space. There's nothing wrong with museums, of course; they permit people to observe and appreciate objects in an important way. But museums often fail to reproduce an artwork's original context and cultural meaning. In that sense museums can diminish understanding as much as they contribute to it. Contextual rhetorical analysis is an attempt to understand communications through the lens of their environments, examining the setting or scene out of which any communication emerges.

Similar to textual analysis, contextual analysis may be conducted in any number of ways. But contextual rhetorical analysis always proceeds from a description of the **rhetorical situation** that motivated the event in question. It demands an appreciation of the social circumstances that call rhetorical events into being and that orchestrate the course of those events. It regards communications as anything but self-contained:

- Each communication is considered as a response to other communications and to other social practices.
- Communications, and social practices more generally, are considered to reflect the attitudes and values of the communities that sustain them.
- Analysts seek evidence of how those other communications and social practices are reflected in texts.

Rhetorical analysis from a contextualist perspective understands individual pieces as parts of ongoing conversations.

The challenge is to reconstruct the conversation surrounding a specific piece of writing or speaking. Sometimes it is easy to do so. You may have appropriate background information on the topic, as well as a feel for what is behind what people are writing or saying about it. People who have strong feelings about the environment, stem cell research, same-sex marriage, or any number of other current issues are well informed about the arguments that are converging around those topics.

But other times it takes some research to reconstruct the conversations and social practices related to a particular issue. If the issue is current, you need to see how the debate is conducted in current magazines, newspapers, talk shows, movies and TV shows, Web sites, and so forth. If the issue is from an earlier time, you must do archival research into historical collections of newspapers, magazines, books, letters, and other documentary sources. Archival research usually involves libraries, special research collections, or film and television archives where it is possible to learn quite a bit about context.

An example will clarify how contextual analysis works to open up an argument to analysis. Let's return to a discussion of Silko's "The Border Patrol State" on pages 160–166. It will take a bit of research to reconstruct some of the "conversations" that Silko is participating in, but the result will be an enhanced understanding of the essay as well as an appreciation for how you might do a contextual rhetorical analysis.

Silko's life and works

You can begin by learning more about Silko herself. The essay provides some facts about her (e.g., that she is a Native American writer of note who is from the Southwest). The headnote on page 160 gives additional information (that her writing usually develops out of Native American traditions and tales). You can learn more about Silko using the Internet and your library's Web site. Silko's credibility, her ethos, is established not just by her textual decisions but also by her prior reputation, especially for readers of *The Nation* who would recognize and appreciate her accomplishments.

Perhaps the most relevant information on the Web is about *Almanac of the Dead*, the novel Silko refers to in paragraph 3. The novel, set mainly in Tucson, involves a Native American woman psychic who is in the process of transcribing the lost histories of her dead ancestors into "an almanac of the dead"—a history of her people. This history is written from the point of view of the conquered, not the conqueror. "The Border Patrol State," it seems, is an essay version of *Almanac of the Dead* in that Silko protests what has been lost—and what is still being lost—in the clash between white and Native American cultures. It is a protest against the tactics of the border police. Or is it?

The context of publication

Through a consideration of the conversations swirling around it, contextual analysis actually suggests that "The Border Patrol State" is just as much about immigration policy as it is about the civil rights of Native Americans. The article first appeared in *The Nation*, a respected, politically progressive magazine that has been appearing weekly for decades. Published in New York City, it is a magazine of public opinion that covers theater, film, music, fiction, and other arts; politics and public affairs; and contemporary culture. If you want to know what left-leaning people are thinking about an issue, *The Nation* is a good magazine to consult. You can imagine that Silko's essay therefore reached an audience of sympathetic readers—people who would be receptive to her message. They would be inclined to sympathize with Silko's complaints and to heed her call for a less repressive Border Patrol.

What is more interesting is that Silko's essay appeared on October 17, 1994, in a special issue of *The Nation* devoted to "The Immigration Wars," a phrase prominent on the magazine's cover. Silko's essay was one of several articles that appeared under that banner, an indication that Silko's argument is not just about the violation of the civil rights of Native Americans but also about the larger issue of immigration policy. "The Border Patrol State" appeared after David Cole's "Five Myths about Immigration," Elizabeth Kadetsky's "Bashing Illegals in California," Peter Kwong's "China's Human Traffickers," two editorials about immigration policy, and short columns on immigration by *Nation* regulars Katha Pollitt, Aryeh Neier, and Christopher Hitchens. Together the articles in this issue of *The Nation* mounted a sustained argument in favor of a liberal immigration policy.

The larger conversation

Why did *The Nation* entitle its issue "The Immigration Wars"? Immigration was a huge controversy in October 1994, just before the 1994 elections. When the 1965 Immigration Act was amended in 1990, the already strong flow of immigrants to the United States became a flood. While many previous immigrants came to the United States from Europe, most recent immigrants have come from Asia, Latin America, the Caribbean islands, and Africa. While earlier immigrants typically passed through Ellis Island and past the Statue of Liberty that welcomed them, most recent immigrants in 1994 were coming to Florida, Texas, and California. The arrival of all those new immigrants revived old fears that have been in the air for decades (that they take away jobs from native-born Americans, that they undermine national values by resisting assimilation and clinging to their own cultures, that they reduce standards of living by putting stress on education and social-welfare budgets). Many people countered those fears by pointing out that immigrants create jobs and wealth, enhance the vitality of American culture, become among the proudest of Americans, and contribute to the tax base of their communities. But those counterarguments were undermined when a tide of illegal immigrants—up to 500,000 per year—was arriving at the time Silko was writing.

The Immigration Wars were verbal wars. In the 1994 election, Republicans had united under the banner of a "Contract with America." Some 300 Republican congressional candidates, drawn together by conservative leader Newt Gingrich, agreed to run on a common platform in an ultimately successful effort to gain control of the House of Representatives. Among a number of initiatives, the Contract with America proposed changes in laws in order to curtail immigration, to reduce illegal immigration, and to deny benefits such as health care, social services, and education to illegal residents.

The Contract with America offered support for California's Proposition 187, another important 1994 proposal. This so-called "Save Our State" initiative was designed to "prevent California's estimated 1.7 million undocumented immigrants from partaking of every form of public welfare including nonemergency medical care, prenatal clinics and public schools," as Kadetsky explained in her essay in *The Nation*. The Republican Contract with America and California's Proposition 187 together constituted the nation's leading domestic issue in October 1994. The war of words about the issue was evident in the magazines, books, newspapers, talk shows, barber shops, and hair salons of America—much as it is today.

Silko's political goals

In this context, it is easy to see that Silko's essay is against more than the Border Patrol. It is an argument in favor of relatively unrestricted immigration, especially for Mexicans and Native Americans. Moreover, it is a direct refutation of the Contract with America and Proposition 187. Proposition 187 states "that [the People of California] have suffered and are suffering economic hardship caused by the presence of illegal aliens in this state, that they have suffered and are suffering personal injury and damage caused by the criminal conduct of illegal aliens, [and] that they have a right to the protection of their government from any person or persons entering this country illegally."

Silko turns the claim around. It is the Border Patrol that is behaving illegally. It is the Border Patrol that is creating economic hardship. It is the border police that are inflicting personal injury and damage through criminal conduct. Finally, it is the U.S. government that is acting illegally by ignoring the treaty of Guadalupe Hidalgo, which "recognizes the right of the Tohano O'Odom (Papago) people to move freely across the U.S.-Mexico border without documents," as Silko writes in a footnote. Writing just before the election of 1994 and in the midst of a spirited national debate, Silko had specific political goals in mind. A contextual analysis of "The Border Patrol State" reveals that the essay is, at least in part, an eloquent refutation of the Contract with America and Proposition 187—two items that are not even named explicitly in the essay!

We could do more contextual analysis here. There is no need to belabor the point, however; our purpose has been simply to illustrate that contextual analysis of a piece of rhetoric can enrich our understanding.

Write a Rhetorical Analysis

Effective rhetorical analysis, as we have seen, can be textual or contextual in nature. But we should emphasize again that these two approaches to rhetorical analysis are not mutually exclusive. Indeed, many if not most analysts operate between these two extremes; they consider the details of the text, but they also attend to the particulars of context. Textual analysis and contextual analysis inevitably complement each other. Getting at what is at stake in "The Border Patrol State" or any other sophisticated argument takes patience and intelligence. Rhetorical analysis, as a way of understanding how people argue, is both enlightening and challenging.

Try to use elements of both kinds of analysis whenever you want to understand a rhetorical event more completely. Rhetoric is "inside" texts, but it is also "outside" them. Specific rhetorical performances are an irreducible mixture of text and context, and so interpretation and analysis of those performances must account for both as well. Remember, however, the limitations of your analysis. Realize that your analysis will always be somewhat partial and incomplete, ready to be deepened, corrected, modified, and extended by the insights of others. Rhetorical analysis can itself be part of an unending conversation—a way of learning and teaching within a community.

Steps to Writing a Rhetorical Analysis

Step 1 Select an Argument to Analyze

Find an argument to analyze—a speech or sermon, an op-ed in a newspaper, an ad in a magazine designed for a particular audience, or a commentary on a talk show.

Examples

- Editorial pages of newspapers (but not letters to the editor unless you can find a long and detailed letter)
- Opinion features in magazines such as *Time, Newsweek*, and *U.S. News & World Report*
- Magazines that take political positions such as *National Review, Mother Jones, New Republic, Nation*, and *Slate*
- Web sites of activist organizations (but not blog or newsgroup postings unless they are long and detailed)

Step 2 Analyze the context

Who is the author?

Through research in the library or on the Web, learn all you can about the author.

- How does the argument you are analyzing repeat arguments previously made by the author?
- What motivated the author to write? What is the author's purpose for writing this argument?

Who is the audience?

Through research, learn all you can about the publication and the audience.

- Who is the anticipated audience?
- How do the occasion and forum for writing affect the argument?

What is the larger conversation?

Through research, find out what else was being said about the subject of your selection. Track down any references made in the text you are examining.

- When did the argument appear?
- What other concurrent pieces of "cultural conversation" (e.g., TV shows, other articles, speeches, Web sites) does the item you are analyzing respond to or "answer"?

Step 3 Analyze the text

Summarize the argument

- What is the main claim?

- What reasons are given in support of the claim?
- How is the argument organized? What are the components, and why are they presented in that order?

What is the medium and genre?

- What is the medium? A newspaper? a scholarly journal? a Web site?
- What is the genre? An editorial? an essay? a speech? an advertisment? What expectations does the audience have about this genre?

What appeals are used?

- Analyze the ethos. How does the writer represent himself or herself? Does the writer have any credentials as an authority on the topic? Do you trust the writer?
- Analyze the logos. Where do you find facts and evidence in the argument? What kinds of facts and evidence does the writer present? Direct observation? statistics? interviews? surveys? quotations from authorities?
- Analyze the pathos. Does the writer attempt to invoke an emotional response? Where do you find appeals to shared values?

How would you characterize the style?

- Is the style formal, informal, satirical, or something else?
- Are any metaphors used?

Step 4 Write a draft

Introduction

- Describe briefly the argument you are analyzing, including where it was published, how long it is, and who wrote it.
- If the argument is about an issue unfamiliar to your readers, supply the necessary background.

Body

- Analyze the context, following Step 2.
- Analyze the text, following Step 3.

Conclusion

- Do more than simply summarize what you have said. You might, for example, end with an example that typifies the argument.
- You don't have to end by either agreeing or disagreeing with the writer. Your task in this assignment is to analyze the strategies the writer uses.

Step 5 Revise, edit, proofread

For detailed instructions, see Chapter 4.
  For a checklist to evaluate your draft, see pages 48–49.

Barbara Jordan

Statement on the Articles of Impeachment

Barbara Jordan (1936–1996) grew up in Houston and received a law degree from Boston University in 1959. Working on John F. Kennedy's 1960 presidential campaign stirred an interest in politics, and Jordon became the first African American woman elected to the Texas State Senate in 1966. In 1972 she was elected to the United States House of Representatives and thus became the first African American woman from the South ever to serve in Congress. Jordan was appointed to the House Judiciary Committee. Soon she was in the national spotlight when that committee considered articles of impeachment against President Richard Nixon, who had illegally covered up a burglary of Democratic Party headquarters during the 1972 election. When Nixon's criminal acts reached to the Judiciary Committee, Jordan's opening speech on July 24, 1974, set the tone for the debate and established her reputation as a moral beacon for the nation. Nixon resigned as president on August 9, 1974, when it was evident that he would be impeached.

Thank you, Mr. Chairman.

Mr. Chairman, I join my colleague Mr. Rangel in thanking you for giving the junior members of this committee the glorious opportunity of sharing the pain of this inquiry. Mr. Chairman, you are a strong man and it has not been easy, but we have tried as best we can to give you as much assistance as possible.

2   Earlier today, we heard the beginning of the Preamble to the Constitution of the United States: "We, the people." It's a very eloquent beginning. But when that document was completed on the seventeenth of September in 1787, I was not included in that "We, the people." I felt somehow for many years that George Washington and Alexander Hamilton just left me out by mistake. But through the process of amendment, interpretation, and court decision, I have finally been included in "We, the people."

3   Today I am an inquisitor. Any hyperbole would not be fictional and would not overstate the solemnness that I feel right now. My faith in the Constitution is whole; it is complete; it is total. And I am not going to sit here and be an idle spectator to the diminution, the subversion, the destruction, of the Constitution.

4   "Who can so properly be the inquisitors for the nation as the representatives of the nation themselves?" "The subjects of its jurisdiction are those offenses which proceed from the misconduct of public men." And that's what we're talking about. In other words, [the jurisdiction comes] from the abuse or violation of some public trust.

5   It is wrong, I suggest, it is a misreading of the Constitution for any member here to assert that for a member to vote for an article of impeachment means that that member must be convinced that the President should be removed from office. The Constitution doesn't say that. The powers relating to impeachment are an essential check in the hands of the body of the legislature against and upon the encroachments of the executive. [By creating] the division between the two branches of the legislature, the House and the Senate, assigning to the one the right to accuse and to the other the right to judge, the framers of this Constitution were very astute. They did not make the accusers and the judgers the same person.

6   We know the nature of impeachment. We've been talking about it awhile now. It is chiefly designed for the President and his high ministers to somehow be called into account. It is designed to "bridle" the executive if he engages in excesses. "It is designed as a method of national inquest into the conduct of public men." The framers confided in the Congress the power, if need be, to remove the President in order to strike a delicate balance between a President swollen with power and grown tyrannical, and preservation of the independence of the executive.

7   The nature of impeachment: [it is] a narrowly channeled exception to the separation-of-powers maxim. The Federal Convention of 1787 said that. It limited impeachment to high crimes and misdemeanors and discounted and opposed the term *maladministration*. "It is to be used only for great misdemeanors," so it was said in the North Carolina ratification convention. And in the Virginia ratification convention: "We do not trust our liberty to a particular branch. We need one branch to check the other."

8   "No one need be afraid"—the North Carolina ratification convention—"No one need be afraid that officers who commit oppression will pass with immunity." "Prosecutions of impeachments will seldom fail to agitate the passions of the whole community," said Hamilton in the Federalist Papers, number 65. "We divide into parties more or less friendly or inimical to the accused." I do not mean political parties in that sense.

9   The drawing of political lines goes to the motivation behind impeachment; but impeachment must proceed within the confines of the constitutional term "high crime[s] and misdemeanors." Of the impeachment process, it was Woodrow Wilson who said that "Nothing short of the grossest offenses against the plain law of the land will suffice to give them speed and effectiveness. Indignation so great as to overgrow party interest may secure a conviction; but nothing else can."

10   Common sense would be revolted if we engaged upon this process for petty reasons. Congress has a lot to do: Appropriations, Tax Reform, Health Insurance, Campaign Finance Reform, Housing, Environmental Protection, Energy Sufficiency, Mass Transportation. Pettiness cannot be allowed to stand in the face of such overwhelming problems. So today we are not being petty. We are trying to be big, because the task we have before us is a big one.

11   This morning, in a discussion of the evidence, we were told that the evidence which purports to support the allegations of misuse of the CIA by the President is thin.

We're told that that evidence is insufficient. What that recital of the evidence this morning did not include is what the President did know on June the 23rd, 1972.

12   The President did know that it was Republican money, that it was money from the Committee for the Re-Election of the President, which was found in the possession of one of the burglars arrested on June the 17th. What the President did know on the 23rd of June was the prior activities of E. Howard Hunt, which included his participation in the break-in of Daniel Ellsberg's psychiatrist, which included Howard Hunt's participation in the Dita Beard ITT affair, which included Howard Hunt's fabrication of cables designed to discredit the Kennedy Administration.

13   We were further cautioned today that perhaps these proceedings ought to be delayed because certainly there would be new evidence forthcoming from the President of the United States. There has not even been an obfuscated indication that this committee would receive any additional materials from the President. The committee subpoena is outstanding, and if the President wants to supply that material, the committee sits here. The fact is that only yesterday, the American people waited with great anxiety for eight hours, not knowing whether their President would obey an order of the Supreme Court of the United States.

14   At this point, I would like to juxtapose a few of the impeachment criteria with some of the actions the President has engaged in. Impeachment criteria: James Madison, from the Virginia ratification convention: "If the President be connected in any suspicious manner with any person and there be grounds to believe that he will shelter him, he may be impeached."

15   We have heard time and time again that the evidence reflects the payment to defendants' money. The President had knowledge that these funds were being paid and these were funds collected for the 1972 presidential campaign. We know that the President met with Mr. Henry Petersen 27 times to discuss matters related to Watergate, and immediately thereafter met with the very persons who were implicated in the information Mr. Petersen was receiving. The words are: "If the President is connected in any suspicious manner with any person and there be grounds to believe that he will shelter that person, he may be impeached."

16   Justice Story: "Impeachment is intended for occasional and extraordinary cases where a superior power acting for the whole people is put into operation to protect their rights and rescue their liberties from violations." We know about the Huston plan. We know about the break-in of the psychiatrist's office. We know that there was absolute complete direction on September 3rd when the President indicated that a surreptitious entry had been made in Dr. Fielding's office, after having met with Mr. Ehrlichman and Mr. Young. "Protect their rights." "Rescue their liberties from violation."

17   The Carolina ratification convention impeachment criteria: those are impeachable "who behave amiss or betray their public trust." Beginning shortly after the Watergate break-in and continuing to the present time, the President has engaged in a series of public statements and actions designed to thwart the lawful investigation by government prosecutors. Moreover, the President has made public announcements and assertions bearing on the Watergate case, which the evidence will show he knew to be false. These assertions, false assertions, impeachable, those who misbehave. Those who "behave amiss or betray the public trust."

18   James Madison again at the Constitutional Convention: "A President is impeachable if he attempts to subvert the Constitution." The Constitution charges the President with the task of taking care that the laws be faithfully executed, and yet the President has counseled his aides to commit perjury, willfully disregard the secrecy of grand jury proceedings, conceal surreptitious entry, attempt to compromise a federal judge, while publicly displaying his cooperation with the processes of criminal justice. "A President is impeachable if he attempts to subvert the Constitution."

19   If the impeachment provision in the Constitution of the United States will not reach the offenses charged here, then perhaps that 18th-century Constitution should be abandoned to a 20th-century paper shredder.

20   Has the President committed offenses, and planned, and directed, and acquiesced in a course of conduct which the Constitution will not tolerate? That's the question. We know that. We know the question. We should now forthwith proceed to answer the question. It is reason, and not passion, which must guide our deliberations, guide our debate, and guide our decision.

21   I yield back the balance of my time, Mr. Chairman.

Sample Student Rhetorical Analysis

T. Jonathan Jackson

Dr. Netaji

English 1102

11 October 2010

An Argument of Reason and Passion: Barbara Jordan's

"Statement on the Articles of Impeachment"

Barbara Jordan's July 24, 1974 speech before the U.S. House Judiciary Committee helped convince the House of Representatives, and the American public, that President Richard Nixon should be impeached. Nixon was under investigation for his role in the cover-up of the Watergate scandal. He knew about the burglary of Democratic Party headquarters, but denied having any knowledge of it and illegally shielded those responsible. Jordan used her speech to argue that the president should be impeached because his actions threatened the Constitution and the people of the United States; however, Jordan never explicitly states this position in her speech. Instead, she establishes her credibility and then uses logic to set out the evidence against the president. •————

> Jonathan Jackson provides background information in the first paragraph and his thesis at the end.

In one sense, the audience of Jordan's speech consisted of the other 34 members of the House Judiciary Committee, gathered together to decide whether or not to recommend impeachment. And yet Jordan was not speaking just to a committee meeting; her speech was very public. The Senate Watergate hearings had been televised during the months before her speech, and millions of Americans watched sensational testimony by a host of witnesses. The Senate hearings produced charges that Nixon authorized break-ins at Democratic campaign headquarters in Washington during the 1972 election and that the White House was involved in many political dirty tricks and improprieties.

But the accusations remained only accusations—and Americans remained deeply divided about them—until it was discovered that Nixon had himself collected possible hard evidence: he had taped many conversations in the Oval Office, tapes that could support or refute the charges against the president. Nixon engaged in a protracted legal battle to keep the tapes from being disclosed, on the grounds that they were private

Jackson 2

conversations protected under "executive privilege," and he released only partial and edited transcripts. Finally on July 24, 1974, the courts ruled that Nixon had to turn all his remaining tapes over. That same day, knowing that hard evidence was now at hand, the House Judiciary Committee immediately went into session to vote whether to impeach Nixon. Each member of the committee was given fifteen minutes for an opening statement.

Nixon was a Republican and Jordan, like the majority of the committee, was a Democrat. Jordan had to convince her audience she was not biased against the president simply because of her party affiliation. Jordan was also new to Congress, relatively unknown outside of Texas, and a low-ranking member of the committee. Consequently, she had to establish her ethos to the committee as well as to the television audience. She had to present herself as fair, knowledgeable, and intellectually mature.

Jackson observes that Jordan had a formidable assignment in establishing her ethos in a short speech.

At the heart of Jordan's argument is her faith in the Constitution. She begins her speech from a personal perspective, pointing out that the Constitution is not perfect because it originally excluded African Americans like her. But now that the Constitution recognizes her as a citizen, Jordan says, her faith in it "is whole, it is complete, it is total." She even implies that, as a citizen, she has a moral duty to protect the Constitution, saying, "I am not going to sit here and be an idle spectator to the diminution, the subversion, the destruction of the Constitution." Jordan's emotional connection to the Constitution shows the audience that she is motivated by a love of her country, not by party loyalty. She establishes herself as someone fighting to defend and protect American values.

Jackson analyzes how Jordan's fervent allegiance to the Constitution made her appear unbiased.

Jordan describes the Constitution as the accepted authority on the laws related to impeachment. She shows the audience how the Constitution gives her the authority to act as an "inquisitor," or judge. She depicts the Constitution and the American people as potential victims, and the president as the potential criminal. She warns of the need to remove "a President swollen with power and grown tyrannical."

Jackson 3

The appeals to pathos and ethos in the opening of the speech establishes Jordan's motivations and credibility, allowing her to next lay out her logical arguments. Jordan proceeds to explain how the Constitution defines impeachment, and fleshes out this brief definition with evidence from several state Constitutional Conventions. She also quotes Supreme Court Justice Joseph Story. Using evidence from the North Carolina and Virginia Constitutional Conventions, Jordan shows that impeachment was intended only for "great misdemeanors," and that the branches of government were intended to act as a check upon one another.

Next Jordan uses quotations from James Madison, Justice Story, and others to define impeachable offenses. For each offense, Jordan provides an example of an act that President Nixon was known to have committed, and she shows how his actions meet the definition of impeachable offenses. She compares Nixon's meetings with Watergate suspects to Madison's statement that "if the President is connected in any suspicious manner with any person and there be grounds to believe that he will shelter that person, he may be impeached." She pairs Justice Story's statement that impeachment should "protect [citizens'] rights and rescue their liberties from violation" with Nixon's knowledge of the burglary of a private psychiatrist's office. She links Nixon's attempts to bribe a judge and thwart grand jury proceedings with Madison's statement that "a President is impeachable if he attempts to subvert the Constitution."

> Jordan uses quotations from respected figures in American history to apply to Nixon's misdeeds.

> Jordan had to confront a legal issue: Were the actions of President Nixon serious enough to justify impeachment?

Throughout this section, Jordan repeats the historical quotes before and after her descriptions of the president's acts. This repetition makes the connections stronger and more memorable for the audience. Jordan also contrasts the formal, high-toned language of the Founders and the Constitution with descriptions that make President Nixon's actions sound sordid and petty: He knew about money "found in the possession of one of the burglars arrested on June the 17th," about "the break-in of Daniel Ellsberg's psychiatrist," about "the fabrication of cables designed to discredit the Kennedy Administration." Words like "burglars," "arrested," "break-in," and "fabrication," sound like evidence in a criminal trial. These words are not the kind of language Americans want to hear describing the actions of their president.

Jackson 4

Jordan then adds another emotional appeal, implying that the
Constitution is literally under attack. "If the impeachment provisions will
not reach the offenses charged here," she says, "then perhaps that
18th-century Constitution should be abandoned to a 20th-century paper
shredder." This dramatic image encourages the audience to imagine
President Nixon shredding the Constitution just as he had destroyed
other evidence implicating him in the Watergate scandal. It implies that
if the president is not stopped, he will commit further abuses of power.
Jordan also makes the American people responsible for this possible outcome, saying that "we" may as well shred the Constitution if it cannot be
used to impeach Nixon. This emotional appeal has the effect of shaming
those say they can't or shouldn't vote for impeachment.

Jordan concludes her speech not by calling for impeachment, but by
calling for an answer to the question, "Has the President committed
offenses, and planned, and directed, and acquiesced in a course of conduct
which the Constitution will not tolerate?" It almost seems like Jordan is
being humble and trying not to judge by not stating her position
outright. However, the reverse is true: Jordan doesn't state her position
because she doesn't need to. The evidence she presented led Congress
and the American public inescapably to one conclusion: That President
Nixon had committed impeachable offenses. Just two week later, Nixon
resigned from office. Jordan had made her point.

*Jackson notes
that the
metaphor of the
paper shredder
adds emotional
force.*

*In his conclu-
sion Jackson
points out how
Jordan shifts
the focus to her
audience in her
conclusion.*

Jackson 5

Works Cited

Jordan, Barbara. "Statement on the Articles of Impeachment." *American
     Rhetoric: Top 100 Speeches*. American Rhetoric, 25 July 1974.
     Web. 25 Sept. 2010.

For support in learning this chapter's content, follow this path in MyCompLab:

⊳Resources ⊳Writing ⊳Writing Purposes ⊳Writing to Analyze.

Review the Instruction and Multimedia resources, then complete the Exercises and click on Gradebook to measure your progress.

6 Analyzing Visual and Multimedia Arguments

QUICK TAKE

In this chapter, you will learn that

1. Visual arguments have similarities and differences with verbal arguments (see below)
2. Photos and videos used as evidence in visual arguments need to be evaluated critically (see pages 79–81)
3. Visual arguments can be analyzed using strategies similar to those used to analyze a written argument (see pages 81–82)
4. An effective visual analysis takes into account the context of the image as well as its visual elements and any surrounding text (see pages 83–86)

What Is a Visual Argument?

We live in a world flooded with images. They pull on us, compete for our attention, push us to do things. But how often do we think about how they work?

Can there be an argument without words?

Arguments in written language are visual in one sense: we use our eyes to read the words on the page. But without words, can there be a visual argument? Certainly some visual symbols take on conventional meanings. Signs in airports or other public places, for example, are designed to communicate with speakers of many languages.

Some visual symbols even make explicit claims. A one-way street sign says that drivers should travel only in the one direction. But are such signs arguments? In Chapter 3 we point out that scholars of argument do not believe that everything *is* an argument. Most scholars define an argument as a claim supported by one or more reasons. A one-way sign has a claim: all drivers should go in the same direction. But is there a reason? We all know an unstated reason the sign carries: drivers who go the wrong way violate the law and risk a substantial fine (plus they risk a head-on collision with other drivers).

Visual arguments require viewer participation

The *Deepwater Horizon* oil spill (also known as the BP oil spill) was the largest off-shore oil spill in the history of the United States. Caused by an explosion on April 20, 2010, the spill dumped millions of gallons of oil every day for months in spite of efforts to contain it. People around the world were reminded of the spill when they turned on their televisions and saw video of the oil gushing from the well, and nearly everyone was outraged.

People interpreted the oil flowing from the pipe quite differently, inferring multiple because clauses. Citizens were angry for different reasons.

The *Deepwater Horizon* oil spill was a disaster because

- eleven workers were killed and seventeen were injured.
- enormous harm was done to Gulf wetlands, birds, fish, turtles, marine mammals, and other animals.
- the tourism industry suffered another major blow just five years after Hurricane Katrina.
- the fishing and shrimping industries suffered huge losses.

The main oil leak from the *Deepwater Horizon* wellhead. © BP p.l.c.

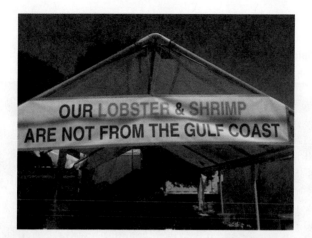

Photograph of a booth at the Taste of Chicago that was sent on Twitter and enraged people in New Orleans.

- President Obama declared a moratorium on deep-water drilling, threatening the loss of jobs.
- BP and its partners were negligent in drilling the well.
- the spill was an unfortunate act of God like Hurricane Katrina.

Differing interpretations of visual arguments extended beyond the spill itself. A news producer in Chicago took the photo below at the Taste of Chicago festival, sent it to a friend in New Orleans, who sent it to a food writer, who posted it on Twitter. The mayor of New Orleans called it "disgraceful."

Talks shows in both Chicago and New Orleans ranted for a few days about the other city. One comment was perhaps telling about the source of the rage: a menu disclaimer would have been acceptable, but a prominent visual argument, even in text form, was hitting below the belt.

What Is a Multimedia Argument?

Multimedia describes the use of multiple content forms including text, voice and music audio, video, still images, animation, and interactivity. Multimedia goes far back in human history (texts and images were combined at the beginnings of writing), but digital technologies and the Web have made multimedia the fabric of our daily lives. But what exactly are multimedia arguments?

For example, games provide intense multimedia experiences, but are they arguments? Game designers such as Jane McGonigal believe they are arguments. McGonigal maintains that games make people more powerful because they connect them into larger wholes.

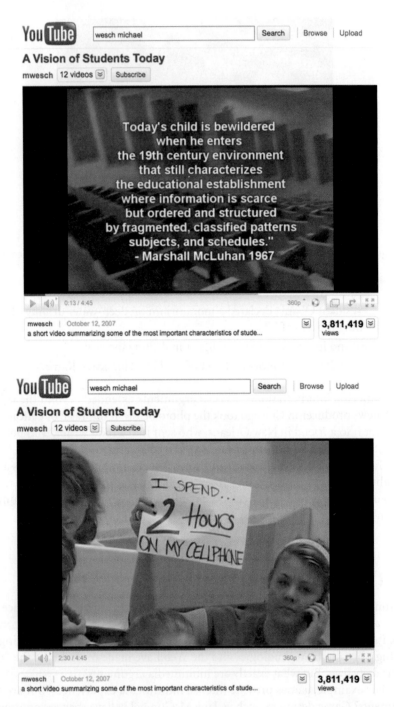

Images from Michael Wesch's *A Vision of Students Today*

Thousands of multimedia arguments have been posted on YouTube. One frequently viewed video is Michael Wesch's *A Vision of Students Today*, posted in October 2007. Wesch's point is that today's education is ill-suited for most students. He enlisted his students to make the point with text and video.

Analyze Visual Evidence

Videos without narration, images, and graphics seldom make arguments on their own, but they are frequently used to support arguments.

Evaluate photographs and videos as evidence

Almost from the beginnings of photography, negatives were manipulated but realistic results required a high skill level. In the digital era anyone can alter photographs. Perhaps there's nothing wrong with using Photoshop to add absent relatives to family photographs or remove ex-boyfriends and ex-girlfriends. But where do you draw the line? Not only do many videos on YouTube use outright deception, but newsmagazines and networks have also been found guilty of these practices.

Ask questions about what you view.

- Who created the image or video? What bias might the creator have?
- Who published the image or video? What bias might the publisher have?
- Who is the intended audience? For example, political videos often assume that the viewers hold the same political views as the creators.
- What is being shown, and what is not being shown? For example, a video ad promoting tourism for the Gulf of Mexico will look very different from a video showing sources of pollution.
- Who is being represented, and who is not being represented? Who gets left out is as important as who gets included.

The ease of cropping digital photographs reveals an important truth about photography: a photograph represents reality from a particular viewpoint. A high-resolution picture of a crowd can be divided into many smaller images that each say something different about the event. The act of pointing the camera in one direction and not in another shapes how photographic evidence will be interpreted. (See the examples on page 80.)

Evaluate charts and graphs

Statistical information is frequently used as evidence in arguments. The problem with giving many statistics in sentence form, however, is that readers shortly lose track of the numbers. Charts and graphs present statistics visually, allowing readers to take in trends and relationships at a glance.

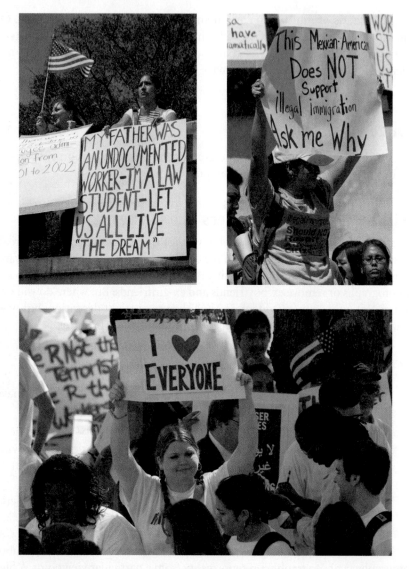

A photographer's choices about who and what to photograph shapes how we see an event.

However, charts and graphs can also be misleading. For example, a chart that compares the amounts of calories in competing brands of cereal might list one with 70 calories and another with 80 calories. If the chart begins at zero, the difference looks small. But if the chart starts at 60, the brand with 80 calories appears to have twice the calories of the brand with 70. Furthermore, the chart is worthless if the data is inaccurate or comes from an unreliable source. Creators of charts and graphs have an ethical obligation to present data as fairly and accurately as possible and to provide the sources of the data.

Ask these questions when you are analyzing charts and graphs

- Is the type of chart appropriate for the information presented?

 Bar and column charts make comparisons in particular categories. If two or more charts are compared, the scales should be consistent.

 Line graphs plot variables on a vertical and a horizontal axis. They are useful for showing proportional trends over time.

 Pie charts show the proportion of parts in terms of the whole. Segments must add up to 100 percent of the whole.

- Does the chart have a clear purpose?
- Does the title indicate the purpose?
- What do the units represent (dollars, people, voters, percentages, and so on)?
- What is the source of the data?
- Is there any distortion of information?

Evaluate informational graphics

Informational graphics more sophisticated than standard pie and bar charts have become a popular means of conveying information. Many are interactive, allowing viewers of a Web site to select the information they want displayed. These information graphics are a form of narrative argument, and the stories they tell have a rhetorical purpose. (See the examples on page 82.)

Build a Visual Analysis

It's one thing to construct a visual argument yourself; it's another thing to analyze visual arguments that are made by someone else. Fortunately, analyzing arguments made up of images and graphics is largely a matter of following the same strategies for rhetorical analysis that are outlined in Chapter 5—except that you must analyze images instead of (or in addition to) words. To put it another way, when you analyze

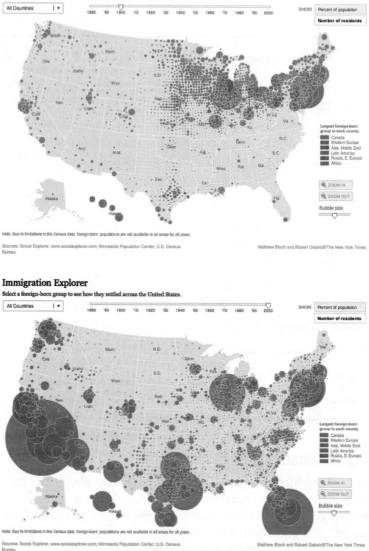

This set of information graphics on immigration tells a story. In 1900 the great majority of immigrants were from Western and Eastern Europe and Russia, and the majority settled in the Northeast and Midwest. In 2000 most immigrants came from Latin America, and they settled in Florida, Texas, and the West Coast along with the metropolitan areas of Chicago and New York City.

a visual argument, think about the image itself as well as its relationship to other images (and discourses). The arguments implied by visual images, like the arguments made through text alone, are carried both by the context and by the image.

Determination and hard work, at any age, can lead to being the best.
Hofstra University, just 50 years old, is already among the
top ten percent of American colleges and universities in
almost all academic criteria and resources.

Professionally accredited programs in such major areas as business,
engineering, law, psychology and education.

A library with over 1.1 million volumes *on campus*—a collection
larger than that of 95% of American universities.

Record enrollments with students from 31 states and 59 countries—
with a student-faculty ratio of only 17 to 1.

The largest, most sophisticated non-commercial television facility
in the East. A high technology undergraduate teaching
resource with broadcast-quality production capability.

A ranking in *Barron's Guide to the Most Prestigious Colleges*—one of
only 262 colleges and universities chosen from almost 4,000.

At Hofstra, determination, inspiration and hard work are qualities
our faculty demands in itself and instills in our students.

These qualities are what it takes to be the best. In anything.

HOFSTRA UNIVERSITY
WE TEACH SUCCESS.
50th Anniversary
Hempstead, L.I., New York 11550

Ad for Hofstra University, 1989

Analyze context

A critical analysis of a visual image, like the analyses of written arguments that we
discuss in the previous chapter, must include a consideration of context. Consider,
for example, the above advertisement for Hofstra University. The context for the ad
is not difficult to uncover through a bit of research. The ad appeared in 1989 and
1990 when Hofstra, located on Long Island 25 miles from New York City, was celebrating its fiftieth anniversary and hoping to use the occasion to enhance its esteem.
At the time, Hofstra enjoyed a good reputation for its professional programs, particularly in education and business (which one-third of the 7,500 students were

majoring in). However, it was not as highly regarded in the core science and humanities disciplines that are often associated with institutional prestige. In addition, Hofstra was quite well known in the New York metropolitan area—half its students were commuting to school rather than living in dormitories—but it was not attracting many students from outside the region, and its campus life was consequently regarded as mediocre. Its student body was generally well prepared, hardworking, and capable, but its most outstanding applicants were too often choosing other universities.

Feeling that its performance was exceeding its reputation and that it was capable of attracting a more diverse and talented student body, Hofstra developed a national ad campaign designed to change the opinions of prospective students and their parents, as well as the general public. It placed the ads—the ad reproduced here is one of a series—in several magazines and newspapers in order to persuade people that Hofstra was an outstanding university not just in the professions but in all fields, and that the opportunities available to its students were varied and valuable.

Analyze visual and textual elements

Ads make arguments, and the message of the Hofstra ad is something like this: "Hofstra is a prestigious, high-quality institution that brings out the best in students because of its facilities, its academic reputation, its student body, and the strength of its faculty and academic programs." The text of the Hofstra ad expresses that argument specifically: "The best" and "we teach success" are prominently displayed; the size of the print visually reinforces the message; and the fine print supports the main thesis by mentioning Hofstra's facilities (the large library with "a collection [of volumes] larger than that of 95% of American universities," the "television facility . . . with broadcast quality production capability"); its reputation (its ranking in *Barron's Guide to the Most Prestigious Colleges* and its "professionally accredited programs"); and its faculty and students. The ad works by offering good reasons and supporting arguments that are based on logical reasoning and evidence, as well as appeals to our most fervently held values. By placing the ad in prestigious publications, Hofstra enhanced its credibility even further.

In this chapter, however, we are emphasizing visuals in arguments. What kind of argument is made and supported by the image of the young girl with the flute? The photo of the girl is black and white, so that it can be printed easily and inexpensively in newspapers and magazines. But the black and white format also contributes a sense of reality and truthfulness, in the manner of black and white photos or documentary films. (Color images, on the other hand, can imply flashiness or commercialism.) Even in black and white, the image is quite arresting. In the context of an ad for Hofstra, the image is particularly intriguing. The girl is young—does she seem about ten or twelve years of age?—and her readiness for distinguished performance suggests that she is a prodigy, a genius—in other words, the kind of person that Hofstra attracts and sustains. The ad implies that you might encounter her on the Hofstra campus sometime: if she is not a student at Hofstra now, she soon will be. Come to Hofstra, and you too can acquire the traits associated with excellence and success.

The girl is dressed up for some kind of musical performance, and the details of her costume imply that the performance is of a high order: it is not just any costume, but one associated with professional performances of the most rarefied kind, a concert that calls for only the best musicians. The delicacy and refinement of the girl are implied by the posture of her fingers, the highly polished flute that she holds with an upright carriage, and the meticulousness of her tie, shirt, and coat. The girl's expression suggests that she is serious, sober, disciplined, but comfortable—the kind of student (and faculty member) that Hofstra features. (The layout and consistent print style used in the ad reinforce that impression: by offering a balanced and harmonious placement of elements and by sticking to the same type style throughout, the ad stands for the values of balance, harmony, consistency, and order.) The girl is modest and unpretentious in expression, yet she looks directly at the viewer with supreme self-confidence. Her age suggests innocence, yet her face proclaims ambition; her age and the quasi-masculine costume (note that she wears neither a ring nor earrings) give her a sexual innocence that is in keeping with the contemplative life. Come to Hofstra, the image proclaims, and you will meet people who are sober and graceful, self-disciplined and confident, ambitious without being arrogant. The ad is supporting its thesis with good reasons implied by its central image—good reasons that we identified with logos and pathos in the previous chapter.

Speaking of pathos, what do you make of the fact that the girl is Asian? On one hand, the Asian girl's demeanor reinforces cultural stereotypes. Delicate, small, sober, controlled, even humorless, she embodies characteristics that recall other Asian American icons (particularly women), especially icons of success through discipline and hard work. On the other hand, the girl speaks to the Asian community. It is as if she is on the verge of saying, "Come and join me at Hofstra, where you too can reach the highest achievement. And read the copy below me to learn more about what Hofstra has to offer." In this way the girl participates in Hofstra's ambition to attract highly qualified, highly motivated, and high-performing minority students—as well as any other high-performing student, regardless of ethnicity or gender, who values hard work, academic distinction, and the postponement of sensual gratification in return for long-term success.

If she is Asian, the girl is also thoroughly American. She appears not to be an international student but an American of immigrant stock. Her costume, her controlled black hair, and her unmarked face and fingers identify her as achieving the American dream of material success, physical health and well being, and class advancement. If her parents or grandparents came to New York or California as immigrants, they (and she) are now naturalized—100 percent American, completely successful. The social class element to the image is unmistakable: the entire ad speaks of Hofstra's ambition to be among the best, to achieve an elite status. When the ad appeared in 1989, Hofstra was attracting few of the nation's elite students. The girl signals a change. She displays the university's aspiration to become among the nation's elite—those who enjoy material success as well as the leisure, education, and sophistication to appreciate the finest music. That ambition is reinforced by the university's emblem in the lower right-hand corner of the ad. It resembles a coat of arms and is associated with royalty. Hofstra may be a community that is strong in the professions, but it also values the arts.

No doubt there are other aspects of the image that work to articulate and to support the complex argument of the ad. There is more to be said about this ad, and you may disagree with some of the points we have offered. But consider this: By 2009, twenty years after the ad was run, Hofstra's total enrollment had climbed above 12,000, with 7,500 undergraduates. Its admissions were more selective, its student body was more diverse and less regional in character, its graduation rate had improved, its sports teams had achieved national visibility, and its minority student population had grown. Many factors contributed to the university's advancement, but it seems likely that this ad was one of them.

Write a Visual Analysis

Like rhetorical analysis, effective visual analysis takes into account the context of the image as well as its visual elements and any surrounding text. When you analyze a visual image, look carefully at its details and thoroughly consider its context. What visual elements grab your attention first, and how do other details reinforce that impression—what is most important and less important? How do color and style influence impressions? How does the image direct the viewer's eyes and reinforce what is important? What is the relationship between the image and any text that might accompany it? Consider the shapes, colors, and details of the image, as well as how the elements of the image connect with different arguments and audiences.

Consider also what you know or can learn about the context of an image and the design and text that surround it. Try to determine why and when it was created, who created it, where it appeared, and the target audience. Think about how the context of its creation and publication affected its intended audience. What elements have you seen before? Which elements remind you of other visuals?

Sample Student Visual Analysis

Discussion board posts are a frequent assignment in writing classes. Usually they are short essays, no more than 300 words. Sources of any information still need to be cited.

The assignment for this post was to find and analyze an example of a visual metaphor.

Thread: "Use Only What You Need" : The Denver Water Conservation
Campaign
Author: Chrissy Yao
Posted Date: March 1, 2010 1:12 PM

Partial bus bench from Denver Water's conservation campaign

In 2006, Denver Water, the city's oldest water utility, launched a
water ten-year conservation plan based on using water efficiently
("Conservation"). Denver Water teamed up with the Sukle Advertising
firm and produced the "Use Only What You Need Campaign" to help
alleviate the water crisis that the city was enduring (Samuel). The
campaign uses billboard advertising, magazine ads, and even stripped-
down cars to impart messages of water conservation and efficiency. •——

> Yao describes the ad campaign which uses the partial bus bench.

Clever visual metaphors are at the heart of the campaign. One
example is a park bench with available seating only for one individual.
The words, "USE ONLY WHAT YOU NEED," are stenciled in on the back of
the bench. The bench, which can actually be used for sitting, conveys the
idea that if only one person were using the bench, that would only need
a small area to sit on, not the whole thing. The bench makes concrete •——
the concept of water conservation.

> Yao analyzes the visual metaphor.

The innovative ad campaign that uses objects in addition to
traditional advertising has proven successful. The simplicity and minimal-
ist style of the ads made a convincing argument about using resources
sparingly. The average water consumption of Denver dropped between
18% and 21% annually from 2006 to 2009.

Works Cited

"Conservation." *Denver Water*. Denver Water, 2010. Web. 23 Feb. 2010.

Samuel, Frederick. "Denver Water." *Ad Goodness*. N.p., 16 Nov. 2006. Web. 24 Feb. 2010.

PEARSON
mycomplab

For support in learning this chapter's content, follow this path in MyCompLab:
> Resources > Media Index > Visual Analysis and Rhetoric.

Review the Instruction and Multimedia resources, then complete the Exercises and click on Gradebook to measure your progress.

Writing Arguments

7 | Putting Good Reasons into Action

QUICK TAKE

In this chapter, you will learn that

1. Most arguments use multiple approaches to achieve a specific purpose (see below)
2. Thinking explicitly about the structure of arguments can help identify different ways to approach your topic (see below)
3. Using different kinds of arguments can help you get started writing about a complex topic (see page 92)

Find a Purpose for Writing an Argument

Imagine that you bought a new car in June and you are taking some of your friends to your favorite lake over the Fourth of July weekend. You have a great time until, as you are heading home, a drunk driver—a repeat offender—swerves into your lane and totals your new car. You and your friends are lucky not to be hurt, but you're outraged because you believe that repeat offenders should be prevented from driving, even if that means putting them in jail. You also remember going to another state that had sobriety checkpoints on holiday weekends. If such a checkpoint had been at the lake, you might still be driving your new car. You live in a town that encourages citizens to contribute to the local newspaper, and you think you could get a guest editorial published. The question is, how do you want to write the editorial?

- You could tell your story about how a repeat drunk driver endangered the lives of you and your friends.
- You could define driving while intoxicated (DWI) as a more legally culpable crime.
- You could compare the treatment of drunk drivers in your state with the treatment of drunk drivers in another state.
- You could cite statistics that alcohol-related accidents killed 13,846 people in 2008.
- You could evaluate the present drunk-driving laws as insufficiently just or less than totally successful.

- You could propose taking vehicles away from repeat drunk drivers and forcing them to serve mandatory sentences.
- You could argue that your community should have sobriety checkpoints at times when drunk drivers are likely to be on the road.
- You could do several of the above.

Finding Good Reasons

What do we mean by diversity?

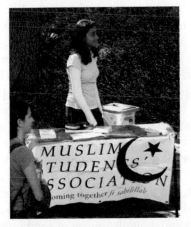

Colleges and universities talk a great deal about diversity nowadays, but what exactly do they mean by *diversity*? If diversity is connected with people, do they mean diversity of races and ethnicities? Is it diversity of nations and cultures represented among the students? Should the numbers of students of different races, ethnicities, or family income levels be roughly equal to the population of the state where the school is located? Is a campus diverse if about 60 percent of the students are women and 40 percent men, as many campuses now are? Or if diversity is connected with ideas, what makes for a diverse intellectual experience on a college campus?

Write about it

1. Formulate your own definition of what diversity means on a college campus (see Chapter 8).
2. Evaluate diversity on your campus according to your definition. Is your campus good or bad in its diversity (see Chapter 10)?
3. What are the effects of having a diverse campus, however you define diversity (see Chapter 9)? What happens if a campus isn't diverse?
4. If you consider diversity desirable, write a proposal that would increase diversity on your campus, whether it's interacting with people of different backgrounds or encountering a variety of ideas (see Chapter 13). Or if you think too much emphasis is being placed on diversity, write a rebuttal argument against proponents of diversity (see Chapter 12).

Get Started Writing About Complex Issues

You're not going to have much space in the newspaper, so you decide to argue for sobriety checkpoints. You know that they are controversial. One of your friends who was in the car with you said that the checkpoints are unconstitutional because they involve search without cause. However, after doing some research to find out whether checkpoints are defined as legal or illegal, you learn that on June 14, 1990, the U.S. Supreme Court upheld the constitutionality of using checkpoints as a deterrent and enforcement tool against drunk drivers.

But you still want to know whether most people would agree with your friend that sobriety checkpoints are an invasion of privacy. You find opinion polls and surveys going back to the 1980s that show that 70 to 80 percent of those polled support sobriety checkpoints. You also realize that you can argue by analogy that security checkpoints for alcohol are similar in many ways to airport security checkpoints that protect passengers. You decide you will finish by making an argument from consequence. If people who go to the lake with plans to drink know in advance that there will be checkpoints, they will find a designated driver or some other means of safe transportation, and everyone else will also be a lot safer.

The point of this example is that people very rarely set out to define something in an argument for the sake of definition, to compare for the sake of comparison, or to adopt any of the other ways of structuring an argument. Instead, they have a purpose in mind, and they use the kinds of arguments that are discussed in Chapters 8–13—most often in combination—as means to an end. Most arguments use multiple approaches and multiple sources of good reasons.

PEARSON
mycomplab

For support in learning this chapter's content, follow this path in MyCompLab:
⟩Resources ⟩Writing ⟩The Writing Process ⟩Planning.
Review the Instruction and Multimedia resources, then complete the Exercises and click on Gradebook to measure your progress.

8 | Definition Arguments

QUICK TAKE

In this chapter, you will learn that

1. Definition arguments set out criteria and argue that something meets or doesn't meet those criteria (see page 94)
2. Definitions work by classification and example (see page 95)
3. Because definition arguments are the most powerful arguments, they are often at the center of the most important debates in American history (see page 96)

Graffiti dates back to the ancient Egyptian, Greek, Roman, and Mayan civilizations. Is graffiti vandalism? Or is it art? The debate has gone on for three decades. In the 1980s New York City's subways were covered with graffiti. Many New Yorkers believe that removing graffiti from subway cars was a first step toward the much-celebrated social and economic recovery of the city. For them graffiti was a sign that the subways were not safe. But at the same time, Martha Cooper and Henry Chalfant released a book titled *Subway* Art—a picture book—that celebrated graffiti-covered subways as an art form. Should we appreciate graffiti as the people's art or should graffiti be removed as quickly as possible, which many cities advocate?

Understand How Definition Arguments Work

Definition arguments set out criteria and then argue that whatever is being defined meets or does not meet those criteria.

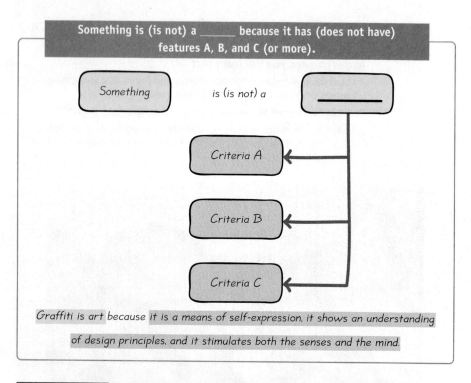

Something is (is not) a _____ because it has (does not have) features A, B, and C (or more).

Something | is (is not) a | _____

Criteria A

Criteria B

Criteria C

Graffiti is art because it is a means of self-expression. it shows an understanding of design principles. and it stimulates both the senses and the mind.

Recognize Kinds of Definitions

Rarely do you get far into an argument without having to define something. Imagine that you are writing an argument about the decades-old and largely ineffective "war on drugs" in the United States. We all know that the war on drugs is being waged against drugs that are illegal, like cocaine and marijuana, and not against the legal drugs produced by the multibillion-dollar drug industry. Our society classifies drugs into two categories: "good" drugs, which are legal, and "bad" drugs, which are illegal.

How exactly does our society arrive at these definitions? Drugs would be relatively easy to define as good or bad if the difference could be defined at the molecular level. Bad drugs would contain certain molecules that define them as bad. The history of drug use in the United States, however, tells us that it is not so simple. In the twentieth century alcohol was on the list of illegal drugs for over a decade, while opium was considered a good drug and was distributed in many patent medicines by pharmaceutical companies. Similarly, LSD and MDMA (methylenedioxymethamphetamine, known better by its street name *ecstasy*) were developed by the pharmaceutical industry but later made illegal. In a few states marijuana is now legal for medicinal use.

If drugs cannot be classified as good or bad by their molecular structure, then perhaps society classifies them by their effects. It might be reasonable to assume that addictive drugs are illegal, but that's not the case. Nicotine is highly addictive and is a legal drug, as are many prescription medicines. Drugs taken for the purpose of pleasure are not necessarily illegal (think of alcohol and Viagra), nor are drugs that alter consciousness or change personality (such as Prozac).

How a drug is defined as legal or illegal apparently is determined by example. The nationwide effort to stop Americans from drinking alcohol during the first decades of the twentieth century led to the passage of the Eighteenth Amendment and the ban on sales of alcohol from 1920 to 1933, known as Prohibition. Those who argued for Prohibition used examples of drunkenness, especially among the poor, to show how alcohol broke up families and left mothers and children penniless in the street. Those who opposed Prohibition initially pointed to the consumption of beer and wine in many cultural traditions. Later they raised examples of the bad effects of Prohibition—the rise of organized crime, the increase in alcohol abuse, and the general disregard for laws.

When you make a definition argument, it's important to think about what kind of definition you will use. Descriptions of three types follow.

Formal definitions

Formal definitions typically categorize an item into the next-higher classification and provide criteria that distinguish the item from other items within that classification. Most dictionary definitions are formal definitions. For example, fish are cold-blooded aquatic vertebrates that have jaws, fins, and scales and are distinguished from other cold-blooded aquatic vertebrates (such as sea snakes) by the presence of gills. If you can construct a formal definition with a specific classification and differentiating criteria that your audience will accept, then likely you will have a strong argument. The key is to get your audience to agree to your classification and criteria. Often your argument will amount to revising your audience's view of the classification or criteria (or both). For instance, imagine that you want to change your audience's view of contemporary universities. You might construct a thesis statement something like this: "While most people still think of universities as institutions [classification] of higher learning that prepare people for citizenship and the workplace [differentiating criteria], they are actually nothing more than big businesses" [revised classification].

Operational definitions

Many concepts cannot be easily defined by formal definitions. Researchers in the natural and social sciences must construct **operational definitions** that they use for their research. For example, researchers who study binge drinking among college students define a binge as five or more drinks in one sitting for a man, and four or more drinks for a woman. Some people think this standard is too low and should be raised to six to eight drinks to distinguish true problem drinkers from the general college population. No matter what the number, researchers must argue that the particular definition is one that suits the concept.

Definitions from example

Many human qualities such as honesty, courage, creativity, deceit, and love must be defined by examples that the audience accepts as representative of the concept. Few would not call the firefighters who entered the World Trade Center on September 11, 2001, courageous. Most people would describe someone with a diagnosis of terminal cancer who refuses to feel self-pity as courageous. But what about a student who declines to go to a concert with her friends so she can study for an exam? Her behavior might be admirable, but most people would hesitate to call it courageous. The key to arguing a **definition from example** is that the examples must strike the audience as typical of the concept, even if the situation is unusual.

Build a Definition Argument

Because definition arguments are so powerful, they are found at the center of some of the most important debates in American history. Definition arguments were at the heart of the abolition of slavery, for example, and many of the major arguments of the civil rights movement were based on definitions. Martin Luther King, Jr.'s, "Letter from Birmingham Jail" is one eloquent example.

King was jailed in April 1963 for leading a series of peaceful protests in Birmingham, Alabama. While he was being held in solitary confinement, Rev. King wrote a letter to eight white Birmingham clergymen. These religious leaders had issued a statement urging an end to the protests in their city. King argued that it was necessary to act now rather than wait for change. His purpose in writing the argument was to win acceptance for the protests and protestors and to make his audience see that the anti-segregationists were not agitators and rabble-rousers,

U.S. National Guard troops block off Beale Street in Memphis, Tennessee, as striking sanitation workers wearing placards reading, "I AM A MAN" pass by on March 29, 1968. Rev. Martin Luther King, Jr., returned to Memphis to lead the march and was assassinated a week later on April 4.

but citizens acting responsibly to correct a grave injustice. A critical part of King's argument is his definition of "just" and "unjust" laws.

Supporters of segregation in Birmingham had obtained a court order forbidding further protests, and the eight white clergymen urged King and his supporters to obey the courts. Our society generally assumes that laws, and the courts that enforce them, should be obeyed. King, however, argues that there are two categories of laws, and that citizens must treat one category differently from the other. Morally just laws, King argues, should be obeyed, but unjust ones should not. By distinguishing two different kinds of laws, King creates a rationale for obeying some laws and disobeying others. He then completes his definitional argument by showing how segregation laws fit the definition of "unjust." Once his audience accepts his placement of segregation laws in the "unjust" category, they must also accept that King and his fellow protestors were right to break those laws.

King maintains in his letter that people have a moral responsibility to obey just laws, and, by the same logic, "a moral responsibility to disobey unjust laws." His argument rests on the clear moral and legal criteria he uses to define just and unjust laws. Without these criteria, people could simply disobey any law they chose, which is what King's detractors accused him of advocating. King had to show that he was in fact acting on principle, and that he and his supporters wanted to establish justice, not cause chaos.

Here's how King makes the distinction between just and unjust laws:

> A just law is a man-made code that squares with the moral law of God. An unjust law is a code that is out of harmony with the moral law. . . . Any law that uplifts human personality is just. Any law that degrades human personality is unjust. All segregation statutes are unjust because segregation distorts the soul and damages the personality. It gives the segregator a false sense of superiority and the segregated a false sense of inferiority.

According to King, a just law meets the criteria of being consistent with moral law and uplifting human personality. An unjust law does not meet these criteria. Instead, it is out of harmony with moral law and damages human personality. King's claim that

> "All segregation laws are unjust because segregation distorts the soul and damages the personality"

uses the structure described at the beginning of this chapter:

Something is (or is not) a ___ because it has (does not have) features A, B, and C.

Building an extended definition argument like King's is a two-step process. First, you have to establish the criteria for the categories you wish to define. In King's letter, consistency with moral law and uplifting of the human spirit are set forth as criteria for a just law. King provides arguments from St. Thomas Aquinas, a religious authority likely to carry significant weight with Birmingham clergymen and others who will read the letter.

Second, you must convince your audience that the particular case in question meets or doesn't meet the criteria. King cannot simply state that segregation laws are unjust; he must provide evidence showing how they fail to meet the criteria for a just law. Specifically, he notes the segregation "gives the segregator a false sense of superiority and the segregated a false sense of inferiority." These false senses of self are a distortion or degradation of the human personality.

Sometimes definition arguments have to argue for the relevance of the criteria. King, in fact, spent a great deal of his letter laying out and defending his criteria for just and unjust laws. While he addressed his letter to clergymen, he knew that it would find a wider audience. Therefore, he did not rely solely on criteria linked to moral law, or the "law of God." People who were not especially religious might not be convinced by those parts of his argument. King presents two additional criteria for just laws that he knows will appeal to those who value the democratic process. He argues that "an unjust law is a code that a numerical or power majority group compels a minority group to obey but does not make binding on itself." In other words, a just law is the law for everyone. It is fairly easy to show how segregation laws fail to meet this criterion. These laws commonly prevented African Americans from using certain facilities reserved for whites, for example, but did not compel whites to stay out of African American seating areas on buses.

King also argues that a just law is a law created by representatives of the people the law will affect. He shows how segregation laws fail to match this criterion by pointing out that many African Americans had been denied the right to vote in Alabama. Consequently, the legislature that passed the segregation laws was not democratically elected.

When you build a definition argument, often you must put much effort into identifying and explaining your criteria. You must convince your readers that your criteria are the best ones for what you are defining and that they apply to the case you are arguing.

King's Extended Definition Argument

After establishing criteria for two kinds of laws, *just* and *unjust*, King argues that citizens must respond differently to laws that are unjust, by disobeying them. He then shows how the special case of *segregation laws* meets the criteria for unjust laws. If readers accept his argument, they will agree that segregation laws belong in the category of unjust laws, and therefore must be disobeyed.

Criteria for Just Laws	Criteria for Unjust Laws	Segregation Laws
Consistent with moral law	Not consistent with moral law	✓
Uplift human personality	Damage human personality	✓
Must be obeyed by all people	Must be obeyed by some people, but not others	✓
Made by democratically elected Representatives	Not made by democratically elected representatives	✓
Appropriate Response to Just Laws: All citizens should obey them.	Appropriate Response to Unjust Laws: All citizens should disobey them.	

Finding Good Reasons

What is Parody?

YouTube parody of an Apple iPad commercial as a "Big Ol' iPod Touch"

Downfall, a German film released in 2004 about Hitler's last days, has been used for hundreds of popular YouTube parodies. Most parodies use the same scene of a defeated Hitler, played by Bruno Ganz, unleashing a furious speech to his staff in German with YouTubers adding English subtitles on topics as varied as the plot of *Avatar*, the upgrade to Windows 7, Apple's iPad, academic grant reviews, and the failure of various sports teams to win big games.

The owner of the rights to the film, Constantin Films, demanded that YouTube take down the parodies in April 2010, and YouTube complied. Critics of the move complained that Constantin Films used YouTube's Content ID filter to determine what is acceptable rather than the fair use provisions of copyright law. They argue that fair-use law allows a film clip, a paragraph from an article, or a short piece of music to be adapted if the purpose is to create commentary or satire.

Write about it

1. Which of the following criteria do you think must be present for a work to be considered a parody? Are there any criteria you might change or add?
   - the work criticizes a previous work
   - the work copies the same structure, details, or style of the previous work
   - the connections to the previous work are clear to the audience
   - the work is humorous
   - the title is a play on the previous work
   - the work is presented in either a print, visual, or musical medium

2. Do the various uses of the *Downfall* clip meet the criteria above? Would you define them as parodies? Why or why not?

Steps to Writing a Definition Argument

Step 1 Make a Claim

Make a definitional claim on a controversial issue that focuses on a key term.

Template

_____ is (or is not) a _____ because it has (or does not have) features A, B, and C (or more).

Examples

- Hate speech (or pornography, literature, films, and so on) is (or is not) free speech protected by the First Amendment because it has (or does not have) these features.

- Hunting (or using animals for cosmetics testing, keeping animals in zoos, wearing furs, and so on) is (or is not) cruelty to animals because it has (or does not have) these features.

Step 2 Think About What's at Stake

- Does nearly everyone agree with you? If so, then your claim probably isn't interesting or important. If you can think of people who disagree, then something is at stake.
- Who argues the opposite of your claim?
- Why or how do they benefit from a different definition?

Step 3 List the Criteria

- Which criteria are necessary for _____ to be a _____?
- Which are the most important?
- Does your case in point meet all the criteria?

Step 4 Analyze Your Potential Readers

- Who are your readers?
- How does the definitional claim you are making affect them?
- How familiar are they with the issue, concept, or controversy that you're writing about?
- Which criteria are they most likely to accept with little explanation, and which will they disagree with?

Step 5 Write a Draft

Introduction
- Set out the issue, concept, or controversy.
- Give the background that your intended readers need.

Body
- Set out your criteria and argue for the appropriateness of the criteria.
- Anticipate where readers might question either your criteria or how they apply to your subject.
- Address opposing viewpoints by acknowledging how their definitions differ and by showing why your definition is better.

Conclusion
- Do more than simply summarize. You can, for example, go into more detail about what is at stake or the implications of your definition.

Step 6 Revise, Edit, Proofread

- For detailed instructions, see Chapter 4.
- For a checklist to use to evaluate your draft, see pages 48–49.

Michael
Pollan

Eat Food: Food Defined

Michael Pollan is a journalism professor at the University of California, Berkeley, and the author of *In Defense of Food: An Eater's Manifesto* (2008), from which this excerpt is taken. *In Defense of Food* received many prizes and was named one of the ten best books of the year by the *New York Times* and the *Washington Post*. Pollan is also the author of *Second Nature* (1991), *A Place of My Own* (1997), *The Botany of Desire: A Plant's Eye View of the World* (2001), *The Omnivore's Dilemma: A Natural History of Four Meals* (2006), and *Food Rules* (2010). He is also a contributing writer for the *New York Times Magazine*.

Pollan asks why Americans worry so much about nutrition and yet seem so unhealthy. The title, *In Defense of Food*, is one of the many paradoxes that Pollan examines in the book. After all, why should food need defending if it is plentiful and we eat so much of it? Pollan argues that the answer lies in how we define food.

Pollan begins by asking why does food need to be defined?

The first time I heard the advice to "just eat food" it was in a speech by Joan Gussow, and it completely baffled me. Of course you should eat food—what else is there to eat? But Gussow, who grows much of her own food on a flood-prone finger of land jutting into the Hudson River, refuses to dignify most of the products for sale in the supermarket with that title. "In the thirty-four years I've been in the field of nutrition," she said in the same speech, "I have watched real food disappear from large areas of the supermarket and from much of the rest of the eating world." Taking food's place on the shelves has been an unending stream of foodlike substitutes, some seventeen thousand new ones every year—"products constructed largely around commerce and hope, supported by frighteningly little actual knowledge." Ordinary food is still out there, however, still being grown and even occasionally sold in the supermarket, and this ordinary food is what we should eat.

Pollan claims that everything that pretends to be food really isn't food, thus establishing the need for a definition.

2   But given our current state of confusion and given the thousands of products calling themselves food, this is more easily said than done. So consider these related rules of thumb. Each proposes a different sort of map to the contemporary food landscape, but all should take you to more or less the same place.

Don't eat anything your great grandmother wouldn't recognize as food.

3   Why your great grandmother? Because at this point your mother and possibly even your grandmother is as confused as the rest of us; to be safe we need to go back at least a couple generations, to a time before the advent of most modern foods. So depending on your age (and your grandmother), you may need to

go back to your great- or even great-great grandmother. Some nutritionists recommend going back even further. John Yudkin, a British nutritionist whose early alarms about the dangers of refined carbohydrates were overlooked in the 1960s and 1970s, once advised, "Just don't eat anything your Neolithic ancestors wouldn't have recognized and you'll be OK."

Pollan's first criterion of what is food offers a simple concept.

4   What would shopping this way mean in the supermarket? Well, imagine your great grandmother at your side as you roll down the aisles. You're standing together in front of the dairy case. She picks up a package of Go-Gurt Portable Yogurt tubes—and has no idea what this could possibly be. Is it a food or a toothpaste? And how, exactly, do you introduce it into your body? You could tell her it's just yogurt in a squirtable form, yet if she read the ingredients label she would have every reason to doubt that that was in fact the case. Sure, there's some yogurt in there, but there are also a dozen other things that aren't remotely yogurt like, ingredients she would probably fail to recognize as foods of any kind, including high-fructose corn syrup, modified corn starch, kosher gelatin, carrageenan, tri-calcium phosphate, natural and artificial flavors, vitamins, and so forth. (And there's a whole other list of ingredients for the "berry bubblegum bash" flavoring, containing everything but berries or bubblegum.) How did yogurt, which in your great grandmother's day consisted simply of milk inoculated with a bacterial culture, ever get to be so complicated? Is a product like Go-Gurt Portable Yogurt still a whole food? A food of any kind? Or is it just a food product?

Another way of defining food is to define what isn't food, but what Pollan calls "food products."

5   There are in fact hundreds of foodish products in the supermarket that your ancestors simply wouldn't recognize as food: breakfast cereal bars transected by bright white veins representing, but in reality having nothing to do with, milk; "protein waters" and "nondairy creamer"; cheeselike food-stuffs equally innocent of any bovine contribution; cakelike cylinders (with creamlike fillings) called Twinkies that never grow stale. Don't eat anything incapable of rotting is another personal policy you might consider adopting.

6   There are many reasons to avoid eating such complicated food products beyond the various chemical additives and corn and soy derivatives they contain. One of the problems with the products of food science is that, as Joan Gussow has pointed out, they lie to your body; their artificial colors and flavors and synthetic sweeteners and novel fats confound the senses we rely on to assess new foods and prepare our bodies to deal with them. Foods that lie leave us with little choice but to eat by the numbers, consulting labels rather than our senses.

7   It's true that foods have long been processed in order to preserve them, as when we pickle or ferment or smoke, but industrial processing aims to do much more than extend shelf life. Today foods are processed in ways specifically designed to sell us more food by pushing our evolutionary buttons—our inborn preferences

for sweetness and fat and salt. These qualities are difficult to find in nature but cheap and easy for the food scientist to deploy, with the result that processing induces us to consume much more of these ecological rarities than is good for us. "Tastes great, less filling!" could be the motto for most processed foods, which are far more energy dense than most whole foods: They contain much less water, fiber, and micronutrients, and generally much more sugar and fat, making them at the same time, to coin a marketing slogan, "More fattening, less nutritious!"

8   The great grandma rule will help keep many of these products out of your cart. But not all of them. Because thanks to the FDA's willingness, post–1973, to let food makers freely alter the identity of "traditional foods that everyone knows" without having to call them imitations, your great grandmother could easily be fooled into thinking that that loaf of bread or wedge of cheese is in fact a loaf of bread or a wedge of cheese. This is why we need a slightly more detailed personal policy to capture these imitation foods; to wit:

What food is can also be defined by what it isn't, hence a list of criteria for what isn't food.

Avoid food products containing ingredients that are a) unfamiliar set, b) unpronounceable, c) more than five in number, or that include d) high-fructose corn syrup.

9   None of these characteristics, not even the last one, is necessarily harmful in and of itself, but all of them are reliable markers for foods that have been highly processed to the point where they may no longer be what they purport to be. They have crossed over from foods to food products.

Pollan points out that the language used for food products is as convoluted as the ingredients.

10   Consider a loaf of bread, one of the "traditional foods that everyone knows" specifically singled out for protection in the 1938 imitation rule. As your grandmother could tell you, bread is traditionally made using a remarkably small number of familiar ingredients: flour, yeast, water, and a pinch of salt will do it. But industrial bread— even industrial whole-grain bread—has become a far more complicated product of modern food science (not to mention commerce and hope). Here's the complete ingredients list for Sara Lee's Soft & Smooth Whole Grain White Bread. (Wait a minute—isn't "Whole Grain White Bread" a contradiction in terms? Evidently not any more.)

> Enriched bleached flour [wheat flour, malted barley flour, niacin, iron, thiamin mononitrate (vitamin B), riboflavin (vitamin B_2), folic acid], water, whole grains [whole wheat flour, brown rice flour (rice flour, rice bran)], high fructose corn syrup [hello!], whey, wheat gluten, yeast, cellulose. Contains 2% or less of each of the following: honey, calcium sulfate, vegetable oil (soybean and/or cottonseed oils), salt, butter (cream, salt), dough conditioners (may contain one or more of the following: mono- and diglycerides, ethoxylated mono- and diglycerides, ascorbic acid, enzymes, azodicarbonamide),

guar gum, calcium propionate (preservative), distilled vinegar, yeast nutrients (monocalcium phosphate, calcium sulfate, ammonium sulfate), corn starch, natural flavor, beta-carotene (color), vitamin D_3, soy lecithin, soy flour.

11   There are many things you could say about this intricate loaf of "bread," but note first that even if it managed to slip by your great grandmother (because it is a loaf of bread, or at least is called one and strongly resembles one), the product fails every test proposed under rule number two: It's got unfamiliar ingredients (monoglycerides I've heard of before, but ethoxylated monoglycerides?); unpronounceable ingredients (try "azodicarbonamide"); it exceeds the maximum of five ingredients (by roughly thirty-six); and it contains high-fructose corn syrup. Sorry, Sara Lee, but your Soft & Smooth Whole Grain White Bread is not food and if not for the indulgence of the FDA could not even be labeled "bread."

12   Sara Lee's Soft & Smooth Whole Grain White Bread could serve as a monument to the age of nutritionism. It embodies the latest nutritional wisdom from science and government (which in its most recent food pyramid recommends that at least half our consumption of grain come from whole grains) but leavens that wisdom with the commercial recognition that American eaters (and American children in particular) have come to prefer their wheat highly refined—which is to say, cottony soft, snowy white, and exceptionally sweet on the tongue. In its marketing materials, Sara Lee treats this clash of interests as some sort of Gordian knot—it speaks in terms of an ambitious quest to build a "no compromise" loaf—which only the most sophisticated food science could possibly cut.

13   And so it has, with the invention of whole-grain white bread. Because the small percentage of whole grains in the bread would render it that much less sweet than, say, all-white Wonder Bread—which scarcely waits to be chewed before transforming itself into glucose—the food scientists have added high-fructose corn syrup and honey to to make up the difference; to overcome the problematic heft and toothsomeness of a real whole grain bread, they've deployed "dough conditioners," including guar gum and the aforementioned azodicarbonamide, to simulate the texture of supermarket white bread. By incorporating certain varieties of albino wheat, they've managed to maintain that deathly but apparently appealing Wonder Bread pallor.

14   Who would have thought Wonder Bread would ever become an ideal of aesthetic and gustatory perfection to which bakers would actually aspire—Sara Lee's Mona Lisa?

15   Very often food science's efforts to make traditional foods more nutritious make them much more complicated, but not necessarily any better for you. To make dairy products low fat, it's not enough to remove the fat. You then have to go to great lengths to

preserve the body or creamy texture by working in all kinds of food additives. In the case of low-fat or skim milk that usually means adding powdered milk. But powdered milk contains oxidized cholesterol, which scientists believe is much worse for your arteries than ordinary cholesterol, so food makers sometimes compensate by adding antioxidants, further complicating what had been a simple one-ingredient whole food. Also, removing the fat makes it that much harder for your body to absorb the fat-soluble vitamins that are one of the reasons to drink milk in the first place.

16   All this heroic and occasionally counterproductive food science has been undertaken in the name of our health—so that Sara Lee can add to its plastic wrapper the magic words "good source of whole grain" or a food company can ballyhoo the even more magic words "low fat." Which brings us to a related food policy that may at first sound counterintuitive to a health-conscious eater:

Avoid Food Products That Make Health Claims.

17   For a food product to make health claims on its package it must first have a package, so right off the bat it's more likely to be a processed than a whole food. Generally speaking, it is only the big food companies that have the wherewithal to secure FDA-approved health claims for their products and there trumpet them to the world. Recently, however, some of the tonier fruits and nuts have begun boasting about their health-enhancing properties, and there will surely be more as each crop council scrounges together the money to commission its own scientific study. Because all plants contain antioxidants, all these studies are guaranteed to find something on which to base a health oriented marketing campaign.

18   But for the most part it is the products of food science that make the boldest health claims, and these are often founded on incomplete and often erroneous science—the dubious fruits of nutritionism. Don't forget that trans-fat-rich margarine, one of the first industrial foods to claim it was healthier than the traditional food it replaced, turned out to give people heart attacks. Since that debacle, the FDA, under tremendous pressure from industry, has made it only easier for food companies to make increasingly doubtful health claims, such as the one Frito-Lay now puts on some of its chips—that eating them is somehow good for your heart. If you bother to read the health claims closely (as food marketers make sure consumers seldom do), you will find that there is often considerably less to them than meets the eye.

19   Consider a recent "qualified" health claim approved by the FDA for (don't laugh) corn oil. ("Qualified" is a whole new category of health claim, introduced in 2002 at the behest of industry.) Corn oil, you may recall, is particularly high in the omega-6 fatty acids we're already consuming far too many of.

Very limited and preliminary scientific evidence suggests that eating about one tablespoon (16 grams) of corn oil daily may reduce the risk of heart disease due to the unsaturated fat content in corn oil.

20 The tablespoon is a particularly rich touch, conjuring images of moms administering medicine, or perhaps cod-liver oil, to their children. But what the FDA gives with one hand, it takes away with the other. Here's the small-print "qualification" of this already notably diffident health claim:

> [The] FDA concludes that there is little scientific evidence supporting this claim.
>
> To achieve this possible benefit, corn oil is to replace a similar amount of saturated fat and not increase the total number of calories you eat in a day.

Close reading of labels undercuts health claims of food products.

21 This little masterpiece of pseudoscientific bureaucratese was extracted from the FDA by the manufacturer of Mazola corn oil. It would appear that "qualified" is an official FDA euphemism for "all but meaningless." Though someone might have let the consumer in on the game: The FDA's own research indicates that consumers have no idea what to make of qualified health claims (how would they?), and its rules allow companies to promote the claims pretty much any way they want—they can use really big type for the claim, for example, and then print the disclaimers in teeny-tiny type. No doubt we can look forward to a qualified health claim for high-fructose corn syrup, a tablespoon of which probably does contribute to your health—as long as it replaces a comparable amount of, say, poison in your diet and doesn't increase the total number of calories you eat in a day.

22 When corn oil and chips and sugary breakfast cereals can all boast being good for your heart, health claims have become hopelessly corrupt. The American Heart Association currently bestows (for a fee) its heart-healthy seal of approval on Lucky Charms, Cocoa Puffs, and Trix cereals, Yoo-hoo lite chocolate drink, and Healthy Choice's Premium Caramel Swirl Ice Cream Sandwich—this at a time when scientists are coming to recognize that dietary sugar probably plays a more important role in heart disease than dietary fat. Meanwhile, the genuinely heart-healthy whole foods in the produce section, lacking the financial and political clout of the packaged goods a few aisles over, are mute. But don't take the silence of the yams as a sign that they have nothing valuable to say about health.

Pollan adds a playful touch by echoing the title of a popular movie to make a point.

Sample Student Definition Argument

Conley 1

Patrice Conley
Professor Douglas
English 101
15 Nov. 2010

Flagrant Foul: The NCAA's Definition of Student Athletes as Amateurs

Every year, thousands of student athletes across America sign the National Collegiate Athletic Association's Form 08-3a, the "Student-Athlete" form, waiving their right to receive payment for the use of their name and image (McCann). The form defines student athletes as amateurs, who cannot receive payment for playing their sports. While their schools and coaches may make millions of dollars in salaries and endorsement deals and are the highest-paid public employees in many states, student athletes can never earn a single penny from their college athletic careers.

Make no mistake: college athletics are big business. The most visible college sports—big-time men's football and basketball—generate staggering sums of money. For example, the twelve universities in the Southeastern Conference receive $205 million each year from CBS and ESPN for the right to broadcast its football games (Smith and Ourand). Even more money comes in from video games, clothing, and similar licenses. In 2010, the *New York Times* reported, "the NCAA's licensing deals are estimated at more than $4 billion" per year (Thamel). While the staggering executive pay at big corporations has brought public outrage, coaches' salaries are even more outlandish. Kentucky basketball coach, John Calipari, is paid over $4 million a year for a basketball program that makes about $35-40 million a year, more than 10% of the entire revenue. Tom Van Riper observes that no corporate CEO commands this large a share of the profits. He notes that if Steve Ballmer, the CEO at Microsoft, had Calipari's deal, Ballmer would make over $6 billion a year.

How can colleges allow advertisers, arena operators, concession owners, athletic gear manufacturers, retailers, game companies, and media moguls, along with coaches and university officials, to make millions and pay the stars of the show nothing? The answer is that colleges define

Patrice Conley sets out the definition she is attempting to rectify: amateurs are athletes who aren't paid.

Conley identifies what's at st[...]

Conley disputes t[...] definition [...] college sp[...] are amate[...] sports.

The huge salaries p[...] to college[...] coaches a[...] comparab[...] to those i[...] professio[...] sports.

Conley 2

athletes as amateurs. Not only are student athletes not paid for playing their sport, they cannot receive gifts and are not allowed to endorse products, which may be a violation of their right to free speech. The NCAA, an organization of colleges and schools, forces student athletes to sign away their rights because, it says, it is protecting the students. If student athletes could accept money from anyone, the NCAA argues, they might be exploited, cheated, or even bribed. Taking money out of the equation is supposed to let students focus on academics and preserve the amateur status of college sports.

The definition of amateur arose in the nineteenth century in Britain, when team sports became popular. Middle-class and upper-class students in college had ample time to play their sports while working-class athletes had only a half-day off (no sports were played on Sundays in that era). Teams began to pay top working-class sportsmen for the time they had to take off from work. Middle-class and upper-class sportsmen didn't want to play against the working-class teams, so they made the distinction between amateurs and professionals. The definition of amateur crossed the Atlantic to the United States, where college sports became popular in the 1880s. But it was not long until the hypocrisy of amateurism undermined the ideal. Top football programs like Yale had slush funds to pay athletes, and others used ringers—players who weren't students—and even players from other schools (Zimbalist 7). The Olympic Games maintained the amateur-professional distinction until 1988, but it was long evident that Communist bloc nations were paying athletes to train full-time and Western nations were paying athletes through endorsement contracts. The only Olympic sport that now requires amateur status is boxing. The college sports empire in the United States run by the NCAA is the last bastion of amateurism for sports that draw audiences large enough to be televised.

Colleges might be able to defend the policy of amateurism if they extended this definition to all students. A fair policy is one that treats all students the same. A fair policy doesn't result in some students getting paid for professional work, while other students do not. Consider the

Conley 3

students in the Butler School of Music at the University of Texas at Austin, for example. Many student musicians perform at the professional level. Does the school prevent them from earning money for their musical performances? No. In fact, the school runs a referral service that connects its students with people and businesses who want to hire professional musicians. The university even advises its students on how to negotiate a contract and get paid for their performance ("Welcome").

> Comparisons show that colleges do not apply the definition of amateur consistently.

Likewise, why are student actors and actresses allowed to earn money from their work and images, while student athletes are not? Think about actress Emma Watson, who enrolled at Brown University in Rhode Island. Can you imagine the university officials at Brown telling Watson that she would have to make the next two *Harry Potter* films for free, instead of for the $5 million she has been offered? Can you imagine Brown University telling Watson that all the revenue from Harry Potter merchandise bearing her likeness would have to be paid directly to the university for the rest of her life? They would if Watson were an athlete instead of an actress.

> Do you think this analogy is effective?

In fact, compared to musicians and actors, student athletes have an even greater need to earn money while they are still in college. Athletes' professional careers are likely to be much shorter than musicians' or actors'. College may be the only time some athletes have the opportunity to capitalize on their success. (Indeed, rather than focusing student athletes on their academic careers, the NCAA policy sometimes forces students to leave college early, so they can earn a living before their peak playing years are over.) Student athletes often leave school with permanent injuries and no medical insurance or job prospects, whereas student musicians and actors rarely suffer career-ending injuries on the job.

Student athletes are prevented from profiting from their name and image. The NCAA says this rule preserves their standing as amateurs and protects them from the celebrity and media frenzy surrounding professional sports stars. Search for a "Tim Tebow Jersey" online, and you can buy officially branded Florida Gators shirts, ranging in price from $34.99 to $349.99 (autographed by Tebow). The NCAA, the University of Florida, Nike, and the other parties involved in the production and sale of these products get around the problem of using an amateur's name by

Conley 4

using his team number instead. Tebow's name doesn't appear anywhere on the jerseys—just his number, 15. Yet all these jerseys are identified as "Official Tim Tebow Gators merchandise," and they are certainly bought by fans of Tebow rather than by people who just happen to like the number fifteen. Nobody is saying how much money these jerseys have made for Nike, or for the NCAA. What we do know for sure is the amount Tim Tebow has made off the jerseys: nothing.

Defenders of the current system argue that student athletes on scholarships are paid with free tuition, free room and board, free books, and tutoring help. The total package can be the equivalent of $120,000 over four years. For those student athletes who are motivated to take advantage of the opportunity, the lifetime benefits can be enormous. Unfortunately, too few student athletes do take advantage of the opportunity. Seldom does a major college football and men's basketball program have graduation rates at or close to overall student body. A study by the University of North Carolina's College Sports Research Institute released in 2010 accuses the NCAA of playing fast and loose with graduation rates by counting part-time students in statistics for the general student body, making graduation rates for athletes look better in a comparison. Student athletes must be full-time students, thus they should be compared to other full-time students. The North Carolina Institute reports that 54.8% of major college (Football Bowl Subdivision) football players at 117 schools graduated within six years, compared to 73.7% of other full-time students. The gap between basketball players was even greater, with 44.6% of athletes graduating compared to 75.7% of the general student body (Zaiger). For the handful of talented athletes who can play in the National Football League or the National Basketball Association, college sports provide training for their future lucrative, although short-lived, profession. But as the NCAA itself points out in its ads, the great majority of student athletes "go pro in something other than sports." For the 55% of college basketball players who fail to graduate, the supposed $120,000 package is an air ball.

The NCAA would be wise to return to the older definition of *amateur*, which comes from Latin through old French, meaning "lover of." It doesn't

example of Tebow [illus]trates how [de]finition of [ama]teur works [agai]nst college [athl]etes.

[Con]ley gives [evid]ence that [unde]rcuts the [argu]ment that [colle]ge athletes [are] compen[sate]d with a [colle]ge degree.

[A] clever use [of "a]ir ball" [rein]forces [Con]ley's argu[men]t that the [NCA]A's defini[tion] of amateur [is ou]tdated and [unfa]ir.

Conley 5

necessarily have to have anything to do with money. Whether it's a jazz performer or a dancer or an athlete, an amateur ought to be considered someone in love with an activity—someone who cares deeply about the activity, studies the activity in depth, and practices in order to be highly proficient. NBA players, Olympians, college athletes, high school players, and even bird watchers, star gazers, and open-source programmers: they're all amateurs. If they are lucky enough to be paid, so be it.

Conley concludes w her main cla She propose new definiti of amateur, that would permit salar and royalties to go to the college athle

Conley 6

Works Cited

McCann, Michael. "NCAA Faces Unspecified Damages, Changes in Latest Anti-Trust Case." *SI.com*. Time, Inc., 21 July 2009. Web. 3 Nov. 2010.

National Collegiate Athletic Association. Advertisement. *NCAA.org*. NCAA, 13 Mar. 2007. Web. 3 Nov. 2010.

Smith, Michael, and John Ourand. "ESPN Pays $2.25B for SEC Rights." *SportsBusiness Journal*. Smith and Street, 25 Aug. 2008. Web. 1 Nov. 2010.

Thamel, Pete. "N.C.A.A. Fails to Stop Licensing Lawsuit." *New York Times*. New York Times, 8 Feb. 2010. Web. 1 Nov. 2010.

Van Riper, Thomas. "The Highest-Paid College Basketball Coaches." *Forbes.com*. Forbes, 8 Mar. 2010. Web. 3 Nov. 2010.

"Welcome to the Music Referral Service." *Butler School of Music*. Univ. of Texas at Austin, n.d. Web. 5 Nov. 2010.

Zaiger, Alan Scher. "Study: NCAA Graduation Rate Comparisons Flawed." *ABC News*. ABC News, 20 Apr. 2010. Web. 1 Nov. 2010.

Zimbalist, Andrew. *Unpaid Professionals: Commercialism and Conflict in Big-Time College Sports*. Princeton UP, 2001. Print.

PEARSON
mycomplab

For support in learning this chapter's content, follow this path in MyCompLab:
> Resources > Writing > Writing Purposes > Writing to Argue or Persuade.
Review the Instruction and Multimedia resources, then complete the Exercises and click on Gradebook to measure your progress.

9 | Causal Arguments

QUICK TAKE

In this chapter, you will learn that

1. Causal arguments take three basic forms (see page 114)
2. Causes can be identified using four methods (see page 115)
3. Effective causal arguments go beyond the obvious causes to explore complex relationships (see page 117)

Each year, we hear that American students are falling behind their international peers. Different groups argue that the solution lies in investing more in funding for additional teacher training, or smaller classrooms, or more technology in the classroom. Yet America invests billions more in education than some nations whose students surpass American students in achievement rankings. Still others have suggested that America's problem lies in a wide-scale cultural shift that has created an American student who is less motivated than those of the past. How can America's schools become world leaders again?

Understand How Causal Arguments Work

Causal claims can take three basic forms:

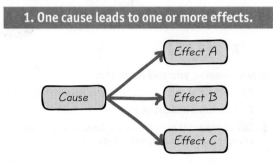

1. One cause leads to one or more effects.

The invention of the telegraph led to the commodities market, the establishment of standard time zones, and news reporting as we know it today.

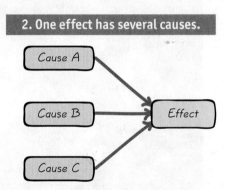

2. One effect has several causes.

Hurricanes are becoming more financially destructive to the United States because of the greater intensity of recent storms, an increase in the commercial and residential development of coastal areas, and a reluctance to enforce certain construction standards in coastal residential areas.

3. A series of events form a chain, where one event causes another, which then causes a third, and so on.

Making the HPV vaccination mandatory for adolescent girls will make unprotected sex seem safer, leading to greater promiscuity, ultimately resulting in more teenage pregnancies.

Find Causes

The causal claim is at the center of the causal argument. Writing a clear claim about cause and effect can be difficult because if a cause is worth writing about, it is likely to be complex. Obvious cases of cause and effect (staying out in the sun too long without skin protection causes sunburn) usually do not require written arguments because everyone is convinced that the causal relationship exists. Many of the causal claims that most people now accept without question—smoking causes cancer, shifting plates on the Earth's crust cause earthquakes, DDT causes eggshell thinning in bald eagles—were "settled" only after long and complex arguments.

The philosopher John Stuart Mill devised four ways for an investigator to go about finding causes.

- **The Common Factor Method.** Sometimes causes can be identified because two or more similar events share a common factor. The common factor may be the cause. For example, if two people in two different states both develop a rare disease, and both of them recently traveled to Madagascar, they were probably exposed to the illness while there.

- **The Single Difference Method.** Causes can often be identified when two situations or events have different outcomes. If there is a single difference in the two scenarios, that difference may be the cause. At the 1998 Winter Olympics in Nagano, Japan, the speed skating team from the Netherlands introduced a technological innovation to the sport— clap skates, which improve skaters' performance by keeping the skate blade in contact with the ice longer. Racing against the best skaters in the world, the Dutch on their clap skates won eleven of thirty medals, five of which were gold. By the 2002 Winter Olympics, all speed skaters had switched over to the new skates, and the medal count was much more evenly distributed. That year the United States, Netherlands, and Germany each won three gold medals, and a total of eight medals apiece. Clap skates were the most likely cause of the Netherlands' dominance four years earlier.

- **Concomitant Variation.** Some causes are discovered by observing a shared pattern of variation in a possible cause and possible effect. For example, scientists noticed that peaks in the 11-year sunspot cycle match disruptions in high-frequency radio transmission on earth, leading them to conclude that the solar activity somehow causes the disruptions.

- **Process of Elimination.** Another way to establish causation is to identify all the possible causes of something, and then test them one by one to eliminate those that can't be the cause. When an electrical appliance stops working, electricians often trace the problem this way, by checking switches one at a time to see if current can flow across them. The switch that doesn't show a continuous flow of current is the one that needs replacing.

A frequent error of people looking for cause and effect is to mistake correlation for causation. Just because one event happens after or at the same time as another one, you cannot assume that the first one caused the second. Sometimes it's just a coincidence. For example, you may observe that every time the mail carrier comes to your door, your dog barks at him, and then the mail carrier leaves. You might assume that your dog's barking causes the mail carrier to leave (your dog is probably convinced of this). However, the more likely cause is that the carrier has finished delivering your mail, so he goes on to the next house. Using Mills's methods will help you avoid mistaking correlation for causation in your own causal arguments.

To understand how you might use Mills's methods of identifying causes, suppose you want to research the cause of the increase in legalized lotteries in the United States. You research the history of lotteries in order to look for possible causes. You would discover that lotteries go back to colonial times, but were controversial because they were run by private companies that sometimes failed to pay the winners. Laws against lotteries were passed in 1840, but after the Civil War, the defeated states of the Confederacy needed money to rebuild bridges, buildings, and schools. Southerners ran lotteries and sold tickets throughout the nation. But once again, these lotteries were run by private companies, and some of them simply took people's money without paying out winnings. Eventually, lotteries were banned again.

In 1964, New Hampshire became the first state to authorize a lottery to fund the state's educational system. Soon other states, realizing that their citizens were spending their money on lottery tickets from New Hampshire, established lotteries of their own. During the 1980s, states began approving other forms of state-run gambling such as keno and video poker. By 1993 only Hawaii and Utah had no legalized gambling of any kind.

Knowing this background, you can begin using Mills's methods to look for the causes of lotteries' recent popularity. Using the common factor method, you consider what current lotteries have in common with earlier lotteries. That factor is easy to identify: It's economic. The early colonies and later the states have turned to lotteries again and again as a way of raising money without raising taxes. But, you wonder, why have lotteries spread so quickly since 1964, and raised so little concern? The single difference method shows you the likely reason: Lotteries in the past were run by private companies, and inevitably someone took off with the money instead of paying it out. Today's lotteries are operated by state agencies or contracted under state control. While they are not immune to scandal, they are much more closely monitored than lotteries in the past.

Mills's other methods might also lead you to potential causes. If you find, for example, that lotteries grow in popularity in the aftermath of wars, this concomitant variation might lead you to suspect that the economic damage of war can be one cause of lotteries' popularity. This in turn might suggest inflation caused by the Vietnam War as a possible contributing cause to the rise of state lotteries in the '60s and '70s. The process of elimination could also lead you to some probable causes for lotteries' popularity, though for such a complex topic, it would be time-consuming. You might begin by making a list of all the reasons you could think of: Perhaps people these days are more economically secure, and don't mind risking a few dollars on lottery tickets? Or maybe people are more desperate now, and lotteries represent one of the few ways they can accumulate wealth? Each of these possibilities would require research into history, economics, and psychology, but this might lead you to some interesting conclusions on the complex forces contributing to today's extensive lottery system.

Build a Causal Argument

Effective causal arguments move beyond the obvious to get at underlying causes. One great causal mystery today is global warming. Scientists generally agree that the average surface temperature on Earth has gone up by 1.3 degrees Fahrenheit or 0.7 degrees Celsius over the last hundred years, and that the amount of carbon dioxide in the atmosphere has increased by 25 percent since 1960. But the causes of those phenomena are disputed. Some people argue that the rise in temperature is caused by natural climate variations, and that the increase in carbon dioxide has little or nothing to do with it. Others argue that the rise in carbon dioxide traps heat in the atmosphere and has increased the earth's temperature. They argue further that the increased carbon dioxide is the result of human activity, especially the burning of fossil fuels and the destruction of tropical forests. The debate over global warming continues because the causation at work is not simple or easy to prove.

There are many events that may be caused by global warming, and they are more dramatically evident in arctic and subarctic regions. The decade from January 2000 to December 2009 is the warmest decade since modern temperature records began in the 1880s. Arctic sea ice shrank by 14 percent—an area the size of Texas—from 2004 to 2005, and Greenland's massive ice sheet has been thinning by more than 3 feet a year.

Many scientists consider these phenomena to be effects of global warming. They argue that a single cause—the rise in the Earth's temperature—has led to many dire effects, and will lead to more. If you wanted to make an argument along these lines, you would need to construct a causal chain:

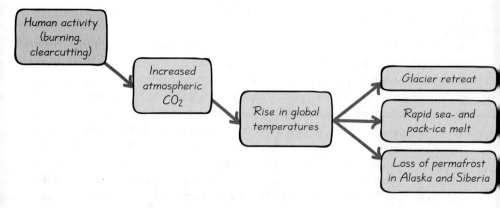

At each step, you would need to show the links between an event and its consequences, and you would need to convince readers that that link is real, not mere coincidence. You might find common factors, single differences, or concomitant variation that supports each causal link. You would also need to use a process of elimination to show that other possible causes are not in fact involved in your causal chain.

Some climate scientists have doubts about all these causal links. While the observable events—the loss of sea ice, glacier retreat, and so on—may be caused by human activity, they may be caused instead by naturally recurring cycles.

Or, the effects could be caused partly by natural cycles and partly by humans.

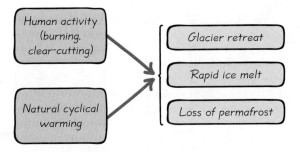

It is difficult to say for certain because much of the detailed data about the great melt in the north goes back only to the early 1990s—not long enough to rule out short-term climate cycles. However, computer models suggest a very low probability that such rapid change could occur naturally. So even if we are in a natural, short-term warming cycle, we still must ask if human activities are contributing to the documented warming, and making it even worse.

Identifying the causes of global warming is important because if we do not know the real causes, we cannot make the necessary changes to stop, reduce, or reverse it. If global warming continues unabated, the economic and human costs will be disastrous. But efforts to stop it are expensive and politically risky. Thus correctly establishing the causes of global warming is a crucial first step in solving the problem.

Glaciers in many parts of the world are melting at rates faster than scientists thought possible just a few years ago. Even major oil companies have acknowledged that global warming is real. Yet the American public has taken little notice of world climate change—perhaps because it's difficult to get excited about the mean temperature rising a few degrees and the sea level rising a few feet. What would get Americans thinking seriously about global warming?

Steps to Writing a Causal Argument

Step 1 Make a Claim

Make a causal claim on a controversial trend, event, or phenomenon.

Template

> SOMETHING does (or does not) cause SOMETHING ELSE.

—or—

> SOMETHING causes SOMETHING ELSE, which, in turn, causes SOMETHING ELSE.

Examples

- One-parent families (or television violence, bad diet, and so on) are (or are not) the cause of emotional and behavioral problems in children.
- Firearms control laws (or right-to-carry-handgun laws) reduce (or increase) violent crimes.
- Putting grade school children into competitive sports teaches them how to succeed in later life (or puts undue emphasis on winning and teaches many who are slower to mature to have a negative self-image).

Step 2 What's at Stake in Your Claim?

- If the cause is obvious to everyone, then it probably isn't worth writing about.

Step 3 Think of Possible Causes

- Which are the immediate causes?
- Which are the background causes?
- Which are the hidden causes?
- Which are the causes that most people have not recognized?

Step 4 Analyze Your Potential Readers

- Who are your readers?
- How familiar will they be with the trend, event, or phenomenon that you're writing about?
- What are they likely to know and not know?
- How likely are they to accept your causal explanation?
- What alternative explanation might they argue for?

Step 5 Write a Draft

Introduction

- Describe the controversial trend, event, or phenomenon.
- Give the background that your intended readers will need.

Body

- Explain the cause or chain of causation of a trend, event, or phenomenon that is unfamiliar to your readers.
- Set out the causes that have been offered and reject them one by one. Then you can present the cause that you think is most important.
- Treat a series of causes one by one, analyzing the importance of each.

Conclusion

- Do more than simply summarize. Consider describing additional effects beyond those that have been noted previously.

Step 6 Revise, Edit, Proofread

- For detailed instructions, see Chapter 4.
- For a checklist to use to evaluate your draft, see pages 48–49.

Finding Good Reasons

Why Are Americans Gaining Weight?

Eric Schlosser, author of *Fast Food Nation* (2001), chows down on a grilled cheese sandwich, fries, and a soda. *Fast Food Nation* traces the rise of fast-food restaurants against the background of American culture based on the automobile. Schlosser claims that one of the effects of fast food is the increase in the number of overweight Americans.

There is no doubt that Americans have grown larger. A 2004 survey of Americans published in *JAMA: The Journal of the American Medical Association* found that nearly one-third (32.5 percent) of adults are obese and two-thirds (66.3 percent) are overweight. An especially disturbing aspect of this trend is that children are increasingly obese. The Center for Disease Control and Prevention reports that the percentage of obese children aged 6 to 11 almost quadrupled from 4 percent in 1974 to 15 percent in 2000, and the percentage of obese children aged 12 to 19 increased from 6 percent in 1974 to 15 percent in 2000.

Write about it

1. To what extent do you think fast food is the cause of the trend toward excess weight? To what extent do you think lifestyle changes and the content of food are causes? In addition to the amount of fast food Americans consume, consider the following:

   - more sedentary lifestyle with more driving and less walking
   - more time spent watching television, using computers, and playing video games
   - introduction of high-fructose corn syrup in many foods, from ketchup and peanut butter to chocolate milk and yogurt
   - inadequate physical education and reduced outdoor recess periods in schools
   - more food advertising directed at children

Emily
Raine

Why Should I Be Nice to You? Coffee Shops and the Politics of Good Service

Emily Raine recently received a master's degree in communication studies at McGill University in Montreal. She writes about graffiti and street art. This article appeared in the online journal *Bad Subjects* in 2005.

In this article, Raine explains why work in a coffee chain is worse than work in other kinds of service jobs. She also outlines the causes for what she sees as a destructive dynamic in the coffee chain culture and provides a possible alternative.

> "There is no more precious commodity than the relationship of trust and confidence a company has with its employees."
> —*Starbucks Coffee Company chairman Howard Schultz*

I actually like to serve. I'm not sure if this comes from some innate inclination to mother and fuss over strangers, or if it's because the movement and sociability of service work provides a much-needed antidote to the solitude of academic research, but I've always found something about service industry work satisfying. I've done the gamut of service jobs, from fine dining to cocktail waitressing to hip euro-bistro counter work, and the only job where I've ever felt truly whipped was working as a barista at one of the now-ubiquitous specialty coffee chains, those bastions of jazz and public solitude that have spread through urban landscapes over the last ten years or so. The pay was poor, the shifts long and oddly dispersed, the work boring and monotonous, the managers demanding, and the customers regularly displayed that unique spleen that emerges in even the most pleasant people before they've had the morning's first coffee. I often felt like an aproned Coke machine, such was the effect my sparkling personality had on the clientele. And yet, some combination of service professionalism, fear of termination and an imperative to be "nice" allowed me to suck it up, smile and continue to provide that intangible trait that the industry holds above all else, good service.

Raine establishes a credible, ethical stance in her introduction.

2   Good service in coffee shops doesn't amount to much. Unlike table service, where interaction with customers spans a minimum of half an hour, the average contact with a café customer lasts less than ten seconds. Consider how specialty cafés are laid

Even before identifying the effect that she intends to analyze, Raine identifies the cause—an efficient but impersonal assembly-line approach to service.

3

out: the customer service counter is arranged in a long line that clients move along to "use" the café. The linear coffee bar resembles an assembly line, and indeed, café labor is heavily grounded in the rationalism of Fordist manufacturing principles, which had already been tested for use in hospitality services by fast food chains. Each of the café workers is assigned a specific stage in the service process to perform exclusively, such as taking orders, using the cash registers, or handing clients cups of brewed coffee.

4

The specialization of tasks increases the speed of transactions and limits the duration of any one employee's interaction with the clientele. This means that in a given visit a customer might order from one worker, receive food from the next, then brewed coffee or tea from yet another, then pay a cashier before proceeding down the line of the counter, finishing the trip at the espresso machine which is always situated at its end. Ultimately, each of the café's products is processed and served by a different employee, who repeats the same preparation task for hours and attends to each customer only as they receive that one product.

Raine argues that the assembly-line service model precludes real interaction with customers.

Needless to say, the productive work in cafés is dreary and repetitive. Further, this style of service severely curtails interaction with the clientele, and the very brevity of each transaction precludes much chance for authentic friendliness or conversation—even asking about someone's day would slow the entire operation. The one aspect of service work that can be unpredictable—people—becomes redundant, and interaction with customers is reduced to a fatiguing eight-hour-long smile and the repetition of sentiments that allude to good service, such as injunctions to enjoy their purchases or to have a nice day. Rather than friendly exchanges with customers, barista workers' good service is reduced to a quick rictus in the customer's direction between a great deal of friendly interaction with the espresso machine.

Do you agree with this description of a typical coffee shop?

5

As the hospitality industry really took off in the sixties, good service became one of the trademarks of its advertising claims, a way for brands to distinguish themselves from the rest of the pack. One needn't think too hard to come up with a litany of service slogans that holler the good graces of their personnel—at Starbucks where the baristas make the magic, at Pacific Southwest Airlines where smiles aren't just painted on, or at McDonald's where smiles are free. Employee friendliness emerged as one of the chief distinguishing brand features of personal services, which means that the workers themselves become an aspect of the product for sale.

6

Our notions of good service revolve around a series of platitudes about professionalism—we're at your service, with a smile, where the customer's always right—each bragging the centrality of the customer to everything "we" do. Such claims imply an easy and equal exchange between two parties: the "we" that gladly serves and the "you" that happily receives. There is, however, always a third party involved in the service exchange, and that's whoever has hired the server, the body that ultimately decides just what the dimensions of good service will be.

This "third party"—management, ownership—is the ultimate cause of the phenomenon under discussion.

7   Like most employees, a service worker sells labor to an employer at a set rate, often minimum wage, and the employer sells the product of that labor, the service itself, at market values. In many hospitality services, where gratuities make up the majority of employment revenue, the worker directly benefits from giving good service, which of course translates to good tips. But for the vast majority of service staff, and particularly those employed in venues yielding little or no gratuities—fast food outlets, café chains, cleaning and maintenance operations—this promises many workers little more than a unilateral imperative to be perpetually bright and amenable.

8   The vast majority of service personnel do not spontaneously produce an unaffected display of cheer and good will continuously for the duration of a shift. When a company markets its products on servers' friendliness, they must then monitor and control employees' friendliness, so good service is defined and enforced from above. Particularly in chains, which are premised upon their consistent reproduction of the same experience in numerous locations, organizations are obliged to impose systems to manage employees' interaction with their customers. In some chains, namely the fast food giants such as McDonald's and Burger King, employee banter is scripted into cash registers, so that as soon as a customer orders, workers are cued to offer, "would you like a dessert with that?" (an offer of dubious benefit to the customer) and to wish them a nice day. Ultimately, this has allowed corporations to be able to assimilate "good service"—or, friendly workers—into their overall brand image.

Does your experience as a customer (or worker) at fast food chains match this description?

9   While cafés genuflect toward the notion of good service, their layouts and management styles preclude much possibility of creating the warmth that this would entail. Good service is, of course, important, but not if it interferes with throughput. What's more, these cafés have been at the forefront of a new wave of organizations that not only market themselves on service quality but also describe employees' job satisfaction as the seed from which this flowers.

10   Perhaps the most glaring example of this is Starbucks, where cheerful young workers are displayed behind elevated

counters as they banter back and forth, calling out fancy Italian drink names and creating theatre out of their productive labor. Starbucks' corporate literature gushes not only about the good service its customers will receive, but about the great joy that its "partners" take in providing it, given the company's unique ability to "provide a great work environment and treat each other with respect and dignity," and where its partners are "emotionally and intellectually committed to Starbucks success." In the epigraph to this essay, Starbucks' chairman even describes the company's relationship with its workers as a commodity. Not only does Starbucks offer good service, but it attempts to guarantee something even better: good service provided by employees that are genuinely happy to give it.

The creation of this new kind of worker is in effect a public relations gimmick.

11   Starbucks has branded a new kind of worker, the happy, wholesome, perfume-free barista. The company offers unusual benefits for service workers, including stock options, health insurance, dental plans and other perks such as product discounts and giveaways. Further, they do so very, very publicly, and the company's promotional materials are filled with moving accounts of workers who never dreamed that corporate America could care so much. With the other hand, though, the company has smashed unionization drives in New York, Vancouver and at its Seattle roaster; it schedules workers at oddly timed shifts that never quite add up to full-time hours; the company pays only nominally more than minimum wage, and their staffs are still unable to subsist schlepping lattes alone.

12   Starbucks is not alone in marketing itself as an enlightened employer. When General Motors introduced its Saturn line, the new brand was promoted almost entirely on the company's good relations with its staff. The company's advertising spots often featured pictures of and quotes from the union contract, describing their unique partnership between manufacturer, workers and union, which allowed blue-collar personnel to have a say in everything from automobile designs to what would be served for lunch. The company rightly guessed that this strategy would go over well with liberal consumers concerned about the ethics of their purchases. Better yet, Saturn could market its cars based on workers' happiness whether personnel were satisfied or not, because very few consumers would ever have the chance to interact with them.

13   At the specialty coffee chains, however, consumers *have* to talk to employees, yet nobody ever really asks. The café service counter runs like a smooth piece of machinery, and I found that most people preferred to pretend that they were interacting with an appliance. In such short transactions, it is exceedingly difficult

for customers to remember the humanity of each of the four to seven people they might interact with to get their coffees. Even fast food counters have one server who processes each customer's order, yet in cafés the workers just become another gadget in the well-oiled café machine. This is a definite downside for the employees—clients are much ruder to café staff than in any other sector of the industry I ever worked in. I found that people were more likely to be annoyed than touched by any reference to my having a personality, and it took no small amount of thought on my part to realize why.

14   Barista workers are hired to represent an abstract category of worker, not to act as individuals. Because of the service system marked by short customer interaction periods and a homogenous staff, the services rendered are linked in the consumer imagination to the company and not to any one individual worker. Workers' assimilation into the company image makes employees in chain service as branded as the products they serve. The chain gang, the workers who hold these eminently collegiate after-school jobs, are proscribed sales scripts and drilled on customer service scenarios to standardize interactions with customers. The company issues protocols for hair length, color and maintenance, visible piercings and tattoos as well as personal hygiene and acceptable odorific products. Workers are made more interchangeable by the use of uniforms, which, of course, serve to make the staff just that. The organization is a constant intermediary in every transaction, interjecting its presence in every detail of the service experience, and this standardization amounts to an absorption of individuals' personalities into the corporate image.

Raine spells out her thesis in this paragraph.

15   Many of the measures that chains take to secure the homogeneity of their employees do not strike us as particularly alarming, likely because similar restrictions have been in place for several hundred years. Good service today has inherited many of the trappings of the good servant of yore, including prohibitions against eating, drinking, sitting or relaxing in front the served, entering and exiting through back doors, and wearing uniforms to visually mark workers' status. These measures almost completely efface the social identities of staff during work hours, providing few clues to workers' status in their free time. Contact between service workers and their customers is thus limited to purely functional relations, so that the public only see them as workers, as makers of quality coffee, and never as possible peers.

16   Maintaining such divisions is integral to good service because this display of class distinctions ultimately underlies our

notions of service quality. Good service means not only serving well, but also allowing customers to feel justified in issuing orders, to feel okay about being served—which, in turn, requires demonstrations of class difference and the smiles that suggest servers' comfort with having a subordinate role in the service exchange.

17   Unlike the penguin-suited household servant staffs whose class status was clearly defined, service industry workers today often have much more in common from a class perspective with those that they serve. This not only creates an imperative for them to wear their class otherness on their sleeves, as it were, but also to accept their subordinate role to those they serve by being unshakably tractable and polite.

18   Faith Popcorn has rather famously referred to the four-dollar latte as a "small indulgence," noting that while this is a lot to pay for a glass of hot milk, it is quite inexpensive for the feeling of luxury that can accompany it. In this service climate, the class status of the server and the served—anyone who can justify spending this much on a coffee—is blurry, indeed. Coffee shops that market themselves on employee satisfaction assert the same happy servant that allows politically conscientious consumers, who are in many cases the workers' own age and class peers, to feel justified in receiving good service. Good service—as both an apparent affirmation of subordinate classes' desire to serve and as an enforced one-sided politeness—reproduces the class distinctions that have historically characterized servant-served relationships so that these are perpetuated within the contemporary service market.

Raine begins to shift attention to the customers' role in coffee shop culture.

19   The specialty coffee companies are large corporations, and for the twenty-somethings who stock their counters, barista work is too temporary to bother fighting the system. Mostly, people simply quit. Dissatisfied workers are stuck with engaging in tactics that will change nothing but allow them to make the best of their lot. These include minor infractions such as taking liberties with the uniforms or grabbing little bits of company time for their own pleasure, what Michel de Certeau calls *la perruque* and the companies themselves call "time theft." As my time in the chain gang wore on, I developed my own tactic, the only one I found that jostled the customers out of their complacency and allowed me to be a barista and a person.

20   There is no easy way to serve without being a servant, and I have always found that the best way to do so is to show my actual emotions rather than affecting a smooth display of interminable patience and good will. For café customers, bettering baristas' lots can be as simple as asking about their day,

addressing them by name—any little gesture to show that you noticed the person behind the service that they can provide. My tactic as a worker is equally simple, but it is simultaneously an assertion of individual identity at work, a refusal of the class distinctions that characterize the service environment and a rebuttal to the companies that would promote my satisfaction with their system: be rude. Not arbitrarily rude, of course—customers are people, too, and nobody gains anything by spreading bad will. But on those occasions when customer or management behavior warranted a zinging comeback, I would give it.

Were you expecting this "solution" to the situation Raine presents?

21   Rudeness, when it is demanded, undermines companies' claims on workers' personal warmth and allows them to retain their individuality by expressing genuine rather than affected feelings in at-work interpersonal exchanges. It is a refusal of the class distinctions that underlie consumers' unilateral prerogative of rudeness and servers' unilateral imperative to be nice. It runs contrary to everything that we have been taught, not only about service but about interrelating with others. But this seems to be the only method of asserting one's person-hood in the service environment, where workers' personalities are all too easily reduced to a space-time, conflated with the drinks they serve. Baristas of the world, if you want to avoid becoming a green-aproned coffee dispensary, you're just going to have to tell people off about it.

Raine reveals her specific audience, "baristias of the world," only at the end of her argument.

Sample Student Causal Argument

Tansal 1

Armadi Tansal

Professor Stewart

English 115

29 October 2010

Modern Warfare: Video Games' Link to Real-World Violence

"John" is a nineteen-year-old college student who gets decent grades. He comes from a typical upper-middle-class family and plans to get his MBA after he graduates. John is also my friend, which is why I'm not using his real name.

John has been playing moderately violent video games since he was nine years old. I started playing video and console games around that age too, and I played a lot in junior high, but John plays more than anyone I know. John says that over the past year he has played video games at least four hours every day, and "sometimes all day and night on the weekends." I have personally witnessed John play *Call of Duty: Modern Warfare 2* for six hours straight, with breaks only to use the bathroom or eat something.

> Armadi Tansal establishes a personal relationship to his subject and audience.

I've never seen John act violently, and he's never been in trouble with the law. But new research on violent video games suggests that John's gaming habit puts him at risk for violent or aggressive behavior. Dr. Craig Anderson, a psychologist at the University of Iowa, says "the active role required by video games . . . may make violent video games even more hazardous than violent television or cinema." When people like John play these games, they get used to being rewarded for violent behavior. For example, in the multiplayer version of *Modern Warfare 2*, if the player gets a five-kill streak, he can call in a Predator missile strike. If you kill 25 people in a row, you can call in a tactical nuclear strike. Missile strikes help you advance toward the mission goals more quickly, so the more people you kill, the faster you'll win.

Along with *Modern Warfare 2*, John plays games like *Left 4 Dead, Halo,* and *Grand Theft Auto*. All these games are rated M for Mature, which according to the Entertainment Software Rating Board means they "may contain intense violence, blood and gore, sexual content and/or strong

Tansal 2

language." Some M-rated games, like *Grand Theft Auto,* feature random violence, where players can run amok in a city, beat up and kill people, and smash stuff for no reason. In others, like *Modern Warfare 2*, the violence takes place in the context of military action. To do well in all of these games, you have to commit acts of violence. But does acting violently in games make you more violent in real life?

Anderson says studies show that "violent video games are significantly associated with: increased aggressive behavior, thoughts, and affect [feelings]; increased physiological arousal; and decreased prosocial (helping) behavior." He also claims that "high levels of violent video game exposure have been linked to delinquency, fighting at school and during free play periods, and violent criminal behavior (e.g., self-reported assault, robbery)."

Being "associated with" and "linked to" violent behavior doesn't necessarily mean video games cause such behavior. Many people have argued that the links Anderson sees are coincidental, or that any effects video games might have on behavior are so slight that we shouldn't worry about them. Christopher Ferguson and John Kilburn, professors of Criminal Justice at Texas A&M International University, feel that the existing research does not support Anderson's claims. In a report published in the *Journal of Pediatrics*, they point out that in past studies, "the closer aggression measures got to actual violent behavior, the weaker the effects seen" (762).

From what I can tell, John doesn't have any more violent thoughts and feelings than most men his age. When I asked him if he thought the games had made him more violent or aggressive in real life, he said, "I'm actually less violent now. When we were kids we used to play 'war' with fake guns and sticks, chasing each other around the neighborhood and fighting commando-style. We didn't really fight but sometimes kids got banged up. No one ever gets hurt playing a video game."

Anderson admits that "a healthy, normal, nonviolent child or adolescent who has no other risk factors for high aggression or violence is not going to become a school shooter simply because they play five hours or 10 hours a week of these violent video games" (qtd. in St. George). But just because violent video games don't turn all players into

> Tansal identifies the causal question at the heart of his argument.

> Direct quotations from published sources build credibility.

> Tansal is careful not to accept the easy answer that video games cause everyone to be more violent.

Tansal 3

Here Tansal hints at his thesis, which will be explicitly stated at the end of his argument.

mass murderers, that doesn't mean they have no effect on a player's behavior and personality. For example, my friend John doesn't get into fights or rob people, but he doesn't display a lot of prosocial "helping" behaviors either. He spends most of his free time gaming, so he doesn't get out of his apartment much. Also, the friends he does have mostly play video games with him.

Even though the games restrict his interactions with other humans and condition him to behave violently onscreen, John is probably not at high risk of becoming violent in real life. But according to researchers, this low risk of becoming violent is because none of the dozens of other risk factors associated with violent behavior are present in his life (Anderson et al. 160). If John was a high school dropout, came from a broken home, or abused alcohol and other drugs, his game playing might be more likely to contribute to violent behavior.

Tansal clarifies his thesis that games can be a contributing cause of violent behavior.

Anderson contends that violent video games are a "causal risk factor" for violence and aggression—not that they cause violent aggression. In other words, the games are a small piece of a much larger problem. People like my friend John are not likely to become violent because of the video games they play. But Anderson's research indicates that some people do. Although there is no simple way to tell who those people are, we should include video games as a possible risk factor when we think about who is likely to become violent.

Even if the risk contributed by violent video games is slight for each individual, the total impact of the games on violence in society could be huge. *Call of Duty: Modern Warfare 2* is the third-best-selling video game in the United States (Orry). Its creator, Activision Blizzard, had $1.3 billion dollars in sales in the just first three months of 2010 (Pham). Millions of people play this game, and games like it, and they aren't all as well-adjusted as John. If video games contribute to violent tendencies in only a small fraction of players, they could still have a terrible impact.

Tansal concludes by arguing that video games may not cause many people to become more violent, but it doesn't take many to be a big problem.

Tansal 4

Works Cited

Anderson, Craig. "Violent Video Games: Myths, Facts, and Unanswered Questions." *Psychological Science Agenda* 16.5 (2003): n. pag. Web. 6 Oct. 2010.

Anderson, Craig, et al. "Violent Video Game Effects on Aggression, Empathy, and Prosocial Behavior in Eastern and Western Countries." *Psychological Bulletin* 136 (2010): 151–73. Print.

Entertainment Software Rating Board. *Game Ratings and Descriptor Guide*. Entertainment Software Association, n. d. Web. 7 Oct. 2010.

Ferguson, Christopher J. and John Kilburn. "The Public Health Risks of Media Violence: A Meta-Analytic Review." *Journal of Pediatrics* 154.5 (2009): 759–63. Print.

John (pseudonym). Personal interview. 4 Oct. 2010.

Orry, James. "*Modern Warfare 2* the 3rd Best-Selling Game in the US." *Videogamer.com*. Pro-G Media Ltd., 12 Mar. 2010. Web. 6 Oct. 2010.

Pham, Alex. "Call of Duty: Modern Warfare 2 Propels Revenue, Profit for Activision Blizzard." *Los Angeles Times*. Los Angeles Times, 6 May 2010. Web. 7 Oct. 2010.

St. George, Donna. "Study Links Violent Video Games, Hostility." *Washington Post*. Washington Post, 3 Nov. 2008. Web. 5 Oct. 2010.

PEARSON
mycomplab

For support in learning this chapter's content, follow this path in MyCompLab:
> Resources > Writing > Writing Purposes > Writing to Analyze.

Review the Instruction and Multimedia resources, then complete the Exercises and click on Gradebook to measure your progress.

10 | Evaluation Arguments

QUICK TAKE

In this chapter, you will learn that

1. Evaluation arguments set out criteria and then judge something to be good or bad according to those criteria (see page 135)
2. Evaluation arguments are based on practical, aesthetic, and ethical criteria (see page 137)
3. Evaluation arguments often use comparisons (see page 138)

By some estimates, as many as five million animals are killed in shelters each year. Are "no-kill" shelters a good idea? Advocates of no-kill shelters argue that alternatives to euthanizing animals can be created by working to increase adoption demand for shelter animals. No-kill shelters also work to promote spaying and neutering to decrease the number of animals sent to shelters in the first place. Others argue that the term "no-kill" is divisive because it implies that some shelters are "kill" shelters and suggests that many shelter workers are cruel or uncaring. Are no-kill shelters an effective solution? What kind of evaluations would support or oppose the concept of the "no-kill" shelter? How can evaluation arguments be used to support more humane treatment of shelter animals?

People make evaluations all the time. Newspapers, magazines, and television have picked up on this love of evaluation by running "best of" polls. They ask their readers to vote on the best Chinese restaurant, the best pizza, the best local band, the best coffeehouse, the best dance club, the best neighborhood park, the best swimming hole, the best bike ride (scenic or challenging), the best volleyball court, the best place to get married, and so on. If you ask one of your friends who voted in a "best" poll why she picked a particular restaurant as the best of its kind, she might respond by saying simply, "I like it." But if you ask her why she likes it, she might start offering good reasons such as these: the food is good, the service prompt, the prices fair, and the atmosphere comfortable. It's really not a mystery why these polls are often quite predictable or why the same restaurants tend to win year after year. Many people think that evaluations are matters of personal taste, but when we begin probing the reasons, we often discover that different people use similar criteria to make evaluations.

The key to convincing other people that your judgment is sound is establishing the criteria you will use to make your evaluation. Sometimes it will be necessary to argue for the validity of the criteria that you think your readers should consider. If your readers accept your criteria, it's likely they will agree with your conclusions.

Understand How Evaluation Arguments Work

Evaluation arguments set out criteria and then judge something to be good or bad (or better, or best) according to those criteria.

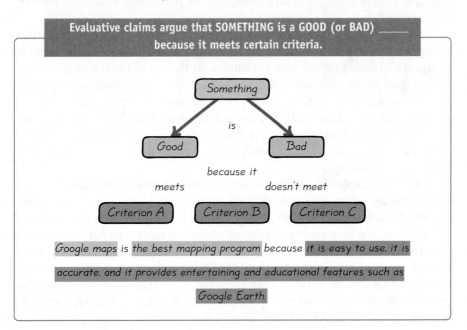

Recognize Kinds of Evaluations

Arguments of evaluation are structured much like arguments of definition. Recall that the criteria in arguments of definition are set out in because clauses:

People often disagree about the relevance and appropriateness of criteria in an evaluation. Take as an example the question of which colleges are good schools. Until twenty years ago, most of the information that people used to evaluate a college came from the college itself. You could find out the price of tuition and what courses were offered, but other information was difficult to find, and it was hard to compare one college with another.

In 1983 the magazine *U.S. News & World Report* began ranking U.S. colleges and universities from a consumer's perspective. These rankings have remained controversial ever since. *U.S. News* evaluates schools using a complex set of criteria. Twenty-five percent of a school's ranking is based on a survey of reputation in which officials at each college rate the quality of schools in the same category as their own school. The remaining 75 percent is based on six kinds of statistical data. These measure retention of students, faculty resources, student selectivity, financial resources, alumni giving, and, for some schools, graduation rates (the difference between the number of students expected to graduate and the number who actually do).

U.S. News chooses specific types of information to look at in each category. For example, "faculty resources" are measured by the size of classes, average faculty pay, the percentage of professors with the highest degree in their field, the overall student-faculty ratio, and the percentage of faculty who are full-time.

Many college officials have criticized the criteria *U.S. News* uses to evaluate colleges. In an August 1998 *U.S. News* article, Gerhard Casper, the president of Stanford University (which is consistently near the top of the rankings), writes, "Much about these rankings—particularly their specious formulas and spurious precision—is utterly misleading." Casper argues that using graduation rates as a criterion rewards schools that pass low-achieving students. Other college presidents have argued that the magazine should use different criteria or weight the criteria differently, and some have called (without much success) for a boycott of the *U.S. News* rankings.

U.S. News replies in its defense that colleges and universities themselves do a lot of ranking, using data and methods that can be questioned. Schools rank students for admission, using SAT or ACT scores, high school GPA, class rank, and other factors, and then grade students and rank them against each other once they are enrolled in college. Schools also evaluate their faculty and take great interest in the national ranking of their departments. They care very much about how they stand in relation to one another. Why, then, *U.S. News* argues, shouldn't people be able to evaluate colleges and universities, since colleges and universities are in the business of evaluating people?

The magazine and the colleges have very different ideas about what constitute fair and relevant criteria for evaluating a college. But the *U.S. News* college rankings generate a tremendous amount of income for the magazine, suggesting that students and their parents agree with the criteria, and use them to help make their own decisions about college.

Some evaluation arguments rely more heavily on certain types of criteria than others. For example, a movie review (_____ is a good movie) is likely to focus most closely on aesthetic considerations: Engaging characters, an exciting story, beautiful cinematography. Ethical considerations may be relevant—say, if the film is exceptionally violent, or celebrates antisocial behavior—but usually don't predominate in a movie review. Practical considerations will probably be least important, since anyone reading a movie review is presumably willing to spend the price of admission to see a film.

Build an Evaluation Argument

Although evaluation arguments seem very similar to definition arguments, there is a key difference. Definition arguments seek to place something in the correct category by observing its qualities. They hinge on our judgments about similarity and difference. Evaluation arguments focus instead on what we value. Because of this, the criteria you choose when making an evaluation argument are very important. If your criteria do not appeal to the values of your audience, your readers will not feel that your evaluation is accurate.

Suppose that a city task force on downtown revitalization has a plan to demolish the oldest commercial building in your city. Your neighborhood association wants to preserve the building, perhaps by turning it into a museum. To persuade officials to do this, you must show that your plan for preservation is a good one, while the taskforce's plan for demolition is a bad one. You might argue that a museum would attract visitors to the downtown area, bringing in revenue. You might argue that the elaborately carved stone facade of the building is a rare example of a disappearing craft. Or you might argue that it is only fair to preserve the oldest commercial building in town, since the city's oldest house and other historic buildings have been saved.

Each of these arguments uses different criteria. The argument that a museum will bring in money is based on practical considerations. The argument about the rare and beautiful stonework on the building is based on aesthetic (artistic) considerations. The argument that an old commercial building deserves the same treatment as other old buildings is based on fairness, or ethical concerns. Depending on your audience, you might use all three kinds of criteria, or you might focus more on one or two kinds. If your city is in the middle of a budget crisis, it might be wise to stress the practical, economic benefits of a museum. If several City Council members are architects or amateur historians, your argument

Windmills produce energy without pollution and reduce dependence on foreign oil. Do you agree or disagree with people who do not want windmills built near them because they find them ugly?

might focus on the aesthetic criteria. You have to make assumptions about what your audience will value most as they consider your evaluation.

Evaluative arguments can look at just one case in isolation, but often they make comparisons. You could construct an argument about the fate of the old building that only describes your plan and its benefits. Or, you might also directly address the demolition proposal, showing how it lacks those benefits. Then your argument might be structured like this:

Finding Good Reasons

What's the best alternative fuel?

Biodiesel is an alternative fuel source that is made from vegetable oil (or animal fats) and alcohol. While biodiesel can be used alone, it is often mixed with petroleum diesel. Blends of up to 20 percent biodiesel can be used in a standard diesel engine without modifications—meaning that many cars on the road today would be capable of using biodiesel if it were to become widely available.

But is biodiesel a realistic solution to the world's dependence on fossil fuels? Many think yes. Proponents point to the reduction in greenhouse gas emissions and the lower dependence on foreign oil that would accompany wide-scale biodiesel adoption. Detractors point to millions of acres of land, which would typically be used for food production, that would be converted to fuel production, inevitably causing shortages and an overall rise in food prices.

Write about it

1. One way to assess a complicated issue like alternative fuel technologies is to evaluate each technology against a set of common criteria. Which of the following criteria are useful for evaluating fuel-efficient cars? Why are they useful?
   - cost of development and production
   - sticker price of cars using the technology
   - how long it takes for cars to reach the market
   - efficiency and reliability of cars using the technology
   - environmental impact
   - convenience of refueling and maintenance
   - driver's aesthetic experience

2. Are any of the above criteria more important than the others? If so, how would you rank them? Why? Are there any criteria you would add?

Steps to Writing an Evaluation Argument

Step 1 Make a Claim

Make an evaluative claim based on criteria.

Template

> SOMETHING is good (bad, the best, the worst) if measured by certain criteria (practicality, aesthetics, ethics).

Examples

- A book or movie review.
- An evaluation of a controversial aspect of sports (e.g., the current system of determining who is champion in Division I college football by a system of bowls and polls) or a sports event (e.g., this year's WNBA playoffs) or a team.
- An evaluation of the effectiveness of a social policy or law such as legislating 21 as the legal drinking age, current gun control laws, or environmental regulation.

Step 2 Think About What's at Stake

- Does nearly everyone agree with you? Then your claim probably isn't interesting or important. If you can think of people who disagree, then something is at stake.
- Who argues the opposite of your claim?
- Why do they make a different evaluation?

Step 3 List the Criteria

- Which criteria make something either good or bad?
- Which criteria are the most important?
- Which criteria are fairly obvious, and which will you have to argue for?

Step 4 Analyze Your Potential Readers

- Who are your readers?
- How familiar will they be with what you are evaluating?
- Which criteria are they most likely to accept with little explanation, and which will they disagree with?

Step 5 Write a Draft

Introduction

- Introduce the person, group, institution, event, or object that you are going to evaluate. You might want to announce your stance at this point or wait until the concluding section.
- Give the background that your intended readers will need.

Body

- Describe each criterion and then analyze how well what you are evaluating meets that criterion.
- If you are making an evaluation according to the effects someone or something produces, describe each effect in detail.
- Anticipate where readers might question either your criteria or how they apply to your subject.
- Address opposing viewpoints by acknowledging how their evaluations might differ and by showing why your evaluation is better.

Conclusion

- If you have not yet announced your stance, conclude that, on the basis of the criteria you set out or the effects you have analyzed, something is good (bad, the best, the worst).
- If you have made your stance clear from the beginning, end with a compelling example or analogy.

Step 6 Revise, Edit, Proofread

- For detailed instructions, see Chapter 4.
- For a checklist to use to evaluate your draft, see pages 48–49.

P. J. O'Rourke

The End of the Affair

P. J. O'Rourke is a humorist and satirist who follows in the tradition of the New Journalism where there is no pretense of objectivity and the biases of the writer are in the foreground. Even those who don't agree with his libertarian conservative political views still find him funny, like Bill Maher, who invites O'Rourke on his HBO show. O'Rourke was editor-in-chief of the satirical *National Lampoon* magazine and worked at *Rolling Stone* from 1986 to 2001. The titles of his book suggest his sense of humor: *Modern Manners: An Etiquette Book for Rude People* (1983), *The Bachelor's Home Companion: A Practical Guide to Keeping House like a Pig* (1987), *Holidays in Hell* (1988), *Parliament of Whores: A Lone Humorist Attempts to Explain the Entire U.S. Government* (1991), *Give War a Chance: Eyewitness Accounts of Mankind's Struggle against Tyranny, Injustice, and Alcohol-free Beer* (1992), and *Peace Kills: America's Fun New Imperialism* (2004). O'Rourke's humor is infused with outrage over the influence of government in ordinary life, which you will find in this evaluation argument.

O'Rourke begins by announcing that he is from an older generation. What does he gain and lose from this strategy?

2   The phrase "bankrupt General Motors," which we expect to hear uttered on Monday, leaves Americans my age in economic shock. The words are as melodramatic as "Mom's nude photos." And, indeed, if we want to understand what doomed the American automobile, we should give up on economics and turn to melodrama.

Politicians, journalists, financial analysts and other purveyors of banality have been looking at cars as if a convertible were a business. Fire the MBAs and hire a poet. The fate of Detroit isn't a matter of financial crisis, foreign competition, corporate greed, union intransigence, energy costs or measuring the shoe size of the footprints in the carbon. It's a tragic romance—unleashed passions, titanic clashes, lost love and wild horses. Foremost are the horses. Cars can't be comprehended without them. A hundred and some years ago Rudyard Kipling wrote "The Ballad of the King's Jest," in which an Afghan tribesman avers: Four things greater than all things are—Women and Horses and Power and War.

Note how his favored criteria—romance, passion, horses—have to do with aesthetics, not practical issues like safety or environmental impact.

3   Insert another "power" after the horse and the verse was as true in the suburbs of my 1950s boyhood as it was in the Khyber Pass.

4   Horsepower is not a quaint leftover of linguistics or a vague metaphoric anachronism. James Watt, father of the steam engine

and progenitor of the industrial revolution, lacked a measurement for the movement of weight over distance in time—what we call energy. (What we call energy wasn't even an intellectual concept in the late 18th century—in case you think the recent collapse of global capitalism was history's most transformative moment.)

Note how this paragraph establishes O'Rourke's expertise, his credibility.

Mr. Watt did research using draft animals and found that, under optimal conditions, a dray horse could lift 33,000 pounds one foot off the ground in one minute. Mr. Watt—the eponymous watt not yet existing—called this unit of energy "1 horse-power."

O'Rourke's favored criteria—status and being cool—have nothing to do with practicality and everything to do with aesthetics.

5   In 1970 a Pontiac GTO (may the brand name rest in peace) had horsepower to the number of 370. In the time of one minute, for the space of one foot, it could move 12,210,000 pounds. And it could move those pounds down every foot of every mile of all the roads to the ends of the earth for every minute of every hour until the driver nodded off at the wheel. Forty years ago the pimply kid down the block, using $3,500 in saved-up soda-jerking money, procured might and main beyond the wildest dreams of Genghis Khan, whose hordes went forth to pillage mounted upon less oomph than is in a modern leaf blower.

6   Horses and horsepower alike are about status and being cool. A knight in ancient Rome was bluntly called "guy on

horseback," Equesitis. Chevalier means the same, as does Cavalier. Lose the capitalization and the dictionary says, "insouciant and debonair; marked by a lofty disregard of others' interests, rights, or feelings; high-handed and arrogant and supercilious." How cool is that? Then there are cowboys—always cool—and the U.S. cavalry that coolly comes to their rescue plus the proverbially cool-handed "Man on Horseback" to whom we turn in troubled times.

O'Rourke uses predominantly male references. Do you think he was writing only for men?

7   Early witnesses to the automobile urged motorists to get a horse. But that, in effect, was what the automobile would do—get a horse for everybody. Once the Model T was introduced in 1908 we all became Sir Lancelot, gained a seat at the Round Table and were privileged to joust for the favors of fair maidens (at drive-in movies). The pride and prestige of a noble mount was vouchsafed to the common man. And woman, too. No one ever tried to persuade ladies to drive sidesaddle with both legs hanging out the car door.

More "status" and "being cool."

"Schlub" is Yiddish slang for an unattractive person. Why does O'Rourke use this term?

8   For the purpose of ennobling us schlubs, the car is better than the horse in every way. Even more advantageous than cost, convenience and not getting kicked and smelly is how much easier it is to drive than to ride. I speak with feeling on this subject, having taken up riding when I was nearly 60 and having begun to drive when I was so small that my cousin Tommy had to lie on the transmission hump and operate the accelerator and the brake with his hands.

9   After the grown-ups had gone to bed, Tommy and I shifted the Buick into neutral, pushed it down the driveway and out of earshot, started the engine and toured the neighborhood. The sheer difficulty of horsemanship can be illustrated by what happened to Tommy and me next. Nothing. We maneuvered the car home, turned it off and rolled it back up the driveway. (We were raised in the blessedly flat Midwest.) During our foray the Buick's speedometer reached 30. But 30 miles per hour is a full gallop on a horse. Delete what you've seen of horse riding in movies. Possibly a kid who'd never been on a horse could ride at a gallop without killing himself. Possibly one of the Jonas Brothers could land an F-14 on a carrier deck.

Cars in the 1950s and 1960s represented the triumph of aesthetics over practical issues like gas mileage and safety.

10   Thus cars usurped the place of horses in our hearts. Once we'd caught a glimpse of a well-turned Goodyear, checked out the curves of the bodywork and gaped at that swell pair of headlights, well, the old gray mare was not what she used to be. We embarked upon life in the fast lane with our new paramour. It was a great love story of man and machine. The road to the future was paved with bliss.

11   Then we got married and moved to the suburbs. Being away from central cities meant Americans had to spend more of their

time driving. Over the years away got farther away. Eventually this meant that Americans had to spend all of their time driving. The play date was 40 miles from the Chuck E. Cheese. The swim meet was 40 miles from the cello lesson. The Montessori was 40 miles from the math coach. Mom's job was 40 miles from Dad's job and the three-car garage was 40 miles from both.

O'Rourke describes how practicality gained the upper hand over aesthetics.

12   The car ceased to be object of desire and equipment for adventure and turned into office, rec room, communications hub, breakfast nook and recycling bin—a motorized cup holder. Americans, the richest people on Earth, were stuck in the confines of their crossover SUVs, squeezed into less space than tech-support call-center employees in a Mumbai cubicle farm. Never mind the six-bedroom, eight-bath, pseudo-Tudor with cathedral-ceilinged great room and 1,000-bottle controlled-climate wine cellar. That was a day's walk away.

O'Rourke mocks how practicality rules—that the romance of cars is reduced to cup holders.

13   We became sick and tired of our cars and even angry at them. Pointy-headed busybodies of the environmentalist, new urbanist, utopian communitarian ilk blamed the victim. They claimed the car had forced us to live in widely scattered settlements in the great wasteland of big-box stores and the Olive Garden. If we would all just get on our Schwinns or hop a trolley, they said, America could become an archipelago of cozy gulags on the Portland, Oregon, model with everyone nestled together in the most sustainably carbon-neutral, diverse and ecologically unimpactful way.

14   But cars didn't shape our existence; cars let us escape with our lives. We're way the heck out here in Valley Bottom Heights and Trout Antler Estates because we were at war with the cities. We fought rotten public schools, idiot municipal bureaucracies, corrupt political machines, rampant criminality and the pointy-headed busybodies. Cars gave us our dragoons and hussars, lent us speed and mobility, let us scout the terrain and probe the enemy's lines. And thanks to our cars, when we lost the cities we weren't forced to surrender, we were able to retreat.

Note how O'Rourke charac-terizes the unfortunate practicalities of modern life.

15   But our poor cars paid the price. They were flashing swords beaten into dull plowshares. Cars became appliances. Or worse. Nobody's ticked off at the dryer or the dishwasher, much less the fridge. We recognize these as labor-saving devices. The car, on the other hand, seems to create labor. We hold the car responsi-ble for all the dreary errands to which it needs to be steered. Hell, a golf cart's more fun. You can ride around in a golf cart with a six-pack, safe from breathalyzers, chasing Canada geese on the fairways and taking swings at gophers with a mashie.

O'Rourke reverses the usual positive meaning of the metaphor of turning swords into plowshares.

Now the new cars are tied explicitly to "busybodies"—the practical-minded regulators that O'Rourke despises.

16   We've lost our love for cars and forgotten our debt to them and meanwhile the pointy-headed busybodies have been exacting their revenge. We escaped the poke of their noses once, when we lived downtown, but we won't be able to peel out so fast the next time. In the name of safety, emissions control and fuel economy, the simple mechanical elegance of the automobile has been rendered ponderous, cumbersome and incomprehensible. One might as well pry the back off an iPod as pop the hood on a contemporary motor vehicle. An aging shade-tree mechanic like myself stares aghast and sits back down in the shade. Or would if the car weren't squawking at me like a rehearsal for divorce. You left the key in. You left the door open. You left the lights on. You left your dirty socks in the middle of the bedroom floor.

17   I don't believe the pointy-heads give a damn about climate change or gas mileage, much less about whether I survive a head-on with one of their tax-sucking mass-transit projects. All they want to is to make me hate my car. How proud and handsome would Bucephalas look, or Traveler or Rachel Alexandra, with seat and shoulder belts, air bags, 5-mph bumpers and a maze of pollution-control equipment under the tail?

It's romantic aesthetics vs. ugly practicality.

18   And there's the end of the American automobile industry. When it comes to dull, practical, ugly things that bore and annoy me, Japanese things cost less and the cup holders are more conveniently located.

19   The American automobile is—that is, was—never a product of Japanese-style industrialism. America's steel, coal, beer, beaver pelts and PCs may have come from our business plutocracy, but American cars have been manufactured mostly by romantic fools. David Buick, Ransom E. Olds, Louis Chevrolet, Robert and Louis Hupp of the Hupmobile, the Dodge brothers, the Studebaker brothers, the Packard brothers, the Duesenberg brothers, Charles W. Nash, E. L. Cord, John North Willys, Preston Tucker and William H. Murphy, whose Cadillac cars were designed by the young Henry Ford, all went broke making cars. The man who founded General Motors in 1908, William Crapo (really) Durant, went broke twice. Henry Ford, of course, did not go broke, nor was he a romantic, but judging by his opinions he certainly was a fool.

20 America's romantic foolishness with cars is finished, however, or nearly so. In the far boondocks a few good old boys haven't got the memo and still tear up the back roads. Doubtless the Obama administration's Department of Transportation is even now calculating a way to tap federal stimulus funds for mandatory OnStar installations to locate and subdue these reprobates.

Is O'Rourke himself one of those good old boys?

21 Among certain youths—often first-generation Americans—there remains a vestigial fondness for Chevelle low-riders or Honda "tuners." The pointy-headed busybodies have yet to enfold these youngsters in the iron-clad conformity of cultural diversity's embrace. Soon the kids will be expressing their creative energy in a more constructive way, planting bok choy in community gardens and decorating homeless shelters with murals of Che.

22 I myself have something old-school under a tarp in the basement garage. I bet when my will has been probated, some child of mine will yank the dust cover and use the proceeds of the eBay sale to buy a mountain bike. Four things greater than all things are, and I'm pretty sure one of them isn't bicycles. There are those of us who have had the good fortune to meet with strength and beauty, with majestic force in which we were willing to trust our lives. Then a day comes, that strength and beauty fails, and a man does what a man has to do. I'm going downstairs to put a bullet in a V-8.

Sample Student Evaluation Argument

Rashaun Giddens

Professor Chen

English 1302

21 April 2009

Stop Loss or "Loss of Trust"

Looking back on my high school career, my social and extracurricular lives were filled with countless highs: hanging out with my friends, prom, and varsity track to name a few. My academic career, however, was a bit shakier. So busy with what I saw then as the important things in life, I often procrastinated or altogether avoided my schoolwork. My senior year, the recruiter from the U.S. Army Reserves spoke at a school assembly. He asked that we as seniors consider the prospect of becoming "weekend warriors." In the wake of September 11, we could help protect our country and simultaneously work toward paying for a college education, which seemed like a great idea to many students. For those who could not otherwise afford college, the prospect of receiving a higher education in return for patriotism and some good hard work sounded fair enough. My life, however, took a different turn. When I received my track scholarship, I decided to head off to college right away. Many of my friends, however, heeded the call to service. So far, their realities have been far from the lives that were pitched to them; rather, this was the beginning of a path to broken dreams and broken promises.

My cousin, moved to action by a charismatic recruiter, an Army announcement of fifteen-month active tours, and the prospect of a paid college education, chose to join the United States Army Reserves. The Army, suffering from a recruitment shortfall, had recently announced a policy that would allow recruits to serve in active duty for a mere fifteen months. For serving for just over a year, my cousin could do his national duty and put himself on a path to self-improvement. The recruiter did not, however, highlight the fine print to this new program. No one told my cousin that he could be called back to active duty for up to eight years under the government's "stop loss" policy. Further, no one told him that just one day after the Army announced the incentive program, an

Note how the introduction creates a connection with the audience; while anyone can be persuaded by this essay, Giddens is especially addressing people around his own age.

Here the Giddens names the specific issue, "stop loss," and indicates some of what is at stake.

Giddens 2

appeals court ruled that the Army could, under stop loss, compel soldiers to remain beyond the initial eight-year obligation (Wickham).

The stop loss policy forces thousands of soldiers to serve beyond their volunteer enlistment contracts. The all-volunteer Army—on which the government prides itself—is slowly developing into a disgruntled mass of men and women being held against their will. These men and women wanted to serve their countries and their families, and they signed what they believed were binding agreements with a trustworthy employer—the United States government—only to find that their government didn't bargain in good faith.

> "Against their will" raises an ethical issue.

> Giddens announces the point he will defend and that his argument will be based in part on ethical considerations.

As far back as the Civil War, the government needed incentives to retain its troops. (Although we all want freedom, few actually want to put our own lives on the line in the pursuit of that goal.) Both the Union and the Confederacy needed to make tough decisions to maintain strong armed forces when soldiers' contracts were expiring. The Union chose to offer financial incentives to keep its young men in uniform, while the Confederacy instituted a series of (not so) "voluntary" reenlistment policies (Robertson). During World War II all soldiers were forced to remain active until they reached a designated number of points. Vietnam saw the last stage of a mandatory draft, with soldiers serving one-year tours (Hockstader). Today's military relies on stop loss, making soldiers stay in the military after their commitment ends. Congress first gave the military the authority to retain soldiers after the Vietnam War when new volunteers were too few to replace departing soldiers. In November 2002, the Pentagon gave stop loss orders for Reserve and National Guard units activated to fight terrorism (Robertson).

> The research in this paragraph builds Giddens's credibility. He has done his homework.

> The definition of "stop loss" is embedded in the larger argument.

This policy is neither forthcoming, safe, nor compassionate toward those most directly impacted—the soldiers and their families. As the United States became more and more entrenched in the conflicts in Iraq and later in Afghanistan, the military was stretched thinner and thinner. By 2004, approximately 40% of those serving in Iraq and Afghanistan came from the ranks of the part-time soldiers: the Reserves and the National Guard (Gerard). While these individuals did know that their countries could call if they enlisted, they continue to bear an inordinate burden of actual combat time, and this new policy continues

> This specific thesis defines the three criteria that the essay will discuss, in order.

Giddens presents his first criterion in this paragraph: the "stop loss" policy is not forthcoming.

to create situations further removed from the job for which they enlisted. Recruiters often pitch the military—including the Reserves and the Guard—to young, impressionable, and often underprivileged kids. I have experienced this pitch firsthand and have seen the eyes of my classmates as the recruiter promised them a better and richer tomorrow. Seeing a golden opportunity for self-respect and achievement, young men and women sign on the dotted line. Today, other young men and women are buying a bill of goods. These recruits—and those who came before them—deserve to have an honest relationship with the government they protect. As policymakers tout the all-volunteer Army, those who serve find their rights threatened. The military claims to teach soldiers respect and honor. Is misleading your employees honest?

Giddens argues that if the policy is not forthcoming, it isn't fair.

Giddens introduces his second criterion—the "stop loss" policy isn't safe.

Aside from being less than forthright, stop loss may be putting our soldiers in harm's way. The policy forces these soldiers to suffer the strain of combat for extended periods of time. Because of the way the policy works, troops may learn of tour extensions mere hours before they had planned to return stateside to lower-stress positions and their loved ones. These troops need to be ready, alert, and equipped with a morale which allows them to fight effectively. Stop loss instead forces these soldiers—often those trained for short stints—to work beyond their experience and training. This policy may prove to overextend, both emotionally and physically, our fighting men and women. As they repeatedly suffer disappointment because of changes in their orders and delays of departure, morale is likely to drop. Based on reports from families, this practice has been devastating to their soldiers. Nancy Durst, wife of United States Reservist Staff Sergeant Scott Durst, told *Talk of the Nation*'s Neal Conan that the military detained her husband's unit just thirty minutes before it was to board the bus scheduled to deliver it to a stateside flight. The unit was later informed that tours had been extended for another four months (Durst). War breeds stress, but how can soldiers be expected to function at an optimal level when forced to suffer disappointments at the hands of their own government?

This second criterion, safety, is based on practicality—on the policy's negative consequences.

Finally, this policy simply runs contrary to the current administration's stated interest in the preservation of family and the bolstering of small

Giddens 4

businesses. First (and most obviously), this less-than-forthright policy keeps families separated. Husbands, wives, and children find themselves separated for longer periods of time, left with uncertainty and ambiguity for comfort. How does this aid in preserving the family? Second, when the government deploys reservists, soldiers often take a severe pay cut. Forced to leave their regular jobs, soldiers—and their families—must survive on an often much smaller government wage. Stop loss extends tours of duty and consequently the economic struggles of the families in question. Third, the policy has proven detrimental to the small-business owner. Men and women have used their military experience, discipline, and training to further themselves economically. The United States prides itself on the power of the small businessman; however, individuals such as Chief Warrant Officer Ronald Eagle have been hurt by this policy. After twenty years of service, Eagle was set to retire from the Army and focus on his aircraft-maintenance business. Instead, the Army has indefinitely moved his retirement date. As a consequence, Eagle has taken a $45,000 pay cut and wonders whether his business will survive his hiatus (Hockstader). Is this the way the government and military fight to preserve the family—emotionally and economically?

> Giddens's third criterion maintains that the policy hurts families and small businesses.

> Giddens raises the practical consequences on individual soldiers.

> This third criterion is not just a matter of impracticality; it's also a matter of fairness.

Because American men and women risk their lives in the name of bettering those of Iraqis and Afghans, the military should think about how their policy affects the lives of their soldiers and those back home. While the stop loss policy does allow the armed forces to build a larger active force without the public backlash (and political suicide) of instituting the draft, this policy comes at a cost. Those who have chosen to serve their country—whether for the training, educational possibilities, economic support, or expression of patriotism—are being bamboozled.

> Giddens sums up what is at stake.

Watch the television commercials that, even now, tout training and part-time service. Read the stories of those serving and the families left behind. The sales pitch and the real picture do not match. The United States is undeniably one of the strongest nations in the world and a bastion of freedom. For these very reasons, the armed forces and the United States government, which represents all citizens, must find a way to lead this war (or conflict or crusade) honestly. If we have to pay soldiers double what they currently make in order to get them to reenlist, we should

Giddens 5

Giddens ends by emphasizing the ethical issue because ethical consideration typically are the strongest ones to include in an evaluation argument.

do so. Even a draft would at least be aboveboard and honest. But we cannot continue to trick people into risking their lives for our national security. Our country must show the honor and respect deserved by those who fight, and stop loss undeniably dishonors and shows disrespect to our soldiers. The military must take a cue from its own advertising and "be all they can be." Be honest.

Giddens 6

Works Cited

Durst, Nancy. Interview with Neal Conan. *Talk of the Nation*. Natl. Public Radio. WNYC, New York. 19 Apr. 2004. Radio.

Gerard, Philip. "When the Cry Was 'Over the Hill in October.'" *Charleston Gazette* 16 May 2004: 1E. *LexisNexis Academic*. Web. 6 Apr. 2009.

Hockstader, Lee. "Army Stops Many Soldiers from Quitting; Orders Extend Enlistments to Curtail Troop Shortages." *WashingtonPost* 29 Dec. 2003: A01. *LexisNexis Academic*. Web. 8 Apr. 2009.

Robertson, John. "The Folly of Stop Loss." *Pittsburgh Post-Gazette* 19 Dec. 2004: J1. *LexisNexis Academic*. Web. 7 Apr. 2009.

Wickham, DeWayne. "A 15-Month Enlistment? Check Army's Fine Print." *USA Today* 17 May 2005: 13A. *LexisNexis Academic*. Web. 6 Apr. 2009.

PEARSON
mycomplab

For support in learning this chapter's content, follow this path in MyCompLab:
▶Resources ▶Writing ▶Writing Purposes ▶Writing to Evaluate.
Review the Instruction and Multimedia resources, then complete the Exercises and click on Gradebook to measure your progress.

11 | Narrative Arguments

QUICK TAKE

In this chapter, you will learn that

1. Narrative arguments rely on concrete individual stories rather than large-scale statistics (see below)
2. Narrative arguments should allow readers to draw their own conclusions (see page 154)
3. Narrative arguments must strike readers as truthful and representative of larger issues (see page 156)

Charity: water understands the persuasive power of personal stories. Their online campaign features narratives like the story of Louis Mackenzie, a young boy who lost his father in the January 2010 earthquake in Haiti. "I cried and cried and cried when my mom told me he died," the text reads. As many organizations have learned, people often feel more compelled to donate money when they read personal stories like Louis's than when they are barraged with abstract numbers and statistics. Why are such stories effective as arguments? What makes some stories more compelling than others? © 2010 Charitywater.org. Used with permission.

Understand How Narrative Arguments Work

A single, detailed personal story sometimes makes a stronger case than large-scale statistical evidence. The Annenberg Public Policy Center reported that an estimated 1.6 million of 17 million U.S. college students gambled online in 2005, but it was the story of Greg Hogan that made the problem real for many Americans. Hogan, the son of a Baptist minister, was an extraordinarily talented musician, who played onstage twice at Carnegie Hall by age 13. He chose to attend Lehigh University in Pennsylvania, where he was a member of the orchestra and class president. At Lehigh he also acquired an addiction to online poker. He lost $7,500, much of which he borrowed from fraternity brothers. To pay them back, he robbed a bank, only to be arrested a few hours later. Eventually he received a long prison sentence. Hogan's story helped to influence Congress to pass the Unlawful Internet Gambling Enforcement Act, which requires financial institutions to stop money transfers to gambling sites.

Successful narrative arguments typically don't have a thesis statement but instead tell a compelling story. From the experience of one individual, readers infer a claim and the reasons that support the claim.

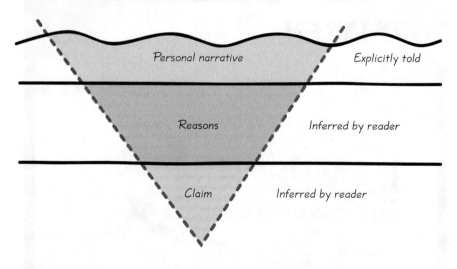

Recognize Kinds of Narrative Arguments

Using narrative to make an argument is part of human nature. As far back as we have records, we find people telling stories and singing songs that argue for change. During periods of history where explicit arguments are dangerous to make, stories allow people to safely criticize authority or imagine how life could be different. The history of folk music is a continuous recycling of old tunes, phrases, and narratives to engage new political situations. Anti-war ballads popular in Ireland in the 1840s were sung in the 1960s by Americans protesting their country's involvement in Vietnam. All the popular narrative genres—short stories, novels, movies, and theater—have been used as ways to make arguments for change.

Singer/songwriter Shawn Colvin is one of many contemporary folk, blues, rock, and rap artists who continue the tradition of making narrative arguments in their songs. Can you think of a song that makes a narrative argument?

Narrative arguments allow readers to fill in the good reasons, and come to their own conclusions. The personal connection readers can feel with the writer of a narrative argument makes this strategy a compelling means of persuasion. Moreover, because the writer usually refrains from making an outright claim, people reading narrative arguments are more likely to feel that they are "making up their own minds" rather than being reluctantly persuaded.

Narrative arguments can be representative anecdotes or they can be longer accounts of particular events that express larger ideas. One such story is George Orwell's account of a hanging in Burma (the country now known as Myanmar) while he was a British colonial administrator in the late 1920s. In "A Hanging," first published in 1931, Orwell narrates the story of an execution of a nameless prisoner who was convicted of a nameless crime. Everyone present quietly and dispassionately performs his job—the prison guards, the hangman, the superintendent, and even the prisoner, who offers no resistance when he is bound and led to the gallows. All is totally routine until a very small incident makes Orwell realize what is happening:

> It was about forty yards to the gallows. I watched the bare brown back of the prisoner marching in front of me. He walked clumsily with his bound arms, but quite steadily, with that bobbing gait of the Indian who never straightens his knees. At each step his muscles slid neatly into place, the lock of hair on

his scalp danced up and down, his feet printed themselves on the wet gravel. And once, in spite of the men who gripped him by each shoulder, he stepped slightly aside to avoid a puddle on the path.

It is curious, but till that moment I had never realized what it means to destroy a healthy, conscious man. When I saw the prisoner step aside to avoid the puddle, I saw the mystery, the unspeakable wrongness, of cutting a life short when it is in full tide. This man was not dying, he was alive just as we were alive. All the organs of his body were working—bowels digesting food, skin renewing itself, nails growing, tissues forming—all toiling away in solemn foolery. His nails would still be growing when he stood on the drop, when he was falling through the air with a tenth of a second to live. His eyes saw the yellow gravel and the grey walls, and his brain still remembered, foresaw, reasoned— reasoned even about puddles. He and we were a party of men walking together, seeing, hearing, feeling, understanding the same world; and in two minutes, with a sudden snap, one of us would be gone—one mind less, one world less.

Orwell's narrative leads to a dramatic moment of recognition, which gives this story its lasting power. His sudden realization of what execution means to both the prisoner and his executioners is a powerful argument to reconsider the morality of the death penalty.

Build a Narrative Argument

Because storytelling is such a familiar activity, it is easy for writers to get carried away with their narrative, and lose sight of the point they are trying to make. Readers find narrative compelling, but not if the narrative is long-winded, full of unnecessary detail, or has no obvious point. Furthermore, readers are quickly put off if they feel they are being given a lecture.

There are two keys to making effective narrative arguments: establishing that the narrative is truthful, and showing its relevance to a wider problem or question. Writing from personal experience can increase the impact of your argument, but that impact diminishes greatly if readers doubt you are telling the truth. And while the story you tell may be true, it is important that it also be representative— something that has happened to many other people, or something that could happen to your readers. Narrative arguments are useful for illustrating how people are affected by particular issues or events, but they are more effective if you have evidence that goes beyond a single incident.

One rule of thumb that you can keep in mind when building a narrative argument is to start out with as much detail and as many events as you can recall, then revise and edit heavily. It's hard to select the best details and events for your argument until you have written them all down, and often the process of writing and remembering will bring up new details that you had forgotten, or hadn't seen the relevance of before. Once you can see the big picture you have painted with your narrative, it is easier to see what your readers do not need, and remove it. This strategy brings your story, and your argument, into sharper focus.

Finding Good Reasons

Can a Story Make an Argument?

This photo shows two polar bears standing atop a small ice flow in the Arctic Ocean. The National Wildlife Foundation describes the plight of the polar bear, struggling to survive in the face of a changing climate.

As climate change melts sea ice, the U.S. Geological Survey projects that two-thirds of polar bears will disappear by 2050. This dramatic decline of polar bears is occurring in our lifetime, which is but a minuscule fraction of the time polar bears have roamed the vast Arctic seas. The retreat of ice has implications beyond the obvious habitat loss. The larger gap of open water between the ice and land also contributes to rougher wave conditions, making the bears' swim from shore to sea ice more hazardous. Exacerbating the problems of the loss of hunting areas, the shrinking polar ice cap will also cause a decline in polar bears' prey—seals. The polar bear is the proverbial "canary in the coal mine" of the serious threat global warming poses to wildlife species around the world, unless we take immediate and significant action to reduce global warming pollution.

The National Wildlife Foundation

Write about it

1. What argument might the National Wildlife Foundation be making about the state of climate change? What details reveal their argument?

2. Why might the National Wildlife Foundation have chosen the polar bear to personify the effects of climate change? What other types of animals would have made good choices? Poor choices?

3. How does the National Wildlife Foundation's account of climate change differ from other accounts that you have heard? What is the other side of this issue? Does this story change your thinking about climate change? Why or why not?

Steps to Writing a Narrative Argument

Step 1 Identify an Experience That Makes an Implicit Argument

Think about experiences that made you realize that something is wrong or that things need to be changed. The experience does not have to be one that leads to a moral lesson at the end, but it should be one that makes your readers think.

Examples

- Being accused of and perhaps even arrested and hauled to jail for something you didn't do or for standing up for something you believed in.
- Moving from a well-financed suburban school to a much poorer rural or urban school in the same state.
- Experiencing stereotyping or prejudice in any way—for the way you look, the way you act, your age, your gender, your race, or your sexual orientation.

Step 2 List All the Details You Can Remember

- When did it happen?
- How old were you?
- Why were you there?
- Who else was there?
- Where did it happen? If the place is important, describe what it looked like.

Step 3 Examine the Significance of the Event

- How did you feel about the experience when it happened?
- How did it affect you then?
- How do you feel about the experience now?
- What long-term effects has it had on your life?

Step 4 Analyze Your Potential Readers

- Who are your readers?
- How much will your readers know about the background of the experience you are describing?
- Would anything similar ever likely have happened to them?
- How likely are they to agree with your feelings about the experience?

Step 5 Write a Draft

- You might need to give some background first, but if you have a compelling story, often it's best to launch right in.
- You might want to tell the story as it happened (chronological order), or you might want to begin with a striking incident and then go back to tell how it happened (flashback).
- You might want to reflect on your experience at the end, but you want your story to do most of the work. Avoid drawing a simple moral lesson. Your readers should share your feelings if you tell your story well.

Step 6 Revise, Edit, Proofread

- For detailed instructions, see Chapter 4.
- For a checklist to use to evaluate your draft, see pages 48–49.

Leslie
Marmon
Silko

The Border Patrol State

Leslie Marmon Silko (1948–) was born in Albuquerque and graduated from the University of New Mexico. She has received much critical acclaim for her writings about Native Americans. Her first novel, *Ceremony* (1977), describes the struggles of a veteran returning home after World War II to civilian life on a New Mexico reservation. Her incorporation of Indian storytelling techniques in *Ceremony* drew strong praise. One critic called her "the most accomplished Indian writer of her generation." She has since published two more novels, *Almanac of the Dead* (1991) and *Gardens in the Dunes* (1999); a collection of essays, *Yellow Woman* and a *Beauty of the Spirit: Essays on Native American Life Today* (1996); two volumes of poems and stories; and many shorter works. Silko's talents as a storyteller are evident in this essay, which first appeared in the magazine *The Nation* in 1994.

I used to travel the highways of New Mexico and Arizona with a wonderful sensation of absolute freedom as I cruised down the open road and across the vast desert plateaus. On the Laguna Pueblo reservation, where I was raised, the people were patriotic despite the way the U.S. government had treated Native Americans. As proud citizens, we grew up believing the freedom to travel was our inalienable right, a right that some Native Americans had been denied in the early twentieth century. Our cousin, old Bill Pratt, used to ride his horse 300 miles overland from Laguna, New Mexico, to Prescott, Arizona, every summer to work as a fire lookout.

Silko establishes freedom of travel 2 as a fundamental human, as well as American, right—an important assumption underlying her argument. 3

In school in the 1950s, we were taught that our right to travel from state to state without special papers or threat of detainment was a right that citizens under communist and totalitarian governments did not possess. That wide open highway told us we were U.S. citizens; we were free. . . .

Not so long ago, my companion Gus and I were driving south from Albuquerque, returning to Tucson after a book promotion for the paperback edition of my novel *Almanac of the Dead*. I had settled back and gone to sleep while Gus drove, but I was awakened when I felt the car slowing to a stop. It was nearly midnight on New Mexico State Road 26, a dark, lonely stretch of two-lane highway between Hatch and Deming. When I sat up, I saw the headlights and emergency flashers of six vehicles—Border Patrol cars and a van were blocking both lanes of the highway. Gus stopped the car and rolled down the window to ask what was wrong. But the closest Border Patrolman and his companion did not reply; instead, the first agent ordered us to "step out of the car." Gus asked why, but his question seemed to set them off. Two more Border Patrol agents immediately approached our car, and one of them snapped, "Are you looking for trouble?" as if he would relish it.

Specific details paint a vivid picture of the experience and establish credibility.

4   I will never forget that night beside the highway. There was an awful feeling of menace and violence straining to break loose. It was clear that the uniformed men would be only too happy to drag us out of the car if we did not speedily comply with their request (asking a question is tantamount to resistance, it seems). So we stepped out of the car and they motioned for us to stand on the shoulder of the road. The night was very dark, and no other traffic had come down the road since we had been stopped. All I could think about was a book I had read—*Nunca Mas*—the official report of a human rights commission that investigated and certified more than 12,000 "disappearances" during Argentina's "dirty war" in the late 1970s.

5   The weird anger of these Border Patrolmen made me think about descriptions in the report of Argentine police and military officers who became addicted to interrogation, torture and the murder that followed. When the military and police ran out of political suspects to torture and kill, they resorted to the random abduction of citizens off the streets. I thought how easy it would be for the Border Patrol to shoot us and leave our bodies and car beside the highway, like so many bodies found in these parts and ascribed to "drug runners."

Silko connects her experience with border patrol to more extreme incidents to establish the potential danger inherent in these searches.

6   Two other Border Patrolmen stood by the white van. The one who had asked if we were looking for trouble ordered his partner to "get the dog," and from the back of the van another patrolman brought a small female German shepherd on a leash. The dog apparently did not heel well enough to suit him, and the handler jerked the leash. They opened the doors of our car and pulled the dog's head into it, but I saw immediately from the expression in her eyes that the dog hated them, and that she would not serve them. When she showed no interest in the inside of the car, they brought her around back to the trunk, near where we were standing. They half-dragged her up into the trunk, but still she did not indicate any stowed-away human beings or illegal drugs.

7   The mood got uglier; the officers seemed outraged that the dog could not find any contraband, and they dragged her over to us and commanded her to sniff our legs and feet. To my relief, the

strange violence the Border Patrol agents had focused on us now seemed shifted to the dog. I no longer felt so strongly that we would be murdered. We exchanged looks—the dog and I. She was afraid of what they might do, just as I was. The dog's handler jerked the leash sharply as she sniffed us, as if to make her perform better, but the dog refused to accuse us: She had an innate dignity that did not permit her to serve the murderous impulses of those men. I can't forget the expression in the dog's eyes; it was as if she were embarrassed to be associated with them. I had a small amount of medicinal marijuana in my purse that night, but she refused to expose me. I am not partial to dogs, but I will always remember the small German shepherd that night.

> Silko implicitly asks, if even the dog recognizes the border patrol's barbarity, how can any reasonable person defend their actions?

8   Unfortunately, what happened to me is an everyday occurrence here now. Since the 1980s, on top of greatly expanding border checkpoints, the Immigration and Naturalization Service and the Border Patrol have implemented policies that interfere with the rights of U.S. citizens to travel freely within our borders. I.N.S. agents now patrol all interstate highways and roads that lead to or from the U.S.–Mexico border in Texas, New Mexico, Arizona and California. Now, when you drive east from Tucson on Interstate 10 toward El Paso, you encounter an I.N.S. check station outside Las Cruces, New Mexico. When you drive north from Las Cruces up Interstate 25, two miles north of the town of Truth or Consequences, the highway is blocked with orange emergency barriers, and all traffic is diverted into a two-lane Border Patrol checkpoint—ninety-five miles north of the U.S.–Mexico border.

9   I was detained once at Truth or Consequences, despite my and my companion's Arizona driver's licenses. Two men, both Chicanos, were detained at the same time, despite the fact that they too presented ID and spoke English without the thick Texas accents of the Border Patrol agents. While we were stopped, we watched as other vehicles—whose occupants were white—were waved through the checkpoint. White people traveling with brown people, however, can expect to be stopped on suspicion they work with the sanctuary movement, which shelters refugees. White people who appear to be clergy, those who wear ethnic clothing or jewelry and women with very long hair or very short hair (they could be nuns) are also frequently detained; white men with beards or men with long hair are likely to be detained, too, because Border Patrol agents have "profiles" of "those sorts" of white people who may help political refugees. (Most of the political refugees from Guatemala and El Salvador are Native American or mestizo because the indigenous people of the Americas have continued to resist efforts by invaders to displace them from their

ancestral lands.) Alleged increases in illegal immigration by people of Asian ancestry mean that the Border Patrol now routinely detains anyone who appears to be Asian or part Asian, as well.

10   Once your car is diverted from the Interstate Highway into the checkpoint area, you are under the control of the Border Patrol, which in practical terms exercises a power that no highway patrol or city patrolman possesses: They are willing to detain anyone, for no apparent reason. Other law-enforcement officers need a shred of probable cause in order to detain someone. On the books, so does the Border Patrol; but on the road, it's another matter. They'll order you to stop your car and step out; then they'll ask you to open the trunk. If you ask why or request a search warrant, you'll be told that they'll have to have a dog sniff the car before they can request a search warrant, and the dog might not get there for two or three hours. The search warrant might require an hour or two past that. They make it clear that if you force them to obtain a search warrant for the car, they will make you submit to a strip search as well.

11   Traveling in the open, though, the sense of violation can be even worse. Never mind high-profile cases like that of former Border Patrol agent Michael Elmer, acquitted of murder by claiming self-defense, despite admitting that as an officer he shot an "illegal" immigrant in the back and then hid the body, which remained undiscovered until another Border Patrolman reported the event. (Last month, Elmer was convicted of reckless endangerment in a separate incident, for shooting at least ten rounds from his M-16 too close to a group of immigrants as they were crossing illegally into Nogales in March 1992.) Or that in El Paso a high school football coach driving a vanload of players in full uniform was pulled over on the freeway and a Border Patrol agent put a cocked revolver to his head. (The football coach was Mexican-American, as were most of the players in his van; the incident eventually caused a federal judge to issue a restraining order against the Border Patrol.) We've a mountain of personal experiences like that which never make the newspapers. A history professor at U.C.L.A. told me she had been traveling by train from Los Angeles to Albuquerque twice a month doing research. On each of her trips, she had noticed that the Border Patrol agents were at the station in Albuquerque scrutinizing the passengers. Since she is six feet tall and of Irish and German ancestry, she was not particularly concerned. Then one day when she stepped off the train in Albuquerque, two Border Patrolmen accosted her, wanting to know what she was doing, and why she was traveling between Los Angeles and Albuquerque twice a month. She

Have you ever crossed an international border? What experiences have you had?

In paragraphs 11 and 12, Silko offers additional stories to exemplify the unnerving nature of these searches.

presented identification and an explanation deemed "suitable" by the agents, and was allowed to go about her business.

12   Just the other day, I mentioned to a friend that I was writing this article and he told me about his 73-year-old father, who is half Chinese and who had set out alone by car from Tucson to Albuquerque the week before. His father had become confused by road construction and missed a turnoff from Interstate 10 to Interstate 25; when he turned around and circled back, he missed the turnoff a second time. But when he looped back for yet another try, Border Patrol agents stopped him and forced him to open his trunk. After they satisfied themselves that he was not smuggling Chinese immigrants, they sent him on his way. He was so rattled by the event that he had to be driven home by his daughter.

13   This is the police state that has developed in the southwestern United States since the 1980s. No person, no citizen, is free to travel without the scrutiny of the Border Patrol. In the city of South Tucson, where 80 percent of the respondents were Chicano or Mexicano, a joint research project by the University of Wisconsin and the University of Arizona recently concluded that one out of every five people there had been detained, mistreated verbally or nonverbally, or questioned by I.N.S. agents in the past two years.

14   Manifest Destiny may lack its old grandeur of theft and blood—"lock the door" is what it means now, with racism a trump card to be played again and again, shamelessly, by both major political parties. "Immigration," like "street crime" and "welfare fraud," is a political euphemism that refers to people of color. Politicians and media people talk about "illegal aliens" to dehumanize and demonize undocumented immigrants, who are for the most part people of color. Even in the days of Spanish and Mexican rule, no attempts were made to interfere with the flow of people and goods from south to north and north to south. It is the U.S. government that has continually attempted to sever contact between the tribal people north of the border and those to the south.

15   Now that the "Iron Curtain" is gone, it is ironic that the U.S. government and its Border Patrol are constructing a steel wall ten feet high to span sections of the border with Mexico. While politicians and multinational corporations extol the virtues of NAFTA and "free trade" (in goods, not flesh), the ominous curtain is already up in a six-mile section at the border crossing at Mexicali; two miles are being erected but are not yet finished at Naco; and at Nogales, sixty miles south of Tucson, the steel wall has been

---

Silko uses statistics from a research study conducted by respected universities as evidence for her claim.

Having established the injustice of U.S. methods for defending its borders, Silko changes her focus to question the idea of borders themselves.

all rubber-stamped and awaits construction likely to begin in March. Like the pathetic multimillion-dollar "antidrug" border surveillance balloons that were continually deflated by high winds and made only a couple of meager interceptions before they blew away, the fence along the border is a theatrical prop, a bit of pork for contractors. Border entrepreneurs have already used blowtorches to cut passageways through the fence to collect "tolls," and are doing a brisk business. Back in Washington, the I.N.S. announces a $300 million computer contract to modernize its record-keeping and Congress passes a crime bill that shunts $255 million to the I.N.S. for 1995, $181 million earmarked for border control, which is to include 700 new partners for the men who stopped Gus and me in our travels, and the history professor, and my friend's father, and as many as they could from South Tucson.

16   It is no use; borders haven't worked, and they won't work, not now, as the indigenous people of the Americas reassert their kinship and solidarity with one another. A mass migration is already under way; its roots are not simply economic. The Uto–Aztecan languages are spoken as far north as Taos Pueblo near the Colorado border, all the way south to Mexico City. Before the arrival of the Europeans, the indigenous communities throughout this region not only conducted commerce, the people shared cosmologies, and oral narratives about the Maize Mothers, the Twin Brothers and their Grandmother, Spider Woman, as well as Quetzalcoatl the benevolent snake. The great human migration within the Americas cannot be stopped; human beings are natural forces of the Earth, just as rivers and winds are natural forces.

17   Deep down the issue is simple: The so-called "Indian Wars" from the days of Sitting Bull and Red Cloud have never really ended in the Americas. The Indian people of southern Mexico, of Guatemala and those left in El Salvador, too, are still fighting for their lives and for their land against the "cavalry" patrols sent out by the governments of those lands. The Americas are Indian country, and the "Indian problem" is not about to go away.

18   One evening at sundown, we were stopped in traffic at a railroad crossing in downtown Tucson while a freight train passed us, slowly gaining speed as it headed north to Phoenix. In the twilight I saw the most amazing sight: Dozens of human beings, mostly young men, were riding the train; everywhere, on flat cars, inside open boxcars, perched on top of boxcars, hanging off ladders on tank cars and between boxcars. I couldn't count fast

Silko extends her thesis further.

Silko concludes with another story as evidence for her thesis that people cannot be bound by artificial borders.

enough, but I saw fifty or sixty people headed north. They were dark young men, Indian and mestizo; they were smiling and a few of them waved at us in our cars. I was reminded of the ancient story of Aztlán, told by the Aztecs but known in other Uto–Aztecan communities as well. Aztlán is the beautiful land to the north, the origin place of the Aztec people. I don't remember how or why the people left Aztlán to journey farther south, but the old story says that one day, they will return.

PEARSON
mycomplab

For support in learning this chapter's content, follow this path in MyCompLab:
▷ Resources ▷ Writing ▷ Writing Purposes ▷ Writing to Describe.
Review the Instruction and Multimedia resources, then complete the Exercises and click on Gradebook to measure your progress.

12 | Rebuttal Arguments

QUICK TAKE

In this chapter, you will learn that

1. Rebuttal arguments use two basic strategies: refutation and counter-argument (see page 168)
2. Refutation arguments focus on the shortcomings of the opposing argument (see page 169)
3. Counterarguments acknowledge opposing positions but go on to maintain that the writer has the better argument (see page 170)

Whaling is an ancient form of hunting that greatly expanded in the nineteenth century due to a worldwide demand for whale oil. By 1986 the worldwide whale populations were so seriously depleted that the International Whaling Committee banned commercial whaling to allow whale populations to replenish. Limited whaling continues for scientific research, but environmental organizations such as Greenpeace insist that "science" is a guise for the continuation of commercial whaling. Greenpeace protests all whaling vigorously—both by peaceful means and by open ocean confrontations with whaling vessels. Could their protests at sea be considered a rebuttal argument?

Understand How Rebuttal Arguments Work

There are two basic approaches to rebutting an argument: you can refute the argument, or you can counterargue. In the first case, **refutation**, you demonstrate the shortcomings of the argument you wish to discredit, and you may or may not offer a positive claim of your own. In the second case, **counterargument**, you focus on the strengths of the position you support, and spend little time on the specifics of the argument you are countering. There can be substantial overlap between these two tactics, and good rebuttal arguments often employ both refutation and counterargument.

Because they focus on the shortcomings in the opposition's argument, a refutation argument often takes much of its structure from the argument being refuted.

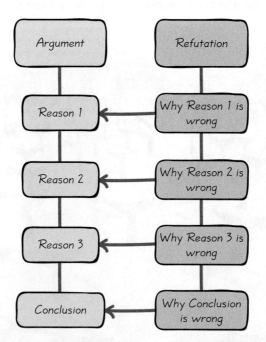

Many college students believe that using technology to "multitask" makes them more productive, believing that studying, texting a friend, and listening to music all at once is an efficient use of their time. But research shows that engaging in multiple tasks is distracting, interferes with memory, and makes it difficult to switch from one task to another, making multitaskers less productive than people focusing on one task at a time.

Counterarguments more often take up ideas the opposing claims has not addressed at all, or they take a very different approach to the problem. By largely ignoring the specifics of the argument being countered, they make the implicit claim that the counterargument is superior.

Those who argue for tariffs on goods from China claim that tariffs will protect American manufacturing jobs, but tariffs are a bad idea because they would increase prices on clothing, furniture, toys, and other consumer goods for everyone, and would cause the loss of retailing jobs as well.

Recognize Kinds of Rebuttal Arguments

Refutation

A refutation can either challenge the assumptions underlying a claim, or it can question the evidence supporting a claim. Until about five hundred years ago, people believed that the sky, and everything in it, moved, while the Earth remained still. They observed the stars moving from west to east in a regular, circular motion, and concluded that all the heavenly bodies orbited around an axis between Earth and Polaris, the northern star. This theory, however, did not explain the movement of the planets. If you watch the path of Mars over several nights, for example, you will notice that it moves, like the stars, from east to west. But occasionally, it will appear to move backward, from west to east, before reversing itself and resuming an east-to-west course. This phenomenon is called retrograde motion, and it is exhibited by all the planets in our solar system. In fact, our word *planet* derives from the Greek term *planetes*, meaning "wanderer." The ancient Greeks assumed that the planets and stars orbited the Earth, but that the planets sometimes wandered from their paths.

In the second century CE, the Greek astronomer Ptolemy made precise and detailed observations of the planets and created a model to predict their retrograde motion. In his treatise, the *Almagest*, he theorized that Mars and the other "wanderers" periodically deviated from their path around the Earth, making small circles, or epicycles, before moving on again. It was a complicated system, but it predicted the movements of the planets very accurately, and so it went unchallenged for over a thousand years.

In the early sixteenth century, the Polish astronomer Nicolaus Copernicus recognized that Ptolemy's observations could be explained more simply if the Earth and other planets circled the Sun. Copernicus's theory, later confirmed by the German astronomer Johannes Kepler, eventually replaced the Ptolemaic model of the solar system as the accepted explanation for observed planetary motion.

Copernicus did not question Ptolemy's evidence—the data he had collected showing where the stars and planets appear in the sky to an Earth-bound observer. Instead, he questioned Ptolemy's central assumption that Earth is the center of the solar system. Because evidence of the planet's retrograde motion had been observed by people over such a long period of time, it was unlikely to be wrong. Instead, it was the theory Ptolemy constructed to explain his data that was incorrect.

But sometimes evidence is wrong. Sometimes, too, evidence is incomplete or not representative, and sometimes counterevidence can be found. People who are bent on persuading others may leave out information that weakens their case, or employ evidence in questionable ways to try to bolster their claims. Dermatologists argue that indoor tanning is harmful to people's health because it exposes them to ultraviolet radiation, a known cause of cancer. The tanning industry, not surprisingly, disagrees, arguing that indoor tanning is safer than outdoor tanning because it assures safe levels of UV radiation exposure. While sunbathers often get sunburned, indoor tanners only get safe levels of radiation. This is an intriguing claim, but the AMA has discovered that in fact people who use tanning beds *do* get burned—as many of 50 percent of them. The tanning industry also claims indoor tanning provides people with a "protective" tan that reduces the amount of harmful UV radiation they absorb when they do go out in the sun. Doctors counter this claim by pointing out that a "base tan" provides only as much protection as a sunblock with a Sun Protection Factor, or SPF, of 3, and that the minimum recommended SPF for sunscreen is 15. The protection offered by an indoor tan is minimal at best. Both sides continue to argue over what evidence is valid, and accurate, when assessing the safety of indoor tanning.

Counterargument

Another way to rebut is to counterargue. In a counterargument, you might acknowledge an opposing point of view, but you might not consider it in detail. Rather, you put the main effort into your own argument. A counterarguer, in effect, says, "I hear your argument. But there is more to it than that. Now listen while I explain why another position is stronger." Counterargument is an effective way of persuading audiences, but sometimes it is used as a way to avoid addressing opposing views honestly. People's tendency to be persuaded by counterargument also makes them susceptible to red herrings, when an irrelevant but dramatic detail is put forward as if it were important, or *ad hominem* attacks, where someone makes spurious accusations about an opponent instead of engaging in real debate.

The counterarguer depends on the wisdom of his or her audience members to hear all sides of an issue and make up their own minds about the merits of the case. In the following short poem, Wilfred Owen, a veteran of the horrors of World War I trench warfare, offers a counterargument to those who argue that war is noble, to those who believe along with the poet Horace that "dulce et decorum est pro patria mori"—that it is sweet and fitting to die for one's country. This poem gains in popularity whenever there is an unpopular war for it rebuts the belief that it is noble to die for one's country in modern warfare.

Dulce Et Decorum Est

Bent double, like old beggars under sacks,
Knock-kneed, coughing like hags, we cursed through sludge,
Till on the haunting flares we turned our backs
And towards our distant rest began to trudge.
Men marched asleep. Many had lost their boots
But limped on, blood-shod. All went lame; all blind;
Drunk with fatigue; deaf even to the hoots
Of tired, outstripped Five-Nines that dropped behind.

Gas! Gas! Quick, boys! — An ecstasy of fumbling,
Fitting the clumsy helmets just in time;
But someone still was yelling out and stumbling,
And flound'ring like a man in fire or lime . . .
Dim, through the misty panes and thick green light,
As under a green sea, I saw him drowning.
In all my dreams, before my helpless sight,
He plunges at me, guttering, choking, drowning.

If in some smothering dreams you too could pace
Behind the wagon that we flung him in,
And watch the white eyes writhing in his face,
His hanging face, like a devil's sick of sin;
If you could hear, at every jolt, the blood
Come gargling from the froth-corrupted lungs,
Obscene as cancer, bitter as the cud
Of vile, incurable sores on innocent tongues,
My friend, you would not tell with such high zest
To children ardent for some desperate glory,
The old Lie; Dulce et Decorum est
Pro patria mori.

Owen does not summarize the argument in favor of being willing to die for one's country and then refute that argument point by point. Rather, his poem presents an opposing argument, supported by a narrative of the speaker's experience in a poison-gas attack, that he hopes will more than counterbalance what he calls "the old Lie." Owen simply ignores the reasons people give for being willing to die for one's country and argues instead that there are good reasons not to do so. And he hopes that the evidence he summons for his position will outweigh for his audience (addressed as "My friend,") the evidence in support of the other side.

Rebuttal arguments frequently offer both refutation and counterargument. Like attorneys engaged in a trial, people writing rebuttals must make their own cases based on good reasons and hard evidence, but they also do what they can to undermine their opponent's case. In the end the jury—the audience—decides.

Build a Rebuttal Argument

As you prepare to rebut an argument, look closely at what your opponent says. What exactly are the claims? What is the evidence? What are the assumptions? What do you disagree with? Are there parts you agree with? Are there assumptions you share? Do you agree that the evidence is accurate?

Knowing where you agree with someone helps you focus your rebuttal on differences. Having points of agreement can also help you build credibility with your audience, if you acknowledge that your opponent makes some logical points, or makes reasonable assumptions.

Consider using counterargument if you generally agree with a claim but do not think it goes far enough, if you feel an argument proposes the wrong solution to a problem, or if you think that, while accurate, it misses the "big picture." Counterargument lets you frame your own, stronger take on the question at hand without spending a lot of time trying to find flaws in the opposing position when there may not be many there.

If you do have serious objections to an argument, plan to refute it, and start by looking for the most important differences in your respective positions. What are the biggest "red flags" in the argument you disagree with? What are the weakest points of your opponent's argument? What are the strongest points of your own? You will probably want to highlight these differences in your rebuttal. You may find many problems with evidence and logic, in which case you will probably want to prioritize them. You do not necessarily need to point out the flaws in every single element of an argument. Direct your audience to the ones that matter the most.

You can also use counterargument in combination with refutation, first showing why an existing argument is wrong, and then offering an alternative. This is one of the more common forms of rebuttal. As you examine your opponent's claims and evidence, look closely for fallacies and faulty logic (see pages 17–19). How do these distort the problem or lead the audience to mistaken conclusions? Pointing them out to your readers will strengthen your position.

Look too at sources. Check your opponent's facts. Scrutinize the experts he or she relies on. And consider the purpose and motivation behind arguments you rebut. Groups funded by major industries, political parties, and special interest groups may have hidden or not-so-hidden agendas driving the arguments they make. Pointing these out to your readers can strengthen your own position.

Finding Good Reasons

Can the Web be trusted for research?

Most Web users are familiar with the huge and immensely popular Wikipedia, the online encyclopedia. What makes Wikipedia so different from traditional, print encyclopedias is that entries can be contributed or edited by anyone.

In 2007, Jimmy Wales, president of Wikimedia and one of its founders, debated the legitimacy of Wikipedia with Dale Hoiberg, editor-in-chief of *Encyclopedia Britannica*. Hoiberg's main criticism of Wikipedia is that its structure—an open-source wiki without the formal editorial control that shapes traditional, print encyclopedias—allows for inaccurate entries.

In response, Wales argues that *Britannica* and newspapers also contain errors, but Wikipedia has the advantage that they are easily corrected. Furthermore, he asserts that Wikipedia's policy of using volunteer administrators to delete irrelevant entries and requiring authors of entries to cite reliable, published sources ensures quality. Nonetheless, some universities including UCLA and the University of Pennsylvania along with many instructors strongly discourage and even ban students from citing Wikipedia in their work. (Wikipedia also cautions against using its entries as a primary source for serious research.)

Write about it

1. If your college decided to ban the use of Wikipedia as a reference because it lacked the authority of a traditional encyclopedia, would you want to challenge it? Why or why not?

2. If you chose to challenge the college's policy, how would you do so? Would it be effective to refute the college's claims point by point, noting fallacies in logic and reasoning? Would it be effective to build a counterargument in which you examine the assumptions on which the college's claims are based? Which strategy would you choose, and why?

Steps to Writing a Rebuttal Argument

1	2	3
Identify an Argument to Argue Against as Well as Its Main Claim(s)	Examine the Facts on Which the Claim Is Based	Examine the Assumptions on Which the Claim Is Based

Step 1 Identify an Argument to Argue Against as Well as Its Main Claim(s)

- What exactly are you arguing against?
- Are there secondary claims attached to the main claim?
- Include a fair summary of your opponent's position in your finished rebuttal.

Examples

- Arguing against raising taxes for the purpose of building a new sports stadium (examine how proponents claim that a new sports facility will benefit the local economy).
- Arguing for raising the minimum wage (examine how opponents claim that a higher minimum wage isn't necessary and negatively affects small-business owners).

Step 2 Examine the Facts on Which the Claim Is Based

- Are the facts accurate, current, and representative?
- Is there another body of facts that you can present as counterevidence?
- If the author uses statistics, can the statistics be interpreted differently?
- If the author quotes from sources, how reliable are those sources?
- Are the sources treated fairly, or are quotations taken out of context?

Step 3 Examine the Assumptions on Which the Claim Is Based

- What are the primary and secondary assumptions of the claim you are rejecting?
- How are those assumptions flawed?
- Does the author resort to name calling, use faulty reasoning, or ignore key facts (see pages 17–19)?

Step 4 Analyze Your Potential Readers

- To what extent do your potential readers support the claim that you are rejecting?
- If they strongly support that claim, how might you appeal to them to change their minds?
- What common assumptions and beliefs do you share with them?

Step 5 Write a Draft

Introduction

Identify the issue and the argument you are rejecting.

- Provide background if the issue is unfamiliar to most of your readers.
- Give a quick summary of the competing positions even if the issue is familiar to your readers.
- Make your aim clear in your thesis statement.

Body

Take on the argument that you are rejecting. Consider questioning the evidence that is used to support the argument by doing one or more of the following.

- Challenge the facts and the currency and relevance of examples.
- Present counterevidence and countertestimony.
- Challenge the credibility of sources cited.
- Question the way in which statistical evidence is presented and interpreted.
- Argue that quotations are taken out of context.

Conclusion

- Conclude on a firm note by underscoring your objections.
- Consider closing with a counterargument or counterproposal.

Step 6 Revise, Edit, Proofread

- For detailed instructions, see Chapter 4.
- For a checklist to use to evaluate your draft, see pages 48–49.

Dan Stein

Crossing the Line

Dan Stein is president of the Federation for American Immigration Reform, a Washington D.C.–based nonprofit organization that seeks to stop illegal immigration. He frequently speaks and writes about immigration issues. "Crossing the Line" was published in the *Los Angeles Business Journal* in February 2007.

Stein uses a fact from a respected polling agency to bolster his assumption that the majority of Americans strongly oppose illegal immigration.

The timing could not have been worse for Bank of America to announce that it would begin issuing credit cards to illegal aliens in Los Angeles. News of Bank of America's decision was published in the *Wall Street Journal* on February 13, the same day that a new Harris Poll revealed that Americans perceive the two greatest threats to their security to be illegal immigration and the outsourcing of American jobs.

2   Even more than the prospect of the Iranians or the North Koreans with nukes, Americans believe that their security is threatened by millions of people pouring across our borders and by corporations that appear willing to sell out the interests of American workers. In one decision, Bank of America managed to pluck two raw nerves by appearing to encourage illegal immigration, while sending the message that it would not let any national interest stand in the way of it making a buck.

3   The Bank of America decision and the overwhelming negative public reaction to it illustrates the growing disconnect between the elite and everyone else in this country. To the elite—including the current occupant of the White House—the traditional idea of the nation has become a bothersome anachronism. To the extent that the entity known as the United States has any relevance at all to them, it is to secure their ability to conduct business and maximize their corporate bottom lines. Concepts of patriotism and loyalty are marketing tools and nothing more.

Stein connects his argument to other issues his audience is likely to relate to.

4   To Bank of America and other large corporations, illegal immigrants are a source of low wage labor and an untapped customer market. It matters not that illegal immigrants are breaking the laws of the United States, taking jobs from and driving down wages for middle class workers, burdening schools (not the ones the children of Bank of America executives attend, of course) and other vital public services. What matters to the banking industry is that the estimated 12 to 15 million illegal aliens living in the United States have purchasing power and that there is money to be made off of serving them.

5   It is true that Bank of America did not create the illegal immigration crisis in the United States, although banking industry
decisions to allow illegal aliens to open bank accounts, take out
home mortgages and now obtain credit cards has certainly added
to the problem. But the fact that the federal government has done
little to resolve the problem of illegal immigration does not mean
that banks and other business interests have an unfettered right
to profit from illegal immigration. Bank of America did not create
the illegal drug problem in the United States, but that does not entitle it to market services to the drug cartels, even though it would
be enormously profitable to do so.

Stein alludes to the drug industry to assert that corporations' obligation to respect the laws of the country trump their obligation to make a profit.

OVERTLY DISCRIMINATORY

6   The plan to issue credit cards to illegal aliens is also overtly
discriminatory, giving a new meaning to their corporate slogan:
"Bank of America, Higher Standards" (for some). While American
citizens and legal U.S. residents are held to one standard in order
to obtain credit, illegal aliens will be held to a lower standard. The
plastic that any of us tote around in our wallets required us to open
our entire lives to our creditors and to provide verification of our
identities and credit-worthiness. In their hunger to make money off
of illegal aliens Bank of America is prepared to accept easily counterfeited Mexican matricula cards as proof of identity, and maintaining a checking account for three months as a credit history.

7   Bank of America has obviously felt the sting of a public
backlash, as evidenced by their sudden reluctance to discuss
it in the media. Some people have gone so far as to pull their
accounts out of Bank of America. But given the consolidation of
the banking industry generally, and the fact that a handful of
banks have a corner on the credit card market, it will require government action to stop financial institutions from pursuing profits
in blatant disregard of the law and the public interest.

Stein uses refutation heavily in his rebuttal, never straying too far from the issue: the legality and morality of Bank of America's new policy.

8   Existing federal law clearly prohibits "encouraging or induc-
ing unauthorized aliens to enter the United States, and engaging
in a conspiracy or aiding and abetting" people who violate U.S.
immigration laws. Products and services specifically marketed to
illegal aliens, intended to make it easier to live and work in the
U.S. illegally, violate the spirit if not the letter of the law.

9   To Bank of America, illegal aliens are just customers and
the United States nothing more than a market. To the American
people, illegal immigration and corporate greed are seen as serious threats to their security. Bank of America has provided the
proof that both are inexorably intertwined.

Stein summarizes his thesis in the conclusion.

Gregory Rodriguez

Illegal Immigrants—They're Money

Gregory Rodriguez is a Los Angeles–based Irvine Senior Fellow at the New America Foundation, a nonpartisan think tank in Washington, D.C. He has written widely about issues of national identity, social cohesion, assimilation, race relations, religion, immigration, demographics, and social and political trends. He published "Illegal Immigrants— They're Money," a rebuttal to Dan Stein's article about the Bank of America, as a column in the Los Angeles Times on March 4, 2007.

Dan Stein, the premier American nativist and president of the Federation for American Immigration Reform, is shocked, shocked. He's mad at Bank of America for issuing credit cards to illegal immigrants. He says that to Bank of America "and other large corporations, illegal immigrants are a source of low-wage labor and an untapped customer market." You bet they are, and that's the American way.

In paragraphs 2 and 3, Rodriguez defines his vision of the realities of the American dream.

2   Sure, I'm proud to be a citizen of a nation that portrays itself as a refuge for the "tired," "the poor" and the "huddled masses yearning to breathe free." But let's face it, Emma Lazarus, the poet who wrote those words, may have laid it on a bit thick. The truth, no less beautiful in its way, is a little more crass and self-serving. But it wouldn't have sounded nearly as poetic to say, "bring us your able-bodied, poor, hardworking masses yearning for a chance to climb out of poverty, establish a credit history and. . . ." We all love to rhapsodize about immigrants' embrace of the American dream, but it's more like a hard-nosed American deal— you come here, you work your tail off under grueling conditions, and you can try your damnedest to better your lot over time.

3   In their generational struggle for acceptance and security, from outsider to insider and, dare I say, from exploited to exploiter, immigrants could avail themselves of those inalienable rights that stand at the core of our national political philosophy—life, liberty and the pursuit of happiness.

Rodriguez makes a transition to his thesis by pointing out that illegal immigration is a recent construct.

4   But that, of course, was before the invention of illegal immigration.

5   Until the early 1900s, pretty much anybody who wasn't diseased, a criminal, a prostitute, a pauper, an anarchist or a Chinese laborer could gain entrance to the U.S. Between 1880 and 1914, only 1% of a total of 25 million European immigrants were excluded from this country. But after transatlantic crossings had already been halted by World War I, Congress buckled to anti-foreign sentiment and closed the proverbial Golden Door by passing a series of restrictionist laws in 1917, 1921 and 1924.

6   Yet even as the historical front door of the nation was being closed, business interests were busy prying open a new side-door. Only three months after the passage of the Immigration Act of 1917, which required all newcomers to pass a literacy test and pay a head tax, the U.S. Secretary of Commerce waived the regulations for Mexican workers. Thus began America's dishonorable relationship with Mexican immigrant labor.

7   For the next several decades, Mexican workers were brought in when the economy expanded and kicked out when times got bad. They were recruited in the 1920s, only to be deported in the 1930s. They were brought in again during the labor shortage in the 1940s. By the 1950s, one branch of the government recruited Mexican workers, under the illusion that they were "temporary," while another sought to keep them out.

Rodriguez establishes a longstanding tradition of fairweather treatment of Mexican immigrants by U.S. policy.

8   The *piece de resistance* in the creation of the illegal immigrant is the Immigration Act of 1965. Although touted as a great piece of liberal legislation that ended discriminatory immigration barriers, it imposed an annual cap on migrants from the Western Hemisphere that was 40% less than the number that had been arriving yearly before 1965. A decade later, Congress placed a 20,000 limit per country in this hemisphere.

9   In other words, after importing millions of Mexicans over the decades, particularly during the bracero guest-worker program from 1942 to 1963, and establishing well-trod routes to employment north of the border, the U.S. drastically reduced the number of visas available to Mexicans. This reduction, of course, coincided with a rapid rise in Mexico's population. And guess what? When jobs were available on this side of the border, Mexicans just kept coming, whether they had papers or not.

10   Clearly, today as ever, mass migration to the U.S. is being driven by economic need—the immigrants' and our economy's. But the hard-nosed American deal has become unfair because, on top of the handicaps we have always imposed on new arrivals, we've added a rather brutal one—criminal status. Good luck with that pursuit of happiness as you engage in backbreaking labor when your place in society is summed up with that one cutting word, "illegal."

Rodriguez asserts his thesis in this paragraph.

11   No, I'm not advocating open borders. Nor do I believe that immigrants should be guaranteed anything but a chance to achieve their end of the nation's cruel bargain. For hardworking illegal immigrants who've established roots here, we should uphold our end of the bargain and give them a chance to achieve their piece of the American dream. Bank of America is not wrong to give illegal immigrants the tools with which to compete legitimately in the marketplace. We as a nation are wrong for treating all these people as illegitimate.

Rodriguez addresses Stein only briefly in the introduction and here in the conclusion. Why?

Sample Student Rebuttal Argument

Ramos 1

Marta Ramos
Professor Jacobs
English 1010
30 April 2010

Oversimplifying the Locavore Ethic

James McWilliams's argument in his essay "On Locavorism" is based on an overly simplistic understanding of the locavore ethic. His claim, that eating locally is an unrealistic goal, fails to take into account the flexibility of locavorism, the ways consumer food preferences drive the free market system, and the realities of food processing infrastructure.

McWilliams's criticism of locavorism would make sense if, as he implies, locavores were a single-minded group of people demanding the complete conversion of the agricultural systems to uniform, regimented local production and consumption. In fact, there is no reason that locavorism has to completely replace the existing agricultural system, and hardly any locavores advocate this. Locavorism, the practice of eating food that is grown locally and in season, is not an all-or-nothing policy. It is a direction in which individuals and communities can move. Locavores.com, a Web site run by the chef Jessica Prentice, who coined the term "locavore," spells out local-eating strategies:

> If not LOCALLY PRODUCED, then ORGANIC.
> If not ORGANIC, then FAMILY FARM.
> If not FAMILY FARM, then LOCAL BUSINESS.
> If not LOCAL BUSINESS, then TERROIR—foods famous for the region they are grown in. ("Guidelines")

This hierarchy of food sources prefers local sources over distant ones, and prioritizes local farms and businesses to receive local food dollars. Eating locally, according to Locavores, represents "A step toward regional food self reliance" ("Top"). Given the political instability of many areas of the world that grow our food and the way energy costs can drastically affect food prices, it makes sense to reduce our dependence on distant food sources. As Jennifer Maiser, one of the founders of the locavore movement, puts it,

Ramos identifies the source that she will refute and the source's claim in the first paragraph.

Ramos defines the term "locavore" and asserts that McWilliams misunderstands the movement.

Ramos uses a direct quotation from a respected voice in the locavore community to build credibility.

Ramos 2

> Locavores are people who pay attention to where their food
> comes from and commit to eating local food as much as
> possible. The great thing about eating local is that it's not
> an all-or-nothing venture. Any small step you take helps the
> environment, protects your family's health and supports
> small farmers in your area.

The goal is not to end completely our importation of food.

McWilliams cites Phoenix as an example of why locavorism won't work. Certainly cities like Phoenix, which lacks the water to grow much food, will always rely on external supply chains to feed their populations. But the obstacles to local eating in Phoenix should not prevent residents of San Francisco, Sarasota, or Charleston from eating locally grown foods. Locavorism doesn't have to work everywhere to be beneficial.

In addition to misrepresenting locavorism's goals, McWilliams illogically claims that it cannot meet people's food needs. "At current levels of fruit production," he warns, "apples are the only crop that could currently feed New Yorkers at a level that meets the U.S. Recommended Dietary Allowances." McWilliams is wrong when he claims that if New Yorkers ate locally grown fruits, they could "rarely indulge in a pear, peach, or basket of strawberries." That might be the case if New York farmers continued to grow nothing but apples and grapes. But if some of those crops were replaced with other fruits, New York could have a very diverse supply of produce that would come reasonably close to meeting the nutritional needs of its citizens. In fact, if committed locavores seek out locally grown strawberries, peaches, and pears, and are willing to pay more money for them than they do for apples, local farmers will have sound economic reasons for replacing some of their aging apple trees with peach and pear trees instead. McWilliams makes locavorism sound impractical because he tries to imagine it working within current agricultural realities. In fact, locavores seek to change the way food is produced and consumed. Moreover, locavorism works toward this change not, as McWilliams suggests, by advocating laws that restrict food producers but by encouraging consumers to vote with their wallets.

McWilliams's argument about New York also rests on the peculiar assumption that every person in the state has to eat the same fruits in

---

her refuta-
n Ramos ad-
esses
cWilliams's
gument point
point.

---

amos quotes
cWilliams
d then dis-
oves the
oted claim.

Ramos 3

the same amounts in order for locavorism to work. He points out that except for apples and grapes, "every other fruit the state produces is not being harvested at a level to provide all New Yorkers with an adequate supply." McWilliams implies that if you can't grow enough of a crop to supply every single person in the state, there is no point in growing it; however, the goal of locavorism is choice, not total local supply of all food, a fact McWilliams seems to willfully ignore.

Ramos questions McWilliams's assumptions and finds them lacking.

Finally, McWilliams claims that the cost and inconvenience of processing food locally will prevent communities from moving toward local eating. He notes that "whereas the conventional system of production and distribution has in place a series of large-scale processing centers capable of handling these tasks in a handful of isolated locations," smaller communities do not. There are two problems with this argument. First, many of the "processing centers" McWilliams is thinking of *aren't* capable of handling the task of food production. The National Resources Defense Council reports that "from 1995 to 1998, 1,000 spills or pollution incidents occurred at livestock feed-lots in 10 states and 200 manure-related fish kills resulted in the death of 13 million fish" ("Facts"). In 2009, Fairbank Farms recalled over half a million pounds of ground beef after nineteen people were hospitalized and two died from E. coli bacteria in the meat (United States). Also in 2009, the King Nut Companies of Solon, Ohio, sickened over 400 people, including three who died, by producing and distributing peanut butter infected with salmonella ("Virginia"). Large-scale processing plants are not a solution to our food security needs. They are part of the problem.

Ramos addresses the claim that she takes greatest issue with last. She then gives it further emphasis by providing two distinct counterarguments.

Second, the cost of changing the country's food-processing system from large-scale to small-scale is not as prohibitive as McWilliams makes it sound. Factories age. Machines wear out and have to be replaced. Food production facilities are replaced all the time. Newer facilities could easily be built on a smaller, more regional scale. In fact, given the cost of recalls and lawsuits when tainted food is distributed over a large area, food producers have good reason to think about smaller, more localized production and distribution.

McWilliams either does not understand locavorism or understands it and prefers to misrepresent its goals and methods. His arguments in favor of our current food production system ignore both the very real benefits of local eating, and the considerable cost of the existing system.

Ramos closes with an appeal to the benefits of locavorism.

Ramos 4

Works Cited

"Facts about Pollution from Livestock Farms." *Natural Resources Defense Council*. Natural Resources Defense Council, 15 July 2005. Web. 7 Apr. 2010.

"Guidelines for Eating Well." *Locavores*. Locavores, 3 June 2009. Web. 9 Apr. 2010.

Maiser, Jennifer. "10 Steps to Becoming a Locavore." *PBS: NOW*. Jump Start Productions, 2 Nov. 2007. Web. 8 Apr. 2010.

McWilliams, James. "On Locavorism." *New York Times*. New York Times, 26 Aug. 2008. Web. 8 Apr. 2010.

"Top Twelve Reasons to Eat Locally." *Locavores*. Locavores, 3 June 2009. Web. 9 Apr. 2010.

United States. Dept. of Health and Human Services. "Multistate Outbreak of E. coli O157:H7 Infections Associated with Beef from Fairbanks Farms." *Centers for Disease Control and Prevention*. Dept. of Health and Human Services, 24 Nov. 2009. Web. 8 Apr. 2010.

"Virginia, Minnesota Confirms Salmonella Deaths Related to Tainted Peanut Butter." *Fox News*. Fox News Network, 13 Jan. 2009. Web. 10 Apr. 2010.

PEARSON
mycomplab

For support in learning this chapter's content, follow this path in MyCompLab:
> Resources > Writing > Writing Purposes > Writing to Argue or Persuade.
Review the Instruction and Multimedia resources, then complete the Exercises and click on Gradebook to measure your progress.

13 | Proposal Arguments

QUICK TAKE

In this chapter, you will learn that

1. Proposal arguments identify a problem and offer a solution (see page 185)

2. Successful proposal arguments convince readers that the solution will work (see page 186)

3. Successful proposal arguments acknowledge other possible solutions and argue why the proposed solution is better (see page 186)

The San Francisco Bicycle Coalition, "dedicated to creating safer streets and more livable communities," is an organization whose primary goal is to build a citywide bike network in San Francisco. The success of the coalition's efforts to increase bicycle ridership for commuters created its own problem: Caltrain commuter trains ran out of room for bicycles, and riders were "bumped" because the trains' bike storage cars were filled to capacity. The coalition crafted a new proposal called Bikes On Board to persuade Caltrain to add more bike storage capacity on its trains. The coalition's proposal encourages riders to report "bumps" in order to document exactly how many times cyclists are denied rides on trains due to limited bike storage. This well-defined proposal forms part of a larger campaign and organizational mission encompassing environmental, economic, and personal fitness issues. What local issues inspire you to propose action? How would you go about crafting a proposal argument to promote interest in a cause or solution?

Understand How Proposal Arguments Work

Proposal arguments make the case that someone should do something: "The federal government should raise grazing fees on public lands." "The student union should renovate the old swimming pool in Butler Gymnasium." "All parents should secure their children in booster seats when driving, even for short distances." Proposals can also argue that something should *not* be done, or that people should stop doing something: "The plan to extend Highway 45 is a waste of tax dollars and citizens should not vote for it." "Don't drink and drive."

The challenge for writers of proposal arguments is to convince readers to take action. It's easy for readers to agree that something should be done, as long as they don't have to do it. It's much harder to get readers involved with the situation or convince them to spend their time or money trying to carry out the proposal. A successful proposal argument conveys a sense of urgency to motivate readers, and describes definite actions they should take.

The key to a successful proposal is using good reasons to convince readers that if they act, something positive will happen (or something negative will be avoided). If your readers believe that taking action will benefit them, they are more likely to help bring about what you propose.

Proposal arguments take the form shown here.

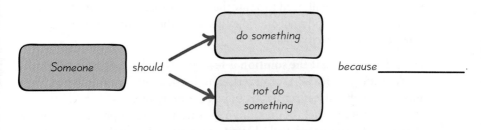

We should convert existing train tracks in the downtown areas to a light-rail system and build a new freight track around the city because we need to relieve traffic and parking congestion downtown.

Recognize Components of Proposal Arguments

Most successful proposals have four major components:

■ **Identifying and defining the problem.** Sometimes, your audience is already fully aware of the problem you want to solve. If your city frequently tears up streets and then leaves them for months without fixing them, you shouldn't have much trouble convincing citizens that streets should be repaired more quickly. But if you raise a problem unfamiliar to your readers, first you will have to convince them that the problem is real. Citizens will not see the need to replace miles of plumbing lines running under the streets, for example, unless you convince them that the pipes are old and corroded and are a risk to everyone's safety. You will also need to define the scope of the problem—does every single pipe need replacing, or only those more than forty years old? Is this a job for the city, or do federal clean water regulations mean that other government officials must be involved? The clearer you are about what must be done, and by whom, the stronger your argument will be.

- **Stating a proposed solution.** A strong proposal offers a clear, definite statement of exactly what you are proposing. Vague statements that "Something must be done!" may get readers stirred up about the issue, but are unlikely to lead to constructive action. A detailed proposal also adds credibility to your argument, showing that you are concerned enough to think through the nuts and bolts of the changes to be made. You can state your proposed solution near the beginning of your argument, or introduce it later—for example, after you have considered and rejected other possible solutions.

- **Convincing readers that the proposed solution is fair and will work.** Once your readers agree that a problem exists and a solution should be found, you have to convince them that your solution is the best one. Perhaps you want your city to fire the planning committee members who are responsible for street repair. You will need to show that those officials are indeed responsible for the delays, and that, once they are fired, the city will be able to quickly hire new, more effective planners.

- **Demonstrating that the solution is feasible.** Your solution not only has to work; it must be feasible, or practical, to implement. You might be able to raise money for street repairs by billing property owners for repairs to the streets in front of their houses, but opposition to such a proposal would be fierce. Most Americans will object to making individuals responsible for road repair costs when roads are used by all drivers.

You may also have to show how your proposal is better than other possible actions that could be taken. Perhaps others believe your city should hire private contractors to repair the streets more quickly, or reward work crews who finish quickly with extra pay or days off. If there are multiple proposed solutions, all perceived as equally good, then there is no clear course of action for your audience to work for. Very often, that means nothing will happen.

Build a Proposal Argument

At this moment, you might not think that you feel strongly enough about anything to write a proposal argument. But if you write a list of things that make you mad or at least a little annoyed, then you have a start toward writing a proposal argument. Some things on your list are not going to produce proposal arguments that many people would want to read. If your roommate is a slob, you might be able to write a proposal for that person to start cleaning up more, but who else would be interested? Similarly, it might be annoying to you that where you live is too far from the ocean, but it is hard to imagine making a serious proposal to move your city closer to the coast. Short of those extremes, however, are many things that might make you think, "Why hasn't someone done something about this?" If you believe that others have something to gain if a problem is solved, or at least that the situation can be made a little better, then you might be able to develop a good proposal argument.

For instance, suppose you are living off campus, and you buy a student parking sticker when you register for courses so that you can park in the student lot. However, you quickly find out that there are too many cars and trucks for the number of available spaces, and unless you get to campus by 8:00 A.M., you aren't going to find a place to park in your assigned lot. The situation makes you angry because you believe that if you pay for a sticker, you should have a reasonable chance of finding a place to park. You see that there are unfilled lots reserved for faculty and staff next to the student parking lot, and you wonder why more spaces aren't allotted to students. You decide to write to the president of your college. You want her to direct parking and traffic services to give more spaces to students or else to build a parking garage that will accommodate more vehicles.

When you start talking to other students on campus, however, you begin to realize that the problem may be more complex than your first view of it. Your college has taken the position that if fewer students drive to campus, there will be less traffic on and around your campus. The administration wants more students to ride shuttle buses, to form car pools, or to bicycle to campus instead of driving alone. You also find out that faculty and staff members pay ten times as much as students for their parking permits, so they pay a very high premium for a guaranteed space—much too high for most students. If the president of your college is your primary audience, you first have to argue that a problem really exists. You have to convince the president that many students have no choice but to drive if they are to attend classes. You, for example, are willing to ride the shuttle buses, but they don't run often enough for you to make your classes, get back to your car that you left at home, and then drive to your job.

Next, you have to argue that your solution will solve the problem. An eight-story parking garage might be adequate to park all the cars of students who want to drive, but parking garages are very expensive to build. Even if a parking garage is the best solution, the question remains: who is going to pay for it? Many problems in life could be solved if you had access to unlimited resources, but very few people—or organizations—have such resources at their command. It's not enough to propose a solution that can resolve the problem. You have to be able to argue for the feasibility of your solution. If you want to argue that a parking garage is the solution to the parking problem on your campus, then you must also propose how to finance the garage.

Steps to Writing a Proposal Argument

Step 1 Make a Claim

Make a proposal claim advocating a specific change or course of action.

Template

We should (or should not) do SOMETHING.

Examples

- Redesigning the process of registering for courses, getting e-mail, or making appointments to be more efficient.
- Creating bicycle lanes to make cycling safer and to reduce traffic.
- Streamlining the rules for recycling newspapers, bottles, and cans to encourage increased participation.

Step 2 Identify the Problem

- What exactly is the problem, what causes it, and who is most affected?
- Has anyone tried to do anything about it? If so, why haven't they succeeded?
- What is likely to happen in the future if the problem isn't solved?

Step 3 Propose Your Solution

State your solution as specifically as you can.

- What exactly do you want to achieve?
- How exactly will your solution work? Can it be accomplished quickly, or will it have to be phased in over a few years?
- Has anything like it been tried elsewhere? If so, what happened?
- If your solution costs money, how do you propose to pay for it?

Step 4 Consider Other Solutions
- What other solutions have been or might be proposed for this problem, including doing nothing?
- Why is your solution better?

Step 5 Write a Draft

Introduction
- Set out the issue or problem, perhaps by telling about your experience or the experience of someone you know.
- Argue for the seriousness of the problem.
- Give some background about the problem if necessary.

Body
- Present your solution. Consider setting out your solution first, explaining how it will work, discussing other possible solutions, and arguing that yours is better. Or consider discussing other possible solutions first, arguing that they don't solve the problem or are not feasible, and then presenting your solution.
- Make clear the goals of your solution. Many solutions cannot solve problems completely.
- Describe in detail the steps in implementing your solution and how they will solve the problem you have identified.
- Explain the positive consequences that will follow from your proposal. What good things will happen, and what bad things will be avoided, if your advice is taken?

Conclusion
- Issue a call to action—if your readers agree with you, they will want to take action.
- Restate and emphasize exactly what readers need to do to solve the problem.

Step 6 Revise, Edit, Proofread
- For detailed instructions, see Chapter 4.
- For a checklist to use to evaluate your draft, see pages 48–49.

Finding Good Reasons

Who should make decisions about economic development?

Cape Cod, Massachusetts, is a peninsula that expands from the southern portion of Massachusetts into the Atlantic Ocean. Famous for its beautiful shoreline, Cape Cod is a popular destination for summer vacationers. The Cape Wind Project is a proposed 24-square-mile offshore wind farm that would be built beginning a little less than 5 miles off of the Cape's southern coast. Proponents of the plan cite the benefits of clean energy. Strong opposition, however, has been voiced by the Alliance to Protect Nantucket Sound, which claims that the proposed wind farm will not only destroy property values, but also irrevocably damage the Cape's priceless views, threaten the vital tourist industry, dislocate necessary shipping lanes, disrupt fish populations, and pose a hazard to birds. The Cape Wind Project has brought a prolonged battle in Massachusetts courts that no doubt will continue with a series of appeals.

Write about it

1. If you were the spokesperson for the Cape Wind Project, what reasons would you give to the Massachusetts State Courts to persuade them to begin construction of the wind farm?

2. If you were the spokesperson for the Alliance to Protect Nantucket Sound, what reasons would you give to the Massachusetts State Courts to persuade them to block the construction of the wind farm?

3. If you were a judge on the Massachusetts State Bench, what reasons might you expect to hear from these two groups? Draft a proposal that would win your vote.

Glenn Loury

A Nation of Jailers

Glenn Loury is Merton P. Stoltz Professor of the Social Sciences at Brown University and a guest on many television and radio news programs. He is the author of *One by One, From the Inside Out: Essays and Reviews on Race and Responsibility in America* (1995), *Anatomy of Racial Inequality* (2001), *Ethnicity, Social Mobility and Public Policy: Comparing the US and the UK* (2005), and over two hundred essays and reviews on racial inequality and social policy.

Instead of immediately announcing his thesis, Loury asks the big question: what is our ideal vision of society?

The most challenging problems of social policy in the modern world are never merely technical. In order properly to decide how we should govern ourselves, we must take up questions of social ethics and human values. What manner of people are we Americans? What vision would we affirm, and what example would we set, before the rest of the world? What kind of society would we bequeath to our children? How shall we live? Inevitably, queries such as these lurk just beneath the surface of the great policy debates of the day. So, those who would enter into public argument about what ails our common life need make no apology for speaking in such terms.

In paragraph 2, Loury narrows the focus to the massive-scale imprisonment of poor Americans.

2   It is precisely in these terms that I wish to discuss a preeminent moral challenge for our time — that imprisonment on a massive scale has become one of the central aspects of our nation's social policy toward the poor, powerfully impairing the lives of some of the most marginal of our fellow citizens, especially the poorly educated black and Hispanic men who reside in large numbers in our great urban centers.

3   The bare facts of this matter — concerning both the scale of incarceration and its racial disparity — have been much remarked upon of late. Simply put, we have become a nation of jailers and, arguably, racist jailers at that. The past four decades have witnessed a truly historic expansion, and transformation, of penal institutions in the United States — at every level of government, and in all regions of the country. We have, by any measure, become a vastly more punitive society. Measured in constant dollars and taking account of all levels of government, spending on corrections and law enforcement in the United States has more than quadrupled over the last quarter century. As a result, the American prison system has grown into a leviathan unmatched in human history. This development should be deeply troubling to anyone who professes to love liberty.

4   Here, as in other areas of social policy, the United States is a stark international outlier, sitting at the most rightward end of

the political spectrum: We imprison at a far higher rate than the other industrial democracies — higher, indeed, than either Russia or China, and vastly higher than any of the countries of Western Europe. According to the International Centre for Prison Studies in London, there were in 2005 some 9 million prisoners in the world; more than 2 million were being held in the United States. With approximately one twentieth of the world's population, America had nearly one fourth of the world's inmates. At more than 700 per 100,000 residents, the U.S. incarceration rate was far greater than our nearest competitors (the Bahamas, Belarus, and Russia, which each have a rate of about 500 per 100,000.) Other industrial societies, some of them with big crime problems of their own, were less punitive than we by an order of magnitude: the United States incarcerated at 6.2 times the rate of Canada, 7.8 times the rate of France, and 12.3 times the rate of Japan.

Comparisons with other nations make a strong argument that the United States has an incarceration problem.

5   The demographic profile of the inmate population has also been much discussed. In this, too, the U.S. is an international outlier. African Americans and Hispanics, who taken together are about one fourth of the population, account for about two thirds of state prison inmates. Roughly one third of state prisoners were locked up for committing violent offenses, with the remainder being property and drug offenders. Nine in ten are male, and most are impoverished. Inmates in state institutions average fewer than eleven years of schooling.

6   The extent of racial disparity in imprisonment rates exceeds that to be found in any other arena of American social life: at eight to one, the black to white ratio of male incarceration rates dwarfs the two to one ratio of unemployment rates, the three to one non-marital child bearing ratio, the two to one ratio of infant mortality rates and the one to five ratio of net worth. More black male high school dropouts are in prison than belong to unions or are enrolled in any state or federal social welfare programs. The brute fact of the matter is that the primary contact between black American young adult men and their government is via the police and the penal apparatus. Coercion is the most salient feature of their encounters with the state. According to estimates compiled by sociologist Bruce Western, nearly 60% of black male dropouts born between 1965 and 1969 had spent at least one year in prison before reaching the age of 35.

Statistics show the degree to which the problem applies to black men.

7   For these men, and the families and communities with which they are associated, the adverse effects of incarceration will extend beyond their stays behind bars. My point is that this is not merely law enforcement policy. It is social policy writ large. And no other country in the world does it quite like we do.

8   This is far more than a technical issue — entailing more, that is, than the task of finding the most efficient crime control policies. Consider, for instance, that it is not possible to conduct a cost-benefit analysis of our nation's world-historic prison buildup over the past 35 years without implicitly specifying how the costs imposed on the persons imprisoned, and their families, are to be reckoned. Of course, this has not stopped analysts from pronouncing on the purported net benefits to "society" of greater incarceration without addressing that question! Still, how — or, indeed, whether — to weigh the costs born by law-breakers — that is, how (or whether) to acknowledge their humanity — remains a fundamental and difficult question of social ethics. Political discourses in the United States have given insufficient weight to the collateral damage imposed by punishment policies on the offenders themselves, and on those who are knitted together with offenders in networks of social and psychic affiliation.

Loury asserts that imprisonment policies cause far greater costs than simply keeping criminals in jail.

9   Whether or not one agrees, two things should be clear: social scientists can have no answers for the question of what weight to put on a "thug's," or his family's, well-being; and a morally defensible public policy to deal with criminal offenders cannot be promulgated without addressing that question. To know whether or not our criminal justice policies comport with our deepest values, we must ask how much additional cost borne by the offending class is justifiable per marginal unit of security, or of peace of mind, for the rest of us. This question is barely being asked, let alone answered, in the contemporary debate.

10   Nor is it merely the scope of the mass imprisonment state that has expanded so impressively in the United States. The ideas underlying the doing of criminal justice — the superstructure of justifications and rationalizations — have also undergone a sea change. Rehabilitation is a dead letter; retribution is the thing. The function of imprisonment is not to reform or redirect offenders. Rather, it is to keep *them* away from *us*. "The prison," writes sociologist David Garland, "is used today as a kind of reservation, a quarantine zone in which purportedly dangerous individuals are segregated in the name of public safety." We have elaborated what are, in effect, a "string of work camps and prisons strung across a vast country housing millions of people drawn mainly from classes and racial groups that are seen as politically and economically problematic." We have, in other words, marched quite a long way down the punitive road, in the name of securing public safety and meting out to criminals their just deserts.

11   And we should be ashamed of ourselves for having done so. Consider a striking feature of this policy development, one that is

crucial to this moral assessment: the ways in which we now deal with criminal offenders in the United States have evolved in recent decades in order to serve expressive and not only instrumental ends. We have wanted to "send a message," and have done so with a vengeance. Yet in the process we have also, in effect, provided an answer for the question: who is to blame for the maladies that beset our troubled civilization? That is, we have constructed a narrative, created scapegoats, assuaged our fears, and indulged our need to feel virtuous about ourselves. We have met the enemy and the enemy, in the now familiar caricature, is *them* — a bunch of anomic, menacing, morally deviant "thugs." In the midst of this dramaturgy — unavoidably so in America — lurks a potent racial subplot.

Loury introduces a personal narrative argument to give a concrete example to the statistics he has provided.

12   This issue is personal for me. As a black American male, a baby-boomer born and raised on Chicago's South Side, I can identify with the plight of the urban poor because I have lived among them. I am related to them by the bonds of social and psychic affiliation. As it happens, I have myself passed through the courtroom, and the jailhouse, on my way along life's journey. I have sat in the visitor's room at a state prison; I have known, personally and intimately, men and women who lived their entire lives with one foot to either side of the law. Whenever I step to a lectern to speak about the growth of imprisonment in our society, I envision voiceless and despairing people who would have me speak on their behalf. Of course, personal biography can carry no authority to compel agreement about public policy. Still, I prefer candor to the false pretense of clinical detachment and scientific objectivity. I am not running for high office; I need not pretend to a cool neutrality that I do not possess. While I recognize that these revelations will discredit me in some quarters, this is a fate I can live with.

13   So, my racial identity is not irrelevant to my discussion of the subject at hand. But, then, neither is it irrelevant that among the millions now in custody and under state supervision are to be found a vastly disproportionate number of the black and the brown. There is no need to justify injecting race into this discourse, for prisons are the most race-conscious public institutions that we have. No big city police officer is "colorblind" nor, arguably, can any afford to be. Crime and punishment in America have a color — just turn on a television, or open a magazine, or listen carefully to the rhetoric of a political campaign — and you will see what I mean. The fact is that, in this society as in any other, order is maintained by the threat and the use of force. We enjoy our good lives because we are shielded by the forces of law and order upon which we rely to keep the unruly at bay. Yet, in this society to an extent unlike virtually any other, those bearing the

heavy burden of order-enforcement belong, in numbers far exceeding their presence in the population at large, to racially defined and historically marginalized groups. Why should this be so? And how can those charged with the supervision of our penal apparatus sleep well at night knowing that it is so?

14   This punitive turn in the nation's social policy is intimately connected, I would maintain, with public rhetoric about responsibility, dependency, social hygiene, and the reclamation of public order. And such rhetoric, in turn, can be fully grasped only when viewed against the backdrop of America's often ugly and violent racial history: There is a reason why our inclination toward forgiveness and the extension of a second chance to those who have violated our behavioral strictures is so stunted, and why our mainstream political discourses are so bereft of self-examination and searching social criticism. An historical resonance between the stigma of race and the stigma of prison has served to keep alive in our public culture the subordinating social meanings that have always been associated with blackness. Many historians and political scientists — though, of course, not all — agree that the shifting character of race relations over the course of the nineteenth and twentieth centuries helps to explain why the United States is exceptional among democratic industrial societies in the severity of its punitive policy and the paucity of its social-welfare institutions. Put directly and without benefit of euphemism, the racially disparate incidence of punishment in the United States is a morally troubling residual effect of the nation's history of enslavement, disenfranchisement, segregation, and discrimination. It is not merely the accidental accretion of neutral state action, applied to a racially divergent social flux. It is an abhorrent expression of who we Americans are as a people, even now, at the dawn of the twenty-first century.

In this paragraph, Loury makes a causal argument: the present situation is the result of a history of racism in the United States.

15   My recitation of the brutal facts about punishment in today's America may sound to some like a primal scream at this monstrous social machine that is grinding poor black communities to dust. And I confess that these facts do at times leave me inclined to cry out in despair. But my argument is intended to be moral, not existential, and its principal thesis is this: we law-abiding, middle-class Americans have made collective decisions on social and incarceration policy questions, and we benefit from those decisions. That is, we benefit from a system of suffering, rooted in state violence, meted out at our behest. Put differently our society — the society we together have made — first tolerates crime-promoting conditions in our sprawling urban ghettos, and then goes on to act out rituals of punishment against them as some awful form of human sacrifice.

After expressing anger Loury returns to a reasoned argument about public policy.

16   It is a central reality of our time that a wide racial gap has opened up in cognitive skills, the extent of law-abidingness, stabil-

ity of family relations, and attachment to the work force. This is the basis, many would hold, for the racial gap in imprisonment. Yet I maintain that this gap in human development is, as a historical matter, rooted in political, economic, social, and cultural factors peculiar to this society and reflective of its unlovely racial history. That is to say, *it is a societal, not communal or personal, achievement.* At the level of the individual case we must, of course, act as if this were not so. There could be no law, and so no civilization, absent the imputation to persons of responsibility for their wrongful acts. But the sum of a million cases, each one rightly judged fairly on its individual merits, may nevertheless constitute a great historic wrong. This is, in my view, now the case in regards to the race and social class disparities that characterize the very punitive policy that we have directed at lawbreakers. And yet, the state does not only deal with individual cases. It also makes policies in the aggregate, and the consequences of these policies are more or less knowable. It is in the making of such aggregate policy judgments that questions of social responsibility arise.

17   This situation raises a moral problem that we cannot avoid. We cannot pretend that there are more important problems in our society, or that this circumstance is the necessary solution to other, more pressing problems — unless we are also prepared to say that we have turned our backs on the ideal of equality for all citizens and abandoned the principles of justice. We ought to be asking ourselves two questions: Just what manner of people are we Americans? And in light of this, what are our obligations to our fellow citizens — even those who break our laws?

Loury returns to the question that he set out in the opening paragraph: what is our collective vision of the ideal society?

18   Without trying to make a full-fledged philosophical argument here, I nevertheless wish to gesture — in the spirit of the philosopher John Rawls — toward some answers to these questions. I will not set forth a policy manifesto at this time. What I aim to do is suggest, in a general way, how we ought to be thinking differently about this problem. Specifically, given our nation's history and political culture, I think that there are severe limits to the applicability in this circumstance of a pure ethic of personal responsibility, as the basis for distributing the negative good of punishment in contemporary America. I urge that we shift the boundary toward greater acknowledgment of social responsibility in our punishment policy discourse — even for wrongful acts freely chosen by individual persons. In suggesting this, I am not so much making a "root causes" argument — he did the crime, but only because he had no choice — as I am arguing that the society at large is implicated in his choices because we have acquiesced in structural arrangements which work to our benefit and his detriment, and yet which shape his consciousness and sense of identity in such a way that

the choices he makes. We condemn those choices, but they are nevertheless compelling to him. I am interested in the moral implications of what the sociologist Loïc Wacquant has called the "double-sided production of urban marginality." I approach this problem of moral judgment by emphasizing that closed and bounded social structures — like racially homogeneous urban ghettos — create contexts where "pathological" and "dysfunctional" cultural forms emerge, but these forms are not intrinsic to the people caught in these structures. Neither are they independent of the behavior of the people who stand outside of them.

19   Several years ago, I took time to read some of the nonfiction writings of the great nineteenth-century Russian novelist Leo Tolstoy. Toward the end of his life he had become an eccentric pacifist and radical Christian social critic. I was stunned at the force of his arguments. What struck me most was Tolstoy's provocative claim that the core of Christianity lies in Jesus' Sermon on the Mount: You see that fellow over there committing some terrible sin? Well, if you have ever lusted, or allowed jealousy, or envy or hatred to enter your own heart, then you are to be equally condemned! This, Tolstoy claims, is the central teaching of the Christian faith: we're all in the same fix.

Loury makes a surprising move by appealing to the teachings of Jesus.

20   Now, without invoking any religious authority, I nevertheless want to suggest that there is a grain of truth in this religious sentiment that is relevant to the problem at hand: That is, while the behavioral pathologies and cultural threats that we see in society — the moral erosions "out there" — the crime, drug addiction, sexually transmitted disease, idleness, violence and all manner of deviance — while these are worrisome, nevertheless, our moral crusade against these evils can take on a pathological dimension of its own. We can become self-righteous, legalistic, ungenerous, stiff-necked, and hypocritical. We can fail to see the beam in our own eye. We can neglect to raise questions of social justice. We can blind ourselves to the close relationship that actually exists between, on the one hand, behavioral pathology in the so-called urban underclass of our country and, on the other hand, society-wide factors — like our greed-driven economy, our worship of the self, our endemic culture of materialism, our vacuous political discourses, our declining civic engagement, and our aversion to sacrificing private gain on behalf of much needed social investments. We can fail to see, in other words, that the problems of the so-called underclass — to which we have reacted with a massive, coercive mobilization — are but an expression, at the bottom of the social hierarchy, of a more profound and widespread moral deviance — one involving all of us.

21   Taking this position does not make me a moral relativist. I merely hold that, when thinking about the lives of the disadvantaged in our society, the fundamental premise that should guide us is that we are all in this together. *Those* people languishing in the corners of our society are *our* people — they are *us* – whatever may be their race, creed, or country of origin, whether they be the crack-addicted, the HIV-infected, the mentally ill homeless, the juvenile drug sellers, or worse. Whatever the malady, and whatever the offense, we're all in the same fix. We're all in this thing together.

22   Just look at what we have wrought. We Americans have established what, to many an outside observer, looks like a system of racial caste in the center of our great cities. I refer here to millions of stigmatized, feared, and invisible people. The extent of disparity in the opportunity to achieve their full human potential, as between the children of the middle class and the children of the disadvantaged — a disparity that one takes for granted in America — is virtually unrivaled elsewhere in the industrial, advanced, civilized, free world.

23   Yet too many Americans have concluded, in effect, that those languishing at the margins of our society are simply reaping what they have sown. Their suffering is seen as having nothing to do with us — as not being evidence of systemic failures that can be corrected through collective action. Thus, as I noted, we have given up on the ideal of rehabilitating criminals, and have settled for simply warehousing them. Thus we accept — despite much rhetoric to the contrary — that it is virtually impossible effectively to educate the children of the poor. Despite the best efforts of good people and progressive institutions — despite the encouraging signs of moral engagement with these issues that I have seen in my students over the years, and that give me hope — despite these things, it remains the case that, speaking of the country as a whole, there is no broadly based demand for reform, no sense of moral outrage, no anguished self-criticism, no public reflection in the face of this massive, collective failure.

The main work of the essay is getting readers to acknowledge the problem. If the problem is recognized, then various solutions will follow.

24   The core of the problem is that the socially marginal are not seen as belonging to the same general public body as the rest of us. It therefore becomes impossible to do just about anything with them. At least implicitly, our political community acts as though some are different from the rest and, because of their culture — because of their bad values, their self-destructive behavior, their malfeasance, their criminality, their lack of responsibility, their unwillingness to engage in hard work — they *deserve* their fate.

25   But this is quite wrongheaded. What we Americans fail to recognize — not merely as individuals, I stress, but as a political

community — is that these ghetto enclaves and marginal spaces of our cities, which are the source of most prison inmates, are products of our own making: Precisely because we do not want those people near us, we have structured the space in our urban environment so as to keep *them* away from *us*. Then, when they fester in their isolation and their marginality, we hypocritically point a finger, saying in effect: "Look at those people. They threaten to the civilized body. They must therefore be expelled, imprisoned, controlled." It is not *we* who must take social responsibility to reform our institutions but, rather, it is *they* who need to take personal responsibility for their wrongful acts. It is not we who must set our *collective* affairs aright, but they who must get their *individual* acts together. This posture, I suggest, is inconsistent with the attainment of a just distribution of benefits and burdens in society.

26   Civic inclusion has been the historical imperative in Western political life for 150 years. And yet — despite our self-declared status as a light unto the nations, as a beacon of hope to freedom-loving peoples everywhere — despite these lofty proclamations, which were belied by images from the rooftops in flooded New Orleans in September 2005, and are contradicted by our overcrowded prisons — the fact is that this historical project of civic inclusion is woefully incomplete in these United States.

27   At every step of the way, reactionary political forces have declared the futility of pursuing civic inclusion. Yet, in every instance, these forces have been proven wrong. At one time or another, they have derided the inclusion of women, landless peasants, former serfs and slaves, or immigrants more fully in the civic body. Extending to them the franchise, educating their children, providing health and social welfare to them has always been controversial. But this has been the direction in which the self-declared "civilized" and wealthy nations have been steadily moving since Bismarck, since the revolutions of 1848 and 1870, since the American Civil War with its Reconstruction Amendments, since the Progressive Era and through the New Deal on to the Great Society. This is why we have a progressive federal income tax and an estate tax in this country, why we feed, clothe and house the needy, why we (used to) worry about investing in our cities' infrastructure, and in the human capital of our people. What the brutal facts about punishment in today's America show is that *this American project of civic inclusion remains incomplete*. Nowhere is that incompleteness more evident than in the prisons and jails of America. And this as yet unfulfilled promise of American democracy reveals a yawning chasm between an ugly and uniquely American reality, and our nation's exalted image of herself.

Loury proposes that if Americans would embrace the ideals of the United States, the conditions that lead to massive-scale imprisonment would change.

Sample Student Proposal Argument

Lee 1

Kim Lee
Professor Patel
RHE 306
31 March 2009

Let's Make It a Real Melting Pot with Presidential Hopes for All

The image the United States likes to advertise is a country that
embraces diversity and creates a land of equal opportunity for all. As the
Statue of Liberty cries out, "give me your tired, your poor, your huddled
masses yearning to breathe free," American politicians gleefully evoke
such images to frame the United States as a bastion for all things good,
fair, and equal. As a proud American, however, I must nonetheless highlight one of the cracks in this façade of equality. Imagine that an infertile couple decides to adopt an orphaned child from China. They follow
all of the legal processes deemed necessary by both countries. They fly
abroad and bring home their (once parentless) six-month-old baby boy.
They raise and nurture him, and while teaching him to embrace his ethnicity, they also teach him to love Captain Crunch, baseball, and *The
Three Stooges*. He grows and eventually attends an ethnically diverse
American public school. One day his fifth-grade teacher tells the class
that anyone can grow up to be president. To clarify her point, she turns
to the boy, knowing his background, and states, "No, you could not be
president, Stu, but you could still be a senator. That's something to
aspire to!" How do Stu's parents explain this rule to this American-raised
child? This scenario will become increasingly common, yet as the Constitution currently reads, only "natural-born" citizens may run for the
offices of president and vice president. Neither these children nor the
thousands of hardworking Americans who chose to make America their official homeland may aspire to the highest political position in the land.
While the huddled masses may enter, it appears they must retain a
second-class citizen ranking.

> Lee sets out
> the problem
> with a
> concrete
> scenario.

The "natural-born" stipulation regarding the presidency stems from
the self-same meeting of minds that brought the American people the
Electoral College. During the Constitutional Convention of 1787, the

Lee 2

Congress formulated the regulatory measures associated with the office of the president. A letter sent from John Jay to George Washington during this period reads as follows:

> "Permit me to hint," Jay wrote, "whether it would not be wise and seasonable to provide a strong check to the admission of foreigners into the administration of our national government; and to declare expressly that the Commander in Chief of the American army shall not be given to, nor devolve on, any but a natural-born citizen." (Mathews A1)

Shortly thereafter, Article II, Section I, Clause V, of the Constitution declared that "No Person except a natural born Citizen, or a Citizen of the United States at the time of the Adoption of this Constitution, shall be eligible to the Office of President." Jill A. Pryor states in the *Yale Law Journal* that "some writers have suggested that Jay was responding to rumors that foreign princes might be asked to assume the presidency" (881). Many cite disastrous examples of foreign rule in the eighteenth century as the impetus for the "natural-born" clause. For example, in 1772—only fifteen years prior to the adoption of the statute—Poland had been divided up by Prussia, Russia, and Austria (Kasindorf). Perhaps an element of self-preservation and not ethnocentrism led to the questionable stipulation. Nonetheless, in the twenty-first century this clause reeks of xenophobia.

> Lee gives the historical background of the "natural-born" restriction.

The Fourteenth Amendment clarified the difference between "natural-born" and "native-born" citizens by spelling out the citizenship status of children born to American parents outside of the United States (Ginsberg 929). This clause qualifies individuals such as Senator John McCain—born in Panama—for presidency. This change, however, is not adequate. I propose that the United States abolish the natural-born clause and replace it with a stipulation that allows naturalized citizens to run for president. This amendment would state that a candidate must have been naturalized and must have lived in residence in the United States for a period of at least twenty-five years. The present time is ideal for this change. This amendment could simultaneously honor the spirit of the Constitution, protect and ensure the interests of the United States, promote an international image of

> Lee states her proposal in this paragraph.

inclusiveness, and grant heretofore-withheld rights to thousands of legal and loyal United States citizens.

In our push for change, we must make clear the importance of this amendment. It would not provide special rights for would-be terrorists. To the contrary, it would fulfill the longtime promises of the nation. The United States claims to allow all people to blend into the great stew of citizenship. It has already suffered embarrassment and international cries of ethnic bias as a result of political moves such as Japanese American internment and the Guantanamo Bay detention center. This amendment can help mend the national image as every American takes one more step toward equality. Naturalized citizens have been contributing to the United States for centuries. Many nameless Mexican, Irish, and Asian Americans sweated and toiled to build the American railroads. The public has welcomed naturalized Americans such as Bob Hope, Albert Pujols, and Peter Jennings into their hearts and living rooms. Individuals such as German-born Henry Kissinger and Czechoslovakian-born Madeleine Albright have held high posts in the American government and have served as respected aides to its presidents. The amendment must make clear that it is not about one man's celebrity. Approximately seven hundred foreign-born Americans have won the Medal of Honor and over sixty thousand proudly serve in the United States military today (Siskind 5). The "natural-born" clause must be removed to provide each of these people—over half a million naturalized in 2003 alone—with equal footing to those who were born into citizenship rather than working for it (United States).

Since the passing of the Bill of Rights, only seventeen amendments have been ratified. This process takes time and overwhelming congressional and statewide support. To alter the Constitution, a proposed amendment must pass with a two-thirds "super-majority" in both the House of Representatives and the Senate. In addition, the proposal must find favor in two-thirds (38) of state legislatures. In short, this task will not be easy. In order for this change to occur, a grassroots campaign must work to dispel misinformation regarding naturalized citizens and to force the hands of senators and representatives wishing to retain their congressional seats. We must take this proposal to ethnicity-specific political

> Lee gives examples of people who are qualified to become president yet are ineligible.

> Lee explains the process of amending the Constitution and ends with a call for action.

Lee 4

groups from both sides of the aisle, business organizations, and community activist groups. We must convince representatives that this issue matters. Only through raising voices and casting votes can the people enact change. Only then can every American child see the possibility for limitless achievement and equality. Only then can everyone find the same sense of pride in the possibility for true American diversity in the highest office in the land.

Lee 5

Works Cited

Ginsberg, Gordon. "Citizenship: Expatriation: Distinction between Naturalized and Natural Born Citizens." *Michigan Law Review* 50 (1952): 926–29. *JSTOR*. Web. 6 Mar. 2009.

Kasindorf, Martin. "Should the Constitution Be Amended for Arnold?" *USA Today* 2 Dec. 2004. *LexisNexis Academic*. Web. 8 Mar. 2009.

Mathews, Joe. "Maybe Anyone Can Be President." *Los Angeles Times* 2 Feb. 2005: A1. *LexisNexis Academic*. Web. 6 Mar. 2009.

Pryor, Jill A. "The Natural Born Citizen Clause and Presidential Eligibility: An Approach for Resolving Two Hundred Years of Uncertainty." *Yale Law Journal* 97.5 (1988): 881–99. Print.

Siskind, Lawrence J. "Why Shouldn't Arnold Run?" *Recorder* 10 Dec. 2004: 5. *LexisNexis Academic*. Web. 10 Mar. 2009.

United States. Dept. of Commerce. Census Bureau. "The Fourth of July 2005." *Facts for Features*. US Dept. of Commerce, 27 June 2005. Web. 17 Mar. 2009.

PEARSON
mycomplab

For support in learning this chapter's content, follow this path in MyCompLab:
> Resources > Writing > Writing Samples: Technical and Workplace Writing
> Writing Samples: Proposals. Review the Instruction and Multimedia resources, then complete the Exercises and click on Gradebook to measure your progress.

Designing and Presenting Arguments

PART

4

14 | Designing Multimedia Arguments

QUICK TAKE

In this chapter, you will learn that

1. The choice of media is critical for persuading particular audiences (see below)
2. Images and graphics, when used purposefully, can be used as evidence to support your argument (see page 208)
3. Printed documents need to be carefully designed to engage and persuade your audience (see page 209)
4. Multimedia arguments can be designed and delivered to meet the needs of college audiences (see page 210)

Arguments do not communicate with words alone. Even written arguments that do not contain graphics or images have a look and feel that also communicate meaning. Many arguments depend on presenting information visually, in multimedia, or in images, in addition to using written language. Using effective design strategies will make your arguments more engaging and compelling.

Think About Which Media Will Reach Your Audience

Before you graduate from college, likely you will find occasions when you want to persuade an audience beyond your teacher, classmates, and friends—possibly for your work, possibly for an organization you belong to, or possibly because an issue concerns you. You may have a clear sense of your message and the good reasons to support that message. But no matter how good your argument, nothing will happen unless you can command the scarcest commodity in our multitasking world—the attention of your audience.

Most college assignments specify the medium, which is typically a printed paper that you submit to the instructor. In the workplace and in life outside college, the choice of medium often isn't immediately evident. For example, if you want to address a neighborhood issue, would a brochure or a Web site be more effective?

Think about your options.

PRINTED TEXT

- Advantages: Low technological requirements to produce; complex, in-depth arguments are possible.
- Disadvantages: Unless published in an established forum like a newspaper, it can be difficult to get people to read the argument.

WEB SITE

- Advantages: Inexpensive to create and allows images, video, audio, and animations to be embedded.
- Disadvantages: How do people find your Web site among the millions of other sites?

BLOG

- Advantages: Inexpensive to create and many sites host blogs.
- Disadvantages: Requires frequent, interesting content to keep readers coming back.

AUDIO PODCAST

- Advantages: Inexpensive to create and can be downloaded from a Web site.
- Disadvantages: Requires some audio editing skills. Like other Web-based media, you have to have a strategy for getting people to listen.

VIDEO

- Advantages: Can be uploaded to sites like YouTube and Vimeo.
- Disadvantages: Producing quality original video takes time, equipment, and editing skills.

Know When to Use Visual Evidence

Personal computers, digital cameras, scanners, printers, and the Web have made it easy to include images and graphics in writing and link to audio and video. But these technologies don't tell you if, when, or how images and graphics should be used.

Think about what an image or graphic communicates

- **What are your readers' expectations for the medium you are using?** Most essays don't include images; most Web sites and brochures do.

- **What is the purpose for an image or graphic?** Does it illustrate a concept? Does it highlight an important point? Does it show something that is hard to explain with words alone? If you don't know the purpose, you may not need the image.

- **Where should an image or graphic be placed in your text?** Images should be as close as possible to the relevant point in your text.

- **What will readers focus on when they see the image?** Will they focus on the part that matters? If not, you may need to crop the image.

- **What explanation do readers need in order to understand the image?** Provide informative captions for the images and graphics you use, and refer to them in your text.

Think About the Argument an Image Makes

Images don't speak for themselves, but if they are referenced in your text and captioned, they can make supporting arguments. Think strategically when you include arguments.

Say, for example, you are making a proposal argument for more students to become more involved in feeding homeless people in your city. Students are aware that there are homeless people, but many students are not aware of organizations that deliver food to hungry people. You might want to photograph the volunteers instead of homeless people.

Volunteers work to make sandwiches that will be distributed by a food truck to homeless people.

Think about the argument a chart or graph makes

Charts and graphs are useful for visually representing statistical trends and for making comparisons. For example, the rising national debt became a hotly debated issue during the administrations of George H. W. Bush and Barack Obama. Many graphs were used in the debate to show the dramatic rise of federal debt. But if you want to make a causal argument that lowering the income tax rate for the rich contributed to the rise in the debt, you might use a line graph.

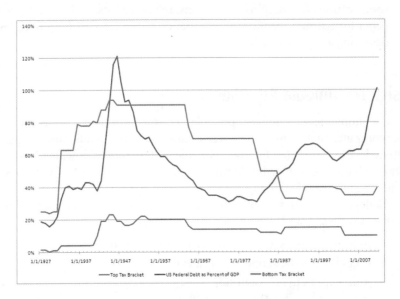

Line graph comparing the national debt with the highest and lowest income tax rates.

Design Arguments for Print

Writing on a computer gives you a range of options for designing a page that is appropriate to your assignment. Thinking about design will lead to a more effective presentation of your argument.

- **Choose the orientation, size of your page, and number of columns.** You can usually use the defaults on your computer for academic essays (remember to select double-spacing for line spacing if the default is single-spaced). For other kinds of texts you may want a horizontal rather than a vertical orientation, a size other than a standard sheet of paper, and two or more columns rather than one.

- **Divide your text into units.** The paragraph is the basic unit of extended writing, but also think about when to use lists. This list is a bulleted list. You can also use a numbered list.

- **Use left-aligned text with a ragged-right margin.** Fully justified text aligns the right margin, which gives a more formal look but can also leave unsightly rivers of extra white space running through the middle of your text. Ragged-right text is easier to read.

- **Be conscious of white space.** White space can make your text more readable and set off more important elements. Headings stand out more with white space surrounding them. Leave room around graphics. Don't crowd words too close to graphics because both the words and the visuals will become hard to read.

- **Be aware of MLA and APA design specifications.** MLA and APA styles have specifications for margins, indentions, reference lists, and other aspects of paper formatting. See the sample paper on pages 276–282 for guidelines on designing a paper using MLA style.

Design Multimedia Arguments

Digital technologies now make it possible to create multimedia projects on your home computer that formerly required entire production staffs. You can publish multimedia projects on the Internet (either as Web sites or as downloadable files), as stand-alone media distributed on CDs and DVDs, or in print with posters, brochures, and essays with images.

College viewers and listeners have the expectations of multimedia projects that they do of essays and research papers. They expect

- your project to be well organized and free of errors,
- your claims to be supported with evidence,
- your analysis to be insightful,
- your sources to be documented, and
- your work clearly distinguished from the work of others.

Creating multimedia projects

If you decide to create a multimedia project, find out what resources are available for students on your campus. Many colleges and universities have digital media labs, which offer workshops and can provide video and audio studios, technical assistance, equipment, and software. Look for links to digital media services on your college's Web site.

Oral presentation with visuals (see Chapter 15)
Essay with images

- **Example project**: Evaluation argument concerning the poor condition of parks in your city
- Plan: Visit several parks, make notes, and take photographs.
- Produce: Write the project. Edit your images with an image editor and insert them in your project with captions.
- Edit: Revise with the comments of classmates and your instructor.

Web site production

- **Example project**: Web site making a definition argument that censorship of the Internet is a violation of the right to free speech
- Plan: Collect all the materials you will need for your site including text; digital images; graphics; and audio, video, and animation files.
- Produce: If you don't have a Web editor on your computer, find a campus lab that has Dreamweaver or similar software. Upload your site to a server. Many colleges offer server space to host student Web sites.
- Edit: Test your site to ensure that all links are working and all images and other files are showing up correctly. Edit with a Web editor.

Audio production

- **Example project**: Oral history of neighborhood residents making a causal argument about why a neighborhood declined after a freeway was built through the middle of it
- Plan: Arrange and record interviews and write a script.
- Produce: Reserve a campus audio production lab or record on your computer. Create an audio file by combining the interviews with your narration.
- Edit: Edit with an audio editor. Export the video into a format such as WAV or MP3 that you can put on the Web or share as a downloadable file.

Video production

- **Example project**: Proposal to create bike lanes on a busy street near your campus
- Plan: Identify locations, get permission to film if necessary, and write a script.
- Produce: Shoot video of the street with cars and bikes competing. Interview cyclists, drivers, and local business owners about their sense of urgency of the problem and the effects of creating bike lanes.
- Edit: Edit with a video editor. Export the video into a format such as QuickTime that you can put on the Web or share as a downloadable file.

PEARSON

mycomplab

For support in learning this chapter's content, follow this path in MyCompLab:

> Resources > Writing > Writing Samples: Technical and Workplace Writing
> Writing Samples: Presentation. Review the Instruction and Multimedia resources, then complete the Exercises and click on Gradebook to measure your progress.

15 | Presenting Arguments

QUICK TAKE

In this chapter, you will learn that

1. Planning an effective presentation requires putting the audience first (see below)
2. Simple slides with visual impact work best (see page 214)
3. Delivering an effective presentation is all about you (see page 216)
4. When converting a written text into a presentation, avoid the temptation to dump sentences and paragraphs onto the slides (see page 217)

Plan a Presentation

If you are assigned to give a presentation, look carefully at the assignment for guidance on finding a topic. The process for finding a topic is similar to a written assignment (see Chapter 3). If your assignment requires research, you will need to document the sources of information just as you do for a research paper (see Chapters 16–19).

Start with your goal in mind

What is the real purpose of your presentation? Are you informing, persuading, or motivating? Take the elevator test. Imagine you are in an elevator with the key people who can approve or reject your ideas. Their schedule is very tight. You have only thirty seconds to convince them. Can you make your case?

This scenario is not far-fetched. One executive demanded that every new idea had to be written in one sentence on the back of a business card. What's your sentence?

It's all about your audience

Who is your audience? In college your audience is often your instructor and fellow students—an audience you know well. Many times you will not have this advantage.

Take a few minutes to answer these questions.

- Will my audience be interested in the topic?
- Why does it matter to them?
- What are they likely to know and believe about the topic?
- What are they likely to not know?
- Where are they likely to disagree?
- What do I want them to do?
- How much time do I have?
- If they remember only one thing, what should it be?

Get organized

Start with pen and paper before you begin creating slides. Post-it notes are another useful planning tool.

- **Make a list of key points.** Think about the best order for your major points.
- **Plan your introduction.** Your success depends on your introduction. You must gain the attention of your audience, introduce your topic, indicate why it's important, and give a sense of where you are headed. It's a tall order, but if you don't engage your audience in the first two minutes, you will lose them.
- **Plan your conclusion.** You want to end on a strong note. Stopping abruptly or rambling on only to tail off leaves your audience with a bad impression. Give your audience something to take away, a compelling example or an idea that captures the gist of your presentation.

Build content

Content alone does not make a presentation successful, but you cannot succeed without solid content. Support your major points with relevant evidence.

- **Facts.** Speakers who know their facts build credibility.
- **Statistics.** Effective use of statistics can give the audience the impression that you have done your homework. Statistics can also indicate that a particular example is representative.
- **Statements by authorities.** Quotations from credible experts can support key points.
- **Narratives.** Narratives are brief stories that illustrate key points. Narratives can hold the attention of the audience—but keep them short or they will become a distraction.

Design Visuals for a Presentation

Less is more with slides. One text-filled slide after another is mind-numbingly dull. Presentations using slides don't have to be this bad.

Keep it simple

Imagine you are making an argument that fewer animals would be euthanized at animal shelters if more people in your city knew that they could save a pet's life by adopting it. You could fill your slides with statistics alone. Or you tell your audience the facts while showing them slides that give emotional impact to your numbers.

Simple design rules! Keep in mind these principles.

- One point per slide
- Very few fonts
- Quality photos, not clipart
- Less text, more images
- Easy on the special effects

Compare the following examples.

Pet Overpopulation in the United States

- Estimated number of animals that enter shelters each year: 6-8 million
- Estimated number of animals euthanized at shelters each year: 3-4 million
- Estimated number of animals adopted at shelters each year: 3-4 million

Source: "HSUS Pet Overpopulation Estimates." *Humane Society of the U.S.* Humane Society of the U.S., 9 Nov. 2009. 18 Oct. 2010.

Pet Overpopulation in the United States

- Estimated number of animals entering shelters each year: 6-8 million
- Estimated number of animals euthanized at shelters each year: 3-4 million
- Estimated number of animals adopted at shelters: 3-4 million

Source: "HSUS Pet Overpopulation Estimates." *Humane Society of the U.S.* Humane Society of the U.S., 9 Nov. 2009. Web. 18 Oct. 2010.

Save a pet

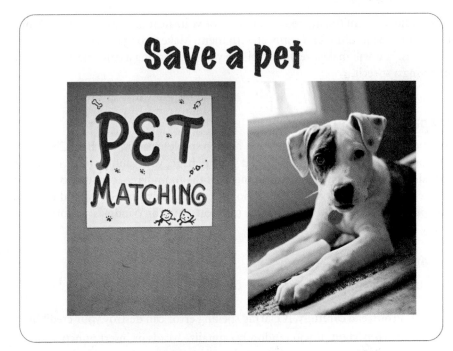

Which slide makes the point most effectively?

But what if you have a lot of data to show? Make a handout that the audience can study later. They can make notes on your handout, which gives them a personal investment. Keep your slides simple and emphasize the main points in the presentation.

Use audio and video clips strategically

Short audio and video clips can offer concrete examples and add some variety to your presentation. An audience appreciates hearing and even seeing the people you interview. PowerPoint makes it simple to embed the files within a presentation. Be careful, however, in using the built-in sound effects in PowerPoint such as canned applause. Most sound effects are annoying and make you come off as inexperienced.

Deliver an Effective Presentation

If you are not passionate about your subject, you will never get your audience committed to your subject, no matter how good your slides. Believe in what you say; enthusiasm is contagious.

It's all about you

The audience didn't come to see the back of your head in front of slides. Move away from the podium and connect with them. Make strong eye contact with individuals. You will make everyone feel like you were having a conversation instead of giving a speech.

Prepare in advance

Practice your presentation, even if you have to speak to an empty chair. Check out the room and equipment in advance. If you are using your laptop with a projector installed in the room, make sure it connects. If the room has a computer connected to the projector, bring your presentation on a flash drive and download it to the computer. PowerPoint works much the same on a Mac or Windows platform.

Be professional

Pay attention to the little things.

- **Proofread carefully.** A glaring spelling error can destroy your credibility.
- **Be consistent.** If you randomly capitalize words or insert punctuation, your audience will be distracted.

- **Pay attention to the timing of your slides.** Stay in sync with your slides. Don't leave a slide up when you are talking about something else.
- **Use the "B" key.** If you get sidetracked, press the "B" key, which makes the screen go blank so the audience can focus on you. When you are ready to resume, press the "B" key again and the slide reappears.
- **Involve your audience.** Invite response during your presentation where appropriate, and leave time for questions at the end.
- **Add a bit of humor.** Humor can be tricky, especially if you don't know your audience well. But if you can get your audience to laugh, they will be on your side.
- **Slow down.** When you are nervous, you tend to go too fast. Stop and breathe. Let your audience take in what's on your slides.
- **Finish on time or earlier.** Your audience will be grateful.
- **Be courteous and gracious.** Remember to thank anyone who helped you and the audience for their comments. Eventually you will run into someone who challenges you, sometimes politely, sometimes not. If you remain cool and in control, the audience will remember your behavior long after the words are forgotten.

Convert a Written Text into a Presentation

The temptation when converting a written text into a presentation is to dump sentences and paragraphs onto the slides. Indeed, it's simple enough to cut and paste big chunks of text, but you risk losing your audience.

Make a list of the main points in your written text, and then decide which ones you need to show on slides and which you can tell the audience. Your voice supplies most of the information; your slides help your audience to remember and organize your presentation.

People learn better when your oral presentation is accompanied by engaging images and graphics. Slides can also add emotional involvement.

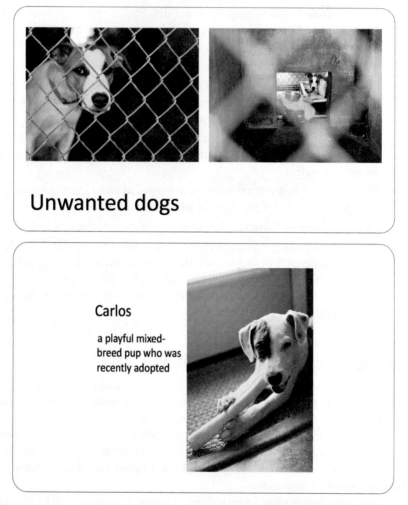

Arrange your slides so they tell a story. For example, if you are arguing that fewer dogs would be euthanized if your city were more active in promoting adoption, you can show slides that give statistics, or you can report statistics in your presentation while letting your audience identify with individual dogs.

For support in learning this chapter's content, follow this path in MyCompLab:
> Resources > Writing > Writing Samples: Technical and Workplace Writing
> Writing Samples: Presentation. Review the Instruction and Multimedia resources, then complete the Exercises and click on Gradebook to measure your progress.

Researching Arguments

PART

5

16 | Planning Research

QUICK TAKE

In this chapter, you will learn that
1. Analyzing the assignment is the first step in completing a research project (see below)
2. The next step is finding a topic and asking a research question (see page 221)
3. For local and campus issues, you may need to conduct field research, including interviews, surveys, and observations (see page 222)
4. Your preliminary research should lead to a working thesis, which will guide you through further research and the development of your argument (see page 225)

Analyze the Research Task

Research is a creative process, which is another way of saying it is a messy process. Even though the process is complex, your results will improve if you keep the big picture in mind while you are immersed in research. If you have an assignment that requires research, look closely at what you are being asked to do.

Look for key words

Often the assignment will tell you what is expected.

- An assignment that asks you, for example, how the usual *definition* of intellectual property applies to YouTube invites you to write a definition argument (see Chapter 8).
- An *analysis of causes* requires you to write a causal argument (see Chapter 9).
- An *evaluation* requires you to make critical judgments based on criteria (see Chapter 10).
- A *proposal* requires you to assemble evidence in support of a solution to a problem or a call for the audience to do something (see Chapter 13).

Identify your potential readers

- How familiar are your readers with your subject?
- What background information will you need to supply?
- If your subject is controversial, what opinions or beliefs are your readers likely to hold?
- If some readers are likely to disagree with you, how can you convince them?

Assess the project's length, scope, and requirements

- What kind of research are you being asked to do?
- What is the length of the project?
- What kinds and number of sources or field research are required?
- Which documentation style is required such as MLA (see Chapter 20) or APA (see Chapter 21)?

Set a schedule

- Note the due dates on the assignment for drafts and final versions.
- Set dates for yourself on finding and evaluating sources, drafting your thesis, creating a working bibliography, and writing a first draft.
- Give yourself enough time to do a thorough job.

Find a Subject

One good way to begin is by browsing, which may also show you the breadth of possibilities included in a topic and possibly lead you to new topics (see Chapter 3).

You might begin browsing by doing one or more of the following.

- **Visit "Research by Subject" on your library's Web site.** Clicking on a subject such as "African and African American Studies" will take you to a list of online resources. Often you can find an e-mail link to a reference librarian who can assist you.
- **Look for topics in your courses.** Browse your course notes and readings. Are there any topics you might want to explore in greater depth?
- **Browse a Web subject directory.** Web subject directories, including Yahoo Directory (dir.yahoo.com), are useful when you want to narrow a topic or learn what subcategories a topic might contain. In addition to

the Web subject directories, your library's Web site may have a link to the *Opposing Viewpoints* database.

- **Look for topics as you read.** When you read actively, you ask questions and respond to ideas in the text. Review what you wrote in the margins or the notes you have made about something you read that interested you. You may find a potential topic.

Ask a Research Question

Often you'll be surprised by the amount of information your initial browsing uncovers. Your next task will be to identify a question for your research project within that mass of information. This **researchable question** will be the focus of the remainder of your research and ultimately of your research project or paper. Browsing on the subject of organic foods, for example, might lead you to one of the following researchable questions.

- How do farmers benefit from growing organic produce?
- Why are organic products more expensive than nonorganic products?
- Are Americans being persuaded to buy more organic products?

Once you have formulated a research question, you should begin thinking about what kind of research you will need to do to address the question.

Gather Information About the Subject

Most researchers rely partly or exclusively on the work of others as sources of information. Research based on the work of others is called **secondary research**. In the past this information was contained almost exclusively in collections of print materials housed in libraries, but today enormous amounts of information are available through library databases and on the Web (see Chapter 17).

Much of the research done at a university creates new information through **primary research**—experiments, examination of historical documents—and **field research**, including data-gathering surveys, interviews, and detailed observations, described below.

Conducting field research

Sometimes you may be researching a question that requires you to gather first-hand information with field research. For example, if you are researching a campus issue such as the impact of a new technology fee on students' budgets, you may need to conduct interviews, make observations, and give a survey.

Interviews

College campuses are a rich source of experts in many areas, including people on the faculty and in the surrounding community. Interviewing experts on your research subject can help build your knowledge base. You can use interviews to discover what the people most affected by a particular issue are thinking, such as why students object to some fees and not others.

Arrange interviews

Before you contact anyone, think carefully about your goals. Knowing what you want to find out through your interviews will help you determine whom you need to interview and what questions you need to ask. Use these guidelines to prepare for an interview.

- Decide what you want or need to know and who best can provide that for you.
- Schedule each interview in advance, and let the person know why you are conducting the interview. Estimate how long your interview will take, and tell your subject how much of her or his time you will need.
- Choose a location that is convenient for your subject but not too chaotic or loud. An office or study room is better than a noisy cafeteria.
- Plan your questions in advance. Write down a few questions and have a few more in mind.
- If you want to record the interview, ask for permission in advance. A recording device sometimes can intimidate the person you are interviewing.

Conduct interviews

- Come prepared with your questions, a notebook, and a pen or pencil.
- If you plan to record the interview (with your subject's permission), make sure whatever recording device you use has an adequate power supply and will not run out of tape, disc space, or memory.
- Listen carefully so you can follow up on key points. Make notes when important questions are raised or answered, but don't attempt to transcribe every word the person is saying.
- When you are finished, thank your subject, and ask his or her permission to get in touch again if you have additional questions.

Surveys

Extensive surveys that can be projected to large populations, like the ones used in political polls, require the effort of many people. Small surveys, however, often can provide insight on local issues, such as what percentage of students might be affected if library hours were reduced.

Plan surveys

What information do you need for your research question? Decide what exactly you want to know and design a survey that will provide that information. Likely you will want both close-ended questions (multiple choice, yes or no, rating scale) and open-ended questions that allow detailed responses. To create a survey, follow these guidelines.

- Write a few specific, unambiguous questions. People will fill out your survey quickly, and if the questions are confusing, the results will be meaningless.
- Include one or two open-ended questions, such as "What do you like about X?" or "What don't you like about X?" Open-ended questions can be difficult to interpret, but sometimes they turn up information you had not anticipated.
- Test the questions on a few people before you conduct the survey.
- Think about how you will interpret your survey. Multiple-choice formats make data easy to tabulate, but often they miss key information. Open-ended questions will require you to figure out a way to sort responses into categories.

Administer surveys

- Decide on who you need to survey and how many respondents your survey will require. For example, if you want to claim that the results of your survey represent the views of residents of your dormitory, your method of selecting respondents should give all residents an equal chance to be selected. Don't select only your friends.
- Decide how you will contact participants in your survey. If you are conducting your survey on private property, you will need permission from the property owner. Likewise, e-mail lists and lists of mailing addresses are usually guarded closely to preserve privacy. You will need to secure permission from the appropriate parties if you want to contact people via an e-mail list.
- If you mail or e-mail your survey, include a statement about what the survey is for.

Observations

Observing can be a valuable source of data. For example, if you are researching why a particular office on your campus does not operate efficiently, observe what happens when students enter and how the staff responds to their presence.

Make observations

- Choose a place where you can observe with the least intrusion. The less people wonder about what you are doing, the better.
- Carry a notebook and write extensive field notes. Record as much information as you can, and worry about analyzing it later.
- Record the date, exactly where you were, exactly when you arrived and left, and important details like the number of people present.
- Write on one side of your notebook so you can use the facing page to note key observations and analyze your data later.

Analyze observations

You must interpret your observations so they make sense in the context of your argument. Ask yourself the following questions.

- What patterns of behavior did you observe?
- How was the situation you observed unique? How might it be similar to other locations?
- What constituted "normal" activity during the time when you were observing? Did anything out of the ordinary happen?
- Why were the people there? What can you determine about the purposes of the activities you observed?

Draft a Working Thesis

Once you have done some preliminary research into your question, you can begin to craft a working thesis. Let's take one topic as an example—the increasing popularity of organic products, including meat, dairy products, and produce. If you research this topic, you will discover that due to this trend, large corporations such as Walmart are beginning to offer organic products in their stores. However, the enormous demand for organic products is endangering smaller organic farmers and producers. As you research the question of why small farmers and producers in the United States are endangered and what small farmers and producers in other countries have done to protect themselves, a working thesis begins to emerge.

Write your subject, research question, and working thesis on a note card or sheet of paper. Keep your working thesis handy. You may need to revise it several times until the wording is precise. As you research, ask yourself, does this information tend to support my thesis? Information that does not support your thesis is still important! It may lead you to adjust your thesis or even to abandon it altogether. You may need to find another source or reason that shows your thesis is still valid.

Example

SUBJECT: Increased demand for organic products endangering smaller farmers and producers

RESEARCH QUESTION: How can smaller organic farms and producers protect themselves from becoming extinct?

WORKING THESIS: In order to meet the increasing demand for organic products that has been created by larger corporations such as Walmart, smaller organic farmers and producers should form regional co-ops. These co-ops will work together to supply regional chains, much as co-ops of small farmers and dairies in Europe work together, thereby cutting transportation and labor costs and ensuring their survival in a much-expanded market.

PEARSON
mycomplab

For support in learning this chapter's content, follow this path in MyCompLab:
❯Resources ❯Research ❯The Research Assignment ❯Understanding a Research Assignment. Review the Instruction and Multimedia resources, then complete the Exercises and click on Gradebook to measure your progress.

17 | Finding Sources

QUICK TAKE

In this chapter, you will learn that

1. Developing a search strategy at the beginning will get you to quality sources faster (see below)
2. Using your working thesis to generate a list of keywords will enable you to search library databases, the Web, and print sources in your library (see page below)
3. Library sources, including databases, online references, and printed books and journals offer the highest quality because they have been screened by reference librarians (see page 228 and page 236)
4. Valuable sources are also on the Web, but you have to know how and where to find them (see page 231)

Develop Strategies for Finding Sources

The distinction between doing research online and in the library is blurring as more and more libraries make their collections accessible on the Web. Nevertheless, libraries still contain many resources not available on the Web. Even more important, libraries have professional research librarians who can help you locate sources quickly.

Determine where to start looking

Searches using *Google* or *Yahoo!* turn up thousands of items, many of which are often not useful for research. Considering where to start is the first step.

Scholarly books and articles in scholarly journals often are the highest-quality sources, but the lag in publication time makes them less useful for very current topics. Newspapers cover current issues, but often not in the depth of books and scholarly journals. Government Web sites and publications are often the best for finding statistics and are also valuable for researching science and medicine.

Learn the art of effective keyword searches

Keyword searches take you to the sources you need. Start with your working thesis and generate a list of possible keywords for researching your thesis.

First, think of keywords that make your search more specific. For example, a search for sources related to Internet privacy issues might focus more specifically on privacy *and*

Internet
cookies
Web profiling
Flash
spyware

You should also think about more general ways to describe what you are doing—what synonyms can you think of for your existing terms? Other people may have discussed the topic using those terms instead. Instead of relying on "privacy," you can also try keywords like

identity theft
data protection
electronic records

You can even search using terms that refer to related people, events, or movements that you are familiar with.

Facebook
Internet vigilantism
MySpace
phishing

Many databases have a thesaurus that can help you find more keywords.

Find Sources in Databases

Sources found through library **databases** have already been filtered for you by professional librarians. They will include some common sources like popular magazines and newspapers, but the greatest value of database sources are the many journals, abstracts, studies, e-books, and other writing produced by specialists whose work has been scrutinized and commented on by other experts. When you read a source from a library database, chances are you are hearing an informed voice in an important debate.

Locate databases

You can find databases on your library's Web site. Sometimes you will find a list of databases. Sometimes you select a subject, and then you are directed to databases. Sometimes you select the name of a database vendor such as EBSCO or ProQuest. The vendor is the company that provides databases to the library.

Use databases

Your library has a list of databases and indexes by subject. If you can't find this list on your library's Web site, ask a **reference librarian** for help. Follow these steps to find articles.

1. Select a database appropriate to your subject or a comprehensive database like *Academic Search Complete, Academic Search Premier,* or *LexisNexis Academic.*
2. Search the database using your list of keywords.
3. Once you have chosen an article, print or e-mail to yourself the complete citation to the article. Look for the e-mail link after you click on the item you want.
4. Print or e-mail to yourself the full text if it is available. The full text is better than cutting and pasting because you might lose track of which words are yours, leading to unintended plagiarism.
5. If the full text is not available, check the online library catalog to see if your library has the journal.

Your library will probably have printed handouts or information on the Web that tells you which database to use for a particular subject. Ask a librarian who works at the reference or information desk to help you.

If you wish to get only full-text articles, you can check that option. Full-text documents give you the same text you would find in print. Sometimes the images are not reproduced in the HTML versions, but the PDF versions show the actual printed copy. Get the PDF version if it is available. Articles in HTML format usually do not contain the page numbers.

Common Databases

Academic OneFile	Indexes periodicals from the arts, humanities, sciences, social sciences, and general news, with full-text articles and images. (*Formerly Expanded Academic ASAP*)
Academic Search Premier and Complete	Provide full-text articles for thousands of scholarly publications, including social sciences, humanities, education, computer sciences, engineering, language and linguistics, literature, medical sciences, and ethnic-studies journals.

(*Continued*)

Common Databases

ArticleFirst	Indexes journals in business, the humanities, medicine, science, and social sciences.
EBSCOhost Research Databases	Gateway to a large collection of EBSCO databases, including *Academic Search Premier* and *Complete, Business Source Premier* and *Complete, ERIC,* and *Medline.*
Factiva	Provides full-text articles on business topics, including articles from the *Wall Street Journal.*
Google Books	Allows you to search within books and gives you snippets surrounding search terms for copyrighted books. Many books out of copyright have the full text. Available for everyone.
Google Scholar	Searches scholarly literature according to criteria of relevance. Available for everyone.
General OneFile	Contains millions of full-text articles about a wide range of academic and general-interest topics.
LexisNexis Academic	Provides full text of a wide range of newspapers, magazines, government and legal documents, and company profiles from around the world.
Opposing Viewpoints Resource Center	Provides full-text articles representing differing points of view on current issues.
ProQuest Databases	Like EBSCOhost, ProQuest is a gateway to a large collection of databases with over 100 billion pages, including the best archives of doctoral dissertations and historical newspapers.

Find Sources on the Web

Because anyone can publish on the Web, there is no overall quality control and there is no system of organization—two strengths we take for granted in libraries. Nevertheless, the Web offers you some resources for current topics that would be difficult or impossible to find in a library. The key to success is knowing where you are most likely to find current and accurate information about the particular question you are researching, and knowing how to access that information.

Use search engines wisely

Search engines designed for the Web work in ways similar to library databases and your library's online catalog but with one major difference. Databases typically do some screening of the items they list, but search engines potentially take you to everything on the Web—millions of pages in all. Consequently, you have to work harder to limit searches on the Web or you can be deluged with tens of thousands of items.

Kinds of search engines

A search engine is a set of programs that sort through millions of items at incredible speed. There are four basic kinds of search engines.

1. **Keyword search engines** (e.g., *Bing, Google, Yahoo!*). Keyword search engines give different results because they assign different weights to the information they find.
2. **Meta-search engines** (e.g., *Dogpile, MetaCrawler, Surfwax*). Meta-search engines allow you to use several search engines simultaneously. While the concept is sound, metasearch agents are limited because many do not access *Google* or *Yahoo!*
3. **Web directories** (e.g., *Britannica.com, Yahoo! Directory*). Web directories classify Web sites into categories and are the closest equivalent to the cataloging system used by libraries. On most directories professional editors decide how to index a particular Web site. Web directories also allow keyword searches.
4. **Specialized search engines** are designed for specific purposes:

   - regional search engines (e.g., *Baidu* for China)
   - medical search engines (e.g., *WebMD*)
   - legal search engines (e.g., *Lexis*)
   - job search engines (e.g., *Monster.com*)
   - property search engines (e.g., *Zillow*)

Advanced searches

Search engines often produce too many hits and are therefore not always useful. If you look only at the first few items, you may miss what is most valuable. The alternative is to refine your search. Most search engines offer you the option of an advanced search, which gives you the opportunity to limit numbers.

The advanced searches on *Google* and *Yahoo!* give you the options of using a string of words to search for sites that contain (1) all the words, (2) the exact phrase, (3) any of the words, or (4) that do not contain certain words. They also allow you to specify the site, the date range, the file format, and the domain. For example, if you want to limit a search for *identity theft statistics* to reliable government Web sites, you can specify the domain as **.gov**.

An advanced search on *Google* for government (.gov) sites only.

The **OR** operator is useful if you don't know exactly which term will get the results you want, especially if you are searching within a specific site. For example, you could try this search: "face-to-face OR f2f site:webworkerdaily.com."

You can also exclude terms by putting a minus sign before the term. If you want to search for social network privacy, but not *Facebook*, try "social network privacy–Facebook."

Find online government sources

The federal government has made many of its publications available on the Web. Also, many state governments now publish important documents on the Web. Often the most current and most reliable statistics are government statistics. Among the more important government resources are the following.

- **Bureau of Labor Statistics** (www.bls.gov/). Source for official U.S. government statistics on employment, wages, and consumer prices
- **Census Bureau** (www.census.gov/). Contains a wealth of links to sites for population, social, economic, and political statistics, including the *Statistical Abstract of the United States* (www.census.gov/compendia/statab/)
- **Centers for Disease Control** (www.cdc.gov/). Authoritative and trustworthy source for health statistics
- **CIA World Factbook** (www.cia.gov/library/publications/the-world-factbook/). Resource for geographic, economic, demographic, and political information on the nations of the world
- **Library of Congress** (www.loc.gov/). Many of the resources of the largest library in the world are available on the Web
- **National Institutes of Health** (www.nih.gov/). Extensive health information including MedlinePlus searches
- **NASA** (www.nasa.gov/). A rich site with much information and images concerning space exploration and scientific discovery
- **Thomas** (thomas.loc.gov/). The major source of legislative information, including bills, committee reports, and voting records of individual members of Congress
- **USA.gov** (www.usa.gov/). The place to start when you are not sure where to look for government information

Find online reference sources

Your library's Web site has a link to reference sites, either on the main page or under another heading like "research tools."

Reference sites are usually organized by subject, and you can find resources under the subject heading.

- **Business information** (links to business databases and sites like *Hoover's* that profiles companies)
- **Dictionaries** (including the *Oxford English Dictionary* and various subject dictionaries and language dictionaries)
- **Education** (including *The College Blue Book* and others)
- **Encyclopedias** (including *Britannica Online* and others)
- **Government information** (links to federal, state, and local Web sites)
- **Reference books** (commonly used books like atlases, almanacs, biographies, handbooks, and histories)
- **Statistics and demographics** (links to federal, state, and local government sites; *FedStats* [www.fedstats.gov/] is a good place to start)

Search interactive media

The Internet allows you to access other people's opinions on thousands of topics. Millions of people post messages on discussion lists and groups, *Facebook* groups, blogs, RSS feeds, *Twitter*, and so on. Much of what you read on interactive media sites is undocumented and highly opinionated, but you can still gather important information about people's attitudes and get tips about other sources, which you can verify later.

Several search engines have been developed for interactive media. *Facebook* and *Twitter* also have search engines for their sites.

Discussion list search engines

- **Big Boards** (www.big-boards.com). Tracks over two thousand of the most active discussion forums
- **Google Groups** (groups.google.com). Archives discussion forums dating back to 1981
- **Yahoo Groups** (groups.yahoo.com). A directory of groups by subject

Blog search engines

- **Bloglines** (www.bloglines.com). Web-based aggregator that delivers RSS feeds
- **Google Blog Search** (blogsearch.google.com). Searches blogs in several languages besides English
- **IceRocket** (blogs.icerocket.com). Searches blogs, *MySpace*, and *Twitter*
- **Technorati** (www.technorati.com). Searches blogs and other user-generated content

Know the limitations of Wikipedia

Wikipedia is a valuable resource for current information and for popular culture topics that are not covered in traditional encyclopedias. You can find out, for example, that SpongeBob SquarePants's original name was "SpongeBoy," but it had already been copyrighted.

Nevertheless, many instructors and the scholarly community in general do not consider *Wikipedia* a reliable source of information for a research paper. The fundamental problem with *Wikipedia* is stability, not whether the information is correct or incorrect. *Wikipedia* and other wikis constantly change. The underlying idea of documenting sources is that readers can consult the same sources that you consulted. Consult other sources to confirm what you find on Wikipedia and cite those sources.

Find Multimedia Sources

Massive collections of images; audio files including music, speeches, and podcasts; videos; maps, charts, and graphs; and other resources are now available on the Web.

Find images

The major search engines for images include the following.

- **Bing Images** (www.bing.com/images/)
- **Google Image Search** (images.google.com/)
- **Picsearch** (www.picsearch.com/)
- **Yahoo! Image Search** (images.search.yahoo.com)

Libraries and museums also offer large collections. For example, the American Memory collection in the Library of Congress offers an important visual record of the history of the United States (memory.loc.gov/ammem/).

Find videos

- **Bing Videos** (www.bing.com/videos/)
- **blinkx** (www.blinkx.com/)
- **Google Videos** (video.google.com/)
- **Yahoo! Video Search** (video.search.yahoo.com)
- **YouTube** (www.youtube.com)

Find podcasts

- **iTunes Podcast Resources** (www.apple.com/itunes/podcasts/)
- **PodcastDirectory.com** (http://www.podcastdirectory.com/)

Find charts, graphs, and maps

You can find statistical data represented in charts and graphs on many government Web sites.

- **Statistical Abstract of the United States** (www.census.gov/compendia/statab/)
- **Google Earth** (earth.google.com/)

- National Geographic Map Machine
  (mapmachine.nationalgeographic.com/)
- Perry Casteñada Map Collection, University of Texas (www.lib.utexas.edu/maps/map_sites/map_sites.html)

Respect copyright

Just because images, videos, and other multimedia files are easy to download from the Web does not mean that everything is available for you to use. Look for the creator's copyright notice and suggested credit line. This notice will tell you if you can reproduce the multimedia file.

Find Print Sources

Print sources may seem "old fashioned" if you grew up with the Internet. You might even feel a little bit intimidated by them. But they are the starting point for much of the research done by experts. In college and beyond, they are indispensable. No matter how current the topic you are researching, you will likely find information in print sources that is simply not available online.

Print sources have other advantages as well.

- Books are shelved according to subject, allowing easy browsing.
- Books often have bibliographies, directing you to other research on the subject.
- You can search for books in multiple ways: author, title, subject, or call letter.
- The majority of print sources have been evaluated by scholars, editors, and publishers, who decided whether they merited publication.

Find books

Nearly all libraries now shelve books according to the Library of Congress Classification System, which uses a combination of letters and numbers to give you the book's unique location in the library. The Library of Congress call number begins with a letter or letters that represent the broad subject area into which the book is classified.

Locating books in your library

The floors of your library where books are shelved are referred to as the stacks. The call number will enable you to find the item in the stacks. You will need to consult the locations guide for your library, which gives the level and section where an item is shelved.

Locating e-books

Use your library's online catalog to find e-books the same way you find printed books. You'll see on the record "e-book" or "electronic resource." Click on the link and you can read the book and often download a few pages.

Find journal articles

Like books, **scholarly journals** provide in-depth examinations of subjects. The articles in scholarly journals are written by experts, and they usually contain lists of references that can guide you to other research on a subject.

Popular journals are useful for gaining general information. Articles in popular magazines are usually short with few, if any, source references and are typically written by journalists. Some instructors frown on using popular magazines, but these journals can be valuable for researching current opinion on a particular topic.

Many scholarly journals and popular magazines are available on your library's Web site. Find them the same way you look for books, using your library's online catalog. Databases increasingly contain the full text of articles, allowing you to read and copy the contents onto your computer. If the article you are looking for isn't available online, the paper copy will be shelved with the books in your library.

PEARSON
mycomplab

For support in learning this chapter's content, follow this path in MyCompLab:
> Resources > Research > The Research Assignment > Finding Sources.
Review the Instruction and Multimedia resources, then complete the Exercises and click on Gradebook to measure your progress.

18 | Evaluating and Recording Sources

QUICK TAKE

In this chapter, you will learn that

1. Your working thesis will help you to determine the relevance of sources (see below)
2. Librarians have developed methods for evaluating the quality of library database and print sources (see page 241)
3. Evaluating the quality of Web sources presents special challenges (see page 243)
4. Recording all the information you need to cite a source is critical to the research process (see page 244)

Determine the Relevance of Sources

Whether you use print or online sources, a successful search will turn up many more items than you can expect to use in your final product. You have to make a series of decisions as you evaluate your material. Use your research question and working thesis to create guidelines for yourself about importance and relevance.

If you ask a research question about contemporary events such as the NCAA's policy on compensating student athletes (see pages 108–112), you will need to find both background information and current information. You will need to know, for example, the most recent statistics on how many scholarship athletes actually graduate because the NCAA's main defense of not paying scholarship athletes is that they get a free education.

Use these guidelines to determine the importance and relevance of your sources to your research question.

- Does your research question require you to consult primary or secondary sources?
- Does a source you have found address your question?
- Does a source support or disagree with your working thesis? (You should not throw out work that challenges your views. Representing opposing views accurately enhances your credibility.)
- Does a source add significant information?

- Is the source current? (For most topics try to find the most up-to-date information.)
- What indications of possible bias do you note in the source?

Determine the Quality of Sources

In the Internet era, we don't lack for information, but we do lack filters for finding quality information. Two criteria will help you to make a beginning assessment of quality: individual vs. edited sources and popular vs. scholarly sources.

Distinguish individual and anonymous sources from edited sources

Anyone with a computer and access to the Internet can put up a Web site. Furthermore, they can put up sites anonymously or under an assumed name. It's no wonder that so many Web sites contain misinformation or are intentionally deceptive.

In general, sources that have been edited and published in scholarly journals, scholarly books, major newspapers, major online and print magazines, and government Web sites are considered of higher quality than what an individual might put on a personal Web site, a Facebook page, a user review, or in a blog.

Edited sources can have biases, and indeed some are quite open about their perspectives. *National Review* offers a conservative perspective, the *Wall Street Journal* is pro-business, and *The Nation* is a liberal voice. The difference from individual and anonymous sites is that we know the editorial perspectives of these journals, and we expect the editors to check the facts. On self-published Web sites and in self-published books, anything goes.

Distinguish popular sources from scholarly sources

Scholarly books and **scholarly journals** are published by and for experts. Scholarly books and articles published in scholarly journals undergo a **peer review** process in which a group of experts in a field reviews them for their scholarly soundness and academic value. Scholarly books and articles in scholarly journals include

- author's name and academic credentials and
- a list of works cited.

Newspapers, **popular books**, and **popular magazines** vary widely in quality. Newspapers and popular magazines range from highly respected publications such as the *Los Angeles Times*, *Scientific American*, and the *Atlantic Monthly* to the sensational tabloids at grocery-store checkouts. Popular sources are not peer reviewed and require more work on your part to determine their quality. EBSCO-host databases allow you to limit searches to scholarly journals.

Distinguish primary sources from secondary sources

Another key distinction for researchers is primary versus secondary sources. In the humanities and fine arts, **primary sources** are original, creative works and original accounts of events written close to the time they occurred. **Secondary sources** interpret creative works and primary sources of events.

In the sciences, **primary sources** are the factual results of experiments, observations, clinical trials, and other factual data. **Secondary sources** analyze and interpret those results.

Read sources critically

Evaluating sources requires you to read critically, which includes the following.

- Identifying the source, which is not always easy on the Web
- Identifying the author and assessing the author's credentials
- Understanding the content—what the text says
- Recognizing the author's purpose—whether the author is attempting to reflect, inform, or persuade
- Recognizing biases in the choices of words, examples, and structure
- Recognizing what the author does not include or address
- Developing an overall evaluation that takes into account all of the above

Evaluate the quality of visual sources

Evaluating the quality of visual sources involves skills similar to critical reading. Similar to critical reading, you should

- identify and assess the source,
- identify the creator,
- identify the date of creation,
- describe the content,
- assess the purpose, and
- recognize how the purpose influences the image, graphic, or video.

For graphics including charts and graphs, pay attention to the source of any data presented and see that the data are presented fairly.

Evaluate Database and Print Sources

Books are expensive to print and distribute, so book publishers generally protect their investment by providing some level of editorial oversight. Printed and on-line materials in your library undergo another review by professional librarians who select them to include in their collections.

This initial screening doesn't free you, however, from the responsibility of evaluating the quality of the sources. Many printed and database sources contain their share of inaccurate, misleading, and biased information. Also, all sources carry the risk of becoming outdated if you are looking for current information.

Checklist for evaluating database and print sources

Over the years librarians have developed a set of criteria for evaluating sources, and you should apply them in your research.

1. **Source.** Who published the book or article? Enter the publisher's name on Google or another search engine to learn about the publisher. Scholarly books and articles in scholarly journals are generally more reliable than popular maga-zines and books, which tend to emphasize what is sensational or entertaining at the expense of accuracy and comprehensiveness.

2. **Author.** Who wrote the book or article? What are the author's qualifications? Enter the author's name on Google or another search engine to learn more about him or her. Does the author represent an organization?

3. **Timeliness.** How current is the source? If you are researching a fast-developing subject such as treating ADHD, then currency is very important, but even histor-ical topics are subject to controversy or revision.

4. **Evidence.** Where does the evidence come from—facts, interviews, observations, surveys, or experiments? Is the evidence adequate to support the author's claims?

5. **Biases.** Can you detect particular biases of the author? How do the author's bi-ases affect the interpretation offered?

6. **Advertising.** For print sources, is advertising a prominent part of the journal or newspaper? How might the ads affect the credibility or the biases of the informa-tion that gets printed?

Evaluate Web Sources

Researching on the Web has been compared to drinking from a fire hose. The key to success is not only getting the torrent down to the size of a glass, but also making sure the water in the glass is pure enough to drink.

Pay attention to domain names

Domain names can give you clues about the quality of a Web site.

- **.com** Commercial site. The information on a .com site is generally about a product or company. While the information may be accurate, keep in mind that the purpose of the site is to sell a product or service.
- **.edu** Educational institution. The suffix tells you the site is on a school server, ranging from kindergarten to higher education. If the information is from a department or research center, it is generally credible, but if the site is an individual's, treat it as you would other kinds of self-published information.
- **.gov** Government. If you see this suffix, you're viewing a federal government site. Most government sites are considered credible sources.
- **.org** Nonprofit organization. Initially, nonpartisan organizations like the Red Cross used this domain, but increasingly partisan political groups and commercial interests have taken the .org suffix. Treat this domain with scrutiny.
- **.mil** Military. This domain suffix is owned by the various branches of the armed forces.
- **.net** Network. Anyone can use this domain.

Be alert for biased Web sites

Nearly every large company and political and advocacy organization has a Web site. We expect these sites to represent the company or the point of view of the organization. Many sites on the Web, however, are not so clearly labeled.

For example, if you do a search for "Sudden Infant Death Syndrome (SIDS)" and "vaccines," you'll find near the top of the list an article titled "Vaccines and Sudden Infant Death Syndrome (SIDS): A Link?" (www.thinktwice.com/sids.htm). The article concludes that vaccines cause SIDS. If you look at the home page—www.thinktwice.com—you'll find that the site's sponsor, Global Vaccine Institute, opposes all vaccinations of children.

Always look for other objective sources for verification of your information. The U.S. Centers for Disease Control publishes fact sheets with the latest information about diseases and their prevention (www.cdc.gov/vaccinesafety/

Concerns/sids_faq.html). The fact sheet on SIDS and vaccines reports that people associate sudden infant death syndrome with vaccinations because babies begin vaccinations between 2 and 4 months, the same age babies die of SIDS. There is no scientific evidence that vaccines cause SIDS.

Checklist for evaluating Web sources

Web sources present special challenges for evaluation. When you find a Web page by using a search engine, you will often go deep into a complex site without having any sense of the context for that page. To evaluate the credibility of the site, you would need to examine the home page, not just the specific page you get to first.

Use these criteria for evaluating Web sites.

1. **Source.** What organization sponsors the Web site? Look for the site's owner at the top or bottom of the home page or in the Web address. Enter the owner's name on *Google* or another search engine to learn about the organization. If a Web site doesn't indicate ownership, then you have to make judgments about who put it up and why.

2. **Author.** Is the author identified? Look for an "About Us" link if you see no author listed. Enter the author's name on *Google* or another search engine to learn more about the author. Often Web sites give no information about their authors other than an e-mail address, if that. In such cases it is difficult or impossible to determine the author's qualifications. Be cautious about information on an anonymous site.

3. **Purpose.** Is the Web site trying to sell you something? Many Web sites are infomercials that might contain useful information, but they are no more trustworthy than other forms of advertising. Is the purpose to entertain? to inform? to persuade?

4. **Timeliness.** When was the Web site last updated? Look for a date on the home page. Many Web pages do not list when they were last updated; thus you cannot determine their currency.

5. **Evidence.** Are sources of information listed? Any factual information should be supported by indicating where the information came from. Reliable Web sites that offer information will list their sources.

6. **Biases.** Does the Web site offer a balanced point of view? Many Web sites conceal their attitude with a reasonable tone and seemingly factual evidence such as statistics. Citations and bibliographies do not ensure that a site is reliable. Look carefully at the links and sources cited, and peruse the "About Us" link if one is available.

Keep Track of Sources

As you begin to collect your sources, make sure you get full bibliographic information for everything you might want to use in your project. Decide which documentation style you will use. (Two major documentation styles—MLA and APA—are explained in detail in Chapters 20 and 21.)

Locate elements of a citation in database sources

For any sources you find on databases, MLA style requires you to provide the full print information, the name of the database in italics, the medium of publication (*Web*), and the date you accessed the database. If page numbers are not included, use *n. page*. Do not include the URL of the database.

See pages 262-263 for detailed coverage.

Author's name	Shaughnessy, Dan
Title of article	"They've Had Some Chief Concerns"
Publication information	
Name of periodical	*Boston Globe*
Date of publication	12 Oct. 2007
Section and page number	C5
Database information	
Name of database	*LexisNexis Academic*
Medium of publication	Web
Date you accessed the site	19 Apr. 2010

Citation in MLA-style list of works cited

Shaughnessy, Dan. "They've Had Some Chief Concerns." *Boston Globe* 12 Oct. 2007: C5. *LexisNexis Academic*. Web. 19 Apr. 2010.

Locate elements of a citation in Web sources

As you conduct your online research, make sure you collect the necessary bibliographic information for everything you might want to use as a source. Because of the potential volatility of Web sources (they can and do disappear overnight), their citations require extra information. Depending on the citation format you use, you'll arrange this information in different ways.

See pages 263 for detailed coverage.

Author's name	Zaiger, Alan Scher
Title of work	"Study: NCAA Graduation Rate Comparisons Flawed"
Title of the overall Web site	*ABC News*
Publication information	
Publisher or sponsor	ABC News
Date of publication	20 Apr. 2010
Medium of publication	Web
Date you accessed the site	1 Nov. 2010

Citation in MLA-style list of works cited

Zaiger, Alan Scher. "Study: NCAA Graduation Rate Comparisons Flawed." *ABC News*. ABC News, 20 Apr. 2010. Web. 1 Nov. 2010.

Locate elements of a citation in print sources

For books you will need, at minimum, the following information, which can typically be found on the front and back of the title page.

See page 263 for detailed coverage.

Author's name	Fleitz, David L.
Title of the book	Louis Sockalexis: The First Cleveland Indian
Publication information	
Place of publication	Jefferson
Name of publisher	McFarland
Date of publication	2002
Medium of publication	Print

Citation in MLA-style list of works cited

Fleitz, David L. *Louis Sockalexis: The First Cleveland Indian*. Jefferson: McFarland, 2002. Print.

See pages 261–262 for detailed coverage.

For support in learning this chapter's content, follow this path in MyCompLab:
⊙ Resources ⊙ Research ⊙ The Research Assignment ⊙ Evaluating Sources.
Review the Instruction and Multimedia resources, then complete the Exercises and click on Gradebook to measure your progress.

19 Writing the Research Project

QUICK TAKE

In this chapter, you will learn that

1. Before you begin writing, you need to take time to review your thesis and determine your contribution and your main points (see below)
2. Plagiarism means claiming credit for someone else's intellectual work (see page 248)
3. The best way to avoid unintentional plagiarism is to take care to distinguish source words from your own words (see page 250)
4. All quotations should be well integrated into your text (see page 255)

Review Your Goals and Plan Your Organization

If you have chosen a subject you're interested in, asked questions about it, and researched it thoroughly, you have a wealth of ideas and information to communicate to your audience.

Review your assignment and thesis

Before you begin writing a research project, review the assignment to remind you of the purpose of your argument, your potential readers, and the requested length.

By now you should have formulated a **working thesis**, which will be the focus of your project. You also should have located, read, evaluated, and taken notes on enough source material to write your project, and perhaps have conducted field research. At this stage in the writing process, your working thesis may be rough and may change as you write your draft, but having a working thesis will help keep your project focused.

Determine your contribution

A convincing and compelling source-based argument does not make claims based solely on the word of you, the writer. To be persuasive, it must draw on the expertise and reputations of others as well. However, you must also demonstrate that you have thought about and synthesized the evidence you have gathered from your sources, and you must show your readers which elements of your project represent your original thinking.

Determine exactly what you are adding to the larger conversation about your subject by answering these questions.

- Whom do you agree with?
- Whom do you disagree with?
- Which positions do you agree with but can add an additional point or example to?
- What original analysis or theorizing do you have to offer?

See pages 31–34 for examples of how to identify your contribution in relation to your sources.

Determine your main points

Look back over your notes on your sources and determine how to group the ideas you researched. Decide what your major points will be and how those points support your thesis. Group your research findings so that they match up with your major points.

Now it is time to create a working outline. Always include your thesis at the top of your outline as a guiding light. Some writers create formal outlines with roman numerals and the like; others compose the headings for the paragraphs of their project and use them to guide their draft; still others may start writing and then determine how they will organize their draft when they have a few paragraphs written. Experiment and decide which method works best for you.

Avoid Plagiarism

Plagiarism means claiming credit for someone else's intellectual work no matter whether it's to make money or get a better grade. Intentional or not, plagiarism has dire consequences. Reputable authors have gotten into trouble through carelessness by copying passages from published sources without acknowledging those sources. A number of famous people have had their reputations tarnished by accusations of plagiarism, and several prominent journalists have lost their jobs and careers for copying the work of other writers and passing it off as their own.

Deliberate plagiarism

If you buy a paper on the Web, copy someone else's paper word for word, or take an article off the Web and turn it in as yours, it's plain stealing, and people who take that risk should know that the punishment can be severe—usually failure for the course and sometimes expulsion. Deliberate plagiarism is easy for your instructors to spot because they recognize shifts in style, and it is easy for them to use search engines to find the sources of work stolen from the Web.

Patch plagiarism

The use of the Web has increased instances of plagiarism in college. Some students view the Internet as a big free buffet where they can grab anything, paste it in a file, and submit it as their own work. Other students intend to submit work that is their own, but they commit patch plagiarism because they aren't careful in taking notes to distinguish the words of others from their own words.

What you are not required to acknowledge

Fortunately, common sense governs issues of academic plagiarism. The standards of documentation are not so strict that the source of every fact you cite must be acknowledged. You do not have to document the following.

- **Facts available from many sources.** For example, many reference sources report that the death toll of the sinking of the *Titanic* on April 15, 1912, was around 1,500.
- **Results of your own field research.** If you take a survey and report the results, you don't have to cite yourself. You do need to cite individual interviews.

What you are required to acknowledge

The following sources should be acknowledged with an in-text citation and an entry in the list of works cited (MLA style) or the list of references (APA style).

- **Quotations.** Short quotations should be enclosed within quotation marks, and long quotations should be indented as a block. See page 256 for how to integrate quotations with signal phrases.
- **Summaries and paraphrases.** Summaries represent the author's argument in miniature as accurately as possible. Paraphrases restate the author's argument in your own words.
- **Facts that are not common knowledge.** For facts that are not easily found in general reference works, cite the source.
- **Ideas that are not common knowledge.** The sources of theories, analyses, statements of opinion, and arguable claims should be cited.
- **Statistics, research findings, examples, graphs, charts, and illustrations.** As a reader you should be skeptical about statistics and research findings when the source is not mentioned. When a writer does not cite the sources of statistics and research findings, there is no way of knowing how reliable the sources are or whether the writer is making them up.

Plagiarism in college writing

If you find any of the following problems in your academic writing, you may be guilty of plagiarizing someone else's work. Because plagiarism is usually inadvertent, it is especially important that you understand what constitutes using sources responsibly. Avoid these pitfalls.

- **Missing attribution.** Make sure the author of a quotation has been identified. Include a lead-in or signal phrase that provides attribution to the source, and identify the author in the citation.

- **Missing quotation marks.** You must put quotation marks around material quoted directly from a source.

- **Inadequate citation.** Give a page number to show where in the source the quotation appears or where a paraphrase or summary is drawn from.

- **Paraphrase relies too heavily on the source.** Be careful that the wording or sentence structure of a paraphrase does not follow the source too closely.

- **Distortion of meaning.** Don't allow your paraphrase or summary to distort the meaning of the source, and don't take a quotation out of context, resulting in a change of meaning.

- **Missing works-cited entry.** The Works Cited page must include all the works cited in the project.

- **Inadequate citation of images.** A figure or photo must appear with a caption and a citation to indicate the source of the image. If material includes a summary of data from a visual source, an attribution or citation must be given for the graphic being summarized.

Avoid plagiarism when taking notes

The best way to avoid unintentional plagiarism is to take care to distinguish source words from your own words. Don't mix words from the source with your own words.

- **Create a working bibliography and make separate files for content notes.** Create a file for each source and label it clearly with the author's name. If you work on paper, use a separate page for each source. At the top of each page, write down all the information you need for a list of works cited or a list of references in your working bibliography.

- **If you copy anything from a source when taking notes, place those words in quotation marks and note the page number(s) where those words appear.** If you copy words from an online source, take special care to note the source. You could easily copy online material and later not be able to find where it came from.

■ **Print out the entire source so you can refer to it later.** Having photocopies or complete printed files allows you to double-check later that you haven't used words from the source by mistake and that any words you quote are accurate.

Avoid Plagiarism When Quoting Sources

Effective research writing builds on the work of others. You can summarize or paraphrase the work of others, but often it is best to let the authors speak in your text by quoting their exact words. Indicate the words of others by placing them inside quotation marks.

Most people who get into plagiarism trouble lift words from a source and use them without quotation marks. Look carefully at this example to see where the line is drawn. In the following passage, Steven Johnson takes sharp issue with the metaphor of surfing applied to the Web:

> The concept of "surfing" does a terrible injustice to what it means to navigate around the Web. . . .What makes the idea of cybersurf so infuriating is the implicit connection drawn to television. Web surfing, after all, is a derivation of channel surfing—the term thrust upon the world by the rise of remote controls and cable panoply in the mid-eighties. . . . Applied to the boob tube, of course, the term was not altogether inappropriate. Surfing at least implied that channel-hopping was more dynamic, more involved, than the old routine of passive consumption. Just as a real-world surfer's enjoyment depended on the waves delivered up by the ocean, the channel surfer was at the mercy of the programmers and network executives. The analogy took off because it worked well in the one-to-many system of cable TV, where your navigational options were limited to the available channels.
>
> But when the term crossed over to the bustling new world of the Web, it lost a great deal of precision. . . . Web surfing and channel surfing are genuinely different pursuits; to imagine them as equivalents is to ignore the defining characteristics of each medium. Or at least that's what happens in theory. In practice, the Web takes on the greater burden. The television imagery casts the online surfer in the random, anesthetic shadow of TV programming, roaming from site to site like a CD player set on shuffle play. But what makes the online world so revolutionary is the fact that there *are* connections between each stop on a Web itinerant's journey. The links that join those various destinations are links of association, not randomness. A channel surfer hops back and forth between different channels because she's bored. A Web surfer clicks on a link because she's interested.
>
> —Steven Johnson. *Interface Culture: How New Technology Transforms the Way We Create and Communicate.* New York: Harper, 1997. 107–09.

If you were writing a paper or creating a Web site that concerns Web surfing, you might want to mention the distinction that Johnson makes between channel surfing and surfing on the Web.

Quoting directly

If you quote directly, you must place quotation marks around all words you take from the original:

> One observer marks this contrast: "A channel surfer hops back and forth between different channels because she's bored. A Web surfer clicks on a link because she's interested" (Johnson 109).

Notice that the quotation is introduced and not just dropped in. This example follows MLA style, where the citation—(Johnson 109)—goes outside the quotation marks but before the final period. In MLA style, source references are made according to the author's last name, which refers you to the full citation in the list of works cited at the end. Following the author's name is the page number where the quotation can be located. (Notice that there is no comma after the name.)

Attributing every quotation

If the author's name appears in the sentence, cite only the page number, in parentheses:

> According to Steven Johnson, "A channel surfer hops back and forth between different channels because she's bored. A Web surfer clicks on a link because she's interested" (109).

Quoting words that are quoted in your source

Use single quotation marks to quote material that is already quoted in your source:

> Steven Johnson uses the metaphor of a Gothic cathedral to describe a computer interface: "'The principle of the Gothic architecture,' Coleridge once said, 'is infinity made imaginable.' The same could be said for the modern interface" (42).

Avoid Plagiarism When Summarizing and Paraphrasing

Summarizing

When you summarize, you state the major ideas of an entire source or part of a source in a paragraph or perhaps even a sentence. The key is to put the summary in your own words. If you use words from the source, you must put those words within quotation marks.

Plagiarized

> Steven Johnson argues in *Interface Culture* that the concept of "surfing" is misapplied to the Internet because channel surfers hop back and forth between different channels because they're bored, but Web surfers click on links because they're interested. [Most of the words are lifted directly from the original; see page 251.]

Acceptable summary

> Steven Johnson argues in *Interface Culture* that the concept of "surfing" is misapplied to the Internet because users of the Web consciously choose to link to other sites while television viewers mindlessly flip through the channels until something catches their attention.

Paraphrasing

When you paraphrase, you represent the idea of the source in your own words at about the same length as the original. You still need to include the reference to the source of the idea. The following example illustrates an unacceptable paraphrase.

Plagiarized

> Steven Johnson argues that the concept of "surfing" does a terrible injustice to what it means to navigate around the Web. What makes the idea of Web surfing infuriating is the association with television. Surfing is not a bad metaphor for channel hopping, but it doesn't fit what people do on the Web. Web surfing and channel surfing are truly different activities; to imagine them as the same is to ignore their defining characteristics. A channel surfer skips around because she's bored while a Web surfer clicks on a link because she's interested (107–09).

Even though the source is listed, this paraphrase is unacceptable. Too many of the words in the original are used directly here, including much or all of entire sentences. When a string of words is lifted from a source and inserted without quotation marks, the passage is plagiarized. Changing a few words in a sentence is not a paraphrase. Compare these two sentences.

Source

> Web surfing and channel surfing are genuinely different pursuits; to imagine them as equivalents is to ignore the defining characteristics of each medium.

Unacceptable paraphrase

> Web surfing and channel surfing are truly different activities; to imagine them as the same is to ignore their defining characteristics.

The paraphrase takes the structure of the original sentence and substitutes a few words. It is much too similar to the original.

> **A true paraphrase represents an entire rewriting of the idea from the source.**

Acceptable paraphrase

> Steven Johnson argues that "surfing" is a misleading term for describing how people navigate on the Web. He allows that "surfing" is appropriate for clicking across television channels because the viewer has to interact with what the networks and cable companies provide, just as the surfer has to interact with what the ocean provides. Web surfing, according to Johnson, operates at much greater depth and with much more consciousness of purpose. Web surfers actively follow links to make connections (107-09).

Even though this paraphrase contains a few words from the original, such as *navigate* and *connections*, these sentences are original in structure and wording while accurately conveying the meaning of the source.

Decide When to Quote and When to Paraphrase

The general rule in deciding when to include direct quotations and when to paraphrase lies in the importance of the original wording.

- If you want to refer to an idea or fact and the original wording is not critical, make the point in your own words.
- Save direct quotations for language that is memorable or conveys the character of the source.

Use quotations effectively

Quotations are a frequent problem area in research projects. Review every quotation to ensure that each is used effectively and correctly.

- **Limit the use of long quotations.** If you have more than one block quotation on a page, look closely to see if one or more can be paraphrased or summarized. Use direct quotations only if the original wording is important.
- **Check that each quotation is supporting your major points rather than making major points for you.** If the ideas rather than the original wording are what's important, paraphrase the quotation and cite the source.
- **Check that each quotation is introduced and attributed.** Each quotation should be introduced and the author or title named. Check for signal phrases that signal a quotation: Smith *claims*, Jones *argues*, Brown *states*.
- **Check that each quotation is properly formatted and punctuated.** Prose quotations longer than four lines (MLA) or forty words (APA) should be indented one inch in MLA style or one-half inch in APA style. Shorter quotations should be enclosed within quotation marks.
- **Check that you cite the source for each quotation.** You are required to cite the sources of all direct quotations, paraphrases, and summaries.
- **Check the accuracy of each quotation.** It's easy to leave out words or mistype a quotation. Compare what is in your project to the original source. If you need to add words to make the quotation grammatical, make sure the added words are in brackets. Use ellipses to indicate omitted words.
- **Read your project aloud to a classmate or a friend.** Each quotation should flow smoothly when you read your project aloud. Put a check beside rough spots as you read aloud so you can revise later.

Use signal phrases

Signal verbs often indicate your stance toward a quotation. Introducing a quotation with "X says" or "X believes" tells your readers nothing. Find a livelier verb that suggests how you are using the source. For example, if you write "X contends," your reader is alerted that you likely will disagree with the source. Be as precise as possible.

Signal phrases that report information or a claim

> X argues that . . .
> X asserts that . . .
> X claims that . . .
> X observes that . . .
> As X puts it, . . .
> X reports that . . .
> As X sums it up, . . .

Signal phrases when you agree with the source

> X affirms that . . .
> X has the insight that . . .
> X points out insightfully that . . .
> X theorizes that . . .
> X verifies that . . .

Signal phrases when you disagree with the source

> X complains that . . .
> X contends that . . .
> X denies that . . .
> X disputes that . . .
> X overlooks that . . .
> X rejects that . . .
> X repudiates that . . .

Signal phrases in the sciences

Signal phrases in the sciences often use the past tense, especially for interpretations and commentary.

> X described . . .
> X found . . .
> X has suggested . . .

Introduce block quotations

Long direct quotations, called **block quotations**, are indented from the margin instead of being placed in quotation marks. In MLA style, a quotation longer than four lines should be indented 1 inch. A quotation of forty words or longer is indented 1/2 inch in APA style. In both MLA and APA styles, long quotations are double-spaced. You still need to integrate a block quotation into the text of your project by mentioning who wrote or said it.

- No quotation marks appear around the block quotation.
- Words quoted in the original retain the double quotation marks.
- The page number appears in parentheses after the period at the end of the block quotation.

It is a good idea to include at least one or two sentences following the quotation to describe its significance to your thesis.

Double-check quotations

Whether they are long or short, you should double-check all quotations you use to be sure they are accurate and that all words belonging to the original are set off with quotation marks or placed in a block quotation. If you wish to leave out words from a quotation, indicate the omitted words with ellipses (. . .), but make sure you do not alter the meaning of the original quotation. If you need to add words of your own to a quotation to make the meaning clear, place your words in square brackets.

Write a Draft

Some writers begin by writing the title, first paragraph, and concluding paragraph.

Write a specific title

A bland, generic title says to readers that you are likely to be boring.

Generic

Good and Bad Fats

Specific titles are like tasty appetizers; if you like the appetizer, you'll probably like the main course.

Specific

> The Secret Killer: Hydrogenated Fats

Write an engaging introduction

Get off to a fast start. If, for example, you want to alert readers to the dangers of partially hydrogenated oils in the food we eat, you could begin by explaining the difference in molecular structure between natural unsaturated fatty acids and trans fatty acids. And you would probably lose your readers by the end of the first paragraph.

Instead, let readers know what is at stake along with giving some background and context. State your thesis early on. Then go into the details in the body of your project.

Write a strong conclusion

The challenge in writing ending paragraphs is to leave the reader with something provocative, something beyond pure summary of the previous paragraphs. Connect back to your thesis, and use a strong concluding image, example, question, or call to action to leave your readers with something to remember and think about.

Review and Revise

After you've gone through the peer editing process or assessed your own draft, sit down with your project and consider the changes you need to make. Start from the highest level, reorganizing paragraphs and possibly even cutting large parts of your project and adding new sections. If you make significant revisions, likely you will want to repeat the overall evaluation of your revised draft when you finish (see Chapter 4).

When you feel your draft is complete, begin the editing phase. Use the guidelines on pages 51–52 to revise style and grammatical errors. Finally, proofread your project, word by word, checking for mistakes.

PEARSON
mycomplab

> For support in learning this chapter's content, follow this path in MyCompLab:
> ⬗ Resources ⬗ Research ⬗ The Research Assignment ⬗ Integrating Sources.
> Review the Instruction and Multimedia resources, then complete the Exercises and click on Gradebook to measure your progress.

20 | Documenting Sources in MLA Style

QUICK TAKE

In this chapter, you will learn that

1. Citing sources in MLA style is a two-part process, including in-text references and a Works Cited page at the end of your paper (see below)

2. Works cited entries for different kinds of sources follow a basic pattern (see page 261)

3. Research papers using MLA style are formatted according to a few basic conventions (see page 276)

The two styles of documentation used most frequently are APA style and MLA style. APA stands for American Psychological Association, which publishes a style manual used widely in the social sciences and education (see Chapter 21). MLA stands for the Modern Language Association, and its style is the norm for the humanities and fine arts, including English and rhetoric and composition. If you have questions that this chapter does not address, consult the *MLA Handbook for Writers of Research Papers*, Seventh Edition (2009), and the *MLA Style Manual and Guide to Scholarly Publishing*, Third Edition (2008).

Elements of MLA Documentation

Citing a source in your paper

Citing sources is a two-part process. When readers find a reference to a source (called an in-text or parenthetical citation) in the body of your paper, they can turn to the works-cited list at the end and find the full publication information. Place the author's last name and the page number inside parentheses at the end of the sentence.

Anticipating the impact of Google's project of digitally scanning books in major research libraries, one observer predicts that "the real magic will come in the second act, as each word in each book is cross-linked, clustered, cited, extracted, indexed, analyzed, annotated, remixed, re-assembled and woven deeper into the culture than ever before" (Kelly 43).

Author not mentioned in text

If you mention the author's name in the sentence, you do not have to put the name in the parenthetical reference at the end. Just cite the page number.

> Anticipating the impact of Google's project of digitally scanning books in major research libraries, Kevin Kelly predicts that "the real magic will come in the second act, as each word in each book is cross-linked, clustered, cited, extracted, indexed, analyzed, annotated, remixed, re-assembled and woven deeper into the culture than ever before" (43).

Author mentioned in text

The corresponding entry in the work-cited list at the end of your paper would be as follows.

Works Cited

> Kelly, Kevin. "Scan This Book!" *New York Times* 14 May 2006, late ed., sec 6: 43+. Print.

Entry in the works-cited list

Citing an entire work, a Web site, or another electronic source

If you wish to cite an entire work (a book, a film, a performance, and so on), a Web site, or an electronic source that has no page numbers or paragraph numbers, MLA style instructs that you mention the name of the person (for example, the author or director) in the text with a corresponding entry in the works-cited list. You do not need to include the author's name in parentheses. If you cannot identify the author, mention the title in your text.

> Joel Waldfogel discusses the implications of a study of alumni donations to colleges and universities, observing that parents give generously to top-rated colleges in the hope that their children's chances for admission will improve.

Author mentioned in text

Works Cited

> Waldfogel, Joel. "The Old College Try." *Slate.* Washington Post Newsweek Interactive, 6 July 2007. Web. 27 Jan. 2010.

MLA style now requires the medium of publication (print, Web, performance, etc.) to be included in each citation.

Creating an MLA-style works-cited list

To create your works-cited list, go through your paper and find every reference to the sources you consulted during your research. Each in-text reference must have an entry in your works-cited list.

Organize your works-cited list alphabetically by authors' last names or, if no author is listed, the first word in the title other than *a*, *an*, or *the*. (See pages 281–282 for a sample works-cited list.) MLA style uses four basic forms for entries in the works-cited list: books, periodicals (scholarly journals, newspapers, magazines), online library database sources, and other online sources (Web sites, discussion forums, blogs, online newspapers, online magazines, online government documents, and e-mail messages).

Works-cited entries for books

Entries for books have three main elements.

> Pollan, Michael. *In Defense of Food: An Eater's Manifesto.* New York: Penguin, 2008. Print.

1. Author's name.
- List the author's name with the last name first, followed by a period.

2. *Title of book.*
- Find the exact title on the title page, not the cover.
- Separate the title and subtitle with a colon.
- Italicize the title and put a period at the end.

3. Publication information.
- Give the city of publication and a colon.
- Give the name of the publisher, using accepted abbreviations, and a comma.
- Give the date of publication, followed by a period.
- Give the medium of publication (Print), followed by a period.

Works-cited entries for periodicals

Entries for periodicals (scholarly journals, newspapers, magazines) have three main elements.

Pilgrim, Sarah, David Smith, and Jules Pretty. "A Cross-Regional Assessment of the Factors Affecting Ecoliteracy: Implications for Policy and Practice." *Ecological Applications* 17.6 (2007): 1742-51. Print.

1. **Author's name.**
   - List the author's name with the last name first, followed by a period.

2. **"Title of article."**
   - Place the title of the article inside quotation marks.
   - Insert a period before the closing quotation mark.

3. **Publication information.**
   - Italicize the title of the journal.
   - Give the volume number.
   - List the date of publication, in parentheses, followed by a colon.
   - List the page numbers, followed by a period.
   - Give the medium of publication (Print), followed by a period.

Works-cited entries for library database sources

Basic entries for library database sources have four main elements.

Damiano, Jessica. "Growing Vegetables in Small Spaces: Train Them up Trellises and Plant Crops in Succession." *Newsday* 2 May 2010: G107. *LexisNexis Academic*. Web. 8 Apr. 2010.

1. **Author's name.**
   - List the author's name with the last name first, followed by a period.

2. **"Title of article."**
   - Place the title of the article inside quotation marks.
   - Insert a period before the closing quotation mark.

3. **Print publication information**
   - Give the print publication information in standard format, in this case for a periodical (see pages 270–272).

4. Database information
- Italicize the name of the database, followed by a period.
- List the medium of publication, followed by a period. For all database sources, the medium of publication is *Web*.
- List the date you accessed the source (day, month, and year), followed by a period.

Works-cited entries for other online sources

Basic entries for online sources (Web sites, discussion forums, blogs, online newspapers, online magazines, online government documents, and e-mail messages) have three main elements. Sometimes information such as the author's name or the date of publication is missing from the online source. Include the information you are able to locate.

There are many formats for the different kinds of electronic publications. Here is the format of an entry for an online article.

Jacobs, Ruth. "Organic Garden Gives Back." Colby Magazine 99:1 (2010): n.pag. Web. 2 Apr. 2010.

1. Author's name.
- List the author's name with the last name first, followed by a period.

2. "Title of work"; Title of the overall Web site
- Place the title of the work inside quotation marks if it is part of a larger Web site.
- Italicize the name of the overall site if it is different from the title of the work.
- Some Web sites are updated periodically, so list the version if you find it (e.g., 2010 edition).

3. Publication information.
- List the publisher or sponsor of the site, followed by a comma. If not available, use *N.p.* (for *no publisher*).
- List the date of publication if available; if not, use *n.d.*
- List the medium of publication (*Web*).
- List the date you accessed the source (day, month, and year).

MLA In-Text Citations

1. Author named in your text

Put the author's name in a signal phrase in your sentence.

> Sociologist Daniel Bell called this emerging U.S. economy the "postindustrial society" (3).

2. Author not named in your text

Put the author's last name and the page number inside parentheses at the end of the sentence.

> In 1997, the Gallup poll reported that 55% of adults in the United States think secondhand smoke is "very harmful," compared to only 36% in 1994 (Saad 4).

3. Work by a single author

The author's last name comes first, followed by the page number. There is no comma.

> (Bell 3)

4. Work by two or three authors

The authors' last names follow the order of the title page. If there are two authors, join the names with *and*. If there are three authors, use a comma between the first two names and a comma with *and* before the last name.

> (Francisco, Vaughn, and Lynn 7)

5. Work by four or more authors

You may use the phrase *et al.* (meaning "and others") for all names but the first, or you may write out all the names. Make sure you use the same method for both the in-text citations and the works-cited list.

> (Abrams et al. 1653)

6. Work by an unnamed author

Use a shortened version of the title that includes at least the first important word. Your reader will use the shortened title to find the full title in the works-cited list.

> A review in the *New Yorker* of Ryan Adams's new album focuses on the artist's age ("Pure" 25).

Notice that "Pure" is in quotation marks because it is the shortened title of an article. If it were a book, the short title would be in italics.

7. Work by a group or organization

Treat the group or organization as the author, but try to identify the group author in the text and place only the page number in parentheses. Shorten terms that are commonly abbreviated.

> According to the *Irish Free State Handbook*, published by the Ministry for Industry and Finance, the population of Ireland in 1929 was approximately 4,192,000 (23).

8. Quotations longer than four lines

When using indented (block) quotations of more than four lines, place the period *before* the parentheses enclosing the page number.

> In her article "Art for Everybody," Susan Orlean attempts to explain the popularity of painter Thomas Kinkade:
>> People like to own things they think are valuable. . . .
>> The high price of limited editions is part of their appeal:
>> it implies that they are choice and exclusive, and that
>> only a certain class of people will be able to
>> afford them. (128)
>
> This same statement could possibly also explain the popularity of phenomena like PBS's *Antiques Road Show*.

If the source is longer than one page, provide the page number for each quotation, paraphrase, and summary.

9. Web sources including Web pages, blogs, podcasts, wikis, videos, and other multimedia sources

Give the author in the text instead of putting the author's name in parentheses.

> Andrew Keen ironically used his own blog to claim that "blogs are boring to write (yawn), boring to read (yawn) and boring to discuss (yawn)."

If you cannot identify the author, mention the title in your text.

> The podcast "Catalina's Cubs" describes the excitement on Catalina Island when the Chicago Cubs went there for spring training in the 1940s.

10. Work in an anthology

Cite the name of the author of the work within an anthology, not the name of the editor of the collection. Alphabetize the entry in the list of works cited by the author, not the editor.

> In "Beard," Melissa Jane Hardie explores the role assumed by Elizabeth Taylor as the celebrity companion of gay actors including Rock Hudson and Montgomery Cliff (278–79).

11. Two or more works by the same author

When an author has two or more items in the works-cited list, distinguish which work you are citing by using the author's last name and then a shortened version of the title of each source.

> The majority of books written about coauthorship focus on partners of the same sex (Laird, *Women* 351).

Note that *Women* is italicized because it is the name of a book; if an article were named, quotation marks would be used.

12. Different authors with the same last name

If your list of works cited contains items by two or more different authors with the same last name, include the initial of the first name in the parenthetical reference.

> Web surfing requires more mental involvement than channel surfing (S. Johnson 107).

Note that a period follows the initial.

13. Two or more sources within the same sentence

Place each citation directly after the statement it supports.

> In the 1990s, many sweeping pronouncements were made that the Internet is the best opportunity to improve education since the printing press (Ellsworth xxii) or even in the history of the world (Dyrli and Kinnaman 79).

14. Two or more sources within the same citation

If two sources support a single point, separate them with a semicolon.

> (McKibbin 39; Gore 92)

15. Work quoted in another source

When you do not have access to the original source of the material you wish to use, put the abbreviation *qtd. in* (quoted in) before the information about the indirect source.

> National governments have become increasingly what Ulrich Beck, in a 1999 interview, calls "zombie institutions"—institutions that are "dead and still alive" (qtd. in Bauman 6).

16. Literary works

To supply a reference to a literary work, you sometimes need more than a page number from a specific edition. Readers should be able to locate a quotation in any edition of the book. Give the page number from the edition that you are using, then a semicolon and other identifying information.

> "Marriage is a house" is one of the most memorable lines in *Don Quixote* (546; pt. 2, bk. 3, ch. 19).

MLA Works-Cited List: Books

One author

17. Book by one author

The author's last name comes first, followed by a comma, the first name, and a period.

> Doctorow, E. L. *The March*. New York: Random, 2005. Print.

18. Two or more books by the same author

In the entry for the first book, include the author's name. In the second entry, substitute three hyphens and a period for the author's name. List the titles of books by the same author in alphabetical order.

> Grimsley, Jim. *Boulevard*. Chapel Hill: Algonquin, 2002. Print.
> ---. *Dream Boy*. New York: Simon, 1995. Print.

Multiple authors

19. Book by two or three authors

Second and subsequent authors' names appear first name first. A comma separates the authors' names.

> Chapkis, Wendy, and Richard J. Webb. *Dying to Get High: Marijuana as Medicine*. New York: New York UP, 2008. Print.

20. Book by four or more authors

You may use the phrase *et al.* (meaning "and others") for all authors but the first, or you may write out all the names. Use the same method in the in-text citation as you do in the works-cited list.

> Zukin, Cliff, et al. *A New Engagement? Political Participation, Civic Life, and the Changing American Citizen*. New York: Oxford UP, 2006. Print.

Anonymous and group authors

21. Book by an unknown author

Begin the entry with the title.

> *Encyclopedia of Americana*. New York: Somerset, 2001. Print.

22. Book by a group or organization

Treat the group as the author of the work.

> United Nations. *The Charter of the United Nations: A Commentary*. New York: Oxford UP, 2000. Print.

23. Religious texts

Do not italicize the title of a sacred text, including the Bible, unless you are citing a specific edition.

> Holy Bible. King James Text: Modern Phrased Version. New York: Oxford UP, 1980. Print.

Imprints, reprints, and undated books

24. Book with no publication date

If no year of publication is given but can be approximated, put a *c.* ("circa") and the approximate date in brackets: [c. 2009]. Otherwise, put *n.d.* ("no date"). For works before 1900, you do not need to list the publisher.

> O'Sullivan, Colin. *Traditions and Novelties of the Irish Country Folk*. Dublin, [c. 1793]. Print.

> James, Franklin. *In the Valley of the King*. Cambridge: Harvard UP, n.d. Print.

25. Reprinted works

For works of fiction that have been printed in many different editions or reprints, give the original publication date after the title.

Wilde, Oscar. *The Picture of Dorian Gray*. 1890. New York: Norton, 2001. Print.

Parts of books

26. Introduction, foreword, preface, or afterword

Give the author and then the name of the specific part being cited. Next, name the book. Then, if the author for the whole work is different, put that author's name after the word *By*. Place inclusive page numbers at the end.

Benstock, Sheri. Introduction. *The House of Mirth*. By Edith Wharton. Boston: Bedford-St. Martin's, 2002. 3–24. Print.

27. Single chapter written by same author as the book

Ardis, Ann L. "Mapping the Middlebrow in Edwardian England." *Modernism and Cultural Conflict: 1880-1922*. Cambridge: Cambridge UP, 2002. 114–42. Print.

28. Selection from an anthology or edited collection

Sedaris, David. "Full House." *The Best American Nonrequired Reading 2004*. Ed. Dave Eggers. Boston: Houghton, 2004. 350–58. Print.

29. Article in a reference work

You can omit the names of editors and most publishing information for an article from a familiar reference work. Identify the edition by date. There is no need to give the page numbers when a work is arranged alphabetically. Give the author's name, if known.

"Utilitarianism." *The Columbia Encyclopedia*. 6th ed. 2001. Print.

Editions and translations

30. Book with an editor

List an edited book under the editor's name if your focus is on the editor. Otherwise, cite an edited book under the author's name as shown in the second example below.

Lewis, Gifford, ed. *The Big House of Inver*. By Edith Somerville and Martin Ross. Dublin: Farmar, 2000. Print.

> Somerville, Edith, and Martin Ross. *The Big House of Inver*. Ed. Gifford Lewis. Dublin: Farmar, 2000. Print.

31. Book with a translator

> Benjamin, Walter. *The Arcades Project*. Trans. Howard Eiland and Kevin McLaughlin. Cambridge: Harvard UP, 1999. Print.

32. Second or subsequent edition of a book

> Hawthorn, Jeremy, ed. *A Concise Glossary of Contemporary Literary Theory*. 3rd ed. London: Arnold, 2001. Print.

Multivolume works

33. Multivolume work

Identify both the volume you have used and the total number of volumes in the set.

> Samuel, Raphael. *Theatres of Memory*. Vol. 1. London: Verso, 1999. 2 vols. Print.

If you refer to more than one volume, identify the specific volume in your in-text citations, and list the total number of volumes in your list of works cited.

> Samuel, Raphael. *Theatres of Memory*. 2 vols. London: Verso, 1999. Print.

MLA Works-Cited List: Periodicals

Journal articles

34. Article by one author

> Mallory, Anne. "Burke, Boredom, and the Theater of Counterrevolution." *PMLA* 118.2 (2003): 329–43. Print.

35. Article by two or three authors

> Miller, Thomas P., and Brian Jackson. "What Are English Majors For?" *College Composition and Communication* 58.4 (2007): 825–31. Print.

36. Article by four or more authors

You may use the phrase *et al.* (meaning "and others") for all authors but the first, or you may write out all the names.

> Breece, Katherine E., et al. "Patterns of mtDNA Diversity in Northwestern North America." *Human Biology* 76.1 (2004): 33–54. Print.

Pagination in journals

37. Article in a scholarly journal

List the volume and issue number after the name of the journal.

> Duncan, Mike. "Whatever Happened to the Paragraph?" *College English* 69.5 (2007): 470–95. Print.

38. Article in a scholarly journal that uses only issue numbers

List the issue number after the name of the journal.

> McCall, Sophie. "Double Vision Reading." *Canadian Literature* 194 (2007): 95–97. Print.

Magazines

39. Monthly or seasonal magazines

Use the month (or season) and year in place of the volume. There is no comma before the date. Abbreviate the names of all months except May, June, and July.

> Barlow, John Perry. "Africa Rising: Everything You Know about Africa Is Wrong." *Wired* Jan. 1998: 142–58. Print.

40. Weekly or biweekly magazines

Give both the day and the month of publication, as listed on the issue.

> Brody, Richard. "A Clash of Symbols." *New Yorker* 25 June 2007: 16. Print.

Newspapers

41. Newspaper article by one author

The author's last name comes first, followed by a comma and the first name.

> Marriott, Michel. "Arts and Crafts for the Digital Age." *New York Times* 8 June 2006, late ed.: C13. Print.

42. Article by two or three authors

The second and subsequent authors' names are printed in regular order, first name first:

> Schwirtz, Michael, and Joshua Yaffa. "A Clash of Cultures at a Square in Moscow." *New York Times* 11 July 2007, late ed.: A9. Print.

43. Newspaper article by an unknown author

Begin the entry with the title.

> "The Dotted Line." *Washington Post* 8 June 2006, final ed.: E2. Print.

Reviews, editorials, letters to the editor

44. Review

If there is no title, just name the work reviewed.

> Mendelsohn, Daniel. "The Two Oscar Wildes." Rev. of *The Importance of Being Earnest*, dir. Oliver Parker. *The New York Review of Books* 10 Oct. 2002: 23–24. Print.

45. Editorial

> "Hush-hush, Sweet Liberty." Editorial. *Los Angeles Times* 7 July 2007: A18. Print.

46. Letter to the editor

> Doyle, Joe. Letter. *Direct* 1 July 2007: 48. Print.

MLA Works-Cited List: Library Database Sources

47. Work from a library database

Begin with the print publication information, then the name of the database (italicized), the medium of publication (*Web*), and the date of access.

> Snider, Michael. "Wired to Another World." *Maclean's* 3 Mar. 2003: 23–24. *Academic Search Premier*. Web. 14 Jan. 2010.

MLA Works-Cited List: Online Sources

Web publications

When do you list a URL? MLA style no longer requires including URLs of Web sources. URLs are of limited value because they change frequently and they can be specific to an individual search. Include the URL as supplementary information only when your readers probably cannot locate the source without the URL.

48. Publication by a known author

> Boerner, Steve. "Leopold Mozart." *The Mozart Project: Biography*. The Mozart
>   Project, 21 Mar. 1998. Web. 30 Oct. 2010.

49. Publication by a group or organization
If a work has no author's or editor's name listed, begin the entry with the title.

> "State of the Birds." *Audubon*. National Audubon Society, 2008. Web.
>   19 Aug. 2010.

50. Article in a scholarly journal on the Web
Some scholarly journals are published on the Web only. List articles by author, title, name of journal in italics, volume and issue number, and year of publication. If the journal does not have page numbers, use *n. pag.* in place of page numbers. Then list the medium of publication (*Web*) and the date of access (day, month, and year).

> Fleckenstein, Kristie. "Who's Writing? Aristotelian Ethos and the Author Position
>   in Digital Poetics." *Kairos* 11.3 (2007): n. pag. Web. 6 Apr. 2010.

51. Article in a newspaper on the Web
The first date is the date of publication; the second is the date of access.

> Brown, Patricia Leigh. "Australia in Sonoma." *New York Times*. New York
>   Times, 5 July 2008. Web. 3 Aug. 2010.

52. Article in a magazine on the Web

> Brown, Patricia Leigh. "The Wild Horse Is Us." *Newsweek*. Newsweek,
>   1 July 2008. Web. 12 Dec. 2010.

53. Book on the Web

> Prebish, Charles S., and Kenneth K. Tanaka. *The Faces of Buddhism in*
> *America*. Berkeley: U of California P, 2003. *eScholarship Editions*.
> Web. 2 May 2010.

Other online sources

54. Blog entry

If there is no sponsor or publisher for the blog, use *N.p.*

> Arrington, Michael. "Think Before You Voicemail." *TechCrunch*. N.p., 5 July
> 2008. Web. 10 Sept. 2010.

55. E-mail

Give the name of the writer, the subject line, a description of the message, the date, and the medium of delivery (*E-mail*).

> Ballmer, Steve. "A New Era of Business Productivity and Innovation."
> Message to Microsoft Executive E-mail. 30 Nov. 2010. E-mail.

56. Video on the Web

Video on the Web often lacks a creator and a date. Begin the entry with a title if you cannot find a creator. Use *n.d.* if you cannot find a date.

> Wesch, Michael. *A Vision of Students Today*. *YouTube*. YouTube, 2007.
> Web. 28 May 2010.

57. Personal home page

List *Home page* without quotation marks in place of the title. If no date is listed, use *n.d.*

> Graff, Harvey J. Home page. Dept. of English, Ohio State U, n.d. Web.
> 15 Nov. 2010.

58. Wiki entry

A wiki is a collaborative writing and editing tool. Although some topic-specific wikis are written and carefully edited by recognized scholars, the more popular wiki sites—such as *Wikipedia*—are often considered unreliable sources for academic papers.

> "Snowboard." *Wikipedia*. Wikimedia Foundation, 2009. Web. 30 Jan. 2010.

59. Podcast

> Sussingham, Robin. "All Things Autumn." No. 2. *HighLifeUtah*. N.p.,
> 20 Nov. 2006. Web. 28 Feb. 2010.

60. PDFs and digital files

PDFs and other digital files can often be downloaded through links. Determine the kind of work you are citing, include the appropriate information for the particular kind of work, and list the type of file.

> Glaser, Edward L., and Albert Saiz. "The Rise of the Skilled City." Discussion
> Paper No. 2025. Harvard Institute of Economic Research. Cambridge:
> Harvard U, 2003. PDF file.

MLA Works-Cited List: Other Sources

61. Sound recording

> McCoury, Del, perf. "1952 Vincent Black Lightning." By Richard Thompson.
> *Del and the Boys*. Ceili, 2001. CD.

62. Film

Begin with the title in italics. List the director, the distributor, the date, and the medium. Other data, such as the names of the screenwriters and performers, is optional.

> *Wanted*. Dir. Timur Bekmambetov. Perf. James McAvoy, Angelina Jolie, and
> Morgan Freeman. Universal, 2008. Film.

63. DVD

> *No Country for Old Men*. Dir. Joel Coen and Ethan Coen. Perf. Tommy Lee
> Jones, Javier Bardem, and Josh Brolin. Paramount, 2007. DVD.

64. Television or radio program

> "Kaisha." *The Sopranos*. Perf. James Gandolfini, Lorraine Bracco, and Edie
> Falco. HBO. 4 June 2006. Television.

Sample MLA paper

Include your last name and page number as page header, beginning with the first page, 1/2" from the top.

Witkowski 1

MLA style does not require a title page. Ask your instructor whether you need one.

Brian Witkowski

Professor Mendelsohn

RHE 309K

3 May 2010

Center your title. Do not put the title in quotation marks or type it in all capital letters.

Need a Cure for Tribe Fever?

How About a Dip in the Lake?

Use 1" margins all around. Double-space everything.

Everyone is familiar with the Cleveland Indians' Chief Wahoo logo—and I do mean everyone, not just Clevelanders. Across America people wear the smiling mascot on Cleveland Indians caps and jerseys, and recent trends in sports merchandise have popularized new groovy multicolored Indians sportswear. Because of lucrative contracts between major league baseball and Little League, youth teams all over the country don Cleveland's famous (or infamous) smiling Indian each season as fresh-faced kids scamper onto the diamonds looking like mini major leaguers (Liu). Various incarnations of the famous Chief Wahoo—described by writer Ryan Zimmerman as "a grotesque caricature grinning idiotically through enormous bucked teeth"—have been around since the 1940s. Now redder and even more cartoonish than the original hook-nosed, beige Indian with a devilish grin, Wahoo often passes as a cheerful baseball buddy like the San Diego Chicken or the St. Louis Cardinals' Fredbird.

Cite publications by the name of the author (or authors).

Though defined by its distinctive logo, Cleveland baseball far preceded its famous mascot. The team changed from the Forest Citys to the Spiders to the Bluebirds/Blues to the Broncos to the Naps and finally to the Indi-ans. Dubbed the Naps in 1903 in honor of its star player and manager Napoleon Lajoie, the team gained their current appellation in 1915. After Lajoie was traded, the team's president challenged sportswriters to devise a suitable "temporary" label for the floundering club. Publicity material claims that the writers decided on the Indians to celebrate Louis Sockalexis, a Penobscot Indian who played for the team from 1897 to 1899. With a high batting average and the notability of being the first Na-tive American in professional baseball, Sockalexis was immortalized by the new Cleveland label (Schneider 10-23). (Contrary to popular lore, some cite alternative—and less reverent—motivations behind the team's

Indent each paragraph 1/2" on the ruler in your word pro-cessing program.

naming and point to a lack of Sockalexis publicity in period newspaper articles discussing the team's naming process [Staurowsky 95-97].) Almost ninety years later, the "temporary" name continues to raise eyebrows, in both its marketability and its ideological questionability.

Today the logo is more than a little embarrassing. Since the high-profile actions of the American Indian Movement (AIM) in the 1970s, sports teams around the country—including the Indians—have been criticized for their racially insensitive mascots. Native American groups question these caricatured icons—not just because of grossly stereotyped mascots, but also because of what visual displays of team support say about Native American culture. Across the country, professional sporting teams, as well as high schools and colleges, perform faux rituals in the name of team spirit. As Tim Giago, publisher of *The Lakota Times*, a weekly South Dakotan Native American newspaper, has noted,

> The sham rituals, such as the wearing of feathers, smoking of so-called peace pipes, beating of tomtoms, fake dances, horrendous attempts at singing Indian songs, the so-called war whoops, and the painted faces, address more than the issues of racism. They are direct attacks upon the spirituality of the Indian people. (qtd. in Wulf).

Controversy over such performances still fuels the fire between activists and alumni at schools such as the University of Illinois at Champaign-Urbana, where during many decades of football halftimes fans cheered the performance of a student (often white) dressed as Chief Illiniwek. In March of 2007, the University of Illinois board of trustees voted in a nearly unanimous decision to retire the mascot's name, regalia and image ("Illinois").

Since 1969, when Oklahoma disavowed its "Little Red" mascot, more than 600 school and minor league teams have followed a more ethnically sensitive trend and ditched their "tribal" mascots (Price). High-profile teams such as Stanford, St. Johns University, and Miami (Ohio) University have changed their team names from the Indians to the Cardinal (1972), the Redmen to the Red Storm (1993), and the Redskins to the Redhawks (1996), respectively. In 2005, the NCAA officially ruled that "colleges whose nicknames or mascots refer to American Indians will not be permitted to hold National Collegiate Athletic Association tournament events" (Wolverton). By September 2005, only seventeen schools remained in violation (Wolverton). While many people see such controversies as mere bowing to the pressures of the late twentieth and early twenty-first centuries, others see the mascot issue as a topic well worthy of debate.

Cleveland's own Chief Wahoo has far from avoided controversy. Multiple conflicts between Wahoo devotees and dissenters occur annually during the baseball season. At the opening game of 1995, fifty Native Americans and supporters took stations around Jacobs Field to demonstrate against the use of the cartoonish smiling crimson mascot (Kropk). Arrests were made in 1998 when demonstrators from the United Church of Christ burned a three-foot Chief Wahoo doll in effigy ("Judge"). Opinions on the mascot remain mixed. Jacoby Ellsbury, outfielder for the Boston Red Sox and a member of the Colorado River Indian Tribes, said in 2007, "I'm not offended [by the mascot]. You can look at it two different ways. You can look at it that it's offensive or you can look at it that they are representing Native Americans. Usually I'll try to take the positive out of it" (Shaughnessy). Nonetheless, Ellsbury still acknowledges that he "can see both sides of [the controversy]" (Shaughnessy). Wedded to their memorabilia, fans proudly stand behind their Indian as others lobby vociferously for its removal, splitting government officials, fans, and social and religious groups.

In 2000 Cleveland mayor Michael White came out publicly against the team mascot, joining an already established group of religious leaders, laypersons, and civil rights activists who had demanded Wahoo's retirement. African American religious and civic leaders such as Rev. Gregory A. Jacobs pointed to the absurdity of minority groups who embrace the Wahoo symbol. "Each of us has had to fight its [sic] own battle, quite frankly," Jacobs stated. "We cannot continue to live in this kind of hypocrisy that says, Yes, we are in solidarity with my [sic] brothers and sisters, yet we continue to exploit them" (qtd. in Briggs).

This controversy also swirls outside of the greater Cleveland area. In 2009 the image of Wahoo was removed from the team's training complex in Goodyear, Arizona ("Cleveland"), while the *Seattle Times* went so far as to digitally remove the Wahoo symbol from images of the Cleveland baseball cap ("Newspaper"). As other teams make ethnically sensitive and image-conscious choices to change their mascots, Cleveland stands firm in its resolve to retain Chief Wahoo. Despite internal division and public ridicule fueled by the team icon, the city refuses to budge.

Cleveland's stubbornness on the issue of Wahoo runs contrary to the city's recently improved image and downtown revitalization. As a native of Cleveland, I understand the power of "Tribe Fever" and the unabashed pride one feels when wearing Wahoo garb during a winning (or losing) season. Often it is not until we leave northeastern Ohio that we realize the negative image that Wahoo projects. What then can Cleveland do to simultaneously save face and bolster its burgeoning positive city image? I propose that the team finally change the "temporary" Indians label. In a city so proud of its diverse ethnic heritage—African American, Italian American, and Eastern European American to name a few examples—why stand as a bearer of retrograde ethnic politics? Cleveland should take this opportunity to link its positive Midwestern image to the team of which it is so proud. I propose changing the team's name to the Cleveland Lakers.

The city's revival in the last twenty years has embraced the geographic and aesthetic grandeur of Lake Erie. Disavowing its "mistake on the lake" moniker of the late 1970s, Cleveland has traded aquatic pollution fires for a booming lakeside business district. Attractions such as the Great Lakes Science Center, the Rock and Roll Hall of Fame, and the new Cleveland Browns Stadium take advantage of the beauty of the landscape and take back the lake. Why not continue this trend through one of the city's biggest and highest-profile moneymakers: professional baseball? By changing the team's name to the Lakers, the city would gain national advertisement for one of its major selling points, while simultaneously announcing a new ethnically inclusive image that is appropriate to our wonderfully diverse city. It would be a public relations triumph for the city.

Of course this call will be met with many objections. Why do we have to buckle to pressure? Do we not live in a free country? What fans and citizens alike need to keep in mind is that ideological pressures would not be the sole motivation for this move. Yes, retiring Chief Wahoo would take Cleveland off AIM's hit list. Yes, such a move would promote a kinder and gentler Cleveland. At the same time, however, such a gesture would work toward uniting the community. So much civic division exists over this issue that a renaming could help start to heal these old wounds.

Additionally, this type of change could bring added economic prosperity to the city. First, a change in name will bring a new wave of team merchandise. Licensed sports apparel generates more than a 10-billion-dollar annual retail business in the United States, and teams have proven repeatedly that new uniforms and logos can provide new capital. After all, a new logo for the Seattle Mariners bolstered severely slumping merchandise sales (Lefton). Wahoo devotees need not panic; the booming vintage uniform business will keep him alive, as is demonstrated by the current ability to purchase replica 1940s jerseys with the old Indians logo. Also, good press created by this change will hopefully help increase tourism in Cleveland. If the goodwill created by the Cleveland Lakers can prove half as profitable as the Rock and Roll Hall of Fame, then local businesses will be humming a happy tune. Finally, if history repeats itself, a change to a more culturally inclusive logo could, in and of itself, prove to be a cash cow. When Miami University changed from the Redskins to the Redhawks, it saw alumni donations skyrocket (Price). A less divisive mascot would prove lucrative to the ball club, the city, and the players themselves. (Sluggers with inoffensive logos make excellent spokesmen.)

Perhaps this proposal sounds far-fetched: Los Angeles may seem to have cornered the market on Lakers. But where is their lake? (The Lakers were formerly the Minneapolis Lakers, where the name makes sense in the "Land of 10,000 Lakes.") Various professional and collegiate sports teams—such as baseball's San Francisco Giants and football's New York Giants—share a team name, so licensing should not be an issue. If Los Angeles has qualms about sharing the name, perhaps Cleveland could persuade Los Angeles to become the Surfers or the Stars; after all, Los Angeles players seem to spend as much time on the big and small screens as on the court.

Witkowski 6

Now is the perfect time for Cleveland to make this jump. Perhaps a
new look will help usher in a new era of Cleveland baseball and a World
Series ring to boot. Through various dry spells, the Cleveland Indians institution has symbolically turned to the descendants of Sockalexis, asking
for goodwill or a latter-generation Penobscot slugger (Fleitz 3). Perhaps
the best way to win goodwill, fortunes, and the team's first World Series
title since 1948 would be to eschew a grinning life-size Chief Wahoo for
the new Cleveland Laker, an oversized furry monster sporting water
wings, cleats, and a catcher's mask. His seventh-inning-stretch show
could include an air-guitar solo with a baseball bat as he quietly reminds
everyone that the Rock Hall is just down the street.

Witkowski 7

Center
"Works
Cited" on a
new page.

Works Cited

Briggs, David. "Churches Go to Bat Against Chief Wahoo." *Cleveland
Plain Dealer* 25 Aug. 2000: 1A. *LexisNexis Academic*. Web. 19 Apr.
2010.

ouble-space
ll entries. In-
ent all but the
rst line in
ach entry one-
alf inch.

"Cleveland Indians' Chief Wahoo Logo Left Off Team's Ballpark, Training
Complex in Goodyear, Arizona." *Cleveland.com*. Cleveland Plain
Dealer, 12 Apr. 2009. Web. 23 Apr. 2010.

Fleitz, David L. *Louis Sockalexis: The First Cleveland Indian*. Jefferson:
McFarland, 2002. Print.

"Illinois Trustees Vote to Retire Chief Illiniwek." *ESPN*. ESPN Internet
Ventures, 13 Mar. 2007. Web. 26 Apr. 2010.

"Judge Dismisses Charges Against City in Wahoo Protest." *Associated
Press* 6 Aug. 2001. *LexisNexis Academic*. Web. 19 Apr. 2010.

lphabetize en-
ies by the last
ames of the
uthors or by
ie first impor-
ant word in the
tle if no au-
nor is listed.

Kropk, M. R. "Chief Wahoo Protestors Largely Ignored by Fans." *Austin
American Statesman* 6 May 1995: D4. Print.

Lefton, Terry. "Looks Are Everything: For New Franchises, Licensing Battles Must Be Won Long Before the Team Even Takes the Field."
Sport 89 (May 1998): 32. Print.

Witkowski 8

Liu, Caitlin. "Bawl Game." *Portfolio.com*. Condé Nast, 21 Oct. 2008.
Web. 28 Apr. 2009.

"Newspaper Edits Cleveland Indian Logo from Cap Photo." *Associated
Press* 31 Mar. 1997. *LexisNexis Academic*. Web. 27 Apr. 2010.

Price, S. L. "The Indian Wars." *Sports Illustrated* 4 Mar. 2002: 66+.
Academic OneFile. Web. 20 Apr. 2010.

Schneider, Russell. *The Cleveland Indians Encyclopedia*. Philadelphia:
Temple UP, 1996. Print.

Shaughnessy, Dan. "They've Had Some Chief Concerns." *Boston Globe* 12
October 2007: C5. *LexisNexis Academic*. Web. 19 Apr. 2010.

Staurowsky, Ellen J. "Sockalexis and the Making of the Myth at the Core of
the Cleveland's 'Indian' Image." *Team Spirits: The Native American
Mascots Controversy*. Eds. C. Richard King and Charles Fruehling
Springwood. Lincoln: U of Nebraska P, 2001. 82-106. Print.

Wolverton, Brad. "NCAA Restricts Colleges With Indian Nicknames and
Mascots." *Chronicle of Higher Education* 2 Sept. 2005: A65.
ProQuest. Web. 25 Apr. 2010.

Wulf, Steve. "A Brave Move." *Sports Illustrated* 24 Feb. 1992: 7. Print.

Zimmerman, Ryan. "The Cleveland Indians' Mascot Must Go." *Christian
Science Monitor* 15 Oct. 2007: 5. *LexisNexis Academic*. Web. 19
Apr. 2010.

Italicize the titles of books and periodicals.

Check to make sure all the sources you have cited in your text are in the list of works cited.

PEARSON
mycomplab

For support in learning this chapter's content, follow this path in MyCompLab:
Resources Research Citing Sources MLA (2009 updates).
Review the Instruction and Multimedia resources, then complete the Exercises and
click on Gradebook to measure your progress.

21 | Documenting Sources in APA Style

QUICK TAKE

In this chapter, you will learn that

1. APA documentation style uses a name + date system to cite sources in the body of a paper (see below)
2. Every source used in a paper needs to be included in a References list at the end of the paper (see page 284)
3. Reference list entries for different kinds of source follow a basic pattern (see page 284)

Papers written for the social sciences, including government, linguistics, psychology, sociology, and education, frequently use the APA documentation style. For a detailed treatment of APA style, consult the *Publication Manual of the American Psychological Association*, sixth edition (2010).

Elements of APA Documentation

Citing a source in your paper

APA style emphasizes the date of publication. When you cite an author's name in the body of your paper, always include the date of publication. Notice too that APA style includes the abbreviation for page "(p.)" in front of the page number. A comma separates each element of the citation.

> Zukin (2004) observes that teens today begin to shop for themselves at age 13 or 14, "the same age when lower-class children, in the past, became apprentices or went to work in factories" (p. 50).

If the author's name is not mentioned in the sentence, cite the author, date, and page number inside parentheses.

> One sociologist notes that teens today begin to shop for themselves at age 13 or 14, "the same age when lower-class children, in the past, became apprentices or went to work in factories" (Zukin, 2004, p. 50).

The corresponding entry in the references list would be as follows.

Zukin, S. (2004). *Point of purchase: How shopping changed American culture.* New York, NY: Routledge.

Creating an APA-style references list

To create your references list, go through your paper and find every reference to the sources you consulted during your research. Each in-text citation must have an entry in your references list.

Organize your references list alphabetically by authors' last names or, if no author is listed, the first word in the title other than *a, an,* or *the.* APA style uses three basic forms for entries in the references list: books, periodicals (scholarly journals, newspapers, magazines), and online sources (online library database sources, Web sites, blogs, online newspapers, online magazines, and online government documents).

References entries for books

Orum, A. M., & Chen, X. (2003). *The world of cities: Places in comparative and historical perspective.* Malden, MA: Blackwell.

1. Author's or editor's name.
- List the author's name with the last name first, followed by a comma and the author's initials.
- Join two authors' names with an ampersand.
- If an editor, put "(Ed.)" after the name: Kavanaugh, P. (Ed.).

2. (Year of publication).
- Give the year of publication in parentheses. If no year of publication is given, write *(n.d.)* ("no date") : Smith, S. (n.d.).
- If it is a multivolume edited work, published over a period of more than one year, put the time span in parentheses: Smith, S. (1999–2001).

3. Title of book.
- Italicize the title.
- Capitalize only the first word, proper nouns, and the first word after a colon.
- If the title is in a foreign language, copy it exactly as it appears on the title page.

4. Publication information.

- For all books list the city with a two-letter state abbreviation (or full country name) after the city name. If more than one city is given on the title page, list only the first.
- Do not shorten or abbreviate words like *University* or *Press*. Omit words such as *Co.*, *Inc.*, and *Publishers*.

References entries for periodicals

Lee, E. (2007). Wired for gender: Experientiality and gender-stereotyping in computer-mediated communication. *Media Psychology, 10,* 182–210.

1. Author's name.

- List the author's name, last name first, followed by the author's initials.
- Join two authors' names with a comma and an ampersand.

2. (Year of publication).

- Give the year the work was published in parentheses.

3. Title of article.

- Do not use quotation marks. If there is a book title in the article title, italicize it.
- Capitalize only the first word of the title, the first word of the subtitle, and any proper nouns in the title.

4. Publication information.

- Italicize the journal name.
- Capitalize all nouns, verbs, and pronouns, and the first word of the journal name. Do not capitalize any article, preposition, or coordinating conjunction unless it is the first word of the title or subtitle.
- Put a comma after the journal name.
- Italicize the volume number and follow it with a comma.
- If each issue of the journal begins on page 1, give the issue number in parentheses, followed by comma.
- Give page numbers of the article (see sample references 19 and 20 for more on pagination).

References entries for online sources

> Department of Justice. Federal Bureau of Investigation. (2004). Hate crime statistics 2004: Report summary. Retrieved from http://www.fbi.gov /ucr/hc2004/openpage.htm

1. Author's name, associated institution, or organization.

- List the author's name, if given, with the last name first, followed by the author's initials.
- If the only authority you find is a group or organization (as in this example), list its name as the author.
- If the author or organization is not identified, begin the reference with the title of the document.

2. (Date of publication).

- List the date the site was produced, last revised, or copyrighted.

3. Title of page or article.

- If you are citing a page or article that has a title, treat the title like an article in a periodical. If you are citing an entire Web site, treat the name like a book.
- If the Web site has no title, list it by author or creator.

4. Retrieval information

- If your source has been assigned a DOI (Digital Object Identifier), list it after the title. Do not add a period at the end of a DOI.
- If the source does not have a DOI, list the URL of the journal's home page.

APA In-Text Citations

1. Author named in your text

> Influential sociologist Daniel Bell (1973) noted a shift in the United States to the "postindustrial society" (p. 3).

2. Author not named in your text

> In 1997, the Gallup poll reported that 55% of adults in the United States think secondhand smoke is "very harmful," compared to only 36% in 1994 (Saad, 1997, p. 4).

3. Work by a single author

(Bell, 1973, p. 3)

4. Work by two authors
Notice that APA uses an ampersand (&) with multiple authors' names rather than *and*.

(Suzuki & Irabu, 2002, p. 404)

5. Work by three to five authors
The authors' last names follow the order of the title page.

(Francisco, Vaughn, & Romano, 2001, p. 7)

Subsequent references can use the first name and *et al.*

(Francisco et al., 2001, p. 17)

6. Work by six or more authors
Use the first author's last name and *et al.* for all in-text references.

(Swallit et al., 2004, p. 49)

7. Work by a group or organization
Identify the group author in the text and place only the page number in parentheses.

The National Organization for Women (2001) observed that this "generational shift in attitudes towards marriage and childrearing" will have profound consequences (p. 325).

8. Work by an unknown author
Use a shortened version of the title (or the full title if it is short) in place of the author's name. Capitalize all key words in the title. If it is an article title, place it in quotation marks.

("Derailing the Peace Process," 2003, p. 44)

9. Quotations of 40 words or longer

Indent long quotations 1/2 inch and omit quotation marks. Note that the period appears before the parentheses in an indented block quote.

> Orlean (2001) has attempted to explain the popularity of the painter Thomas Kinkade:
>
> > People like to own things they think are valuable. . . . The high price of limited editions is part of their appeal; it implies that they are choice and exclusive, and that only a certain class of people will be able to afford them. (p. 128)

APA References List: Books

10. Book by one author

The author's last name comes first, followed by a comma and the author's initials.

> Ball, E. (2000). *Slaves in the family*. New York, NY: Ballantine Books.

If an editor, put "(Ed.)" in parentheses after the name.

> Kavanagh, P. (Ed.). (1969). *Lapped furrows*. New York, NY: Hand Press.

11. Book by two authors

Join two authors' names with a comma and ampersand.

> Hardt, M., & Negri, A. (2000). *Empire*. Cambridge, MA: Harvard University Press.

If editors, use "(Eds.)" after the names.

> McClelland, D., & Eismann, K. (Eds).

12. Book by three or more authors

List last names and initials for up to seven authors, with an ampersand between the last two names. For works with eight or more authors, list the first six names, then an ellipsis, then the last author's name.

> Anders, K., Child, H., Davis, K., Logan, O., Petersen, J., Tymes, J., . . . Johnson, S.

13. Chapter in an edited collection

Add "In" after the selection title and before the names of the editor(s).

> Howard, A. (1997). Labor, history, and sweatshops in the new global
> economy. In A. Ross (Ed.), *No sweat: Fashion, free trade, and the rights
> of garment workers* (pp. 151–172). New York, NY: Verso.

14. Published dissertation or thesis

If the dissertation you are citing is published by University Microfilms International (UMI), provide the order number as the last item in the entry.

> Price, J. J. (1998). Flight maps: Encounters with nature in modern American
> culture. *Dissertation Abstracts International, 59*(5), 1635. (UMI No.
> 9835237)

15. Government document

When the author and publisher are identical, use "Author" as the name of the publisher.

> U.S. Environmental Protection Agency. (2002). *Respiratory health effects of
> passive smoking: Lung cancer and other disorders.* (EPA Publication No.
> 600/6-90/006 F). Washington, DC: Author.

APA References List: Periodicals

16. Article by one author

> Kellogg, R. T. (2001). Competition for working memory among writing
> processes. *American Journal of Psychology, 114,* 175–192.

17. Article by multiple authors

Write out all of the authors' names, up to seven authors. For works with eight or more authors, list the first six names, then an ellipsis, then the last author's name.

> Blades, J., & Rowe-Finkbeiner, K. (2006). The motherhood manifesto. *The
> Nation, 282*(20) 11–16.

18. Article by a group or organization

> National Organization for Women (2002). Where to find feminists in Austin. *The NOW guide for Austin women*. Austin, TX: Chapter Press.

19. Article in a journal with continuous pagination
Include the volume number and the year, but not the issue number.

> Engen, R., & Steen, S. (2000). The power to punish: Discretion and sentencing reform in the war on drugs. *American Journal of Sociology*, *105*, 1357–1395.

20. Article in a journal paginated by issue
List the issue number in parentheses (not italicized) after the volume number. For a popular magazine that does not commonly use volume numbers, use the season or date of publication.

> McGinn, D. (2006, June 5). Marriage by the numbers. *Newsweek*, 40–48.

21. Monthly publication

> Barlow, J. P. (1998, January). Africa rising: Everything you know about Africa is wrong. *Wired*, 142–158.

22. Newspaper article

> Hagenbaugh, B. (2005, April 25). Grads welcome an uptick in hiring. *USA Today*, p. A1.

APA References List: Library Database Sources

23. Document from a library database
Increasingly, articles are accessed online. Because URLs frequently change, many scholarly publishers have begun to use a Digital Object Identifier (DOI), a unique alphanumeric string that is permanent. If a DOI is available, use the DOI.

APA no longer requires listing the names of well-known databases. The article below was retrieved from the PsychARTICLES database, but there is no need to list the database, the retrieval date, or the URL if the DOI is listed.

> Erdfelder, E. (2008). Experimental psychology: Good news. *Experimental Psychology, 55*(1), 1–2. doi: 0.1027/1618-3169.55.1.1

APA References List: Online Sources

24. Online publication by a known author

Authorship is sometimes hard to discern for online sources. If you do have an author or creator to cite, follow the rules for periodicals and books.

> Carr, A. (2003. May 22). AAUW applauds senate support of title IX resolution. Retrieved from http://www.aauw.org/about/newsroom/press_releases /030522.cfm

25. Online publication by a group or organization

If the only authority you find is a group or organization, list its name as the author.

> Girls Incorporated. (2003). Girls' bill of rights. Retrieved from http://www.girlsinc.org/gc/page.php?id=9

26. Article in an online scholarly journal

> Brown, B. (2004). The order of service: the practical management of customer interaction. *Sociological Research Online, 9*(4). Retrieved from http://www.socresonline.org.uk/9/4/brown.html

27. Article in an online newspaper

> Slevin, C. (2005, April 25). Lawmakers want to put limits on private toll roads. *Boulder Daily Camera.* Retrieved from http://www.dailycamera.com

28. Article in an online magazine

> Pein, C. (2005, April 20). Is Al-Jazeera ready for prime time? *Salon.* Retrieved from http://www.salon.com

APA References List: Other Sources

29. Television program

> Burgess, M., & Green, M. (Writers). (2004). Irregular around the margins. [Television series episode]. In D. Chase (Producer), *The sopranos.* New York: HBO.

30. Film, Video, or DVD

> Kaurismäki, A. (Director). (1999). *Leningrad cowboys go America* [DVD]. United States: MGM.

31. Musical recording

List both the title of the song and the title of the album or CD. In the in-text citation, include side or track numbers.

> Lowe, N. (2001). Lately I've let things slide. On *The convincer* [CD]. Chapel Hill, NC: Yep Roc Records.

For support in learning this chapter's content, follow this path in MyCompLab:

⊳Resources ⊳Research ⊳Citing Sources ⊳APA (2010 Updates).

Review the Instruction and Multimedia resources, then complete the Exercises and click on Gradebook to measure your progress.

Contemporary Arguments

PART

6

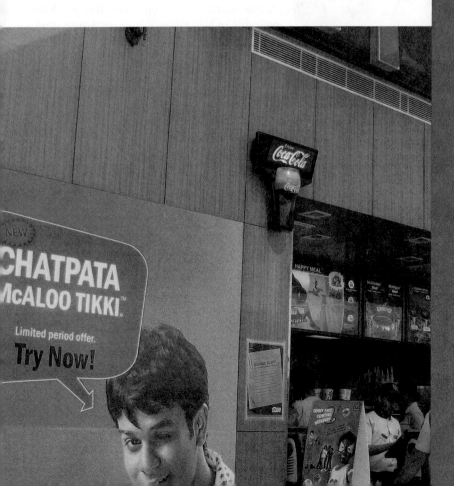

22 | Negotiating the Environment

American Environmentalism

Most people agree that the modern environmental movement emerged from the work of two people: Aldo Leopold, who outlined a "land ethic" in his 1948 book *A Sand County Almanac;* and Rachel Carson, whose 1962 book *Silent Spring* sounded a national alarm against pesticides commonly used in the agriculture industry, particularly DDT. Together Leopold and Carson argued persuasively for a new sense of our relationship to our environment, for the conviction that we should be living in balance with nature, not in domination over it. Both books ultimately influenced not only agricultural practice but also efforts to protect endangered species, to regulate population growth, and to clean up our air and water resources. When President Richard Nixon created the Environmental Protection Agency in 1973, environmental concern became institutionalized in the United States; most states created their own departments of natural resources or environmental protection soon afterward.

Dams on the Klamath River in Oregon provide water to power plants, which in turn supply clean electricity. But dams also affect fish and other wildlife, farmers, and Native Americans who live along the river. When people decide to build a dam, whose priorities should be considered?

In part, Aldo Leopold and Rachel Carson were successful because their appeals struck a chord deep within many Americans. For in a very real sense environmentalism is anything but modern. Ingrained deep within the American character, it derives from a respect for the land—the American Eden—that is evident in the legend of Rip Van Winkle, in the work of Hudson River painters such as Thomas Cole, in the landscape architecture of Frederick Law Olmsted, in Henry David Thoreau's *Walden*

> We are the most dangerous species of life on the planet, and every other species, even the earth itself, has cause to fear our power to exterminate.
> But we are also the only species which, when it chooses to do so, will go to great effort to save what it might destroy.
>
> —WALLACE STEGNER

and in Ralph Waldo Emerson's Transcendentalist writings in the 1850s, in John Muir's testimonials about Yosemite, and in Theodore Roosevelt's withdrawals into the Badlands and his campaign to begin a system of national parks. Of course, the exploitation of the American green world for profit is also ingrained in our national character. Even as some Americans were revering the land as a special landscape that sustained them physically and spiritually, pioneers moving westward were subduing it for their own purposes, in the process spoiling rivers and air and virgin forests—and native peoples—in the name of development.

In this photograph of an environmental rally in Washington, D.C., what images evoke environmental themes?

Contemporary Arguments

Today, tensions between preserving nature and using nature are perhaps as high as they have ever been. When the BP spill dumped millions of gallons of crude oil into the Gulf of Mexico in 2010, the debate between exploiters of nature and preservers of nature became particularly fierce. The tensions inherent in the two positions help to explain why environmental issues remain so prevalent in public discourse.

- What are—and what should be—the proper relationships among science, technology, and the environment?
- What is the appropriate relationship between people and the natural environment?
- How can humans balance resource development and resource protection—with "resources" including everything from timber and coal to streams and animals?
- What are the nature and extent of global warming, and what human actions does it require?
- How can poorer nations develop economically without negative global environmental repercussions?

Such questions are debated each day in all media, especially as organized environmental groups are legion, ranging from the activist Earth First! (whose 10,000 members sometimes advocate direct action in support of environmental aims) to more mainstream groups such as the Sierra Club or the Nature

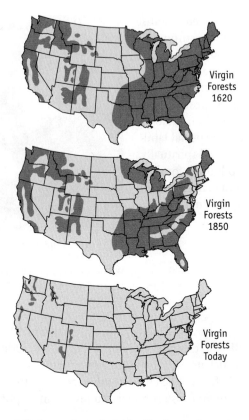

How virgin forests have diminished in the continental United States.

Conservancy. The Nature Conservancy has created a membership of about a million in an explicit effort to create partnerships between scientists and businesspeople in the interests of environmental reform. On the other hand, conservatives such as Rush Limbaugh and Sarah Palin have often ridiculed the efforts of environmentalists in the interest of a relatively unbridled developmentalism that is in the optimistic tradition of nineteenth-century free enterprise.

Debates about environmental issues are part and parcel of American culture. In the following pages you will find a sampling of the arguments concerning our relationship to the natural world. Three selections (by Rachel Carson, Edward O. Wilson, and Wendell Berry) offer philosophical perspectives and relate environmental ethics to human societies and practices—thereby providing context for a host of specific arguments, such as those about global warming. We also present an argument and counter-argument (by Chris Packham and Mark Wright) on an issue of expediency: Do we have the financial resources to spend on saving exotic animal species (like pandas) when there are so many other pressing environmental issues before us?

Then this chapter focuses at length on the issue of global warming, from Al Gore's moral appeal to Americans to dramatically change their energy habits to Christopher Horner's exhortation that global warming is merely a phenomenon in Earth's history that bears little or no relationship to human practices. The Issue in Focus on global warming also includes a kind of debate between George Will and Chris Mooney on the seriousness of global warming. How reliable is the scientific evidence that shows warming in the Earth's atmosphere? How responsible are humans for climate changes? This section also offers advice on coping with global warming from a conservative commentator and from a journalist who questions the efficacy of so-called "green consumerism." Do some creature comforts have to be given up in order for people to survive in a healthy environment? What choices must we make among economic growth, technological advancement and innovation, the preservation of green spaces, environmental quality, and biodiversity—and what should be our priorities?

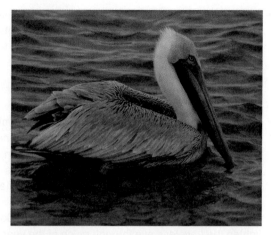

Brown pelicans are common along the coasts of the South and California, but they were headed toward extinction by 1970 because the pesticide DDT caused their eggs to be too thin to support developing chicks to maturity. Although DDT was banned in the United States, many countries continue to use it for agricultural spraying and malaria control even though insects and mosquitoes have developed resistance to it.

Rachel Carson

The Obligation to Endure

Rachel Carson (1907–1964) was raised in Springdale, Pennsylvania, 18 miles up the Allegheny River from Pittsburgh, where she developed the love of nature that she maintained throughout her life. At age 22 she began her career as a marine biologist at Woods Hole, Massachusetts, and she later went to graduate school at Johns Hopkins University in Baltimore. In 1936 she began working in the agency that later became the U.S. Fish and Wildlife Service. A meticulous scientist, Carson wrote three highly praised books about the sea and wetlands: *Under the Sea Wind* (1941), *The Sea Around Us* (1951), and *The Edge of the Sea* (1954).

When Carson decided to write *Silent Spring* (published in 1962), it marked a great change in her life. For the first time, she became an environmental activist in addition to being an enthusiastic writer about nature. During the 1950s she had grown progressively alarmed at the effects of the chemical DDT on fish, waterfowl, and birds. When her initial alarms went unheard, because DDT was contributing to substantial increases in agricultural production and controlling disease-spreading insects, she decided to write a short book to raise public consciousness. That book was *Silent Spring*, one of the most important books of the past century.

What follows are the famous first chapter and beginning sections of the second chapter of *Silent Spring*. Notice how the two chapters use very different rhetorical tactics in order to persuade readers and move them to act.

I.

There was once a town in the heart of America where all life seemed to live in harmony with its surroundings. The town lay in the midst of a checkerboard of prosperous farms, with fields of grain and hillsides of orchards where, in spring, white clouds of bloom drifted above the green fields. In autumn, oak and maple and birch set up a blaze of color that flamed and flickered across a backdrop of pines. Then foxes barked in the hills and deer silently crossed the fields, half hidden in the mists of the fall mornings.

2   Along the roads, laurel, viburnum and alder, great ferns and wildflowers delighted the traveler's eye through much of the year. Even in winter the roadsides were places of beauty, where countless birds came to feed on the berries and on the seed heads of the dried weeds rising above the snow. The countryside was, in fact, famous for the abundance and the variety of its bird life, and when the flood of migrants was pouring through in spring and fall people traveled from great distances to observe them. Others came to fish the streams, which flowed clear and cold out of the hills and contained shady pools where trout lay. So it had been from the days many years ago when the first settlers raised their houses, sank their wells, and built their barns.

3   Then a strange blight crept over the area and everything began to change. Some evil spell had settled on the community: mysterious maladies swept the flocks of chickens; the cattle and sheep sickened and died. Everywhere was a shadow of death. The farmers spoke of much illness among their families. In the town the doctors had become more and more puzzled by new kinds of sickness appearing among their patients. There had been several sudden and unexpected deaths not only among adults but even among children, who would be stricken suddenly while at play and die within a few hours.

4   There was a strange stillness. The birds, for example—where had they gone? Many people spoke of them, puzzled and disturbed. The feeding stations in the backyards were deserted. The few birds seen anywhere were moribund; they trembled violently and could not fly. It was a spring without voices. On the mornings that had once throbbed with the dawn chorus of robins, catbirds, doves, jays, wrens, and scores of other bird voices there was now no sound; only silence lay over the fields and woods and marsh.

5   On the farms the hens brooded, but no chicks hatched. The farmers complained that they were unable to raise any pigs—the litters were small and the young survived only a few days. The apple trees were coming into bloom but no bees droned among the blossoms, so there was no pollination and there would be no fruit.

6   The roadsides, once so attractive, were now lined with browned and withered vegetation as though swept by fire. These, too, were silent, deserted by all living things. Even the streams were now lifeless. Anglers no longer visited them, for all the fish had died.

7   In the gutters under the eaves and between the shingles of roofs, a white granular powder still showed a few patches; some weeks before it had fallen like snow upon the roofs and the lawns, the fields and the streams.

8   No witchcraft, no enemy action had silenced the rebirth of new life in this stricken world. The people had done it themselves.

9   This town does not actually exist, but it might easily have a thousand counterparts in America or elsewhere in the world. I know of no community that has experienced all the misfortunes I describe. Yet every one of these disasters has actually happened somewhere, and many real communities have already suffered a substantial number of them. A grim specter has crept upon us almost unnoticed, and this imagined tragedy may easily become a stark reality we all shall know

       What has already silenced the voices of spring in countless towns in America? This book is an attempt to explain.

II.

The history of life on earth has been a history of interaction between living things and their surroundings. To a large extent, the physical form and the habits of the earth's vegetation and its animal life have been molded by the environment. Considering the whole span of earthly time, the opposite effect, in which life actually modifies its surroundings, has been relatively slight. Only within the moment of time represented by the present century has one species—man—acquired significant power to alter the nature of his world.

2   During the past quarter century this power has not only increased to one of disturbing magnitude but it has changed in character. The most alarming of all man's assaults upon the environment is the contamination of air, earth, rivers, and sea with dangerous and even lethal materials. This pollution is for the most part irrecoverable; the chain of evil it initiates not only in the world that must support life but in living tissues is for the most part irreversible. In this now universal contamination of the environment, chemicals are the sinister and little-recognized partners of radiation in changing the very nature of the world—the very nature of its life. Strontium 90, released through nuclear explosions into the air, comes to earth in rain or drifts down as fallout, lodges in soil, enters into the grass or corn or wheat grown there, and in time takes up its abode in the bones of a human being, there to remain until his death. Similarly, chemicals sprayed on croplands or forests or gardens lie long in soil, entering into living organisms, passing from one to another in a chain of poisoning and death. Or they pass mysteriously by underground streams until they emerge and, through the alchemy of air and sunlight, combine into new forms that kill vegetation, sicken cattle, and work unknown harm on those who drink from once pure wells. As Albert Schweitzer has said, "Man can hardly even recognize the devils of his own creation."

3   It took hundreds of millions of years to produce the life that now inhabits the earth—eons of time in which that developing and evolving and diversifying life reached a state of adjustment and balance with its surroundings. The environment, rigorously shaping and directing the life it supported, contained elements that were hostile as well as supporting. Certain rocks gave out dangerous radiation; even within the light of the sun, from which all life draws its energy, there were short-wave radiations with power to injure.

Given time—time not in years but in millennia—life adjusts, and a balance has been reached. For time is the essential ingredient; but in the modern world there is no time.

4   The rapidity of change and the speed with which new situations are created follow the impetuous and heedless pace of man rather than the deliberate pace of nature. Radiation is no longer merely the background radiation of rocks, the bombardment of cosmic rays, the ultraviolet of the sun that have existed before there was any life on earth; radiation is now the unnatural creation of man's tampering with the atom. The chemicals to which life is asked to make its adjustment are no longer merely the calcium and silica and copper and all the rest of the minerals washed out of the rocks and carried in rivers to the sea; they are the synthetic creations of man's inventive mind, brewed in his laboratories, and having no counterparts in nature.

5   To adjust to these chemicals would require time on the scale that is nature's; it would require not merely the years of a man's life but the life of generations. And even this, were it by some miracle possible, would be futile, for the new chemicals come from our laboratories in an endless stream; almost five hundred annually find their way into actual use in the United States alone. The figure is staggering and its implications are not easily grasped—500 new chemicals to which the bodies of men and animals are required somehow to adapt each year, chemicals totally outside the limits of biologic experience.

6   Among them are many that are used in man's war against nature. Since the mid-1940's over 200 basic chemicals have been created for use in killing insects, weeds, rodents, and other organisms described in the modern vernacular as "pests"; and they are sold under several thousand different brand names.

7   These sprays, dusts, and aerosols are now applied almost universally to farms, gardens, forests, and homes—nonselective chemicals that have the power to kill every insect, the "good" and the "bad," to still the song of birds and the leaping of fish in the streams, to coat the leaves with a deadly film, and to linger on in soil—all this though the intended target may be only a few weeds or insects. Can anyone believe it is possible to lay down such a barrage of poisons on the surface of the earth without making it unfit for all life? They should not be called "insecticides," but "biocides."

8   The whole process of spraying seems caught up in an endless spiral. Since DDT was released for civilian use, a process of escalation has been going on in which ever more toxic materials must be found. This has happened because insects, in a triumphant vindication of Darwin's principle of the survival of the fittest, have evolved super races immune to the particular insecticide used, hence a deadlier one has always to be developed—and then a deadlier one than that. It has happened also because, for reasons to be described later, destructive insects often undergo a "flareback," or resurgence, after spraying, in numbers greater than before. Thus the chemical war is never won, and all life is caught in its violent crossfire.

9   Along with the possibility of the extinction of mankind by nuclear war, the central problem of our age has therefore become the contamination of man's total environment with such substances of incredible potential for harm—substances that accumulate in the tissues of plants and animals and even penetrate the germ cells to shatter or alter the very material of heredity upon which the shape of the future depends.

10   Some would-be architects of our future look toward a time when it will be possible to alter the human germ plasm by design. But we may easily be doing so now by

inadvertence, for many chemicals, like radiation, bring about gene mutations. It is ironic to think that man might determine his own future by something so seemingly trivial as the choice of an insect spray.

11   All this has been risked—for what? Future historians may well be amazed by our distorted sense of proportion. How could intelligent beings seek to control a few un-wanted species by a method that contaminated the entire environment and brought the threat of disease and death even to their own kind? Yet this is precisely what we have done. We have done it, moreover, for reasons that collapse the moment we examine them. We are told that the enormous and expanding use of pesticides is necessary to maintain farm production. Yet is our real problem not one of *overproduction*? Our farms, despite measures to remove acreages from production and to pay farmers *not* to produce, have yielded such a staggering excess of crops that the American taxpayer in 1962 is paying out more than one billion dollars a year as the total carrying cost of the surplus-food storage program. And is the situation helped when one branch of the Agriculture Department tries to reduce production while another states, as it did in 1958, "It is believed generally that reduction of crop acreages under provisions of the Soil Bank will stimulate interest in use of chemicals to obtain maximum production on the land retained in crops."

12   All this is not to say there is no insect problem and no need of control. I am say-ing, rather, that control must be geared to realities, not to mythical situations, and that the methods employed must be such that they do not destroy us along with the insects. . . .

Edward O. Wilson

The Conservation Ethic

Edward O. Wilson, a long-time Harvard professor and an entomologist with a special interest in ants, is one of the world's leading naturalists. He has won the Pulitzer Prize (twice) and the National Medal of Science, among other awards. Many of his books, in-cluding *The Diversity of Life, Naturalist,* and *Biophilia*, emphasize the vitality of species diversity and decry activities that cause the extinction of particular species. Wilson points out the value of even the smallest bugs and plants as integral parts of life sys-tems. The following text, from *Biophilia* (1984), outlines important connections between ecology and ethics.

When very little is known about an important subject, the questions people raise are almost invariably ethical. Then as knowledge grows, they become more concerned with information and amoral, in other words more narrowly intellectual. Finally, as understanding becomes sufficiently complete, the questions turn ethical again. Environmentalism is now passing from the first to the second phase, and there is reason to hope that it will proceed directly on to the third.

2   The future of the conservation movement depends on such an advance in moral reasoning. Its maturation is linked to that of biology and a new hybrid field, bioethics, that deals with the many technological advances recently made possible by biology. Philosophers and scientists are applying a more formal analysis to such complex problems as the allocations of scarce organ transplants, heroic but extremely expensive efforts to prolong life, and the possible use of genetic engineering to alter human heredity. They have only begun to consider the relationships between human beings and organisms with the same rigor. It is clear that the key to precision lies in the understanding of motivation, the ultimate reasons why people care about one thing but not another—why, say, they prefer a city with a park to a city alone. The goal is to join emotion with the rational analysis of emotion in order to create a deeper and more enduring conservation ethic.

3   Aldo Leopold, the pioneer ecologist and author of *A Sand County Almanac*, defined an ethic as a set of rules invented to meet circumstances so new or intricate, or else encompassing responses so far in the future, that the average person cannot foresee the final outcome. What is good for you and me at this moment might easily sour within ten years, and what seems ideal for the next few decades could ruin future generations. That is why any ethic worthy of the name has to encompass the distant future. The relationships of ecology and the human mind are too intricate to be understood entirely by unaided intuition, by common sense—that overrated capacity composed of the set of prejudices we acquire by the age of eighteen.

4   Values are time-dependent, making them all the more difficult to carve in stone. We want health, security, freedom, and pleasure for ourselves and our families. For distant generations we wish the same but not at any great personal cost. The difficulty created for the conservation ethic is that natural selection has programmed people to think mostly in physiological time. Their minds travel back and forth across hours, days, or at most a hundred years. The forests may all be cut, radiation slowly rise, and the winters grow steadily colder, but if the effects are unlikely to become decisive for a few generations, very few people will be stirred to revolt. Ecological and evolutionary time, spanning centuries and millennia, can be conceived in an intellectual mode but has no immediate emotional impact. Only through an unusual amount of education and reflective thought do people come to respond emotionally to far-off events and hence place a high premium on posterity.

5   The deepening of the conservation ethic requires a greater measure of evolutionary realism, including a valuation of ourselves as opposed to other people. What do we really owe our remote descendants? At the risk of offending some readers I will suggest: Nothing. Obligations simply lose their meaning across centuries. But what do we owe ourselves in planning for them? Everything. If human existence has any verifiable meaning, it is that our passions and toil are enabling mechanisms to continue that existence unbroken, unsullied, and progressively secure. It is for ourselves, and not for them or any abstract morality, that we think into the distant future. The precise manner in which we take this measure, how we put it into words, is crucially important. For if the whole process of our life is directed toward preserving our species and personal genes, preparing for future generations is an expression of the highest morality of which human beings are capable. It follows that the destruction of

the natural world in which the brain was assembled over millions of years is a risky step. And the worst gamble of all is to let species slip into extinction wholesale, for even if the natural environment is conceded more ground later, it can never be reconstituted in its original diversity. The first rule of the tinkerer, Aldo Leopold reminds us, is to keep all the pieces.

6   This proposition can be expressed another way. What event likely to happen during the next few years will our descendants most regret? Everyone agrees, defense ministers and environmentalists alike, that the worst thing possible is global nuclear war. If it occurs the entire human species is endangered; life as normal human beings wish to live it would come to an end. With that terrible truism acknowledged, it must be added that if no country pulls the trigger the worst thing that will *probably* happen—in fact is already well underway—is not energy depletion, economic collapse, conventional war, or even the expansion of totalitarian governments. As tragic as these catastrophes would be for us, they can be repaired within a few generations. The one process now going on that will take millions of years to correct is the loss of genetic and species diversity by the destruction of natural habitats. This is the folly our descendants are least likely to forgive us.

7   Extinction is accelerating and could reach ruinous proportions during the next twenty years. Not only are birds and mammals vanishing but such smaller forms as mosses, insects, and minnows. A conservative estimate of the current extinction rate is one thousand species a year, mostly from the destruction of forests and other key habitats in the tropics. By the 1990s the figure is expected to rise past ten thousand species a year (one species per hour). During the next thirty years fully one million species could be erased.

8   Whatever the exact figure—and the primitive state of evolutionary biology permits us only to set broad limits—the current rate is still the greatest in recent geological history. It is also much higher than the rate of production of new species by ongoing evolution, so that the net result is a steep decline in the world's standing diversity. Whole categories of organisms that emerged over the past ten million years, among them the familiar condors, rhinoceros, manatees, and gorillas, are close to the end. For most of their species, the last individuals to exist in the wild state could well be those living there today. It is a grave error to dismiss the hemorrhaging as a "Darwinian" process, in which species autonomously come and go and man is just the latest burden on the environment. Human destructiveness is something new under the sun. Perhaps it is matched by the giant meteorites thought to smash into the Earth and darken the atmosphere every hundred million years or so (the last one apparently arrived 65 million years ago and contributed to the extinction of the dinosaurs). But even that interval is ten thousand times longer than the entire history of civilization. In our own brief lifetime humanity will suffer an incomparable loss in aesthetic value, practical benefits from biological research, and worldwide biological stability. Deep mines of biological diversity will have been dug out and carelessly discarded in the course of environmental exploitation, without our even knowing fully what they contained.

9   The time is late for simple answers and divine guidance, and ideological confrontation has just about run its course. Little can be gained by throwing sand in the gears of industrialized society, even less by perpetuating the belief that we can solve

Aldo Leopold

Excerpts from "The Land Ethic"

Aldo Leopold (1887–1948) was one of the most influential nature writers of the twentieth century and one of the founders of modern ecology. He was completing his essay "The Land Ethic" when he died while fighting a brushfire in a neighbor's field. It appeared in Leopold's posthumously published A Sand County Almanac *(1949). As the following excerpts illustrate, the essay offers a new way of understanding our relationship with the environment—an understanding that has powerfully influenced environmental policy debates in the United States.*

The Ethical Sequence

The first ethics dealt with the relation between individuals; the Mosaic Decalogue is an example. Later accretions dealt with the relation between the individual and society. The Golden Rule tries to integrate the individual to society; democracy to integrate social organization to the individual.

There is as yet no ethic dealing with man's relation to land and to the animals and plants which grow upon it.

The Community Concept

All ethics so far evolved rest upon a single premise: that the individual is a member of a community of interdependent parts. His instincts prompt him to compete for his place in that community, but his ethics prompt him also to cooperate (perhaps in order that there may be a place to compete for).

The land ethic simply enlarges the boundaries of the community to include soils, waters, plants, and animals, or collectively: the land.

any problem created by earlier spasms of human ingenuity. The need now is for a great deal more knowledge of the true biological dimensions of our problem, civility in the face of common need, and the style of leadership once characterized by Walter Bagehot as agitated moderation.

10   Ethical philosophy is a much more important subject than ordinarily conceded in societies dominated by religious and ideological orthodoxy. It faces an especially severe test in the complexities of the conservation problem. When the time scale is expanded to encompass ecological events, it becomes far more difficult to be certain about the wisdom of any particular decision. Everything is riddled with ambiguity; the middle way turns hard and general formulas fail with dispiriting consistency. Consider that a man who is a villain to his contemporaries can become a hero to his descendants. If a tyrant were to carefully preserve his nation's land and natural resources for his personal needs while keeping his people in poverty, he might unintentionally be-

The Ecological Conscience
Obligations have no meaning without conscience, and the problem we face is the extension of the social conscience from people to land.

Substitutes for a Land Ethic
A system of conservation based solely on economic self-interest is hopelessly lopsided. It tends to ignore, and thus eventually to eliminate, many elements in the land community that lack commercial value, but that are (as far as we know) essential to its healthy functioning.

The Land Pyramid
Land, then, is not merely soil; it is a fountain of energy flowing through a circuit of soils, plants, and animals. Food chains are the living channels which conduct energy upward; death and decay return it to the soil.

Land Health and the A–B Cleavage
We see repeated the same basic paradoxes: man the conqueror *versus* man the biotic citizen; science the sharpener of his sword *versus* science the searchlight on his universe; land the slave and servant *versus* land the collective organism.

The Outlook
Examine each question in terms of what is ethically and esthetically right, as well as what is economically expedient. A thing is right when it tends to preserve the integrity, stability, and beauty of the biotic community. It is wrong when it tends otherwise.

queath a rich, healthful environment to a reduced population for enjoyment in later, democratic generations. This caudillo will have improved the long-term welfare of his people by giving them greater resources and more freedom of action. The exact reverse can occur as well: today's hero can be tomorrow's destroyer. A popular political leader who unleashes the energies of his people and raises their standard of living might simultaneously promote a population explosion, overuse of resources, flight to the cities, and poverty for later generations. Of course these two extreme examples are caricatures and unlikely to occur just so, but they suffice to illustrate that, in ecological and evolutionary time, good does not automatically flow from good or evil from evil. To choose what is best for the near future is easy. To choose what is best for the distant future is also easy. But to choose what is best for both the near and distant futures is a hard task, often internally contradictory, and requiring ethical codes yet to be formulated.

Many species of frogs and toads are disappearing throughout the world at a rapid rate. The causes of this decline appear to be numerous, but in the Amazon basin, the primary cause is loss of habitat from deforestation. Frogs and toads occupy an important niche on the food chain, and their loss negatively affects all other species.

Chris Packham and Mark Wright

Should Pandas Be Left to Face Extinction?

In September 2009 the well known British naturalist, photographer, and writer Chris Packham (born 1961) created an international furor when during a radio interview he proposed that giant pandas ought to be allowed to go extinct. A fierce advocate for nature and wildlife, he nevertheless contends that so-called "T-shirt animals" (like pandas) get far too much attention and draw resources from far more critical environmental concerns. On September 23, 2009, the British newspaper *The Guardian* carried a debate between Packham and Mark Wright that we reprint below. Wright, a leading scientist at the

World Wide Fund for Nature, was one of a great many who disagreed with Packham. Scientists are estimating that half the species on earth may become extinct in the next century. After the debate, we reprint several blog postings from around the world that commented on Packham's position. The blogs appeared on the *RadioTimes* Web site in the final days of September.

Yes, says Chris Packham

I don't want the panda to die out. I want species to stay alive—that's why I get up in the morning. I don't even kill mosquitoes or flies. So if pandas can survive, that would be great. But let's face it: conservation, both nationally and globally, has a limited amount of resources, and I think we're going to have to make some hard, pragmatic choices.

2   The truth is, pandas are extraordinarily expensive to keep going. We spend millions and millions of pounds on pretty much this one species, and a few others, when we know that the best thing we could do would be to look after the world's biodiversity hotspots with greater care. Without habitat, you've got nothing. So maybe if we took all the cash we spend on pandas and just bought rainforest with it, we might be doing a better job.

3   Of course, it's easier to raise money for something fluffy. Charismatic megafauna like the panda do appeal to people's emotional side, and attract a lot of public attention. They are emblematic of what I would call single-species conservation: i.e., a focus on one animal. This approach began in the 1970s with Save the Tiger, Save the Panda, Save the Whale, and so on, and it is now out of date. I think pandas have had a valuable role in raising the profile of conservation, but perhaps "had" is the right word.

4   Panda conservationists may stand up and say, "It's a flagship species. We're also conserving Chinese forest, where there is a whole plethora of other things." And when that works, I'm not against it. But we have to accept that some species are stronger than others. The panda is a species of bear that has gone herbivorous, and that eats a type of food that isn't all that nutritious, and that dies out sporadically. It is susceptible to various diseases, and, up until recently, it has been almost impossible to breed in captivity. They've also got a very restricted range, which is ever decreasing, due to encroachment on their habitat by the Chinese population. Perhaps the panda was already destined to run out of time.

5   Extinction is very much a part of life on earth. And we are going to have to get used to it in the next few years because climate change is going to result in all sorts of disappearances. The last large mammal extinction was another animal in China—the Yangtze river dolphin, which looked like a worn-out piece of pink

soap with piggy eyes and was never going to make it on to anyone's T-shirt. If that had appeared beautiful to us, then I doubt very much that it would be extinct. But it vanished, because it was pig-ugly and swam around in a river where no one saw it. And now, sadly, it has gone for ever.

6   I'm not trying to play God; I'm playing God's accountant. I'm saying we won't be able to save it all, so let's do the best we can. And at the moment I don't think our strategies are best placed to do that. We should be focusing our conservation endeavours on biodiversity hotspots, spreading our net more widely and looking at good-quality habitat maintenance in order to preserve as much of the life as we possibly can, using hard science to make educated decisions as to which species are essential to a community's maintenance. It may well be that we can lose the cherries from the cake. But you don't want to lose the substance. Save the Rainforest, or Save the Kalahari: that would be better.

No, says Mark Wright

7   You are reading this because it is about giant pandas. We could have this argument about the frogs of the rainforest and the issues would be identical, but the ability to get people's attention would be far lower. So in that sense, yes, you could argue that conservationists capitalize on the panda's appeal.

8   And, to be fair, I can understand where Chris Packham is coming from. Everywhere you look on this planet there are issues to be addressed, and we have finite resources. So we do make really horrible choices. But nowadays, almost exclusively, when people work in conservation they focus on saving habitats.

9   Chris has talked about pandas being an evolutionary cul-de-sac, and it's certainly unusual for a carnivore to take up herbivory. But there are many, many other species that live in a narrowly defined habitat. When he says that if you leave them be, they will die out, that's simply not true. If we don't destroy their habitat they will just chunter along in the same way that they have for the thousands of years.

10   And besides, in terms of its biodiversity and the threats it faces, I think that the part of China where pandas live should be on the preservation list anyway. The giant panda shares its habitat with the red panda, golden monkeys, and various birds that are found nowhere else in the world. The giant panda's numbers are increasing in the wild, so I don't see them dying out, and I haven't heard anything to suggest that other biodiversity isn't thriving equally.

11   It is true, though, that there some cases where preserving an animal is not the best use of resources. If you asked 100 conservationists—even at the World Wide Fund—you would proba-

bly get 90 different answers, but look at what happened with the northern white rhino in Africa, which we're pretty sure has died out. We lament its loss. But at the same time it had gotten to the stage where the likelihood of success was at a critically low level. If you were doing a battlefield triage system, the rhino would probably have had to be a casualty.

12   Otherwise, charismatic megafauna can be extremely useful. Smaller creatures often don't need a big habitat to live in, so in conservation terms it's better to go for something further up the food chain, because then by definition you are protecting a much larger area, which in turn encompasses the smaller animals.

13   And of course they are an extraordinarily good vehicle for the messages we want to put out on habitat conservation. Look at Borneo, where you instantly think of the orangutans. In the southern oceans, you think of the blue whale. Then there are polar bears in the north. There are things you pull out from the picture because people can relate to them. And it does make a difference.

A giant panda, an example of what Chris Packham calls "T-shirt animals."

Web postings

14   Lay off them! They haven't done anything to you! They are already nearly extinct [so] let them die naturally. How would you like it if they told you to go die? You wouldn't like it, would you? (**Nicola-Lucy**)

15   Nice to hear someone with such a public profile expressing the honest view of the majority within conservation circles. It's long been widely agreed that the long-term success of [conservation] efforts depends on promoting sustainable environments, where the natural world (including all the animals, plants, etc.) will find its own balance without us—as opposed to the reactive preservation on total global numbers of individual species, without regards to impact on local environments.

16   Nicola-Lucy: breathe and relax. I think you may have misread Chris's views on pandas. I think he meant we should 'pull the plug' on plowing so much money into a campaign that has seen no marked improvement for decades now, not go round culling the remaining population. (**Sam**)

17   [Packham's] comments have clearly been made through a lack of understanding of wider conservation projects. By protecting the

panda you are protecting its habitat and environment and therefore protecting the entire ecosystem that it lives within, including the people that need sustainable livelihoods. He's clearly missed the bigger picture that species and humans are intrinsically linked and by saving one you are protecting the longevity of the other. (**Becki**)

18   We pour millions into cats and dogs. Why not get rid of cats and dogs and save the panda! (**Sally**)

19   Becki misses the point spectacularly. Protecting ecosystems is certainly an excellent cause, but there is no need to link that to pandas who seem to have a darwinian instinct for self-elimination. It isn't about money plowed into conservation of habitats. . . . It is more about the ridiculous lengths we humans are going to get them to mate. (**Peter**)

20   This man is an evil, disgusting specimen of humanity. Is this what it's come down to? We can ignore the fact that the economy spends millions on cigarettes every year and this is causing more damage to the universal economy than the pandas are! We were put on this earth to do whatever we can to preserve the earth that we were put on and the animals that we share it with. (**Amy**)

21   I suppose I sit on the fence. I can see both points of view. If it is us humans causing the extinction, then we have a responsibility to do all we can reasonably do to prevent this. . . . However, it does seem to me that the panda has itself chosen to take a path which because of its diet would in any event lead to extinction. So should we step in and do something or allow nature to take its course? (**John**)

22   I think it is terrible that anyone can say that pandas should be left to die. The human race really is arrogant, greedy, etc. Glad I do not eat meat. (**Sue**)

23   I have to admit I've had an unreasonable hatred of pandas ever since I failed to see one in the Quinling Mountains in central China, but even I wouldn't agree that we should let it go extinct. It is certainly an environmental oddity, but before humans impacted on its life it would have been quite a widespread and successful species with a good chance of carrying on for the 3 million years or so that is the average life expectancy of a vertebrate species. To call it an evolutionary failure because human-induced habitat destruction had vastly reduced its range seems a little unfair. Like gorillas and tigers it is a flagship species and as we approach the point of total destruction of most of the world's ecosystems it would seem the best chance for any of them to survive is if they are home to some big charismatic animal. Conserve the panda and you conserve the Golden Takin, the Golden Pheasant, the Golden Snub-Nosed Monkey, not to mention all the other thousands of species that live in the area. (**Julian**)

Wendell Berry

Manifesto: The Mad Farmer Liberation Front

Writer, teacher, and land lover Wendell Berry (born 1934) grew up (and still lives) on a farm in Kentucky. His poetry and essays explore the connections between people and nature and typically endorse a simple lifestyle, at odds with new technologies that threaten agrarian ways. His many published works include the essays "What Are People For?" and "Why I Am Not Going to Buy a Computer." His books of poetry include *Sabbaths* and *The Country of Marriage* (1973), from which the following poetic argument is taken.

Love the quick profit, the annual raise,
vacation with pay. Want more
of everything ready-made. Be afraid
to know your neighbors and to die.

5 And you will have a window in your head.
Not even your future will be a mystery
any more. Your mind will be punched in a card
and shut away in a little drawer.

When they want you to buy something
10 they will call you. When they want you
to die for profit they will let you know.
So, friends, every day do something
that won't compute. Love the Lord.
Love the world. Work for nothing.
15 Take all that you have and be poor.
Love someone who does not deserve it.

Denounce the government and embrace
the flag. Hope to live in that free
republic for which it stands.
20 Give your approval to all you cannot
understand. Praise ignorance, for what man
has not encountered he has not destroyed.

Ask the questions that have no answers.
Invest in the millennium. Plant sequoias.
25 Say that your main crop is the forest
that you did not plant,
that you will not live to harvest.

Say that the leaves are harvested
when they have rotted into the mold.
30 Call that profit. Prophesy such returns.
Put your faith in the two inches of humus

that will build under the trees
every thousand years.

Listen to carrion—put your ear
35   close, and hear the faint chattering
of the songs that are to come.
Expect the end of the world. Laugh.

Laughter is immeasurable. Be joyful
though you have considered all the facts.
40   So long as women do not go cheap
for power, please women more than men.

Ask yourself: Will this satisfy
a woman satisfied to bear a child?
Will this disturb the sleep
45   of a woman near to giving birth?

Go with your love to the fields.
Lie down in the shade. Rest your head
in her lap. Swear allegiance
to what is nighest your thoughts.

50   As soon as the generals and the politicos
can predict the motions of your mind,
lose it. Leave it as a sign
to mark the false trail, the way
you didn't go.

55   Be like the fox
who makes more tracks than necessary,
some in the wrong direction.
Practice resurrection.

ISSUE IN FOCUS

Climate Change

Climate change gets considerable attention in political and social debates today: that's an understatement. The broad term *climate change* refers to variability over time within Earth's atmospheric conditions as well as to recorded alterations within regional temperatures and climate patterns. While the vast majority of scientists agree that climates are always changing, debates nevertheless still arise about the consequences of those changes and their causes: are the changes serious, and are they the result of natural causes and cycles or human activities? Scientists, activists, and policy makers also dispute about the degree of damage (if any) that is caused by climate change, and about the kinds of changes humans need to make in response to climate change.

Some scientists and political leaders assert the need to completely overhaul human habits—from our dependency on fossil fuels to heat our homes and the kinds of cars we drive to the kinds of lightbulbs we use and the kinds of clothes we wear. Other voices publicly assert that global warming, with its emphasis on endangered species, severe storms, and devastation to impoverished regions, is simply stirring up drama and debate when we're actually seeing merely the cyclical and natural patterns of Earth.

The most visible public figure to emerge in the climate change conversation is former U.S. vice president Al Gore. In his 2006 film *An Inconvenient Truth,* Gore strives to make the complex science behind this issue clear and spur his audience to action. Certainly, the widespread distribution, compelling visuals (particularly the footage of a polar bear stranded on melting ice), and impassioned arguments of the film make *An Inconvenient Truth* a stirring statement of the position of many environmentalists on climate change and its negative consequences. The issue reached a public milestone at the 2007 Academy Awards ceremony (where *An Inconvenient Truth* won an Oscar for best documentary) as Gore and actor Leonardo DiCaprio bantered about politics and climate change—demonstrating very visible faces in the conversation about climate change. It reached an additional milestone when Gore was awarded the Nobel Peace Prize in recognition of his efforts. (He shared the prize with the Intergovernmental Panel on Climate Change, a United Nations network of scientists, in October 2007.)

In short, the debates about climate change continue—debates not only about whether or not it exists, but also about whether and to what extent people should respond. Skeptics (such as George Will, in an essay printed below) argue that there is not enough measurable data to support *any* action. They contend that scientists have captured only a glimpse of Earth's long-standing history of temperature, atmospheric, and climate variation. They wonder whether global warming is natural and inevitable—not the result of human activity after all. If human activity is the primary cause, then why did global temperatures seem to decrease in the 1950s and 1960s, when carbon dioxide emissions were already increasing greatly—and why did *Newsweek* publish a cover story on global *cooling* in 1975? If temperature changes occur cyclically, why worry, particularly because attempted interventions on such a large phenomenon would only be futile—and because there could be as many benefits to global warming as problems associated with it? Skeptics on the subject of climate change question scientists' ability to forecast vast,

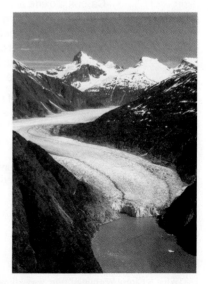

Sawyer Glacier, Alaska

long-term climatic conditions when even highly trained meteorologists sometimes struggle to predict the next day's weather. They question the motivations of politicians like Gore, the costs of a "cleanup," and the impact of those costs on the poor.

Perhaps there is only one thing that everyone can agree on: the debate will continue. In this section, you'll find images and words that illustrate the arguments in the complicated conversations about climate change. On the one hand, we include Christopher Horner's "Top Ten 'Global-Warming' Myths," and George Will's "Dark Green Doomsayers," to demonstrate the arguments of the skeptics. On the other hand, to represent the arguments of those concerned about climate change, we include a feature from Al Gore's "climate crisis" Web site, Chris Mooney's rejoinder to Will, James Murdoch's advice on the conservative approach to global warming, a cartoon that supports climate change in visual (and satiric) form, and Alex Williams's account about how even the fashion industry factors into climate change. At their heart, all of these arguments require us to think about how we live on our planet and how we care for it, as well as the legacy we wish to leave future generations. As readers and writers, you too may feel strongly about humans' influence and your own role in climate change. Pay attention to how the arguers that follow construct their presentations in essays, cartoons, and photographs. Focus on what makes a text effective or ineffective, regardless of what position you take with regard to climate change.

Al Gore

What Is Global Warming?

Carbon dioxide and other gases warm the surface of the planet naturally by trapping solar heat in the atmosphere. This is a good thing because it keeps our planet habitable. However, by burning fossil fuels such as coal, gas and oil and clearing forests we have dramatically increased the amount of carbon dioxide in the Earth's atmosphere and temperatures are rising.

The vast majority of scientists agree that global warming is real, it's already happening, and that it is the result of our activities and not a natural occurrence.[1] The evidence is overwhelming and undeniable.

The number of Category 4 and 5 hurricanes has almost doubled in the last 30 years.[2]

"What Is Global Warming?" from www.climatecrisis.net. Courtesy of Participant Productions.

Malaria has spread to higher altitudes in places like the Colombian Andes, 7,000 feet above sea level.[3]

The flow of ice from glaciers in Greenland has more than doubled over the past decade.[4]

At least 279 species of plants and animals are already responding to global warming by moving closer to the poles.[5]

If the warming continues, we can expect catastrophic consequences.

Deaths from global warming will double in just 25 years—to 300,000 people a year.[6]

Global sea levels could rise by more than 20 feet with the loss of shelf ice in Greenland and Antarctica, devastating coastal areas worldwide.[7]

Heat waves will be more frequent and more intense.

Droughts and wildfires will occur more often.

The Arctic Ocean could be ice-free in summer by 2050.[8]

More than a million species worldwide could be driven to extinction by 2050.[9]

We're already seeing changes. Glaciers are melting, plants and animals are being forced from their habitat, and the number of severe storms and droughts is increasing.

There is no doubt we can solve this problem. In fact, we have a moral obligation to do so. Small changes to your daily routine can add up to big differences in helping to stop global warming. The time to come together to solve this problem is now—TAKE ACTION.

---

[1] According to the Intergovernmental Panel on Climate Change (IPCC), this era of global warming "is unlikely to be entirely natural in origin" and "the balance of evidence suggests a discernible human influence of the global climate."

[2] Emanuel, K. 2005. Increasing destructiveness of tropical cyclones over the past 30 years. *Nature* 436: 686–688.

[3] World Health Organization.

[4] Krabill, W., E. Hanna, P. Huybrechts, W. Abdalati, J. Cappelen, B. Csatho, E. Frefick, S. Manizade, C. Martin, J, Sonntag, R. Swift, R. Thomas, and J. Yungel. 2004. Greenland Ice Sheet: Increased coastal thinning. *Geophysical Research Letters* 31.

[5] *Nature.*

[6] World Health Organization.

[7] *Washington Post*, Debate on Climate Shifts to Issue of Irreparable Change, Juliet Eilperin, January 29, 2006, Page A1.

[8] Arctic Climate Impact Assessment. 2004. Impacts of a Warming Arctic. Cambridge, UK: Cambridge University Press. Also quoted in *Time Magazine,* Vicious Cycles, Missy Adams, March 26, 2006.

[9] *Time Magazine,* Feeling the Heat, David Bjerklie, March 26, 2006.

Al Gore

Ten Things to Do to Help Stop Global Warming

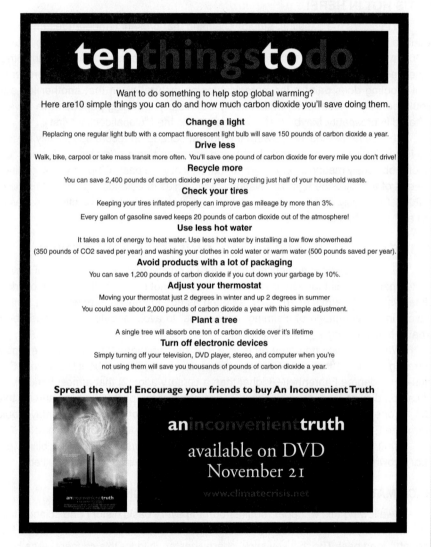

Want to do something to help stop global warming?
Here are 10 simple things you can do and how much carbon dioxide you'll save doing them.

Change a light
Replacing one regular light bulb with a compact fluorescent light bulb will save 150 pounds of carbon dioxide a year.

Drive less
Walk, bike, carpool or take mass transit more often. You'll save one pound of carbon dioxide for every mile you don't drive!

Recycle more
You can save 2,400 pounds of carbon dioxide per year by recycling just half of your household waste.

Check your tires
Keeping your tires inflated properly can improve gas mileage by more than 3%.

Every gallon of gasoline saved keeps 20 pounds of carbon dioxide out of the atmosphere!

Use less hot water
It takes a lot of energy to heat water. Use less hot water by installing a low flow showerhead
(350 pounds of CO2 saved per year) and washing your clothes in cold water or warm water (500 pounds saved per year).

Avoid products with a lot of packaging
You can save 1,200 pounds of carbon dioxide if you cut down your garbage by 10%.

Adjust your thermostat
Moving your thermostat just 2 degrees in winter and up 2 degrees in summer
You could save about 2,000 pounds of carbon dioxide a year with this simple adjustment.

Plant a tree
A single tree will absorb one ton of carbon dioxide over it's lifetime

Turn off electronic devices
Simply turning off your television, DVD player, stereo, and computer when you're
not using them will save you thousands of pounds of carbon dioxide a year.

Spread the word! Encourage your friends to buy An Inconvenient Truth

aninconvenient**truth**
available on DVD
November 21
www.climatecrisis.net

"The Ten Things to Do to Stop Global Warming" from www.climatecrisis.net. Courtesy of Participant Productions.

Christopher C. Horner

Top Ten "Global-Warming" Myths

1. IT'S HOT IN HERE!

2   In fact, "It's the baseline, stupid." Claiming that present temperatures are warm requires a starting point at, say, the 1970s, or around the Little Ice Age (approximately 1200 A.D. to the end of the 19th century), or thousands of years ago. Select many other baselines, for example, such as the 1930s, or 1000 A.D.—or 1998—and it is presently cool. Cooling does paint a far more frightening picture, given that another ice age would be truly catastrophic, while throughout history, warming periods have always ushered in prosperity. Maybe that's why the greens tried "global cooling" first.

3   The claim that the 1990s were the hottest decade on record specifically targets the intellectually lazy and easily frightened, ignoring numerous obvious factors. "On record" obviously means a very short period, typically the past 100-plus years, or since the end of the Little Ice Age. The National Academies of Science debunked this claim in 2006. Previously, rural measuring stations registered warmer temps after decades of "sprawl" (growth), cement being warmer than a pasture.

2. THE SCIENCE IS SETTLED—CO_2 CAUSES GLOBAL WARMING.

4   Al Gore shows his audience a slide of CO_2 concentrations, and a slide of historical temperatures. But for very good reason he does not combine them in one overlaid slide: historically, atmospheric CO_2, as often as not, increases after warming. This is typical in the campaign of claiming "consensus" to avoid debate (consensus about what is being left unspoken or distorted).

5   What scientists do agree on is little and says nothing about man-made global warming, to wit: (1) that global average temperature is probably about 0.6 degree Celsius—or 1 degree Fahrenheit—higher than a century ago; (2) that atmospheric levels of carbon dioxide have risen by about 30 percent over the past 200 years; and (3) that CO_2 is one greenhouse gas, some level of an increase of which presumably would warm the Earth's atmosphere were all else equal, which it demonstrably is not.

6   Until scientists are willing to save the U.S. taxpayers more than $5 billion per year thrown at researching climate, it is fair to presume the science is not settled.

3. CLIMATE WAS STABLE UNTIL MAN CAME ALONG.

7   Swallowing this whopper requires burning every basic history and science text, just as "witches" were burned in retaliation for changing climates in ages (we had thought) long past. The "hockey stick" chart—poster child for this concept—has been disgraced and air-brushed from the UN's alarmist repertoire.

4. THE GLACIERS ARE MELTING!

8   As good fortune has it, frozen things do in fact melt or at least recede after cooling periods mercifully end. The glacial retreat we read about is selective, however.

Glaciers are also advancing all over, including lonely glaciers nearby their more popular retreating neighbors. If retreating glaciers were proof of global warming, then advancing glaciers are evidence of global cooling. They cannot both be true, and in fact, neither is. Also, retreat often seems to be unrelated to warming. For example, the snow-cap on Mount Kilimanjaro is receding—despite decades of cooling in Kenya due to regional land use and atmospheric moisture.

5. CLIMATE CHANGE IS RAISING THE SEA LEVELS.

9   Sea levels rise during interglacial periods such as that in which we (happily) find ourselves. Even the distorted United Nations Intergovernmental Panel on Climate Change reports refute the hysteria, finding no statistically significant change in the rate of increase over the past century of man's greatest influence, despite green claims of massive melting already occurring. Small island nations seeking welfare and asylum for their citizens such as in socially generous New Zealand and Australia have no sea-level rise at all and in some cases see instead a drop. These societies' real problem is typically that they have made a mess of their own situation. One archipelago nation is even spending lavishly to lobby the European Union for development money to build beachfront hotel resorts, at the same time it shrieks about a watery and imminent grave. So, which time are they lying?

Images of polar bears have become popular in the arguments made by those working to spur people to take action to slow global warming. As large predators, polar bears need vast ice scapes for hunting, but these icy spaces are dwindling.

"Some say it's irrevocable, others say it's irreversible. Given such an absence of consensus I suggest we do nothing drastic."

6. GLOBAL WARMING HAS DOOMED THE POLAR BEARS!

10   For some reason, Al Gore's computerized polar bear can't swim, unlike the real kind, as one might expect of an animal named Ursa Maritimus. On the whole, these bears are thriving, if a little less well in those areas of the Arctic that are cooling (yes, cooling). Their biggest threat seems to be computer models that air-brush them from the future, the same models that tell us it is much warmer now than it is. As usual in this context, you must answer the question: Who are you going to believe—me or your lying eyes?

7. GLOBAL WARMING MEANS MORE FREQUENT, MORE SEVERE STORMS.

11   Here again the alarmists cannot even turn to the wildly distorted and politicized "Summary for Policy Makers" of the UN's IPCC to support this favorite chestnut of the press.

8. CLIMATE CHANGE IS THE GREATEST THREAT TO THE WORLD'S POOR.

12   Climate—or more accurately, weather—remains one of the greatest challenges facing the poor. Climate change adds nothing to that calculus, however. Climate and weather patterns have always changed, as they always will. Man has always best dealt with this through wealth creation and technological advance—a.k.a. adaptation—and most poorly through superstitious casting of blame, such as burning "witches." The wealthiest societies have always adapted best. One would prefer to face a similar storm in Florida than Bangladesh. Institutions, infrastructure and affordable energy are key to dealing with an ever-changing climate, not rationing energy.

9. GLOBAL-WARMING PROPOSALS ARE ABOUT THE ENVIRONMENT.

13   Only if this means that they would make things worse, given that "wealthier is healthier and cleaner." Even accepting every underlying economic and alarmist environmentalist assumption, no one dares say that the expensive Kyoto Protocol would detectably affect climate. Imagine how expensive a pact must be—in both financial and human costs—to so severely ration energy use as the greens demand. Instead, proponents candidly admit desires to control others' lifestyles, and supportive industries all hope to make millions off the deal. Europe's former environment commissioner admitted that Kyoto is "about leveling the playing field for big businesses worldwide" (in other words, bailing them out).

10. THE U.S. IS GOING IT ALONE ON KYOTO AND GLOBAL WARMING.

14   Nonsense. The U.S. rejects the Kyoto Protocol's energy-rationing scheme, along with 155 other countries, representing most of the world's population, economic activity, and projected future growth. Kyoto is a European treaty with one dozen others, none of whom is in fact presently reducing its emissions. Similarly, claims that Bush refused to sign Kyoto, and/or he withdrew, not only are mutually exclusive but also false. We signed it, Nov. 11, 1998. The Senate won't vote on it. Ergo, the (Democratic) Senate is blocking Kyoto. Gosh.

15   Don't demand they behave otherwise, however. Since Kyoto was agreed, Europe's CO_2 emissions are rising twice as fast as those of the climate-criminal United States, a gap that is widening in more recent years. So we should jump on a sinking ship?

16   Given Al Gore's proclivity for invoking Winston Churchill in this drama, it is only appropriate to summarize his claims as such: Never in the field of political conflict has so much been asked by so few of so many . . . for so little.

Sea ice in the Arctic Ocean has been shrinking at a rate of 9% per decade. The image on the left shows the minimum sea ice concentration for the year 1979, and the image on the right shows the minimum sea ice concentration in 2003. Are these photographs more or less effective than the photographs of polar bears, such as the one on page 319, in getting people to take action to slow global warming?

George Will

Dark Green Doomsayers

A corollary of Murphy's Law ("If something can go wrong, it will") is: "Things are worse than they can possibly be." Energy Secretary Steven Chu, an atomic physicist, seems to embrace that corollary but ignores Gregg Easterbrook's "Law of Doomsaying": Predict catastrophe no sooner than five years hence but no later than 10 years away, soon enough to terrify but distant enough that people will forget if you are wrong.

2   Chu recently told the *Los Angeles Times* that global warming might melt 90 percent of California's snowpack, which stores much of the water needed for agriculture. This, Chu said, would mean "no more agriculture in California," the nation's leading food producer. Chu added: "I don't actually see how they can keep their cities going."

3   No more lettuce or Los Angeles? Chu likes predictions, so here is another: Nine decades hence, our great-great-grandchildren will add the disappearance of California artichokes to the list of predicted planetary calamities that did not happen. Global cooling recently joined that lengthening list.

4   In the 1970s, "a major cooling of the planet" was "widely considered inevitable" because it was "well established" that the Northern Hemisphere's climate "has been getting cooler since about 1950" (*New York Times*, May 21, 1975). Although some disputed that the "cooling trend" could result in "a return to another ice age" (the *Times*, Sept. 14, 1975), others anticipated "a full-blown 10,000-year ice age" involving "extensive Northern Hemisphere glaciation" (*Science News*, March 1, 1975, and *Science* magazine, Dec. 10, 1976, respectively). The "continued rapid cooling of the Earth" (*Global Ecology*, 1971) meant that "a new ice age must now stand alongside nuclear war as a likely source of wholesale death and misery" (*International Wildlife*, July 1975). "The world's climatologists are agreed" that we must "prepare for the next ice age" (*Science Digest*, February 1973). Because of "ominous signs" that "the Earth's climate seems to be cooling down," meteorologists were "almost unanimous" that "the trend will reduce agricultural productivity for the rest of the century," perhaps triggering catastrophic famines (*Newsweek* cover story, "The Cooling World," April 28, 1975). Armadillos were fleeing south from Nebraska, heat-seeking snails were retreating from Central European forests, the North Atlantic was "cooling down about as fast as an ocean can cool," glaciers had "begun to advance" and "growing seasons in England and Scandinavia are getting shorter" (*Christian Science Monitor*, Aug. 27, 1974).

5   Speaking of experts, in 1980 Paul Ehrlich, a Stanford scientist and environmental Cassandra who predicted calamitous food shortages by 1990, accepted a bet with economist Julian Simon. When Ehrlich predicted the imminent exhaustion of many nonrenewable natural resources, Simon challenged him: Pick a "basket" of any five such commodities, and I will wager that in a decade the price of the basket will decline, indicating decreased scarcity. Ehrlich picked five metals—chrome, copper, nickel, tin and tungsten—that he predicted would become more expensive. Not only did the price of the basket decline, the price of *all five* declined.

6   An expert Ehrlich consulted in picking the five was John Holdren, who today is President Obama's science adviser. Credentialed intellectuals, too—actually, *especially*—illustrate Montaigne's axiom: "Nothing is so firmly believed as what we least know."

7   As global levels of sea ice declined last year, many experts said this was evidence of man-made global warming. Since September, however, the increase in sea ice has been the fastest change, either up or down, since 1979, when satellite record-keeping began. According to the University of Illinois' Arctic Climate Research Center, global sea ice levels now equal those of 1979.

8   An unstated premise of eco-pessimism is that environmental conditions are, or recently were, optimal. The proclaimed faith of eco-pessimists is weirdly optimistic: These optimal conditions must and can be preserved or restored if government will make us minimize our carbon footprints and if government will "remake" the economy.

9   Because of today's economy, another law—call it the Law of Clarifying Calamities—is being (redundantly) confirmed. On graphs tracking public opinion, two lines are moving in tandem and inversely: The sharply rising line charts public concern about the economy, the plunging line follows concern about the environment. A recent Pew Research Center poll asked which of 20 issues should be the government's top priorities. Climate change ranked 20th.

10   Real calamities take our minds off hypothetical ones. Besides, according to the U.N. World Meteorological Organization, there has been no recorded global warming for more than a decade, or one-third of the span since the global cooling scare.

Chris Mooney

Climate Change Myths and Facts

A recent controversy over claims about climate science by *Washington Post* op-ed columnist George F. Will raises a critical question: Can we ever know, on any contentious or politicized topic, how to recognize the real conclusions of science and how to distinguish them from scientific-sounding spin or misinformation?

2   Congress will soon consider global-warming legislation, and the debate comes as contradictory claims about climate science abound. Partisans of this issue often wield vastly different facts and sometimes seem to even live in different realities. In this context, finding common ground will be very difficult. Perhaps the only hope involves taking a stand for a breed of journalism and commentary that is not permitted to simply say anything; that is constrained by standards of evidence, rigor and reproducibility that are similar to the canons of modern science itself.

3   Consider a few of Will's claims from his February 15 column, "Dark Green Doomsayers": In a long paragraph quoting press sources from the 1970s, Will suggested that widespread scientific agreement existed at the time that the world faced potentially catastrophic cooling. Today, most climate scientists and climate journalists consider this a timeworn myth. Just last year, the *Bulletin of the American Meteorological Society* published a peer-reviewed study examining media coverage at the time and the

contemporary scientific literature. While some media accounts did hype a cooling scare, others suggested more reasons to be concerned about warming. As for the published science? Reviewing studies between 1965 and 1979, the authors found that "emphasis on greenhouse warming dominated the scientific literature even then."

4   Yet there's a bigger issue: It's misleading to draw a parallel between "global cooling" concerns articulated in the 1970s and global warming concerns today. In the 1970s, the field of climate research was in a comparatively fledgling state, and scientific understanding of 20th-century temperature trends and their causes was far less settled. Today, in contrast, hundreds of scientists worldwide participate in assessments of the state of knowledge and have repeatedly ratified the conclusion that human activities are driving global warming—through the U.N. Intergovernmental Panel on Climate Change, the scientific academies of various nations (including our own), and leading scientific organizations such as the American Association for the Advancement of Science, the American Geophysical Union and the American Meteorological Society.

5   Will wrote that "according to the University of Illinois' Arctic Climate Research Center, global sea ice levels now equal those of 1979." It turns out to be a relatively meaningless comparison, though the Arctic Climate Research Center has clarified that global sea ice extent was "1.34 million sq. km less in February 2009 than in February 1979." Again, though, there's a bigger issue: Will's focus on "global" sea ice at two arbitrarily selected points of time is a distraction. Scientists pay heed to long-term trends in sea ice, not snapshots in a noisy system. And while they expect global warming to reduce summer Arctic sea ice, the global picture is a more complicated matter; it's not as clear what ought to happen in the Southern Hemisphere. But summer Arctic sea ice is indeed trending downward, in line with climatologists' expectations, according to the Arctic Climate Research Center.

6   Will also wrote that "according to the U.N. World Meteorological Organization, there has been no recorded global warming for more than a decade." The World Meteorological Organization (WMO) is one of many respected scientific institutions that support the consensus that humans are driving global warming. Will probably meant that since 1998 was the warmest year on record according to the WMO—NASA, in contrast, believes that that honor goes to 2005—we haven't had any global warming since. Yet such sleight of hand would lead to the conclusion that "global cooling" sets in immediately after every new record temperature year, no matter how frequently those hot years arrive or the hotness of the years surrounding them. Climate scientists, knowing that any single year may trend warmer or cooler for a variety of reasons—1998, for instance, featured an extremely strong El Niño—study globally averaged temperatures over time. To them, it's far more relevant that out of the 10 warmest years on record, at least seven have occurred in the 2000s, according to the WMO.

7   Readers and commentators must learn to share some practices with scientists—following up on sources, taking scientific knowledge seriously rather than cherry-picking misleading bits of information, and applying critical thinking to the weighing of evidence. That, in the end, is all that good science really is. It's also what good journalism and commentary alike must strive to be—now more than ever.

James Murdoch

Clean Energy That Conservatives Can Embrace

Conservatives champion the essential characteristics of America: liberty, enterprise and ingenuity. As world leaders consider how to transform the way we make and use energy in the face of a changing climate, it's time for an energy policy true to that spirit— and it shouldn't be anathema to the American right. Conservatives have a robust tradition of principled concern for the environment. It was, after all, Teddy Roosevelt who created five national parks and signed the Antiquities Act. It was Richard Nixon who established the Environmental Protection Agency, and George H.W. Bush who ushered in one of the greatest environmental success stories, the 1990 cap-and-trade plan to take on acid rain.

2   Today, Americans of all political persuasions want to see their country on a path toward an economy powered by energy that is clean, safe, secure and stable. With climate legislation pending and a binding global treaty being negotiated, conservative leadership is critical because the only way to get the job done is with broad bipartisan agreement. How can they do it? By establishing a Red-Blue-Green agenda on whose principles conservatives, Democrats and independents can all agree. Which Americans would argue against energy that meets the following five principles?

1. *Freedom from national insecurity.* The Western world's dependence on oil means transferring billions of dollars to nations whose interests are at odds with democratic ideals. This makes for geopolitical instability and forces the United States to compromise its role as a beacon of freedom just to secure traditional fuels.

2. *A return to economic strength.* Ultimately, the question is: Which countries will lead the world to a clean-energy future—and reap the benefits? The United States is already falling behind. It has lost its dominance in solar manufacturing and ranks 22nd in energy efficiency. The Chinese market for clean tech is forecast to grow to as much as $1 trillion per year. America cannot afford to cede new markets and the jobs they create without even trying.

3. *New employment, with lower long-term costs.* Much of the U.S. debate focuses on the short-term costs associated with the transition to a clean-energy economy without considering its long-term benefits or without calculating the costs of continuing business as usual. The wave of innovations around clean energy will not only create new industries and jobs but

also allow businesses to have increasingly efficient—and therefore more profitable—operations.

4. *Cleaner, healthier communities.* Republicans once played a leading role in cleaning up our air and water, and conservatives of all stripes should champion that role again. The manufacturing booms that built cities such as Detroit and Cleveland left environmental degradation in their wake. Good climate legislation will bring jobs back to hard-hit areas, but this time factories will not pollute the groundwater or make the air unsafe to breathe.

5. *Competition trumps regulation.* A sensible clean-energy policy should free, rather than constrain, markets. Smart policy corrects market failures and provides certainty, stimulating investment in the technology and infrastructure necessary to build an economy based on clean energy. Washington must ensure that such investment will be rewarded. The government shouldn't "pick winners"—it should unleash competition, ensuring that the cleanest businesses thrive and the dirtiest are held accountable. A well-crafted federal law to limit pollution is better than unfettered regulation by the EPA or ever-changing regulation by the states.

3   The seeds of these opportunities have already been planted. And companies that have taken the lead are prospering. At News Corporation, we have saved millions by becoming more energy-efficient, overhauling a range of systems from the production of such shows as "American Idol" and "24" to energy usage in our buildings around the world. This has yielded savings that help us invest more in talent and has inspired us to look for further opportunities to improve.

4   You do not need to believe that all climate science is settled or every prediction or model is perfect to understand the benefits of limiting pollution and transforming our energy policies—as a gradually declining cap on carbon pollution would do. This is the moment to champion policies that yield new industries, healthy competition, cleaner air and water, freedom from petroleum politics, and reduced costs for businesses.

5   Through market-based incentives we can achieve clean energy at the lowest cost and with the strongest incentives for innovation—ensuring that the energy solution will help, not harm, the economy. Republicans such as Senator Lindsey Graham (South Carolina) get this and are working across party lines to build support for new legislation. Previously conservation-minded conservatives are missing in the heated partisanship of today's politics. It's time they found their voice again.

Alex Williams

Buying into the Green Movement

Here's one popular vision for saving the planet: Roll out from under the sumptuous hemp-fiber sheets on your bed in the morning and pull on a pair of $245 organic cotton Levi's and an Armani biodegradable knit shirt. Stroll from the bedroom in your eco-McMansion, with its photovoltaic solar panels, into the kitchen remodeled with reclaimed lumber. Enter the three-car garage lighted by energy-sipping fluorescent bulbs and slip behind the wheel of your $104,000 Lexus hybrid. Drive to the airport, where you settle in for an 8,000-mile flight—careful to buy carbon offsets beforehand—and spend a week driving golf balls made from compacted fish food at an eco-resort in the Maldives.

2   That vision of an eco-sensitive life as a series of choices about what to buy appeals to millions of consumers and arguably defines the current environmental movement as equal parts concern for the earth and for making a stylish statement. Some 35 million Americans regularly buy products that claim to be earth-friendly, according to one report, everything from organic beeswax lipstick from the west Zambian rain forest to Toyota Priuses. With baby steps, more and more shoppers browse among the 60,000 products available under Home Depot's new Eco Options program.

3   Such choices are rendered fashionable as celebrities worried about global warming appear on the cover of *Vanity Fair*'s "green issue," and pop stars like Kelly Clarkson and Lenny Kravitz prepare to be headline acts on July 7 at the Live Earth concerts at sites around the world. Consumers have embraced living green, and for the most part the mainstream green movement has embraced green consumerism. But even at this moment of high visibility and impact for environmental activists, a splinter wing of the movement has begun to critique what it sometimes calls "light greens."

4   Critics question the notion that we can avert global warming by buying so-called earth-friendly products, from clothing and cars to homes and vacations, when the cumulative effect of our consumption remains enormous and hazardous. "There is a very common mind-set right now which holds that all that we're going to need to do to avert the large-scale planetary catastrophes upon us is make slightly different shopping decisions," said Alex Steffen, the executive editor of Worldchanging.com, a Web site devoted to sustainability issues. The genuine solution, he and other critics say, is to significantly reduce one's consumption of goods and resources. It's not enough to build a vacation home of recycled lumber; the real way to reduce one's carbon footprint is to only own one home. Buying a hybrid car won't help if it's the aforementioned Lexus, the luxury LS 600h L model, which gets 22 miles to the gallon on the highway; the Toyota Yaris ($11,000) gets 40 highway miles a gallon with a standard gasoline engine. It's as though the millions of people whom environmentalists have successfully prodded to be concerned about climate change are experiencing a SnackWell's moment: confronted with a box of fat-free devil's food chocolate cookies, which seem deliciously guilt-free, they consume the entire box, avoiding any fats but loading up on calories.

5   The issue of green shopping is highlighting a division in the environmental movement: "the old-school environmentalism of self-abnegation versus this camp of buying

your way into heaven," said Chip Giller, the founder of Grist.org, an online environmental blog that claims a monthly readership of 800,000. "Over even the last couple of months, there is more concern growing within the traditional camp about the Cosmo-izing of the green movement—'55 great ways to look eco-sexy,'" he said. "Among traditional greens, there is concern that too much of the population thinks there's an easy way out."

6   The criticisms have appeared quietly in some environmental publications and on the Web. George Black, an editor and a columnist at *OnEarth,* a quarterly journal of the Natural Resources Defense Council, recently summed up the explosion of high-style green consumer items and articles of the sort that proclaim "green is the new black," that is, a fashion trend, as "eco-narcissism." Paul Hawken, an author and longtime environmental activist, said the current boom in earth-friendly products offers a false promise. "Green consumerism is an oxymoronic phrase," he said. He blamed the news media and marketers for turning environmentalism into fashion and distracting from serious issues. "We turn toward the consumption part because that's where the money is," Mr. Hawken said. "We tend not to look at the 'less' part. So you get these anomalies like 10,000-foot 'green' homes being built by a hedge fund manager in Aspen. Or 'green' fashion shows. Fashion is the deliberate inculcation of obsolescence." He added: "The fruit at Whole Foods in winter, flown in from Chile on a 747—it's a complete joke. The idea that we should have raspberries in January, it doesn't matter if they're organic. It's diabolically stupid."

7   Environmentalists say some products marketed as green may pump more carbon into the atmosphere than choosing something more modest, or simply nothing at all. Along those lines, a company called PlayEngine sells a 19-inch widescreen L.C.D. set whose "sustainable bamboo" case is represented as an earth-friendly alternative to plastic. But it may be better to keep your old cathode-tube set instead, according to "The Live Earth Global Warming Survival Handbook," because older sets use less power than plasma or L.C.D. screens. (Televisions account for about 4 percent of energy consumption in the United States, the handbook says.) "The assumption that by buying anything, whether green or not, we're solving the problem is a misperception," said Michael Ableman, an environmental author and long-time organic farmer. "Consuming is a significant part of the problem to begin with. Maybe the solution is instead of buying five pairs of organic cotton jeans, buy one pair of regular jeans instead."

8   For the most part, the critiques of green consumption have come from individual activists, not from mainstream environmental groups like the Sierra Club, Greenpeace and the Rainforest Action Network. The latest issue of *Sierra,* the magazine of the Sierra Club, has articles hailing an "ecofriendly mall" featuring sustainable clothing (under development in Chicago) and credit cards that rack up carbon offsets for every purchase, as well as sustainably harvested caviar and the celebrity-friendly Tango electric sports car (a top-of-the-line model is $108,000).

9   One reason mainstream groups may be wary of criticizing Americans' consumption is that before the latest era of green chic, these large organizations endured years in which their warnings about climate change were scarcely heard. Much of the public had turned away from the Carter-era environmental

message of sacrifice, which included turning down the thermostat, driving smaller cars and carrying a cloth "Save-a-Tree" tote to the supermarket.

10   Now that environmentalism is high profile, thanks in part to the success of *An Inconvenient Truth,* the 2006 documentary featuring Al Gore, mainstream greens, for the most part, say that buying products promoted as eco-friendly is a good first step. "After you buy the compact fluorescent bulbs," said Michael Brune, the executive director of the Rainforest Action Network, "you can move on to greater goals like banding together politically to shut down coal-fired power plants." John Passacantando, the executive director of Greenpeace USA, argued that green consumerism has been a way for Wal-Mart shoppers to get over the old stereotypes of environmentalists as "tree-hugging hippies" and contribute in their own way. This is crucial, he said, given the widespread nature of the global warming challenge. "You need Wal-Mart and Joe Six-Pack and mayors and taxi drivers," he said. "You need participation on a wide front."

11   It is not just ecology activists with one foot in the 1970s, though, who have taken issue with the consumerist personality of the "light green" movement. Anti-consumerist fervor burns hotly among some activists who came of age under the influence of noisy, disruptive anti-globalization protests. Last year, a San Francisco group called the Compact made headlines with a vow to live the entire year without buying anything but bare essentials like medicine and food. A year in, the original 10 "mostly" made it, said Rachel Kesel, 26, a founder. The movement claims some 8,300 adherents throughout the country and in places as distant as Singapore and Iceland. "The more that I'm engaged in this, the more annoyed I get with things like 'shop against climate change' and these kind of attitudes," said Ms. Kesel, who continues her shopping strike and counts a new pair of running shoes—she's a dog-walker by trade—as among her limited purchases in 18 months. "It's hysterical," she said. "You're telling people to consume more in order to reduce impact."

12   For some, the very debate over how much difference they should try to make in their own lives is a distraction. They despair of individual consumers being responsible for saving the earth from climate change and want to see action from political leaders around the world. Individual consumers may choose more fuel-efficient cars, but a far greater effect may be felt when fuel-efficiency standards are raised for all of the industry, as the Senate voted to do on June 21, the first significant rise in mileage standards in more than two decades. "A legitimate beef that people have with green consumerism is, at end of the day, the things causing climate change are more caused by politics and the economy than individual behavior," said Michel Gelobter, a former professor of environmental policy at Rutgers who is now president of Redefining Progress, a nonprofit policy group that promotes sustainable living. "A lot of what we need to do doesn't have to do with what you put in your shopping basket," he said. "It has to do with mass transit, housing density. It has to do with the war and subsidies for the coal and fossil fuel industry."

13   In fact, those light-green environmentalists who chose not to lecture about sacrifice and promote the trendiness of eco-sensitive products may be on to something. Michael Shellenberger, a partner at American Environics, a market research firm in Oakland, California, said that his company ran a series of focus groups in April for the environmental group Earthjustice, and was surprised by the results. People considered their trip down the Eco Options aisles at Home

Depot a beginning, not an end point. "We didn't find that people felt that their consumption gave them a pass, so to speak," Mr. Shellenberger said. "They knew what they were doing wasn't going to deal with the problems, and these little consumer things won't add up. But they do it as a practice of mindfulness. They didn't see it as antithetical to political action. Folks who were engaged in these green practices were actually becoming more committed to more transformative political action on global warming."

A shopper looks at a display of high-efficiency lightbulbs at a Home Depot store. Products accepted for Home Depot's new Eco Options marketing campaign include solar-powered landscape lighting, biodegradable peat pots, and paints that discharge fewer pollutants. Is buying green the answer or do we need to make due with less?

How "Green" Is Your T-Shirt?

Cotton is cheaper and takes less energy to manufacture than synthetic fibers. But over its lifetime, a cotton T-shirt requires more than twice the energy that is necessary to manufacture and maintain a polyester blouse. The main difference: polyester garments can be washed at a lower temperature, can hang dry and need no ironing.

The list below shows energy used over the lifetime of the garment, in kilowatt hours.*

COTTON T-SHIRT	POLYESTER BLOUSE
Raw material: 4	Raw material: 9
Manufacturing: 7	Manufacturing: 3
Transportation: 2	Transportation: 1
Use: 18	Use: 2

Use assumes 25 washes per garment. The cotton T-shirt is washed at 140 degrees Fahrenheit, followed by tumble-drying and ironing. The polyester blouse is washed at 104 degrees Fahrenheit, hung dry, and not ironed.

*The energy of one kilowatt hour will operate a 40-watt lightbulb for a full day or a 19-inch color television for about four hours.

(*Source:* University of Cambridge Institute for Manufacturing.)

FROM READING TO WRITING

1. Analyze the paired arguments by either Al Gore and Christopher Horner, or by George Will and Chris Mooney: how is each argument the product of its audience and purpose? What sources of argument (ethical appeals, emotional appeals, and logical appeals) does each author choose and why? (See Chapter 5 for more on rhetorical analysis.)

2. Compare the various photos and charts that appear on the preceding pages in this chapter. What visual argument does each photo seem to make? (See Chapter 6 for guidance on analyzing visuals.)

3. Write an argument that makes its point by defining a key term related to environmental concerns. You might choose to change someone's attitude toward a particular practice or concept in order to defend or challenge it, for instance, by defining it in a certain way. For example, you might start with the claim that "Green clothes are just a marketing ploy for the fashion industry to cash in on consumers' increased environmental awareness" or "Global warming is actually a blessing in disguise for some of the world." (See Chapter 8 for strategies for writing definition arguments.)

4. Propose a change in policy related to an environmental issue in your community. (See Chapter 13 for help with writing a proposal argument.)

5. Write a rebuttal of an article related to the environment in your local or school newspaper. Imitate, as appropriate, the moves you see in essays by Horner and Mooney; and see Chapter 12 for advice on rebuttals. Consider whether you wish to show the weaknesses in the article, whether you wish to counterargue, or both.

6. Write an essay that recounts a personal experience of yours to make an argumentative point related to the environment. It could be a story about camping or hiking, for example, or a tale of your encounter with some environmental problem or challenge. (See Chapter 11 for advice on writing narrative arguments.)

23 | Confronting Sexual Difference

Sexual Difference in American Culture

How might these wedding cake-toppers make different arguments about who should be allowed to marry legally?

It happened over a decade ago, but people still talk about it: in 1998 University of Wyoming political science major Matthew Shepard was beaten to a pulp and pistol-whipped to death in the town of Laramie, Wyoming. Russell Henderson, 21, and Aaron McKinney, 20, lured Shepard from a bar (they knew he was gay), drove him to a deserted area, beat him as he begged for mercy, and removed his shoes and tied him to a post, like a coyote, to warn off others. Henderson and McKinney took Shepard's wallet, left him to die, and then attacked two Latino men before they were arrested. Shepard, buried two days later before a crowd of 650 mourners (and a small group of protesters holding signs ridiculing "fags"), became a symbol of growing violence against gays in the United States. His murder and the subsequent trial of the perpetrators led many citizens and legislators to advocate a range of measures to protect gay, lesbian, bisexual, and transgender citizens, and to expand the rights and responsibilities that those citizens might enjoy.

A year before, in 1997, Ellen DeGeneres, star of the comedy series *Ellen*, made public her character's (and her own) lesbianism and redirected her show toward an exploration of gay and lesbian identity. Before the series closed two years later, it consistently treated (typically as the material of comedy) the social and cultural tribulations faced by gays and lesbians, and challenged viewers to confront those tribulations in their own communities. Since then, a number of other television series have pursued the same end—most prominently *Will and Grace, Six Feet Under*, and *Queer as Folk*, but also soap operas, documentaries, variety shows (such as *Saturday Night Live*), and reality shows such as *Survivor* and *Boy Meets Boy*. The televised Miss USA pageant in 2009 became a You Tube sensation when Miss California USA told one of the judges (Perez Hilton, a gay blogger) that she thought "marriage should be between a

Matthew Shepard

man and a woman"—and was subsequently vilified by Perez and praised by the Christian right. Television shows like these, as well as a range of ads, Web sites, podcasts, and movies (e.g., *Milk*), have required American citizens to confront a range of cultural practices involving gay, lesbian, bisexual, and transgender people—practices including service in the military, same-sex marriage and other domestic issues, and even the ordination of priests.

Contemporary Arguments

This section of *Good Reasons* contains a range of arguments related to just those issues. In recent years hate crimes in various communities have focused great attention on the violence that is often leveled at gays and on the issue of rights and protections for gay, lesbian, and bisexual citizens. The question of passing legislation to protect the rights, property, and bodies of gays, lesbians, bisexuals, and transsexuals has animated citizens in many communities. In 2003, in the landmark *Lawrence v. Texas* case, the Supreme Court by a 6–3 margin struck down laws criminalizing consensual sexual relations between people of the same sex. While proponents of such legal maneuvers feel that criminal conduct based on prejudice not only terrorizes victims and strips them of civil rights but also debilitates entire communities, critics note that law enforcement officials may remain indifferent to violence based on sexual orientation—no matter what the laws state. Critics of legislation protecting gays, lesbians, and bisexuals also raise other objections: laws already prohibit violence and excessive harassment; gay rights legislation is really "special rights" legislation as opposed to "civil rights" legislation; sexual preference relates to social behaviors, not inherent and immutable characteristics like gender or race that require protection, and homosexual behaviors can be modified through therapy or even religion; and legal protections might somehow grow into affirmative action for gays, lesbians, and bisexuals.

Thus here in *Good Reasons* we present an argument by Carmen Vazquez about the predicament of gay and lesbian citizens in the United States, an argument that might have implications for legislation. In addition, we offer something of a counterargument: James Kirchick warns readers that the gay community ought to resist special protections and preferences because of their long-term effects. Because many arguments concerning sexual identity depend on an interpretation of biblical passages and Christian tradition, we provide perspective on that tradition in an argument by Peter Gomes. And we offer Ryan Anderson's meditation on the trials of those persons of faith who must wrestle on college campuses with issues of sexual identity.

So-called gay rights legislation might extend the rights of gays, lesbians, and bisexuals to permit a number of practices: serving in the military, getting married, becoming ordained into the clergy, adopting and raising children, sexual freedom, and protection against discrimination based on AIDS. Arguments about the military's so-called "Don't Ask Don't Tell" policy (it permits gay citizens to serve in the military as long as they keep their sexual preferences to themselves) are represented by Andrew Sullivan, who deplores the policy, and by David Horowitz, who defends it. We also include in our sampling several articles relating to culture, sexuality, and gender—including Alexa Hackbarth's lighthearted thoughts on the "metrosexual phenomenon" and a related piece by Heather Havrilesky on "smoothies," both of which reflect on how masculinity is being redefined in the twenty-first century.

But the question of same-sex marriage is the most prominent of those issues right now, so we devote an Issue in Focus segment to it here. The current controversy over gay marriage derives from years of efforts by gay, lesbian, and bisexual activists to achieve family rights on a piecemeal basis—through pressing for domestic partnership laws, for example, or through lawsuits to permit adoption by single persons. While prominent legal cases wind their way to the Supreme Court, citizens are also seeking relief through the ballot box, and it is hard to identify a state in which one or another issue related to gender and sexual preference is not in the news. That's likely to remain the case for some time.

SOME GAY RIGHTS WEB SITES

www.thetaskforce.org	The National Gay and Lesbian Task Force
www.glaad.org	Gay and Lesbian Alliance Against Defamation
www.aclu.org/lgbt/index.html	American Civil Liberties Union
www.advocate.com	The *Advocate* magazine
www.lambdalegal.org	Lambda Legal
www.theweddingparty.org	Seeks to secure equal marriage rights for same-sex couples
www.hrc.org	Human Rights Campaign
www.gmhc.org	Gay Men's Health Crisis organization
www.glsen.org	Gay, Lesbian and Straight Education Network
www.buddybuddy.com	Partners Task Force for Gay and Lesbian Couples
www.actwin.com/cahp	Citizens Against HomoPhobia
www.gay.com	Collects news and commentary

Carmen Vazquez

Appearances

Carmen Vazquez (1949–) was born in Puerto Rico and raised in Harlem, a predominantly African American community in New York City. Active in the gay and lesbian movement for years, she has published many essays. The following piece was included in Warren J. Blumenfeld's 1992 book called *Homophobia: How We All Pay the Price.*

Northern of Market Street and east of Twin Peaks, where you can see the white fog mushroom above San Francisco's hills, is a place called the Castro. Gay men, lesbians, and bisexuals stroll leisurely up and down the bustling streets. They jaywalk with abandon. Night and day they fill the cafés and bars, and on weekends they line up for a double feature of vintage classics at their ornate and beloved Castro theater.

2   The 24 bus line brings people into and out of the Castro. People from all walks of life ride the electric-powered coaches. They come from the opulence of San Francisco's Marina and the squalor of Bayview projects. The very gay Castro is in the middle of its route. Every day, boys in pairs or gangs from either end of the city board the bus for a ride through the Castro and a bit of fun. Sometimes their fun is fulfilled with passionately obscene derision: "Fucking cocksucking faggots." "Dyke cunts." "Diseased butt fuckers." Sometimes, their fun is brutal.

3   Brian boarded the 24 Divisadero and handed his transfer to the driver one late June night. Epithets were fired at him the moment he turned for a seat. He slid his slight frame into an empty seat next to an old woman with silver blue hair who clutched her handbag and stared straight ahead. Brian stuffed his hands into the pockets of his worn brown bomber jacket and stared with her. He heard the flip of a skateboard in the back. The taunting shouts grew louder. "Faggot!" From the corner of his eye, he saw a beer bottle hurtling past the window and crash on the street. A man in his forties, wearing a Giants baseball cap and warmup jacket, yelled at the driver to stop the bus and get the hoodlums off. The bus driver ignored him and pulled out.

4   Brian dug his hands deeper into his pockets and clenched his jaw. It was just five stops to the top of the hill. When he got up to move toward the exit, the skateboard slammed into his gut and one kick followed another until every boy had got his kick in. Despite the plea of the passengers, the driver never called the police.

5   Brian spent a week in a hospital bed, afraid that he would never walk again. A lawsuit filed by Brian against the city states, "As claimant lay crumpled and bleeding on the floor of the bus, the bus driver tried to force claimant off the bus so that the driver could get off work and go home. Claimant was severely beaten by a gang of young men on the #24 Divisadero Bus who perceived that he was gay."

6   On the south side of Market Street, night brings a chill wind and rough trade. On a brisk November night, men with sculptured torsos and thighs wrapped in leather

walked with precision. The clamor of steel on the heels of their boots echoed in the darkness. Young men and women walked by the men in leather, who smiled in silence. They admired the studded bracelets on Mickey's wrists, the shine of his flowing hair, and the rise of his laughter. They were, each of them, eager to be among the safety of like company where they could dance with abandon to the pulse of hard rock, the hypnotism of disco, or the measured steps of country soul. They looked forward to a few drinks, flirting with strangers, finding Mr. or Ms. Right or, maybe someone to spend the night with.

7   At the end of the street, a lone black street lamp shone through the mist. The men in leather walked under the light and disappeared into the next street. As they reached the corner, Mickey and his friends could hear the raucous sounds of the Garden spill onto the street. They shimmied and rocked down the block and through the doors.

8   The Garden was packed with men and women in sweat-stained shirts. Blue smoke stung the eyes. The sour and sweet smell of beer hung in the air. Strobe lights pulsed over the dancers. Mickey pulled off his wash-faded black denim jacket and wrapped it around his waist. An iridescent blue tank top hung easy on his shoulders. Impatient with the wait for a drink, Mickey steered his girlfriend onto the crowded dance floor.

9   Reeling to the music and immersed in the pleasure of his rhythms Mickey never saw the ice pick plunge into his neck. It was just a bump with a drunk yelling, "Lame-assed faggot." "Faggot. Faggot. Faggot. Punk faggot." Mickey thought it was a punch to the neck. He ran after the roaring drunk man for seven steps, then lurched and fell on the dance floor, blood gushing everywhere. His girlfriend screamed. The dance floor spun black.

10   Mickey was rushed to San Francisco General Hospital, where thirty-six stitches were used by trauma staff to close the wound on his neck. Doctors said the pick used in the attack against him was millimeters away from his spinal cord. His assailant, charged with attempted murder, pleaded innocent.

11   Mickey and Brian were unfortunate stand-ins for any gay man. Mickey was thin and wiry, a great dancer clad in black denim, earrings dangling from his ear. Brian was slight of build, wore a leather jacket, and boarded a bus in the Castro. Dress like a homo, dance like a homo, must be a homo. The homophobic fury directed at lesbians, gay men, and bisexuals in America most often finds its target. Ironclad evidence of sexual orientation, however, is not necessary for someone to qualify as a potential victim of deadly fury. Appearances will do.

12   The incidents described above are based on actual events reported to the San Francisco Police and Community United Against Violence (CUAV), an agency serving victims of antilesbian and antigay violence where I worked for four years. The names of the victims have been changed. Both men assaulted were straight.

13   Incidents of antilesbian and antigay violence are not uncommon or limited to San Francisco. A *San Francisco Examiner* survey estimates that over one million hate-motivated physical assaults take place each year against lesbians, gays, and bisexuals. The National Gay and Lesbian Task Force conducted a survey in 1984 that found that 94 percent of all lesbians and gay men surveyed reported being physically assaulted,

threatened, or harassed in an antigay incident at one time or another. The great majority of these incidents go unreported.

14   To my knowledge, no agency other than CUAV keeps track of incidents of antigay violence involving heterosexuals as victims. An average of 3 percent of the over three hundred victims seen by CUAV each year identify as heterosexuals. This may or may not be an accurate gauge of the actual prevalence of antigay violence directed at heterosexuals. Most law enforcement agencies, including those in San Francisco, have no way of documenting this form of assault other than under a generic "harassment" code. The actual incidence of violence directed at heterosexuals that is motivated by homophobia is probably much higher than CUAV's six to nine victims a year. Despite the official paucity of data, however, it is a fact that incidents of antigay and antilesbian violence in which straight men and women are victimized do occur. Shelters for battered women are filled with stories of lesbian baiting of staff and of women whose husbands and boyfriends repeatedly called them "dykes" or "whores" as they beat them. I have personally experienced verbal abuse while in the company of a straight friend, who was assumed to be my lover.

15   Why does it happen? I have no definitive answers to that question. Understanding homophobic violence is no less complex than understanding racial violence. The institutional and ideological reinforcements of homophobia are myriad and deeply woven into our culture. I offer one perspective that I hope will contribute to a better understanding of how homophobia works and why it threatens all that we value as humane.

16   At the simplest level, looking or behaving like the stereotypical gay man or lesbian is reason enough to provoke a homophobic assault. Beneath the veneer of the effeminate gay male or the butch dyke, however, is a more basic trigger for homophobic violence. I call it *gender betrayal.*

17   The clearest expression I have heard of this sense of gender betrayal comes from Doug Barr, who was acquitted of murder in an incident of gay bashing in San Francisco that resulted in the death of John O'Connell, a gay man. Barr is currently serving a prison sentence for related assaults on the same night that O'Connell was killed. He was interviewed for a special report on homophobia produced by ABC's *20/20* (10 April 1986). When asked what he and his friends thought of gay men, he said, "We hate homosexuals. They degrade our manhood. We was brought up in a high school where guys are football players, mean and macho. Homosexuals are sissies who wear dresses. I'd rather be seen as a football player."

18   Doug Barr's perspective is one shared by many young men. I have made about three hundred presentations to high school students in San Francisco, to boards of directors and staff of nonprofit organizations, and at conferences and workshops on the topic of homophobia or "being lesbian or gay." Over and over again, I have asked, "Why do gay men and lesbians bother you?" The most popular response to the question is, "Because they act like girls," or, "Because they think they're men." I have even been told, quite explicitly, "I don't care what they do in bed, but they shouldn't act like that."

19   They shouldn't act like that. Women who are not identified by their relationship to a man, who value their female friendships, who like and are knowledgeable about

sports, or work as blue-collar laborers and wear what they wish are very likely to be "lesbian baited" at some point in their lives. Men who are not pursuing sexual conquests of women at every available opportunity, who disdain sports, who choose to stay at home and be a househusband, who are employed as hairdressers, designers, or housecleaners, or who dress in any way remotely resembling traditional female attire (an earring will do) are very likely to experience the taunts and sometimes the brutality of "fag bashing."

20   The straitjacket of gender roles suffocates many lesbians, gay men, and bisexuals, forcing them into closets without an exit and threatening our very existence when we tear the closet open. It also, however, threatens all heterosexuals unwilling to be bound by their assigned gender identity. Why, then, does it persist?

21   Suzanne Pharr's examination of homophobia as a phenomenon based in sexism and misogyny offers a succinct and logical explanation for the virulence of homophobia in Western civilization:

> It is not by chance that when children approach puberty and increased sexual awareness they begin to taunt each other by calling these names: "queer," "faggot," "pervert." It is at puberty that the full force of society's pressure to conform to heterosexuality and prepare for marriage is brought to bear. Children know what we have taught them, and we have given clear messages that those who deviate from standard expectations are to be made to get back in line. . . .
>
> To be named as lesbian threatens all women, not just lesbians, with great loss. And any woman who steps out of role risks being called a lesbian. To understand how this is a threat to all women, one must understand that any woman can be called a lesbian and there is no real way she can defend herself: there is no real way to credential one's sexuality. (*The Children's Hour,* a Lillian Hellman play, makes this point when a student asserts two teachers are lesbians and they have no way to disprove it.) She may be married or divorced, have children, dress in the most feminine manner, have sex with men, be celibate—but there are lesbians who do all these things. *Lesbians look like all women and all women look like lesbians.*[1]

I would add that gay men look like all men and all men look like gay men. There is no guaranteed method for identifying sexual orientation. Those small or outrageous deviations we sometimes take from the idealized mystique of "real men" and "real women" place all of us—lesbians, gay men, bisexuals, and heterosexuals alike—at risk of violence, derision, isolation, and hatred.

22   It is a frightening reality. Dorothy Ehrlich, executive director of the Northern California American Civil Liberties Union (ACLU), was the victim of a verbal assault in the Castro several years ago. Dorothy lives with her husband, Gary, and her two children, Jill and Paul, in one of those worn and comfortable Victorian homes that grace so many San Francisco neighborhoods. Their home is several blocks from the Castro, but

---

[1]Pharr, Suzanne. *Homophobia: A Weapon of Sexism* (Inverness, CA: Chardon, 1988), 17–19.

Dorothy recalls the many times she and Gary could hear, from the safety of their bedroom, shouts of "faggot" and men running in the streets.

23   When Jill was an infant, Gary and Dorothy had occasion to experience for themselves how frightening even the threat of homophobic violence can be. One foggy, chilly night they decided to go for a walk in the Castro. Dorothy is a small woman whom some might call petite; she wore her hair short at the time and delights in the comfort of jeans and oversized wool jackets. Gary is very tall and lean, a bespectacled and bearded cross between a professor and a basketball player who wears jean jackets and tweed jackets with the exact same slouch. On this night they were crossing Castro Street, huddled close together with Jill in Dorothy's arms. As they reached the corner, their backs to the street, they heard a truck rev its engine and roar up Castro, the dreaded "faggot" spewing from young men they could not see in the fog. They looked around them for the intended victims, but there was no one else on the corner with them. They were the target that night: Dorothy and Gary and Jill. They were walking on "gay turf," and it was reason enough to make them a target. "It was so frightening." Dorothy said. "So frightening and unreal."

24   But it is real. The *20/20* report on homophobia ends with the story of Tom and Jan Matarrase, who are married, have a child, and lived in Brooklyn, New York, at the time of their encounter with homophobic violence. On camera, Tom and Jan are walking down a street in Brooklyn lined with brown townhouses and black wrought-iron gates. It is snowing, and, with hands entwined, they walk slowly down the street where they were assaulted. Tom is wearing a khaki trenchcoat, slacks, and loafers. Snowflakes melt into the tight dark curls on his head. Jan is almost his height, her short bobbed hair moving softly as she walks. She is wearing a black leather jacket, a red scarf, and burnt orange cords. The broadness of her hips and softness of her face belie the tomboy flavor of her carriage and clothes, and it is hard to believe that she was mistaken for a gay man. But she was.

25   They were walking home, holding hands and engrossed with each other. On the other side of the street, Jan saw a group of boys moving toward them. As the gang approached, Jan heard a distinct taunt meant for her and Tom: "Aw, look at the cute gay couple." Tom and Jan quickened their step but it was too late. Before they could say anything, Tom was being punched in the face and slammed against a car. Jan ran toward Tom and the car, screaming desperately that Tom was her husband. Fists pummeled her face as well. Outnumbered and in fear for their lives, Tom yelled at Jan to please open her jacket and show their assailants that she was a woman. The beating subsided only when Jan was able to show her breasts.

26   For the *20/20* interview, Jan and Tom sat in the warmth of their living room, their infant son in Jan's lap. The interviewer asked them how they felt when people said they looked like a gay couple. "We used to laugh," they said. "But now we realize how heavy the implications are. Now we know what the gay community goes through. We had no idea how widespread it was. It's on every level."

27   Sadly, it *is* on every level. Enforced heterosexism and the pressure to conform to aggressive masculine and passive feminine roles place fag bashers and lesbian baiters in the same psychic prison with their victims, gay or straight. Until all children are free to realize their full potential, until all women and men are free from the stigma,

threats, alienation, or violence that come from stepping outside their roles, we are all at risk.

28   The economic and ideological underpinnings of enforced heterosexism and sexism or any other form of systematic oppression are formidable foes and far too complex for the scope of this essay. It is important to remember, however, that bigots are natural allies and that poverty or the fear of it has the power to seduce us all into conformity. In Castro graffiti, *faggot* appears right next to *nigger* and *kike.* Race betrayal or any threat to the sanctimony of light-skinned privilege engenders no less a rage than gender betrayal, most especially when we have a great stake in the elusive privilege of proper gender roles or the right skin color. *Queer lover* and *fag hag* are cut from the same mold that gave us *nigger lover,* a mold forged by fears of change and a loss of privilege.

29   Unfortunately, our sacrifices to conformity rarely guarantee the privilege or protection we were promised. Lesbians, gay men, and bisexuals who have tried to pass know that. Heterosexuals who have been perceived to be gay know that. Those of us with a vision of tomorrow that goes beyond tolerance to a genuine celebration of humanity's diversity have innumerable fronts to fight on. Homophobia is one of them.

30   But how will this front be won? With a lot of help, and not easily. Challenges to homophobia and the rigidity of gender roles must go beyond the visible lesbian and gay movement. Lesbians, gay men, and bisexuals alone cannot defuse the power of stigmatization and the license it gives to frighten, wound, or kill. Literally millions of us are needed on this front, straight and gay alike. We invite any heterosexual unwilling to live with the damage that "real men" or "real women" messages wreak on them, on their children, and on lesbians, gay men, and bisexuals to join us. We ask that you not let queer jokes go unchallenged at work, at home, in the media, or anywhere. We ask that you foster in your children a genuine respect for themselves and their right to be who and what they wish to be, regardless of their gender. We ask that you embrace your daughter's desire to swing a bat or be a carpenter, that you nurture your son's efforts to express affection and sentiment. We ask that you teach your children how painful and destructive words like *faggot* or *bulldyke* are. We ask that you invite your lesbian, gay, and bisexual friends and relatives into the routine of your lives without demanding silence or discretion from them. We invite you to study our history, read the literature written by our people, patronize our businesses, come into our homes and neighborhoods. We ask that you give us your vote when we need it to protect our privacy or to elect open lesbians, gay men, and bisexuals to office. We ask that you stand with us in public demonstrations to demand our right to live as free people, without fear. We ask that you respect our dignity by acting to end the poison of homophobia.

31   Until individuals are free to choose their roles and be bound only by the limits of their own imagination, *faggot, dyke,* and *pervert* will continue to be playground words and adult weapons that hurt and limit far many more people than their intended victims. Whether we like it or not, the romance of virile men and dainty women, of Mother, Father, Dick, Jane, Sally, and Spot is doomed to extinction and dangerous in a world that can no longer meet the expectations conjured by history. There is much to be won and so little to lose in the realization of a world where the dignity of each person is worthy of celebration and protection. The struggle to end homophobia can and must be won, for all our sakes. Personhood is imminent. ■

JAMES **KIRCHICK**

Tripping Over a Leg Up

James Kirchick (born 1983) is an energetic and prolific reporter, essayist, and columnist. He contributes frequently to *The New Republic*, as well as to the *Washington Post*, the *Wall Street Journal*, the *Los Angeles Times*, and a variety of other magazines and newspapers. A respected voice on gay politics, he is a recipient of the National Lesbian and Gay Journalists Association Journalist of the Year Award and a contributing writer to *The Advocate*, the nation's largest gay publication, where the following essay appeared in March 2010.

Last May, Aiden Quinn was texting his girlfriend while operating a moving vehicle—a dangerous activity under any circumstances, but especially reckless considering that Quinn wasn't driving a mere automobile. As a trolley driver for the Massachusetts Bay Transportation Authority, which operates Boston's subway and bus systems nicknamed the "T," Quinn was at the helm of a train carrying dozens of people underground. Buried in his digital billets-doux, he wasn't alert when the train sailed through a red light and rammed into the back of another trolley. Luckily, no one was killed, though nearly 50 people were injured, and the resulting lawsuits could cost the T millions.

2   Media attention slowly drew away from the details of the accident to something far more sensational: Quinn is female-to-male transgender. This immediately provided fodder for all manner of disparaging comments, and given the way in which transgenderism—something of which most Americans are utterly ignorant and view as peculiar—was suddenly thrust into the mainstream media spotlight, it was understandable that transgender organizations would go on the defensive. "Anything related to his gender identity would be irrelevant and further perpetuate unnecessary sensationalism," read a statement from the Massachusetts Transgender Political Coalition. "Media outlets should be reporting on the facts of the case and not using sensationalistic coverage of a person's identity or former name when neither has a bearing on the case."

3   Quinn's trans identity had nothing to do with the collision; being transgender (or gay or female or black or left-handed) does not make one more likely to text while driving. But that doesn't mean that his gender identity was utterly "irrelevant." Indeed, Quinn's transgenderism became fair game when the allegation arose that he had benefited from it to get his job in the first place. "[Quinn] was initially hired as a minority and used her [sic] transgender status," an MBTA source told ABC News. The MBTA rebutted that charge, saying that Quinn was hired through a job lottery, although the T does advertise itself as an "affirmative action employer."

4   Consider the following: Quinn had received three speeding tickets and was involved in a motor vehicle accident during the seven years prior to the accident. Amazingly, these violations do not disqualify one from working for the T, which may say more about lax government hiring standards and the power of public employee unions in Massachusetts than it does about political correctness. But is it not fair to at least raise the question of whether Quinn would have been treated differently were he not transgender?

5   Regardless of the specifics surrounding this particular incident, the prospect of preferential hiring on the basis of homosexuality and transgender identity poses troubling

questions. At this point it's a largely hypothetical issue. In most states employers can fire or refuse to hire LGBTs solely because of their sexual orientation or gender identity. So the idea of asking for special preferences is more than akin to the metaphor of beggars acting like choosers. But in the country's more "progressive" institutions, the notion of gay affirmative action is not so theoretical. At the 2006 annual meeting of the National Association for College Admission Counseling, the subject of affirmative action for gay students came up and found some adherents, including an admissions officer at Vermont's prestigious Middlebury College. The school's assistant director of admissions told the website Inside Higher Ed that gay students bring "a unique quality," which is important as the school tries hard not "to be too homogeneous." Don't be surprised if, within the next few years, the nation's top colleges add homosexuality to their list of applicant "attributes," giving gay students the same leg up that athletes, children of alumni, and some racial minorities also enjoy.

6   Proponents of minority preferences argue that racial or sexual identity has nothing to do with job performance. This was the argument transgender activists made in the wake of the MBTA disaster, when so many opportunistic reactionaries drew attention to Quinn's gender identity. They're absolutely right, which is why factors like race, sex, sexual orientation, and gender identity should have no place in hiring decisions. If gays are asking the government and private institutions to view homosexuality as legally neutral—meaning that one's sexual orientation makes one neither intrinsically good nor bad, neither more nor less qualified—then we cannot simultaneously expect our sexuality to be treated as a bonus quality.

7   Perhaps the greatest achievement of the early gay rights movement was to have homosexuality removed from the list of mental disorders in the American Psychiatric Association's Diagnostic and Statistical Manual. Giving gays a preference would stigmatize homosexuality by treating all of us, regardless of our economic status or upbringing, as inherently disadvantaged.

8   A look at the history of the African-American civil rights movement is instructive. It began as a struggle firmly rooted in the American ideals of personal liberty and equality before the law. It was the courageous actions of Freedom Riders, bus boycotters, and other activists who helped, in the words of Martin Luther King Jr., to slowly bend the moral arc of the universe toward justice. With passage of the Civil Rights Act of 1964, the dream of full legal equality for black people was finally realized.

9   Yet what started as a campaign to end government-sanctioned discrimination turned into a self-perpetuating industry of grievance, victimization, and the institutionalization of government handouts. The Great Society agenda of the 1960s, in which social programs were vastly expanded, created a devastating cycle of dependency. The welfare system grew into a massive bureaucracy that, rather than incentivizing work, encouraged the poor to remain indolent and unwed mothers to have more children. Whole generations of families lived their lives in blighted public housing projects, while crumbling public schools, despite massive infusions of money, continue to be dead ends for most students. These programs came with the noble intention of helping the poor but had the actual effect of keeping them down.

10   Throughout history, when faced with discrimination, gays made progress through private initiative. The power of the "pink dollar" is recognized by corporate America, and gays have risen to the highest levels of industry, politics, media—all without government protection. Affirmative action programs made sense in the early years after the

Civil Rights Act. But today, it is against the law to fire someone because of race or sex. With the passage of the Employment Non-Discrimination Act, a bill being held up not just because of conservative intransigence but also liberal spinelessness, firing someone because of their sexual orientation or gender identity will similarly be prohibited. The mission of organizations representing all minorities should be to ensure that their members get a fair deal—not a preferential one.

11   Homosexuality isn't like race in that it is not apparent at birth and is not tied to specific ethnic communities or economies. So the argument that gays ought to benefit from affirmative action because of historic injustice simply doesn't fly. Not being able to get married hasn't prevented gay people from gaining admission to the best colleges or landing jobs at competitive employers. Unlike those who face economic hardship, for whom a real case can and should be made for affirmative action, gays and lesbians do not have an inherent societal disadvantage so extreme that it requires preferential treatment for them.

12   The other claim commonly used to defend racial preferences, that there is some overriding value of a "diverse" classroom or work environment, also does not hold. Treating homosexuality as a "plus factor" would put a priority on the mere declaration of one's homosexuality rather than on the attributes that distinguish one as an individual. For many of us, being gay or trans is just another fact of life, not something to be prized in the same way as one's true talents. Indeed, the whole point of today's gay rights movement and the attitude of most young people, gay and straight, is to promote the view that homosexuality is unremarkable. In applying for a job, why should the gender of the people to whom one is attracted matter as much as one's unique set of skills? And how would we expect heterosexuals to feel when, through no fault of their own, they're penalized because of their sexual orientation?

13   But the worst aspect of minority preferences isn't the harm they do to those not deemed "disadvantaged," but to their intended recipients. Regardless of how qualified they are, racial minorities on elite college campuses and in high-powered jobs inevitably become subject to the suspicions of some small-minded white peers that their station in society is, at least in part, attributable to the color of their skin. But such (largely unspoken) prejudice is to be expected when an institution acknowledges its partiality to individuals bearing a certain inherent trait. This is the poison that racial preferences introduce into human relationships. And it's why gays, inevitably the next group to become the ostensible recipient of such progressive goodwill, should resist it especially.

PETER J. **GOMES**

Homophobic? Read Your Bible

Peter J. Gomes (1942–) is an American Baptist minister. Widely regarded as one of the most distinguished preachers in the nation, he has served since 1970 in the Memorial Church at Harvard University. Since 1974 he has been Plummer Professor of Christian Morals at Harvard Divinity School as well. On September 15, 2008, he appeared on *The Colbert Report* to promote his most recent book, *The Scandalous Gospel of Jesus*, and that same year he was featured by Henry Louis Gates on the PBS documentary *African American Lives*. He wrote the following essay for the *New York Times* in 1992.

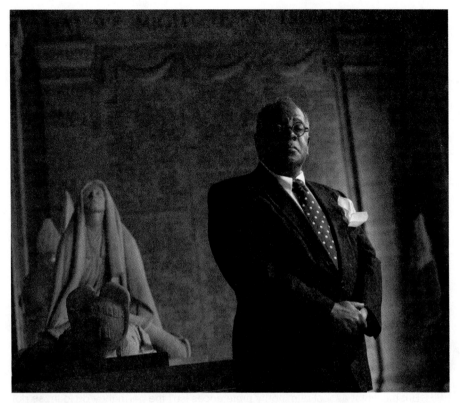

The Reverend Peter J. Gomes

Opposition to gays' civil rights has become one of the most visible symbols of American civic conflict this year, and religion has become the weapon of choice. The army of the discontented, eager for clear villains and simple solutions and ready for a crusade in which political self-interest and social anxiety can be cloaked in morality, has found hatred of homosexuality to be the last respectable prejudice of the century.

2   Ballot initiatives in Oregon and Maine would deny homosexuals the protection of civil rights laws. The Pentagon has steadfastly refused to allow gays into the armed forces. Vice President Dan Quayle is crusading for "traditional family values." And Pat Buchanan, who is scheduled to speak at the Republican National Convention this evening, regards homosexuality as a litmus test of moral purity.

3   Nothing has illuminated this crusade more effectively than a work of fiction, *The Drowning of Stephan Jones,* by Bette Greene. Preparing for her novel, Ms. Greene interviewed more than 400 young men incarcerated for gay-bashing, and scrutinized their case studies. In an interview published in *The Boston Globe* this spring, she said she found that the gay-bashers generally saw nothing wrong in what they did, and, more often than not, said their religious leaders and traditions sanctioned their behavior. One convicted teen-age gay-basher told her that the pastor of his church had said, "Homosexuals represent the devil, Satan," and that the Rev. Jerry Falwell had echoed that charge.

4   Christians opposed to political and social equality for homosexuals nearly always appeal to the moral injunctions of the Bible, claiming that Scripture is very clear on the matter and citing verses that support their opinion. They accuse others of perverting and distorting texts contrary to their "clear" meaning. They do not, however, necessarily see quite as clear a meaning in biblical passages on economic conduct, the burdens of wealth, and the sin of greed.

5   Nine biblical citations are customarily invoked as relating to homosexuality. Four (Deuteronomy 23:17, I Kings 14:24, I Kings 22:46, and II Kings 23:7) simply forbid prostitution, by men and women.

Two others (Leviticus 18:19–23 and Leviticus 20:10–16) are part of what biblical scholars call the Holiness Code. The code explicitly bans homosexual acts. But it also prohibits eating raw meat, planting two different kinds of seed in the same field, and wearing garments with two different kinds of yarn. Tattoos, adultery, and sexual intercourse during a woman's menstrual period are similarly outlawed.

6   There is no mention of homosexuality in the four Gospels of the New Testament. The moral teachings of Jesus are not concerned with the subject.

7   Three references from St. Paul are frequently cited (Romans 1:26–2:1, I Corinthians 6:9–11, and I Timothy 1:10). But St. Paul was concerned with homosexuality only because in Greco-Roman culture it represented a secular sensuality that was contrary to his Jewish-Christian spiritual idealism. He was against lust and sensuality in anyone, including heterosexuals. To say that homosexuality is bad because homosexuals are tempted to do morally doubtful things is to say that heterosexuality is bad because heterosexuals are likewise tempted. For St. Paul, anyone who puts his or her interest ahead of God's is condemned, a verdict that falls equally upon everyone.

8   And lest we forget Sodom and Gomorrah, recall that the story is not about sexual perversion and homosexual practice. It is about inhospitality, according to Luke 10:10–13, and failure to care for the poor, according to Ezekiel 16:49–50: "Behold, this was the iniquity of thy sister Sodom, pride, fullness of bread, and abundance of idleness was in her and in her daughters, neither did she strengthen the hand of the poor and needy." To suggest that Sodom and Gomorrah is about homosexual sex is an analysis of about as much worth as suggesting that the story of Jonah and the whale is a treatise on fishing.

9   Part of the problem is a question of interpretation. Fundamentalists and literalists, the storm troopers of the religious right, are terrified that Scripture, "wrongly interpreted," may separate them from their values. That fear stems from their own recognition that their "values" are not derived from Scripture, as they publicly claim. Indeed, it is through the lens of their own prejudices that they "read" Scripture and cloak their own views in its authority. We all interpret Scripture: Make no mistake. And no one truly is a literalist, despite the pious temptation. The questions are, By what principle of interpretation do we proceed, and by what means do we reconcile "what it meant then" to "what it means now"?

10   These matters are far too important to be left to scholars and seminarians alone. Our ability to judge ourselves and others rests on our ability to interpret Scripture intelligently. The right use of the Bible, an exercise as old as the church itself, means that we confront our prejudices rather than merely confirm them.

For Christians, the principle by which Scripture is read is nothing less than an appreciation of the work and will of God as revealed in that of Jesus. To recover a liberating and inclusive Christ is to be freed from the semantic bondage that makes us curators of a dead culture rather than creatures of a new creation.

11   Religious fundamentalism is dangerous because it cannot accept ambiguity and diversity and is therefore inherently intolerant. Such intolerance, in the name of virtue, is ruthless and uses political power to destroy what it cannot convert. It is dangerous, especially in America, because it is antidemocratic and is suspicious of "the other," in whatever form that "other" might appear. To maintain itself, fundamentalism must always define "the other" as deviant.

12   But the chief reason that fundamentalism is dangerous is that, at the hands of the Rev. Pat Robertson, the Rev. Jerry Falwell, and hundreds of lesser-known but equally worrisome clerics, preachers, and pundits, it uses Scripture and the Christian practice to encourage ordinarily good people to act upon their fears rather than their virtues. Fortunately, those who speak for the religious right do not speak for all American Christians, and the Bible is not theirs alone to interpret. The same Bible that the advocates of slavery used to protect their wicked self-interests is the Bible that inspired slaves to revolt and their liberators to action. The same Bible that the predecessors of Mr. Falwell and Mr. Robertson used to keep white churches white is the source of the inspiration of the Rev. Martin Luther King. Jr., and the social reformation of the 1960's. The same Bible that antifeminists use to keep women silent in the churches is the Bible that preaches liberation to captives and says that in Christ there is neither male nor female, slave nor free.

13   And the same Bible that on the basis of an archaic social code of ancient Israel and a tortured reading of Paul is used to condemn all homosexuals and homosexual behavior includes metaphors of redemption, renewal, inclusion, and love—principles that invite homosexuals to accept their freedom and responsibility in Christ and demands that their fellow Christians accept them as well.

14   The political piety of the fundamentalist religious right must not be exercised at the expense of our precious freedoms. And in this summer of our discontent, one of the most precious freedoms for which we must all fight is freedom from this last prejudice.

RYAN T. ANDERSON

Struggling Alone

Ryan T. Anderson serves as a junior fellow for *First Things*—a magazine published by the Institute on Religion and Public Life, a conservative think tank that offers religious perspectives on social issues. In his work, Anderson has written about issues ranging from stem cell research to Amnesty International's statement on abortion to adoption laws in the United Kingdom. In "Struggling Alone," published in the February 2007 edition of *First Things*, Anderson discusses the loneliness that often challenges homosexuals who strive to live according to the doctrines of their faith.

He came out to me in an email. I've known him for years, long enough that I can't remember when we first met, and we were recently emailing back and forth about our lives, our futures—the kind of stuff separated friends discuss. Along the way he mentioned, in an aside, that he had some lingering troubles he had to work his way through. My reply asked for an explanation—and that's when he told me.

2   Over the past three years, "Chris" (let's call him) has experienced a pronounced attraction to other males—for one old friend from high school in particular. A crush, maybe, or an infatuation. Whatever it was, he knew it wasn't healthy. And though he had never acted on the attraction, he explained, it led to fantasies and lusts he didn't want. So he made a resolution never to embrace them as essential to his identity or accept them as permanent or untreatable—a resolution he has kept practically alone, without the support of community, family, or friends. Over the course of many phone calls and emails, he shared with me his reflections on what he thought had created his problem of same-sex attractions. He described an "exceedingly close, best-friendly relationship" to his mother, often serving the role of her sole confidant, and a subsequent alienation from his father. Relationships with his friends, he thought, also contributed, as he suffered through "deeply hurtful rejection" by male peers, along with "oscillations between reverence for and fear of typically masculine" classmates. Once puberty hit, this took on sexual connotations, as Chris began experiencing "eroticized desire" for traits he found in other males that he himself lacked.

3   All this resulted in his dividing males into those he found "superior and feared (because of their strongly masculine features)," and those he found "inferior and disdained (because of their lack thereof)." But it affected his overall personality, too. He developed, he wrote, a "passive-aggressive, detachedly defensive and otherwise manipulative behavior toward males" and a "woeful inability" to assert himself as others do. The overarching weakness, he thought, was "a deep need to fulfill the emasculating and benign-to-a-fault role of the good little boy who pleases Mom by following all rules (the civil law, school rules, conventional morality, politeness, etc.) [while] remaining unthreatening and unphysical."

4   What he described seemed an accurate summary of the person I have known for years. So when he pointed to the likely causes and said he was seeking help in addressing them, I was supportive. "I would be untrue to myself if I simply accepted this condition right now," he wrote. "I would be denying what I've come to believe—what I believe I know—to be the causes and potential cures of this condition in my case." Some people say that change isn't possible, but he thinks that with God all things are, and he at least wants to try to do his part.

5   Chris' situation is sad, but it seems to be moving somewhere. He told me how he had cried daily for the first two years of his same-sex attractions, knowing that he was becoming someone he didn't want to be. But during the third year he found a good therapist and began making progress. He set out to find "healthy male affirmation through deep, nonerotic same-sex friendships"—along with a "purification of memory regarding the hurts of the past" and a more masculine view of himself. Without any reason to exaggerate his progress, he assured me he is "100 times happier and healthier than before—though not yet whole." Even friends and relatives who do not know about his struggles have remarked on his increased serenity and joy.

6   Other than his confessor and therapist, I'm the only person who knows. His parents would be devastated—his mother wondering whether she had caused it, his father fearing he had failed his son. His roommates and friends wouldn't know how to take it. Others on campus would encourage him to embrace his true self: They'd label him a homosexual and call him gay. But he's not—and neither does he want to be: Sexual attraction, he thinks, doesn't define a person. Indeed, he particularly fears coming out about his attractions while struggling against them, which would get him labeled a repressed homosexual, the gay-basher who himself is queer, the gay kid who thinks it's just some disorder. All he wants is to live chastely and try to make progress in addressing the causes of his same-sex attractions. But at the modern American university, this is anathema. For all their celebrations of diversity and pledges of tolerance, this choice is not to be celebrated or even tolerated.

7   Like many schools, Chris' university has an LGBTQA center (an official office supporting "lesbian, gay, bisexual, transgendered, queer, and allied" students). Had he been seeking advice on how to embrace his same-sex attractions, perform sexually as a gay man, or develop a romantic homosexual relationship, he would have been welcomed. Wanting instead help to live chastely, he found nothing. Worse than nothing, he found rejection. Such centers routinely sponsor public lectures attacking Christian responses to same-sex attractions, calls to chastity, and attempts to seek therapy.

8   You might think Chris could find help at the university's religious-life center. But with pink pride triangles on every interior door, that office, too, has embraced the gay-pride movement. The college hosts an annual Pride Sunday Liturgy in lieu of regular chapel worship—for pride, apparently, is the proper liturgical response to homosexuality—and sponsors public lectures with titles such as "Overcoming Christian Fear of Homosexuality."

9   Fortunately, the Catholic chaplaincy on campus is vibrant and orthodox. The chaplain gave Chris solid if general spiritual advice—regular prayer, reception of the sacraments, and a life of charity—but he wasn't sure how to tailor it to a young Christian experiencing same-sex attractions. So he suggested Chris work with a therapist to address the psychological causes of his attractions.

10   And Chris tried. He went to his school's health center to see a psychologist, but she was hostile. When he asked for a referral to see a Catholic therapist, she all but called him crazy for refusing to give in to his nature as homosexual. In the end, his university health insurance wouldn't cover all the cost of an outside therapist, and he obviously couldn't turn to his parents.

11   Sexual confusion can be found anywhere, but it is particularly pronounced on college campuses, where to the general human confusion is added approved promiscuity and an institutional rejection of anything traditionally Christian or conservative. Is there any student more alienated or marginalized on campus than one who experiences same-sex attractions but who doesn't embrace them? Silence is forced upon him, and his entire life experience is discounted: He suffers same-sex attractions, he doesn't want to, and he seeks to be made whole again. This doesn't seem so extreme a narrative, and yet there are very few, if any, campus groups devoted to supporting these students.

12   While listening to Chris, I grew angrier and angrier about our troubled culture, the sexual chaos our parents' generation bequeathed us, the lack of support the Church provides, and the hostile environment the university maintains. Gradually, however, my anger gave way to sadness. A sadness that Chris struggles almost alone. A sadness

that others like him have no one to turn to. A sadness that universities deliberately reject chaste students with same-sex attractions.

13   In the end, though, I found myself feeling grateful. Grateful for knowing Chris. Grateful for the chance to see him carry a cross he did not choose. Offering up his daily struggles, he strives for holiness, refuses surrender, and resists temptations. He labors to remedy the unwanted causes and side effects of attractions he never desired, aware all the while that a cure isn't certain, that in this fallen world some disorders may always be with us.

14   I am witnessing my friend's unique path to holiness: a remarkable instance of grace working through a broken earthly vessel, making all things new, and leading to fullness of life. I think how blessed I am that I've been fortunate enough to witness it and find inspiration for my life in his struggles.

15   How sad, though, that the rest of the world will never know.

ANDREW SULLIVAN

They Also Served

Andrew Sullivan is one of the leading commentators on gay, lesbian, and bisexual issues in the nation. Openly gay himself, devoutly Catholic, critical of certain aspects of the gay community, and outspokenly politically conservative in many respects, he nevertheless argues for full integration of gays and lesbians into American life. In 1996, Sullivan disclosed that he was receiving treatment for AIDS and entered graduate studies in government at Harvard University, where he eventually completed a PhD in political science. One-time editor of *The New Republic* and author of five books, Sullivan now blogs extensively for *The Atlantic*. The following piece appeared in *The New York Times Magazine* on June 17, 2001. Notice that the following essay in *Good Reasons*, by David Horowitz, is a response to this one.

My favorite character from the old sitcom "M*A*S*H" was Corporal Klinger. Growing up, barely knowing what homosexuality was, I was mesmerized by an ugly, hairy, little man in the Army wearing large floral dresses and boas. It took awhile, but eventually I figured out why he was doing it: he was trying to be discharged! The United States Army being a relatively sensible place, at least in the "M*A*S*H" fantasy about the Korean War, he was forced to stay. In some inchoate way, I took that to be a feature of the way civilized people behaved—even at war. Eccentrics, I mused, aren't always threats. They can even be assets.

2   Klinger (played by Jamie Farr) came back to me while I was watching yet another war epic in these peaceful times. "Pearl Harbor," like many recent war movies, made an effort to look back at old times and see individuals who were invisible in their day. Cuba Gooding, Jr. played the brave, segregated Negro, fighting back for his country. Similarly, in "Saving Private Ryan," the sensibilities of the 1990's were projected backward. We didn't see just soldiers; we saw a Jewish American soldier, an Italian, a WASP and so on. And our acknowledgment of military diversity is no longer restricted to movies. On the Mall in Washington, we have monuments to black soldiers and

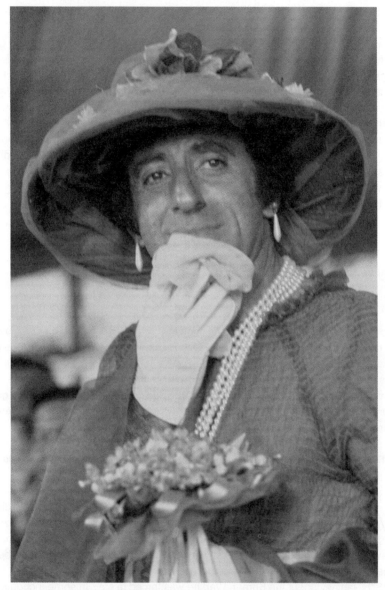

Corporal Maxwell Q. Klinger from the long-running TV show *M*A*S*H*

female soldiers. There are even moving tributes to Japanese-Americans who fought and died for their country.

3   Why no Klinger? I don't mean that literally, of course. Pumps and pearls don't go too well on war memorials. But I do mean some minor recognition in today's war nostalgia of the role that gay men have played in the past in defending their country. Their absence is yet another sign of the ingratitude—that's a mild description, actually—that

we still accord those men who risked their lives for the rest of us and who happened to love other men. Today Klinger would be expelled from the Army, along with countless others.

4 The final figures of President Clinton's "don't ask, don't tell" policy were released recently. Discharges jumped 17 percent from 1999 to 2000. In fact, under the new policy, the rate of expulsion of gay service members has more than doubled in six years, from 0.037 percent of the entire armed services to 0.087 percent. And this, paradoxically, as our culture as a whole has grown more accepting of homosexuals.

5 The Pentagon says these soaring figures are a result not of some new jihad against gay soldiers but of "voluntary" departures. Declaring yourself gay no longer results in a dishonorable discharge, say the top brass, just a handshake and a farewell, so more and more gay and lesbian service members are up and leaving without suffering any penalty or shame. They don't even have to "prove" they're gay. They just have to say they are.

6 But if the Pentagon is right, if there truly is no lasting shame in these discharges, then what's to stop straight soldiers from seeking them also? From "pulling a Klinger," you might say. What easier way to get out of a job you'd otherwise be chained to? There's no way of knowing how many of these supposedly voluntary exits were phony ones. But as the stigma of homosexuality lessens, the numbers can only increase. To be sure, many gay soldiers quit because they're harassed and physically threatened. At the Army base where a soldier perceived to be gay was murdered with a baseball bat in 1999, about 120 soldiers quit the following year. But when quitting is as easy as showing up one day with a rainbow flag, who can blame many, many others for leaping right through the gaping loophole?

7 Other countries, worried about the Klinger Proviso, have simply dropped their bans on gay soldiers—and have found almost no disruption or morale problems as a result. So is it possible the American armed forces could follow suit? Don't bet on it. President Bush has declared that the current policy is workable—even though it was begun as a way to protect gays and has ended up expelling them at twice the previous rate.

8 What few seem to get is that there is also a deeper issue here. At a time when we are rightly celebrating the greatest generation, we are deliberately excluding a part of it. This is particularly odd because the Second World War, as the historian Allan Bérubé has shown, was a time when many American gay men came to terms with their orientation—largely by meeting other homosexuals for the first time, in the military. It was, in its way, the first gay revolution. Back in the 1970's, we at least paid some sort of lip service to a diverse military, even in the comic character of Klinger. Today we seem to be going in reverse—against the trend in the country as a whole and among all our military allies.

9 I remember being intensely moved by the Civil War movie "Glory," about one of the Union Army's first black regiments. It wasn't just the soldiers' courage but the realization that only when those soldiers were allowed to fight for America did it truly become their country. So many decades later, isn't it time that gay Americans were allowed the same privilege? And even given, along with everyone else, a modicum of thanks?

David
Horowitz

Why Gays Shouldn't Serve

One of the first online publications ever produced on the Internet,
Salon.com covers current events, politics, and culture in a
newsmagazine format. In addition to reviews and articles about
movies, music, and books, it offers interactive commentary, with articles like the following one, which was published on June 25, 2001
as a response to the previous selection in *Good Reasons*, by
Andrew Sullivan. Horowitz (b. 1939) for two decades has been a
prominent conservative advocate, watchdog, and gadfly. A prolific
writer, his essays in many magazines and on many Web sites have
opposed affirmative action, opposed reparations to African
Americans descended from slaves, and espoused other causes dear
to the right. Recently he has taken on colleges and universities as
places of liberal indoctrination by founding Students for Academic
Freedom and publishing *The Professors: The 101 Most Dangerous
Academics in America* (2006).

Political correctness is a doctrine widely presumed dead, an
object of ridicule that no one defends these days outside the margins of the ideological left. Yet my recent tour of college campuses
under the necessary armed protection of campus security guards
suggests that it is obviously alive and well—and itself protected—
in certain regions of the political culture.

2   A sure sign of p.c. thinking is when the other side of a
controversial subject is successfully identified as forbidden territory. To cross the invisible boundary that embargoes a politically
incorrect view renders one's motives immediately suspect. To argue the position is a sign of one's indecency. It is to mark the
holder of the position as a bad person, a relic of the reactionary
past, an obstacle on the path to human progress.

3   This was the object of the campaign of vilification I encountered when I suggested that reparations for an injury committed
136 years ago and payable on the basis of skin color instead of
injury was "a bad idea and racist too." For the heresy of opposing
the left on an issue it considered a political litmus, I was accused
of expressing ideas that were "offensive" and then tarred and
feathered as a bonehead "racist." The attacks weren't limited to
me; they were also directed at the journalistic institutions that
printed my ad in the interest of free speech. My Salon colleague
Joan Walsh accurately described these attacks as "political correctness run amok." Yet they were also lent credence and support
by pundits who generally opposed political correctness like
Jonathan Alter, Clarence Page, and the *Washington Post*'s
Richard Cohen.

4   This is a sure sign that the tenets of political correctness are still very much alive and well. An interesting case of this was recently provided by my good and courageous friend Andrew Sullivan in a column that appeared in the *New York Times Magazine*. In it, Sullivan addressed the subject of gays in the military in a way that I found morally persuasive and poignant on the one hand, but politically correct and obtuse on the other.

5   His column was titled "They Also Served," and it asked for "some . . . recognition in today's war nostalgia of the role that gay men have played in the past in defending their country." In the film "Pearl Harbor," for example "Cuba Gooding, Jr. played the brave segregated Negro, fighting back for his country." In "Saving Private Ryan," "the sensibilities of the '90s were projected backward. We didn't see just soldiers; we saw a Jewish American soldier, an Italian, a WASP, and so on." Actually, Sullivan is wrong on that count. This wasn't the sensibility of the '90s. It was the same sensibility I saw as a kid in the 1940s when World War II films invariably featured the identical rainbow and, in features like "Home of the Brave," included black soldiers and was accompanied by a powerful anti-discrimination theme.

6   This is the part of Sullivan's argument I can wholeheartedly embrace—and I believe a majority of Americans do, too. When a socially conservative president appoints an openly gay man to an administration post, it is a sign that things have really changed. But the recognition of gays who served the country was not Sullivan's main agenda in his *New York Times Magazine* essay. Having established the point that we should, but do not, acknowledge the service that gay men have performed for this country, he wants to use it as a wedge for the argument that the armed services should abandon their "Don't ask, don't tell" policy and embrace a gay presence in their ranks. Sullivan calls this goal a "diverse military" and wonders why "we seem to be going in reverse."

7   It is at this point that Sullivan's argument abruptly incorporates the telltale syntax of political correctness. His opponents are reactionaries, prejudiced against "diversity"—i.e., gays. The assumption is that no serious rationale other than lingering social prejudice exists for current military policy. Opposing it requires no military argument, while defending it is a sign of failure to fully qualify for the ranks of the decent and humane. As Sullivan presents the case, no other possibility exists.

8   Sullivan's argument, however, is counterintuitive. Of all social institutions, the military is the most pragmatic. Its task, brutal in its simplicity, is to develop the most efficient killing machine that money can buy and intelligence can devise. This singularity of purpose creates a paradoxical result. The military is indeed retrograde in some of its aspects. (It's not a democratic institution, for example.) On the other hand, it is more progressive in others. Precisely because the military's overriding purpose is to win wars,

free black fighting units were incorporated into its ranks more than a century ago, at a time when slavery was still legal. Less well known is the fact that free black troops and military support units were part of the Confederate war effort as well.

9   For almost a century after that, black soldiers were still segregated and confined to subordinate roles. But in 1947 the military was integrated. That was seven years before the Supreme Court integrated the nation's schools and 18 years before progress in the political realm made it possible to end segregation in the South. (All this military progress was made notwithstanding the fact the military culture is largely a Southern culture.) In short, because of its pragmatic focus, the military—rigid in other areas—in this crucial terrain of social conflict has shown itself to be historically more flexible, progressive, and ready to adapt than the democratic political process itself.

10   Then what is the military's problem with including gays, other than prejudice? It is a sign of the force of political correctness in our culture that there is probably not one among a hundred readers of these words who could answer that question. Because of the embargo that political correctness puts on even considering the arguments of the other side, the conventional "wisdom" is that an institution that pioneered integration is run by individuals—many of whom are themselves minorities—who are more prejudiced against gays than they were against blacks. And by 100 years! Is this an argument that any self-respecting pundit–in other circumstances—would even want to be associated with?

11   Yet it is precisely the argument that all proponents of including gays in the military currently make. For all such advocates, including my friend Sullivan, the "don't ask, don't tell" policy is just a hypocritical attempt to appease lingering social prejudice. That's the voice of political correctness.

12   In fact, there *is* a military argument against the inclusion of gays in combat, which has nothing to do with social prejudice. It may or may not be a sound argument. I am not a military expert, and any opinion I have about the armed forces is necessarily based on intuition rather than experience. I certainly am open to counter arguments. It's just that nobody on the inclusion side is offering any.

13   Sullivan's argument in the *Times* article is more interesting than most in that it credits the Army with having important agendas that are worthy of respect. He observes that the current policy of "don't ask, don't tell" creates a standing loophole for anyone who wants to leave the service. This is bad for the military and an argument for changing the policy. That's well and good, but hardly persuasive for a service that relies on volunteers. To make a credible argument for changing the policy, Andrew and others will have to address the military rationale for the policy itself.

14   "Don't ask, don't tell" is a way of containing the destructive force of sex on a combat capability called "unit cohesion." To create the perfect killing machine, the military works hard to drain re-

cruits of their individuality and their self-interested desires in order to make them think like cogs in a machine. An essential part of the military mind is that the members of fighting units don't think for themselves but do as they are told. They work as a unit in which each performs an appointed task. The mission objective—not personal consideration—guides their actions. Suppose a commander were faced with the choice of risking his unit or risking the life of his own son, for example. Suppose the life of his son were threatened, but to save him would risk the military objective his superiors had set. Suppose he let the human override the imperatives of the machine. He would be doing what was natural, but the military objective he sacrificed might cost the lives of hundreds or thousands.

15   To avoid such breaches of military discipline, military policy does not allow family members to fight in the same unit. The same principle underlies its policy towards gays. Sacrifice of unit cohesion and military order is the threat that sex between soldiers poses for any combat force. The open inclusion of gays in the military is regarded by military men who oppose it a threat to effectiveness of the military as a fighting force.

16   This has nothing to do with the individual fighting capability of gay males. It is about unit cohesion. It's about making every soldier a cog in a machine whose larger purpose he cannot understand, but he is bound to serve. Suppose two men in a five-man unit are sexual partners. What will that do to the cohesiveness and effectiveness of the fighting unit? What impact will it have on its ability to carry out its mission? These are the questions that led to the ban on gays in the military and then to the subsequent "don't ask, don't tell" policy. Because once you are able to tell—and stay—then there is no containing the sexual problem.

17   As a comeback, some may be tempted to ask: What about the fact that women now serve in combat units? Far from taking care of the problem, this comparison only underscores the dangers in letting politicians treat the military as a social experiment. In one sense, of course, we don't really know the magnitude of the threat since we haven't been in a ground war since women were allowed in combat roles. (And there may, indeed, be a connection between the two.) But we do know that every military that has attempted to place women in combat positions—the Israelis, the Germans, and the Russians provide three examples—has abandoned the practice, because of its negative impact on unit cohesion (in part, because men will instinctively sacrifice their tactical missions to protect the women). We do know that since women have been included in these roles, requirements and standards have been dramatically lowered, and along with them morale—a crucial, if immeasurable, element of military success.

18   Moreover, we know that once the politically correct foot is in the door, the possibility of reasserting pragmatic controls

becomes ever more remote. The same "progressive" intolerance that forced the original issue will prevent any rational assessment of the result. The admission of women into the American military was not a military decision but a political act. The Presidential Commission on the Assignment of Women in the Armed Forces, which was created during Bush pére's administration, recommended *against* putting women in combat positions.

19   The Clinton administration ignored the recommendation and slipped the new policy into place without a public discussion or congressional debate. During the Gulf War, women in the armed services failed to report to combat duty at rates many multiples that of men. When you don't show up for your combat assignment, you are effectively sabotaging existing battle plans. On one ship, the Acadia, 36 women in the Persian Gulf war zone over a seven-month period were sent home because they were pregnant. The military looked the other way. None was court-martialed for cowardice or dereliction of duty. In other words, under the force of political correctness, the military has surrendered to the fact that it will be a less effective fighting machine.

20   The integration of women in the military and in combat forces is a politically created debacle that has already weakened America's defenses. The open inclusion of gays in the military could have an even more damaging effect, with unknown consequences for untold lives. If proponents of gay inclusion want to make their case persuasively, they need to make it not on the battlefields of political correctness, but here in the real world.

ALEXA **HACKBARTH**

Vanity, Thy Name Is Metrosexual

In the last several years a new term, metrosexual, has moved toward the center of discussions about sexuality and masculinity. Most likely coined by journalist Mark Simpson in 1994, the term metrosexual has been the subject of many definition arguments on talk radio and TV and in the print media. Alexa Hackbarth, a research assistant and photo technician at the *Washington Post* who has done freelance writing since 1999, invokes the term in her discussion of dating protocols that is reprinted below from the November 17, 2003, *Post*.

At dinner the other night, my date listed the calorie count of the main entrees, raising an eyebrow at my chicken Alfredo selection after he had ordered a salad. I saw him check his reflection in the silver water pitcher three times. During dessert, he looked deeply into my eyes and told me he thought what we have together is very special. It was our third date.

2   It was then that I realized why my dating life has been as mysterious as the Bermuda Triangle since I arrived in Washington. This city, unlike any other place I've lived, is a haven for the metrosexual. A metrosexual, in case you didn't catch any of several newspaper articles about this developing phenomenon (or the recent "South Park" episode on Comedy Central), is a straight man who styles his hair using three different products (and actually calls them "products"), loves clothes and the very act of shopping for them, and describes himself as sensitive and romantic. In other words, he is a man who seems stereotypically gay except when it comes to sexual orientation.

3   Gay men say they actually have a bit of trouble telling the straight from the gay anymore. But at least this new breed of man is more likely to thank the gay man for the compliment than punch him in the face after being approached, which may indicate that metrosexuals are more accepting of other people's sexual preferences. Either that or they're afraid of breaking a nail when their fist makes contact.

4   My primary concern, however, is that women are also having a difficult time telling straight men from gay men. Maybe city girls really do want a boyfriend who can pick out a purse that goes with her outfit, who likes to talk about calorie intake and celebrity hook-ups. But there are just too many men in this city who know all the soap opera story lines and designer labels and too few who associate sweat with hard work instead of a stint in the sauna.

5   In the small western ranching town where I grew up, men wrangle cattle before sitting down to a breakfast of bacon and eggs. They're the strong and silent type, capable and calm in a crisis. They know how to fix a leaky faucet or rewire an electrical outlet. They drive pickup trucks. And when they cook, it's steak and potatoes, not wine-braised duck. They sure don't spend hours in front of the mirror only to emerge with prettier hair than mine.

6   Metrosexuals are overwhelmingly city-dwellers, which makes sense since Diesel, Banana Republic, Gap and Express Men are rarely found down dirt roads. The source of my confusion, however, is the overwhelming abundance of this type of man in Washington. This is a city of transplants, rural and urban alike. But for some reason, each of the nearly two dozen men I have dated over the past eight months has displayed metrosexual traits. I met quite a few of them in bars, some in coffeeshops and grocery stores, and one or two through mutual friends. I figure I've experienced a decent cross-section of the city's dating pool. So where, as Paula Cole sings, have all the cowboys gone?

7   I understand that men, like women, want to look their best in order to convey professionalism, attract lovers and improve their self-image. I just don't think they're going about it the right way. It's as if, in an effort to move far away from the image of a smelly, unshaven man smashing beer cans on his forehead and wiping his nacho cheese down the front of his stained T-shirt, these guys have swung too far in the opposite direction. It makes me uncomfortable when a man can discuss the new season's fashions in intimate detail. Perhaps I am unusually insensitive, but I don't want a man who pours out his heart on the fourth date. I lose interest in men who not only won't make the first move, but hesitate to make the second and third. I don't want my date to be tearing up at the end of a movie when I'm sitting there dry-eyed.

8   We're living in an exciting time. America's social fabric is being unraveled and rewoven as we become more accepting of the differences that make each individual

unique and our country so great. I have no arguments with expressions of individuality. But I will admit to worrying when I read the results of a survey of American men aged 21 to 48, conducted by Euro RSCG Worldwide, that says more than two-thirds of men value love over professional success. As it should be, you say. Perhaps. But only if the men surveyed were just those with families.

9   Who are the young, single men who say they value love over anything else? My guess is they're predominantly members of this new breed called metrosexuals: men in touch with their so-called feminine side who would rather "grow old with the woman they love," even if they haven't met her yet, than "head up a Fortune 500 company." This might be endearing and romantic, but it's not very productive. It doesn't make scientific and medical advances, it doesn't help develop solid foreign policy and it doesn't contribute to the gross national product.

10   So what is the motivation behind this metrosexual trend? A number of close male friends have told me that any secondary reasons for a straight man's behavior are completely overshadowed by their central motivation: to attract women. Men, they tell me, acquire money, status and distinguished job titles to impress and win the ladies, whether in droves or in terms of "till death do us part." They hear women describe the perfect man as being sensitive, sweet and romantic and aspire to that description.

11   But frank, open confessions of emotions on the first date? Poorly written poetry and a closet full of shoes? Plot-line knowledge of "The Bold and the Beautiful"? This just seems like way too much work to get a woman's attention, especially if the man is, indeed, looking to grow old with her. That's a long time to keep up the act. And while the theory that men are changing their images and priorities for love seems terribly flattering to us women, I find it hard to believe.

12   I'd hate to think that this is all the result of marketing and advertising pressure.

13   We all recognize the influence these methods have on people, both individually and en masse. That's why propaganda is an essential part of every war. That's why anorexia and bulimia were, and still are, such a problem in young girls. It is interesting to note that the term "metrosexual" was actually coined a few years ago by a writer in a satirical comment on "consumerism's toll on traditional masculinity." Marketers, like sharks in a feeding frenzy, grabbed on to the term and are currently masticating their way through the attached school of consumers who are willing to pay $150 for a pair of jeans. But even if this explains how a man can rationalize spending $75 on moisturizing cream, it still doesn't explain the mind-set that goes with it.

14   The metrosexual movement can't just be about love. Commercialism also can't be held solely responsible. And it's not just a heightened appreciation of the finer things in life.

15   These are all aspects of what drives this type of man, just as it motivates the women who consider shopping to be a form of therapy, who fall in love every other week, who live vicariously through the characters on TV. We all do this to some extent. But there's something more to it.

16   Perhaps this metrosexual trend indicates how far removed we've become from the real world.

17   Concrete cause-and-effect is becoming more and more disconnected from the lives of those of us fortunate enough to have the resources to be extravagant.

Impracticality has become an indicator of progress. Money can provide every creature comfort, without requiring any skill or knowledge except that which earned the money in the first place. A man with money doesn't need to know how to install a water heater. He doesn't need to know his way around a sawhorse; he can pay someone else to build his cabinets.

Spas for men

18   Maybe the lack of a visible connection between hard work and the fruits of labor means that satisfaction in a job well done is much more elusive today than it used to be. And maybe, if fulfillment isn't being found in work, we end up looking to relationships to provide this sense of satisfaction and contentedness. But while I enjoy being in love as much as the next person, perhaps we shouldn't force its existence simply because we feel disconnected and adrift. It almost seems as if love and money and status are all just flimsy stand-ins for something more.

19   The emergence of metrosexuals, prevalent enough both to warrant a label and provoke discussion, indicates that something has been missing in the lives of these men. I just hope they find what they're looking for.

Heather Havrilesky

Meet the Smoothies

Heather Havrilesky is a senior writer for the online newsmagazine Salon.com, where she covers television and pop culture. She cocreated the cartoon "Filler," which appears on Suck.com, with illustrator Terry Colon; and she has also placed her work in *New York Magazine*, the *Washington Post*, and National Public Radio's *All Things Considered*. On June 30, 2005, Salon.com published the following essay under the teaser, "Metrosexuals, move over. The small towns of America are churning out macho, high-maintenance pretty men who love women and Budweiser—and have perfectly waxed privates."

"I love to dance. I love my body, and I love to take my clothes off."
—*Brian, 28, of VH1's "Strip Search," explaining his life's passions*

2   This guy's a freak, right? Wrong. Let's call him a smoothie, the modern version of a pretty boy, a waxed-chested breed that's

far more prevalent and far more high-maintenance than those dabbling urban metrosexuals. The smoothie transcends the scope of "Queer Eye" and is centered not in the big cities, but in the small towns where decades of boy bands and hair products and Chess King fashions have filtered into the cultural groundwater, until most young men have a grasp of personal hygiene, style, and flamboyant behavior that the older, crustier, and less hygienic among us can hardly fathom.

3   If the heavily primped contestants of VH1's "Strip Search" seem to constitute a particularly skewed sample, take a gander at MTV or the WB or other young channels, where the men not only look uniformly cleaner than they have since the '50s, but their bodies are totally hairless, their hair boasts triple-processed highlights, and their behavior wavers between prancing, posturing, exhibitionism, and Madonna-style outbursts. Next, check out VH1's "Kept," where a gaggle of smoothies competes very sincerely and fiercely for the chance to become Jerry Hall's arm candy, enjoying her wealthy and fabulous lifestyle while presumably accompanying her to events, following her orders, and servicing her engine in exchange.

4   If that doesn't convince you, flip over to "Blow Out," where each week we witness a stiffly gelled yet demonstrably straight hairstylist don the James Dean white-T-and-jeans look that was once a gay club boy staple, start catfights with business partners and stylists in his salons, and then retreat to therapy to cry his eyes out while the cameras roll. Or check out Wes of "The Real World: Austin," whose audition tape included footage of him dancing in a G-string, and a confession that he's always had a secret dream of becoming a male stripper. And if these examples don't convince you that a sea change in the definition of masculinity is reaching the masses and not just the cloistered urban elites, look around your average college campus. These kids keep themselves so trimmed and ironed and clean and buff, even sprawling state campuses have the preening, swaggery feel of a huge outdoor gay nightclub.

5   This vast movement of shiny, swashbuckling heterosexuality engulfs the "metrosexual" tag like the whale swallowing Jonah. While the metrosexual spends a lot at Barney's, shops for heirloom tomatoes at Dean & Deluca, keeps his CD collection carefully alphabetized, and nurtures a wide range of house plants without help from his gay friends, the smoothie is a horse of a different color. He isn't necessarily an effete city dweller; more often than not he lives in Iowa or Florida or Oregon or California. His interest in fashion isn't about keeping up appearances—he's not some slick lawyer with a penchant for Armani or some young actor trying to look appropriately hip. The smoothie's interest in his "look" is more deeply felt and sincere than that, not to mention slightly misguided and disturbingly meticulous: Baseball caps are molded, painstakingly, into the perfect C-shape; stubble is trimmed into the perfect Don Johnson-style 5 o'clock shadow; "distressed" jeans, with their calculated faded patches and hemmed rips, are cleaned and

pressed and tugged just below the waist; eyebrows are waxed, as is back, chest and (gasp) the family jewels to boot. The smoothie spends a lot not just on clothes and haircuts, but on highlights, spray-tans, manicures and pedicures, bodybuilding formulas, gym memberships, dry cleaning bills, man jewelry, and hip-hop classes. Not to put too fine a point on it, but the smoothie is like a cross between a frat boy and Britney Spears.

6   Whether this shiny, pretty new take on masculinity is the product of decades of primped heartthrobs, a redefining of gender roles that's finally come to fruition, or just the result of an endless onslaught of marketing campaigns by the fashion and beauty industries in pursuit of the single male's dollar is anybody's guess. Maybe the definition of masculinity has been so limited for so long that young men have decided to stretch its boundaries in ways that appear daring or even odd to the rest of us. Sure, there have been plenty of boundary-pushing fashion trends for men over the years—the sequins and tight pants and audaciousness of David Bowie and Mick Jagger in the '70s, earrings and tapered pants and blousy rayon shirts of the '80s—but they were adopted by urban hipsters or artists or alternative types. The smoothies aren't on the fringe, they're part of mainstream America.

7   Plenty of pop cultural anthropologists—not to mention the publicists at Bravo—would be happy to sum up this movement as the direct result of the popularity of "Queer Eye," but the shift predates the premiere of "Queer Eye" two years ago. These guys aren't new to the game, having just recently cleaned up and polished their looks. They've been into this stuff since they danced along to "New Kids on the Block" when they were in diapers.

8   Still, when the hosts of "Strip Search" announce that the guys get to go on a shopping trip, and the room explodes into cheering and high-fives, it's like watching the tides change suddenly and drastically. Even the two hosts laugh and look at each other, completely confused. "Oh my god, they're so excited! I had no idea they were gonna get that excited!" Downstairs, we cut to the guys singing together, "We're going shopping! We're going shopping!" as they hurriedly change clothes to leave.

9   What's really interesting about "Strip Search" is that many of the guys aren't dancers, have no experience performing, and didn't necessarily consider becoming strippers before they auditioned in their hometowns. Nonetheless, they're all extremely determined to make the final troupe of seven men, fashioned after the popular male revue "Thunder From Down Under." "I know everybody in this house wants it more than anything," says Jason, 19. "This is everybody's chance. This is everybody's ticket."

10   And so we watch them snap and shimmy through dance routines around the clock, stopping only to swill beer, give each other hell, and rub self-tanning lotion onto each other's backs. Keep in mind, these are guys who actually see the term "pretty boy" as a compliment. "I don't mean to be vain or arrogant but I think myself,

Sean, and Ryan are the pretty boys of the house," says Brian, who's a cable technician from Kentucky, "Because I think that we're probably the top as far as body-wise, and we always have a good time."

11   Shiny, smooth-chested, meticulously styled Danny of "The Real World: Austin" has similar kind words for his buddy in the house, shiny, smooth-chested, meticulously styled Wes. "Wes is a typical frat guy," says Danny, "and I *love* that about him! We get along great." It's no wonder they get along great: They both love ogling the hot girls in the house, high-fiving, getting drunk, and jumping in the hot tub. Does Danny know that Wes gyrated in a G-string in his audition tape, or that his secret dream is to become a stripper? Somehow, given the nature of their friendship, which seems to alternate between macho posturing (puffed chests and "whatever, dude" nonchalance) and girlish gushing (grinning, giggling, and confessional talks about which girls they like the most), this new bit of information shouldn't be a problem.

12   Then there are the boys of VH1's "Kept," who compete with startling sincerity to be Jerry Hall's arm candy. The guys are not only willing to jump through absurd hoops to win Hall's favor, from learning table manners to posing nude, but they become very jealous when one of the other guys has a successful date with Hall—successful meaning that he makes pleasant small talk and kisses up to her fabulous friends with enthusiasm.

13   That's not to say that Hall is looking for a pretty boy: When Ricardo, a self-involved guy who talks endlessly about his good genes, substitutes a strip tease for an improvised dance, Hall and her friends roll their eyes and send him packing. The other guys certainly see Ricardo and his primping sidekick Slavco as a joke, but they've all surrendered themselves to Hall's wishes and don't seem at all ashamed at the thought of assuming a very public role as Hall's trophy boyfriend.

14   You would think that "Average Joe: The Joes Strike Back" might offer one last stronghold against the smoothie onslaught, but no such luck. In its first season, this show was trumpeted as a chance for a regular-looking guy to win the heart of a hot babe, but the producers couldn't help slipping a few smoothies in at the last second. This season, not only is the usual herd of smoothies invading just when the skinny nerds and big, hairy guys are starting to get some game, but each week, one of the rejected regular joes returns after an extreme makeover. The first reject, Nick, a dorky magician, gets a haircut, some new clothes, a little cosmetic dentistry, and plastic surgery to remove extra fat under his eyes and to help define his jaw line. He's also told by a lifestyle coach not to talk about magic or to show girls magic tricks quite so often. In other words, act like your head is made of hamburger, just like a smoothie! The results? Nick doesn't look any better, and now he's sure to have no personality whatsoever.

15   Meanwhile, the herd of smoothies elsewhere on the TV dial are straining their hamburgers just to keep the camera interested

in their empty himbo lives. Take Alec, 29, of SoapNet's "I Wanna Be a Soap Star": "I was blessed with pretty good abs to begin with, and I take care of them," he tells the camera. Then, when pressed, he adds: "Girls often come up to me and ask me about my abs, yes. Yeah, they might want to touch them, too. They're out there, they're there to be seen and touched." Remember how, in the late '80s and early '90s, the camera was attracted to almost any tall, big-breasted blond, and we often had to sit through their rambling thoughts as well? Thanks to the work of pioneers like Fabio, today the camera loves the smoothie even more.

16   Men who indulge in careful grooming and enjoy showing off their bodies aren't limited to reality TV shows, of course—anyone within spitting distance of a college campus or an Abercrombie & Fitch chain can see that. But to really get up-close and personal, rent a copy of "Guys Gone Wild" and check out a steady flow of ripped abs and meat Chiclets, punctuated by the occasional flash of some completely hairless genitalia. After a few such visions, you'll start to think that every guy under 30 gets regular Brazilian waxes.

17   Jonathan of "Blow Out" may be the most shameless smoothie of them all. What he lacks in pumped-up physique he makes up for in behavior, parading his petty grievances, temperamental outbursts, and crying jags like a pampered diva. But all that matters to Jonathan is "beautiful hair"—a fact that he reminds us of over and over as he travels from his West Hollywood salon to his Beverly Hills branch to his therapist's office. Whether he's pitching a fit about the low quality of his product samples or insulting a member of his design team or refusing to follow his fashion-designer client's plans for a fashion show, Jonathan is only doing it, you see, because he cares so *deeply* about beautiful hair. The world is a tough place for Jonathan—we learn this at his therapist's office, where he wipes away tears and says that he feels like he's being pulled in a million directions at once.

18   But it's not the tears or the narcissistic streaks or those tweaks he gives his gelled hair constantly that make Jonathan such a rubbernecker's dream. He's a thoroughly modern character that many of us haven't met before: the swaggering sensitive guy, all raw nerves and sculpted ends and tight T-shirts. He's an unfamiliar type, a sniffling, bossy princess who makes Jessica and Ashlee Simpson look like stoics by comparison. Even his girlfriend is in on the joke: When Jonathan climbs the stairs on the way out of his girlfriend's office and quips, "We're just like Romeo and Juliet!" his girlfriend responds, "Goodbye, Juliet!"

19   So how did the gay male ideal get adopted by so many straight guys? Or more important, how did the smoothie upstage the metrosexual? Well, first of all, the smoothie is actually an exaggeration of the gay male ideal: He's more buff, more hairless, more tan, and yet there are little bits of macho "whatever" clothing thrown in as a hedge, a little signal that he's not, in fact, gay. In a recent *New York Times* article about the rise of this gay-vague

look, Alice Eisenberg, who works the doors at several gay bars in New York, asserted that she can still tell if a guy is straight or gay from this telling "whatever" hedge: "The jeans were right, the loafers were right, and he had a good body," she said of one gay-vague customer, who turned out to be straight. "But the shirt was completely untucked, and I think it was Old Navy."

20   If you're David Beckham, of course, your job is your hedge. British soccer god Beckham, the poster boy for both metrosexuality and smoothiedom, is so confident of his macho image that he has confessed to wearing his wife's panties, he was recently photographed frolicking in a Speedo on a beach in St. Tropez, and last week he lamented that Gavin Henson was supplanting his place as the favorite among gay admirers. "I think I have lost a lot of my gay fans to Welsh rugby star Gavin Henson," said Beckham. "It is a shame as I really love them."

21   Now, maybe Beckham and Jonathan and the guys on "Strip Search" represent a new, more flexible form of masculinity that's wild and free and unafraid of seeming gay. Maybe the smoothie can show off and enjoy being objectified without feeling self-conscious about it. Women have had far more freedom to express themselves or hide in masculine clothing for years; it makes sense that men would follow suit eventually. We should probably applaud the newfound freedom and the joy these young men take in being objectified; we should probably stand up and cheer when these shiny boy toys shake their asses and pout like Britney; we should encourage them to dress with flair and enjoy those spa treatments and dream their big Chippendale's-style dreams.

22   We should, but we can't. Because these men might be looking for visual perfection, but we're not. There's just something a little bit unappealing about men who spend far more time on themselves than most women do. When the previews for next week's "Average Joe" flashed an invasion of blond ab monkeys in matching red sports cars, flashing white teeth and spiked hair and shiny, tan six-packs, all I could think was, Where's the variety? Who wants a bunch of pumped-up clones with the exact same body type?

23   And what's so wrong with a little chest hair, anyway? Doesn't anyone remember Tom Selleck, with his perfect, dark hair-patches that accented his fit-but-not-too-fit barrel chest? To plenty of women and gay men, chest hair gives the bare chest a signature touch or adds a unique feature to an otherwise featureless landscape. Sure, we loved that hairless, buff body in the black-and-white Soloflex ads when we were teenagers, but that was before every third jerk on the street had one.

24   Plus, it's more than a little unnerving to feel disheveled and style-less and hairy in comparison to a man. Even if you're neat and fashionable, there's still something disturbing about the idea of your boyfriend rubbing self-tanning lotions on his biceps, or lying on his back with his legs spread, getting a Brazilian wax.

25   But then, maybe I'm just old-fashioned.

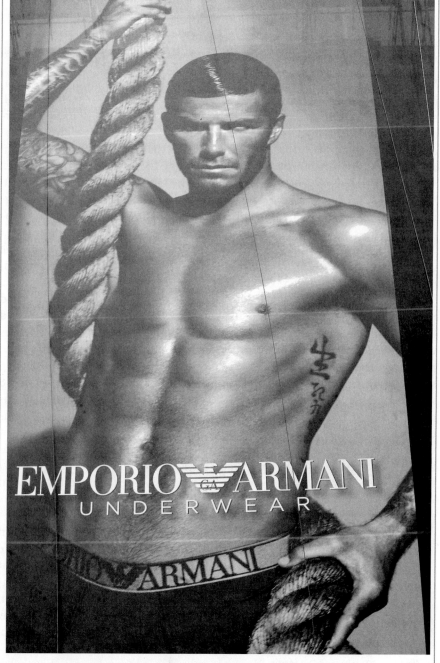

David Beckham in a Times Square billboard.

ISSUE IN FOCUS

Same-Sex Marriage

In 1993, the Hawaii Supreme Court suddenly ruled in support of the recognition of same-sex marriage. Since marriages in one state are usually recognized in all states, the ruling in Hawaii made same-sex marriage into a national issue immediately. A federal law—the Defense of Marriage Act—soon was passed in 1996. Included in this section of *Good Reasons*, it defined marriage as between one man and one woman and stipulated that states are not required to recognize same-sex marriages enacted in other states. Since then the issue has remained significant, however, because each state must now decide whether to permit or at least recognize same-sex marriage. Subsequent court decisions, voter referenda, and proposed new laws have only created additional controversies.

It's been pretty wild. Take California, for example. In February 2004, the newly elected mayor of San Francisco, Gavin Newsom, ordered the issuance of marriage licenses to same-sex couples even though California's Proposition 22 (which defined marriage as exclusively between one man and one woman) had passed with 61 percent of the vote in 2000. Court rulings temporarily stopped the San Francisco marriages, but gay couples again rushed to obtain licenses when the California Supreme Court overturned Proposition 22. That ruling also proved short-lived, however because California's Proposition 8, outlawing same-sex unions, narrowly passed in November 2008—and yet Proposition 8 was also subsequently overturned by U.S. District Judge Vaughn Walker in August 2010. On the other coast, things have been similarly contentious. Massachusetts became the first state to legally sanction gay marriage in 2004, but while some gay couples celebrated on the steps of Boston's City Hall, other citizens fought the decision. These marriages too were stopped temporarily through court actions, but only temporarily, and a subsequent effort to amend the state constitution to forbid same-sex marriage was defeated in 2007.

Phyllis Lyon, 79 (left), and Del Martin, 83, in San Francisco were the first same-sex couple to be officially married in California. (Photo: Liz Margelsdorf in the *San Francisco Chronicle.*)

All these legal actions have drawn continuing national attention to the issue of defining and regulating marriages. At least thirty states have now passed legislation to define marriage as strictly between one man and one woman; five permit gay couples to marry (Massachusetts, Iowa, Vermont, Connecticut, and New Hampshire); and five others have civil-union or domestic partnership laws, which confer some benefits and limited recognition. No constitutional amendment has been ratified, though it has been publicly and persistently debated. Meanwhile a highly visible lawsuit has been filed in California in the hope that it might lead to the same kind of conclusive Supreme Court decision that outlawed segregated schools in 1955 and sodomy laws in 2003.

We include a 2010 argument here by the lawyer who filed that lawsuit, Theodore Olson. A prominent Republican and leading conservative lawyer, he headed the Office of Legal Counsel under President Reagan, later advised Republicans seeking to impeach President Clinton, and served in the George W. Bush administration—and so it surprised many when he filed suit on behalf of two gay couples who are challenging California's Proposition 8, the ballot initiative that outlawed same-sex marriage there. Olson contends that conservatives should endorse same-sex marriage because they are traditionally on the side of personal freedom from government interference. Other proponents of gay marriage, like former *New York Times* and *Newsweek* columnist and novelist Anna Quindlen (whose essay, "Evan's Two Moms," is reprinted here), emphasize the practicality of legalizing same-sex marriages. They argue that legal marriage would recognize and protect personal, lasting, and loving monogamous relationships; shield marital partners from prosecution for sexual behavior; help partners share pensions, insurance, taxes, and inheritances; and guard partners from custody battles.

On the other hand, we also reprint the Defense of Marriage Act, which advocates traditional family arrangements and articulates the case against same-sex marriage. Opponents of same-sex marriage seek to defend traditional perspectives on marriage, to protect children by providing male and female role models within the immediate family unit, to uphold Biblical interpretations of marriage, and to sustain traditional heterosexual marriages already threatened by skyrocketing divorce rates. They call for a constitutional amendment that strictly endorses heterosexual marriage—an amendment like the one reproduced here, which has so far failed to reach the congressional floor for debate.

We close the debate with a proposal by Michael Lindenberger, who contends the entire controversy would be eliminated if we would simply discard the notion of state-sanctioned marriage altogether. But would that idea be practical? All these arguments and proposals and laws—as well as the images you will see in this

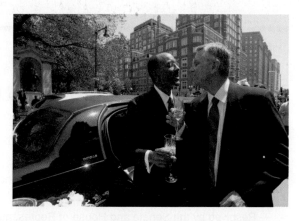

Davis Wilson (left) and Robert Compton were married at the Arlington Street Church in Boston.
(Photo: Deanne Fitzmaurice in the *San Francisco Chronicle*.)

section—hinge on fundamental social concerns: How is and how should marriage be defined? What are and should be social norms in sexual relationships? What kinds of relationships are viable legally and socially—and for whom? As you read, consider how these arguers present their cases and consider entering these conversations yourself, based on what you read here and what you've encountered in your own communities.

U.S. Congress

Proposed Amendment to the U.S. Constitution

108th CONGRESS, 1st Session

RESOLUTION 56 Proposing an amendment to the Constitution of the United States relating to marriage.

Resolved by the Senate and House of Representatives of the United States of America in Congress assembled (two-thirds of each House concurring therein). That the following article is proposed as an amendment to the Constitution of the United States, which shall be valid to all intents and purposes as part of the Constitution when ratified by the legislatures of three-fourths of the several States within seven years after the date of its submission for ratification:

"Article—

"SECTION 1. Marriage in the United States shall consist only of the union of a man and a woman. Neither this Constitution or the constitution of any State, nor state or federal law, shall be construed to require that marital status or the legal incidents thereof be conferred upon unmarried couples or groups."

House of Representatives

The Defense of Marriage Act

Congress of the United States
House of Representatives
AS INTRODUCED ON MAY 7, 1996

SUMMARY OF THE ACT:

The Defense of Marriage Act (DOMA) does two things. First, it provides that no State shall be required to give effect to a law of any other State with respect to a same-sex "marriage." Second, it defines the words "marriage" and "spouse" for purposes of Federal law.

2   The first substantive section of the bill is an exercise of Congress' power under the "Effect" clause of Article IV, section I of the Constitution (the Full Faith and Credit Clause) to allow each State (or other political jurisdiction) to decide for itself whether it wants to grant legal status to same-sex "marriage." This provision is necessary in light of the possibility of Hawaii giving sanction to same-sex "marriage" under its state law, as interpreted by its state courts, and other states being placed in the position of having to give "full faith and credit" to Hawaii's interpretation of what constitutes "marriage." Although so-called "conflicts of law" principles do not necessarily compel such a result, approximately 30 states of the union are sufficiently alarmed by such a prospect to have initiated legislative efforts to defend themselves against any compulsion to acknowledge same sex "marriage."

3   This is a problem most properly resolved by invoking Congress' authority under the Constitution to declare what "effect" one State's acts, records, and judicial proceedings shall have in another State. Congress has invoked this authority recently on two other occasions: in the Parental Kidnapping Prevention Act of 1980, which required each State to enforce child custody determinations made by the home State if made consistently with the provisions of the Act; and in the Full Faith and Credit for Child Support Order Act of 1994, which required each State to enforce child support orders made by the child's State if made consistently with the provisions of the Act.

4   The second substantive section of the bill amends the U.S. Code to make explicit what has been understood under federal law for over 200 years: that a marriage is the legal union of a man and a woman as husband and wife, and a spouse is a husband or wife of the opposite sex. The DOMA definition of marriage is derived most immediately from a Washington state case from 1974, Singer v. Hara, which is included in the 1990 edition of Black's Law Dictionary. More than a century ago, the U.S. Supreme Court spoke of the "union for life of one man and one woman in the holy estate of matrimony." Murphy v. Ramsey, 114 U.S. 15, 45 (1885).

5   DOMA is not meant to affect the definition of "spouse" (which under the Social Security law, for example, runs to dozens of lines). It ensures that whatever definition of "spouse" may be used in Federal law, the word refers only to a person of the opposite sex.

PROVISIONS OF THE ACT

4th CONGRESS 2D SESSION

H.R. 3396

IN THE HOUSE OF REPRESENTATIVES

Mr. BARR of Georgia (for himself, Mr. LARGENT, Mr. SENSENBRENNER, Ms. MYRICK, Mr. VOLKMER, Mr. SKELTON, Mr. BRYANT, and Mr. EMERSON) introduced the following bill, which was referred to the Committee

A BILL To define and protect the institution of marriage.

Be it enacted by the Senate and House of Representatives of the United States of America in Congress assembled,

SECTION 1. SHORT TITLE.
This Act may be cited as the "Defense of Marriage Act."

SECTION 2. POWERS RESERVED TO THE STATES.
(a) IN GENERAL.—Chapter 115 of title 28, United States Code, is amended by adding after section 1738B the following:

Section 1738C. Certain acts, records, and proceedings and the effect thereof "No State, territory, or possession of the United States, or Indian tribe, shall be required to give effect to any public act, record, or judicial proceeding of any other State, territory, possession, or tribe respecting a relationship between persons of the same sex that is treated as a marriage under the laws of such other State, territory, possession, or tribe, or a right or claim arising from such relationship."

(b) CLERICAL AMENDMENT.—The table of sections at the beginning of Chapter 115 of title 28, United States Code, is amended by inserting after the item relating to section 1738B the following new item: "1738C. Certain acts, records, and proceedings and the effect thereof."

SECTION 3. DEFINITION OF MARRIAGE.

(a) IN GENERAL.—Chapter 1 of title 1, United States Code, is amended by adding at the end the following:

"Section 7. Definition of 'marriage' and 'spouse'
"In determining the meaning of any Act of Congress, or of any ruling, regulation, or interpretation of the various administrative bureaus and agencies of the United States, the word 'marriage' means only a legal union between one man and one woman as husband and wife, and the word 'spouse' refers only to a person of the opposite sex who is a husband or a wife." ■

THEODORE OLSON

The Conservative Case for Gay Marriage

Together with my good friend and occasional courtroom adversary David Boies, I am attempting to persuade a federal court to invalidate California's Proposition 8—the voter-approved measure that overturned California's constitutional right to marry a person of the same sex.

My involvement in this case has generated a certain degree of consternation among conservatives. How could a politically active, lifelong Republican, a veteran of the Ronald Reagan and George W. Bush administrations, challenge the "traditional" definition of marriage and press for an "activist" interpretation of the Constitution to create another "new" constitutional right?

My answer to this seeming conundrum rests on a lifetime of exposure to persons of different backgrounds, histories, viewpoints, and intrinsic characteristics, and on my rejection of what I see as superficially appealing but ultimately false perceptions about our Constitution and its protection of equality and fundamental rights.

Many of my fellow conservatives have an almost knee-jerk hostility toward gay marriage. This does not make sense, because same-sex unions promote the values conservatives prize. Marriage is one of the basic building blocks of our neighborhoods and our nation. At its best, it is a stable bond between two individuals who work to create a loving household and a social and economic partnership. We encourage couples to marry because the commitments they make to one another provide benefits not only to themselves but also to their families and communities. Marriage requires thinking beyond one's own needs. It transforms two individuals into a union based on shared aspirations, and in doing so establishes a formal investment in the well-being of society. The fact that individuals who happen to be gay want to share in this vital social institution is evidence that conservative ideals enjoy widespread acceptance. Conservatives should celebrate this, rather than lament it.

Legalizing same-sex marriage would also be a recognition of basic American principles, and would represent the culmination of our nation's commitment to equal rights. It is, some have said, the last major civil-rights milestone yet to be surpassed in our two-century struggle to attain the goals we set for this nation at its formation.

6   This bedrock American principle of equality is central to the political and legal convictions of Republicans, Democrats, liberals, and conservatives alike. The dream that became America began with the revolutionary concept expressed in the Declaration of Independence in words that are among the most noble and elegant ever written: "We hold these truths to be self-evident, that all men are created equal, that they are endowed by their Creator with certain unalienable Rights, that among these are Life, Liberty and the pursuit of Happiness."

7   Sadly, our nation has taken a long time to live up to the promise of equality. In 1857, the Supreme Court held that an African-American could not be a citizen. During the ensuing Civil War, Abraham Lincoln eloquently reminded the nation of its founding principle: "our fathers brought forth on this continent, a new nation, conceived in liberty and dedicated to the proposition that all men are created equal." At the end of the Civil War, to make the elusive promise of equality a reality, the 14th Amendment to the Constitution added the command that "no State shall deprive any person of life, liberty or property, without due process of law; nor deny to any person the equal protection of the laws."

8   Subsequent laws and court decisions have made clear that equality under the law extends to persons of all races, religions, and places of origin. What better way to make this national aspiration complete than to apply the same protection to men and women who differ from others only on the basis of their sexual orientation? I cannot think of a single reason—and have not heard one since I undertook this venture—for continued discrimination against decent, hardworking members of our society on that basis.

9   Various federal and state laws have accorded certain rights and privileges to gay and lesbian couples, but these protections vary dramatically at the state level, and nearly universally deny true equality to gays and lesbians who wish to marry. The very idea of marriage is basic to recognition as equals in our society; any status short of that is inferior, unjust, and unconstitutional.

10   The United States Supreme Court has repeatedly held that marriage is one of the most fundamental rights that we have as Americans under our Constitution. It is an expression of our desire to create a social partnership, to live and share life's joys and burdens with the person we love, and to form a lasting bond and a social identity. The Supreme Court has said that marriage is a part of the Constitution's protections of liberty, privacy, freedom of association, and spiritual identification. In short, the right to marry helps us to define ourselves and our place in a community. Without it, there can be no true equality under the law.

11   It is true that marriage in this nation traditionally has been regarded as a relationship exclusively between a man and a woman, and many of our nation's multiple religions define marriage in precisely those terms. But while the Supreme Court has always previously considered marriage in that context, the underlying rights and liberties that marriage embodies are not in any way confined to heterosexuals.

12   Marriage is a civil bond in this country as well as, in some (but hardly all) cases, a religious sacrament. It is a relationship recognized by governments as providing a privileged and respected status, entitled to the state's support and benefits. The

California Supreme Court described marriage as a "union unreservedly approved and favored by the community." Where the state has accorded official sanction to a relationship and provided special benefits to those who enter into that relationship, our courts have insisted that withholding that status requires powerful justifications and may not be arbitrarily denied.

13   What, then, are the justifications for California's decision in Proposition 8 to withdraw access to the institution of marriage for some of its citizens on the basis of their sexual orientation? The reasons I have heard are not very persuasive.

14   The explanation mentioned most often is tradition. But simply because something has always been done a certain way does not mean that it must always remain that way. Otherwise we would still have segregated schools and debtors' prisons. Gays and lesbians have always been among us, forming a part of our society, and they have lived as couples in our neighborhoods and communities. For a long time, they have experienced discrimination and even persecution; but we, as a society, are starting to become more tolerant, accepting, and understanding. California and many other states have allowed gays and lesbians to form domestic partnerships (or civil unions) with most of the rights of married heterosexuals. Thus, gay and lesbian individuals are now permitted to live together in state-sanctioned relationships. It therefore seems anomalous to cite "tradition" as a justification for withholding the status of marriage and thus to continue to label those relationships as less worthy, less sanctioned, or less legitimate.

15   The second argument I often hear is that traditional marriage furthers the state's interest in procreation—and that opening marriage to same-sex couples would dilute, diminish, and devalue this goal. But that is plainly not the case. Preventing lesbians and gays from marrying does not cause more heterosexuals to marry and conceive more children. Likewise, allowing gays and lesbians to marry someone of the same sex will not discourage heterosexuals from marrying a person of the opposite sex. How, then, would allowing same-sex marriages reduce the number of children that heterosexual couples conceive? This procreation argument cannot be taken seriously. We do not inquire whether heterosexual couples intend to bear children, or have the capacity to have children, before we allow them to marry. We permit marriage by the elderly, by prison inmates, and by persons who have no intention of having children. What's more, it is pernicious to think marriage should be limited to heterosexuals because of the state's desire to promote procreation. We would surely not accept as constitutional a ban on marriage if a state were to decide, as China has done, to discourage procreation.

16   Another argument, vaguer and even less persuasive, is that gay marriage somehow does harm to heterosexual marriage. I have yet to meet anyone who can explain to me what this means. In what way would allowing same-sex partners to marry diminish the marriages of heterosexual couples? Tellingly, when the judge in our case asked our opponent to identify the ways in which same-sex marriage would harm heterosexual marriage, to his credit he answered honestly: he could not think of any.

17   The simple fact is that there is no good reason why we should deny marriage to same-sex partners. On the other hand, there are many reasons why we should formally recognize these relationships and embrace the rights of gays and lesbians to marry and become full and equal members of our society.

18   No matter what you think of homosexuality, it is a fact that gays and lesbians are members of our families, clubs, and workplaces. They are our doctors, our teachers,

our soldiers (whether we admit it or not), and our friends. They yearn for acceptance, stable relationships, and success in their lives, just like the rest of us.

19   Conservatives and liberals alike need to come together on principles that surely unite us. Certainly, we can agree on the value of strong families, lasting domestic relationships, and communities populated by persons with recognized and sanctioned bonds to one another. Confining some of our neighbors and friends who share these same values to an outlaw or second-class status undermines their sense of belonging and weakens their ties with the rest of us and what should be our common aspirations. Even those whose religious convictions preclude endorsement of what they may perceive as an unacceptable "lifestyle" should recognize that disapproval should not warrant stigmatization and unequal treatment.

20   When we refuse to accord this status to gays and lesbians, we discourage them from forming the relationships we encourage for others. And we are also telling them, those who love them, and society as a whole that their relationships are less worthy, less legitimate, less permanent, and less valued. We demean their relationships and we demean them as individuals. I cannot imagine how we benefit as a society by doing so.

21   I understand, but reject, certain religious teachings that denounce homosexuality as morally wrong, illegitimate, or unnatural; and I take strong exception to those who argue that same-sex relationships should be discouraged by society and law. Science has taught us, even if history has not, that gays and lesbians do not choose to be homosexual any more than the rest of us choose to be heterosexual. To a very large extent, these characteristics are immutable, like being left-handed. And, while our Constitution guarantees the freedom to exercise our individual religious convictions, it equally prohibits us from forcing our beliefs on others. I do not believe that our society can ever live up to the promise of equality, and the fundamental rights to life, liberty, and the pursuit of happiness, until we stop invidious discrimination on the basis of sexual orientation.

22   If we are born heterosexual, it is not unusual for us to perceive those who are born homosexual as aberrational and threatening. Many religions and much of our social culture have reinforced those impulses. Too often, that has led to prejudice, hostility, and discrimination. The antidote is understanding, and reason. We once tolerated laws throughout this nation that prohibited marriage between persons of different races. California's Supreme Court was the first to find that discrimination unconstitutional. The U.S. Supreme Court unanimously agreed 20 years later, in 1967, in a case called Loving v. Virginia. It seems inconceivable today that only 40 years ago there were places in this country where a black woman could not legally marry a white man. And it was only 50 years ago that 17 states mandated segregated public education—until the Supreme Court unanimously struck down that practice in Brown v. Board of Education. Most Americans are proud of these decisions and the fact that the discriminatory state laws that spawned them have been discredited. I am convinced that Americans will be equally proud when we no longer discriminate against gays and lesbians and welcome them into our society.

ANNA **QUINDLEN**

Evan's Two Moms

Evan has two moms. This is no big thing. Evan has always had two moms in his school file, on his emergency forms, with his friends. "Ooooh, Evan, you're lucky," they sometimes say. "You have two moms." It sounds like a sitcom, but until last week it was emotional truth without legal bulwark. That was when a judge in New York approved the adoption of a six-year-old boy by his biological mother's lesbian partner. Evan. Evan's mom. Evan's other mom. A kid, a psychologist, a pediatrician. A family.

2   The matter of Evan's two moms is one in a series of events over the last year that led to certain conclusions. A Minnesota appeals court granted guardianship of a woman left a quadriplegic in a car accident to her lesbian lover, the culmination of a seven-year battle in which the injured woman's parents did everything possible to negate the partnership between the two. A lawyer in Georgia had her job offer withdrawn after the state attorney general found out that she and her lesbian lover were planning a marriage ceremony: she's brought suit. The computer company Lotus announced that the gay partners of employees would be eligible for the same benefits as spouses.

3   Add to these public events the private struggles, the couples who go from lawyer to lawyer to approximate legal protections their straight counterparts take for granted, the AIDS survivors who find themselves shut out of their partners' dying days by biological family members and shut out of their apartments by leases with a single name on the dotted line, and one solution is obvious.

4   Gay marriage is a radical notion for straight people and a conservative notion for gay ones. After years of being sledge-hammered by society, some gay men and lesbian women are deeply suspicious of participating in an institution that seems to have "straight world" written all over it.

5   But the rads of twenty years ago, straight and gay alike, have other things on their minds today. Family is one, and the linchpin of family has commonly been a loving commitment between two adults. When same-sex couples set out to make that commitment, they discover that they are at a disadvantage: No joint tax returns. No health insurance coverage for an uninsured partner. No survivor's benefits from Social Security. None of the automatic rights, privileges, and responsibilities society attaches to a marriage contract. In Madison, Wisconsin, a couple who applied at the Y with their kids for a family membership were turned down because both were women. It's one of those small things that can make you feel small.

6   Some took marriage statutes that refer to "two persons" at their word and applied for a license. The results were court decisions that quoted the Bible and embraced circular argument: marriage is by definition the union of a man and a woman because that is how we've defined it.

7   No religion should be forced to marry anyone in violation of its tenets, although ironically it is now only in religious ceremonies that gay people can marry, performed by clergy who find the blessing of two who love each other no sin. But there is no secular reason that we should take a patchwork approach of corporate, governmental,

and legal steps to guarantee what can be done simply, economically, conclusively, and inclusively with the words "I do."

8   "Fran and I chose to get married for the same reasons that any two people do," said the lawyer who was fired in Georgia. "We fell in love; we wanted to spend our lives together." Pretty simple.

9   Consider the case of *Loving v. Virginia*, aptly named. At the time, sixteen states had laws that barred interracial marriage, relying on natural law, that amorphous grab bag for justifying prejudice. Sounding a little like God throwing Adam and Eve out of paradise, the trial judge suspended the one-year sentence of Richard Loving, who was white, and his wife, Mildred, who was black, provided they got out of the State of Virginia.

10   In 1967 the Supreme Court found such laws to be unconstitutional. Only twenty-five years ago it was a crime for a black woman to marry a white man. Perhaps twenty-five years from now we will find it just as incredible that two people of the same sex were not entitled to legally commit themselves to each other. Love and commitment are rare enough; it seems absurd to thwart them in any guise.

MICHAEL **LINDENBERGER**

A Gay-Marriage Solution: End Marriage?

When a Jewish boy turns 13, he heads to a temple for a deeply meaningful rite of passage, his bar mitzvah. When a Catholic girl reaches about the same age, she stands in front of the local bishop, who touches her forehead with holy oil as she is confirmed into a 2,000-year-old faith tradition. But missing in each of those cases—and in countless others of equal religious importance—is any role for government. There is no baptism certificate issued by the local courthouse and no federal tax benefit attached to the confessional booth, the into-the-water-and-out born-again ceremony, or any of the other sacraments that believers hold sacred.

2   Only marriage gets that treatment, and it's a tradition that some legal scholars have been arguing should be abandoned. In a paper published March 2 in the San Francisco *Chronicle,* two law professors from Pepperdine University issued a call to re-examine the role the government plays in marriage. The authors—one of whom voted for and one against Proposition 8, which ended gay marriage in California—say the best way out of the intractable legal wars over gay marriage is to take marriage out of the hands of the government altogether.

3   Instead, give gay and straight couples alike the same license, a certificate confirming them as a family, and call it a civil union—anything, really, other than marriage. For people who feel the word *marriage* is important, the next stop after the courthouse could be the church, where they could bless their union with all the religious ceremony they wanted. Religions would lose nothing of their role in sanctioning the kinds of

unions that they find in keeping with their tenets. And for nonbelievers and those who find the word *marriage* less important, the civil-union license issued by the state would be all they needed to unlock the benefits reserved in most states and in federal law for married couples.

"While new terminology for all may at first seem awkward—mostly in greeting-card shops—[it] dovetails with the court's important responsibility to reaffirm the unfettered freedom of all faiths to extend the nomenclature of marriage as their traditions allow," wrote Douglas W. Kmiec and Shelley Ross Saxer. Kmiec voted for Prop 8 because of his belief in the teachings of the Catholic Church and his notion of religious liberty but has since said he thinks the courts should not allow one group of Californians to marry while denying the privilege to others.

Their idea got a big boost three days later, during the March 5 oral arguments before the California Supreme Court, which is expected to issue a ruling soon in the case brought by gay couples and others who argue the constitutional amendment passed by voters last fall should be invalidated. Justice Ming Chin asked attorneys for each side whether the idea would solve the legal issues connected to gay marriage—issues that at their core revolve around the question of whether allowing some couples to marry but not others violates constitutional guarantees of equal protection under the law.

Both sets of lawyers agreed that the idea would resolve the equal-protection issue. Take the state out of the marriage business, and then both kinds of couples—straight and gay—would be treated the same. Even Ken Starr, the Pepperdine law dean and former Whitewater independent counsel who argued in favor of Prop 8, agreed that the idea would solve the legal issues, though he said it was a solution that lies outside the legal authority of the court. An attorney for the other side, Michael Maroko, didn't expressly endorse the idea, but he told Chin, "If you're in the marriage business, do it equally. And if you're not going to do it equally, get out of the business."

The two Pepperdine professors are arguing that the court should use that line of thinking in crafting its decision in the case before it, short-circuiting the need for a new referendum. Their proposal is aimed at helping speed a resolution on the issue in other states—gay marriage is heating up in Iowa, Connecticut, Vermont and elsewhere—and at the federal level. All sides on the debate expect the issues bubbling up out of the state courts and legislatures to eventually gain traction in federal courts too, ultimately leading to a case before the Supreme Court or efforts to amend the U.S. Constitution or both.

But as Solomonic as the compromise seems, giving up the word *marriage* may be impossible. For many couples joined in matrimony, having the state no longer call them married may make them feel as if something important had been taken away—even if it's hard to define just what was lost. And for many others—the folks who feel most strongly about marriage and most passionately supported the expensive campaign to defeat gay marriage—the issue of nomenclature is only the beginning. They are against not just gay marriage but also gay couples—and especially against government sanctioning of those relationships, no matter what they are called.

And as Chin considers whether he can craft a compromise with his fellow justices that would both uphold Prop 8—and therefore the right of the people to amend the state constitution—and assert the right of gay people to be treated equally, he may find that the folks who cling hardest to *marriage* are gay couples. After all, what was the most sweeping part of the May 2008 decision Ming and his colleagues issued that granted gays the right to marry? It was the idea that the word *marriage* is so strong that denying it to gay couples violates the most sacred right enshrined in the state constitution: the right for all people to be treated with dignity and fairness. Just 10 months later, gay couples—whether or not they are among the 18,000 who married in the state before Prop 8 stopped the ceremonies—are loath to lose a word for which so many fought so hard and so long to have apply to themselves.

10   But the Pepperdine idea puts into a play a new way of thinking—and whether it's part of the court's decision in the Prop 8 case or whether it makes its way into a new referendum, the idea of getting governments out of the marriage business offers a creative way of thinking about a problem that is otherwise likely to be around for a long, long time.

FROM READING TO WRITING

1. Write an essay defining the ideal marriage in order to support or undermine the concept of same-sex marriage. Just what is marriage, anyway? (Chapter 8 has advice on definition arguments.)

2. Just as Anna Quindlen did, write an essay that describes a particular, monogamous, same-sex couple that you know. In your essay, support or undermine the notion of legal same-sex unions.

3. Write a proposal argument (like the ones discussed in Chapter 13) that is based on the positive or negative consequences that would follow from legalizing same-sex unions.

4. Do a rhetorical analysis of an essay or image associated with same-sex marriage. You might use an argument, photo, or cartoon reprinted here; or, you could use another argument with which you are familiar. Consider how the author uses good reasons to support his or her perspective, as well as the completeness of the argument and the credibility of the arguer. (Look again at Chapters 5 and 6 for reminders on effective rhetorical and visual analyses.)

5. Evaluate the Defense of Marriage Act or the proposed constitutional amendment banning same-sex marriage. Based on aesthetic, ethical, and practical criteria, are these good laws or not? Why? (See Chapter 10 for information on forming evaluative arguments.)

6. What alternatives to marriage might make sense? Would civil unions satisfy the political, legal, and moral issues in a way that would lead to a national consensus on the issue?

7. Do some research into the views within the gay, lesbian, bisexual, and transgender community regarding marriage. Does everyone agree that it's a good idea? After you complete your research, write an essay characterizing the views of various constituencies within the community that is fair and balanced.

24 | Globalization: Importing and Exporting America

America meets the world as the iconic golden arches mix with Japanese characters at the world's busiest McDonald's restaurant in Tokyo. Is the world becoming more like America, or is America becoming more global?

America's Place in the World—and the World's Place in America

The place of America and Americans in relation to the rest of the world has always been an important topic in the national conversation. A product itself of globalization (embodied in the figure of Christopher Columbus) and created through the force of European colonialism, the United States has taken an increasing role in international affairs since its founding. But globalization has only grown more important, it seems, since the end of the Cold War (which seemed to leave the United States as the world's only superpower); since the development of economic reforms in China, in the European Union, and in other parts of the world (which are challenging the primacy of American economic power); and especially since the events of September 11 and the subsequent war in Iraq (which have underscored the limits of the American military and compromised our will to work cooperatively with traditional allies). Indeed, according to a survey released on August 18, 2004, by the Pew Research Center for the People and the Press, the American public has a divided, even paradoxical opinion about the place of the United States in the world. On the one hand, Americans agree that the United States has assumed a more powerful role as a world leader, but, on the other hand, they concede that America also seems less respected around the world. Americans reject the role of the United States as a single world leader, but they also reject the pull toward isolation. More generally, then, Americans are confronting the issue of what has come to be known as globalization—that is, the general impact of various nations on each other and more particularly the impact of American culture on other nations and cultures, and their impact on the United States.

Some of those impacts are economic, as the United States outsources manufacturing jobs to other nations, shifts in the direction of a service economy, and exports its ideologies (e.g., representative democracy, women's rights, resistance to sweatshop labor, pluralistic religious tolerance). Other impacts are military and political, as leaders and citizens debate the wisdom of various options. (For example, should our nation behave as a kind of American empire, free to impose its wishes and will on others? Should our foreign policy be an effort to export democracy, even at the point of a gun? Or should we cooperate more broadly with allies, cultivate new friends, and respect the right of each nation to self-determination? Should the United States close off its borders, literally and figuratively, to follow a kind of neo-isolationism?) Yet other impacts are broadly cultural, as Americans import some of the cultural practices and values of others (as in popular songs, films, restaurants, fashions, and so forth) and export our own cultural values and traditions to others. This chapter of *Good Reasons with Contemporary Arguments* offers arguments about one or another aspect of these questions related to globalization.

Workers at a call center in New Delhi, India, take a break between calls.

Contemporary Arguments

The arguments in this chapter focus on the exchange of capital and cultural goods between the United States and other nations. Todd Gitlin's essay uses iconic American cultural signs to argue that the global village today has a distinctly American flavor—though that flavor blends and changes in its new environments. In an essay about WalMart and Mexico, Laura Carlsen (a long-time student of the economic effects of American business on Mexican life) discusses her concern about the broader impact of American economic power on the cultures of other nations. Thomas Friedman explains approvingly the new "flat world" that globalization is creating, and Robyn Meredith and Suzanne Hoppough tout the economic benefits of globalization in a way that counters Carlsen. And Sadanand Dhume interprets the Best Picture of 2008, *Slumdog Millionaire*, as the product of a thoroughly globalized mentality and "a metaphor for India in the age of globalization."

While the topics discussed in this chapter are varied, all of the readings bring up similar questions about the movement between cultures—of people, goods, values, images, and communication. Those questions come together in the Issue in Focus, on the topic of immigration. What are the effects of globalization? What do you think about American importation of cultural forms from other nations? What about exportation of American culture that is welcomed—even sought out—by people in other nations? Is this importation and exportation dangerous, enriching, or some complicated mixture of the two?

Todd Gitlin

Under the Sign of Mickey Mouse & Co.

Todd Gitlin is a professor of journalism and sociology at Columbia University. A leading and longtime culture critic who writes for a variety of publications (including *Mother Jones*, a popular magazine with a left-of-center appeal, especially to younger readers), he has received several prestigious grants and fellowships, including one from the MacArthur Foundation. His books include *Media Unlimited: How the Torrent of Images and Sounds Overwhelms Our Lives* (2002), *Letters to a Young Activist* (2003), and *The Bulldozer and the Big Tent: Blind Republicans, Lame Democrats, and the Recovery of American Ideals* (2007). The selection below comes from the last chapter of *Media Unlimited*.

Everywhere, the media flow defies national boundaries. This is one of its obvious, but at the same time amazing, features. A global torrent is not, of course, the master metaphor to which we have grown accustomed. We're more accus-

AISLIN
THE GAZETTE
Montreal
CANADA

tomed to Marshall McLuhan's *global village.* Those who resort to this metaphor casually often forget that if the world is a global village, some live in mansions on the hill, others in huts. Some dispatch images and sounds around town at the touch of a button; others collect them at the touch of *their* buttons. Yet McLuhan's image reveals an indispensable half-truth. If there is a village, it speaks American. It wears jeans, drinks Coke, eats at the golden arches, walks on swooshed shoes, plays electric guitars, recognizes Mickey Mouse, James Dean, E.T., Bart Simpson, R2-D2, and Pamela Anderson.

2   At the entrance to the champagne cellar of Piper-Heidsieck in Reims, in eastern France, a plaque declares that the cellar was dedicated by Marie Antoinette. The tour is narrated in six languages, and at the end you walk back upstairs into a museum featuring photographs of famous people drinking champagne. And who are they? Perhaps members of today's royal houses, presidents or prime ministers, economic titans or Nobel Prize winners? Of course not. They are movie stars, almost all of them American—Marilyn Monroe to Clint Eastwood. The symmetry of the exhibition is obvious, the premise unmistakable: Hollywood stars, champions of consumption, are the royalty of this century, more popular by far than poor doomed Marie.

3   Hollywood is the global cultural capital—capital in both senses. The United States presides over a sort of World Bank of styles and symbols, an International Cultural Fund of images, sounds, and celebrities. The goods may be distributed by American-, Canadian-, European-, Japanese-, or Australian-owned multinational corporations, but their styles, themes, and images do not detectably change when a new board of directors takes over. Entertainment is one of America's top exports. In 1999, in fact, film, television, music, radio, advertising, print publishing, and computer software together *were* the top export, almost $80 billion worth, and while software alone accounted for $50 billion of the total, some of that category also qualifies as entertainment—video games and pornography, for example. Hardly anyone is exempt from the force of American images and sounds. French resentment of Mickey Mouse, Bruce Willis, and the rest of American civilization is well known. Less well known, and rarely acknowledged by the French, is the fact that *Terminator 2* sold 5 million tickets in France during the month it opened—with no submachine guns at the heads of the customers. The same culture minister, Jack Lang, who in 1982 achieved a moment of predictable notoriety in the United States for declaring that *Dallas* amounted to cultural imperialism, also conferred France's highest honor in the arts on Elizabeth Taylor and Sylvester Stallone. The point is not hypocrisy pure and simple but something deeper, something obscured by a single-minded emphasis on American power: dependency. American popular culture is the nemesis that hundreds of millions—perhaps billions—of people love, and love to hate. The antagonism and the dependency are inseparable, for the media flood—essentially American in its origin, but virtually unlimited in its reach—represents, like it or not, a common imagination.

4   How shall we understand the Hong Kong T-shirt that says "I Feel Coke"? Or the little Japanese girl who asks an American visitor in all innocence, "Is there really a Disneyland in America?" (She knows the one in Tokyo.) Or the experience of a German television reporter sent to Siberia to film indigenous life, who after flying out of Moscow and then traveling for days by boat, bus, and jeep, arrives near the Arctic Sea where live a tribe of Tungusians known to ethnologists for their bearskin rituals. In the community store sits a grandfather with his grandchild on his knee. Grandfather is dressed in traditional Tungusian clothing. Grandson has on his head a reversed baseball cap.

5   American popular culture is the closest approximation today to a global lingua franca, drawing the urban and young in particular into a common cultural zone where they share some dreams of freedom, wealth, comfort, innocence, and power—and perhaps most of all, youth as a state of mind. In general, despite the rhetoric of "identity," young people do not live in monocultures. They are not monocular. They are both local and cosmopolitan. Cultural bilingualism is routine. Just as their "cultures" are neither hard-wired nor uniform, so there is no simple way in which they are "Americanized," though there are American tags on their experience—low-cost links to status and fun. Everywhere, fun lovers, efficiency seekers, Americaphiles, and Americaphobes alike pass through the portals of Disney and the arches of McDonald's wearing Levi's jeans and Gap jackets. Mickey Mouse and Donald Duck, John Wayne, Marilyn Monroe, James Dean, Bob Dylan, Michael Jackson, Madonna, Clint Eastwood, Bruce

Willis, the multicolor chorus of Coca-Cola, and the next flavor of the month or the universe are the icons of a curious sort of one-world sensibility, a global semiculture. America's bid for global unification surpasses in reach that of the Romans, the British, the Catholic Church, or Islam; though without either an army or a God, it requires less. The Tungusian boy with the reversed cap on his head does not automatically think of it as "American," let alone side with the U.S. Army.

6   The misleadingly easy answer to the question of how American images and sounds became omnipresent is: American imperialism. But the images are not even faintly force-fed by American corporate, political, or military power. The empire strikes from inside the spectator as well as from outside. This is a conundrum that deserves to be approached with respect if we are to grasp the fact that Mickey Mouse and Coke are everywhere recognized and often enough *enjoyed.* In the peculiar unification at work throughout the world, there is surely a supply side, but there is not only a supply side. Some things are true even if multinational corporations claim so: there is demand.

7   What do American icons and styles mean to those who are not American? We can only imagine—but let us try. What young people graced with disposable income encounter in American television shows, movies, soft drinks, theme parks, and American-labeled (though not American-manufactured) running shoes, T-shirts, baggy pants, ragged jeans, and so on, is a way of being in the world, the experience of a flow of ready feelings and sensations bobbing up, disposable, dissolving, segueing to the next and the next after that. It is a quality of immediacy and casualness not so different from what Americans desire. But what the young experience in the video game arcade or the music megastore is more than the flux of sensation. They flirt with a loose sort of social membership that requires little but a momentary (and monetary) surrender. Sampling American goods, images, and sounds, they affiliate with an empire of informality. Consuming a commodity, wearing a slogan or a logo, you affiliate with disaffiliation. You make a limited-liability connection, a virtual one. You borrow some of the effervescence that is supposed to emanate from this American staple, and hope to be recognized as one of the elect. When you wear the Israeli version that spells *Coca-Cola* in Hebrew, you express some worldwide connection with unknown peers, or a sense of irony, or both—in any event, a marker of membership. In a world of ubiquitous images, of easy mobility and casual tourism, you get to feel not only local or national but global—without locking yourself in a box so confining as to deserve the name "identity."

8   We are seeing on a world scale the familiar infectious rhythm of modernity. The money economy extends its reach, bringing with it a calculating mentality. Even in the poor countries it stirs the same hunger for private feeling, the same taste for disposable labels and sensations on demand, the same attention to fashion, the new and the now, that cropped up earlier in the West. Income beckons; income rewards. The taste for the marketed spectacle and the media-soaked way of life spreads. The culture consumer may not like the American goods in particular but still acquires a taste for the media's speed, formulas, and frivolity. Indeed, the lightness of American-sponsored "identity" is central to its appeal. It imposes few burdens. Attachments and affiliations coexist, overlap, melt together, form, and re-form.

9   Marketers, like nationalists and fundamentalists, promote "identities," but for most people, the melange is the message. Traditional bonds bend under pressure from imports. Media from beyond help you have your "roots" and eat them, too. You can watch Mexican television in the morning and American in the afternoon, or graze between Kurdish and English. You can consolidate family ties with joint visits to Disney World—making Orlando, Florida, the major tourist destination in the United States, and the Tokyo and Marne-la-Vallée spin-offs massive attractions in Japan and France. You can attach to your parents, or children, by playing oldie music and exchanging sports statistics. You plunge back into the media flux, looking for—what? Excitement? Some low-cost variation on known themes? Some next new thing? You don't know just what, but you will when you see it—or if not, you'll change channels.

10   As devotees of Japanese video games, Hong Kong movies, and Mexican *telenovelas* would quickly remind us, the blends, juxtapositions, and recombinations of popular culture are not just American. American and American-based models, styles, and symbols are simply the most far-flung, successful, and consequential. In the course of a century, America's entertainment corporations succeeded brilliantly in cultivating popular expectations for entertainment—indeed, the sense of a *right* to be entertained, a right that belongs to the history of modernity, the rise of market economies and individualism. The United States, which began as Europe's collective fantasy, built a civilization to deliver the goods for playing, feeling, and meaning. Competitors ignore its success at their own peril, financial and otherwise. ∎

Laura Carlsen

WalMart vs. Pyramids

Laura Carlsen is the director of the Americas Program for the International Relations Center (formerly the Interhemispheric Resource Center), which provides policy analysis and options for economic policy involving North, Central, and South America. A graduate of Stanford University, in 1986 she received a Fulbright Scholarship to study the impact on women of the Mexican economic crisis. She continues to reside in Mexico City. Carlsen has also written about trade agreements and other economic issues impacting Mexico. The article reprinted below appeared in several places in October and November of 2004, including New York University's Global Beat Syndicate, the Common Dreams Web site (www.commondreams.org), and Human Quest, an academic journal of religion and philosophy.

The showdown is rife with symbolism. WalMart's expansion plans in Mexico have brought about a modern-day clash of passions and principles at the site of one of the earth's first great civilizations.

2 Several months ago WalMart, the world's largest retail chain, quietly began constructing a new store in Mexico—the latest step in a phenomenal takeover of Mexico's supermarket sector. But the expansion north of Mexico City is not just part of WalMart's commercial conquest of Mexico. It is infringing on the cultural foundations of the country. The new store is just 3,000 meters from the Pyramid of the Sun, the tallest structure in the ancient city of Teotihuacan.

3 The Teotihuacan Empire is believed to have begun as early as 200 B.C. Its dominion stretched deep into the heart of Mayan country in Guatemala and throughout present-day Mexico. At its peak, Teotihuacan was a thriving city of about 200,000 inhabitants, but the civilization declined in 700 A.D. under circumstances still shrouded in mystery.

4 Since then, other tribes and civilizations, including the Aztecs and contemporary Mexican society, have claimed the "City of the Gods" as their heritage. The grand human accomplishment it represents and the power of its architectural, historical and, for many, spiritual legacy is central to Mexico's history and culture.

5 While little is known for certain about the rise and fall of Teotihuacan, much is known about the rise of the WalMart empire. From a store in Rogers, Arkansas founded by the Walton brothers in 1962, the enterprise grew in the breathtakingly short period of 42 years into the world's largest company.

6 In Mexico, its conquest of the supermarket sector began by buying up the nation's extensive chain, Aurrerá, beginning in 1992. Today, with 657 stores, Mexico is home to more WalMarts and their affiliates than any other country outside the United States. WalMart is now Mexico's largest private employer, with over 100,000 employees. But recent studies in the United States, where resistance to the megastores has been growing, show that job creation is often job displacement, because WalMarts put local stores out of business, leading to net job losses.

7 WalMart has revolutionized the labor and business world by working cheap and growing big. Labor costs are held down through anti-union policies, the hiring of undocumented workers in the United States, alleged discrimination against women and persons with disabilities, and cutbacks in benefits. Prices paid suppliers are driven down by outsourcing competition. Buoyed by $244.5 billion dollars in annual net sales, the chain can afford to make ever deeper incursions into Mexico's retail sector.

8   A diverse group of local merchants, artists, actors, academics and indigenous organizations are leading the opposition, protesting that the store damages Mexico's rich cultural heritage. Through ceremonies, hunger strikes, demonstrations and press coverage, the movement to defend the site has kept the conflict in the public eye and heightened the public-opinion costs to Wal-Mart. Now opponents have taken their concerns to the Mexican Congress and UNESCO.

9   Some ancient ruins have already been found on the store's new site, and WalMart construction workers told the national daily, *La Jornada,* that they had orders to hide any archaeological relics they found. Normally, the presence of relics requires that further excavation be carried out painstakingly or halted altogether. But the booming WalMart corporation clearly has no time for such delays.

10   The dispute in Teotihuacan today is not a battle between the past and the future. It is a struggle over a country's right to define itself. For defenders of the ancient site, the foremost symbol of the nation's cultural heritage also constitutes part of its contemporary integrity. Modern Mexico is still a country that defines itself by legends, and whose collective identity—unlike its neophyte northern neighbor—reaches back thousands of years.

11   In this context, WalMart is a symbol of the cultural insensitivity of rampant economic integration. While its actions may be technically legal, in the end WalMart could pay a high price for this insensitivity . . . and if there is anything WalMart hates, it is high prices.

Thomas Friedman

Why the World Is Flat

The online magazine *Wired* published the following interview in May 2005. Daniel Pink, the author of several books himself on globalization, as well as numerous articles in the *New York Times*, conducted the interview since he is a contributing editor for *Wired*. Friedman, author and syndicated columnist, is described fully in the introduction.

Thirty-five years ago this summer, the golfer Chi Chi Rodriguez was competing in his seventh U.S. Open, played that year at Hazeltine Country Club outside Minneapolis. Tied for second place after the opening round, Rodriguez eventually finished 27th, a few strokes ahead of such golf legends as Jack Nicklaus, Arnold Palmer, and Gary Player. His caddy for the tournament was a 17-year-old local named Tommy Friedman.

2   Rodriguez retired from golf several years later. But his caddy—now known as Thomas L. Friedman, foreign affairs columnist for *The New York Times* and author of the new book *The World Is Flat: A Brief History of the Twenty-First Century*—has spent his career deploying the skills he used on the golf course: describing the terrain, shouting warnings and encouragement, and whispering in the ears of big players. After ten years of writing his twice-weekly foreign affairs column, Friedman has become the most influential American newspaper columnist since Walter Lippmann.

3   One reason for Friedman's influence is that, in the mid-'90s, he staked out the territory at the intersection of technology, financial markets, and world trade, which the foreign policy establishment, still focused on cruise missiles and throw weights, had largely ignored. "This thing called globalization," he says, "can explain more things in more ways than anything else."

4   Friedman's 1999 book, *The Lexus and the Olive Tree: Understanding Globalization*, provided much of the intellectual framework for the debate. "The first big book on globalization that anybody actually read," as Friedman describes it, helped make him a fixture on the Davos-Allen Conference-Renaissance Weekend circuit. But it also made him a lightning rod. He's been accused of "rhetorical hyperventilation" and dismissed as an "apologist" for global capital. The columnist Molly Ivins even dubbed top-tier society's lack of concern for the downsides of globalization "the Tom Friedman Problem."

5   After 9/11, Friedman says, he paid less attention to globalization. He spent the next three years traveling to the Arab and Muslim world trying to get at the roots of the attack on the U.S. His columns on the subject earned him his third Pulitzer Prize. But Friedman realized that while he was writing about terrorism, he missed an even bigger story: Globalization had gone into overdrive. So in a three-month burst last year, he wrote *The World Is Flat* to explain his updated thinking on the subject.

6   Friedman enlisted some impressive editorial assistance. Bill Gates spent a day with him to critique the theory. Friedman presented sections of the book to the strategic planning unit at IBM and to Michael Dell. But his most important tutors were two Indians: Nandan Nilekani, CEO of Infosys, and Vivek Paul, a top executive at Wipro. "They were the guys who really cracked the code for me."

7   *Wired* sat down with Friedman in his office at the *Times*' Washington bureau to discuss the flattening of the world.

8   **WIRED: What do you mean the world is flat?**
FRIEDMAN: I was in India interviewing Nandan Nilekani at Infosys. And he said to me, "Tom, the playing field is being leveled." Indians and Chinese were going to compete for work like never before, and Americans weren't ready. I kept chewing over that phrase—"the playing field is being leveled"—and then it hit me: Holy mackerel, the world is becoming flat. Several technological and political forces have converged, and that has produced a global, Web-enabled playing field that allows for multiple forms of collaboration without regard to geography or distance—or soon, even language.

9 **So, we're talking about globalization enhanced by things like the rise of open source?**
This is Globalization 3.0. In Globalization 1.0, which began around 1492, the world went from size large to size medium. In Globalization 2.0, the era that introduced us to multinational companies, it went from size medium to size small. And then around 2000 came Globalization 3.0, in which the world went from being small to tiny. There's a difference between being able to make long distance phone calls cheaper on the Internet and walking around Riyadh with a PDA where you can have all of Google in your pocket. It's a difference in degree that's so enormous it becomes a difference in kind.

10 **Is that why the Netscape IPO is one of your "10 flatteners"? Explain.**
Three reasons. Netscape brought the Internet alive with the browser. They made the Internet so that Grandma could use it and her grandchildren could use it. The second thing that Netscape did was commercialize a set of open transmission protocols so that no company could own the Net. And the third is that Netscape triggered the dotcom boom, which triggered the dotcom bubble, which triggered the overinvestment of a trillion dollars in fiber-optic cables.

11 **Are you saying telecommunications trumps terrorism? What about September 11? Isn't that as important?**
There's no question flattening is more important. I don't think you can understand 9/11 without understanding flattening.

12 **This is probably the first book by a major foreign affairs thinker that talks about the world-changing effects of . . . supply chains.**
[*Friedman laughs.*]

13 **Why are supply chains so important?**
They're incredible flatteners. For UPS to work, they've got to create systems with customs offices around the world. They've got to design supply chain algorithms so when you take that box to the UPS Store, it gets from that store to its hub and then out. Everything they are doing is taking fat out of the system at every joint. I was in India after the nuclear alert of 2002. I was interviewing Vivek Paul at Wipro shortly after he'd gotten an email from one of their big American clients saying, "We're now looking for an alternative to you. We don't want to be looking for an alternative to you. You don't *want* us to be looking for an alternative to you. Do something about this!" So I saw the effect that India's being part of this global supply chain had on the behavior of the Indian business community, which eventually filtered up to New Delhi.

14 **And that's how you went from your McDonald's Theory of Conflict Prevention—two countries that have a McDonald's will never go to war with each other—to the Dell Theory of Conflict Prevention.**
Yes. No two countries that are both part of a major global supply chain like Dell's will fight against each other as long as they are both part of that supply chain. When I'm managing your back room, when I'm managing your HR, when I'm doing your accounting—that's way beyond selling you burgers. We are intimately in bed with each other. And that has got to affect my behavior.

15 **In some sense, then, the world is a gigantic supply chain. And you don't want to be the one who brings the whole thing down.**
Absolutely.

16 **Unless your goal is to bring the whole thing down. Supply chains work for al Qaeda, too, don't they?**

Al Qaeda is nothing more than a mutant supply chain. They're playing off the same platform as Wal-Mart and Dell. They're just not restrained by it. What is al Qaeda? It's an open source religious political movement that works off the global supply chain. That's what we're up against in Iraq. We're up against a suicide supply chain. You take one bomber and deploy him in Baghdad, and another is manufactured in Riyadh the next day. It's exactly like when you take the toy off the shelf at Wal-Mart and another is made in Shen Zhen the next day.

17 **The book is almost dizzily optimistic about India and China, about what flattening will bring to these parts of the world.**

I firmly believe that the next great breakthrough in bioscience could come from a 15-year-old who downloads the human genome in Egypt. Bill Gates has a nice line: He says, 20 years ago, would you rather have been a B-student in Poughkeepsie or a genius in Shanghai? Twenty years ago you'd rather be a B-student in Poughkeepsie. Today?

18 **Not even close.**

Not even close. You'd much prefer to be the genius in Shanghai because you can now export your talents anywhere in the world.

19 **As optimistic as you are about that kid in Shanghai, you're not particularly optimistic about the US.**

I'm worried about my country. I love America. I think it's the best country in the world. But I also think we're not tending to our sauce. I believe that we are in what Shirley Ann Jackson [president of Rensselaer Polytechnic Institute] calls a "quiet crisis." If we don't change course now and buckle down in a flat world, the kind of competition our kids will face will be intense and the social implications of not repairing things will be enormous.

The 10 Great Levelers

1. **Fall of the Berlin Wall**
   The events of November 9, 1989, tilted the worldwide balance of power toward democracies and free markets.

2. **Netscape IPO**
   The August 9, 1995, offering sparked massive investment in fiber-optic cables.

3. **Work flow software**
   The rise of apps from PayPal to VPNs enabled faster, closer coordination among far-flung employees.

4. **Open-sourcing**
   Self-organizing communities, a la Linux, launched a collaborative revolution.

5. **Outsourcing**
   Migrating business functions to India saved money *and* a third world economy.

20 **You quote a CEO who says that Americans have grown addicted to their high salaries, and now they're going to have to earn them. Are Americans suffering from an undue sense of entitlement?**
Somebody said to me the other day that—I wish I had this for the book, but it's going to be in the paperback—the entitlement we need to get rid of is our sense of entitlement.

21 **Let's talk about the critics of globalization. You say that you don't want the antiglobalization movement to go away. Why?**
I've been a critic of the antiglobalization movement, and they've been a critic of me, but the one thing I respect about the movement is their authentic energy. These are not people who don't care about the world. But if you want to direct your energy toward helping the poor, I believe the best way is not throwing a stone through a McDonald's window or protesting World Bank meetings. It's through local governance. When you start to improve local governance, you improve education, women's rights, transportation.

22 **It's possible to go through your book and conclude it was written by a US senator who wants to run for president. There's a political agenda in this book.**
Yes, absolutely.

23 **You call for portable benefits, lifelong learning, free trade, greater investment in science, government funding for tertiary education, a system of wage insurance. Uh, Mr. Friedman, are you running for president?**
[*Laughs loudly.*] No, I am not running for president!

6. Offshoring
Contract manufacturing elevated China to economic prominence.

7. Supply-chaining
Robust networks of suppliers, retailers, and customers increased business efficiency. See Wal-Mart.

8. Insourcing
Logistics giants took control of customer supply chains, helping mom-and-pop shops go global. See UPS and FedEx.

9. In-forming
Power searching allowed everyone to use the Internet as a "personal supply chain of knowledge." See Google.

10. Wireless
Like "steroids," wireless technologies pumped up collaboration, making it mobile and personal.

24 **Would you accept the vice presidential nomination?**
I just want to get my Thursday column done!

25 **But you are outlining an explicit agenda.**
You can't be a citizen of this country and not be in a hair-pulling rage at the fact that we're at this inflection moment and nobody seems to be talking about the kind of policies we need to get through this flattening of the world, to get the most out of it and cushion the worst. We need to have as focused, as serious, as energetic, as sacrificing a strategy for dealing with flatism as we did for communism. This is the challenge of our day.

26 **Short of Washington fully embracing the Friedman doctrine, what should we be doing? For instance, what advice should we give to our kids?**
When I was growing up, my parents told me, "Finish your dinner. People in China and India are starving." I tell my daughters, "Finish your homework. People in India and China are starving for your job."

27 **Think about your own childhood for a moment. If a teenage Tommy Friedman could somehow have been transported to 2005, what do you think he would have found most surprising?**
That you could go to PGA.com and get the scores of your favorite golfer in real time. That would have been amazing.

ROBYN **MEREDITH** AND SUZANNE **HOPPOUGH**

Why Globalization Is Good

Robyn Meredith is author of the best-selling book *The Elephant and the Dragon: The Rise of India and China and What it Means for All of Us.* She and her colleague at *Forbes* magazine, Suzanne Hoppough, collaborated on the following excerpt from *The Elephant and the Dragon* and published it in *Forbes* on April 16, 2007.

A ragtag army of save-the-world crusaders has spent years decrying multinational corporations as villains in the wave of globalization overwhelming the Third World. This ominous trend would fatten the rich, further impoverish and oppress the poor, and crush local economies.

2 The business-bashing group Public Citizen argued as much in a proclamation signed by almost 1,500 organizations in 89 countries in 1999. Whereupon hundreds of protesters rioted outside a conference of the World Trade Organization in Seattle, shattering windows, blocking traffic, and confronting cops armed with tear gas and pepper spray. Six hundred people were arrested.

3 Cut to 2007, and the numbers are in: The protesters and do-gooders are just plain wrong. It turns out that globalization is good—and not just for the rich, but *especially* for the poor. The booming economies of India and China—the Elephant and the Dragon—have lifted 200 million people out of abject poverty in the 1990s as

globalization took off, the International Monetary Fund says. Tens of millions more have catapulted themselves far ahead into the middle class.

4   It's remarkable what a few container ships can do to make poor people better off. Certainly more than $2 trillion of foreign aid, which is roughly the amount (with an inflation adjustment) that the U.S. and Europe have poured into Africa and Asia over the past half-century.

5   In the next eight years almost a billion people across Asia will take a Great Leap Forward into a new middle class. In China middle-class incomes are set to rise threefold, to $5,000, predicts Dominic Barton, a Shanghai managing partner for McKinsey & Co.

6   As the Chindia revolution spreads, the ranks of the poor get smaller, not larger. In the 1990s, as Vietnam's economy grew 6% a year, the number of people living in poverty (42 million) fell 7% annually; in Uganda, when GDP growth passed 3%, the number fell 6% per year, says the World Bank.

7   China unleashed its economy in 1978, seeding capitalism first among farmers newly freed to sell the fruits of their fields instead of handing the produce over to Communist Party collectives. Other reforms let the Chinese create 22 million new businesses that now employ 135 million people who otherwise would have remained peasants like the generations before them. Foreign direct investment, the very force so virulently opposed by the do-gooders, has helped drive China's gross domestic product to a more than tenfold increase since 1978. Since the reforms started, $600 billion has flooded into the country, $70 billion of it in the past year. Foreigners built hundreds of thousands of new factories as the Chinese government built the coal mines, power grid, airports, and highways to supply them.

8   As China built infrastructure, it created Special Economic Zones where foreign companies willing to build modern factories could hire cheap labor, go years without paying any taxes, and leave it to government to build the roads and other infrastructure they needed. All of that, in turn, drove China's exports from $970 million to $974 billion in three decades. Those container loads make Americans better off, too. You can get a Chinese DVD at Wal-Mart for $28, and after you do you will buy some $15 movies made in the U.S.A.

9   Per-person income in China has climbed from $16 a year in 1978 to $2,000 now. Wages in factory boomtowns in southern China can run $4 a day—scandalously low in the eyes of the protesters, yet up from pennies a day a generation ago and far ahead of increases in living costs. Middle-class Chinese families now own TVs, live in new apartments, and send their children to private schools. Millions of Chinese have traded in their bicycles for motorcycles or cars. McDonald's has signed a deal with Sinopec, the huge Chinese gasoline retailer, to build drive-through restaurants attached to gas stations on China's new roads.

10   Today 254 Starbucks stores serve coffee in the land of tea, including one at the Great Wall and another at the Forbidden Palace. (The latter is the target of protesters.) In Beijing 54 Starbucks shops thrive, peddling luxury lattes that cost up to $2.85 a cup and paying servers $6 for an 8-hour day. That looks exploitative until you peek inside a nearby Chinese-owned teahouse where the staff works a 12-hour day for $3.75. Says one woman, 23, who works for an international cargo shipper in Beijing: "My parents were both teachers when they were my age, and they earned 30 yuan [$3.70] a month.

I earn 4,000 yuan ($500) a month, live comfortably, and feel I have better opportunities than my parents did."

11   Tony Ma, age 51, was an unwilling foot soldier in Mao's Cultural Revolution. During that dark period from 1966 to 1976 universities were closed, and he was sent at age 16 to work in a steel mill for $2 a month. He cut metal all day long for seven years and feared he might never escape. When colleges reopened, he landed a spot to study chemistry, transferred to the U.S., got a Ph.D. in biochemistry, and signed on with Johnson & Johnson at $45,000 a year. Later he returned to the land he fled and now works for B.F. Goodrich in Hong Kong. The young college grads in China today wouldn't bother immigrating to the U.S. for a job that pays $45,000, he says—because now they have better opportunities at home.

12   Capitalism alone, however, isn't enough to remake Third World economies—globalism is the key. A big reason India trails behind its bigger neighbor to the northeast in lifting the lower classes is that, even after embracing capitalism, it kept barriers to the flow of capital from abroad. Thus 77% of Indians live on $2 a day or less, the Asian Development Bank says, down only nine percentage points from 1990. A third of the population is illiterate. In 1980 India had more of its population in urban centers than China did (23% versus 20% for China). But by 2005 China had 41% in cities, where wages are higher; India's urbanites had grown to only 29%.

13   Freed of British colonial rule in 1947 and scarred by its paternalistic effects, India initially combined capitalism with economic isolationism. It thwarted foreign companies intent on investing there and hampered Indian firms trying to sell abroad. This hurt Indian consumers and local biz: A $100 Microsoft operating system got slapped with duties that brought the price to $250 in India, putting imported software and computers further from reach for most people and businesses. Meanwhile, the government granted workers lavish job protections and imposed heavy taxes and regulations on employers. Government jobs usually were by rote and paid poorly, but they guaranteed lifetime employment. They also ensured economic stagnation.

14   Financial crisis struck in 1991. Desperate for cash, India flew a planeload of gold reserves to London and began, grudgingly, to open its economy. Import duties were lowered or eliminated, so India's consumers and companies could buy modern, foreign-made goods and gear. Overseas firms in many industries were allowed to own their subsidiaries in India for the first time since 1977. India all but banned foreign investment until 1991. Since then foreign companies have come back, but not yet on the scale seen in China. Foreign companies have invested $48 billion in India since 1991—$7.5 billion of that just in the last fiscal year—the same amount dumped into China every six weeks. By the mid-1990s the economy boomed and created millions of jobs.

15   By the late 1990s U.S. tech companies began turning to India for software design, particularly in the Y2K crunch. The Indians proved capable and cheap, and the much-maligned offshoring boom began. Suddenly Indian software engineers were programming corporate America's computers. New college graduates were answering America's customer service phone calls. Builders hired construction workers to erect new high-rise buildings suddenly in demand as American and European firms rushed to hire Indian workers. The new college hires, whose older siblings had graduated without finding a job, tell of surpassing their parents' salaries within five years and of

buying cell phones, then motorcycles, then cars and even houses by the time they were 30. All of that would have been impossible had India failed to add globalization to capitalism.

16   Today, despite its still dilapidated airports and pothole-riddled highways, the lumbering Elephant now is in a trot, growing more than 7% annually for the last decade. In 2005, borrowing from the Chinese, India began a five-year, $150 billion plan to update its roads, airports, ports, and electric plants. India is creating free trade zones, like those in China, to encourage exports of software, apparel, auto parts and more. S.B. Kutwal manages the assembly line where Tata Motors builds Safari SUVs. He remembers how, in the 1980s, people waited five years to buy a scooter and cars were only for the rich. "Since we've liberated the economy, lots of companies have started coming into India," says Kutwal. "People couldn't afford cars then. Now the buying power is coming."

17   In Mumbai (formerly Bombay), Delhi, Bangalore, and other big cities, shopping malls have sprung up, selling everything from Levi's jeans to Versace. India still has raggedy street touts, but when they tap on car windows at stoplights, instead of peddling cheap plastic toys, they sell to the new India: copies of *Vogue* and *House & Garden* magazines. Western restaurants are moving in, too: Domino's Pizza and Ruby Tuesday's have come to India, and 107 McDonald's have sprung up, serving veggie burgers in the land where cattle are sacred.

18   None of this gives pause to an entity called International Forum on Globalization. The group declares that globalism's aim is to "benefit transnational corporations over workers; foreign investors over local businesses; and wealthy countries over developing nations. While promoters . . . proclaim that this model is the rising tide that will lift all boats, citizen movements find that it is instead lifting only yachts."

19   "The majority of people in rich and poor countries aren't better off" since the World Trade Organization formed in 1995 to promote global trade, asserts Christopher Slevin, deputy director of Global Trade Watch, an arm of Ralph Nader's Public Citizen. "The breadth of the opposition has grown. It's not just industrial and steel workers and people who care about animal rights. It includes high-tech workers and the offshoring of jobs, also the faith-based community."

20   While well-off American techies may be worried, it seems doubtful that an engineer in Bangalore who now earns $40,000 a year, and who has just bought his parents' house, wants to ban foreign investment.

21   Slevin's further complaint is that globalism is a creature of WTO, the World Bank and other unelected bodies. But no, the people do have a voice in the process, and it is one that is equivocal on the matter of free market capitalism. The Western World's huge agriculture subsidies—$85 billion or more annually, between the U.S., Japan, and the European Union—are decreed by democratically elected legislatures. The EU pays ranchers $2 per cow in daily subsidies, more than most Indians earn. If these farmers weren't getting handouts, and if trade in farm products were free, then poor farmers in the Third World could sell more of their output, and could begin to lift themselves out of poverty.

Sadanand
Dhume

Slumdog Paradox

Sadanand Dhume is a writer who is based in Washington, D.C. Having lived in Asia from 1999 to 2004, he is an expert on Asian affairs and the author of *My Friend the Fanatic: Travels with a Radical Islamist*, a travel narrative about the rise of Muslim fundamentalism in Indonesia. His writing has been published in the *Washington Post, Forbes, Commentary,* and *YaleGlobal Online,* where the following essay appeared on February 9, 2009.

The unexpected international success of *Slumdog Millionaire* has pleased some Indians while provoking unusually strong protests from others. The critical and commercial success of the film, contrasted with sharp criticism and a lackluster run in Indian theaters, captures the inherent contradictions of an increasingly globalized country. India basks in the glow of international recognition, but resents the critical scrutiny that global exposure brings.

2   Not since Sir Richard Attenborough's *Gandhi* has a film about India captured the world's imagination as strongly as *Slumdog Millionaire,* director Danny Boyle's gritty yet uplifting drama about a boy from the slums of Mumbai who makes good as a game-show contestant on the Indian version of *Who Wants to Be a Millionaire.* The low-budget production—which cost $15 million to make, a pittance in Hollywood terms—has garnered both commercial and critical success, grossing $96 million worldwide as of February 1st, and picking up four Golden Globe awards and 10 Oscar nominations. In one among a raft of glowing reviews, the *Wall Street Journal*'s Joe Morgenstern hailed *Slumdog* as "the world's first globalized masterpiece."

3   In India, however, the response to the film has been ambivalent. Commercially, it has failed to replicate its American success. Despite a wave of publicity and an ambitious nationwide rollout, *Slumdog* is showing in half-empty theaters. It trails the box-office receipts of an obscure Hindi horror movie released the same day. And though some Indian reviewers praised the film for everything from inspired casting to an improbable Bollywoodish storyline, it also attracted its share of brickbats. On his blog, Bollywood star Amitabh Bachchan struck a populist note: "If SM projects India as [a] third-world, dirty, underbelly developing nation and causes pain and disgust among nationalists and patriots, let it be known that a murky underbelly exists and thrives even in the most developed nations." The critic Meenakshi Shedde dismissed the film as "a laundry list of India's miseries." Interviewed in the *Los Angeles Times,* film professor Shyamal Sengupta called the film "a white man's imagined India."

Young Jamal (Ayush Mahesh Khedekar) runs through the alleys of Mumbai in a scene from *Slumdog Millionaire* (2008).

4   In many ways, *Slumdog Millionaire* is a metaphor for India in the age of globalization. The director, Danny Boyle, and screenwriter, Simon Beaufoy, are British. The male lead, Dev Patel, who plays the part of the quiz-show contestant Jamal, is a Gujarati whose family migrated to London from Nairobi. His love interest, Latika, is played by Freida Pinto, a Catholic girl from Mumbai, India's most cosmopolitan city. The novel upon which the film is loosely based, *Q and A,* was written by an Indian diplomat currently stationed in South Africa. The television game show *Who Wants to Be a Millionaire,* which supplies the film's narrative backbone, is another British creation. Adapted in more than 50 countries, the show is recognizable to audiences from Beijing to Buenos Aires.

5   The film's success also underscores India's emergence on the world stage. Indeed, the superficial similarities with Ang Lee's *Crouching Tiger, Hidden Dragon,* the 2001 blockbuster set in Qing dynasty China, are striking. Both films draw on the talents of a widespread diaspora: Michelle Yeoh, Dev Patel. Like *Crouching Tiger, Slumdog* taps into Western curiosity about a country whose weight is increasingly felt in ordinary lives. Service workers in the West worry about being "Bangalored," or losing their jobs to less expensive competitors in India. Credit-card and consumer-appliance users routinely deal with customer-service professionals in Gurgaon or Hyderabad. In America, one no longer

has to live in a big city to be familiar with yoga or chicken tikka masala. An Indian company, Tata Motors, owns the iconic automobile brands Jaguar and Land Rover. India-born professionals helm Pepsi and Citibank. Salman Rushdie and Jhumpa Lahiri occupy a similarly exalted place in fiction. To sum up, it seems unlikely that a story set in the slums of Manila or Jakarta would find nearly as large an audience in Boston or Baton Rouge.

6   For India, one of the most autarkic and culturally inward-looking countries in Asia until the advent of economic reforms in 1991, the benefits of globalization are easily apparent. In purchasing power parity terms, per capita income more than doubled from $1,400 in 1991 to $3,800 in 2006. The ranks of the middle class, broadly defined, have swelled to more than 250 million people. More Indians buy cell phones each month than any other people.

7   The same story can be told on the corporate and macroeconomic level. Since liberalization, a dozen Indian firms—spanning banking, pharmaceuticals, software, and services—have listed on the New York Stock Exchange, and three on the technology-heavy NASDAQ. The United Nations Conference on Trade and Development estimates that a record $36.7 billion of foreign direct investment flowed into India in 2008. Foreign-exchange reserves stand at a robust $250 billion.

8   There are less tangible changes as well. For generations after independence from Britain in 1947, more or less the only way for an Indian to make a mark on the world stage was to emigrate. A. R. Rahman, the Chennai-based composer of the *Slumdog* soundtrack, has not needed to change the color of his passport to snag a Golden Globe or multiple Oscar nominations. In a broader sense, the same holds true for many of the scientists and engineers who work for General Electric or Microsoft in Bangalore, or for the employees of a clutch of ambitious homegrown pharmaceutical companies with global ambition. India may not quite be center-stage—its contribution to world trade remains a slender 1.5 percent—but neither is it off-stage anymore. If an ambitious government target is met, the country's share of world trade will more than triple to 5 percent by 2020.

9   Notwithstanding the giant strides made over the past 18 years, Indian criticism of *Slumdog* also reveals the chasm between the country's self-perception and projection and any reasonable measure of its achievements. India may boast homegrown programs in space exploration and nuclear power, but—as a first time visitor to India immediately notices and as the film mercilessly reveals—it also struggles to provide its people with electricity, sanitation, and drinking water. About half of Indian women are illiterate, a higher percentage than in Laos, Cambodia, or Myanmar. It is at number 122—between Nepal and

Lesotho—on the World Bank index that measures ease of doing business, and 85 on the global corruption index maintained by the anti-graft NGO Transparency International. To put it bluntly, the squalor of the slums depicted in *Slumdog* is closer to reality than an elaborately choreographed Bollywood dance sequence shot on location in Switzerland.

10   To sum up, by jettisoning socialism and embracing globalization India has become more prosperous than at any time in more than six decades of independence. But the effects of failed policies pursued between 1947 and 1991 cannot be erased overnight. As *Slumdog* reveals, India is doing better than ever only when benchmarked against its own dismal past. When compared to the West, or to East Asian countries that have truly transformed themselves—Japan, Taiwan, and Korea—the gap between India's rhetoric and its reality remains jarring. *Slumdog* may wound national pride, but the answer is more openness not less. As long as chronic poverty remains a central fact of Indian life, the spotlight that globalization brings will shine on India's software success as well as on its slums.

Jamal Malik (Dev Patel) appears on the game show *Who Wants to Be a Millionaire?* in a scene from *Slumdog Millionaire* (2008).

Immigration

In June 2007, a group called the Fair Immigration Reform Movement organized a march on Washington, D.C., to protest immigration laws that force families to live apart. By using the strollers and the posters, what values are the protesters appealing to?

Just about everyone can quote the famous words that Emma Lazarus wrote for the pedestal of the Statue of Liberty ("Give me your tired, your poor, your huddled masses yearning to breathe free, the wretched refuse of your teeming shore. Send these, the homeless, tempest-tost to me") because the United States prides itself on being a nation of immigrants. And recently we have made good on the promise: more than 10 percent of our people, over 30 million in all (up from 10 million in 1970), were born in other countries. Indeed, according to the most recent census, one in five U.S. citizens was born either abroad or to foreign-born parents. Steady increases in legal immigration after World War II developed into a boom during the 1980s and 1990s in part because the 1965 Immigration Act (amended in 1990) looked favorably on the immigration of relatives of U.S. citizens; repealed quotas on immigrants from certain nations; and therefore encouraged immigration from Asia, Latin America, and Africa. As a result, in 2008 and 2009 well over a million people were still immigrating legally to the United States, despite the economic recession. (An estimated 11 million other people were residing here illegally.) While immigrants in the late nineteenth and early twentieth centuries mostly came from southern and central Europe, most of today's immigrants come from Mexico; the Caribbean islands; the former Soviet Union; and Asian nations such as China, Vietnam, the Philippines, and India. While earlier immigrants typically passed by the Statue of Liberty and were processed at Ellis Island before going on to northern cities, more than half of recent immigrants have been attracted to Florida, Texas, and California.

Nevertheless, there has also been a long history of resistance to immigration in the United States, dating at least to those who proudly enrolled in the Know Nothing political party of the 1840s and 1850s. Members of that political faction resisted the immigrants from Ireland and Germany who were arriving in waves, and they tended to blame all the nation's ills on immigration—crime, economic problems, and social stresses. The questions (and fears) raised by those early critics persist today, except that now they are raised in connection with Asians, Arabs, and Latin Americans. Just what are the social and economic effects of immigration? How quickly and how completely do immigrants become assimilated—learning the majority language, identifying themselves with American cultural values, and participating in American political life? What is our national responsibility to support, educate, and help assimilate immigrants? Do immigrants constitute a threat to the nation's economic well-being because they are commonly poor and less educated, because they take jobs away from native workers, and because they require expensive social services, such as welfare, education, and health? Or do immigrants actually increase the nation's wealth because they are highly motivated and because they supply labor to a perennially labor-hungry economy? Do immigrants endanger our democracy because they cling to

The Statue of Liberty

their original national identities, are slow to learn English, and participate only fitfully in political life—or do immigrants enrich the nation with their values and beliefs, ideas and ideals, and hopes and hard work? Do immigrants pose a threat to national security?

This section provides diverse perspectives on immigration, as do selections included elsewhere in *Good Reasons*. Patrick Buchanan's 1990 speech "To Reunite a Nation," delivered in California while he was a presidential candidate in the Republican party, still represents the point of view of those who have been resisting immigration. In "No Human Being Is Illegal," Mae Ngai (a professor of history at the University of Chicago, where she specializes in immigration studies) takes a balanced look at the stereotypes of immigrants in the United States. The essay, published in Women's *Studies Quarterly* in 2006, challenges readers to rethink the stereotypes we use to label immigrants and raises fundamental questions about what it means to participate in American society with and without the privilege of citizenship. The words to songwriter and singer Phil Ochs's "Bracero" provide an ironic and sarcastic perspective on American treatment of immigrants from Mexico, and the distinguished journalist Lance Morrow, writing in *Smithsonian* magazine in 2009, argues that symbolism associated with immigrants has been absolutely central to our national civic and political identity

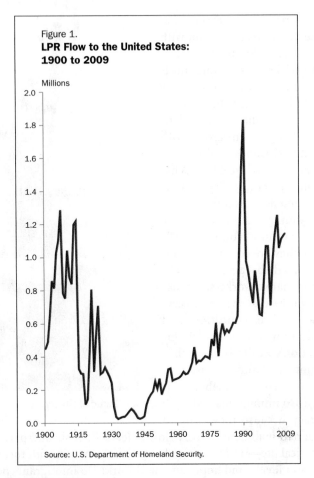

Figure 1.
**LPR Flow to the United States:
1900 to 2009**

Source: U.S. Department of Homeland Security.

Legal immigration, 1900–2009
Source: U.S. Department of Homeland Security

Finally, elsewhere in this book, you will find more voices in the serious debates that surround immigration. In "Crossing the Line" (page 176), Dan Stein argues that illegal immigrants are being dangerously welcomed when banks issue them credit cards. Responding to Stein, Gregory Rodriguez argues in "Illegal Immigrants—They're Money" (page 178) that people who have come to the United States to work should not be denied the opportunity for credit that other Americans enjoy. For a compelling narrative argument about brutalities associated with U.S. immigration policy, turn to Leslie Marmon Silko's "The Border Patrol State" (page 160), which relates the experience of being pulled over by the border police.

Silko's argument, which was written in 1994, gained new resonance in 2010, when the Arizona legislature passed a state law making it a crime to be in the United States illegally. Until that time, illegal immigration was considered a federal matter and enforcement was left to Washington; but the new Arizona law not only transformed police into border patrollers but also required immigrants—indeed, all citizens—to carry proof of their legal status, a requirement that angered even many conservatives (such as the U.S. Catholic bishops). The law also invited racial profiling by police who would have little reason to suspect illegality except for physical appearance. The outraged objections to this law—which were overturned, at least temporarily, by a federal judge on July 28, 2010—and the equally passionate defenses of it once again revealed how deeply divided Americans are over this important issue.

A Time Line on Immigration

1607. The first permanent English settlement at Jamestown, Virginia, is established.

1607–1776. "Open Door" era: individual colonies encourage immigration, restricting only criminals and "undesirables."

1776–1835. The "First Great Lull" in immigration: immigration numbers are low.

1808. Importation of slaves is halted.

1840s. Irish immigration (as a result of famine) initiates an era of mass immigration that lasts until World War I.

1875. The Supreme Court decides that immigration policy is the responsibility of the federal government, not the states.

1882–1917. Asian immigration is effectively interdicted. The 1882 Chinese Exclusion Act bars Chinese in particular.

1892. Ellis Island in New York Harbor becomes the leading entry point for immigrants.

1890–1920. A wave of immigration from southern and eastern Europe peaks at 1.3 million in 1907.

1921. Quotas are initiated to reduce immigration sharply and to make immigration reflect the established face of the American community (i.e., white and European).

1920–1945. Second "Great Lull" in immigration: more restrictive immigration policies, the effects of the Great Depression, and the Second World War limit the number of immigrants who settle in the United States.

1940s. Restrictions on Asian immigration are dropped.

1954. Operation Wetback effectively stops illegal immigration.

1965. The Immigration and Nationality Act increases immigration quotas, abolishes the principle of taking into account immigrants' national origins, and emphasizes family unification.

1986. The Immigration Reform and Control Act provides amnesty for many illegal immigrants.

1990s and 2000s. Immigration numbers increase substantially—for both legal and illegal immigrants.

Basic sources: Peter Brimelow, *Alien Nation; CQ Researcher*

Immigration Web Sites

You can learn more about immigration and read more arguments about it at a number of places on the World Wide Web. Here are a few:

The U. S. Department of Homeland Security, U.S. Citizenship and Immigration Services, administers and enforces U.S. immigration policy. For information check the Office of Immigration Statistics at uscis.gov/graphics/shared/statistics/index.htm.

For information about immigration from the **U.S. Census Bureau,** see www.census.gov/main/www/cen2000.html.

The Cato Institute offers demographic and economic statistics about immigrants: www. cato.org.

The Alexis de Tocqueville Institution works to increase public understanding of the cultural and economic benefits of immigration: www.adti.net.

The Center for Immigration Studies conducts research on the impact of immigration: www.cis.org.

The Federation for American Immigration Reform (FAIR) lobbies in favor of placing restrictions on immigration: www.fairus.org.

The National Council of La Raza lobbies on behalf of Latinos in the United States: www.nclr.org.

The National Immigration Forum builds public support for immigration: www.immigrationforum.org.

The Immigration History Research Center, based at the University of Minnesota, is a substantial resource on American immigration and ethnic history: www. ihrc.umn.edu.

Waiting on the Mexican side of the Rio Grande

Patrick J. Buchanan

To Reunite a Nation

L et me begin with a story: In 1979, Deng Xiaoping arrived here on an official visit. China was emerging from the Cultural Revolution, and poised to embark on the capitalist road. When President Carter sat down with Mr. Deng, he told him he was concerned over the right of the Chinese people to emigrate. The Jackson-Vanik Amendment, Mr. Carter said, prohibited granting most favored nation trade status to regimes that did not allow their people to emigrate.

2   "Well, Mr. President," Deng cheerfully replied, "Just how many Chinese do you want? Ten million? Twenty million? Thirty million?" Deng's answer stopped Carter cold. In a few words, the Chinese leader had driven home a point Mr. Carter seemed not to have grasped: Hundreds of millions of people would emigrate to America in an eyelash, for more than we could take in, far more than our existing population of 270 million, if we threw open our borders. And though the U.S. takes in more people than any other nation, it still restricts immigration to about one million a year, with three or four hundred thousand managing to enter every year illegally.

3   There is more to be gleaned from this encounter. Mr. Carter's response was a patriotic, or, if you will, a nationalistic response. Many might even label it xenophobic. The president did not ask whether bringing in ten million Chinese would be good for them. He had suddenly grasped that the real issue was how many would be good for America? Mr. Carter could have asked another question: Which Chinese immigrants would be best for America? It would make a world of difference whether China sent over ten million college graduates or ten million illiterate peasants, would it not?

4   Since the Carter-Deng meeting America has taken in twenty million immigrants, many from China and Asia, many more from Mexico, Central America and the Caribbean, and a few from Europe. Social scientists now know a great deal about the impact of this immigration.

5   Like all of you, I am awed by the achievements of many recent immigrants. Their contributions to Silicon Valley are extraordinary. The over-representation of Asian-born kids in advanced high school math and science classes is awesome, and, to the extent that it is achieved by a superior work ethic, these kids are setting an example for all of us. The contributions that immigrants make in small businesses and hard work in tough jobs that don't pay well merits our admiration and deepest respect. And many new immigrants show a visible love of the country and an appreciation of freedom that makes you proud to be an American.

6   Northern Virginia, where I live, has experienced a huge and sudden surge in immigration. It has become a better place, in some ways, but nearly unrecognizable in others, and no doubt worse in some realms, a complicated picture overall. But it is clear to anyone living in a state like California or Virginia that the great immigration wave, set in motion by the Immigration Act of 1965, has put an indelible mark upon America.

7   We are no longer a biracial society; we are now a multiracial society. We no longer struggle simply to end the divisions and close the gaps between black and white Americans; we now grapple, often awkwardly, with an unprecedented ethnic diversity. We also see the troubling signs of a national turning away from the idea that we are one people, and the emergence of a radically different idea, that we are separate ethnic nations within a nation.

8   Al Gore caught the change in a revealing malapropism. Mr. Gore translated the national slogan "E Pluribus Unum," which means "Out of many one," into "Out of one, many." Behind it, an inadvertent truth: America is Balkanizing as never before.

9   Five years ago, a bipartisan presidential commission, chaired by Barbara Jordan, presented its plans for immigration reform. The commission called for tighter border controls, tougher penalties on businesses that hire illegal aliens, a new system for selecting legal immigrants, and a lowering of the annual number to half a million. President Clinton endorsed the recommendations. But after ethnic groups and corporate lobbies for foreign labor turned up the heat, he backed away.

10   The data that support the Jordan recommendations are more refined today. We have a National Academy of Sciences report on the economic consequences of immigration, a Rand study, and work by Harvard's George Borjas and other scholars. All agree that new immigration to the United States is heavily skewed to admitting the less skilled. Unlike other industrialized democracies, the U.S. allots the vast majority of its visas on the basis of whether new immigrants are related to recent immigrants, rather than whether they have the skills or education America needs. This is why it is so difficult for Western and Eastern Europeans to come here, while almost entire villages from El Salvador have come in.

11   Major consequences flow from having an immigration stream that ignores education or skills. Immigrants are now more likely than native-born Americans to lack a high school education. More than a quarter of our immigrant population receives some kind of welfare, compared to fifteen percent of native-born. Before the 1965 bill, immigrants were less likely to receive welfare. In states with many immigrants, the fiscal impact is dramatic. The National Academy of Sciences contends that immigration has raised the annual taxes of each native household in California by $1,200 a year. But the real burden is felt by native-born workers, for whom mass immigration means stagnant or falling wages, especially for America's least skilled.

12   There are countervailing advantages. Businesses can hire new immigrants at lower pay; and consumers gain because reduced labor costs produce cheaper goods and services. But, generally speaking, the gains from high immigration go to those who use the services provided by new immigrants.

13   If you are likely to employ a gardener or housekeeper, you may be financially better off. If you work as a gardener or housekeeper, or at a factory job in which unskilled immigrants are rapidly joining the labor force, you lose. The last twenty years of immigration have thus brought about a redistribution of wealth in America, from less-skilled workers and toward employers. Mr. Borjas estimates that one half of the relative fall in the wages of high school graduates since the 1980s can be traced directly to mass immigration.

14   At some point, this kind of wealth redistribution, from the less well off to the affluent, becomes malignant. In the 1950s and '60s, Americans with low reading and math

scores could aspire to and achieve the American dream of a middle class lifestyle. That is less realistic today. Americans today who do poorly in high school are increasingly condemned to a low-wage existence; and mass immigration is a major reason why.

15   There is another drawback to mass immigration: a delay in the assimilation of immigrants that can deepen our racial and ethnic divisions. As in Al Gore's "Out of one, many."

16   Concerns of this sort are even older than the Republic itself. In 1751, Ben Franklin asked: "Why should Pennsylvania, founded by the English, become a Colony of Aliens, who will shortly be so numerous as to Germanize us instead of our Anglifying them?" Franklin would never find out if his fears were justified. German immigration was halted by the Seven Years' War; then slowed by the Great Lull in immigration that followed the American Revolution. A century and half later, during what is called the Great Wave, the same worries were in the air.

17   In 1915 Theodore Roosevelt told the Knights of Columbus: "There is no room in this country for hyphenated Americanism. . . . The one absolutely certain way of bringing this nation to ruin, of preventing all possibility of its continuing to be a nation at all, would be to permit it to become a tangle of squabbling nationalities." Congress soon responded by enacting an immigration law that brought about a virtual forty-year pause to digest, assimilate, and Americanize the diverse immigrant wave that had rolled in between 1890 and 1920.

18   Today, once again, it is impossible not to notice the conflicts generated by a new "hyphenated Americanism." In Los Angeles, two years ago, there was an anguishing afternoon in the Coliseum where the U.S. soccer team was playing Mexico. The Mexican-American crowd showered the U.S. team with water bombs, beer bottles and trash. The "Star Spangled Banner" was hooted and jeered. A small contingent of fans of the American team had garbage hurled at them. The American players later said that they were better received in Mexico City than in their own country.

19   Last summer, El Cenizo, a small town in south Texas, adopted Spanish as its official language. All town documents are now to be written, and all town business conducted, in Spanish. Any official who cooperates with U.S. immigration authorities was warned he or she would be fired. To this day, Governor Bush is reluctant to speak out on this de facto secession of a tiny Texas town to Mexico.

20   Voting in referendums that play a growing part in the politics of California is now breaking down sharply on ethnic lines. Hispanic voters opposed Proposition 187 to cut off welfare to illegal aliens, and they rallied against it under Mexican flags. They voted heavily in favor of quotas and ethnic preferences in the 1996 California Civil Rights Initiative, and, again, to keep bilingual education in 1998. These votes suggest that in the California of the future, when Mexican-American voting power catches up with Mexican-American population, any bid to end racial quotas by referendum will fail. A majority of the state's most populous immigrant group now appears to favor set-asides and separate language programs, rather than to be assimilated into the American mainstream.

21   The list of troubling signs can be extended. One may see them in the Wen Ho Lee nuclear secrets case, as many Chinese-Americans immediately concluded the United States was prosecuting Mr. Lee for racist reasons.

22   Regrettably, a cultural Marxism called political correctness is taking root that makes it impossible to discuss immigration in any but the most glowing terms. In New

York City billboards that made the simple point that immigration increases crowding and that polls show most Americans want immigration rates reduced were forced down under circumstances that came very close to government-sponsored censorship. The land of the free is becoming intolerant of some kinds of political dissent.

23   Sociologist William Frey had documented an out-migration of black and white Americans from California, some of them seeking better labor market conditions, others in search of a society like the one they grew up in. In California and other high-immigration states, one also sees the rise of gated communities where the rich close themselves off from the society their own policies produce.

24   I don't want to overstate the negatives. But in too many cases the American melting pot has been reduced to a simmer. At present rates, mass immigration reinforces ethnic subcultures, reduces the incentives of newcomers to learn English and extends the life of linguistic ghettos that might otherwise be melded into the great American mainstream. If we want to assimilate new immigrants—and we have no choice if we are to remain one nation—we must slow down the peace of immigration.

25   Whatever its shortcomings, the United States has done far better at alleviating poverty than most countries. But an America that begins to think of itself as made up of disparate peoples will find social progress far more difficult. It is far easier to look the other way when the person who needs help does not speak the same language, or share a common culture or common history.

26   Americans who feel it natural and right that their taxes support the generation that fought World War II—will they feel the same way about those from Fukien Province or Zanzibar? If America continues on its present course, it could rapidly become a country with no common language, no common culture, no common memory and no common identity. And that country will find itself very short of the social cohesion that makes compassion possible.

27   None of us are true universalists: we feel responsibility for others because we share with them common bonds—common history and a common fate. When these are gone, this country will be a far harsher place.

28   That is why I am proposing immigration reform to make it possible to fully assimilate the thirty million immigrants who have arrived in the last thirty years. As president, I will ask Congress to reduce new entry visas to 300,000 a year, which is enough to admit immediate family members of new citizens, with plenty of room for many thousands with the special talents or skills our society needs. If after several years, it becomes plain that the United States needs more immigrants because of labor shortages, it should implement a point system similar to that of Canada and Australia, and allocate visas on a scale which takes into account education, knowledge of English, job skills, age, and relatives in the United States.

29   I will also make the control of illegal immigration a national priority. Recent reports of thousands of illegals streaming across the border into Arizona, and the sinister and cruel methods used to smuggle people by ship into the United States, demand that we regain control of our borders. For a country that cannot control its borders isn't fully sovereign; indeed, it is not even a country anymore.

30   Without these reforms, America will begin a rapid drift into uncharted waters. We shall become a country with a dying culture and deepening divisions along the lines of race, class, income and language. We shall lose for our children and for the children of

the thirty million who have come here since 1970 the last best hope of earth. We will betray them all—by denying them the great and good country we were privileged to grow in. We just can't do that.

31   With immigration at the reduced rate I recommend, America will still be a nation of immigrants. We will still have the benefit of a large, steady stream of people from all over the world whose life dream is to be like us—Americans. But, with this reform, America will become again a country engaged in the mighty work of assimilation, of shaping new Americans, a proud land where newcomers give up their hyphens, the great American melting pot does its work again, and scores of thousands of immigrant families annually ascend from poverty into the bosom of Middle America to live the American dream. ■

unitedmedia.com EMAIL: hpayne@detnews.com ©02 DETROIT NEWS

"THE BAD NEWS IS OPERATION ANACONDA DEVASTATED OUR FORCES. THE GOOD NEWS IS THE AMERICAN INS APPROVED YOUR VISA."

Henry Payne reprinted by permission of United Feature Syndicate, Inc.

Mae M. Ngai

No Human Being Is Illegal

Like abortion and guns, immigration has emerged as a hot-button issue in American politics. Because immigration involves concerns in different registers, economic and cultural, it is strangely and perhaps uniquely misaligned in traditional partisan terms (Wong 2006; Zolberg 2006). President Bush cannot manage the split in his own party, between those Republicans who want to exploit immigrants and those who want to expel them. Among Democratic voters, some support cultural diversity and inclusion while others worry that cheaper immigrant labor depresses domestic wages. Political consultants, sensing a no-win situation, are advising Democrats with presidential aspirations to stay clear of the issue altogether.

2   The lack of partisan coherence, however, does not explain why immigration evokes such heated debate. There is a dimension to the debate that seems irrational, impervious to arguments involving empirical data, historical experience, or legal precedent. This was brought home to me after I wrote an op-ed in a major newspaper about how, during the first half of the twentieth century, the U.S. government legalized tens of thousands of illegal European immigrants (Ngai 2006). I received postcards with invectives like, "stupid professor!" I faced similar hostility during a live call-in show on public radio. Confronted with ranting about how immigrants are bad for the United States,

Phil Ochs

Bracero

Wade into the river
Through the rippling shallow water
Steal across the thirsty border
Bracero

Come bring your hungry bodies
To the golden fields of plenty
From a peso to a penny
Bracero

Oh, welcome to California
Where the friendly farmers
Will take care of you
Come labor for your mother
For your father and your brother
For your sisters and your lover
Bracero

Come pick the fruits of yellow
Break the flowers from the berries
Purple grapes will fill your bellies
Bracero

Oh, Welcome to California
Where the friendly farmers
Will take care of you
And the sun will bite your body
As the dust will draw you thirsty
While your muscles beg for mercy
Bracero

I wanted to counter that immigrants are good for the United States. At one level, negative generalizations about immigrants can be refuted point by point: they do not hurt the economy, they expand it; they are more law abiding than the native-born population; they want to learn English and their children all do (Smith and Edmonston 1997; Alba and Nee 2003).

3   But this approach is risky. Generalizations reproduce stereotypes and efface the complexity and diversity of immigrant experience. As Bonnie Honig (2001) has argued, xenophilia is the flip side of xenophobia. In both cases citizens use "immigrants" as a screen onto which they project their own aspirations or frustrations about American democracy. Casting immigrants as bearers of the work ethic, family values, and consensual citizenship renews the tired citizen's faith-liberal capitalism.

In the shade of your sombrero
Drop your sweat upon the soil
Like the fruit your youth can spoil
Bracero

Oh, welcome to California
Where the friendly farmers
Will take care of you
When the weary night embraces
Sleep in shacks that could be cages
They will take it from your wages
Bracero

Come sing about tomorrow
With a jingle of the dollars
And forget your crooked collar
Bracero

Oh, welcome to California
Where the friendly farmers
Will take care of you
And the local men are lazy
And they make too much of trouble
Besides we'd have to pay them double
Bracero

Ah, but if you feel you're fallin'
If you find the pace is killing
There are others who are willing
Bracero

Oh, welcome to California
Where the friendly farmers
Will take care of you

But when the immigrants disappoint or when conditions change, they become easy scapegoats.

4   As Honig suggests, this kind of immigration discourse is an exercise in nationalism. In an important sense, "Are immigrants good or bad for us?" is the wrong question. It takes as its premise that immigrants are not part of "us." The idea falsely posits that non-citizens are not part of American society and leaves them out of the discussion. The mass demonstrations of Mexicans and other immigrants last spring were significant because they showed that immigrants are no longer content to be the object of discussion but have emerged as subjects with voice and agency. It was particularly noteworthy but perhaps not surprising that so many of the participants were female, from older hotel workers to high school students, giving lie to the stereotypes that the "illegal alien" is a solo male laborer or that immigrants are meek. Undocumented immigration involves men, women, and families, and they are all standing up.

5   Further, the question assumes that "we" (the United States, defined by its citizens) have a singular interest above and against the interests of "them" (all non-citizens and the foreign countries from whence they came). To be sure, while human migration is as old as human history, immigration and naturalization are modern phenomena, part of the international system based on nation-states that was consolidated in the period between the late nineteenth century and World War I. In this system, sovereign nations assert their absolute right to determine, in the first instance, who shall be admitted to territory and membership and who shall not.

6   In the United States, immigration was not regulated by the federal government until after the civil war, and not until the late 1880s and 1890s did the U.S. Supreme Court invoke the sovereign principle as the basis for immigration policy. Before that, it considered immigration part of the commerce clause of the Constitution; as laborers, immigrants were easily imagined as "articles of commerce" (Bilder 1996).

7   But Chinese exclusion, first legislated in 1882, required the Court to justify why some laborers were desired and others were not. Was the claim that Chinese were racially inassimilable an acceptable reason? The Court said yes; in fact, it said that Congress did not have to justify itself in terms of the Constitution. In the Chinese Exclusion Case (130 U.S. 518 [1889]) the Court recognized Congress's plenary, or absolute power to regulate immigration as part of its authority over foreign relations, in the same realm as declaring war and making treaties. "Aliens enter and remain in the United States only with the license, permission, and sufferance of Congress," it opined (Fong Yue Ting v. U.S., 149 U.S. 698 [1893]). To this day the plenary power doctrine over immigration stands.

8   American political culture has thoroughly normalized the primacy of national sovereignty in immigration affairs, and with important consequences. Nationalism generates the view that immigration is a zero-sum game among competitive nation-states. Americans like to believe that immigration to the United States proves the superiority of liberal capitalism, that "America" is the object of global envy; we resist examining the role that American world power has played in global structures of migration, including the gendered dimensions of migrant exploitation. Increasing numbers of women from

the global south are leaving their families behind as they migrate to the affluent countries to work as caretakers for other people's children, as hotel-room cleaners, or as indentured sex-workers. We prefer to ignore these realities and to think, instead, that our immigration policy is generous—indeed, too generous, as we also resent the demands made upon us by others and we think we owe outsiders nothing (Ngai 2004).

9   The emphasis on national sovereignty is the basis for the alarm that we've "lost control" of the border and for the draconian proposals against unauthorized immigration: more fencing, criminalization of the undocumented and those who hire or assist them, mass deportations. But many liberals who are sympathetic to Mexican immigrants also want "something done" to stop illegal immigration, although few would actually support turning the entire country into a police state, which is what would be necessary to truly seal the border from unauthorized entry. The cost of viewing sovereignty as the exclusive grounds for immigration policy is that we push to the margins other considerations, such as human rights and global distributive justice. The current debate over immigration policy reform reminds us that sovereignty is not just a claim to national right; it is a theory of power (Carens 1998).

10   Just two months before September 11, 2001, it will be recalled, President Bush announced his intention to legalize undocumented Mexican immigrants and institute a guest-worker program that would offer a path to permanent residency and citizenship. In its details it was not particularly generous and it faced a complex process of legislative negotiation, as have all efforts to reform the immigration laws. But it did not provoke the kind of emotional controversy that we hear today.

11   However, after 9/11 the immigration issue disappeared from the Washington scene. It resurfaced a couple of years ago, with Bush's proposal receiving support from then-president of Mexico, Vicente Fox. But only in the last year has it become an explosive issue in national politics, with vociferous rhetoric like "stop the invasion" and "no amnesty for lawbreakers." It seems no accident that immigration restriction has moved to the fore as public disaffection with the war in Iraq grows. According to Republican strategist Don Allen, immigration is an issue that "gets us talking about security and law and order" (Hulse 2006). House majority leader Dennis Hastert deploys flexible rhetoric of popular sovereignty most succinctly: "We're at war. Our borders are a sieve" (Swarns 2006). Whether mongering terrorism and illegal immigration will result in greater mass support for U.S. wars against both will succeed remains to be seen. But the very connections made between them suggest broad ground for oppositional action.

WORKS CITED

Alba, Richard, and Victor Nee. 2003. *Remaking the American Mainstream.* Cambridge: Harvard University Press.

Bilder, Mary Sarah. 1996. "The Struggle over Immigration: Indentured Servants, Slaves, and Articles of Commerce," *Missouri Law Review.*

Carens, Joseph. 1998. "Aliens and Citizens: The Case for Open Borders," in *The Immigration Reader: America in Multidisciplinary Perspective,* ed. David Jacobson. Malden, MA: Blackwell Publications.

Wiley Miller has been writing *Non Sequitur* since 1991 and has won four National Cartoonist Society awards. This cartoon appeared in 2002.

Honig, Bonnie. 2001. *Democracy and the Foreigner.* Princeton: Princeton University Press.

Hulse, Carl. 2006. "In Bellweather District, GOP Runs on Immigration," *New York Times,* September 6, A1.

Ngai, Mae M. 2004. *Impossible Subjects: Illegal Aliens and the Making of Modern America.* Princeton: Princeton University Press.

———. 2006. "How Granny Got Legal." *Los Angeles Times,* May 18.

Smith, James P., and Barry Edmonston, eds. 1997. *The New Americans: Economic, Demographic, and Fiscal Effects of Immigration.* Washington, DC: National Academy Press.

Swarns, Rachel. 2006. "Immigration Overhaul Takes a Backseat as Campaign Season Begins," *New York Times,* September 8, A1.

Wong, Carolyn. 2006. *Lobbying for Inclusion.* Stanford: Stanford University Press.

Zolberg, Aristide. 2006. *A Nation by Design.* New York: Russell Sage Foundation; Cambridge: Harvard University Press. ■

This tower, near Arivaca, Arizona, is one of many equipped with radar and cameras designed to detect people entering the U.S. illegally. The tower and the fence (in the background) are designed to discourage illegal immigrants: What feelings does the image of this surveillance technology and the desert sunset evoke?

LANCE **MORROW**

Cowboys and Immigrants

At Fort Clark in West Texas one night in the 1870s, my great-grandmother Ella Mollen Morrow was asleep in the officers' quarters. Her husband, Maj. Albert Morrow, was several days' ride away, on patrol with his troop of Fourth U.S. Cavalry. A soldier, probably drunk, crawled into the house through a window. My great-grandmother heard him. She took up a Colt .44 revolver and warned him to get out. He kept coming at her. She warned him again. The man kept coming.

2   She shot him—"between the eyes," as a family history said, adding, "No inquiry was held, or deemed necessary."

3   That was the frontier, all right, and I confess that during the presidential campaign last fall, Sarah Palin—moose hunter, wilderness mom—stirred, for a moment anyway, a genetic current of admiration in my heart. It was an atavistic memory of Ella, of her self-sufficient smoking pistol and its brisk frontier justice, which, on that night in West Texas, pre-emptively brought the bad guy down, dead at her feet. No nonsense.

4   At the time, the McCain-Obama campaign seemed a clash of neat American opposites. John McCain (maverick, ex-fighter pilot, military hero, senator from Geronimo country), with his sidekick Palin (chirpy backwoods deadeye), worked the Frontier story line. Barack Obama came onstage as apotheosis, the multiracial, multicultural evolution of what Ellis Island promised to the Nation of Immigrants long ago.

John Wayne in a scene from *The Searchers* (1956), directed by John Ford, a film widely considered to be one of the greatest Westerns of all time.

5   But in the evolving financial shambles of the months since the election, the conflict between these mystic poles of American history appeared to vanish, or to dissolve in a chaotic nonideological synthesis. Both Ellis Island and the Frontier hated Wall Street, just as passengers in steerage and passengers in first-class unite in despising icebergs. And amid the great federal bailouts, *Newsweek* proclaimed, "We Are All Socialists Now."

6   I wonder. The Frontier and Ellis Island are myths of origin, alternate versions of the American Shinto. They're not likely to disappear anytime soon.

7   The two myths are sentimental and symbolic categories, no doubt—ideas or mere attitudes more than facts: facets of human nature. (Quite often, when given a hard look, myths fall apart: the historical frontier, for example, was demonstrably communitarian as well as individualist.) But like the philosopher Isaiah Berlin's Hedgehog and

Emma Lazarus

The New Colossus

Emma Lazarus (1849–1887) wrote poetry and essays on a wide variety of topics. Her works were published in the best-known magazines of her time, and she became an influential figure in the rapidly changing New York art scene. She was born into a well-established Jewish family in New York City, was well educated, and worked to improve the conditions of Jews both at home and abroad by establishing programs to educate new immigrants and by founding the Society for the Improvement and Colonization of Eastern European Jews. Her most famous sonnet, reprinted here, was written in 1883 to help raise money for the Statue of Liberty Pedestal, and in 1903 it was engraved on a tablet within the pedestal on which the Statue of Liberty now stands.

Fox or literary critic Philip Rahv's Paleface and Redskin, they offer convenient bins in which to sort out tendencies.

8   Both myths owe something of their vividness to Hollywood—one to the films of John Ford and John Wayne, for example, and the other to Frank Capra's parables of the common man. The Frontier is set on the spacious Western side of American memory—a terrain whose official masculinity made my great-grandmother's, and Palin's, Annie Oakley autonomies seem somehow bracing. On the other side (diverse, bubbling away in the "melting pot," vaguely feminine in some *gemütlich* nurturing sense) lies Ellis Island. If Frontier dramas call for big skies, open space and freedom, Ellis Island's enact themselves in cities; their emphasis is human, sympathetic, multilingual, and noisy, alive with distinctive cooking smells and old-country customs. The Frontier is big, open-ended, physically demanding, silent.

9   This bifurcation of American consciousness occurred with a certain chronological neatness—a development "unforeseen, though not accidental," as Trotsky might have said, working his eyebrows. Ellis Island opened for business in 1892 as the gateway for the first of some 12 million immigrants. One year later, the historian Frederick Jackson Turner delivered his "frontier thesis" before the American Historical Society at the World's Columbian Exposition in Chicago. When the Pacific Ocean halted the American frontier on the West Coast, Turner argued, the distinctive urgencies of American destiny closed down. But at just that moment, the East Coast opened up to a powerful flow of new immigrant energies.

10   In the years 1889–96, the gun-toting ranchman-intellectual Theodore Roosevelt published his four-volume history, *The Winning of the West*. The evolution of the Frontier mythology was in some ways an instinctive reaction against all those foreigners. Ellis Island made the Frontier feel claustrophobic, just as the arrival of sodbusters with their plows and fences would incense the free-range cattle people.

11   Starting with Teddy Roosevelt, these two American archetypes have reappeared from time to time as presidential styles and ideological motifs. T.R., the sickly New York City boy who repaired health and heart in the Dakota Badlands, was the first modern Frontier president. His dramatization of Frontier attitude occurred at the moment of the Spanish-American War, of Senator Albert Beveridge's triumphal jingo

> Not like the brazen giant of Greek fame,
> With conquering limbs astride from land to land;
> Here at our sea-washed, sunset gates shall stand
> A mighty woman with a torch, whose flame
> 5   Is the imprisoned lightning, and her name
> Mother of Exiles. From her beacon-hand
> Glows world-wide welcome; her mild eyes command
> The air-bridged harbor that twin cities frame.
> "Keep, ancient lands, your storied pomp!" cries she
> 10 With silent lips. "Give me your tired, your poor,
> Your huddled masses yearning to breathe free,
> The wretched refuse of your teeming shore.
> Send these, the homeless, tempest-tost to me,
> I lift my lamp beside the golden door!"

about "The March of the Flag." In 1899, sixteen of Teddy's Rough Riders joined Buffalo Bill Cody's touring Wild West show. Gaudy Wild Bill in fringed buckskins told an audience at the Trans-Mississippi Exposition in Omaha: "The whistle of the locomotive has drowned the howl of the coyote; the barb-wire fence has narrowed the range of the cow-puncher; but no material evidence of prosperity can obliterate our contribution to Nebraska's imperial progress."

12   But in Frontier rhetoric there was often a paradoxical note of elegy and loss, as if the toughest place and moment of the American story was also the most transient, most fragile. By 1918, the Old Bull Moose, reconciled to the Republican Party, was condemning the "social system . . . of every man for himself" and calling for worker's rights, public housing, and day care for the children of mothers working in factories. In nine months, he was dead.

13   The other Roosevelt, T.R.'s cousin Franklin, became the first Ellis Island president. He came to office not at a moment when America had seemed to triumph, but when it had seemed to fail. In myth, if not in fact, the Frontier sounded the bugle—cavalry to the rescue. Ellis Island's narrative began with Emma Lazarus' disconcerting, hardly welcoming phrases of abjection—"your tired, your poor . . . the wretched refuse . . . " Its soundtrack was the street sounds of the *pluribus*.

14   One of the things that made Lyndon Johnson interesting was that he so thoroughly embodied both the Frontier and Ellis Island—and tried to enact both, in the Great Society and in Vietnam. Perhaps it was the conflict between the two ideals that brought him down. A son of the Texas hill country, with its lingering folklore of the Alamo and of long-ago massacres under the Comanche moon, Johnson was also a New Deal Democrat and FDR protégé with all the activist-government Ellis Island instincts. In an interplay of Ellis and the Frontier, he actually tried to bomb Ho Chi Minh into submission while offering to turn Vietnam into a Great Society, full of New Deal projects (dams and bridges and electrification), if only Uncle Ho would listen to reason.

Thomas Bailey Aldrich

The Unguarded Gates

Thomas Bailey Aldrich (1836–1907) provides a poetic argument from the same time period as Emma Lazarus (his poem was published in 1895—two years after hers), but with a more guarded viewpoint. Aldrich was a prominent and prolific New England writer originally from Portsmouth, New Hampshire; his 1883 book An Old Town by the Sea *was an important regional book. Aldrich's 1870 novel* Story of a Bad Boy *served as one inspiration for Mark Twain's* Tom Sawyer.

Wide open and unguarded stand our gates.
And through them press a wild, a motley throng—
Men from the Volga and the Tartar steppes,
Featureless figures of the Hoang Ho,
5   Malayan, Seythian, Teuton, Kelt, and Slav,
Flying the Old World's poverty and scorn;

15   At the Democratic National Convention in 1984, the perfect Ellis Island man, Gov. Mario Cuomo of New York, conjured up a sweet America that originated in sepia photographs of ships arriving in New York Harbor, the vessels' rails crowded with the yearning faces of people from a dozen countries over there, at the instant of their rebirth, their entry into the American alchemy that would transform them and their children forever. "We speak for the minorities who have not yet entered the mainstream," this son of Italian immigrants proclaimed. "We speak for ethnics who want to add their culture to the magnificent mosaic that is America." He called up Ellis Island that summer of 1984 at the same moment Ronald Reagan of California convinced Americans that they were tall in the saddle again, riding into the sunshine of a new morning in America. The Frontier won that round, by a landslide.

16   Reagan personified the cowboy universe that sees itself as self-reliant, competent, freedom-loving, morally autonomous, responsible. He owned a ranch and wore cowboy clothes, and in the Oval Office he displayed a passel of sculptures of cowboys and Indians and bucking broncos. In Reagan's exercise room in the family quarters of the White House, his wife, Nancy, had hung a favorite Reagan self-image, a framed photograph showing him in bluejeans and work shirt and shield-size belt buckle and a well-aged, handsomely crushed white cowboy hat: Reagan's eyes crinkle at the far horizon. The photo watched from the wall as President Reagan pumped iron.

17   George W. Bush put himself in the Reagan mold. Barack Obama's victory represented, among other things, a repudiation of the Frontier style of Bush and Dick Cheney, in favor of an agenda arising from the Ellis Island point of view, with its emphasis on collective social interests, such as health care and the environment. A civic paradigm seemed to have shifted, and a generational paradigm as well.

18   And yet the future (Obama's hopeful young constituency) found itself boomeranged back to the Great Depression. The simultaneous arrival of Obama and bad financial times elicited perhaps too many articles about Franklin Roosevelt and the New

> These bringing with them unknown gods and rites,
> Those tiger passions, here to stretch their claws.
> In street and alley what strange tongues are these.
> 10 Accents of menace alien to our air,
> Voices that once the tower of Babel knew!
> O, Liberty, white goddess, is it well
> To leave the gate unguarded? On thy breast
> Fold sorrow's children, soothe the hurts of fate,
> 15 Lift the downtrodden, but with the hand of steel
> Stay those who to thy sacred portals come
> To waste the fight of freedom. Have a care
> Lest from thy brow the clustered stars be torn
> And trampled in the dust. For so of old
> 20 The thronging Goth and Vandal trampled Rome,
> And where the temples of the Caesars stood
> The lean wolf unmolested made her lair. ■

Deal. Implicitly, George W. Bush and the Frontier way of doing things seem as discredited today as Herbert Hoover seemed in 1933.

19   *Newsweek's* proclamation notwithstanding, my guess is that the categories of Ellis Island and the Frontier persist—but now, like so much else, have been globalized. In the 21st century, the division between the two mind-sets projects itself into McLuhan's misnamed "global village," which, more accurately, has become a planetary megacity with some wealthy neighborhoods (now not as wealthy as they thought they were) and vast slum districts—a megacity without police force or sanitation department. The messy municipal planet remains in many ways a frontier, a multicultural Dodge City or Tombstone (lawless, with shooting in the streets, dangerous with terrorism and nuclear possibilities, not a fit place for women and children) that has an Ellis Island aspiration to survive and prosper as the family of man.

20   The Frontier and Ellis Island analyze problems in different ways and arrive at different decisions. The Frontier assumes the drunken soldier is a rapist or murderer and shoots him between the eyes. Ellis Island may see him as a confused fool and hope to talk him into a cup of coffee and a 12-step program. Roughly the same choices present themselves to a president: the planet is the Frontier; the planet is Ellis Island. Genius is the ability to hold two contradictory truths in the mind at the same time without going crazy.

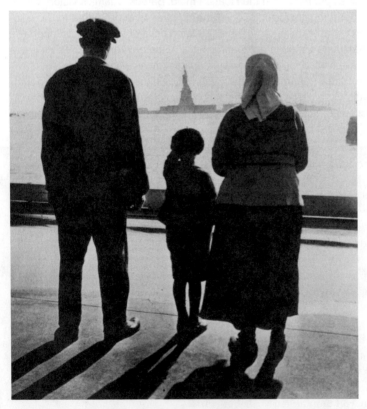

Immigrant families on Ellis Island, 1900, waiting for a ferry to Manhattan.

FROM READING TO WRITING

1. Analyze the argument by Gitlin, Carlson, Ngai, or Morrow: how is that argument the product of its audience and purpose? How would the argument be presented differently if it were directed to a different readership or published in a different forum? How would the argument be different if it were rewritten on this very day? (See Chapter 5 for advice on rhetorical analysis.)

2. Examine the various photos, charts, and other illustration that accompany the selections in this chapter. What visual argument does each one make? (See Chapter 6 for guidance on analyzing visuals.)

3. Write your own argument about some aspect of globalization. Do you see its effects on your campus and in your community? How has immigration impacted your community and your university?

4. Propose your own solution to a problem associated with globalization or immigration. (See Chapter 13 for advice on writing proposals.)

5. Is there a current proposal being considered in Washington to address illegal immigration? Write an essay in support or opposition to the legislation.

6. Or write an essay refuting the argument of someone who is proposing or supporting the legislation. (See Chapter 12 for advice on writing rebuttals.) Consider whether you wish to show the weaknesses in that other argument, or whether you wish to counterargue, or whether you want to do both.

7. Are you an immigrant yourself, or the child (or grandchild) of an immigrant parent or two? Write a narrative argument related to immigration or globalization that is based on, and generalizes from, your own experiences. (See Chapter 11 for advice on writing narrative arguments.)

8. What exactly is "globalization," anyway? Write an essay that defines the term in such a way that persuades readers to sympathize with it—or to oppose it. (See Chapter 8 for advice on writing definition arguments.)

9. Evaluate immigration or globalization, using data from secondary research (or your personal observations) to support your conclusions.

25 | Science and Ethics

The Ethics of Science and Technology

How does the Nuvo robot's appearance meet—or not meet—your notions of what a household robot might look like? What are some of the ethical concerns associated with having robots "living" in the home?

Item: In November 2004, couples with a family history of cancer were given an unusual permission by the Human Fertilization and Embryology Authority in Great Britain—they were allowed to select for human fertilization embryos free of cancer-causing genes. Critics immediately complained about this effort to create "designer babies." They drew comparisons with Adolph Hitler's interest in creating a "super-race" of genetically enhanced Aryans and raised concerns about the possibility that "better" human beings might have advantages over "natural" people.

Item: Early in 2005 in the United States, members of the National Academy of Sciences were finishing a recommendation report on the legal and ethical status of "chimeras"— hybrid creatures created by implanting one animal's stem cells into the fetal matter of a different species. Several living creatures have been "invented" and patented in recent years, raising the question of the possibility of others—mice with human brains? Pigs bioengineered to produce human blood? Or even a genetically plausible hybrid between humans and chimpanzees?

Item: One Thanksgiving Day, teenager Shawn Woolley committed suicide after (his mother claims) weeks of 12-hour stints playing the online role-playing game EverQuest addled his neurochemical condition. Do electronically mediated experiences like playing EverQuest—not to mention similar experiences that may soon make the transition from science fiction to reality— have mind-and-body effects on the human condition? What about the widespread use of Prozac and other mind-altering drugs: do they threaten to change our sense of what human

> "Twenty-first century technologies—genetics, nanotechnology, and robotics—are so powerful they can spawn whole new classes of accidents and abuses."
>
> —BILL JOY, SUN MICROSYSTEMS

nature is at its core? No wonder science fiction movies and narratives are so popular—characters like the Terminator (hybrids of human and nonhuman) seem possible in the not-so-very-distant future.

These three items, brought to our attention by Jeffrey Pruchnic, highlight some of the ethical issues related to science and technology that people are grappling with these days. Science and technology, as central enterprises in our culture, have always raised difficult moral and ethical questions. Science fiction stories and films have frequently addressed those same questions. Whether it is environmental protection (the subject of Chapter 22), medicine, genetic engineering (including stem cell research and cloning), animal rights, the teaching of evolution, computer technologies, space exploration, or military weapons technology, science and technology command our attention and our committed arguments because they challenge our assumptions about what is possible and push the limits of what we think of as ethical.

Contemporary Arguments

Many new technologies are calling into question "the nature of nature," including our human nature. Is the natural world really "natural" when genetic engineers construct new species of plants and animals? And what are we to make of scientific developments that offer the potential for tremendous human benefits if they also have the potential to change our very human natures? Here we include arguments on four especially important and compelling developments related to science and human nature.

The first is robotics. According to Bill Gates, robots have the potential to become as ubiquitous as computers—although he acknowledges that there are as many naysayers about today's robotics developments as there once were about the possibilities of bringing computers into nearly every home. In "A Robot in Every Home," Gates discusses the potential for robotics with enthusiasm, but detractors (represented here by Paul Marks) are raising questions about the ethics of replacing humans and human labor with robots and robotic labor. The rise of robotics lends an almost science-fiction quality to technology and gives rise in the popular imagination to sci-fi's greatest dreams and fears. Will robots turn on their creators, as Frankenstein turned on his? Or will they remain friendly as pets, like C3PO and R2D2?

The second new technology under watch is nanotechnology. MIT researcher K. Eric Drexler coined the term because *nano* literally means "one billionth": nanotechnology refers to the science of creating molecule-sized materials and machines. Occupying the space between biology and engineering, nanotechnologists promise to create new things that fundamentally change the ways we work and live. As *Spiderman, Star-Trek: The Next Generation,* and popular magazines such as *Forbes* and *Wired* all indicate, nanotechnology promises to be the Next Big Thing. Nano skin creams are on the market, nano-enhanced tennis balls are used in the Davis Cup, and microscopic silicon chips run computer games. More important, nanotechnologists are developing micromachines that might radically improve water quality, benefit agriculture, clean up toxic waste, or make obsolete our reliance on oil by improving the efficiency of solar power. Others might enter the human body to repair tissue. Nanomaterials hundreds of times stronger than steel might make possible ten-pound automobiles or airplanes.

But is nanotechnology safe? Could dangerous nanoparticles escape and cause great damage? And what about nanotechnology's implications for the way human beings think of themselves? Will nanotechnology widen the gap between haves and have-nots around the globe? Those very serious questions are raised here in an essay by Bill Joy and in an interview with Ralph C. Merkle.

Third, we invite you to meditate on medical ethics. How do we ethically balance the risks and responsibilities of tampering with the "natural"? No doubt you have read and heard a great deal about stem cell research because of highly publicized appeals on its behalf by very public people: Michael J. Fox (who suffers from Parkinson's disease); Christopher Reeve (who suffered paralyzing, ultimately fatal spine damage in a horseback riding accident); Nancy Reagan (who cared for former president Ronald Reagan during his battle with Alzheimer's); former Senator Arlen Specter (who suffers from cancer); and, at the Democratic National Convention in 2004, the ex-president's son, Ron Reagan. All these people advocate stem cell research.

New scientific advances are creating new ethical issues for consideration. What are the ethical consequences of pursuing genetic engineering or creating robots with humanlike intelligence?

And yet there are many others who find stem cell research to be dangerous and/or unethical, and who find claims of potential miracle cures to be highly exaggerated (and sometimes motivated by the prospect of grant money). Some opponents fear that stem cell research, if approved, would lead to and encourage cloning or the use of aborted fetal tissue—or perhaps even to planned pregnancies and subsequent abortions designed to create the necessary stem cells. If opponents of stem cell research lack high-profile advocates like Fox and the Reagans, they do not lack in fervor and organization. The images and words that follow give you a glimpse of some of the arguments, visual and verbal, that recur in the debate over stem cell research. In addition to photos and cartoons, we include Ron Reagan's highly publicized speech at the 2004 Democratic National Convention and a response to it by Richard M. Doerflinger, an advocate for prolife issues employed by the United States Conference of Catholic Bishops. And we offer a controversial proposal by Sally Satel to permit—under controlled conditions—citizens to sell their organs to people waiting for transplants.

Finally, we close with an Issue in Focus, on genetically modified food—the fourth science-and-ethics controversy represented here. Perhaps you too have personal, moral, religious, or occupational reasons to be concerned about one or another of these controversies. Read the selections that follow with care—and then develop and express your own considered views.

BILL **JOY**

Why the Future Doesn't Need Us

Bill Joy is a cofounder of Sun Microsystems and was the chief scientist there until 2003. He played a major role in developing an early form of UNIX, a computer operating system, as well as other computer technologies, such as the JAVA programming language. "Why the Future Doesn't Need Us" appeared in the April 2000 issue of *Wired* magazine, a monthly periodical that covers cultural, political, and economic impacts of technology. The article, which expresses a surprisingly critical position on technology, created a large stir—see the interview with Ralph C. Merkle that follows the next selection.

From the moment I became involved in the creation of new technologies, their ethical dimensions have concerned me, but it was only in the autumn of 1998 that I became anxiously aware of how great are the dangers facing us in the 21st century. I can date the onset of my unease to the day I met Ray Kurzweil, the deservedly famous inventor of the first reading machine for the blind and many other amazing things.

Ray and I were both speakers at George Gilder's Telecosm conference, and I encountered him by chance in the bar of the hotel after both our sessions were over. I was sitting with John Searle, a Berkeley philosopher who studies consciousness. While we were talking, Ray approached and a conversation began, the subject of which haunts me to this day.

I had missed Ray's talk and the subsequent panel that Ray and John had been on, and they now picked right up where they'd left off, with Ray saying that the rate of improvement of technology was going to accelerate and that we were going to become robots or fuse with robots or something like that, and John countering that this couldn't happen, because the robots couldn't be conscious.

4   While I had heard such talk before, I had always felt sentient robots were in the realm of science fiction. But now, from someone I respected, I was hearing a strong argument that they were a near-term possibility. I was taken aback, especially given Ray's proven ability to imagine and create the future. I already knew that new technologies like genetic engineering and nanotechnology were giving us the power to remake the world, but a realistic and imminent scenario for intelligent robots surprised me.

5   It's easy to get jaded about such breakthroughs. We hear in the news almost every day of some kind of technological or scientific advance. Yet this was no ordinary prediction. In the hotel bar, Ray gave me a partial preprint of his then-forthcoming book *The Age of Spiritual Machines,* which outlined a utopia he foresaw—one in which humans gained near immortality by becoming one with robotic technology. On reading it, my sense of unease only intensified; I felt sure he had to be understating the dangers, understating the probability of a bad outcome along this path.

6   I found myself most troubled by a passage detailing a *dys*topian scenario:

> First let us postulate that the computer scientists succeed in developing intelligent machines that can do all things better than human beings can do them. In that case presumably all work will be done by vast, highly organized systems of machines and no human effort will be necessary. Either of two cases might occur. The machines might be permitted to make all of their own decisions without human oversight, or else human control over the machines might be retained.
>
> If the machines are permitted to make all their own decisions, we can't make any conjectures as to the results, because it is impossible to guess how such machines might behave. We only point out that the fate of the human race would be at the mercy of the machines. It might be argued that the human race would never be foolish enough to hand over all the power to the machines. But we are suggesting neither that the human race would voluntarily turn power over to the machines nor that the machines would willfully seize power. What we do suggest is that the human race might easily permit itself to drift into a position of such dependence on the machines that it would have no practical choice but to accept all of the machines' decisions. As society and the problems that face it become more and more complex and machines become more and more intelligent, people will let machines make more of their decisions for them, simply because machine-made decisions will bring better results than man-made ones. Eventually a stage may be reached at which the decisions necessary to keep the system running will be so complex that human beings will be incapable of making them intelligently. At that stage the machines will be in effective control. People won't be able to just turn the machines off, because they will be so dependent on them that turning them off would amount to suicide.
>
> On the other hand it is possible that human control over the machines may be retained. In that case the average man may have control over certain private machines of his own, such as his car or his personal computer, but control over large systems of machines will be in the hands of a tiny elite—just as it is today, but with two differences. Due to improved techniques the elite will have greater control over the masses; and because human work will no longer be necessary the masses will be superfluous, a useless burden on the system. If the elite is ruthless they may simply decide to exterminate the mass of humanity. If they are humane they may use

propaganda or other psychological or biological techniques to reduce the birth rate until the mass of humanity becomes extinct, leaving the world to the elite. Or, if the elite consists of soft-hearted liberals, they may decide to play the role of good shepherds to the rest of the human race. They will see to it that everyone's physical needs are satisfied, that all children are raised under psychologically hygienic conditions, that everyone has a wholesome hobby to keep him busy, and that anyone who may become dissatisfied undergoes "treatment" to cure his "problem." Of course, life will be so purposeless that people will have to be biologically or psychologically engineered either to remove their need for the power process or make them "sublimate" their drive for power into some harmless hobby. These engineered human beings may be happy in such a society, but they will most certainly not be free. They will have been reduced to the status of domestic animals.[1]

7   In the book, you don't discover until you turn the page that the author of this passage is Theodore Kaczynski—the Unabomber. I am no apologist for Kaczynski. His bombs killed three people during a 17-year terror campaign and wounded many others. One of his bombs gravely injured my friend David Gelernter, one of the most brilliant and visionary computer scientists of our time. Like many of my colleagues, I felt that I could easily have been the Unabomber's next target.

8   Kaczynski's actions were murderous and, in my view, criminally insane. He is clearly a Luddite, but simply saying this does not dismiss his argument; as difficult as it is for me to acknowledge, I saw some merit in the reasoning in this single passage. I felt compelled to confront it.

9   Kaczynski's dystopian vision describes unintended consequences, a well-known problem with the design and use of technology, and one that is clearly related to Murphy's law—"Anything that can go wrong, will." (Actually, this is Finagle's law, which in itself shows that Finagle was right.) Our overuse of antibiotics has led to what may be the biggest such problem so far: the emergence of antibiotic-resistant and much more dangerous bacteria. Similar things happened when attempts to eliminate malarial mosquitoes using DDT caused them to acquire DDT resistance; malarial parasites likewise acquired multi-drug-resistant genes.[2]

10   The cause of many such surprises seems clear: The systems involved are complex, involving interaction among and feedback between many parts. Any changes to such a system will cascade in ways that are difficult to predict; this is especially true when human actions are involved.

11   I started showing friends the Kaczynski quote from *The Age of Spiritual Machines;* I would hand them Kurzweil's book, let them read the quote, and then watch their reaction as they discovered who had written it. At around the same time, I found Hans Moravec's book *Robot: Mere Machine to Transcendent Mind.* Moravec is one of the leaders in robotics research, and was a founder of the world's largest robotics research program, at Carnegie Mellon University. *Robot* gave me more material to try out on my friends—material surprisingly supportive of Kaczynski's argument. For example:

Biological species almost never survive encounters with superior competitors. Ten million years ago, South and North America were separated by a sunken Panama isthmus. South America, like Australia today, was populated by marsupial mammals, including pouched equivalents of rats, deers, and tigers. When the isthmus connecting North and South America rose, it took only a few thousand years for the northern placental species, with slightly more effective metabolisms and reproductive and nervous systems, to displace and eliminate almost all the southern marsupials.

In a completely free marketplace, superior robots would surely affect humans as North American placentals affected South American marsupials (and as humans have affected countless species). Robotic industries would compete vigorously among themselves for matter, energy, and space, incidentally driving their price beyond human reach. Unable to afford the necessities of life, biological humans would be squeezed out of existence.

There is probably some breathing room, because we do not live in a completely free marketplace. Government coerces nonmarket behavior, especially by collecting taxes. Judiciously applied, governmental coercion could support human populations in high style on the fruits of robot labor, perhaps for a long while.

12   A textbook dystopia—and Moravec is just getting wound up. He goes on to discuss how our main job in the 21st century will be "ensuring continued cooperation from the robot industries" by passing laws decreeing that they be "nice,"[3] and to describe how seriously dangerous a human can be "once transformed into an unbounded superintelligent robot." Moravec's view is that the robots will eventually succeed us—that humans clearly face extinction.

13   I decided it was time to talk to my friend Danny Hillis. Danny became famous as the cofounder of Thinking Machines Corporation, which built a very powerful parallel supercomputer. Despite my current job title of Chief Scientist at Sun Microsystems, I am more a computer architect than a scientist, and I respect Danny's knowledge of the information and physical sciences more than that of any other single person I know. Danny is also a highly regarded futurist who thinks long-term: four years ago he started the Long Now Foundation, which is building a clock designed to last 10,000 years, in an attempt to draw attention to the pitifully short attention span of our society.

14   So I flew to Los Angeles for the express purpose of having dinner with Danny and his wife, Pati. I went through my now-familiar routine, trotting out the ideas and passages that I found so disturbing. Danny's answer—directed specifically at Kurzweil's scenario of humans merging with robots—came swiftly, and quite surprised me. He said, simply, that the changes would come gradually, and that we would get used to them.

15   But I guess I wasn't totally surprised. I had seen a quote from Danny in Kurzweil's book in which he said, "I'm as fond of my body as anyone, but if I can be 200 with a body of silicon, I'll take it." It seemed that he was at peace with this process and its attendant risks, while I was not.

16   While talking and thinking about Kurzweil, Kaczynski, and Moravec, I suddenly remembered a novel I had read almost 20 years ago—*The White Plague,* by Frank Herbert—in which a molecular biologist is driven insane by the senseless murder of his family. To seek revenge he constructs and disseminates a new and highly contagious plague that kills widely but selectively. (We're lucky Kaczynski was a mathematician, not a molecular biologist.) I was also reminded of the Borg of *Star Trek,* a hive of partly biological, partly robotic creatures with a strong destructive streak. Borg-like disasters are a staple of science fiction, so why hadn't I been more concerned about such robotic dystopias earlier? Why weren't other people more concerned about these nightmarish scenarios?

17   Part of the answer certainly lies in our attitude toward the new—in our bias toward instant familiarity and unquestioning acceptance. Accustomed to living with almost routine scientific breakthroughs, we have yet to come to terms with the fact that the most compelling 21st-century technologies—robotics, genetic engineering, and nanotechnology—pose a different threat than the technologies that have come before. Specifically, robots, engineered organisms, and nanobots share a dangerous amplifying factor: They can self-replicate. A bomb is blown up only once—but one bot can become many, and quickly get out of control.

18   Much of my work over the past 25 years has been on computer networking, where the sending and receiving of messages creates the opportunity for out-of-control replication. But while replication in a computer or a computer network can be a nuisance, at worst it disables a machine or takes down a network or network service. Uncontrolled self-replication in these newer technologies runs a much greater risk: a risk of substantial damage in the physical world.

19   Each of these technologies also offers untold promise: the vision of near immortality that Kurzweil sees in his robot dreams drives us forward; genetic engineering may soon provide treatments, if not outright cures, for most diseases; and nanotechnology and nanomedicine can address yet more ills. Together they could significantly extend our average life span and improve the quality of our lives. Yet, with each of these technologies, a sequence of small, individually sensible advances leads to an accumulation of great power and, concomitantly, great danger.

20   What was different in the 20th century? Certainly, the technologies underlying the weapons of mass destruction (WMD)—nuclear, biological, and chemical (NBC)—were powerful, and the weapons an enormous threat. But building nuclear weapons required, at least for a time, access to both rare—indeed, effectively unavailable—raw materials and highly protected information; biological and chemical weapons programs also tended to require large-scale activities.

21   The 21st-century technologies—genetics, nanotechnology, and robotics (GNR)—are so powerful that they can spawn whole new classes of accidents and abuses. Most dangerously, for the first time, these accidents and abuses are widely within the reach of individuals or small groups. They will not require large facilities or rare raw materials. Knowledge alone will enable the use of them.

22   Thus we have the possibility not just of weapons of mass destruction but of knowledge-enabled mass destruction (KMD), this destructiveness hugely amplified by the power of self-replication.

23   I think it is no exaggeration to say we are on the cusp of the further perfection of extreme evil, an evil whose possibility spreads well beyond that which weapons of mass destruction bequeathed to the nation-states, on to a surprising and terrible empowerment of extreme individuals.

II

24   Nothing about the way I got involved with computers suggested to me that I was going to be facing these kinds of issues.

25   My life has been driven by a deep need to ask questions and find answers. When I was 3, I was already reading, so my father took me to the elementary school, where I sat on the principal's lap and read him a story. I started school early, later skipped a

grade, and escaped into books—I was incredibly motivated to learn. I asked lots of questions, often driving adults to distraction.

26   As a teenager I was very interested in science and technology. I wanted to be a ham radio operator but didn't have the money to buy the equipment. Ham radio was the Internet of its time: very addictive, and quite solitary. Money issues aside, my mother put her foot down—I was not to be a ham; I was antisocial enough already.

27   I may not have had many close friends, but I was awash in ideas. By high school, I had discovered the great science fiction writers. I remember especially Heinlein's *Have Spacesuit Will Travel* and Asimov's *I, Robot,* with its Three Laws of Robotics. I was enchanted by the descriptions of space travel, and wanted to have a telescope to look at the stars; since I had no money to buy or make one, I checked books on telescope-making out of the library and read about making them instead. I soared in my imagination.

28   Thursday nights my parents went bowling, and we kids stayed home alone. It was the night of Gene Roddenberry's original *Star Trek,* and the program made a big impression on me. I came to accept its notion that humans had a future in space, Western-style, with big heroes and adventures. Roddenberry's vision of the centuries to come was one with strong moral values, embodied in codes like the Prime Directive: to not interfere in the development of less technologically advanced civilizations. This had an incredible appeal to me; ethical humans, not robots, dominated this future, and I took Roddenberry's dream as part of my own.

29   I excelled in mathematics in high school, and when I went to the University of Michigan as an undergraduate engineering student I took the advanced curriculum of the mathematics majors. Solving math problems was an exciting challenge, but when I discovered computers I found something much more interesting: a machine into which you could put a program that attempted to solve a problem, after which the machine quickly checked the solution. The computer had a clear notion of correct and

Science fiction has long toyed with the question of what will happen if robots advance to human (or even above human) reasoning ability. In this film still from *I, Robot,* we see Sonny, a robot with both intelligence and free will.

incorrect, true and false. Were my ideas correct? The machine could tell me. This was very seductive.

30   I was lucky enough to get a job programming early supercomputers and discovered the amazing power of large machines to numerically simulate advanced designs. When I went to graduate school at UC Berkeley in the mid-1970s, I started staying up late, often all night, inventing new worlds inside the machines. Solving problems. Writing the code that argued so strongly to be written.

31   In *The Agony and the Ecstasy,* Irving Stone's biographical novel of Michelangelo, Stone described vividly how Michelangelo released the statues from the stone, "breaking the marble spell," carving from the images in his mind.[4] In my most ecstatic moments, the software in the computer emerged in the same way. Once I had imagined it in my mind I felt that it was already there in the machine, waiting to be released. Staying up all night seemed a small price to pay to free it—to give the ideas concrete form.

32   After a few years at Berkeley I started to send out some of the software I had written—an instructional Pascal system, Unix utilities, and a text editor called vi (which is still, to my surprise, widely used more than 20 years later)—to others who had similar small PDP-11 and VAX minicomputers. These adventures in software eventually turned into the Berkeley version of the Unix operating system, which became a personal "success disaster"—so many people wanted it that I never finished my PhD. Instead I got a job working for Darpa putting Berkeley Unix on the Internet and fixing it to be reliable and to run large research applications well. This was all great fun and very rewarding. And, frankly, I saw no robots here, or anywhere near.

33   Still, by the early 1980s, I was drowning. The Unix releases were very successful, and my little project of one soon had money and some staff, but the problem at Berkeley was always office space rather than money—there wasn't room for the help the project needed, so when the other founders of Sun Microsystems showed up I jumped at the chance to join them. At Sun, the long hours continued into the early days of workstations and personal computers, and I have enjoyed participating in the creation of advanced microprocessor technologies and Internet technologies such as Java and Jini.

34   From all this, I trust it is clear that I am not a Luddite. I have always, rather, had a strong belief in the value of the scientific search for truth and in the ability of great engineering to bring material progress. The Industrial Revolution has immeasurably improved everyone's life over the last couple hundred years, and I always expected my career to involve the building of worthwhile solutions to real problems, one problem at a time.

35   I have not been disappointed. My work has had more impact than I had ever hoped for and has been more widely used than I could have reasonably expected. I have spent the last 20 years still trying to figure out how to make computers as reliable as I want them to be (they are not nearly there yet) and how to make them simple to use (a goal that has met with even less relative success). Despite some progress, the problems that remain seem even more daunting.

36   But while I was aware of the moral dilemmas surrounding technology's consequences in fields like weapons research, I did not expect that I would confront such issues in my own field, or at least not so soon.

37   Perhaps it is always hard to see the bigger impact while you are in the vortex of a change. Failing to understand the consequences of our inventions while we are in the rapture of discovery and innovation seems to be a common fault of scientists and technologists; we have long been driven by the overarching desire to know that is the nature of science's quest, not stopping to notice that the progress to newer and more powerful technologies can take on a life of its own.

38   I have long realized that the big advances in information technology come not from the work of computer scientists, computer architects, or electrical engineers, but from that of physical scientists. The physicists Stephen Wolfram and Brosl Hasslacher introduced me, in the early 1980s, to chaos theory and nonlinear systems. In the 1990s, I learned about complex systems from conversations with Danny Hillis, the biologist Stuart Kauffman, the Nobel-laureate physicist Murray Gell-Mann, and others. Most recently, Hasslacher and the electrical engineer and device physicist Mark Reed have been giving me insight into the incredible possibilities of molecular electronics.

39   In my own work, as codesigner of three microprocessor architectures—SPARC, picoJava, and MAJC—and as the designer of several implementations thereof, I've been afforded a deep and firsthand acquaintance with Moore's law. For decades, Moore's law has correctly predicted the exponential rate of improvement of semiconductor technology. Until last year I believed that the rate of advances predicted by Moore's law might continue only until roughly 2010, when some physical limits would begin to be reached. It was not obvious to me that a new technology would arrive in time to keep performance advancing smoothly.

40   But because of the recent rapid and radical progress in molecular electronics—where individual atoms and molecules replace lithographically drawn transistors—and related nanoscale technologies, we should be able to meet or exceed the Moore's law rate of progress for another 30 years. By 2030, we are likely to be able to build machines, in quantity, a million times as powerful as the personal computers of today—sufficient to implement the dreams of Kurzwell and Moravec.

41   As this enormous computing power is combined with the manipulative advances of the physical sciences and the new, deep understandings in genetics, enormous transformative power is being unleashed. These combinations open up the opportunity to completely redesign the world, for better or worse: The replicating and evolving processes that have been confined to the natural world are about to become realms of human endeavor.

42   In designing software and microprocessors, I have never had the feeling that I was designing an intelligent machine. The software and hardware is so fragile and the capabilities of the machine to "think" so clearly absent that, even as a possibility, this has always seemed very far in the future.

43   But now, with the prospect of human-level computing power in about 30 years, a new idea suggests itself: that I may be working to create tools which will enable the construction of the technology that may replace our species. How do I feel about this? Very uncomfortable. Having struggled my entire career to build reliable software

systems, it seems to me more than likely that this future will not work out as well as some people may imagine. My personal experience suggests we tend to overestimate our design abilities.

44   Given the incredible power of these new technologies, shouldn't we be asking how we can best coexist with them? And if our own extinction is a likely, or even possible, outcome of our technological development, shouldn't we proceed with great caution?

Notes

[1]The passage Kurzweil quotes is from Kaczynski's "Unabomber Manifesto," which was published jointly, under duress, by *The New York Times* and *The Washington Post* to attempt to bring his campaign of terror to an end. I agree with David Gelernter, who said about their decision:

"It was a tough call for the newspapers. To say yes would be giving in to terrorism, and for all they knew he was lying anyway. On the other hand, to say yes might stop the killing. There was also a chance that someone would read the tract and get a hunch about the author; and that is exactly what happened. The suspect's brother read it, and it rang a bell.

"I would have told them not to publish. I'm glad they didn't ask me. I guess."

(*Drawing Life: Surviving the Unabomber.* Free Press, 1997: 120.)

[2]Garrett, Laurie. *The Coming Plague: Newly Emerging Diseases in a World Out of Balance.* Penguin, 1994: 47–52, 414, 419, 452.

[3]Isaac Asimov described what became the most famous view of ethical rules for robot behavior in his book *I, Robot* in 1950, in his Three Laws of Robotics: 1. A robot may not injure a human being, or, through inaction, allow a human being to come to harm. 2. A robot must obey the orders given it by human beings, except where such orders would conflict with the First Law. 3. A robot must protect its own existence, as long as such protection does not conflict with the First or Second Law.

[4]Michelangelo wrote a sonnet that begins:

> Non ha l' ottimo artista alcun concetto
> Ch' un marmo solo in sΠ non circonscriva
> Col suo soverchio; e solo a quello arriva
> La man che ubbidisce all' intelleto.

Stone translates this as:

> The best of artists hath no thought to show
> which the rough stone in its superfluous shell
> doth not include; to break the marble spell
> is all the hand that serves the brain can do.

Stone describes the process: "He was not working from his drawings or clay models; they had all been put away. He was carving from the images in his mind. His eyes and hands knew where every line, curve, mass must emerge, and at what depth in the heart of the stone to create the low relief."

(*The Agony and the Ecstasy.* Doubleday, 1961: 6, 144.)

Ralph C. Merkle

Nanotechnology: Designs for the Future

Ubiquity is a Web-based publication of the Association for Computing Machinery focusing on a variety of issues related to the information technology industry. In 2000, *Ubiquity* interviewed Ralph C. Merkle, a former research scientist at Xerox Parc; advisor at the Foresight Institute; and at the time a nanotechnology theorist at Zyvex, a nanotechnology research and development company. Merkle's main research interests are nanotechnology (also called molecular manufacturing), cryptography, and cryonics. He served as executive editor of the journal *Nanotechnology* for several years. In 1998, Merkle won the Feynman Prize in *Nanotechnology* for his theoretical work. As you will see, the interview excerpted below is partly in response to Bill Joy's "Why the Future Doesn't Need Us," the first selection in this chapter.

UBIQUITY: Bill Joy's recent *Wired* article on the perils of today's advanced technologies—including nanotechnology—has certainly received a lot of attention, and we did a follow-up interview with him in *Ubiquity*. What are your thoughts on that subject?

2 RALPH C.: MERKLE: Well, certainly the idea that nanotechnology would raise concerns is something that actually was a major impetus for the founding of the Foresight Institute back in 1986—and by 1989, Foresight had its first technical conference on nanotechnology, and in fact Bill Joy spoke at that meeting. So one of the things that's a bit surprising is that Bill's concerns about nanotechnology seem to be quite recent—just the last year or two—even though the understanding that this particular technology was going to be very powerful and would raise significant concerns has been around for at least a couple of decades.

3 UBIQUITY: Why don't you take a moment now to tell us about the Foresight Institute?

4 MERKLE: The Foresight Institute (www.foresight.org/guidelines/index.html) was created primarily to guide the development of nanotechnology, and it was founded in large part because, when you look at where the technology is going, you reach the conclusion that, though it has great potential for good, there are also some concerns which need to be addressed. We've been having a series of gatherings at Foresight now for some years where Senior Associates (people who have pledged to support the Foresight Institute) can get together informally and off the record and discuss the various issues.

5 UBIQUITY: What are the meetings like?

6 MERKLE: The most recent gathering had over 250 people—including Bill Joy, as a matter of fact—and one of the sessions was a discussion of the Foresight guidelines for safe development of nanotechnology. A year and a half ago we had a workshop where we discussed the guidelines and

worked out an initial draft, which was discussed at the 1999 gathering at Foresight, and then further modified and updated and then discussed again at the most recent gathering.

7   UBIQUITY: What do you think would explain the sudden increase of concern about this?

8   MERKLE: Well, I can't really address the specifics of Bill Joy's situation. I do know that nanotechnology is an idea that most people simply didn't believe, even though the roots of it go back to a lecture by Richard Feynman in 1959 (www.zyvex.com/nanotech/feynman.html). That was a very famous talk in which he basically said the laws of physics should allow us to arrange things molecule by molecule and even atom by atom, and that at some point it was inevitable that we would develop a technology that would let us do this. I don't think that it was taken very seriously at that time, but as the years progressed it gradually began to be more accepted. If you think the technology is infeasible, you don't worry about what it might do and what its potential is. However, as you begin to internalize the fact that this technology is going to arrive and that we are going to have a very powerful manufacturing technology that will let us build a wide range of remarkable new products, then one of the things that arises is a concern that this new set of capabilities could create new problems, new concerns, and that these should be addressed.

9   UBIQUITY: But not the way Bill Joy is addressing them?

10   MERKLE: One of the things about Bill Joy's original article that concerned me is that he was calling for a relinquishment, as he put it, of research—and I think that's a *very* foolish strategy. If you look at the various strategies available for dealing with a new technology, sticking your head in the sand is not the most plausible strategy and in fact actually makes the situation more dangerous.

11   UBIQUITY: Why so?

12   MERKLE: For at least three reasons. The first, of course, is that we need to have a collective understanding of the new technology in order to ensure that we develop it appropriately. The second reason is that the new technologies that we see coming will have major benefits, and will greatly alleviate human suffering. The third reason is that, if we attempt to block the development of new technology, if we collectively try and say, "These technologies are technologies that are not meant for humans to understand," and we try to back away from them, what we effectively have done is not to block the technologies, we have simply ensured that the most responsible parties will not develop them.

13   UBIQUITY: So you think "relinquishment" is exactly the wrong strategy.

14   MERKLE: Right. Those people who pay no attention to a call for relinquishment, and in particular those people who are least inclined to be concerned about safe development will, in fact, be the groups that eventually develop the technology. In other words, a relinquishment of the new technology, unless it is absolutely 100 percent effective, is not effective at all. If it's 99.99 percent effective, then you simply ensure that the .01 percent

who pays no attention to such calls for relinquishment is the group that will develop it. And that actually creates a worse outcome than if the responsible players move forward and develop the technology with the best understanding that they have and the best efforts to ensure that the technology is developed in a safe and responsible fashion.

15   UBIQUITY: Let's go back to the second reason and expand on that to the extent of enumerating what you consider are the most prominent hopes that it offers.

16   MERKLE: Well, certainly what we see today is an entire planet, which has many limitations. I'm not quite sure how to express it, but certainly if you look at the human condition today, not everyone is well fed. Not everyone has access to good medical care. Not everyone has the basics—the physical basics that provide for a healthy and a happy life. And clearly, if you have a lower cost manufacturing technology, which can build a wide range of products less expensively, it can build, among other things, better medical products. Disease and ill health are caused largely by damage at the molecular and cellular level, yet today's surgical tools are too large to deal with that kind of problem. A molecular manufacturing technology will let us build molecular surgical tools, and those tools will, for the first time, let us directly address the problems at the very root level. So today we see a human population of over six billion people, many of whom have serious medical conditions, which either can't be treated or cannot be treated economically. In other words, we don't have the resources to effectively treat all the conditions that we see. If we can reduce the cost and improve the quality of medical technology through advances in nanotechnology, then we can more widely address the medical conditions that are prevalent and reduce the level of human suf-

This robot, an example of nanotechnology in medicine, is removing plaque from a diseased blood vessel.

fering. (See www.foresight.org/Nanomedicine for more information about medical applications.)

17   UBIQUITY: And besides the opportunities in medicine? What else?

18   MERKLE: On another level, food; the simple process of feeding the human population. Today because of technological limits there is a certain amount of food that we can produce per acre. If we were to have intensive greenhouse agriculture, which would be something we could do economically, if we could economically manufacture the appropriate computer controlled enclosures that would provide protection and would provide a very controlled environment for the growth of food we could have much higher production. It looks as though yields of over 10 times what we can currently grow per acre are feasible if you control, for example, the CO_2 concentration, the humidity, the temperature, all the various factors that plants depend on to grow rapidly. If we control those, if we make those optimal for the growth of various crops then we can grow more per acre. And furthermore, we can grow it less expensively because molecular manufacturing technology is inherently low cost, and therefore it will let us grow more food more easily.

19   UBIQUITY: What are the implications?

20   MERKLE: The first is that it makes food less expensive. The second is that many of the people in the world today who are starving are not starving because there is an inherent inability to produce food, they are starving because they are caught in the middle of political fights and blockades that have been used as political weapons. As a consequence, food is available but it cannot be shipped into an area and so the people in that area suffer the consequences. However, if you have a distributed manufacturing technology, one of the great advantages is that it should let us have a much lower cost infrastructure. In other words, today manufacturing takes place in very large facilities. If you want to build, for example, a computer chip, you need a giant semiconductor fabrication facility. But if you look at nature, nature can grow complex molecular machines using nothing more than a plant.

21   UBIQUITY: Example?

22   MERKLE: Well, a potato, for example, can grow quite easily on a very small plot of land. With molecular manufacturing, in a similar fashion, we'll be able to have distributed manufacturing, which will permit manufacturing at the site using technologies that are low cost and easily available once the core technology has been developed. And as a consequence, you would have people able to build low-cost greenhouse agriculture tools even if there were a blockade because the manufacturing facilities would be widely distributed, and therefore they could avoid the blockade by simply making what they need inside the blockaded region using cheap raw materials and sunlight.

23   UBIQUITY: And if nanotechnology did so much for people's health and food production, what would it do, do you suppose, for their current economic

institution? Would it transition to large-scale nanotechnology? Have un-intended consequences in terms of disrupting the economy?

24 MERKLE: I think we would see changes in the economy. Previous technologies have made major changes. Old companies that have had major advantages in the past certainly find those advantages go away. Certainly as manufacturing becomes less expensive, then today's major manufacturing companies would find that they would be at a disadvantage in the future. Other companies that are producing intellectual products, software companies or companies that are not dealing with material objects—banks and financial institutions, for example—fundamentally are dealing with a flow of information so would be relatively less affected. I think you would see some major shifts in the economy in that manufacturing companies would find that what they were doing was either greatly changed or outright replaced. As in any technological revolution, there will be winners and losers. On balance, everyone will come out ahead, although there will be specific instances where particular companies will have major problems, and in fact, will simply not be able to cope with a new environment and presumably suffer the consequences.

25 UBIQUITY: What about the competition between different countries? Would, for example, the severely underdeveloped countries have an ability to do very rapid catch-up?

26 MERKLE: Yes. I think they would. Also, you have to remember that we are looking at a future where to a first approximation everyone is wealthy. Now, there are certain things that are inherently scarce. For example, there is only a certain amount of beachfront property in California. It is going to be scarce, it is going to be expensive, and only a small percentage of the population will be able to afford it. But if you look at other material possessions—housing or electronics—you find that the only limitation is our ability to manufacture them inexpensively. So the first approximation in this future that we're looking at is that everyone will be physically well off. They will have a great abundance in material goods, and as a consequence, I think that will soften and ease some of the conflicts that we see now. One of the issues facing us today is that there are countries where there is a serious lack of resources, the standards of living are very low, and as a consequence this creates a fundamental unease and discomfort in entire populations. If you have a higher standard of living, at least that source of conflict will be greatly reduced. Now, as we all know, there are many potential sources of conflict in the world, but even easing some of them will be very helpful.

27 UBIQUITY: Give us an example of a product that would be improved using molecular manufacturing?

28 MERKLE: The answer that comes most readily to mind is diamonds. Diamond has a better strength-to-weight ratio than steel or aluminum. Its strength-to-weight ratio is more than 50 times that of steel or aluminum alloy. So, it's much stronger and much lighter. If we had a shatterproof variant of diamond, we would have a remarkably light and strong material from which

to make all of the products in the world around us. In particular, aerospace products—airplanes or rockets—would benefit immensely from having lighter, stronger materials. So one of the things that we can say with confidence is that we will have much lighter, much stronger materials, and this will reduce the cost of air flight, and it will reduce the cost of rockets. It will let us go into space for literally orders of magnitude lower cost.

29   UBIQUITY: Has NASA shown any interest in this?

30   MERKLE: Needless to say, they are pursuing research in nanotechnology with the idea of having lighter, stronger materials as one of the significant objectives. There is a whole range of other capabilities, of course, that would be of interest in NASA. For example, lighter computers and lighter sensors would let you have more function in a given weight, which is very important if you are launching things into space, and you have to pay by the pound to put things there.

31   UBIQUITY: Are there any other areas that would be significantly affected by nanotechnology?

32   MERKLE: The other area is in advanced computer technology. The computer hardware revolution has been continuing with remarkable steadiness over the last few decades. If you extrapolate into the future you find that, in the coming decades, we'll have to build molecular computers to keep the computer hardware revolution on track. Nanotechnology will let us do that, and it will let us build computers that are incredibly powerful. We'll have more power in the volume of a sugar cube than exists in the entire world today.

33   UBIQUITY: Can you put any kind of timeframe on that?

34   MERKLE: We're talking about decades. We're not talking about years; we're not talking about a century. We're talking decades—and probably not many decades.

BILL GATES

A Robot in Every Home

From 1995 to 2009, Bill Gates had been ranked by *Forbes* magazine as the richest person in the world (he has now "fallen" to number 2). Best known for his role with Microsoft, the company he cofounded with Paul Allen, Gates now serves as the primary stockholder for that corporation. He spends most of his time doing philanthropic work with the Gates Foundation, which he and his wife, Melinda, founded in 2000. In "A Robot in Every Home," which first appeared in the December 2006 issue of *Scientific American*, Gates waxes enthusiastic and optimistic about the prospect of bringing robotics into every American household—much as Microsoft did with personal computers.

I magine being present at the birth of a new industry. It is an industry based on groundbreaking new technologies, wherein a handful of well-established corporations sell highly specialized devices for business use and a fast-growing number of start-up companies produce innovative toys, gadgets for hobbyists and other interesting niche products. But it is also a highly fragmented industry with few common standards or platforms. Projects are complex, progress is slow, and practical applications are relatively rare. In fact, for all the excitement and promise, no one can say with any certainty when—or even if—this industry will achieve critical mass. If it does, though, it may well change the world.

2   Of course, the paragraph above could be a description of the computer industry during the mid-1970s, around the time that Paul Allen and I launched Microsoft. Back then, big, expensive mainframe computers ran the back-office operations for major companies, governmental departments and other institutions. Researchers at leading universities and industrial laboratories were creating the basic building blocks that would make the information age possible. Intel had just introduced the 8080 microprocessor, and Atari was selling the popular electronic game Pong. At homegrown computer clubs, enthusiasts struggled to figure out exactly what this new technology was good for.

3   But what I really have in mind is something much more contemporary: the emergence of the robotics industry, which is developing in much the same way that the computer business did 30 years ago. Think of the manufacturing robots currently used on automobile assembly lines as the equivalent of yesterday's mainframes. The industry's niche products include robotic arms that perform surgery, surveillance robots deployed in Iraq and Afghanistan that dispose of roadside bombs, and domestic robots that vacuum the floor. Electronics companies have made robotic toys that can imitate people or dogs or dinosaurs, and hobbyists are anxious to get their hands on the latest version of the Lego robotics system.

4   Meanwhile some of the world's best minds are trying to solve the toughest problems of robotics, such as visual recognition, navigation and machine learning. And they are succeeding. At the 2004 Defense Advanced Research Projects Agency (DARPA) Grand Challenge, a competition to produce the first robotic vehicle capable of navigating autonomously over a rugged 142-mile course through the Mojave Desert, the top competitor managed to travel just 7.4 miles before breaking down. In 2005, though, five vehicles covered the complete distance, and the race's winner did it at an average speed of 19.1 miles an hour. (In another intriguing parallel between the robotics and computer industries, DARPA also funded the work that led to the creation of Arpanet, the precursor to the Internet.)

5   What is more, the challenges facing the robotics industry are similar to those we tackled in computing three decades ago. Robotics companies have no standard operating software that could allow popular application programs to run in a variety of devices. The standardization of robotic processors and other hardware is limited, and very little of the programming code used in one machine can be applied to another. Whenever somebody wants to build a new robot, they usually have to start from square one.

6   Despite these difficulties, when I talk to people involved in robotics—from university researchers to entrepreneurs, hobbyists and high school students—the level of excitement and expectation reminds me so much of that time when Paul Allen and I

looked at the convergence of new technologies and dreamed of the day when a computer would be on every desk and in every home. And as I look at the trends that are now starting to converge, I can envision a future in which robotic devices will become a nearly ubiquitous part of our day-to-day lives. I believe that technologies such as distributed computing, voice and visual recognition, and wireless broadband connectivity will open the door to a new generation of autonomous devices that enable computers to perform tasks in the physical world on our behalf. We may be on the verge of a new era, when the PC will get up off the desktop and allow us to see, hear, touch and manipulate objects in places where we are not physically present.

From Science Fiction to Reality

7   The word "robot" was popularized in 1921 by Czech playwright Karel Capek, but people have envisioned creating robot-like devices for thousands of years. In Greek and Roman mythology, the gods of metalwork built mechanical servants made from gold. In the first century A.D., Heron of Alexandria—the great engineer credited with inventing the first steam engine—designed intriguing automatons, including one said to have the ability to talk. Leonardo da Vinci's 1495 sketch of a mechanical knight, which could sit up and move its arms and legs, is considered to be the first plan for a humanoid robot.

8   Over the past century, anthropomorphic machines have become familiar figures in popular culture through books such as Isaac Asimov's *I, Robot*, movies such as *Star Wars* and television shows such as *Star Trek*. The popularity of robots in fiction indicates that people are receptive to the idea that these machines will one day walk among us as helpers and even as companions. Nevertheless, although robots play a vital role in industries such as automobile manufacturing—where there is about one robot for every 10 workers—the fact is that we have a long way to go before real robots catch up with their science-fiction counterparts.

9   One reason for this gap is that it has been much harder than expected to enable computers and robots to sense their surrounding environment and to react quickly and accurately. It has proved extremely difficult to give robots the capabilities that humans take for granted—for example, the abilities to orient themselves with respect to the objects in a room, to respond to sounds and interpret speech, and to grasp objects of varying sizes, textures and fragility. Even something as simple as telling the difference between an open door and a window can be devilishly tricky for a robot.

10   But researchers are starting to find the answers. One trend that has helped them is the increasing availability of tremendous amounts of computer power. One megahertz of processing power, which cost more than $7,000 in 1970, can now be purchased for just pennies. The price of a megabit of storage has seen a similar decline. The access to cheap computing power has permitted scientists to work on many of the hard problems that are fundamental to making robots practical. Today, for example, voice-recognition programs can identify words quite well, but a far greater challenge will be building machines that can understand what those words mean in context. As computing capacity continues to expand, robot designers will have the processing power they need to tackle issues of ever greater complexity.

11   Another barrier to the development of robots has been the high cost of hardware, such as sensors that enable a robot to determine the distance to an object as well as motors and servos that allow the robot to manipulate an object with both strength and

delicacy. But prices are dropping fast. Laser range finders that are used in robotics to measure distance with precision cost about $10,000 a few years ago; today they can be purchased for about $2,000. And new, more accurate sensors based on ultrawide-band radar are available for even less.

12   Now robot builders can also add Global Positioning System chips, video cameras, array microphones (which are better than conventional microphones at distinguishing a voice from background noise) and a host of additional sensors for a reasonable expense. The resulting enhancement of capabilities, combined with expanded processing power and storage, allows today's robots to do things such as vacuum a room or help to defuse a roadside bomb—tasks that would have been impossible for commercially produced machines just a few years ago.

A BASIC Approach

13   In February 2004 I visited a number of leading universities, including Carnegie Mellon University, the Massachusetts Institute of Technology, Harvard University, Cornell University and the University of Illinois, to talk about the powerful role that computers can play in solving some of society's most pressing problems. My goal was to help students understand how exciting and important computer science can be, and I hoped to encourage a few of them to think about careers in technology. At each university, after delivering my speech, I had the opportunity to get a firsthand look at some of the most interesting research projects in the school's computer science department. Almost without exception, I was shown at least one project that involved robotics.

14   At that time, my colleagues at Microsoft were also hearing from people in academia and at commercial robotics firms who wondered if our company was doing any work in robotics that might help them with their own development efforts. We were not, so we decided to take a closer look. I asked Tandy Trower, a member of my strategic staff and a 25-year Microsoft veteran, to go on an extended fact-finding mission and to speak with people across the robotics community. What he found was universal enthusiasm for the potential of robotics, along with an industry-wide desire for tools that would make development easier. "Many see the robotics industry at a technological turning point where a move to PC architecture makes more and more sense," Tandy wrote in his report to me after his fact-finding mission. "As Red Whittaker, leader of [Carnegie Mellon's] entry in the DARPA Grand Challenge, recently indicated, the hardware capability is mostly there; now the issue is getting the software right."

15   Back in the early days of the personal computer, we realized that we needed an ingredient that would allow all of the pioneering work to achieve critical mass, to coalesce into a real industry capable of producing truly useful products on a commercial scale. What was needed, it turned out, was Microsoft BASIC. When we created this programming language in the 1970s, we provided the common foundation that enabled programs developed for one set of hardware to run on another. BASIC also made computer programming much easier, which brought more and more people into the industry. Although a great many individuals made essential contributions to the development of the personal computer, Microsoft BASIC was one of the key catalysts for the software and hardware innovations that made the PC revolution possible.

16   After reading Tandy's report, it seemed clear to me that before the robotics industry could make the same kind of quantum leap that the PC industry made 30 years

ago, it, too, needed to find that missing ingredient. So I asked him to assemble a small team that would work with people in the robotics field to create a set of programming tools that would provide the essential plumbing so that anybody interested in robots with even the most basic understanding of computer programming could easily write robotic applications that would work with different kinds of hardware. The goal was to see if it was possible to provide the same kind of common, low-level foundation for integrating hardware and software into robot designs that Microsoft BASIC provided for computer programmers.

17 Tandy's robotics group has been able to draw on a number of advanced technologies developed by a team working under the direction of Craig Mundie, Microsoft's chief research and strategy officer. One such technology will help solve one of the most difficult problems facing robot designers: how to simultaneously handle all the data coming in from multiple sensors and send the appropriate commands to the robot's motors, a challenge known as concurrency. A conventional approach is to write a traditional, single-threaded program—a long loop that first reads all the data from the sensors, then processes this input and finally delivers output that determines the robot's behavior, before starting the loop all over again. The shortcomings are obvious: if your robot has fresh sensor data indicating that the machine is at the edge of a precipice, but the program is still at the bottom of the loop calculating trajectory and telling the wheels to turn faster based on previous sensor input, there is a good chance the robot will fall down the stairs before it can process the new information.

18 Concurrency is a challenge that extends beyond robotics. Today as more and more applications are written for distributed networks of computers, programmers have struggled to figure out how to efficiently orchestrate code running on many different servers at the same time. And as computers with a single processor are replaced by machines with multiple processors and "multicore" processors—integrated circuits with two or more processors joined together for enhanced performance—software designers will need a new way to program desktop applications and operating systems. To fully exploit the power of processors working in parallel, the new software must deal with the problem of concurrency.

19 One approach to handling concurrency is to write multi-threaded programs that allow data to travel along many paths. But as any developer who has written multi-threaded code can tell you, this is one of the hardest tasks in programming. The answer that Craig's team has devised to the concurrency problem is something called the concurrency and coordination runtime (CCR). The CCR is a library of functions—sequences of software code that perform specific tasks—that makes it easy to write multithreaded applications that can coordinate a number of simultaneous activities. Designed to help programmers take advantage of the power of multicore and multiprocessor systems, the CCR turns out to be ideal for robotics as well. By drawing on this library to write their programs, robot designers can dramatically reduce the chances that one of their creations will run into a wall because its software is too busy sending output to its wheels to read input from its sensors.

20 In addition to tackling the problem of concurrency, the work that Craig's team has done will also simplify the writing of distributed robotic applications through a technology called decentralized software services (DSS). DSS enables developers to create applications in which the services—the parts of the program that read a sensor, say, or

control a motor—operate as separate processes that can be orchestrated in much the same way that text, images and information from several servers are aggregated on a Web page. Because DSS allows software components to run in isolation from one another, if an individual component of a robot fails, it can be shut down and restarted—or even replaced—without having to reboot the machine. Combined with broadband wireless technology, this architecture makes it easy to monitor and adjust a robot from a remote location using a Web browser.

21   What is more, a DSS application controlling a robotic device does not have to reside entirely on the robot itself but can be distributed across more than one computer. As a result, the robot can be a relatively inexpensive device that delegates complex processing tasks to the high-performance hardware found on today's home PCs. I believe this advance will pave the way for an entirely new class of robots that are essentially mobile, wireless peripheral devices that tap into the power of desktop PCs to handle processing-intensive tasks such as visual recognition and navigation. And because these devices can be networked together, we can expect to see the emergence of groups of robots that can work in concert to achieve goals such as mapping the seafloor or planting crops.

22   These technologies are a key part of Microsoft Robotics Studio, a new software development kit built by Tandy's team. Microsoft Robotics Studio also includes tools that make it easier to create robotic applications using a wide range of programming languages. One example is a simulation tool that lets robot builders test their applications in a three-dimensional virtual environment before trying them out in the real world. Our goal for this release is to create an affordable, open platform that allows robot developers to readily integrate hardware and software into their designs.

Robots like this vacuum by IRobot are already in use in households around the world.

Should We Call Them Robots?

23 How soon will robots become part of our day-to-day lives? According to the International Federation of Robotics, about two million personal robots were in use around the world in 2004, and another seven million will be installed by 2008. In South Korea the Ministry of Information and Communication hopes to put a robot in every home there by 2013. The Japanese Robot Association predicts that by 2025, the personal robot industry will be worth more than $50 billion a year worldwide, compared with about $5 billion today.

24 As with the PC industry in the 1970s, it is impossible to predict exactly what applications will drive this new industry. It seems quite likely, however, that robots will play an important role in providing physical assistance and even companionship for the elderly. Robotic devices will probably help people with disabilities get around and extend the strength and endurance of soldiers, construction workers and medical professionals. Robots will maintain dangerous industrial machines, handle hazardous materials and monitor remote oil pipelines. They will enable health care workers to diagnose and treat patients who may be thousands of miles away, and they will be a central feature of security systems and search-and-rescue operations.

25 Although a few of the robots of tomorrow may resemble the anthropomorphic devices seen in *Star Wars*, most will look nothing like the humanoid C-3PO. In fact, as mobile peripheral devices become more and more common, it may be increasingly difficult to say exactly what a robot is. Because the new machines will be so specialized and ubiquitous—and look so little like the two-legged automatons of science fiction— we probably will not even call them robots. But as these devices become affordable to consumers, they could have just as profound an impact on the way we work, communicate, learn and entertain ourselves as the PC has had over the past 30 years.

Paul Marks

Armchair Warlords and Robot Hordes

Paul Marks is a technology correspondent for *New Scientist*, an international weekly science magazine and Web site that covers issues in science and technology. In 2007, Marks won the BT IT Security Journalist of the Year Award. His portfolio included the article below, published in *New Scientist* on October 28, 2006, which examines the development of lethal robot soldiers and the risks attached to their use.

It sounds like every general's dream: technology that allows a nation to fight a war with little or no loss of life on its side. It is also a peace-seeking citizen's nightmare. Without the politically embarrassing threat of soldiers returning home in flag-wrapped coffins, governments would find it far easier to commit to military action. The consequences for countries on the receiving end—and for world peace—would be immense.

2   This is not a fantasy scenario. Over the coming years, the world's most powerful military machine, the U.S. Department of Defense, aims to replace a large proportion of its armed vehicles and weaponry with robotized technologies. By 2010, a third of its "deep-strike" aircraft will be unmanned aerial vehicles (UAVs), according to a Congressional Research Service report issued in July (http://tinyurl.com/yafoht). In a further five years a similar proportion of the U.S. army's ground combat vehicles will be remote-controlled robots varying in size from supermarket carts to trucks. The U.S. navy, too, will have fleets of uncrewed boats and submarines.

3   The U.S. military is already using robots in various roles. In November 2002, for example, an armed UAV destroyed a car in Yemen carrying the suspected chief of Al-Qaida in that country, killing him and five others. In Iraq and Afghanistan, robots are proving highly successful in neutralizing roadside bombs and other small-scale explosives.

4   This is only the start. One of the next steps is to give robotic ground vehicles the attack power of UAVs, arming them with weapons such as machine guns, grenade launchers and anti-tank rockets (*New Scientist,* 21 September, p. 28). They could then be sent into places that were particularly dangerous for troops, such as booby-trapped or ambush-vulnerable buildings.

5   After that the plan is to take things to a whole new level, with unmanned planes and ground robots able to communicate with each other and act in concert. A reconnaissance UAV could signal swarms of robots to attack an enemy position, for example, or an unmanned ground vehicle might call in an air strike from UAVs.

6   All uncrewed vehicles are remote-controlled at present, but the Pentagon's Office of Naval Research is planning to develop technology that it hopes will enable a robot to determine whether a person it comes across is a threat, using measures such as the remote sensing of their heartbeat—though whether these kinds of methods can be made reliable is highly questionable.

7   "Teleoperation [remote control] is the norm, but semi-autonomous enhancements are being added all the time," says Bob Quinn of Foster-Miller, a technology firm in Waltham, Massachusetts, owned by the UK defense research company Qinetiq. Foster-Miller, like its main rival iRobot, was set up by roboticists from the Massachusetts Institute of Technology. The company's armed robot, dubbed Swords, has just received U.S. army safety certification. Nevertheless, doubts remain over how reliable armed robotic devices will be, especially if they end up operating autonomously. What happens when the software fails?

8   Such fears have persuaded the military to go slow on the use of autonomous weaponry. An early version of one of Foster-Miller's robots was designed to de-mine beaches autonomously

but was later converted to remote control at the navy's request. It is feasible that as safety concerns are addressed, autonomous devices will become increasingly popular, though experts in robotics point out that might be a long time away. An armed robot will not only need to be fail-safe, it must also be able to identify friend and foe just as well as a soldier.

9   Despite these fears, the rise of armed robots seems inevitable. Quinn tells the story of a group of U.S. marines impressed by a Swords robot armed with a machine gun being tested at a U.S. army base. "If they could have, they would have put that robot in their trunk, because they were off to Ramadi, Iraq, and they wanted that robot to [help them] stay alive. When you see that passion, I have no philosophical problems about this technology whatsoever," he says.

10   Outside the military, however, plenty of people beg to differ. Ultimately, these developments will allow the U.S., as well as several NATO countries that are also keen on the technology, to fight wars without suffering anywhere near as many casualties. The idea that warfare can be "clinical" has been found wanting time and again in recent years—think of the current conflicts in Iraq and Afghanistan, and Israel's recent bombardment of Lebanon—but there's no question that reliable autonomous robots deployed on a large scale could make fighting wars a great deal less risky for those that own them.

11   And therein lies the great danger. What are the chances of a less violent world when the powerful nations can make their mark on the less powerful at the flick of a switch? As Quinn puts it: "We are not trying to create a level battlefield here, we are trying to do the opposite: create a very un-level battlefield."

Sally Satel

Organs for Sale

Sally Satel is a practicing psychiatrist, lecturer at the Yale University School of Medicine, and resident scholar at the American Enterprise Institute for Public Policy Research, a nonpartisan, non-profit institution committed to research and education on issues of government, politics, economics, and social welfare. Her work focuses on mental health policy and political trends in medicine. She is the author of several books, including *When Altruism Isn't Enough: The Case for Compensating Kidney Donors*. Her argument below appeared in the *Journal of the American Enterprise Institute* on October 14, 2006.

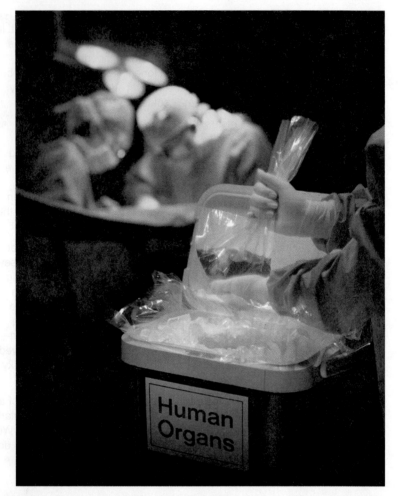

How should we resolve the ever-increasing demand for organs to aid those in need of transplants?

A   year ago, I was searching the Internet for something rare and valuable: a human kidney. In August 2004, I learned I had end-stage renal disease and would need a transplant. At the time, my prospects for a donation from family or friends looked bleak, and I would soon have to begin dialysis. I would be hooked up to a machine three days a week for four hours at a time. This would continue for at least five years—the time it would take for a kidney from a deceased donor to become available. Even with dialysis, the kidneys of many sick people deteriorate so quickly that time runs out. An average of 11 Americans die each day waiting for a renal transplant.

2   Waiting for a kidney from a deceased donor is such a risky business that some people try publicly to convince strangers to give them live organs. Some put up billboards ("I NEED A KIDNEY, CAN YOU HELP? Call . . . "), start websites (GordyNeedsAKidney.org, whose opening page carries the plaintive headline, "Please

Help Our Dad"), or go overseas to become "transplant tourists" on the Chinese black market with the frightful knowledge that the organ they get will almost surely come from an executed political prisoner. The desperation, as I found myself, is perfectly understandable. I have no siblings. Several friends said they would look into it—donors don't need to be genetically related—but they turned out to have disqualifying medical problems or spouses who objected, or they grew scared.

3   Last fall, I turned to a website called MatchingDonors.com—which "matches" mostly prospective kidney donors with recipients—and quickly found a prospective donor. But six weeks later, he changed his mind. Then my wonderful friend Virginia Postrel came along. We are both healthy after a transplant operation on March 4 at the Washington Hospital Center. If Virginia had not donated her kidney, I could have languished on dialysis for years. Indeed, when I joined the national queue in January 2005, there were about 60,000 other people ahead of me, according to the nonprofit United Network for Organ Sharing (UNOS), which maintains the list under a monopoly contract with the federal government.

4   Today, there are 67,600 people waiting for a posthumous kidney. In big cities, where the ratio of needy patients to available organs is highest, the wait—spent on dialysis, a procedure that circulates your blood through a machine that purifies it and returns it to your body—is up to eight years. Last year, only 16,470 people received kidneys; roughly half of the donors were deceased, and half were living. Meanwhile, 4,100 died waiting. By 2010, the wait will be at least ten years, exceeding the average length of time that adults on dialysis survive.

5   Despite decades of public education about the virtues of donating organs at death, the level of such gifts has remained disappointingly steady. Only about one-third of Americans have designated themselves as donors on their driver's licenses or on state-run donor registries. For the rest, the decision to donate organs will fall to family members, who about half the time deny the requests of hospitals. More important, however, is that very few of the Americans who die, perhaps 13,000 a year (or less than 1 percent of all deaths), possess organs healthy enough for transplanting—so even if every family consented, the need for thousands of kidneys would go unmet.

6   The chasm between the number of available kidneys and the number of people needing one will widen each year. This is due to our misplaced faith in the power of altruism. The "transplant community," as it is called—organizations that encourage funding and gifts of organs, and many surgeons and nephrologists—expects people, both living donors and loved ones of the deceased, to give a body part and to receive nothing in return. In fact, it is illegal in the United States to receive money or anything of value ("valuable consideration") in exchange for an organ, a principle set down by Congress in 1984 in the National Organ Transplantation Act.

7   Don't get me wrong. Altruism is a beautiful thing—it's the reason I have a new kidney—but altruism alone cannot resolve the organ shortage. For that reason, more and more physicians, ethicists, economists, and legal scholars are urging the legalization of payments for organs in order to generate more kidneys for transplantation. One doesn't need to be Milton Friedman to know that a price of zero for anything virtually guarantees its shortage.

8   "Is it wrong for an individual . . . who wishes to utilize part of his body for the benefit of another [to] be provided with financial compensation that could obliterate a life of

destitution for the individual and his family?" asked Dr. Richard Fine, president of the American Society of Transplantation, in his address to the World Transplant Congress this year. Supporters of experimenting with a market for organs encounter an array of objections, theoretical and practical. One popular argument, first advanced by Richard M. Titmuss, professor of social administration at the London School of Economics, is that altruism is the sole legitimate impulse behind organ donation. In 1971, Titmuss, a dedicated socialist and member of the Fabian Society, published *The Gift Relationship: From Human Blood to Social Policy*, which rapidly became a U.S. bestseller. He argued that altruistic acts are among the most sensitive indicators of the quality of human relationships and values in a society. Capitalism, on the other hand, is morally bankrupt.

9   This ethic is very much alive among the bureaucrats that run the United Network for Organ Sharing, which manages the transplant list. "Organ transplantation is built upon altruism and public trust. If anything shakes that trust, then everyone loses," says the UNOS website. Yet the trust is already badly rattled. "The current system has degenerated into an equal opportunity to die on the waiting list," observes nephrologist Benjamin Hippen, who advocated compensating donors (or perhaps they should be called "vendors") before the President's Council on Bioethics this summer.

10   Another theoretical objection to compensating donors is the notion that it will "commodify" the body and thus dehumanize the rest of us, let alone the person who gives his kidney in exchange for "valuable consideration." Yet with proper respect for donors and informed consent, it strikes me that careful engagement in financial arrangements is far less distasteful than allowing people to suffer and die. These are not abstract people, mind you, like the ones who may well be helped by stem cell discoveries years down the road, but live humans like the 49-year-old former secretary from the Pentagon I met last summer. For four years now, every Monday, Wednesday, and Friday, she has been sitting in Chair No. 7 in the dialysis center a few blocks from our offices.

11   Others go so far as to reject the very premise that saving lives is a paramount goal of medicine. "If we turn organ procurement into a crusade, we make of death simply a problem to be solved rather than an event to be endured as best we can, with whatever resources of mind and spirit are available to us,"[1] says Gilbert Meilaender, professor of theological ethics at Valparaiso University and a member of the President's Council on Bioethics. Now, it is one thing to question whether we should prolong the life of a vegetative patient, but quite another to abandon treatments for renal failure under circumstances in which a well-established remedy (transplantation) already exists—a remedy whose economic cost to society is lower than the cost of the less effective alternative, dialysis.

12   This is a good time to point out that the live donor—or vendor—of a kidney is exposed to only minor risks, the most significant being those associated with anesthesia and surgery itself—0.03% mortality—comparable to any other operation. Because the surgery is done using a laparoscopic approach, the visible scar is only 2 to 3 inches long. My donor, Virginia, was out of the hospital in three days and back to writing her magazine column a week later.

13   Long-term risks are also low. Typical is a 1997 study from Norway that followed 1,332 kidney donors for an average of 32 years. It found no difference in mortality rates between people who give kidneys and the general population. A 25-year follow-up of

70 donors conducted by the Cleveland Clinic found that the renal function is "well preserved" and that the overall incidence of hypertension was comparable to that of nondonors. The truth is that a normal person can get along perfectly well with one kidney. The risk a donor runs is that his single functioning kidney will become diseased or injured, and he'll need a transplant himself—a highly unlikely event.

14   Perhaps the most vocal critic of compensating donors is the National Kidney Foundation. It is offended by the idea that a donor might benefit in ways other than the psychic reward of pure giving. States NKF chairman Charles Fruit, "Families decide to donate the organs of a loved one for altruistic reasons. Payment is an affront to those who have already donated."[2] Virginia, a take-no-prisoners journalist, responded pointedly to Fruit on her website, <www.dynamist.com>, "The argument that paying organ donors is 'an affront' to unpaid donors is disgusting. Are unpaid donors giving organs to save lives or just to make themselves feel morally superior? Even in the latter case, they shouldn't care if *other* people get paid."

15   In the end, moral objections such as these put us at a standoff. I doubt I could change the mind of Professor Meilaender, who sincerely believes that organ donation violates what it means to be human. And there's nothing he can say to dissuade me from believing that free, informed, and willing individuals should be able to participate in a regulated exchange involving valuable consideration. Thus, the meaningful question becomes how both sides can honor their moral commitments.

16   The best answer is by creating a market arrangement to exist in parallel with altruistic giving. Within such a framework, any medical center or physician who objects to the practice of compensating donors can simply opt out of performing transplants that use such organs. Recipients on the list are free to turn down a paid-for organ and wait for one given altruistically. Choice for all—donors, recipients, and physicians—is enhanced. And it is choice in the greater service of diminishing sickness and death. Paradoxically, the current system based on altruism-or-else undermines the individual autonomy that is at the heart of the most widely held values in bioethics.

17   Not all objections to donor compensation, however, are abstract. A common concern is the potential for exploiting donors—especially low-income donors, who, as the critics reasonably claim, will be the most likely to find incentives attractive. Without question, protecting donors is enormously important. That is why any plan for compensation should be regulated. Potential donors must receive education about what it means to donate a kidney and the risks they run. They must undergo careful medical and psychological screening and receive quality follow-up care.

18   Critics often point to the horror stories from transplant black markets overseas and hold them up as cautionary tales. But the catastrophists have it exactly backward. It is when payment is not an above-board part of the medical system that black markets lead to minimal education of prospective donors, poor post-operative and follow-up care, and failure to honor agreements for payment.

19   Finally, some critics argue we have no evidence that an incentive system would work. True. So we need experimentation. Frankly, I don't know what the perfect kidney market would look like, but let's assume that Congress makes a bold and common-sense move and amends current law to permit the exchange of money or something of value for a kidney. Here are several alternative market systems:

1. A FORWARD MARKET FOR CADAVER ORGANS:

20 Economist Lloyd Cohen proposed one of the first market-based models to increase the number of cadaver organs. Potential donors would either (1) be paid a small amount today by the government or insurance companies to join the current donor registry, or (2) register today in return for the possibility of a much larger payment to their estates should the organs be used at death.

21 The advantage of such a forward-looking approach is that the decision-making burden is taken off family members at a painful time—when they are sitting in the emergency room learning that someone they love is now brain-dead. And, of course, there is no worry of exploiting the donor. A forward market could also help satisfy the 23,000 people waiting for livers, hearts, and lungs.

22 But deceased donors cannot meet the need for kidneys. In addition, kidneys from live donors are healthier than those obtained after death and survive, typically, for 10 to 20 years (or one-third longer). Thus, to mitigate the shortage of kidneys, we must consider offering incentives to people amenable to relinquishing one while they are alive.

2. THE CENTRALIZED SINGLE COMPENSATOR:

23 In this approach, the federal government or a designated agency acts as the only authority with the power to buy and allocate organs for transplants. As is currently the case with cadaver organs, kidneys obtained through compensated donors would be matched with the next best candidate waiting on the national list.

24 Under this scheme, Medicare would underwrite the incentives in light of the fact that it already pays for dialysis treatment under the 1972 End Stage Renal Disease (ESRD) amendment to the Social Security Act. This entitlement provides care for Americans with terminal renal failure regardless of age if they have met required work credits for Social Security. Last year, the ESRD program spent about $16 billion on dialysis, or about $66,000 per patient annually. Since a 35-year-old spends about nine years on dialysis, the total cost is around $600,000; for a 64-year-old, about four years at $300,000. Compare these expenses with the cost of a transplant operation—approximately $75,000 in all for the one-time cost of the surgeries and hospital stays of the donor and recipient, plus the first year of follow-up medical care (including medicine).

25 In most cases, these savings would easily pay for a lifetime supply of the expensive immunosuppressant drugs to prevent rejection of the new kidney. The drugs cost $15,000 to $20,000 a year, and every recipient must take them every day for life. Medicare pays for transplant surgery but stops reimbursing for the drugs, at 80 percent of full price, three years post-transplant if the patient goes back to work.

26 What kinds of compensation should be offered? A reasonable case could be made for an outright payment—after all, it is hard to argue that an individual is competent enough to sell an organ yet unfit to manage the money he receives in exchange for it—but I am partial to a compromise approach in order to defuse those who say that people will sell their organs for quick cash or use it to buy something frivolous. For example, the donor could choose from a menu of options, including a deposit to a 401(k) retirement plan, tax credits, tuition vouchers for the donor's children, long-term nursing

care, family health coverage, life and nonfatal injury insurance, a charitable contribution in the donor's name, or cash payments stretched over time.

27   Donor protection is the linchpin of any compensation model. Standard guidelines for physical and psychological screening, donor education, and informed consent could be formulated by a medical organization, such as the American Society of Transplant Surgeons, or another entity designated by the federal Department of Health and Human Services. A "waiting period" of three to six months could be built in to ensure the prospective donor has ample time to think it through. Monitoring donor health post-transplant is important as well. One idea is to provide lifetime health insurance, through Medicare or a private insurer for the donor. He would receive annual physicals, routine medical screening, and long-term follow-up in addition to standard health coverage. A federally sponsored registry of donors could help us study long-term outcomes for donors and vendors and take steps to remedy physical or psychological difficulties that arise.

3. MULTIPLE COMPENSATORS:

28 In this scheme, donors, compensators (that is, the entities that pay for the transplants), and medical centers (that perform them) would be coordinated with one another through an intermediary broker. Medicare would be one of several possible compensators, along with private insurers, charitable foundations, or a fund established perhaps through a surcharge added to the cost paid by insurers and foundations.

4. PRIVATE CONTRACTS:

29 The easiest way to start a market for organs is simply to change the law to allow someone who needs an organ and someone who wants to sell one to make their own arrangements through contract—as infertile couples currently do with surrogate mothers. But such a system would inevitably attract criticism because it appears to favor well-off sick people over poor.

30   While private contracts may seem unfair because only those with means will be able to purchase directly, poor people who need kidneys would be no worse off—and, very likely, considerably better off—than under the current system. First, a stranger interested in selling a kidney is unlikely to give it away for free to the next person on the list (only 88 donors last year made such anonymous gifts); thus, few poor people would be deprived of kidneys they would otherwise have gotten voluntarily. Second, anyone who gets a kidney by contract is removed from the waiting list, and everyone behind him benefits by moving up. Third, private charities could offer to help subsidize the cost for a needy patient or pay outright.

31   These broad proposals, and variants on them, need considerable elaboration. Many questions remain: How would prices be determined? Would each available kidney be allotted to the next well-matched person on the list? Or should living organs be preferentially allocated to the healthiest people on the list—that is, those who will get the most "life" out of the organ? Could noncitizens be paid donors? Also, could people have a say in who would receive their kidneys? As it currently stands, most living donors give altruistically because they are trying to help a friend or relative, not a stranger. But it is surely possible that the decision of an ambivalent friend could tip in the direction of giving with the promise of compensation. And since each patient on

dialysis is functionally "attached" to a Medicare entitlement, perhaps the recipient could direct a portion of "his" Medicare allotment to his friend as payment.

32   There is no denying the political and practical challenges that come with introducing payment into a 20-year-old scheme built on the premise that generosity is the only legitimate motive for giving. Yet as death and suffering mount, constructing a market-based incentive program to increase the supply of transplantable organs has become a moral imperative. Its architects must give serious consideration to principled reservations and to concerns about donor safety, but repugnance and caution are not in themselves arguments against innovation. They are only reasons for vigilance and care.

Notes

[1] Gilbert Meilaender, "Gifts of the Body," *New Atlantis*, Number 13 (Summer 2006): 25–35.
[2] Letters in response to Richard Epstein, "Kidney Beancounters," *Wall Street Journal*, May 15, 2006 (May 26, 2006). ∎

Ron Reagan

Speech at the Democratic National Convention, July 27, 2004

Ron Reagan is the son of the fortieth president of the United States. In August 1994, at the age of 83, President Reagan was diagnosed with Alzheimer's disease, an incurable neurological disorder that destroys brain cells, and he died of the disease in June 2004. A few months later, on July 27, Ron Reagan offered the following speech to the delegates to the Democratic National Convention and to the millions of Americans watching on television. It was countered the next day by Richard Doerflinger, whose piece follows this one in *Good Reasons*.

G ood evening, ladies and gentlemen.

2   A few of you may be surprised to see someone with my last name showing up to speak at a Democratic Convention. Apparently some of you are not. Let me assure you, I am not here to make a political speech and the topic at hand should not—must not—have anything to do with partisanship.

3   I am here tonight to talk about the issue of research into what may be the greatest medical breakthrough in our or any lifetime: the use of embryonic stem cells—cells created using the material of our own bodies—to cure a wide range of fatal and debilitating illnesses: Parkinson's disease, multiple sclerosis, diabetes, lymphoma, spinal cord injuries, and much more.

4   Millions are afflicted. And every year, every day, tragedy is visited upon families across the country, around the world. Now, it may be within our power to put an end to this suffering. We only need to try.

Some of you already know what I'm talking about when I say embryonic stem cell research. Others of you are probably thinking, that's quite a mouthful. Maybe this is a good time to go for a tall cold one. Well, wait a minute, wait a minute.

Let me try and paint as simple a picture as I can while still doing justice to the science, the incredible science involved. Let's say that ten or so years from now you are diagnosed with Parkinson's disease. There is currently no cure, and drug therapy, with its attendant side-effects, can only temporarily relieve the symptoms.

Now, imagine going to a doctor who, instead of prescribing drugs, takes a few skin cells from your arm. The nucleus of one of your cells is placed into a donor egg whose own nucleus has been removed. A bit of chemical or electrical stimulation will encourage your cell's nucleus to begin dividing, creating new cells which will then be placed into a tissue culture. Those cells will generate embryonic stem cells containing only your DNA, thereby eliminating the risk of tissue rejection. These stem cells are then driven to become the very neural cells that are defective in Parkinson's patients. And finally, those cells—with your DNA—are injected into your brain where they will replace the faulty cells whose failure to produce adequate dopamine led to the Parkinson's disease in the first place.

In other words, you're cured.

And another thing, these embryonic stem cells, they could continue to replicate indefinitely and, theoretically, can be induced to recreate virtually any tissue in your body.

How'd you like to have your own personal biological repair kit standing by at the hospital? Sound like magic? Welcome to the future of medicine.

Now by the way, no fetal tissue is involved in this process. No fetuses are created, none destroyed. This all happens in the laboratory at the cellular level.

Now, there are those who would stand in the way of this remarkable future, who would deny the federal funding so crucial to basic research. They argue that interfering with the development of even the earliest stage embryo, even one that will never be implanted in a womb and will never develop into an actual fetus, is tantamount to murder.

A few of these folks, needless to say, are just grinding a political axe and they should be ashamed of themselves. But many are well-meaning and sincere. Their belief is just that, an article of faith, and they are entitled to it. But it does not follow that the theology of a few should be allowed to forestall the health and well-being of the many.

And how can we affirm life if we abandon those whose own lives are so desperately at risk? It is a hallmark of human intelligence that we are able to make distinctions.

Yes, these cells could theoretically have the potential, under very different circumstances, to develop into human beings—that potential is where their magic lies. But they are not, in and of themselves, human beings. They have no fingers and toes, no brain or spinal cord. They have no thoughts, no fears. They feel no pain.

Surely we can distinguish between these undifferentiated cells multiplying in a tissue culture and a living, breathing person—a parent, a spouse, a child.

I know a child—well, she must be 13 now so I guess I'd better call her a young woman. She has fingers and toes. She has a mind. She has memories. She has hopes. She has juvenile diabetes. Like so many kids with this disease, she's adjusted amazingly well. The insulin pump she wears—she's decorated hers with rhinestones. She

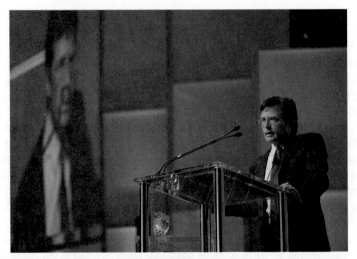

Actor Michael J. Fox, who was diagnosed in 1991 with Parkinson's disease, spoke at the Bio International Convention in 2007. Fox appealed to scientists and investors to aggressively translate scientific research into creative treatments for debilitating diseases, including Parkinson's.

can handle her own catheter needle. She's learned to sleep through the blood drawings in the wee hours of the morning.

18   She's very brave. She is also quite bright and understands full well the progress of her disease and what that might ultimately mean: blindness, amputation, diabetic coma. Every day, she fights to have a future.

19   What excuse will we offer this young woman should we fail her now? What might we tell her children? Or the millions of others who suffer? That when given an opportunity to help, we turned away? That facing political opposition, we lost our nerve? That even though we knew better, we did nothing?

20   And, should we fail, how will we feel if, a few years from now, a more enlightened generation should fulfill the promise of embryonic stem cell therapy? Imagine what they would say of us who lacked the will.

21   No, we owe this young woman and all those who suffer—we owe ourselves— better than that. We are better than that. We are a wiser people, a finer nation.

22   And for all of us in this fight, let me say: we will prevail. The tide of history is with us. Like all generations who have come before ours, we are motivated by a thirst for knowledge and compelled to see others in need as fellow angels on an often difficult path, deserving of our compassion.

23   In a few months, we will face a choice. Yes, between two candidates and two parties, but more than that. We have a chance to take a giant stride forward for the good of all humanity. We can choose between the future and the past, between reason and ignorance, between true compassion and mere ideology.

24   This—this is our moment, and we must not falter.

25   Whatever else you do come November 2, I urge you, please, cast a vote for embryonic stem cell research.

26   Thank you for your time.

Richard M. Doerflinger

Don't Clone Ron Reagan's Agenda

Richard M. Doerflinger is the Secretariat on Pro-life Activities for the United States Conference of Catholic Bishops. In 2009 Doerflinger was awarded an inaugural Life Prize by the Gerard Health Foundation for his work in "preserving and upholding the sanctity of human life" in areas such as public advocacy, legal action, and outreach. A specialist in bioethics, biotechnology, and public policy, he wrote the essay that follows on July 28, 2004, in response to the previous essay in *Good Reasons*, by Ron Reagan.

Ron Reagan's speech at the Democratic convention last night was expected to urge expanded funding for stem cell research using so-called "spare" embryos—and to highlight these cells' potential for treating the Alzheimer's disease that took his father's life.

He did neither. He didn't even mention Alzheimer's, perhaps because even strong supporters of embryonic stem cell research say it is unlikely to be of use for that disease. (Reagan himself admitted this on a July 12 segment of MSNBC's *Hardball*.) And he didn't talk about current debates on funding research using existing embryos. Instead he endorsed the more radical agenda of human cloning—mass-producing one's own identical twins in the laboratory so they can be exploited as (in his words) "your own personal biological repair kit" when disease or injury strikes.

Politically this was, to say the least, a gamble. Americans may be tempted to make use of embryos left over from fertility clinics, but most polls show them to be against human cloning for any purpose. Other advanced nations—Canada, Australia, France, Germany, Norway—have banned the practice completely, and the United Nations may approve an international covenant against it this fall. Many groups and individuals who are "pro-choice" on abortion oppose research cloning, not least because it would require the mass exploitation of women to provide what Ron Reagan casually calls "donor eggs." And the potential "therapeutic" benefits of cloning are even more speculative than those of embryonic stem cell research—the worldwide effort even to obtain viable stem cells from cloned embryos has already killed hundreds of embryos and produced exactly one stem cell line, in South Korea.

But precisely for these reasons, Ron Reagan should be praised for his candor. The scientists and patient groups promoting embryonic stem cell research know that the current debate on funding is a mere transitional step. For years they have supported the mass manufacture of human embryos through cloning, as the logical and necessary goal of their agenda, but lately they have been coy about this as they fight for the more popular slogan of "stem cell research." With his speech Reagan has removed the mask, and allowed us to debate what is really at stake.

He claimed in his speech, of course, that what is at stake in this debate is the lives of millions of patients with devastating diseases. But by highlighting Parkinson's disease and juvenile diabetes as two diseases most clearly justifying the move to human cloning, he failed to do his homework. These are two of the diseases that pro-cloning scientists now admit will probably *not* be helped by research cloning.

6   Scottish cloning expert Ian Wilmut, for example, wrote in the *British Medical Journal* in February that producing genetically matched stem cells through cloning is probably quite unnecessary for treating any neurological disease. Recent findings suggest that the nervous system is "immune privileged," and will not generally reject stem cells from a human who is genetically different. He added that cloning is probably useless for auto-immune diseases like juvenile diabetes, where the body mistakenly rejects its own insulin-producing cells as though they were foreign. "In such cases," he wrote, "transfer of immunologically identical cells to a patient is expected to induce the same rejection."

7   Wilmut's observations cut the ground out from under Ron Reagan's simple-minded claim that cloning is needed to avoid tissue rejection. For some diseases, genetically matched cells are unnecessary; for others, they are useless, because they only replicate the genetic profile that is part of the problem. (Ironically, for Alzheimer's both may be true—cloning may be unnecessary to avoid tissue rejection in the brain, and useless because the cloned cells would have the same genetic defect that may lead to Alzheimer's.) Reagan declared that this debate requires us to "choose between . . . reason and ignorance," but he did not realize which side has the monopoly on ignorance.

8   That ignorance poses an obstacle to real advances that are right before our eyes. Two weeks before Ron Reagan declared that a treatment for Parkinson's may arrive "ten or so years from now," using "the material of our own bodies," a Parkinson's patient and his doctor quietly appeared before Congress to point out that this has already been done. Dennis Turner was treated in 1999 by Dr. Michel Levesque of Cedars-Sinai Medical Center in Los Angeles, using his own adult neural stem cells. Dr. Levesque did not use the Rube Goldberg method of trying to turn those cells into a cloned embryo and then killing the embryo to get stem cells—he just grew Turner's own adult stem cells in the lab, and turned them directly into dopamine-producing cells. And with just one injection, on one side of Turner's brain, he produced an almost complete reversal of Parkinson's symptoms over four years.

9   Turner stopped shaking, could eat without difficulty, could put in his own contact lenses again, and resumed his avocation of big-game photography—on one occasion scrambling up a tree in Africa to escape a charging rhinoceros.

10   Amazingly, while this advance has been presented at national and international scientific conferences and featured on ABC-TV in Chicago, the scientific establishment supporting embryonic stem cell research has almost completely ignored it, and most news media have obediently imposed a virtual news blackout on it. That did not change even after the results were presented to the Senate Commerce Subcommittee on Science, Technology and Space this month. Pro-cloning Senators on the panel actually seemed angry at the witnesses, for trying to distract them from their fixation on destroying embryos.

11   Turner also testified that his symptoms have begun to return, especially arising from the side of his brain that was left untreated, and he would like to get a second treatment. For that he will have to wait. Dr. Levesque has received insufficient appreciation and funding for his technique, and is still trying to put together the funds for broader clinical trials—as most Parkinson's foundations and NIH peer reviewers look into the starry distance of Ron Reagan's dreams about embryonic stem cells.

12   But hey, who cares about real Parkinson's patients when there's a Brave New World to sell? ■

Is stem cell research ethical?

ISSUE IN FOCUS

Is Genetically Modified Food a Boon or a Risk?

Each month, the United States Food and Drug Administration lists on its Web site its latest "food alerts": foods recalled by sellers because of fears about their safety. In the first two weeks of May 2010 alone, the FDA alerted Americans to concerns about certain apricots, breads, sunflower seeds, cheeses, lettuce, bread, and Amish pumpkin butter.

In one sense, fears about food safety have been around since time immemorial; ever since the Garden of Eden, consumers have worried about what they were putting into their mouths. Nevertheless, out of necessity early humans began experimenting with various species to tame for agricultural purposes so that today, just over 100 crop species are grown intensively around the world, and only a handful of these supply us with most of what we now eat. Through a process of trial and error, farmers and scientists developed processes of selection and cross-breeding (or "hybridization") to combine desirable traits from several varieties into elite cross-bred species. When desired characteristics were unavailable in the crop species, farmers introduced genes from wild species into the cultivated plants. The result, as in the case of corn and dairy cows, is the production of highly productive food species that people born two centuries ago could not have envisioned.

And so in a sense the modern use of gene transfer techniques in the development of genetically modified (GM) crops is but a logical extension of a practice that has existed in agriculture for thousands of years. While GM crops are initially more costly to produce, they eventually save farmers money due to the efficiencies created by greater yields and resistance to insects. Biotechnology, its proponents maintain, further benefits our food supply because genetic modification reduces harmful toxic compounds that exist either naturally or unnaturally in the food we eat. Biotechnology may also allow farmers to produce plants that are tolerant to low temperatures, that thrive in poor soil conditions, and that have a longer shelf-life—all of which could benefit the world's hungry.

And yet modern GM processes are decidedly different from their forebears. While the development of new cultivars through classical breeding processes generally takes ten to fifteen years, changes from new gene transfer methods can occur within one generation; and while traditional cross-breeding transfers genes only between similar plants, modern bioengineering can isolate a gene from one type of organism and combine it with the DNA of dissimilar species. Given what is still unknown about the effects of such rapid and dramatic transformation, critics express concern over the rapidity with which GM foods are spreading across the globe. Critics of GM also worry about losses of crop biodiversity—essential for species resilience and the health of surrounding ecosystems—as the popularity of high-yielding varieties limits the genetic variation found in major crops. Should not new species be tested carefully over a long period of time in order that potential risks to health, safety, society, and the environment can be fully assessed?

In the following pages, we present several arguments related to genetically modified food. Mark Anslow, writing in March 2008 for *The Ecologist* (a British publication that promotes ecologically conscious living), summarizes the case against GM foods in his "Ten Reasons Why GM Won't Feed the World." His suspicions are supported by a 2004 argument by Jeffrey Smith (author of *Genetic Roulette: The Documented Health Risks of Genetically Engineered Foods*), who contends that GM foods are influencing behavior; and by a 2009 argument by Ben Burkett, an African American farmer from Mississippi who is president of the National Family Farm. (*The cover of this book also offers a visual argument against GM.*)

By contrast, James Freeman defends GM in an essay that originally appeared in *USA Today* in February 2000. Freeman maintains that biotechnology is nothing more than a highly developed breeding tool, and he labels its opponents "scare mongers" with a limited understanding of the realities of biotechnology and its benefits. Freeman's views are reinforced by Nina Federoff, a leading geneticist and molecular biologist who has assisted in the development of new plants and who has served the past two U.S. secretaries of state as Science and Technology Adviser.

How was your food grown? If you are living in the United States, it is likely that you are consuming genetically modified foods on a regular basis.

Based on her research into how plants adapt to stressful environments (some of it summarized in her book *Mendel in the Kitchen: A Scientist's View of Genetically Modified Foods*), Federoff contends that plant biotechnology can be utilized for positive gains. Finally, we offer Gregory Jaffe's advice on how to "Lessen the Fear of Genetically Engineered Crops." An expert on consumer issues relating to agricultural biotechnology, Jaffe suggests in his essay (which appeared August 8, 2001 in the *Christian Science Monitor*) that "sensible measures" must be developed to ensure that GM foods are safe for public consumption.

So in the end is it ethical and practical for scientists to modify living organisms, to tamper with the food supply? Is the genetic modification of crops inherently hazardous? Could we unwittingly be making our foods and our world unsafe? And what about the long-term consequences of producing and consuming GM foods? Do GM crops affect the environment or the wild ecosystem, reducing crop biodiversity and the persistence of beneficial insects? (Some suspect that the revered monarch butterfly is being compromised by new varieties of corn.) Could new crops lead to the development of noxious "superweeds"? And what about genetic pollution? Should we be concerned that GM genes might be transferred to other organisms, even to humans and other animals? How can scientists allay public concerns considering the complexities of the issues involved?

MARK **ANSLOW**

Ten Reasons Why GM Won't Feed the World

G enetic modification can't deliver a safe, secure future food supply. Here's why.

1. Failure to deliver

2   Despite the hype, genetic modification consistently fails to live up to industry claims. Only two GM traits have ever made it to market: herbicide resistance and BT toxin expression (see below). Other promises of genetic modification have failed to materialize. The much vaunted GM "golden rice"—hailed as a cure to vitamin A deficiency—has never made it out of the laboratory, partly because in order to meet recommended levels of vitamin A intake, consumers would need to eat 12 bowls of the rice every day.[1] In 2004, the Kenyan government admitted that Monsanto's GM sweet potatoes were no more resistant to feathery mottle virus than ordinary strains, and in fact produced lower yields.[2] And in January 2008, news that scientists had modified a carrot to cure osteoporosis by providing calcium had to be weighed against the fact that you would need to eat 1.6 kilograms of these vegetables each day to meet your recommended calcium intake.[3]

2. Costing the Earth

3   GM crops are costing farmers and governments more money than they are making. In 2003, a report by the Soil Association estimated the cost to the US economy of GM crops at around $12 billion (£6 billion) since 1999, on account of inflated farm subsidies, loss of export orders, and various seed recalls.[4] A study in Iowa found that GM soybeans required all the same costs as conventional farming but, because they produced lower yields (see below), the farmers ended up making no profit at all.[5] In India, an independent study found that BT cotton crops were costing farmers 10 per cent more than non-BT variants and bringing in 40 per cent lower profits.[6] Between 2001 and 2005, more than 32,000 Indian farmers committed suicide, most as a result of mounting debts caused by inadequate crops.[7]

3. Contamination and gene escape

4   No matter how hard you try, you can never be sure that what you are eating is GM-free. In a recent article, the *New Scientist* admitted that contamination and cross-fertilization between GM and non-GM crops "has happened on many occasions already."[8] In late 2007, U.S. company Scotts Miracle-Gro was fined $500,000 by the U.S. Department of Agriculture when genetic material from a new golf-course grass was found in native grasses as far as 13 miles away from the test sites, apparently released when freshly cut grass was caught and blown by the wind.[9] In 2006, an analysis of 40 Span-

ish conventional and organic farms found that eight were contaminated with GM corn varieties, including one farmer whose crop contained 12.6 per cent GM plants.

4. Reliance on pesticides

5   Far from reducing dependency on pesticides and fertilizers, GM crops frequently increase farmers' reliance on these products. Herbicide-resistant crops can be sprayed indiscriminately with weedkillers such as Monsanto's Roundup because they are engineered to withstand the effect of the chemical. This means that significantly higher levels of herbicide are found in the final food product, however, and often a second herbicide is used in the late stages of the crop to promote "dessication," or drying, meaning that these crops receive a double dose of harmful chemicals.[10] BT maize, engineered to produce an insecticidal toxin, has never eliminated the use of pesticides,[11] and because the BT gene cannot be switched off, the crops continue to produce the toxin right up until harvest, reaching the consumer at its highest possible concentrations.[12]

5. Frankenfoods

6   Despite the best efforts of the biotech industry, consumers remain staunchly opposed to GM food. In 2007, the vast majority of 11,700 responses to the government's consultation on whether contamination of organic food with traces of GM crops should be allowed were strongly negative. The British government's own "GM Nation" debate in 2003 discovered that half of its participants "never want to see GM crops grown in the United Kingdom under any circumstances," and 96 per cent thought that society knew too little about the health impacts of genetic modification. In India, farmers' experience of BT cotton has been so disastrous that the Maharashtra government now advises that farmers grow soybeans instead. And in Australia, over 250 food companies lodged appeals with the state governments of New South Wales and Victoria over the lifting of bans against growing GM canola crops.[13]

6. Breeding resistance

7   Nature is smart, and there are already reports of species emerging that are resistant to GM crops. This is seen in the emergence of new "superweeds" on farms in North America—plants that have evolved the ability to withstand the industry's chemicals. A report by the conservation body English Nature (now Natural England), in 2002, revealed that oilseed rape plants that had developed resistance to three or more herbicides were "not uncommon" in Canada.[14] The superweeds had been created through random crosses between neighboring GM crops. In order to tackle these superweeds, Canadian farmers were forced to resort to even stronger, more toxic herbicides.[15] Similarly, pests (notably the diamondback moth) have been quick to develop resistance to BT toxin, and in 2007 swarms of mealy bugs began attacking supposedly pestresistant Indian cotton.

7. Creating problems for solutions

8   Many of the so-called "problems" for which the biotechnology industry develops "solutions" seem to be notions of PR rather than science. Herbicide-resistance was sold under the claim that because crops could be doused in chemicals, there would be much

less need to weed mechanically or plough the soil, keeping more carbon and nitrates under the surface. But a new long-term study by the U.S. Agricultural Research Service has shown that organic farming, even with ploughing, stores more carbon than the GM crops save.[16] BT cotton was claimed to increase resistance to pests, but farmers in East Africa discovered that by planting a local weed amid their corn crop, they could lure pests to lay their eggs on the weed and not the crop.[17]

8. Health risks

9 The results of tests on animals exposed to GM crops give serious cause for concern over their safety. In 1998, Scottish scientists found damage to every single internal organ in rats fed blight-resistant GM potatoes. In a 2006 experiment, female rats fed on herbicide-resistant soybeans gave birth to severely stunted pups, of which half died within three weeks. The survivors were sterile. In the same year, Indian news agencies reported that thousands of sheep allowed to graze on BT cotton crop residues had died suddenly. Further cases of livestock deaths followed in 2007. There have also been reports of allergy-like symptoms among Indian laborers in BT cotton fields. In 2002, the only trial ever to involve human beings appeared to show that altered genetic material from GM soybeans not only survives in the human gut, but may even pass its genetic material to bacteria within the digestive system.[18]

9. Left hungry

10 GM crops have always come with promises of increased yields for farmers, but this has rarely been the case. A three-year study of 87 villages in India found that non-BT cotton consistently produced 30 per cent higher yields than the (more expensive) GM alternative.[19] It is now widely accepted that GM soybeans produce consistently lower yields than conventional varieties. In 1992, Monsanto's own trials showed that the company's Roundup Ready soybeans yield 11.5 per cent less on harvest. Later Monsanto studies went on to reveal that some trials of GM canola crops in Australia actually produced yields 16 per cent below the non- GM national average.[20]

10. Wedded to fertilizers and fossil fuels

11 No genetically modified crop has yet eliminated the need for chemical fertilizers in order to achieve expected yields. Although the industry has made much of the possibility of splicing nitrogen-fixing genes into commercial food crops in order to boost yields, there has so far been little success. This means that GM crops are just as dependent on fossil fuels to make fertilizers as conventional agriculture. In addition to this, GM traits are often specifically designed to fit with large-scale industrial agriculture. Herbicide resistance is of no real benefit unless your farm is too vast to weed mechanically, and it presumes that the farmers already farm in a way that involves the chemical spraying of their crops. Similarly, BT toxin expression is designed to counteract the problem of pest control in vast monocultures, which encourage infestations.

12 In a world that will soon have to change its view of farming—facing as it does the twin challenges of climate change and peak oil—GM crops will soon come to look like a relic of bygone practices.

References

[1] http://www.gmwatch.org/archive2.asp?arcid=8521

[2] http://www.greens.org/s-r/35/35-03.html

[3] *Telegraph*, 14th January 2008, http://tinyurl.com/38e2rp

[4] Soil Association, 2007, http://tinyurl.com/33bfuh

[5] http://ianrnews.unl.edu/static/0005161.shtml

[6] http://www.i-sis.org.uk/IBTCF.php

[7] *Indian Muslims*, 20th November 2007, http://tinyurl.com/2u7wy7

[8] *New Scientist*, "Genes for Greens," 5th January 2007, Issue 2637, Vol 197

[9] http://gmfoodwatch.tribe.net/thread/a1b77b8b-15f5-4f1d-86df-2bbca5aaec70

[10] http://www.prospect-magazine.co.uk/article_details.php?id=9927

[11] http://www.btinternet.com/~nlpWESSEX/Documents/usdagmeconomics.htm

[12] http://www.prospect-magazine.co.uk/article_details.php?id=9927

[13] http://www.indybay.org/newsitems/2007/11/27/18463803.php

[14] http://www.english-nature.org.uk/pubs/publication/PDF/enrr443.pdf

[15] *Innovations Report*, 20th June 2005, http://tinyurl.com/3axmln

[16] http://www.gmwatch.org/archive2.asp?arcid=8658

[17] http://www.i-sis.org.uk/GMcropsfailed.php

[18] All references from "GM Food Nightmare Unfolding in the Regulatory Sham," by Mae-Wan Ho, Joe Cummins, and Peter Saunders, ISIS report.

[19] http://www.i-sis.org.uk/IBTCF.php

[20] http://www.gmwatch.org/archive2.asp?arcid=8558

James Freeman

You're Eating Genetically Modified Food

There's no escape. You are consuming mass quantities of genetically modified food. The milk on your Cheerios this morning came from a genetically modified cow, and the Cheerios themselves featured genetically modified whole grain goodness. At lunch you'll enjoy french fries from genetically modified potatoes and perhaps a bucket of genetically modified fried chicken. If you don't have any meetings this afternoon, maybe you'll wash it all down with the finest genetically modified hops, grains, and barley, brewed to perfection—or at least to completion if you're drinking Schaefer.

2   Everything you eat is the result of genetic modification. When a rancher in Wyoming selected his stud bull to mate with a certain cow to produce the calf that ultimately produced the milk on your breakfast table, he was manipulating genes. Sounds delicious, doesn't it? Sorry, but you get the point.

3   Long before you were ever born, farmers were splicing genes and manipulating seeds to create more robust plants. Genetic modification used to be called "breeding," and people have been doing it for centuries. Thomas Jefferson did it at Monticello, as he experimented in his gardens with literally hundreds of varieties of fruits and vegetables. (Hmm, Thomas Jefferson and genes. . . . This column is going to disappoint a lot of people doing Web searches.)

4   Anyway, to return to the topic at hand, breeding isn't a scary word, so people who oppose technology call it "genetic modification." They want to cast biotechnology, which is just a more precise and effective breeding tool, as some kind of threat to our lives, instead of the blessing that it is.

5   Have you ever seen corn in its natural state without genetic modification? It's disgusting. We're talking about that nasty, gnarled, multi-colored garbage used as ornamentation in Thanksgiving displays. The fear mongers should eat that the next time they want to criticize technology. In fact, the fear mongers are waging a very successful campaign against biotechnology, especially in Europe where they've lobbied to limit the availability of "genetically modified" foods. Even in the United States, where we generally embrace technology and its possibilities, the fear is spreading—not because of some horrible event related to the food supply, but because of more aggressive spinning of the media. In fact, you've been enjoying foods enhanced by biotechnology for most of the last decade. And the news is all good—lower prices and more abundant food.

6   As for the future, the potential to eliminate human suffering is enormous. Right now, according to the World Health Organization, more than a million kids die every year because they lack vitamin A in their diets. Millions more become blind. WHO estimates that more than a billion people suffer from anemia, caused by iron deficiency. What if we could develop rice or corn plants with all of the essential vitamins for children? Personally, I'd rather have an entire day's nutrition bio-engineered into a Twinkie or a pan pizza, but I recognize the benefits of more-nutritious crops. Reasonable people can disagree on the best applications for this technology.

7   Still, the critics want to talk about the dangers of genetically modified crops. The Environmental Protection Agency wants to regulate the use of certain bio-engineered corn seeds because they include a resistance to pests. Specifically, the seeds are bred to include a toxin called BT that kills little creatures called corn borers, so farmers don't need to spray pesticides. Turns out, according to the EPA, that the toxin in the corn can kill monarch butterflies, too. The butterflies don't eat corn, but the EPA is afraid that the corn pollen will blow over and land on a milkweed and stick to it and then confused monarch caterpillars will inadvertently eat the pollen. Not exactly the end of the world, but it sounds bad—until you consider the alternatives. According to Professor Nina Fedoroff, "A wide-spectrum pesticide sprayed from a plane is going to kill a lot more insects than will be killed by an in-plant toxin."

8   Of course, the anti-tech crowd will say that they don't like pesticides either. They promote organic farming—meaning we use more land to produce our food and we

clear more wilderness. We also pay more for food, since we're not using the efficiencies that come from technology. Maybe that's not a problem for you or me, but it's bad news for those millions of malnourished kids around the world. Says Fedoroff, "I think that most inhabitants of contemporary urban societies don't have a clue about how tough it is to grow enough food for the human population in competition with bacteria, fungi, insects, and animals and in the face of droughts, floods, and other climatic variations." That may be true, but I do think that most Americans understand the positive impact of technology. And that's why they'll ultimately reject the scare campaign against biotechnology.

Jeffrey Smith

Another Reason for Schools to Ban Genetically Engineered Foods

Before the Appleton, Wisconsin high school replaced their cafeteria's processed foods with wholesome, nutritious food, the school was described as out-of-control. There were weapons violations, student disruptions, and a cop on duty full-time. After the change in school meals, the students were calm, focused, and orderly. There were no more weapons violations, and no suicides, expulsions, dropouts, or drug violations. The new diet and improved behavior has lasted for seven years, and now other schools are changing their meal programs with similar results.

2   Years ago, a science class at Appleton found support for their new diet by conducting a cruel and unusual experiment with three mice. They fed them the junk food that kids in other high schools eat everyday. The mice freaked out. Their behavior was totally different than the three mice in the neighboring cage. The neighboring mice had good karma; they were fed nutritious whole foods and behaved like mice. They slept during the day inside their cardboard tube, played with each other, and acted very mouse-like. The junk food mice, on the other hand, destroyed their cardboard tube, were no longer nocturnal, stopped playing with each other, fought often, and two mice eventually killed the third and ate it. After the three month experiment, the students rehabilitated the two surviving junk food mice with a diet of whole foods. After about three weeks, the mice came around.

3   Sister Luigi Frigo repeats this experiment every year in her second grade class in Cudahy, Wisconsin, but mercifully, for only four days. Even on the first day of junk food, the mice's behavior "changes drastically." They become lazy, antisocial, and nervous. And it still takes the mice about two to three weeks on unprocessed foods to return to normal. One year, the second graders tried to do the experiment again a few months later with the same mice, but this time the animals refused to eat the junk food.

A Conversation with Nina V. Fedoroff

On August 19, 2008, the following interview with Nina Federoff appeared in the regular "Conversations with" feature within the science section of the New York Times. Claudia Dreifus posed the questions and wrote the introduction.

When she was a single mother in the early 1960s, Nina V. Fedoroff, 66, defied odds and conventionality by working her way through college, graduate school and postdoctoral studies. Dr. Fedoroff, a member of the National Academy of Sciences, did fundamental research on plant transposons, or jumping genes, and was among the first to clone plant DNA. She is science adviser to the secretary of state and administrator of the Agency for International Development. We spoke last month in Washington and later on the telephone. An edited version of the conversations follows.

Q. WHEN YOU GAVE A RECENT SPEECH AT COLUMBIA UNIVERSITY ADVOCATING GENETICALLY MODIFIED FOODS, SOMEONE SITTING NEAR ME SAID, "OH GREAT, OUR STATE DEPARTMENT IS PUSHING G.M. FOOD. SHE'S THE AMBASSADOR FROM MONSANTO." WHAT'S YOUR RESPONSE?

A. How do I answer him? My answer is: There's almost no food that isn't genetically modified. Genetic modification is the basis of all evolution.

Things change because our planet is subjected to a lot of radiation, which causes DNA damage, which gets repaired, but results in mutations, which create a ready mixture of plants that people can choose from to improve agriculture.

In the last century, as we learned more about genes, we were able to devise ways of accelerating evolution.

So a lot of modern plant strains were created by applying chemicals or radiation to cause mutations that improved the crop. That's how plant breeding was done in the 20th century. The paradox is that now that we've

4   Across the ocean in Holland, a student fed one group of mice genetically modified (GM) corn and soy, and another group the non-GM variety. The GM mice stopped playing with each other and withdrew into their own parts of the cage. When the student tried to pick them up, unlike their well-behaved neighbors, the GM mice scampered around in apparent fear and tried to climb the walls. One mouse in the GM group was found dead at the end of the experiment.

5   It's interesting to note that the junk food fed to the mice in the Wisconsin experiments also contained genetically modified ingredients. And although the Appleton school lunch program did not specifically attempt to remove GM foods, it happened anyway. That's because GM foods such as soy and corn and their derivatives are largely found in processed foods. So when the school switched to unprocessed alternatives, almost all ingredients derived from GM crops were taken out automatically.

invented techniques that introduce just one gene without disturbing the rest, some people think that's terrible.

Q. WHY DO YOU THINK THERE IS SUCH FIERCE OPPOSITION TO GENETICALLY MODIFIED FOODS?

A. This is an unintended consequence of our success. We've gotten so good at growing food that we've gone, in a few generations, from nearly half of Americans living on farms to 2 percent. We no longer think about how the wonderful things in the grocery store got there, and we'd like to go back to what we think is a more natural way.

But I'm afraid we can't, in part because there are just too many of us in this world. If everybody switched to organic farming, we couldn't support the earth's current population—maybe half.

Q. YOU BELIEVE THAT ENVIRONMENTALISTS SHOULD BE EMBRACING GENETICALLY MODIFIED FOODS. WHAT'S YOUR ARGUMENT?

A. If we put more land under cultivation to feed the world's growing population, we're going to pull down the remaining forests.

And if that happens, it will contribute tremendously to desertification. The more we can grow on already cultivated land, the better. Europe, North America, Australia, Japan—we've been extremely successful in applying science to agriculture and we can afford to say, "Let's go natural." But there's collateral damage.

When I went to Rwanda, you saw farmers with holdings of less than an acre. If their population doubles again, we're looking at more strife. Arguably, Darfur isn't about politics, it's about water. Many of the conflicts in the poorest countries are about too many people chasing too few resources. Do we have time to transition something that looks like Rwanda to a more efficient agriculture and to do it wisely enough to absorb the people? ■

6   Does this mean that GM foods negatively affect the behavior of humans or animals? It would certainly be irresponsible to say so on the basis of a single student mice experiment and the results at Appleton. On the other hand, it is equally irresponsible to say that it doesn't.

7   We are just beginning to understand the influence of food on behavior. A study in *Science* in December 2002 concluded that "food molecules act like hormones, regulating body functioning and triggering cell division. The molecules can cause mental imbalances ranging from attention-deficit and hyperactivity disorder to serious mental illness." The problem is we do not know which food molecules have what effect. The bigger problem is that the composition of GM foods can change radically without our knowledge.

8   Genetically modified foods have genes inserted into their DNA. But genes are not Legos; they don't just snap into place. Gene insertion creates unpredicted,

irreversible changes. In one study, for example, a gene chip monitored the DNA before and after a single foreign gene was inserted. As much as 5 percent of the DNA's genes changed the amount of protein they were producing. Not only is that huge in itself, but these changes can multiply through complex interactions down the line.

9   In spite of the potential for dramatic changes in the composition of GM foods, they are typically measured for only a small number of known nutrient levels. But even if we *could* identify all the changed compounds, at this point we wouldn't know which might be responsible for the antisocial nature of mice or humans. Likewise, we are only beginning to identify the medicinal compounds in food. We now know, for example, that the pigment in blueberries may revive the brain's neural communication system, and the antioxidant found in grape skins may fight cancer and reduce heart disease. But what about other valuable compounds we don't know about that might change or disappear in GM varieties?

10   Consider GM soy. In July 1999, years after it was on the market, independent researchers published a study showing that it contains 12–14 percent less cancer-fighting phytoestrogens. What else has changed that we don't know about? [Monsanto responded with its own study, which concluded that soy's phytoestrogen levels vary too much to even carry out a statistical analysis. They failed to disclose, however, that the laboratory that conducted Monsanto's experiment had been instructed to use an obsolete method to detect phytoestrogens—one that had been replaced due to its highly variable results.]

11   In 1996, Monsanto published a paper in the *Journal of Nutrition* that concluded in the title, "The composition of glyphosate-tolerant soybean seeds is equivalent to that of conventional soybeans." The study only compared a small number of nutrients and a close look at their charts revealed significant differences in the fat, ash, and carbohydrate content. In addition, GM soy meal contained 27 percent more trypsin inhibitor, a well-known soy allergen. The study also used questionable methods. Nutrient comparisons are routinely conducted on plants grown in identical conditions so that variables such as weather and soil can be ruled out. Otherwise, differences in plant composition could be easily missed. In Monsanto's study, soybeans were planted in widely varying climates and geography.

12   Although one of their trials *was* a side-by-side comparison between GM and non-GM soy, for some reason the results were left out of the paper altogether. Years later, a medical writer found the missing data in the archives of the *Journal of Nutrition* and made them public. No wonder the scientists left them out. The GM soy showed significantly lower levels of protein, a fatty acid, and phenylalanine, an essential amino acid. Also, toasted GM soy meal contained nearly twice the amount of a lectin that may block the body's ability to assimilate other nutrients. Furthermore, the toasted GM soy contained as much as seven times the amount of trypsin inhibitor, indicating that the allergen may survive cooking more in the GM variety. (This might explain the 50 percent jump in soy allergies in the UK, just after GM soy was introduced.)

13   We don't know all the changes that occur with genetic engineering, but certainly GM crops are not the same. Ask the animals. Eyewitness reports from all over North America describe how several types of animals, when given a choice, avoided eating GM food. These included cows, pigs, elk, deer, raccoons, squirrels, rats, and mice. In fact, the Dutch student mentioned above first determined that his mice had a

two-to-one preference for non-GM before forcing half of them to eat only the engineered variety.

14   Differences in GM food will likely have a much larger impact on children. They are three to four times more susceptible to allergies. Also, they convert more of the food into body-building material. Altered nutrients or added toxins can result in developmental problems. For this reason, animal nutrition studies are typically conducted on young, developing animals. After the feeding trial, organs are weighed and often studied under magnification. If scientists used mature animals instead of young ones, even severe nutritional problems might not be detected. The Monsanto study used mature animals instead of young ones.

15   They also diluted their GM soy with non-GM protein 10- or 12-fold before feeding the animals. And they never weighed the organs or examined them under a microscope. The study, which is the only major animal feeding study on GM soy ever published, is dismissed by critics as rigged to avoid finding problems.

16   Unfortunately, there is a much bigger experiment going on—an uncontrolled one which we are all a part of. We're being fed GM foods daily, without knowing the impact of these foods on our health, our behavior, or our children. Thousands of schools around the world, particularly in Europe, have decided not to let their kids be used as guinea pigs. They have banned GM foods.

17   The impact of changes in the composition of GM foods is only one of several reasons why these foods may be dangerous. Other reasons may be far worse (see www.seedsofdeception.com). With the epidemic of obesity and diabetes and with the results in Appleton, parents and schools are waking up to the critical role that diet plays. When making changes in what kids eat, removing GM foods should be a priority.

Ben Burkett

Green Revolution a Failure in Africa

The global food crisis and how to stop hunger from escalating in the midst of the current economic crisis will be the subject of a recent G8 meeting of Agricultural ministers in Treviso, Italy. For now, the G8 and the United States continue to advocate the same disastrous policies that got us into the current mess where 1 billion people lack access to adequate food. U.S. agriculture secretary Tom Vilsack has said that biotechnology is necessary to address hunger while the U.S. Senate Foreign Relations Committee recently approved without much public debate the "Global Hunger Security Act" sponsored by Senators Bob Casey and Richard Lugar, that for the first time would mandate the U.S. to fund genetic engineering projects in foreign agriculture research. Meanwhile, the Gates Foundation has billions invested in the "Alliance for a Green Revolution in Africa."

2   As an African American farmer from Mississippi who has visited and traveled to Africa many times, I am stunned that the

real solutions continue to be ignored. We face multiple crises—
financial, climate, energy, and water. Business as usual will not
solve our global hunger crisis. More expensive genetically modified seeds, pesticides, and chemical-intensive practices won't
help the hungry and will only allow more profits and control for
seed companies like Monsanto and Syngenta.

3   While the G8 calls for more "free trade" in agriculture and
more biotechnology, groundbreaking scientific reports and actions
at the United Nations are actively calling for a different vision of
agriculture. This would be based on agroecological methods that
respect our planet's resources and provide a decent living for family farmers. In 2008, the International Assessment of Agricultural
Knowledge, Science and Technology for Development (IAASTD),
backed by United Nations agencies, the World Bank, and over
400 contributing scientists from 80 countries found that the most
promising solutions to the world's food crisis include investing in
agroecological research, extension, and farming. The Congress
and Obama Administration need to take a serious look at the
IAASTD report before funneling scarce resources into another
Green Revolution in Africa.

4   Past public-private partnerships in Africa have proven to be
failures, such as the 14-year project between Monsanto, USAID,
and the Kenyan Agricultural Research Institute to engineer a
virus-resistant sweet potato. The GM sweet potato failed to show
any resistance to the virus while local varieties actually
outperformed the GM variety in field trials. The U.S. approach to
helping Africa should not be a top-down process that excludes
the voices of African farmers who have the knowledge of their
land and what food to grow.

5   The UN is helping to move the discussion towards "food sovereignty" by appointing a Special Rapporteur on the "Right to
Food," and convening a Panel on the Right to Food. I was
privileged to hear General Coordinator of La Via Campesina
Henry Saragih of Indonesia and Professor Olivier De Schutter before the United Nations General Assembly. De Schutter said, "the
right to food is not simply about more production, but about distribution and access. While high food prices are bad for consumers,
so too are depressed prices for farmers who can't make a living.
De Schutter pointed out that 60% of hungry people in the world
are small farmers, pastoralists, fisherfolk, and others who make a
living off the land. An additional 20% are landless agriculture
workers."

6   A "right to food" framework therefore goes deeper than simply the misguided obsession with yields and productivity, and
more fundamentally towards questions regarding democracy and
access to resources, including land, water and credit. A recent re-

port by Union of Concerned Scientists titled "Failure to Yield: Evaluating the Performance of Genetically Engineered Crops," showed that despite 20 years of research and 13 years of commercialization, genetic engineering has failed to significantly increase U.S. crop yields while only driving up costs for farmers. In comparison, traditional breeding continues to deliver better results. The scientific research and renewed focus on the "right to food" exposes why we must move away from Green Revolution monoculture practices and instead embrace ecologically sound practices, more equitable trade rules and local food distribution systems to empower family farmers. Now the governments of the world and the Gates Foundation need to finally get the message as well.

GREGORY **JAFFE**

Lessen the Fear of Genetically Engineered Crops

rotesters carrying signs stating "Biocide is Homicide" and shouting concerns about the risks of eating genetically engineered foods recently demonstrated outside the biotechnology industry's annual convention. Inside the convention center, industry extolled the safety of genetically engineered foods and the benefits of future crops like "golden rice."

2   Neither corporate hyperbole nor radical slogans do much to inform the public. What is needed is the shaping of sensible measures to ensure that genetically engineered foods are safe. The first few first engineered crops are already providing remarkable benefits. Cotton modified to kill insects has greatly diminished farmers' use of toxic insecticides, thereby reducing costs, increasing yields, and, presumably, reducing harm to nontarget species. Likewise, biotech soybeans facilitate no-till farming, which reduces soil erosion and water pollution.

3   Despite such benefits, agricultural biotechnology is under siege for reasons good and bad. Activists have burned fields and bombed labs. Farmers will not plant genetically engineered sweet corn, sugar beets, and apples, for fear of consumer rejection. And countries in Europe and Asia refuse to import U.S.-grown genetically engineered crops. Some countries now require labeling of foods containing engineered ingredients. Those requirements have spurred food processors, who want to avoid negative-sounding labels, to eliminate bioengineered ingredients.

4   Buffeted by the polarized debate, many Americans oppose biotech foods, in part because farmers and seed companies get the benefits while consumers bear the risk. If anti-genetically engineered sentiment increases, U.S. farmers may be forced to forgo

the advantages of engineered crops. And most public and private investment in agricultural biotechnology would dry up.

5   To reap the benefits of agricultural biotechnology, minimize the risks, and boost public confidence, the U.S. must upgrade its flawed regulatory system. Currently, the Food and Drug Administration (FDA) does not formally approve any genetically engineered crops as safe to eat. Instead, it reviews safety data provided voluntarily by seed companies. That consultation process, which the FDA admits is "not a comprehensive scientific review of the data," culminates with the FDA stating only that it has "no further questions . . . at this time." Although no health problems with genetically engineered crops have been detected, that industry-driven process is weak insurance. The recent FDA proposal requiring a formal notification before marketing a biotech food is an improvement.

6   All biotech foods should go through a mandatory approval process with specific testing and data requirements. The National Academy of Sciences should be commissioned to recommend a precise method of assessment.

7   Genetically engineered crops also raise environmental concerns. They could lead to pesticide-resistant insects and weeds and might contaminate plants that are close relatives of the crops. To safeguard our ecosystem, the current laws need fixing. Congress should close regulatory gaps to ensure that all future applications of biotechnology, ranging from fast-growing fish to corn plants that produce industrial chemicals, receive thorough environmental reviews. Also, the Environmental Protection Agency must enforce restrictions it has imposed on bioengineered crops to help prevent emergence of insecticide-resistant pests.

8   Although strong regulations would minimize environmental and safety risks, nothing would boost public confidence more than engineered products that benefit consumers. No beneficial products currently exist.

9   Worldwide acceptance of biotechnology will occur only when other countries reap benefits from this technology. Instead of spending millions of dollars on feel-good advertising campaigns, the biotech industry should train developing-country scientists and fund research in those countries. Companies—and universities—should donate patented crops and processes to developing countries. Agricultural biotechnology is not a panacea for all agricultural problems here or abroad, nor is it free from risk. But, with adequate safeguards, it could provide tremendous benefits for an ever-populous, pesticide-drenched, and water-deficient globe.

FROM READING TO WRITING

1. In this section, you read Bill Joy's written argument for caution in the development of new nanotechnologies, followed by Merkle's reaction to Joy's piece, which takes place in the form of an interview. Conduct a rhetorical analysis of these two forms of argumentation: What are some of the rhetorical differences between arguing through a written essay versus speaking out via a moderated verbal dialogue? Consider questions of audience, the process of argument construction, ethos, rhetorical impact, and so on.

2. In his essay, Bill Gates writes glowingly of the potential for robots to benefit human society. Yet, as you have also seen (in the arguments put forth by Joy and Marks), robots are not without their critics. Exactly what is a robot, anyway? What differentiates robots from other machines? Write an essay that shows your attitude toward robots by defining them in a particular way. (For advice on writing definitions, see Chapter 8.)

3. One of the major methods for convincing people of the need for organ donor compensation or stem cell research is the use of personal examples—narratives—about people who might benefit. Beginning from your own informed beliefs, write a story that illustrates your position on a particular scientific issue—stem cell, organ donation, genetically modified foods, or some other controversial process or technology. If possible, draw from your personal experience with the subject at hand. (For advice on narrative arguments, see Chapter 11.)

4. Conduct a rhetorical analysis of the arguments of Ron Reagan. How is his speech a product of the particular rhetorical situation that he found himself in: in front of the Democratic National Convention, a few weeks after the death of his Republican father, and before a national television audience? How might he have presented his argument if he had appeared before Republicans, or if his speech had not been televised? Do you agree with Reagan's assertion that his speech is not political? (See Chapter 5 for advice on rhetorical analysis.)

5. Evaluate—on the basis of practicality, ethics, or esthetics (or all of them)—one of the scientific processes or technologies discussed in this chapter. (See Chapter 10 for information on how evaluation arguments work.)

6. Based on the guidelines in Chapter 13, write a proposal argument that defends or undermines the practice of genetic modification of food crops *from a human rights perspective*. Is genetic engineering the solution to world hunger (or at least a part of that solution)? Or will it only exacerbate the existing polarization between the "haves" and the "have-nots?" Conduct your own research prior to constructing your argument.

26 | Privacy

New Challenges to Personal Privacy

How does a new bathroom design, like this colored glass structure in the middle of an apartment, reflect (or push for) new attitudes about privacy?

The Dog Poop Girl (as she came to be known) was riding the subway in Seoul, South Korea, one day when her dog decided to "take care of business." According to a *Washington Post* story written by Jonathan Krim on July 7, 2005, the woman (a university student) made no move to clean up the mess, so fellow passengers grew agitated. One of them recorded the scene on a cell phone camera and then posted photos on a Web site. Web surfers came upon the photos and began referring to her as Dog Poop Girl. One thing led to another, and soon her privacy was completely gone: people revealed her true name, began asking for and sharing more information about her, launched blogs commenting about her and her relatives, and generally crackled with gossip about her and her behavior. Ultimately she became the subject of sermons and online discussions, and her story made the national news. In humiliation, Dog Poop Girl withdrew from her university.

According to an American Civil Liberties Union (ACLU) Web posting in May 2010, the Department of Justice was seeking to obtain the contents of a Yahoo! e-mail account without the e-mailer's permission and without a search warrant. Government investigators in the process of building a criminal case were maintaining that because the Yahoo! e-mail had been accessed by the user, it no longer qualified as "in electronic storage" (protected as private property under the Stored Communications Act). But Yahoo! asked a federal court judge to block the government attempt, and the company was supported by the ACLU, the Electronic Frontier Foundation (EFF), Google, and many other public interest organizations. "The government is trying to evade federal privacy law and the Constitution," said EFF Senior Staff Attorney Kevin Bankston. "The Fourth Amendment protects these stored e-mails, just like it does our private papers. We all have a reasonable expectation of privacy in the contents of our e-mail accounts, and the government should have to make a show-

> "You have zero privacy now—get over it."
>
> —SCOTT MCNEALY, CEO OF SUN MICROSYSTEMS

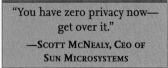

ing of probable cause to a judge before it rifles through our private communications."

A third incident was reported by Felisa Cardona in the *Denver Post* on August 2, 2005. A computer security breach at the University of Colorado left 29,000 students and 7,000 faculty and staff vulnerable to identity theft. It seems that hackers attacked the university computers in order to gain access to the Buff One ID card used by many students and staff. Though no information seems to have been used due to this attack, 6,000 students had to be issued new cards in order to gain access to their dorms. Moreover, after the incident, Colorado officials decided to stop using Social Security number identifications, and many other universities have done the same because they too have been targeted by identity thieves.

These three incidents illustrate some of the new challenges to personal privacy that have been raised in response to technology developments and concerns about secu-

A biometric measuring instrument at Busch Gardens helps staff make sure the same person uses the same ticket each day.

rity that are one legacy of the September 11, 2001, attacks. There is no doubt that electronic technologies have given people a new degree of personal freedom: handheld computers, cell phones, e-mail, and Web shopping are now routine time-savers. But there is also no doubt that a price has been paid for that freedom: That price is the surveillance side of the Internet and other technologies. In the wake of September 11, other terrorist attacks, and the increased attention to security that has ensued, privacy issues have been an increasing concern in American life. Law enforcement officials seek access to information about potential conspiracies, parents are placing devices on their children in order to keep tabs on their whereabouts, and businesses increasingly gather information about people to individualize marketing campaigns, keep an eye out for good (and bad) credit risks, and customize customers. (Businesses and police also increasingly spy on their own employees.)

One emerging technology—biometrics—measures physical and behavioral data, such as fingerprints or keystroke patterns, in order to identify individual human beings. Biometric recognition provides a deeply personalized means of identification that enhances security, say its supporters, but a national biometric database also raises questions of privacy, say its detractors. What would it mean in terms of national security and surveillance to store citizens' inherently unique characteristics in a nationwide database?

And when is freedom too much freedom? If bloggers act as a posse, tracking down criminals and turning them over to law enforcement, is that appropriate action or vigilante action? What about efforts to replicate what was done to the Dog Poop Girl? Should laws prevent people from publicizing and branding people who seem undesirable? Is too much sharing going on via Facebook? Should people who wish to share secrets—whether the secrets are true or not—have the anonymity and apparent protection afforded by the Internet? Must e-mail users simply accept as a fact of life that they are bombarded by hundreds of unauthorized, unsolicited spam messages? And what are the limits of what government officials should be able to do to inspect the personal records of citizens?

Contemporary Arguments

Is it possible, in other words, to have both security and freedom in the United States? What is the proper balance of the two?

On the one hand, some people support a national ID card (like those already used, incidentally, in several European nations) or sign up for in-vehicle security systems such as OnStar (always on the watch!) as a safety feature. They root for police to pursue potential terrorists, they use E-ZPass without giving a thought to the fact that they are giving out their whereabouts, they approve when cameras are mounted to watch over high-crime areas, they wink when Internet service providers disclose customer records to government agents if they feel that a crime

is being committed, and they appreciate being notified that convicted felons have moved into the neighborhood. On the other hand, they also protest when police use wiretaps without explicit legal permission, worry about the ability of global positioning systems to snoop on people from satellites (especially by zeroing in on cell phones or implanted homing devices), and protest when roving surveillance cameras are mounted in stores and at street corners, in public parks and on school playgrounds.

Everyone these days seems to be monitored or monitoring. Online data collectors record which Web sites people visit; airlines record data on people's travels; companies routinely perform background checks on potential employees; bus and train companies

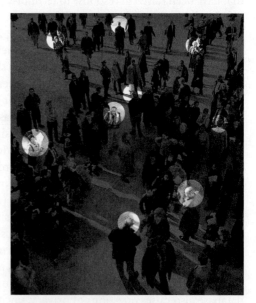

This artistic rendering of the all-seeing eye of surveillance cameras suggests that while such cameras may be designed to provide security, they also intrude on individuals' privacy without their knowledge.

check passenger lists against records of "suspicious" characters; businesses seek to develop systems that can deliver customized marketing information to particular households and commuters; and supermarkets record purchases in order to fine-tune their stocking patterns. In the future, some say, we can look forward to smart cars, smart airports, smart TVs, smart credit cards, and smart homes—all designed to give us certain freedoms, if at the price of losing some of our privacy.

The arguments in this chapter discuss all these questions related to privacy. Adam Penenberg's "The Surveillance Society" overviews the brave new world that is now developing (for better or for worse), and the selections that follow argue about aspects of technology that undermine our privacy. Robert Cringely sounds an alert about Facebook. Jonathan Locker worries about OnStar. Dahlia Lithwick questions the ethics of sexting. Jay Stanley (speaking for the American Civil Liberties Union) contends than body searches of airline passengers are neither effective nor constitutional. And Adam Cohen makes a plea for citizens to be able to walk down the street without being monitored by cameras—to be able to enjoy what he calls "locational privacy." These are just a small sample of the issues that are facing Americans as it becomes easier and easier for us to watch each other.

Because the emerging field of biometrics effectively illustrates the tensions between protection and privacy, we look in detail at this emerging technology in the Issue in Focus. The selections reproduced there describe the technologies (such as signature analysis, keystroke patterns, and vein biometric systems) and dramatize the excitement—and the fears—that accompany them. On one hand, biometric technologies hold out the promise of improved crime fighting and national security. On the other, such technologies inevitably encroach on individuals' privacy and may even open the door to DNA identify theft. What price are we willing to pay for privacy (or security)? At what point does it make sense to forfeit private information for protection and convenience?

ADAM **PENENBERG**

The Surveillance Society

Adam L. Penenberg's Web site indicates that he is assistant director of the Business and Economic Program at New York University. He is the author of several books, including *Spooked: Espionage in Corporate America* and *Viral Loop: From Facebook to Twitter, How Today's Smartest Businesses Grow Themselves*. Formerly senior editor at *Forbes*, Penenberg is now a contributing writer to *Fast Company* and has also written for *Inc.*, the *New York Times*, *Slate*, *Playboy*, *Mother Jones*, and *Wired*, in which the following article appeared in December 2001, shortly after 9-11.

Within hours of the attacks on the World Trade Center and the Pentagon, as federal officials shut down airports and U.S. strategists began plotting a military response, Attorney General John Ashcroft was mobilizing his own forces. In meetings with top aides at the FBI's Strategic Information and Operations Center—during which the

Surveillance cameras have become a part of the urban landscape.

White House as well as the State and Defense departments dialed in via secure video-conference—Ashcroft pulled together a host of antiterrorism measures. Days later, the attorney general sent to Capitol Hill a bill (the Patriot Act) that would make it easier for the government to tap cell phones and pagers, give the Feds broad authority to monitor email and Web browsing, strengthen money-laundering laws, and weaken immigrants' rights. There were whispers of a national identity card and of using face-recognition software and retinal scans at airports and in other public spaces. And high above it all would sit an Office of Homeland Security, run by former Pennsylvania Governor Tom Ridge, who would report directly to the Oval Office.

2   Such talk usually generates fractious debate between privacy hawks and security hounds. By now, most of us can recite the familiar *Nightline* arguments and counterarguments. But this time the acrimony has been muted. The terrorist assault on America shifted the balance between privacy and security. What was considered Orwellian one week seemed perfectly reasonable—even necessary—the next. Politicians who routinely clash were marching in lockstep. "When you're in this type of conflict—when you're at war—civil liberties are treated differently," said Senate Republican Trent Lott. "This event will change the balance between freedom and security," echoed House Democrat Richard Gephardt. "There's a whole range of issues that we're going to be grappling with in the next month that takes us to this basic trade-off."

Almost immediately, there were unmistakable signs that new surveillance tools would be a linchpin in the war on terrorism. The FBI met with AOL, EarthLink, and other large ISPs, and there was renewed talk of using DCS 1000 to let the FBI monitor email traffic. Visionics—a maker of face-recognition software used in surveillance cameras in London and Tampa, Florida, and in the databases of close to a dozen state law enforcement agencies—reported that its switchboards were jammed. The stock prices of some companies in the security business spiked as the rest of the market crumbled.

But truth be told, the U.S. was embracing the Surveillance Society well before September 11. In the name of safety, we have grown increasingly comfortable with cameras monitoring us whenever we stop to buy a Slurpee, grab cash from an ATM, or park in a downtown lot. And in the name of convenience, we've happily accepted a range of products and services, from cell phones to credit cards to Web browsers, that make our lives easier and have the secondary effect of permitting us to be tracked. They're not spy technologies—but they might as well be.

Americans don't seem to be spooked by these incursions. "Apparently, consumers don't feel their privacy is threatened," says Barbara Bellissimo, owner of a now-defunct dotcom that offered anonymous Web browsing. "That's why there are no profitable privacy companies." (It might also be why millions of Americans watch reality-based television shows like *Survivor* that package round-the-clock surveillance as entertainment.)

Just how vast is the new surveillance world? Let's start with cameras. More than 60 communities in a dozen states have set up traffic-light cameras that ticket drivers for running red lights or speeding. Casinos in Las Vegas zoom in on the cards we hold at the blackjack table. Cameras are mounted on police cars, they hang from trees in public parks, they're affixed to the walls in sports stadiums and shopping malls. David Brin, author of *The Transparent Society,* postulates a "Moore's law of cameras." He sees them roughly "halving in size, and doubling in acuity and movement capability and sheer numbers, every year or two."

The surveillance net also has a digital arm. With computers home to the data entrails of half a billion bank accounts, just as many credit card accounts, and hundreds of millions of medical claims, mortgages, and retirement funds, there exists a significant cache of online data about each of us.

Then there's the matter of monitoring our daily travels. Debit cards like New York's E-ZPass deduct a fee as commuters zip through tollbooths *and* track our comings and goings on the road; transit cards chart riders' subway journeys; employee ID cards can show when we arrived at work, when we left, and where we went within the office complex. Phone cards mark who we call and, often, from where. Credit card records etch us in time and space more reliably than any eyewitness. So do airline tickets—even if you pay cash. And as for the cell phone: "If you turn it on, you can be tracked," says Jim Atkinson, a countersurveillance expert who is president of Granite Island Group in Gloucester, Massachusetts.

OnStar, GM's onboard communications system, offers a GPS service to its 1.5 million customers. That means that at any given moment, OnStar can locate each of those 1.5 million cars. (OnStar will track a car only at the request of the driver or, in some instances, the police; the company keeps no historical database of car locations, though if it had the inclination—or was pressured—to gather and store reams of data, it could.) Mercedes' TeleAid and Ford's Wingcast provide similar services. As does

AirIQ, which Hertz, Avis, and Budget use for their premium fleets: If a car is abandoned, AirIQ can locate it; if it's stolen, the company can disable its motor.

10   For now, the information about each of us resides in dozens of separate databases owned by the credit card companies and the phone carriers, the rental car agencies and police departments, the ISPs and the IRS. But the aftermath of September 11 could change all that by creating in many of us an appetite for information and a willingness to be monitored. And this raises a disquieting possibility: Will the disparate elements of our surveillance society be assembled into a surveillance web? Will the private companies and the government agencies come together to create a superdatabase accessible to . . . who? Will it strip us not just of personal privacy—we seem resigned, even OK, with that—but of public anonymity?

11   Worrying is a waste of time. Surveillance is here. It was inevitable. But the surveillance state is not.

12   A few days after September 11, Akram Jaber was driving his Chevy Suburban over the pothole-strewn streets of Chicago's south side. With his 15-month-old son in the backseat, he was heading to the liquor store he owns to lock up for the night. A battered Chevy Caprice sped by, then stopped in front of him at a red light. Two men emerged; one pointed a gun at Jaber. "Take it easy," Jaber called out. "I have my son in the car." He left the keys in the ignition, unhitched his son, and turned over the $50,000 vehicle.

13   As the carjackers sped away, Jaber whipped out his cell phone to dial 911. Then he called an operator at OnStar. (He had been paying $16.95 a month for the basic Safety & Security plan: roadside and emergency assistance, remote lock and unlock, and stolen vehicle tracking.) He gave his name, license plate number, and four-digit PIN. The operator called Jaber's vehicle and requested GPS data, then updated the car's position by pinging it every minute. The operator relayed the car's heading to the police officer on the scene, who forwarded it to a dispatcher. Within minutes, officers swooped in on the vehicle and arrested the men. "The police were amazed at how easy it was," say Jaber, who himself was awfully pleased.

14   What's really amazing is just how many similar tools are becoming available to law enforcement. A suspect's alibi can be checked out by looking at the location data trail created by use of his tollbooth pass, transit card, or credit card. Surveillance cameras capture images that authorities can cross-check against a database of criminals through the use of face-recognition software. And cell phones have become the digital equivalent of Hansel and Gretel's bread crumbs.

15   When a cell phone is turned on, it broadcasts an identification number to the closest antennas, which allow the carrier to chart its customers. It's a simple matter— known as triangulation—to track the signal as it arrives at different towers, then calculate the location of the phone based on time differences. The police have taken full advantage of this tracking trick, though—technically, at least—they need a court order to access the information. Earlier this year, Timothy Crosby, 40, was busted for raping and robbing a Brooklyn woman after the police located him by homing in on his cell phone signal. In November 2000, authorities pursued Kofi Apea Orleans-Lindsay for allegedly killing a Maryland state trooper during a buy-and-bust operation. Police used cell data to track Orleans-Lindsay to Brooklyn, where they arrested him.

16   Then there was the case of Christopher Stewart, a New York subway employee whose alibi in the March slaying of his ex-girlfriend crumbled when police subjected his

MetroCard transit pass to detailed analysis (MetroCard use can be traced by a serial number). Stewart had claimed he was boarding a Staten Island ferry at the time she was killed. But data from the MetroCard, still in his possession, had him exiting a subway station near the crime scene just before the murder. He was arrested and indicted by a grand jury. MetroCard records were also used against Marco Valencia, who was charged in the December 1999 assault and robbery of a supermarket manager in Manhattan. Valencia claimed he was in Staten Island, but his MetroCard told a different tale, and when confronted, he pleaded guilty.

17   In light of the way cell phones and transit cards are being used to track criminals, video cameras seem remarkably, well, obvious. But they're a cornerstone of the surveillance society, and they've proved an important weapon in law enforcement's arsenal. Prior to September 11, such cameras stirred up controversy. When the Tampa Police Department installed face-recognition software in its network last June, the public was outraged, and House majority leader Dick Armey joined with civil rights groups to protest. There was similar push-back in Britain in 1996, when authorities installed 300 cameras in the East London neighborhood of Newham in an effort to gather intelligence on suspected IRA bombings. The cameras didn't help much in the fight on terrorism, but overall crime rates fell 30 percent after they were deployed, according to city figures. Crime dropped an additional 34 percent in 1998, after the cameras were equipped with Visionic's face-recognition software. Last year, illegal activities in surrounding areas increased between 10 and 20 percent, but Newham's inched up less than half a percent. The program has been so successful that Visionics has been retained to hook up closed-circuit TV cameras in five more nearby London neighborhoods.

18   Although face-recognition surveillance systems are not foolproof, most Brits now view "spy" cameras as a part of everyday life, and polls indicate a majority of citizens support their use. England already boasts about 1.5 million police surveillance cameras—more than any other country—and the government plans to double that number within three years. With so many cams, the average city denizen can expect to be taped every five minutes, according to *The Times* of London.

19   Even as new surveillance technologies increase the amount of information available about each of us, there's something reassuring in the fact that this data is extremely far-flung. It would, today, take a considerable amount of sleuthing and multiple search warrants for anyone—individuals, private companies, public agencies—to aggregate the fruits of the surveillance web in any useful way.

20   But there are signs that in the future it might be much easier to access disparate data about individuals—where they've been, what they bought, who they were with, what they were wearing, who they called, what Web sites they visited, what they wrote in email. After all, the information exists, and from a technical perspective, it's easy to tap (cell phones, credit cards, ATMs, tollbooth passes—all are part of the same bitstream of 0s and 1s). The legal protections that might have prevented access to this data are eroding. And as the line between the public and private sectors blurs, the data will likely flow in ways it never has before.

21   So what do we get? Think of all these factoids residing not in some static database but in a dynamic environment in which strands of information can be pulled together from a huge variety of sources based on a user's request. It's not Microsoft Outlook, it's Google. In fact, researchers at Applied Systems Intelligence in Roswell,

Georgia, are working on just such software. Called Karnac (Knowledge Aided Retrieval in Activity Context), the program would scan everything from gun registrations and credit card records to newspapers and Web sites. While Karnac or a similar program may be a long way off, more modest developments provide a glimpse into where we could be headed. In the weeks following the attacks, airport authorities hatched plans for security systems that would link biometric techniques like iris scans with a government database of known or suspected terrorists. Such systems could easily migrate to other public spaces, motivated by a concern for community safety and a desire to catch criminals.

22   Eventually, surveillance cameras in every mom-and-pop store could use face-recognition software and network databases to link you to your Social Security number, consumer profile, credit report, home and work addresses, and criminal and driving records. Networked street cams could track your location—and keep the digital footage on file.

23   The gated communities of tomorrow will be monitored by cameras, motion detectors, and sensors of all kinds embedded in the walls, floors—every surface. Such systems, hyped as smart-house technologies, are already in beta at universities and corporate labs across the country. Tools such as Bluetooth and 802.11 will turn every object and street corner into a node of the wireless Web, aware of and communicating with the Net-connected PDA and cell of every passerby. Like transit cards and toll-booth passes, the wireless Web isn't a surveillance technology per se, but it will have that effect.

24   Look out a few more years and nano-cameras as small as grains of sand will create a world in which the wind has eyes. Fingerprint-scanning doorknobs and steering wheels could know their users by touch.

25   There will be limits, of course—legal mechanisms like search warrants that protect individuals from undue surveillance. But those safeguards will change with the times. In an effort to bring wiretapping laws into the cellular age, Attorney General Ashcroft proposed—and Congress approved—"roving wiretaps" to give the government authority to monitor a suspect's calls from any phone and any jurisdiction. As communications technologies continue to multiply and blur, it will be increasingly difficult to say where the telephone network ends and the Web begins. Cell phones send messages to pagers. Cars log on to the Internet. The search warrants of the surveillance era will need to span multiple technologies and will likely be written with increasingly broad language.

26   If all this raises the specter of Big Brother, well, that's understandable. But it's also wrong. Even as we trade privacy for security and convenience, we're hardly headed toward totalitarianism. Orwell's greatest error, says Peter Huber, author of *Orwell's Revenge,* was his view that the government had a monopoly on surveillance technologies. Says Huber: "If the Thought Police use telescreens, so can others—that's just the way telescreens work, if they work at all."

27   Indeed, citizens have already learned to use surveillance tools to keep government accountable. When motorist Rodney King was beaten by Los Angeles police officers in 1991, a bystander caught the incident on video. Though the subsequent trial ended in acquittal of the officers, it proved the potency of videotape as evidence.

"Video cameras create a potential counterbalance—a kind of ombudsman," says Sam Gregory, a program coordinator for Witness, a New York nonprofit that lends video equipment to human rights activists around the world. "They let citizens protect themselves and hold the state accountable." Recent projects sponsored by Witness include *Operation Fine Girl,* which documents rape as a weapon of war in Sierra Leone, and *Behind the Labels,* an exposé of the clothing-industry sweatshops in Saipan.

28   In Orange County, California, the sheriff's department mounted video cameras on its patrol cars with the idea that footage of arrests could be used to protect against false accusations of excessive force. Not surprisingly, those tapes have been used against the police officers themselves. In June, Robert Delgiudice, who was beaten by police for resisting arrest, had his case dismissed when the video showed that the officer had lied in his police report and preliminary hearing testimony. (Delgiudice is now planning a civil suit.) As Don Landis Jr., the Orange County deputy public defender who argued Delgiudice's case, puts it: "The cameras bring accountability."

29   They also bring transparency, which is almost always a good thing. An antidote to corruption, it keeps financial markets strong, governments honest, and corporations accountable. In public institutions and on city streets, the more transparency the better. Sometimes the reverse is true: The darkness of privacy is essential to the conversations between doctor and patient, to the personal information sent by letter, and to the things we do and say within our bedrooms. In those cases, privacy must be staunchly defended.

30   "Just about the only Fourth Amendment concern that the Supreme Court protects, year after year, decision after decision, is a U.S. citizen's privacy in his own home," says Landis. Earlier this year, the court upheld this principle again, deciding that the police in Florence, Oregon, had violated the Fourth Amendment when, without a warrant, they used thermal imaging technology to detect the heat lamps inside the house of a man they suspected of growing marijuana. Any technology that enables law enforcement to see or hear through walls, the court decreed, required a search warrant; without a warrant, the practice amounted to an unreasonable search.

31   The Constitution itself, therefore, stands in the way of Big Brother. OK, privacy is eroding. But liberty, and the safeguards inherent in due process, remain strong. The government can collect megabytes of information about us, but where and when they do and how that information is used is still subject to the laws designed to keep the state from abusing its power. And of course, even as Congress and the judicial system struggle to maintain the balance of privacy and security, citizens will continue to take technology into their own hands.

32   "Look at all the cameras and cell phones, a gazillion of them, that documented everything on September 11," says David Brin. "The powers of vision and information are expanding exponentially in the hands of the people, far faster than they are being acquired by government." In the long run, Brin predicts, it will be people—empowered by the surveillance web—who thwart the thugs, the tyrants, and even the terrorists.

Mike Luckovich's Pulitzer Prize–winning political cartoons appear in the *Atlanta Journal-Constitution* and are frequently reprinted. This one appear first on May 27, 2010, just after Facebook founder Mark Zuckerberg announced that he was taking steps, in response to criticism, to protect the privacy of Facebook participants.

Robert X. Cringely	# Facebook Puts Your Privacy on Parade

From 1987 to 1995 Robert X. Cringely wrote the "Notes from the Field" column in *InfoWorld,* a weekly computer trade newspaper. More recently, his writing has appeared in the *New York Times, Newsweek, Forbes, Upside, Success,* and *Worth,* among other publications. The argument printed here originally appeared on InfoWorld's Web site in January 2010. In May 2010, Facebook responded to its critics by altering its privacy controls (see the cartoon above), but the criticism has not stopped.

Once again Facebook is involved in a privacy imbroglio, and once again it's because boy-founder Mark Zuckerberg opened his yap and stuck his Keds-clad foot inside.

2   Last week at The Crunchies, the annual awards party thrown by TechCrunch doyenne Michael Arrington, Zuckerberg got on stage briefly and made the following statement (per Gawker):

When I got started in my dorm room at Harvard, the question a lot of people asked was "why would I want to put any information on the Internet at all? Why would I want to have a website?"

And then in the last 5 or 6 years, blogging has taken off in a huge way and all these different services that have people sharing all this information. People have really gotten comfortable not only sharing more information and different kinds, but more openly and with more people. That social norm is just something that's evolved over time.

We view it as our role in the system to constantly be innovating and be updating what our system is to reflect what the current social norms are.

So now, a lot of companies would be trapped by the conventions and their legacies of what they've built, [and so] doing a privacy change for 350 million users is not the type of thing that a lot of companies would do. But we viewed that as a really important thing, to always keep a beginner's mind and think: what would we do if we were starting the company now, and starting the site now, and we decided that these would be the social norms now and we just went for it.

3   Allow me to translate. By "innovating and updating" his system, Zuckerberg means the modifications to user privacy settings Facebook unveiled a few weeks ago that made Facebookers' information more easily accessible by Google et al. by default. And by "current social norms," Zuckerberg means "stuff we think we can get away with today that we couldn't get away with three or four years ago."

Facebook.com founder Mark Zuckerberg at the company's Palo Alto, California headquarters.

4   Interestingly, after Facebook's default settings changed, Zuckerberg's personal profile went from being virtually inaccessible (unless you were the CEO's friend) to nearly wide open, allowing any Facebooker to view the 290 photos he'd posted. These included several of Zucky the Party Animal (the worst of which Gawker happily scooped up and republished). A couple of days later those photos were mysteriously inaccessible again.

5   So much for social norms.

6   After those changes, ten privacy groups banded together and filed a protest with the FTC about Facebook's sudden open-book privacy policy. In response, Facebook also made a few small tweaks to restore some (but not all) of its previous privacy settings.

7   Zuckerberg's comments last week just re-ignited the Facebook privacy debate, including the inevitable responses from knuckleheads like Arrington "that privacy is already really, really dead. . . . We don't really care about privacy anymore. And Facebook is just giving us exactly what we want." (There is, however, no truth to the rumor that Zuckerberg is planning to publish nude pix of himself on his profile as part of Facebook's new "bare it and share it" campaign.)

8   It's almost always the case that people who like to say "privacy is dead, get over it," (a) have a financial interest in buying and selling personal information, and (b) guard their own personal information zealously, even if they live otherwise very public lives. For example: I'm still waiting for Arrington to share his Social Security number with the world, like the Lifelock CEO he seems to like so much, or to post pix from his vacation at that nudist colony (I'm making that last bit up—I hope). Even if he did, that doesn't mean other people should.

9   People may not give a damn about some kinds of personal information, but they care a great deal about other information. The stuff they care about just varies from person to person. In fact, it's usually the most public of us that have the greatest need for privacy. Exotic dancers may take their clothes off in public (or on MySpace), but they don't usually use their real names or broadcast their home address. Their bodies may be public, but not their identities.

10   Likewise, just because women shared their bra colors on Facebook to raise awareness of breast cancer doesn't mean they want to share that information with the marketers at Victoria's Secrets. (Facebook is not explicitly doing this, but opening up people's status updates to searches makes that possible.)

11   I think people want the ability to easily control what information is and isn't private. While Facebook offers a lot of control—you

might even say a confusing amount for most people—it's still doing its best to encourage you to share early and often. If you can't easily determine how someone wants a particular piece of information to be treated, you should assume it is private, not that they want to share it with the world. The latter is the assumption Facebook is making and Zuckerberg was defending.

12   What people really want is not what Facebook is giving us. As Read Write Web's Marshall Fitzpatrick points out, Facebook's popularity stems in part from how carefully it protected its members' information—at first limiting access to college students, then just to your networks of friends. Now it seems to have forgotten all of that, to its detriment.

13   Why? In a word, money. You can't easily monetize data that's private. The more data you can share with the world, the more revenue you can generate. Facebook isn't trying to give users what they want or to conform with "social norms." It's trying to make a buck out of each and every one of its 350 million users, over and over again. Nothing wrong with that, except perhaps how you go about it.

Jonathan Locker

On Star: Big Brother's Eye in the Sky

Jonathan I. Locker contributed the following article to the Web site "The Truth About Cars," which presents automotive news, reviews, and editorials. The article appeared February 14, 2008.

Ever since the Model T hit the silver screen, evading the long arm of the law has been a cinematic theme. From the General Lee locomotive outrunning Boss Hogg, to Smokey being outwitted by Burt Reynolds' mustache, the public imagination has always associated fast cars with police pursuit. While the majority of motorists would never dream of trying to outrun the long arm of the law, soon, they won't have to. It'll be resting on their shoulder.

2   Consider OnStar.

3   OnStar is a telemetry system providing a central data bank with real-time data on virtually every system in your car, including GPS. OnStar's computer knows where you were, when you were there, and how fast you went. It knows if and when you applied the brakes, if and when the air bags deployed, and what speed you were going at the time. It knows if and when your car was

serviced. OnStar operators can determine if you have a passenger in the front seat (airbag detection). All interactions with OnStar's operators are automatically recorded (hence the commercials). By the same token, under certain conditions, OnStar can switch on your GM car's microphone remotely and record any and all sounds within the vehicle (i.e., conversations).

4   But wait, there's more. As of 2009, customers who upgrade to OnStar's "Safe & Sound" plan automatically receive the "Stolen Vehicle Slowdown" service. (Yes, it's an "opt out" deal.) If the OnStar-equipped vehicle is reported stolen and law enforcement has "established a clear line of sight of the stolen vehicle," the police may ask OnStar to slow it down remotely.

5   Many customers find OnStar immensely reassuring; it's their guardian e-angel. No question: OnStar has saved lives and provided its customers with valuable services. Otherwise, they wouldn't be in business.

6   But what if the police are investigating a crime. They ask OnStar where your car was on a certain date and time, to corroborate an alibi. Or what if you're in a crash and the other guy's attorney would like to know how fast you were driving when you ran the red light? Would OnStar surrender the information? GM notes that "OnStar is required to locate the car to comply with legal requirements, including valid court orders showing probable cause in criminal investigations." And OnStar may use gathered information to "protect the rights, property, or safety of you or others."

7   Imagine the following scenario. The FBI shows up at OnStar master command and tells them your car's been stolen by a terrorist, who may be using it to commit a crime at this very moment. Contacting the owner is out of the question; the owner may also be a terrorist. What does OnStar do? They cooperate with the FBI and give them everything they've got on your car. No warrant needed and no notification to you. Hell, you may not even have the service enabled. In other words, you not only have to trust OnStar to protect your privacy, you have to trust the police not to ask the questions in the first place.

8   The Constitution of the United States protects us from the heavy hand of government. However, when it comes to protection from private entities, it does little. Into this void, multiple privacy laws have entered, creating a farrago of local, state, and federal laws which provide limited and haphazard protection to citizens. Whatever privacy protection these laws provide are usually nullified when companies violate them in "good faith" (e.g., while assisting the authorities).

9   So who is going to stop the government from monitoring your car? The Bill of Rights protects you from an unreasonable search and seizure; the government cannot take what belongs to you without a warrant. OnStar can owns the information they collect about your car. In short, there is nothing to stop the police or OnStar from using the information you paid for against you.

10   And the next step is even more insidious. Imagine GPS speed limiters which only allow you to go the speed limit based upon a map uploaded into your car's navigation system. Now Sammy Hagar will only be driving 55 no matter how hard he stomps on the go pedal. This is the ultimate assault on pistonheads. The only place where driving will be fun will be on the track—if OnStar and/or the car's manufacturer (e.g., the Japanese GT-R) let you.

11   There's only one sensible response to this trend: boycott vehicles equipped with OnStar, even if you don't sign up for the service. (Remember: it can be remotely enabled.) If customers actively avoid vehicles that spy on them, manufacturers will have to stop installing the monitoring software and hardware. And law enforcement agencies and prosecutors will have to get their information and apprehend criminals the old-fashioned way: through legally-sanctioned police work.

12   In short, I don't buy OnStar, and neither should you.

DAHLIA **LITHWICK**

Teens, Nude Photos and the Law

Dahlia Lithwick is a contributing editor at *Newsweek* and senior editor at *Slate*, an online current affairs and culture magazine, for which she writes "Supreme Court Dispatches" and "Jurisprudence." Her work has also appeared in *The New Republic*, *ELLE*, the *New York Times*, the *Ottawa Citizen*, and the *Washington Post*. A product of Stanford University's law school, Lithwick worked for a family law firm and clerked for Judge Procter Hug on the United States Court of Appeals for the Ninth Circuit, before turning to a career as a writer. The following article appeared in *Newsweek* in February 2009.

sk yourself: should the police be involved when tipsy teen girls e-mail their boyfriends naughty Valentine's Day pictures?

Say you're a middle-school principal who confiscated a cell phone from a 14-year-old boy, only to discover that it contains a nude photo of his 13-year-old girlfriend. Do you (a) call the boy's parents in despair; (b) call the girl's parents in despair; or (c) call the police? More and more, the answer is (d) all of the above. Which could result in criminal charges for both of your students, and their eventual designation as sex offenders. "Sexting" is the clever new name for the act of sending, receiving, or forwarding naked photos via your cell phone, and I wasn't fully convinced that America was facing a sexting epidemic, as opposed to a journalists-writing-about-sexting epidemic, until I saw a new survey done by the National Campaign to Prevent Teen and Unplanned Pregnancy. One teenager in five reported having sent or posted naked photos of themselves. Whether all this reflects a new child-porn epidemic, or is just a new iteration of the old teen narcissism epidemic, remains unclear.

3   Last month, three girls (ages 14 or 15) in Greensburg, Pa., were charged with disseminating child pornography for sexting their boyfriends. The boys who received the images were charged with possession. A teenager in Indiana faces felony obscenity charges for sending a picture of his genitals to female classmates. A 15-year-old girl in Ohio and a 14-year-old girl in Michigan were charged with felonies for sending nude images of themselves to classmates. Some of these teens have pleaded guilty to lesser charges. Others have not. If convicted, these young people may have to register as sex offenders, in some cases for a decade or two. Similar charges have been brought in cases reported in Alabama, Connecticut, Florida, New Jersey, New York, Pennsylvania, Texas, Utah, and Wisconsin.

4   Want one quick clue that the criminal-justice system is probably not the best venue for addressing sexting? A survey of the charges brought in these cases reflects that—depending on the jurisdiction—prosecutors have charged the senders of smutty photos, the recipients of smutty photos, those who save the smutty photos, and the hapless forwarders of smutty photos with the same crime: child pornography. Who is the victim here? Everybody and nobody.

5   There may be an argument for police intervention in cases that involve a genuine threat or cyberbullying, such as a recent Massachusetts incident in which the picture of a naked 14-year-old girl was allegedly sent to more than 100 cell phones, or a New York case involving a group of boys who turned a nude photo of a 15-year-old girl into crude animations and PowerPoint presentations. But ask yourself whether those cases are the same as the cases in which tipsy teen girls send their boyfriends naughty Valentine's Day pictures.

6   The argument for hammering every such case seems to be that sending naked pictures might have serious consequences, so let's charge these kids with felonies, which will surely have serious consequences. In the Pennsylvania case a police captain explained that the charges were brought because "it's very dangerous. Once it's on a cell phone, that cell phone can be put on the Internet where everyone in the world can get access to that juvenile picture." The argument that we must prosecute kids as the producers and purveyors of kiddie porn because they are too dumb to understand that their seemingly innocent acts can harm them goes beyond paternalism. Child-pornography laws intended to protect children should not be used to prosecute and then label children as sex offenders. We seem to forget that kids can be as tech-savvy as Bill Gates but as gullible as Bambi. Even in the age of the Internet, young people fail to appreciate that naked pictures want to roam free.

7   The real problem with criminalizing teen sexting as a form of child pornography is that the great majority of these kids are not predators. They just think they're being brash and sexy. And while some of the reaction to sexting reflects legitimate concerns about children as sex objects, some also perpetuates legal stereotypes and fallacies.

A recent *New York Times* article quotes the Family Violence Prevention Fund, a non-profit domestic-violence-awareness group, as saying that the sending of nude pictures, even if done voluntarily, constitutes "digital dating violence." But do we truly believe that one in five teens is participating in an act of violence? Experts insist the sexting trend hurts teen girls more than boys, fretting that they feel "pressured" to take and send naked photos. Paradoxically, the girls in the Pennsylvania case were charged with "manufacturing, disseminating, or possessing child pornography" while the boys were merely charged with possession. If the girls are the real victims, why are we treating them more harshly than the boys?

8   Judging from the sexting prosecutions in Pennsylvania, Ohio, and Indiana this year, it's clear that the criminal-justice system is too blunt an instrument to resolve a problem that reflects more about the volatile combination of teens and technology than about some national cybercrime spree. Parents need to remind their teens that a dumb moment can last a lifetime in cyberspace. But judges and prosecutors need to understand that a lifetime of cyberhumiliation shouldn't be grounds for a lifelong real criminal record.

Jay Stanley

ACLU Opposes Body Cavity Searches for Airline Passengers

Jay Stanley works for the American Civil Liberties Union (ACLU) Technology and Liberty Program, and he especially writes and speaks about privacy issues related to technology. He is the coauthor of *Bigger Monster, Weaker Chains: The Growth of an American Surveillance Society*, an ACLU report examining how the government infringes on people's privacy. The following statement was published on the ACLU site December 31, 2009, in response to calls for increased screenings at U.S. airports.

Okay, so no one is explicitly calling for body cavity searches for all airline travelers—yet. But the logic of those pushing for body scanners for all airline passengers, and criticizing the ACLU for opposing that, leads to the inescapable conclusion that these critics would support such a policy.

2   Consider:

1. When Richard Reid brought explosives onto an airliner hidden in his shoes, the authorities began making everyone remove their shoes. When security experts and other critics pointed out that this was "silly security," defenders argued that we must put up with it in order to block that particular kind of plot.

2. Now that a disturbed person has brought explosives onto an airliner in his underwear, panicked voices want the TSA to essentially view naked pictures of every passenger who boards an airline—that's up to 2.5 million people per day on domestic flights alone. When the ACLU and members of Congress object, critics cry that we must abandon our personal dignity and privacy in order to block that particular kind of plot.

How much should airport scanners be able to reveal? Are full-body scanners, which reveal far more than this x-ray scan, ethical?

3. It is far from clear that body scanners will, as so many people seem to be assuming, detect explosives concealed the way that Umar Farouk Abdulmutallab concealed them. Some experts have said plastic explosives can be concealed against the human body. It's not clear how good scanner operators would have been at detecting the "anatomically congruent" explosives Abdulmutallab hid in his underwear (let alone how consistently effective bored operators would be if these $200,000 machines were placed at every screening station in every airport for 2.5 million people a day).

4. However, if terrorists even *perceive* that scanners will work, they take the next logical step and conceal explosives in their body cavities. Al Qaeda has already used this technique; in September a suicide bomber stowed a full pound of high explosives and a detonator inside his rectum, and attempted to assassinate a Saudi prince by blowing himself up. (The prince survived.)

3   So it seems that when the next terrorist tries to blow up an airliner using this technique, all the usual jittery voices surely will once again say that we must abandon our personal dignity and privacy in order to block that particular kind of plot. So we'd just like to get ahead of the game and state right now that the ACLU will be opposed to that.

4   Of course, even if body cavity searches for all were made policy, terrorists would probably shift their efforts to just hiding explosives in their carryon baggage, and the TSA's level of success in catching contraband has always been, shall we say, mixed. And reliably catching every possible means of hiding 50 grams of

explosives is probably impossible given the millions of people who fly each day.

5   Yes, the government must zealously work to make us as safe as possible and must take every reasonable step to make sure security breaches like the ones that led to the Christmas Day attempted attack are not repeated. But we need to act wisely. That means not trading away our privacy for ineffective policies. We should be investing in developing technologies such as trace portal detectors (a.k.a. "puffer machines") that provide a layer of security without invading privacy, and in developing competent law enforcement and intelligence agencies that will stop terrorists *before* they show up at the airport.

6   Ultimately, it is up to the American people to figure out just how much privacy they want to abandon to block a few particular means of carrying out terrorist attacks. The ACLU represents those who value privacy in this debate. But when Americans make that decision, they should do so with their eyes wide open, without any illusions that this will prevent all attacks on airliners, much less attacks on shopping malls or all the infinite number of other plots and targets that terrorists could come up with if they are not stopped by competent law enforcement and intelligence agencies.

ADAM **COHEN**

A Casualty of the Technology Revolution: "Locational Privacy"

Adam Cohen is a member of the *New York Times* editorial board; before that he was a senior writer at Time. Since he holds a law degree, he naturally writes on legal issues, particularly when they involve technology. Among other things, he is the author of *Nothing to Fear: FDR's Inner Circle* and *American Pharaoh: Mayor Richard J. Daley.* The editorial printed below was published by the *New York Times* in September 2009.

When I woke up the other day, I went straight to my computer to catch up on the news and to read e-mail. About 20 minutes later, I walked half a block to the gym, where I exercised for 45 minutes. I took the C train to The New York Times building, and then at the end of the day, I was back on the C train. I had dinner on my friends' (Elisabeth and Dan's) rooftop, then walked home seven blocks.

2   I'm not giving away any secrets here—nothing I did was secret to begin with. Verizon online knows when I logged on, and New York Sports Club knows when I swiped my membership card. The M.T.A. could trace (through the MetroCard I bought with a credit card) when and where I took the subway, and *The Times* knows when I used my ID to enter the building. AT&T could follow me along the way through my iPhone. There may also be videotape of my travels, given the ubiquity of surveillance cameras in New York City. There are thousands of cameras on buildings and lampposts around Manhattan, according to the New York Civil Liberties Union, many near my home and office. Several may have been in a position to film my dinner on Elisabeth and Dan's roof.

3   A little-appreciated downside of the technology revolution is that, mainly without thinking about it, we have given up "locational privacy." Even in low-tech days, our movements were not entirely private. The desk attendant at my gym might have recalled seeing me, or my colleagues might have remembered when I arrived. Now the information is collected automatically and often stored indefinitely.

Location-aware cell phones, iPads, and other mobile devices make it easy for anyone to track your location and movements. Privacy advocates are concerned; are you?
© 2010 Google-Map Data © Google, Sanborn

4   Privacy advocates are rightly concerned. Corporations and the government can keep track of what political meetings people attend, what bars and clubs they go to, whose homes they visit. It is the fact that people's locations are being recorded "pervasively, silently, and cheaply that we're worried about," the Electronic Frontier Foundation said in a recent report.

5   People's cellphones and E-ZPasses are increasingly being used against them in court. If your phone is on, even if you are not on a call, you may be able to be found (and perhaps picked up) at any hour of the day or night. As disturbing as it is to have your private data breached, it is worse to think that your physical location might fall into the hands of people who mean you harm.

6   This decline in locational privacy, from near-absolute to very little in just a few years, has not generated much outrage, or even discussion. That is partly because so much of it is a side-effect of technology that people like. Drivers love E-ZPasses. G.P.S. enables all sorts of cool smart phone applications, from driving directions and find-a-nearby-restaurant features to the ever-popular "Take Me to My Car."

7   And people usually do not know that they are being monitored. The transit authority does not warn buyers that their MetroCards track their subway use (or that the police have used the cards in criminal investigations). Cameras that follow people on the street are placed in locations that are hard to spot. It is difficult for cellphone users to know precisely what information their devices are sending about their current location, when they are doing it, and where that information is going. Some privacy advocates were upset by recent reports that the Palm Pre, which has built-in G.P.S., has a feature that regularly sends its users' location back to Palm without notifying them at the time.

8   What can be done? As much as possible, location-specific information should not be collected in the first place, or not in personally identifiable form. There are many ways, as the Electronic Frontier Foundation notes, to use cryptography and anonymization to protect locational privacy. To tell you about nearby coffee shops, a cellphone application needs to know where you are. It does not need to know who you are.

9   In addition, when locational information is collected, people should be given advance notice and a chance to opt out. Data should be erased as soon as its main purpose is met. After you pay your E-ZPass bill, there is no reason for the government to keep records of your travel.

10   The idea of constantly monitoring the citizenry's movements used to conjure up images of totalitarian states. Now, technology does the surveillance—generally in the name of being helpful. It's time for a serious conversation about how much of our privacy of movement we want to give up.

ISSUE IN FOCUS

BIOMETRICS: Measuring the Body for Identity

The 1997 film *Gattaca,* starring Ethan Hawke and Uma Thurman, features the supposedly futuristic plot of a "natural" man stealing genetic information to pose as an elite citizen—someone who was genetically engineered before birth. Using stolen biometric identifiers, Hawke's character poses as another person, but the

Tom Cruise in *Minority Report* (2002)

film's final message just may be that the "natural" man still triumphs: spirit trumps technology. Another relatively recent film, *Minority Report* (2002), starring Tom Cruise, also involves biometric technologies. Cruise's character takes someone else's retinas in order to clear his name of a crime he supposedly commits in the future. Like *Gattaca, Minority Report* employs futuristic biometric technologies that today are not entirely feasible but are no longer beyond the realm of possibility. Indeed, both films characterize the possibilities—fascinating and frightening—of biometrics that no longer belong exclusively to the realm of science fiction.

2   Biometrics encompasses a variety of identification strategies. You've seen them on TV shows like *CSI* and *24*. Biometric devices can record physical characteristics such as irises, retinas, fingerprints, hands, knuckles, palms, veins, faces, DNA, sweat, pores, lips, odors, and voices. In addition, biometric technologies can analyze human behavior patterns such as signatures, keyboard keystroke patterns, and gaits. Some of these technologies are more advanced and more feasible than others, but the goal of biometrics is to conclusively determine individual identity and thus remove the element of human error that comes with lost, stolen, hacked, copied, or shared passwords and tokens. Biometrics helps us bypass these pitfalls by securing data that belongs exclusively to one person—since that data is actually part of the person.

3   There are more everyday problems with biometrics than *CSI* and *24*, *Gattaca,* and *Minority Report* suggest. For one thing, in large-scale uses of biometrics, there are likely to be portions of the population for whom some facets

of the technology simply don't work, as well as small percentages of overlap that make identity difficult to determine. In addition to concerns about the cleanliness and safety of the machinery used to collect and measure biometric data, some detractors raise concerns about security and privacy: if biometric data is stolen, individuals can be permanently vulnerable because, unlike passwords and tokens, biometric information is difficult, if not impossible, to change. Furthermore, biometrics incites fears that individuals who protect valuable property with biometrics might be physically harmed or endangered if someone tries to steal the property. These concerns about biometrics extend beyond the cost and logistics to the ways in which we use, store, and manipulate our bodies for security's sake.

4   The reading selections in this section describe the range of types and uses of biometrics and argue about advantages and disadvantages that accompany this emerging technology. Because biometric recognition technologies effectively illustrate the tensions between protection and privacy, we include images and articles that dramatize the excitement and fear surrounding them.

5   The section opens with an article by Steven C. Bennett, a partner in a law firm who teaches a course in privacy law at Hunter College. He gives an even-handed discussion of the pros and cons of biometric technologies and goes on to argue that the biometrics industry should set standards that protect the privacy of individuals. Less even-handed is a page from the FBI Web site, which extols the benefits of these technologies. Paul Saffo, the Roy Amara Fellow at the Institute for the Future and a writer whose essays have appeared in *Fortune,* *The Harvard Business Review,* the *Los Angeles Times, Newsweek,* the *New York Times,* the *Washington Post,* and *Wired,* explains the not-so-science-fiction possibility of DNA identity theft and cautions against blind faith in biometrics. We conclude with Ben Goldacre lamenting "the biometric blues": A physician and medical researcher in Britain, Goldacre contributes frequently to the British national newspaper *The Guardian*—especially in a regular column entitled "Bad Science."

6   As you read and analyze the texts and images, consider the desirability of biometrics—a technology that started as science fiction but has been studied and advanced by the U.S. military in efforts to secure the nation and catch terrorists. What about this technology captivates our imaginations in so many different ways? What balance are we willing to strike between personal privacy and national security, or even personal protection? How does biometrics alter our sense of ourselves as unique individuals—both in terms of what information we would share publicly and in terms of identity theft? These selections introduce you to a complex and significant technological advance, and they can prompt further thinking, reading, research, and writing as you enter this important contemporary debate about security and privacy.

STEVEN C. **BENNETT**

Privacy Implications of Biometrics

<p>B roadly speaking, biometrics is a term for any measurement of individuals used either to identify or authenticate their claimed identity. Fingerprints and wanted posters, for example, are well-established biometric methods used by law enforcement to track down, identify, and authenticate suspects. Modern information technology has added a number of new machine-based identification techniques, such as facial scanning and recognition, and improved the older techniques. These mechanical innovations offer a host of benefits, chiefly speed, efficiency, and vast analytical power. Several nations, including the United States and most of Europe, have begun to take advantage of the security benefits of these advances by issuing passports and other forms of identification encoded with biometric information. With such benefits, however, may come significant risks to the privacy and data security rights of consumers, workers, and citizens at large. The development of "best practices" in managing the use of biometrics is essential to strike an appropriate balance, ensuring proper use of these techniques and safeguards against abuse. If industry does not develop and follow such guidelines, more stringent regulations may be imposed.</p>

2   A prime example of both the potential benefits and the threats of rapidly evolving biometric technology appears in the use of facial scanning technology at several recent NFL Superbowls. Before the 2001 Superbowl in Tampa, over 30 closed-circuit television cameras were installed to monitor the crowd and compare images of spectators to images of known criminals. Approximately 20 matches were made, several during the game. There was a widespread outcry, including dramatic media accounts labeling the game the "Snooper Bowl," disparaging the Orwellian overtones, after this use of biometrics became public knowledge. These complaints were muted at the New Orleans Superbowl in 2002, perhaps as a consequence of the September 11th attacks. Nonetheless, the use of facial recognition technology during the Superbowl has since been abandoned.

WHAT IS BIOMETRICS?

3   Essentially, biometrics is the use of human physical characteristics as identifiers. While any trait can be used, several specific types have proven to be most useful. The three most common genres of biometric identifiers are appearance, physiography, and bio-dynamics. Physical appearance is primarily judged through the use of photographs or other still images, but can also be validated through written descriptions of an individual's height, weight, coloration, hair, and visible markings. Physiography, on the other hand, requires some form of measurement—such as fingerprints, dental measurements, optical scans of the retina or iris, hand geometry, or DNA testing. As opposed to these two static characteristics, bio-dynamics measures patterned active behavior—voice fluctuation, keystroke tendencies, manner of writing a signature, and habituated body signals such as gait.

4   To perform the task of identification or authentication, biometrics relies on the comparison of live data supplied—voluntarily or not—by the subject to a dataset or template containing pre-existing information. The prime difference between the objectives of identification and authentication lies in the scope of pre-existing information required for each

task. Identification can assign a name or other value to a previously anonymous person by comparing the live data to a large number of samples, a "1:N search," to determine whether there is a match. Authentication, on the other hand, merely requires confirmation that individuals are who they claim to be. The comparison, then, is between the live data and previously supplied data from a single individual, or a "1:1 search." Both searches can either be positive or negative; they can ensure either that a person is already within the database and permitted access (positive) or, as in the Superbowl example, that a person is not within a database and therefore permitted access (negative).

5   Basic forms of biometrics are all around us. The typical driver's license or state identification card, for example, contains a photograph and some form(s) of physical description (such as height and eye color). The license often also contains a sample signature from the individual; and the individual's address. All of these, in some ways, are forms of biometrics:

- The photograph may be compared to the individual carrying the license;
- The physical characteristics described on the license may also be compared to those of the individual;
- The individual may be asked for a signature sample, and that sample compared to the license sample;
- The individual may be asked to recall (unaided) his or her address, and that answer compared to the license information.

What Is Different About Machine Biometrics?

6   Biometrics standing alone are just characteristics; they neither protect nor threaten individual privacy. As the license example suggests, the use of biometrics has been accepted and commonplace for over 100 years. It is how biometric technologies are used that determines their effect on privacy. The rise of mechanical biometric technology, especially computers and computerized databases, and the consequent automation of the identification process have radically increased both the ability to identify individuals biometrically and the potential for abuse of biometrics. These changes extend to almost every aspect of biometrics—data capture, analysis, communication, and storage—and must be understood before analyzing their implications for privacy and data security rights of individuals.

Data Capture

7   Technological advances now allow for involuntary or unknowing capture of biometric characteristics. The Superbowl provides an example—if the security firm had chosen to store the captured images rather than merely test and destroy them, it would have created the possibility for biometric identification of all who attended the game. Even when the submission of information is voluntary, many biometrics are very difficult for a human to gather unaided. For example, scanning the retina of the human eye requires light-producing and magnification devices, and meaningful analysis of the results requires imaging and comparison technology. These techniques, however, may offer highly individualized identification when used properly. Even biometric methods that can be performed competently by humans (such as fingerprint or hand shape identification) can be greatly improved through machine operation.

Data Analysis

8 Though Moore's law of increasing computer capacity is only observational, the exponential growth of computing power has allowed for ever more rapid identification searches, even as databases expand. Fingerprinting technology provides the perfect lens through which to view this growth. Originally, fingerprinting could only be used to authenticate the identity of criminals who had left their prints at a crime scene, noting any 1:1 matches. Gradually, a classification system (the Henry system) developed, which allowed for identification searches, but these searches required significant amounts of time to perform. By 1971, the FBI possessed over 200 million paper fingerprint files, including records on 30 million criminals, and J. Edgar Hoover had unsuccessfully promoted universal fingerprinting. The true technological shift, however, came in the 1990s, when new fingerprint scanners cut the time to identify prints from months to hours.

Data Communication

9 Many forms of biometrics were impossible to communicate until recently. Before the creation of reasonably high quality photographs and copies, accurate re-creation of most biometrics via transmission was impossible. The year 1924 witnessed the first transmission of fingerprints from Australia to Scotland Yard via telegraph. Since then, modern communication has dramatically enhanced the efficiency of biometrics. Just as computational analysis has followed the predictions of Moore's law, so too the field of communications has lived up to the even more aggressive predictions of the "Photon Law"—that bandwidth will more than double every year. As bandwidth increases, more biometrics can be transmitted, and data transfer is faster. This allows for linkage of varied biometric data sets, as well as non-biometric information.

Data Storage

10 Finally, the ability to reduce biometrics to electronic datasets of relatively small size has allowed for construction of large, searchable electronic databases. As a result of the falling costs of electronic data storage and the rising ability to transmit that data rapidly across long distances, technological shifts have allowed for creation of massive interlinked databases of biometric information. The FBI's Integrated Automated Fingerprint Identification System ("IAFIS") is the largest biometric database in the world, containing the fingerprints and related criminal history of over 47 million individuals. Remote electronic submissions for criminal inquiries can receive a response from IAFIS within two hours. The IAFIS data illustrate a final observational law of technology, Metcalfe's law, which states that the power of a network increases (exponentially, though this value is debated) as every node is added. Thus, the ability to integrate and store information from many different databases dramatically increases the value of biometric data.

THE VALUE OF MACHINE BIOMETRICS

11 The efficiency gained from mechanization of biometrics is clear. Fingerprint searches that a decade ago took three months to complete now can be completed in under two hours. Biometrics also has an intrinsic value in its ability to function as

(potentially) the most effective security safeguard, restricting access to sensitive information or physical areas. To secure such access, authorization (or identity) must be validated. The rise in identity theft demonstrates the weakness of validating systems based purely on possession of particular information about the individual. These faults have caused many in business to turn to biometrics as a more secure method of identifying or authenticating individuals.

12   In response to digital hackers, many password systems now require frequent changes or the use of special symbols and non-repetitive character strings. These shifts, designed to protect security, tend instead to undermine it as users often write their passwords on a sticky note by their desks. Relying on access cards is equally problematic—such cards can be lost, stolen, or left right by the computer to which they provide access. A recent survey, moreover, found that 70 percent of Americans, in response to an unsolicited email or phone call, would share information such as an account number, or provide the answer to a security code question. A majority also indicated they would not want their accounts locked after three failed attempts to verify the identity of someone trying to gain access. More than two-thirds of respondents in this survey were open to using biometric technologies—they want technology that is as secure as it is convenient.

13   The weaknesses and security lapses in other validation mechanisms have increasingly caused industry innovators to turn to biometrics. Banco Azteca was created in 2001 by the massive Grupo Elektra, to target the previously untapped 70 percent of Mexico's population that did not use banks at all. One of the problems the new bank confronted in enrolling customers in underserved communities was the lack of any form of secure identification papers, driver's licenses, or the like. In response, the bank turned to biometrics and fingerprint scans. Over seven million Banco Azteca customers have enrolled in the biometric identification program; more than 75 percent of the bank's business comes from customers who have dealt with a bank for the first time due to this program.

HOW CAN MACHINE BIOMETRICS THREATEN PRIVACY?

14   Although biometrics techniques may provide new opportunities for security, these techniques also present the potential for abuse. Biometric information is inherently linked to individuality and functions as a unique identifier in a way that would make its loss irreplaceable. The potentially unrestrained scope of data collecting, sharing, linking, and warehousing also may invite misuse. Finally, the potential for pervasive monitoring of movement and activities may chill discourse and protest.

15   Identity theft in a biometric world may be particularly problematic. When a check is lost or stolen, one immediately requests a stop payment order. When a credit card is taken, one calls the company to freeze the account and order a new card. What does one do when biometric information is stolen? Once biometric information is reduced to electronic data, that data can be captured or altered by hackers. Hackers can then reproduce the data in a way that convinces biometric scanners that they are authorized, and thereby gain access to supposedly secure information or locations. Essentially, biometrics are the equivalent of a PIN that is impossible to change. The theft of biometric information amounts to permanent identity theft, and thus may be extremely difficult to counteract.

16   Use of biometrics also risks the problem of data creep, in which information given voluntarily to one recipient for one purpose may be transferred, without permission or knowledge, to another recipient, linked with other data, or applied to a new purpose. The average American's personal information is now available in approximately 50 different commercial databases. Linkage of such information could permit discrimination based on physical characteristics that might otherwise remain unknown.

17   Followed to its logical extreme, moreover, the linkage of digital images into a single database with facial recognition technology would permit the tracking of everyone's movements. The possibility of such tracking, however remote, epitomizes the threat that widespread use of biometrics poses for personal privacy. If an organization or government can monitor movement and actions, it could discriminate against individuals based on their associations. As anonymous behavior becomes less possible, dissent may be suppressed.

WHAT FORM OF REGULATION IS APPROPRIATE?

18   Individual autonomy is the cornerstone of the American legal and social structure. The free flow of information, however, is equally essential to a functioning democracy. The challenge of regulating biometrics lies in resolving the tension between the rights to privacy, free speech, and information security.

19   Americans generally disfavor broad government regulation of industry practices regarding personal information. Congress prefers to rely on industry self-regulation when possible. Nevertheless, the government will step in to regulate a market when the market clearly has failed to provide adequate safeguards. Notable examples of such government intervention include the Child Online Protection Act, the Graham-Leach-Bliley Act, and the Health Insurance Portability and Accountability Act. If the biometrics industry wishes to avoid potentially strict sector-specific government regulations, it must self-regulate, to harmonize the tensions between the fundamental benefits of biometrics while limiting the potential for abuse. In establishing such best practices, the industry must proceed from two basic principles: notice and security.

Notice

20   Individuals must know when data collection occurs. A notice requirement recognizes the importance of individual autonomy and enables people to choose whether to participate. Notice, however, means more than simply saying "surveillance cameras are in use," when police apply facial recognition software at the Superbowl. When any biometric system is used, there should ideally be an open statement of its scope, purpose, function, and application, including the system's potential uses. The evaluation of potential uses is beneficial because biometric systems rarely threatens abuse in themselves. The true threat to privacy comes from the mission creep permitted by latent capabilities. Biometric systems should be narrowly tailored to the job they are to perform. Participation, if at all possible, should be optional. Any change in scope once in use should have the same public disclosure, and participants should be given the option to unroll from the system.

21   While enrolled within a system, participants should be able to access and correct their personal information contained within the system. Failure to provide for access and correction will increase error in the program and may violate privacy principles.

22   The final notice element of a good self-regulatory program is third-party over-sight. Some independent oversight should be implemented to ensure conformity with "best practices," and to suggest other improvements. Periodic audits of the scope and operation of the system coupled with public disclosure of the results of the audits may provide particular deterrence against abuse.

Security

23   To ensure adequate security of biometric information requires both limits on construction of system capabilities as well as protections for data use. System operators should inform participants of the different security measures a biometric identification system will undertake.

24   Data collected should be protected by techniques such as encryption, data hashing, and the use of closed networks and secure facilities. Wireless transmissions of data, even when encrypted, should be avoided. To the extent possible, data should not be stored in a warehouse or database but rather with the individual participant, by means of an encrypted smart card. If storage is necessary, the initial collection of biometric data should be used to generate templates of authorized people and not linked to any one individual.

Government Oversight

25   If the biometrics industry establishes adequate notice and security practices, it may avoid potentially more restrictive governmental regulations. Some system of enforcement of best practice principles may be necessary. The Federal Trade Commission's power to prosecute unfair, deceptive, or fraudulent business activities may help prevent violations of security procedures or unannounced expansions of a biometric system's purview. The FTC already leads in the data protection field, having developed its own set of information practice principles.

WHAT IS THE FUTURE OF BIOMETRICS?

26   A decade ago, Bill Gates forecast that biometrics would be among "the most important IT innovations of the next several years." Technological innovation has dramatically increased the breadth, depth, and speed with which disparate data sets can be connected and analyzed. Recent developments demonstrate the widespread growth and potential power of biometrics. Use of this technology will certainly continue to grow in the next decade. Taken on its own, biometrics is neither a friend nor a foe to privacy rights; their relationship depends on the manner in which the technology is used.

27   If the biometrics industry wishes to maintain its current flexibility and avoid overly stringent regulations, it must respond to the potential threats to privacy by formulating and adopting best practice principles, keeping in mind the essential need for notice and security. Such self-regulation in managing the use of biometrics will allow the market to strike an appropriate balance between the rights to privacy, free speech, and effective use of information technology.

PAUL **SAFFO**

A Trail of DNA and Data

I f you're worried about privacy and identity theft, imagine this:
The scene: Somewhere in Washington. The date: April 3, 2020.

3 You sit steaming while the officer hops off his electric cycle and walks up to the car window. "You realize that you ran that red light again, don't you, Mr. Witherspoon?" It's no surprise that he knows your name; the intersection camera scanned your license plate and your guilty face, and matched both in the DMV database. The cop had the full scoop before you rolled to a stop.

4 "I know, I know, but the sun was in my eyes," you plead as you fumble for your driver's license.

5 "Oh, don't bother with that," the officer replies, waving off the license while squinting at his hand-held scanner. Of course. Even though the old state licensing system had been revamped back in 2014 into a "secure" national program, the new licenses had been so compromised that the street price of a phony card in Tijuana had plummeted to five euros. In frustration, law enforcement was turning to pure biometrics.

6 "Could you lick this please?" the officer asks, passing you a nanofiber blotter. You comply and then slide the blotter into the palm-sized gizmo he is holding, which reads your DNA and runs a match against a national genomic database maintained by a consortium of drug companies and credit agencies. It also checks half a dozen metabolic fractions looking for everything from drugs and alcohol to lack of sleep.

7 The officer looks at the screen, and frowns, "Okay. I'll let you off with a warning, but you really need more sleep. I also see that your retinal implants are past warranty, and your car tells me that you are six months overdue on its navigation firmware upgrade. You really need to take care of both or next time it's a ticket."

8 This creepy scenario is all too plausible. The technologies described are already being developed for industrial and medical applications, and the steadily dropping cost and size of such systems will make them affordable and practical police tools well before 2020. The resulting intrusiveness would make today's system of search warrants and wiretaps quaint anachronisms.

9 Some people find this future alluring and believe that it holds out the promise of using sophisticated ID techniques to catch everyone from careless drivers to bomb-toting terrorists in a biometric dragnet. We have already seen places such as Truro, Mass., Baton Rouge, La. and Miami ask hundreds or thousands of citizens to submit to DNA mass-testing to catch killers. Biometric devices sensing for SARS symptoms are omnipresent in Asian airports. And the first prototypes of systems that test in real time for SARS, HIV and bird flu have been deployed abroad.

10 The ubiquitous collection and use of biometric information may be inevitable, but the notion that it can deliver reliable, theft-proof evidence of identity is pure science fiction. Consider that oldest of biometric identifiers—fingerprints. Long the exclusive domain of government databases and FBI agents who dust for prints at crime scenes,

fingerprints are now being used by electronic print readers on everything from ATMs to laptops. Sticking your finger on a sensor beats having to remember a password or toting an easily lost smart card.

11   But be careful what you touch, because you are leaving your identity behind every time you take a drink. A Japanese cryptographer has demonstrated how, with a bit of gummi bear gelatin, some cyanoacrylic glue, a digital camera and a bit of digital fiddling, he can easily capture a print off a glass and confect an artificial finger that foils fingerprint readers with an 80 percent success rate. Frightening as this is, at least the stunt is far less grisly than the tale, perhaps apocryphal, of some South African crooks who snipped the finger off an elderly retiree, rushed her still-warm digit down to a government ATM, stuck it on the print reader and collected the victim's pension payment. (Scanners there now gauge a finger's temperature, too.)

12   Today's biometric advances are the stuff of tomorrow's hackers and clever crooks, and anything that can be detected eventually will be counterfeited. Iris scanners are gaining in popularity in the corporate world, exploiting the fact that human iris patterns are apparently as unique as fingerprints. And unlike prints, iris images aren't left behind every time someone gets a latte at Starbucks. But hide something valuable enough behind a door protected by an iris scanner, and I guarantee that someone will figure out how to capture an iris image and transfer it to a contact lens good enough to fool the readers. And capturing your iris may not even require sticking a digital camera in your face—after all, verification requires that the representation of your iris exist as a cloud of binary bits of data somewhere in cyberspace, open to being hacked, copied, stolen and downloaded. The more complex the system, the greater the likelihood that there are flaws that crooks can exploit.

13   DNA is the gold standard of biometrics, but even DNA starts to look like fool's gold under close inspection. With a bit of discipline, one can keep a card safe or a PIN secret, but if your DNA becomes your identity, you are sharing your secret with the world every time you sneeze or touch something. The novelist Scott Turow has already written about a hapless sap framed for a murder by an angry spouse who spreads his DNA at the scene of a killing.

14   The potential for DNA identity theft is enough to make us all wear a gauze mask and keep our hands in our pockets. DNA can of course be easily copied—after all, its architecture is designed for duplication—but that is the least of its problems. Unlike a credit card number, DNA can't be retired and swapped for a new sequence if it falls into the hands of crooks or snoops. Once your DNA identity is stolen, you live with the consequences forever.

15   This hasn't stopped innovators from using DNA as an indicator of authenticity. The artist Thomas Kinkade signs his most valuable paintings with an ink containing a bit of his DNA. (He calls it a "forgery-proof DNA Matrix signature.") We don't know how much of Tom is really in his paintings, but perhaps it's enough for forgers to duplicate the ink, as well as the distinctive brush strokes.

16   The biggest problem with DNA is that it says so much more about us than an arbitrary serial number does. Give up your Social Security number and a stranger can inspect your credit rating. But surrender your DNA and a snoop can discover your in-

nermost genetic secrets—your ancestry, genetic defects and predispositions to certain diseases. Of course we will have strong genetic privacy laws, but those laws will allow consumers to "voluntarily" surrender their information in the course of applying for work or pleading for health care. A genetic marketplace not unlike today's consumer information business will emerge, swarming with health insurers attempting to prune out risky individuals, drug companies seeking customers and employers managing potential worker injury liability.

17   Faced with this prospect, any sensible privacy maven would conclude that DNA is too dangerous to collect, much less use for a task as unimportant as turning on a laptop or working a cash machine. But society will not be able to resist its use. The pharmaceutical industry will need our DNA to concoct customized wonder drugs that will fix everything from high cholesterol to halitosis. And crime fighters will make giving DNA information part of our civic duty and national security. Once they start collecting, the temptation to use it for other purposes will be too great.

18   Moreover, snoops won't even need a bit of actual DNA to invade our privacy because it will be so much easier to access its digital representation on any number of databanks off in cyberspace. Our Mr. Witherspoon will get junk mail about obscure medical conditions that he's never heard of because some direct marketing firm "bot" will inspect his digital DNA and discover that he has a latent disease or condition that his doctor didn't notice at his annual checkup.

19   It is tempting to conclude that Americans will rise up in revolt, but experience suggests otherwise. Americans profess a concern for privacy, but they happily reveal their deepest financial and personal secrets for a free magazine subscription or cheesy electronic trinket. So they probably will eagerly surrender their biometric identities as well, trading fingerprint IDs for frequent shopper privileges at the local supermarket and genetic data to find out how to have the cholesterol count of a teenager.

20   Biometric identity systems are inevitable, but they are no silver bullet when it comes to identity protection. The solution to identity protection lies in the hard work of implementing system-wide and nationwide technical and policy changes. Without those changes, the deployment of biometric sensors will merely increase the opportunities for snoops and thieves—and escalate the cost to ordinary citizens.

21   It's time to fix the problems in our current systems and try to anticipate the unique challenges that will accompany the expanded use of biometrics. It's the only way to keep tomorrow's crooks from stealing your fingers and face and, with them, your entire identity.

FBI

Using Technology to Catch Criminals

The FBI's enthusiasm for biometric technologies is reflected on its Web site. The page shown here was posted on December 27, 2005.

Home | Site Map | FAQs

FEDERAL BUREAU OF INVESTIGATION

Celebrating a Century 1908-2008

SEARCH

Contact Us
- Your Local FBI Office
- Overseas Offices
- Submit a Crime Tip
- Report Internet Crime
- More Contacts

Learn About Us
- Quick Facts
- What We Investigate
- Natl. Security Branch
- Information Technology
- Fingerprints & Training
- Laboratory Services
- Reports & Publications
- History
- More About Us

Get Our News
- Press Room
- E-mail Updates
- News Feeds

Be Crime Smart
- Wanted by the FBI
- More Protections

Use Our Resources
- For Law Enforcement
- For Communities
- For Researchers
- More Services

Visit Our Kids' Page

Apply for a Job

Headline Archives

USING TECHNOLOGY TO CATCH CRIMINALS
Fingerprint Database "Hits" Felons at the Border

12/27/05

A CBP officer takes a passenger's fingerprint scan to compare with the IAFIS database.

When U.S. Customs and Border Protection installed technology that can quickly check the fingerprints of illegal immigrants against the FBI's massive biometric database, its chief called the measure "absolutely critical."

"This technology helps...shed light on those with criminal backgrounds we could never have identified before," Commissioner Robert C. Bonner said in a press statement in October, a month after our Integrated Automated Fingerprint Identification System (IAFIS) became fully available in all 136 border patrol stations.

A very bright light, it turns out. Since last September, IAFIS has returned "hits" on 118,557 criminal subjects who were trying to enter this country illegally, according to Customs and Border Protection officials.

Many of the "hits"—a match of an individual's 10 fingerprints—led to arrests of dangerous criminal suspects, including:

- 460 individuals for homicide
- 155 for kidnapping
- 599 for sexual assault
- 970 for robbery
- 5,919 for assault
- 12,077 for drug-related charges

Border Patrol officials began using our biometric tool in the summer of 2001, connecting two of their facilities in San Diego to our Criminal Justice Information Services Division facility in Clarksburg, West Virginia. Congress sought the deployment to supplement the Border Patrol's 10-year-old biometric database called IDENT, which relies on matching an individual's index fingers, rather than the comprehensive 10-finger prints made by IAFIS.

With IAFIS in place, Border Patrol agents can simultaneously check IDENT's specialized databases and IAFIS's 49 million sets of prints.

Voice Verification for Transactions

VoiceVerified's patent-pending Point Service Provider (PSP) platform uses voice verification to help businesses secure remote transactions, protect consumer data, and combat identity fraud. During the verification process, a user is prompted to repeat five random numeric digits to create a voice sample that is compared to a previously enrolled voiceprint to determine a match.

Somerset, Pa.–based Somerset Trust has purchased the PSP to secure wire transfers, and the bank envisions future usage across all banking services requiring multifactor authentication. VoiceVerified is currently in discussions with several other financial institutions as banks seek to comply with the Federal Financial Institutions Examination Council's recent guidelines advocating multifactor user authentication during electronic transactions.

BEN **GOLDACRE**

Now for ID Cards—and the Biometric Blues

S ometimes just throwing a few long words about can make people think you know what you're talking about. Words like "biometric."

2   When Alistair Darling was asked if the government will ditch ID cards in the light of this week's data crack-up, he replied: "The key thing about identity cards is, of course, that information is protected by personal biometric information. The problem at present is that, because we do not have that protection, information is much more vulnerable than it should be."

3   Yes, that's the problem. We need biometric identification. Fingerprints. Iris scans. Gordon Brown says so too: "What we must ensure is that identity fraud is avoided, and the way to avoid identity fraud is to say that for passport information we will have the biometric support that is necessary."

4   Tsutomu Matsumoto is a Japanese mathematician, a cryptographer who works on security, and he decided to see if he could fool the machines which identify you by your fingerprint. This home science project costs about £20. Take a finger and make a cast with the moulding plastic sold in hobby shops. Then pour some liquid gelatin (ordinary food gelatin) into that mould and let it harden. Stick this over your finger pad: it fools fingerprint detectors about 80% of the time. The joy is, once you've fooled the machine, your fake fingerprint is made of the same stuff as fruit pastilles, so you can simply eat the evidence.

5   But what if you can't get the finger? Well, you can chop one off, of course—another risk with biometrics. But there is an easier way. Find a fingerprint on glass. Sorry, I should have pointed out that every time you touch something, if your security systems rely on biometric ID, then you're essentially leaving your pin number on a post-it note.

You can make a fingerprint image on glass more visible by painting over it with some cyanoacrylate adhesive. That's a posh word for superglue. Photograph that with a digital camera. Improve the contrast in a picture editing program, print the image on to a transparency sheet, and then use that to etch the fingerprint on to a copper-plated printed circuit boar. (It sounds difficult, but you can buy a beginner's etching set for about for £10.) This gives an image with some three-dimensional relief. You can now make your gelatin fingerpad using this as a mould.

Should I have told you all that, or am I very naughty? Yes to both.

It's well known that security systems which rely on secret methods are less secure than open systems, because the greater the number of people who know about the system, the more people there are to spot holes in it, and it is important that there are no holes. If someone tells you their system is perfect and secret, that's like quacks who tell you their machine cures cancer but they can't tell you how. Open the box, quack. In fact you might sense that the whole field of biometrics and ID is rather like medical quackery: as usual, on the one hand we have snake oil salesmen promising the earth, and on the other a bunch of humanities graduates who don't understand technology, science, or even human behaviour: buying it; bigging it up; thinking it's a magic wand.

But it's not. Leaks occur not because of unauthorized access, and they can't be stopped with biometrics; they happen because of authorized access, often ones which are managed with contemptible, cavalier incompetence. The damaging repercussions will not be ameliorated by biometrics.

So will biometrics prevent ID theft? Well, it might make it more difficult for you to prove your innocence. And once your fingerprints are stolen, they are harder to replace than your pin number. But here's the final nail in the coffin. Your fingerprint data will be stored in your passport or ID card as a series of numbers, called the "minutiae template." In the new biometric passport with its wireless chip, remember, all your data can be read and decrypted with a device near you, but not touching you.

What good would the data be, if someone lifted it? Not much, insisted Jim Knight, the minister for schools and learners, in July: "It is not possible to recreate a fingerprint using the numbers that are stored. The algorithm generates a unique number, producing no information of any use to identity thieves." Crystal clear, Jim.

Unfortunately, a team of mathematicians published a paper in April this year, showing that they could reconstruct a fingerprint from this data alone. In fact, they printed out the images they made, and then—crucially, completing the circle—used them to fool fingerprint readers.

Ah biometrics. Such a soothingly technical word. Repeat it to yourself.

Fujitsu Computer Products of America recently launched its palm vein authentication device. The device captures a person's palm vein pattern and checks it against a preregistered palm vein pattern from that individual. The device offers users a high level of accuracy and security. It is already in use at some of Asia's leading financial institutions.

FROM READING TO WRITING

1. Examine the outcries of biometrics critics and consider writing a rebuttal of one or more of their arguments. (Consult Chapter 12 on writing a rebuttal.)

2. In a causal argument (see Chapter 9), consider how the technological age in which we live exacerbates issues of privacy.

3. Evaluate any one of the technologies described in this chapter, based on practicality and/or constitutional principles.biometrics according to its effects. Has the technology actually helped in the war on terrorism? Has it actually led to significant privacy violations? (See Chapter 10 for advice on evaluation.)

4. Consider popular portrayals of security technologies and biometrics (like those in *CSI* or *24*). Why are these technologies so fascinating within the realm of science fiction? What qualities do these popular versions exaggerate, and why? What effect might these popular images have on viewers' opinions of real-life technologies, and why?

5. Analyze the visual images associated with this issue, building on Chapter 6 of this text. What is the nature of the arguments made in these visuals? How do they work to persuade an audience?

6. Write a narrative argument (such as the ones described in Chapter 11) that contributes to the debates represented in this chapter. How does a single incident—drawn from the news, an interview, or your own experience—contribute to this conversation? Alternatively, write a short story portraying the issue with a science fiction or futuristic slant.

27 | Regulating Substances, Regulating Bodies

Private Bodies, Public Controls

Regulation is often about deciding where lines may be crossed—and where they should not be crossed. How would we decide which burgers or fries (if any) should be regulated?

The U.S. prison population—now at 2.3 million, the Justice Department reported in 2008—has more than quadrupled since the early 1980s, which means that our nation now has the highest rate of incarceration in the world. Although only 4 percent of the world population is in the United States, the United States has a quarter of the entire world's prison population, and 1 in every 31 American adults is now in prison, on probation, or on parole. A great many of those in prison are nonviolent drug offenders, usually small-timers who need help with their own addictions. In the late 1980s, in the face of a cocaine epidemic that was ravaging the nation's cities and claiming the lives of citizens as prominent as Boston Celtics first-round draftee Len Bias, legislators and law enforcement agents cracked down by instituting mandatory minimum sentences. Because people who inform on others can often secure reduced sentences, small-time drug violators often get stiffer sentences than major dealers. According to *Newsweek*, 6 percent of inmates in state prisons in 1980 were there for drug violations; in 1996 the figure was 23 percent. In 1980, 25 percent of inmates in federal prisons were drug violators, while in 2005 the figure had risen to over 60 percent.

Should we be so hard on drug dealers and abusers? Is the state and federal governments' "war on drugs" going so poorly that it should be abandoned? Many people think so. Critics call attention not only to the figures on incarceration but also to the other social costs associated with strict drug laws. For example, many addicts resist treatment because they fear punishment; instead, they commit crimes to support their bad habits. Widespread urine testing and seizures of drug-related property have threatened basic civil rights and undermined respect for police. Extensions of the drug war have led to conflicts with

Number of inmates in U.S. prisons, 1920 to 2006. The number of inmates in U.S. prisons has more than quadrupled since the early 1980s.

other nations where drugs are produced. Moreover, if drugs were considered a medical and social problem rather than a criminal one, citizens could be helped rather than sent to prison. Needle-exchange programs could help check the spread of AIDS by reducing the incidence of shared needles. Recognizing that illegal drugs often are no worse and no better than alcohol (legal since the disastrous 1920s experiment known as Prohibition), Californians voted to legalize marijuana use for cancer and AIDS patients. Many people, drawing from the experiences of other nations, are now calling for moves to decriminalize some kinds of drug use, or at least to reduce penalties and increase treatment. In other words, the war on drugs might be maintained—but without quite so much prison warehousing.

On the other hand, many people argue for a continuing hard line on drugs (including alcohol) because of the damage that illegal drugs do. They point to the health risks and social costs—to early deaths, lost work days, rapes and assaults and broken lives attributable to substance abuse. In the tradition of Carry Nation and other temperance warriors who successfully lobbied for prohibition

An estimated 80–100 million Americans have tried marijuana.

Of every one hundred people who have smoked marijuana, twenty-eight have tried cocaine—but only one uses cocaine weekly.

of alcohol in the 1920s, they have evidence that drug use (especially cocaine use) has decreased during the years of the war on drugs, that marijuana may be a "gateway drug" to more dangerous substances (because marijuana smokers are far more likely to try other drugs, such as cocaine), and that the war on drugs is worth waging for all sorts of other reasons.

Advocates of a hard line on drugs sometimes take on not only drug kingpins but also others—alcohol producers, Big Tobacco, performance-enhancing drug users. For example, they promote stiff taxes on cigarettes and alcohol on the grounds that making harmful substances expensive discourages use and pays for the social costs involved. And they are often proponents of testing athletes for the use of unfair and dangerous performance-enhancing substances, such as steroids (which promote muscle growth but have harmful side effects), synthetic forms of testosterone (for which 2006 Tour de France winner Floyd Landis tested positive, causing him to be stripped of his title), and creatine (a dietary supplement that many athletes feel helps their training). They point to the popularity of such substances among young people. They also work to combat binge drinking on campuses because they see it as a frightening epidemic that encourages date rape, promotes vandalism, and otherwise ruins or undermines the lives of countless college students.

Reformer Carry Nation holding the weapons of her trade: a hatchet for destroying liquor containers and a copy of the Bible

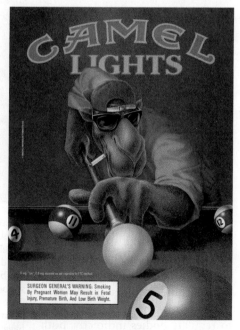

Contemporary Arguments

Should certain substances be regulated—and, if so, which ones? Is substance abuse a victimless crime that we have to live with in order to preserve a free society? Is education the only proper approach to the problem? If not, what exactly should be done about various drugs, alcohol, tobacco, and other controversial and harmful practices and substances? Just how should we weigh the risks of drug and alcohol use against the social costs of overzealous law enforcement?

The essays in this section provide a number of perspectives on public control over private bodies. Consider, for instance, the debate between Joe Klein and Bernadine Healy concerning the legalization of marijuana. Each writer looks at the legalization and criminalization of marijuana from a different perspective and with a different ultimate proposal. Then consider the argument about steroid use that follows: celebrated baseball analyst Bill James asks on his Web site whether our collective condemnation of performance enhancing drugs (PEDs) will soften in the coming years, offering his own perspective on the dangers posed by PEDs and the issues of fairness and consequence that are raised when professional athletes use such substances. Where exactly should lines be drawn between personal freedom—what we choose to do with our own bodies—and government intervention on behalf of health and public safety? That question underlies the other arguments, verbal and visual, that we present for your consideration in this chapter—arguments about body weight and body image, controlling tobacco, body modification through tattoos and piercing, and disability. We conclude the chapter with an Issue in Focus that has particular relevance: What, if anything, should be done to regulate excessive and dangerous alcohol consumption by college students?

Finally, consider as you read this chapter how visuals can serve to regulate bodies indirectly, both

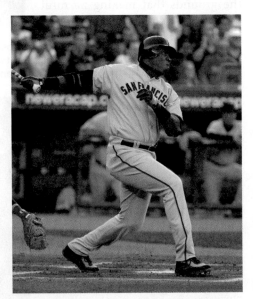

When Barry Bonds hit his 756th Major League Baseball home run on August 7, 2007, he broke the all-time record held by Henry Aaron. Although Bonds has never failed an official steroid test, he has been implicated frequently in the taking of steroids, and his home run record is embroiled in controversy. Other prominent players, most famously Roger Clemens and Alex Rodriguez, also have been implicated.

through the ideals that are presented and the concepts and values that are omitted. Photos, cartoons, ads, and other visuals in this chapter suggest that our identifications with certain body types can influence our behaviors; that argument also applies to television shows and movies. These issues concerning written and visual arguments arise especially in the essays by Terrence Rafferty (on film and body image), Rebecca Traister (on the Dove Campaign for Real Beauty), Pippa Wysong (on tattoos), and James Hibberd (on the employment of college students as "beer boys" and girls).

JOE **KLEIN**

Why Legalizing Marijuana Makes Sense

Joe Klein (born 1946) is journalist, a member of the Council on Foreign Relations, and a former Guggenheim Fellow. He has been a contributor to *Time* since 2003 and has also been published in *The New Republic*, the *New York Times*, the *Washington Post*, and *Rolling Stone*. He is the author of *Primary Colors*, an "anonymously" written exposé novel about Bill Clinton's first presidential campaign that later became a movie, as well as a follow-up entitled *Running Mate*. He contributed the following article to *Time* in April 2009.

For the past several years, I've been harboring a fantasy, a last political crusade for the baby-boom generation. We who started on the path of righteousness, marching for civil rights and against the war in Vietnam, need to find an appropriately high-minded approach to life's exit ramp. In this case, I mean the high-minded part literally. And so, a deal: give us drugs, after a certain age—say, 80—all drugs, any drugs we want. In return, we will give you our driver's licenses. (I mean, can you imagine how terrifying a nation of decrepit, solipsistic 90-year-old boomers behind the wheel would be?) We'll let you proceed with your lives—much of which will be spent paying for our retirement, in any case—without having to hear us complain about our every ache and reflux. We'll be too busy exploring altered states of consciousness. I even have a slogan for the campaign: "Tune in, turn on, drop dead."

2   A fantasy, I suppose. But beneath the furious roil of the economic crisis, a national conversation has quietly begun about the irrationality of our drug laws. It is going on in state legislatures, like New York's, where the draconian Rockefeller drug laws are up for review; in other states, from California to Massachusetts, various forms of marijuana decriminalization are being enacted. And it has reached the floor of Congress, where Senators Jim Webb and Arlen Specter have proposed a major prison-reform package, which would directly address drug-sentencing policies.

3   There are also more puckish signs of a zeitgeist shift. A few weeks ago, the White House decided to stage a forum in which the President would answer questions submitted by the public; 92,000 people responded—and most of them seemed obsessed with the legalization of marijuana. The two most popular questions about "green jobs and energy," for example, were about pot. The President dismissed the

outpouring—appropriately, I guess—as online ballot-stuffing and dismissed the legalization question with a simple: "No."

4 This was a rare instance of Barack Obama reacting reflexively, without attempting to think creatively, about a serious policy question. He was, in fact, taking the traditional path of least resistance: an unexpected answer on marijuana would have launched a tabloid firestorm, diverting attention from the budget fight and all those bailouts. In fact, the default fate of any politician who publicly considers the legalization of marijuana is to be cast into the outer darkness. Such a person is assumed to be stoned all the time, unworthy of being taken seriously. Such a person would be lacerated by the assorted boozehounds and pill poppers of talk radio. The hypocrisy inherent in the American conversation about stimulants is staggering.

5 But there are big issues here, issues of economy and simple justice, especially on the sentencing side. As Webb pointed out in a cover story in *Parade* magazine, the U.S. is, by far, the most "criminal" country in the world, with 5% of the world's population and 25% of its prisoners. We spend $68 billion per year on corrections, and one-third of those being corrected are serving time for nonviolent drug crimes. We spend about $150 billion on policing and courts, and 47.5% of all drug arrests are marijuana-related. That is an awful lot of money, most of it nonfederal, that could be spent on better schools or infrastructure—or simply returned to the public.

6 At the same time, there is an enormous potential windfall in the taxation of marijuana. It is estimated that pot is the largest cash crop in California, with annual revenues approaching $14 billion. A 10% pot tax would yield $1.4 billion in California alone. And that's probably a fraction of the revenues that would be available—and of the economic impact, with thousands of new jobs in agriculture, packaging, marketing and advertising. A veritable marijuana economic-stimulus package!

7 So why not do it? There are serious moral arguments, both secular and religious. There are those who believe—with some good reason—that the accretion of legalized vices is debilitating, that we are a less virtuous society since gambling spilled out from Las Vegas to "riverboats" and state lotteries across the country. There is a medical argument, though not a very convincing one: alcohol is more dangerous in a variety of ways, including the tendency of some drunks to get violent. One could argue that the abuse of McDonald's has a greater potential health-care cost than the abuse of marijuana. (Although it's true that with legalization, those two might not be unrelated.) Obviously, marijuana can be abused. But the costs of criminalization have proved to be enormous, perhaps unsustainable. Would legalization be any worse?

8 In any case, the drug-reform discussion comes just at the right moment. We boomers are getting older every day. You're not going to want us on the highways. Make us your best offer.

Bernadine Healy

Legalize Marijuana? Obama Was Right to Say No

Dr. Bernadine Healy (born 1944), a cardiologist, formerly headed the National Institutes of Health (NIH) and was once president of the American Red Cross. Currently she is health editor and columnist for *U.S. News & World Report.* The following column appeared February 4, 2009, on the *U.S. News* Web site.

Puff the Magic Dragon—in his naughtier incarnation—bit the dust when President Barack Obama recently made it clear that he is against legalizing marijuana. His message was delivered on his website, Change.gov, even before he placed his hand on the Lincoln Bible. Astonishingly, legalization of marijuana ranked as Priority No. 1 for the new administration among the thousands of possible actions voted upon on the website by the public—yes, even above stem cell research, the war in Iraq, and Wall Street bailouts. Obama's prompt no to the query "Will you consider legalizing marijuana so that the government can regulate it, tax it, put age limits on it, and create millions of new jobs and create a billion-dollar industry right here in the U.S.?" dashed the hopes of many who thought our young, hip, new president—who long ago dabbled in the stuff and, by his own admission, inhaled—would come to marijuana's rescue.

2   Listen to the president's inauguration speech, and it seems clear why he's unwilling. In a "new era of responsibility," somehow a fat new billion-dollar U.S. marijuana industry doesn't quite square with a world that almost universally outlaws the stuff. Making weed as accessible to our children as cigarettes doesn't fit with Obama's words to parents about nurturing their children, as he and Michelle so sweetly do their own little girls. And it would be the antithesis of the inaugural pledge he made to respect science.

3   Scientific research from the National Institute on Drug Abuse and elsewhere leaves little doubt that marijuana abuse is bad for brains, particularly younger ones. The psychoactive chemical in weed, THC (short for delta-9-tetrahydrocannabinol), binds to a class of receptors known as cannabinoids that are dense on neurons in brain areas associated with thinking, memory, concentration, sensation, time perception, and emotions like fear, anxiety, and pleasure. Once THC has delivered its buzz, it hangs around for days, if not many weeks, accumulating with regular use. The lingering chemical makes drug testing possible long after the last

puff, and it also means that weekend joints carry a low-grade marijuana haze into the next week, perhaps contributing to marijuana's so-called amotivational syndrome.

4   Researchers remain unsure whether the residual effects of cannabis on intellectual performance, attention span, and learning ability now identified in users (including college students) represent lingering drug, withdrawal symptoms, or toxic damage. Evidence is accumulating, however, that heavy drug use is associated with lasting damage. Just published in the journal *Pediatrics* is a preliminary study of young men who had been heavy marijuana users starting in their early teens. MRI scans showed disrupted neural development in the brain areas that influence memory, attention, and high level decision making, areas known to develop and mature during adolescence.

5   As for marijuana's association with anxiety, depression, and suicidal or even psychotic thinking, it's hard to say whether the mental disturbances are caused by the drug or are the trigger for its use in those already struggling with a mental illness. But however it's argued, academic stars are rarely potheads, and regular exposure to this powerful psychoactive drug is a nasty idea for developing young minds trying to study hard, mature emotionally, and get started in life.

6   Moreover, contrary to popular thought, NIDA stresses that marijuana can be physiologically and psychologically addictive. And Australian scientists recently reported that cannabis junkies hooked for more than 10 years develop brain injury. Compared with matched controls, users in this relatively small but provocative study scored lower on mental health and cognitive performance measures, and their MRI scans showed brain shrinkage in regions targeted by cannabis. Face it: Were the crude, dried, ground weed reviewed by the Food and Drug Administration for safety, it would flunk on its brain effects alone.

7   Yet cannabis has adverse effects on more than the brain. The heart is stressed by marijuana, which for one thing elevates serum triglycerides that bring coronary disease risk. Marijuana is a serious respiratory irritant that serves up more carcinogenic hydrocarbons than tobacco smoke. When pregnant women smoke, the drug gets into the fetus; in nursing mothers, it enters breast milk. And in the cannabis-receptor-laden testicles, there is growing evidence from the laboratory and in humans that THC causes mutant sperm, which among other things can't swim right—thus impairing male fertility, at least while the male and his sperm are under the influence.

8   Clearly, legalization of medical marijuana use is a more persuasive battle cry than that of recreational highs. The FDA has al-

ready approved synthetic THC in pill and suppository form to stimulate appetite (the marijuana "munchies") and to ease the nausea of chemotherapy in seriously ill or terminal patients. Anti-inflammatory and pain-perception benefits may be important as well.

9   All that said, the science remains immature and stymied by ideological and moral objections, at a time when there is much to be learned both about a drug that's so commonly used and about the body's own natural and still-mysterious cannabinoid receptor network. In the spirit of honoring science and an open mind, such work should be pursued—and, I might add, compassion and consideration afforded the sick and dying who use marijuana under a doctor's care.

10   As for the rest of society, arguments for legalization will rage: End the criminal underground that prohibition fosters; let adults be free to grow and smoke whatever they wish; or, lamely, pot's no worse than other—legal—vices. But as I see it, in an age of responsibility, protecting our young people's health is the stronger imperative and should rightfully keep policymakers from cozying up to this brain-toxic drug.

Bill James

Cooperstown and the 'Roids

Bill James (born 1949) is one of the most influential people in baseball history—though he never played the game professionally. A statistician who has brought social science methods, an open mind, and excellent writing ability to the study of professional baseball, James since the late 1970s has written many books and articles about baseball history and the performance of baseball players and teams. As a result of his work and the work of like-minded individuals affiliated with the Society for American Baseball Research, people now consider ballpark factors when they evaluate players, newspapers publish "onbase plus slugging percentages" as well as batting averages, and teams look at hard numbers (not just what they see with the naked eye) when they evaluate prospects. Amazingly, *Time* named him one of the one hundred most influential people in the world in 2006. James now serves as an adviser to the Boston Red Sox and maintains a Web site, billjamesonline.com, where the essay below appeared in July 2009.

For the last ten years or so people have been asking me to comment on the issue of steroids and the Hall of Fame. To this point I have resisted addressing these questions, arguing—as I do with the Hall of Fame status of active players—that there is nothing to be gained by trying to guess where objects still in motion will eventually land. With the passage of time the dust will settle, and we will see the issue more clearly.

2   After ten years, however, the dust does not seem to be settling very rapidly. There seem to be as many different and contradictory opinions on the issue now as there were five or eight years ago. We are all tired of arguing about it, but we still don't agree. In any case, I am finally ready to say what I have to say about it. It is my opinion that, in time, the use of steroids or other Performance Enhancing Drugs will mean virtually nothing in the debate about who gets into the Hall of Fame and who does not.

3   The process of arriving at this conclusion began when I was studying aging patterns in the post-steroid era. One of the characteristics of the steroid era was that we had several dozen players who continued to improve beyond the normal aging time frame, so that many of them had their best seasons past the age of 32. This is historically not normal. In the post-steroid era we are returning to the historic norm in which players hit a wall sometime in their early thirties. But what does this mean?

4   It means that *steroids keep you young.* You may not like to hear it stated that way, because steroids are evil, wicked, mean and nasty and youth is a good thing, but...that's what it means. Steroids help the athlete resist the effects of aging.

5   Well, if steroids help keep you young, what's wrong with that?

6   What's wrong with that is that steroids may help keep players "young" at some risk to their health, and the use of steroids by athletes may lead non-athletes to risk their health as well. But the fact is that, with time, the use of drugs like steroids will not disappear from our culture. It will, in fact, grow, eventually becoming so common that it might almost be said to be ubiquitous. *Everybody wants to stay young.* As we move forward in time, more and more people are *going* to use more and more drugs in an effort to stay young. Many of these drugs are going to be steroids or the descendants of steroids.

7   If we look into the future, then, we can reliably foresee a time in which *everybody is going to be using steroids* or their pharmaceutical descendants. We will learn to control the health risks of these drugs, or we will develop alternatives to them. Once that happens, people will start living to age 200 or 300 or 1,000, and

doctors will begin routinely prescribing drugs to help you live to be 200 or 300 or 1,000. If you look into the future 40 or 50 years, I think it is quite likely that every citizen will routinely take anti-aging pills every day.

8   How, then, are those people of the future—who are taking ' steroids every day—going to look back on base-ball players who used steroids? They're going to look back on them as pioneers. They're going to look back at it and say "So what?"

9   The argument for discriminating against PED users rests upon the assumption of the moral superiority of non-drug users. But in a culture in which *everyone* routinely uses steroids, that argument cannot possibly prevail. You can like it or you can dislike it, but your grandchildren are going to be steroid users. Therefore, they are very likely to be people who do not regard the use of steroids as a moral failing. They are more likely to regard the banning of steroids as a bizarre artifice of the past.

10   Let us suppose that I am entirely wrong about all of that; let us suppose that our grandchildren do *not* wind up regularly ingesting chemicals to extend their youth. I would still argue that, in the long run, the use of steroids will eventually become a non-issue in who gets into the Hall of Fame.

11   My second argument is this:

   1. Eventually, *some* players who have been associated with steroids are going to get into the Hall of Fame. This is no longer at issue. One cannot keep Barry Bonds, Roger Clemens, A-Rod, Manny Ramirez, Mark McGwire, Sammy Sosa and all of the others out of the Hall of Fame forever. *Some* of them have to get in. If nothing else, somebody will eventually get in and *then* acknowledge that he used steroids.

   2. Once *some* players who have been associated with steroids are in the Hall of Fame, the argument against the others will become un-sustainable.

12   When the time comes at which two or three or four players are in the Hall of Fame who have acknowledged some steroid use, the barrier to other steroid users rests upon some sort of balancing test. Did this player use *too many* steroids to be considered legiti-mate? Is his career a creation of the steroids? Would he have been a Hall of Fame player without the steroids?

13   I am not suggesting that it is inappropriate for any one sportswriter or any one Hall of Fame voter to balance these consid-erations as best he can. But one does not build a house upon a well-balanced rock. The way that each sportswriter looks at these

issues is going to be different from the way that each other looks at them. There can only be a consensus on one of two positions:

a. that steroid users should not be in the Hall of Fame,

b. that steroid use is not an issue in the debate.

or

14   Between the two extreme positions, it becomes a fluid discussion. Once we move away from the one extreme, in my view, we will begin to drift inevitably toward the other.

15   I would liken this to attitudes about sexuality and television. At one point there was a firm consensus that there was no place for sex on TV. Married couples, on TV, slept in twin beds. The first departures from this firm position were small and insignificant...PBS specials on prostitution, chewing gum and soft drink commercials that pushed the boundaries of "taste", and edited-for-TV movies that were not quite as edited as they would have been a few years ago. Once there was no longer a firm consensus at an extreme position, there was a fluid standard that moved inevitably toward more and more openness about sexuality.

16   I will note that this happened without the consent and without the approval of most of the American public. It was never true that *most* people wanted to see more sex on TV. Probably it was generally true that most Americans disliked what they regarded as the erosion of standards of decency. But it was always true that *some* people wanted to see more sex on TV, and that was all that mattered, because that created a market for shows that pushed the envelope, and thus eroded the barriers. It was like a battle line that disintegrated once the firing started. The importance of holding the battle line, in old-style military conflict, was that once the line was breached, there was no longer an organized point of resistance. Once the consensus against any sexual references on TV was gone, there was no longer any consensus about what the standards should be—thus, a constant moving of the standards.

17   I think the same thing will happen here: Once there is no longer a firm consensus against steroid users in the Hall of Fame, there will be a fluid situation which moves inevitably in the direction of more and more inclusiveness. It is not necessary that people approve of this movement in principle. It is only necessary that there be advocates for those who are still on the outside looking in...for Sammy Sosa, let's say, and Manny Ramirez. And there is no question that there will be those advocates.

18   Third argument. History is forgiving. Statistics endure.

19   At the time that Dick Allen left the major leagues, virtually no one thought of him as a Hall of Fame player. In his first year of

eligibility for the Hall of Fame, he received the support of a little less than 4% of the voters. In his fifteen years of eligibility for BBWAA selection, he never reached 20% in the voting.

20 Dick Allen did not have imaginary sins or imaginary failings as a player. He had very real offenses. But as time passes, the details of these incidents (and eventually the incidents themselves) are forgotten, and it becomes easier for Allen's advocates to re-interpret them as situations in which Allen was the victim, rather than the aggressor or offender. The people who were there die off. A certain number of people want to play the role of Dick Allen's advocate. No one—including me—wants to play the role of persistently denigrating Dick Allen; in fact, I'm pretty sure you can go to hell for that. People who were friends of Dick Allen speak up; the dozens or hundreds of exteammates who despised Dick Allen keep silent, or speak of him as well as they can manage.

21 For very good reasons, we do not nurture hatred. We let things pass. This leads history to be forgiving. Perhaps it is right, perhaps it is wrong, but that is the way it is. Sometime between 2020 and 2030, Dick Allen will be elected to the Hall of Fame.

22 The same thing has happened, more slowly, with the Black Sox. In 1950 no one thought Joe Jackson should be in the Hall of Fame. Now it is a common opinion—perhaps a majority opinion—that he should. People question whether he "really" did the things that he clearly admitted doing. His virtues are celebrated; his sins are minimized. Perhaps this is right; perhaps it is wrong. It is the way of history.

23 History will rally on the side of the steroid users in the same way that it has rallied on the side of Dick Allen, Joe Jackson, Orlando Cepeda, Hack Wilson and many others. But with the steroid users, we are not talking about a single isolated "offender", but about a large group of them, representing the bulk of the dominant players of their generation. The forces that push for their acceptance will get organized much more quickly and will move with much greater force. This, in my view, will make the use of steroids a non-factor in Hall of Fame discussions within 30 to 40 years.

24 Fourth argument. Old players play a key role in the Hall of Fame debate. It seems unlikely to me that aging ballplayers will divide their ex-teammates neatly into classes of "steroid users" and "non-steroid users."

25 One of the key reasons that Dick Allen will eventually be in the Hall of Fame is that one of his ex-teammates—Goose Gossage—feels strongly that he should be, and is outspoken on this issue. Goose Gossage is now a Hall of Famer. His voice carries weight.

26   Eventually, younger players who were teammates of Mark McGwire, Sammy Sosa, A-Rod and Roger Clemens are going to be in the Hall of Fame. Andy Pettitte is probably going to be in the Hall of Fame. When he is in the Hall of Fame—if he gets there before Roger—he is *going* to speak up for Roger Clemens. Hell, somebody might even speak up for Barry Bonds.

27   Once this happens, it will erode the prejudice against steroid users in the Hall of Fame, to the extent that that prejudice might otherwise exist. *You* might choose to divide the world of baseball players into steroid users and non-steroid users, but this is not a division that makes intuitive sense when you know the people involved. Therefore, this is not the division that will ultimately endure, once the long historical sorting-out process that makes Goose Gossage relevant and Lindy McDaniel irrelevant has run its course.

28   I have a fifth argument here, but before I get to that, let me speak for a moment on the other side of the issue. Let us adopt, as the face of the non-steroid user, Will Clark. Will Clark and Rafael Palmeiro were college teammates, and apparently were not the best of friends. As players they were rivals. Texas had Palmeiro (1989-1993) and then had Clark (1994-1998), while Palmeiro went to Baltimore. After the 1998 season the Orioles—then a strong franchise—signed Clark, while Palmeiro went back to the Rangers. Later on Palmeiro went back to the Orioles, so that both the Rangers and the Orioles had Palmeiro, then Clark, then Palmeiro. There was always a debate about which was the better player.

29   I've always been a great admirer of Will Clark, who I think was a great player and is a historically under-rated player in part because his numbers are dimmed by comparison to the steroid-inflated numbers that came just after him. Will Clark, in the pre-steroid era, was a much better player than Palmeiro, although Palmeiro was good. Palmeiro, as we entered the steroid era, gradually pulled ahead of Clark. I have no idea whether Will Clark ever used steroids or not, but let us use Will Clark as the face of the player who chose *not* to use steroids in order to stay in the game, the player who chose the natural route and suffered the consequences of that.

30   Is it fair to Will Clark to compare him to players who chose to cheat in order to move beyond that level? No, it is not. Absolutely, it is not. But the critical issue is, Is this cheating? If you choose to regard it as cheating, if you choose not to support the Hall of Fame candidacy of a steroid user because you regard it as cheating, I would not argue with you. I think that Will Clark has a perfect right to feel that he was cheated out of a fair chance to compete for honors in his time, and, if you choose to look at it

from the standpoint of Will Clark, I don't think that you are wrong to do so.

31   But at the same time, I do not believe that history will look at this issue from the standpoint of Will Clark. I don't see how it can. What it seems to me that the Will Clark defenders have not come to terms with is the breadth and depth of the PED problem, which began in the 1960s and expanded without resistance for almost 40 years, eventually involving generations of players. It seems to me that the Will Clark defenders are still looking at the issue as one of "some" players gaining an advantage by using Performance Enhancing Drugs. But it wasn't really an issue of *some* players gaining an advantage by the use of performance Enhancing Drugs; it is an issue of *many* players using Performance Enhancing drugs in competition with one another. Nobody knows how many. It would be my estimate that it was somewhere between 40 and 80%.

32   The discrimination against PED users in Hall of Fame voting rests upon the perception that this was *cheating.* But is it cheating if one violates a rule that nobody is enforcing, and which one may legitimately see as being widely ignored by those within the competition?

33   It seems to me that, at some point, this becomes an impossible argument to sustain—that all of these players were "cheating," in a climate in which most everybody was doing the same things, and in which there was either no rule against doing these things or zero enforcement of those rules. If one player is using a corked bat, like Babe Ruth, clearly, he's cheating. But if 80% of the players are using corked bats and no one is enforcing any rules against it, are they all cheating? One better: if 80% of the players are using corked bats and it is unclear whether there are or are not any rules against it, is that cheating?

34   And... was there really a rule against the use of Performance Enhancing Drugs? At best, it is a debatable point. The Commissioner issued edicts banning the use of Performance Enhancing Drugs. People who were raised on the image of an all-powerful commissioner whose every word was law are thus inclined to believe that there was a rule against it.

35   But "rules," in civilized society, have certain characteristics. They are agreed to by a process in which all of the interested parties participate. They are included in the rule book. There is a process for enforcing them. Someone is assigned to enforce the rule, and that authority is given the powers necessary to enforce the rule. There are specified and reasonable punishments for violation of the rules.

36   The "rule" against Performance Enhancing Drugs, if there was such a rule before 2002, by-passed all of these gates. It was never

agreed to by the players, who clearly and absolutely have a right to participate in the process of changing any and all rules to which they are subject. It was not included in any of the various rule books that define the conduct of the game from various perspectives. There was no process for enforcing such a rule. The punishments were draconian in theory and non-existent in fact.

37   It seems to me that, with the passage of time, more people will come to understand that the commissioner's periodic spasms of self-righteousness do not constitute baseball law. It seems to me that the argument that it is cheating must ultimately collapse under the weight of carrying this great contradiction—that 80% of the players are cheating against the other 20% by violating some "rule" to which they never consented, which was never included in the rule books, and which for which there was no enforcement procedure. History is simply *not* going to see it that way.

38   The end of the day here is about the year 2040, perhaps 2050. It will come upon us in a flash. And, at the end of the day, Mark McGwire is going to be in the Hall of Fame, and Roger Clemens, and Sammy Sosa, and Rafael Palmeiro, and probably even Barry Bonds. I am not especially advocating this; I simply think that is the way it is. I only hope that, when all of these players are enshrined, they will extend a hand up to a few players from the Will Clark division of the game.

Star MLB pitcher Roger Clemens and others are sworn in prior to their testimony before the U.S. House Oversight and Government Reform Committee investigation into allegations of widespread performance-enhancing drug use in Major League Baseball.

Barry Blitt's art has appeared in many publications, including the *New York Times*, *Entertainment Weekly*, the *Chicago Tribune*, and *The New Yorker*, which published this art on its March 26, 2007, cover. Blitt comments on the inaccessibility of many spaces for individuals with physical disabilities—in this case, a soldier who has returned wounded from the war in Iraq.

TERRENCE **RAFFERTY**

Kate Winslet, Please Save Us!

Brooklyn native Terrence Rafferty is a film critic whose articles have appeared in the *Atlantic*, the *Village Voice*, *Film Quarterly*, the *New York Times*, and many other publications. He also has been the "critic-at-large" for *GQ* (short for *Gentleman's Quarterly*), a fashion and culture magazine geared to young professional men. *GQ* carried the following argument in May 2001. Do you think the argument would have been constructed differently if it had been published elsewhere?

When I go to the movies these days, I sometimes find myself gripped by a very peculiar sort of nostalgia: I miss flesh. I see skin, I see bones, I see many rocklike outcroppings of muscle, but I rarely see, in the angular bodies up there on the screen—either the hard, sculpted ones or the brittle, anorexic ones— anything extra, not even a hint of the soft layer of fatty tissue that was once an essential component of the movies' romantic fantasy, the cushion that made encounters between the sexes seem like pleasant, sensual experiences rather than teeth-rattling head-on collisions. The sleek form-follows-function physiques of today's film stars suggest a world in which power and brutal efficiency are all that matter, in the bedroom no less than in the pitiless, sun-seared arena of Gladiator. This may well be an accurate reflection of our anxious time, but it's also mighty depressing. When I come out of the multiplex now, I often feel like the archetypal ninety-eight-pound weakling in the old Charles Atlas ads—like big bullies have been kicking sand in my face for two hours. And that's just the women.

Kate Moss, waiflike

2   This is a touchy area, I realize. Where body type is concerned, an amazingly high percentage of social and cultural commentary is fueled by simple envy, resentment of the young and the buff. A few years ago, when Calvin Klein ads featuring the stunning, wai-flike Kate Moss appeared on the sides of New York City buses, they were routinely defaced with bitter-sounding graffiti—FEED ME was the most popular—which was, you had to suspect, largely the product of women who were enraged by her distinctive beauty. (Men, to my knowledge, had few complaints about having to see Moss in her underwear whiz past them on Madison Avenue.) Protesters insisted that images such as those in the Klein ads promote eating disorders in impressionable teenage girls. Maybe that's so—I don't have the statistics—but the sheer violence of the attacks on Moss, along with the fact that they seemed to be directed more at the model herself than at the marketing wizards who exploited her, strongly suggested another, less virtuous agenda. The taste of sour grapes was unmistakable.

3   I happened to think Moss looked great—small, but well-proportioned, and mercifully lacking the ropy musculature that had begun to creep into pop-culture images of femininity, in the cunning guise of "empowerment." The Bionic Woman could only dream of the bulging biceps sported by Linda Hamilton in *Terminator 2: Judgment Day* (1991); and Ginger Rogers, even when she was struggling to match steps with Astaire, never had the calf muscles of the mighty Madonna. (Nor would she have wanted them: She was a dancer and not, like Mrs. Ritchie or any of her brood of MTV chicks, a kinky aerobics instructor.) It's understandable, I suppose, that women might have felt the impulse to bulk up during the might-makes-right regimes of Ronald Reagan and George Herbert Walker Bush, when the rippling behemoths of machismo, Arnold and Sly, ruled the screen; in that context, working on one's abs and pecs could be considered a prudent strategy of self-defense. But the arms buildup in the Cold War between the sexes was not a pretty sight. Applied to sex, the doctrine of Mutually Assured Destruction is kind of a bummer. The wages of sinew is the death of romance.

4   At least that's how it looks to people of my generation, whose formative years were the '60s, and to many of Moss's generation (the one commonly designated "X"), who in their youth embraced, for a while, the antipower aesthetic of grunge. What we oversaturated pop-culture consumers consider attractive— i.e., what's sexy in the

opposite gender and worth aspiring to in one's own—usually develops in adolescence, as the relevant body parts do, and doesn't change much thereafter. For men older than I am, the perfect woman might have been Sophia Loren or Elizabeth Taylor or Marilyn Monroe or Rita Hayworth or the wartime pinup Betty Grable or (reaching back to the hugely eroticized flapper era) the original It girl, Clara Bow. And for them, the image of the ideal masculine self might have been Cary Grant or Clark Gable or Henry Fonda or Gary Cooper or even, for the less physically prepossessing—OK, shorter—guys, Cagney or Bogart or Tracy. By the time the '60s rocked and rolled into history, some subtle transformations had occurred, primarily in female sexual iconography. While the male stars of that decade remained more or less within the range of body types of their predecessors—Steve McQueen and Sean Connery might have looked a bit more athletic than the old norms demanded, but they wouldn't qualify as hard-bodies by today's standards—the shape of desirability in women distinctly altered, to something less voluptuous and more elongated. The fashions of the era tended to shift the erotic focus southward, from the breasts and the hips down to the legs, which, in a miniskirt, did rather overwhelm all other possible indicators of a woman's sexual allure. Although smaller-chested, leaner-hipped women, such as Julie Christie, stole some thunder from the conspicuously curvaceous, a certain amount of flesh was still required. Minis didn't flatter skinny legs any more than they did chubby ones.

5   So there was, to the avid eyes of teenage boys like me, a fine balance struck in the body aesthetic of the '60s, between, so to speak, length and width, Giacometti and Rubens. And muscles weren't part of the equation. He-men such as Steve Reeves— whose 1959 *Hercules,* a cheap Italian import initiated a spate of "sword and sandal" epics—seemed, to both sexes, ridiculous, vain rather than truly manly. (It's worth noting that in those days it was widely perceived that the primary market for body-building magazines was gay men.) And women? Forget it. The epitome of the muscular gal was the Russian or East German Olympic athlete, an Olga or a Helga, whose gender identity was frequently, and often justly, a matter of some dispute. There's an echo of that attitude in Ridley Scott's 1997 *G.I. Jane,* in which a feminist senator played by Anne Bancroft, trying to select a candidate for the first woman to undergo Navy SEAL training, summarily dismisses several of the beefier applicants on the grounds of ambiguous sexuality. She settles on Demi Moore, who is slender and pretty and, on the evidence of a spectacularly obvious boob job, unquestionably straight.

6   But bodies like Moore's puzzle me. What, exactly, is the empowering element here—the iron she's pumped or the silicone that's been pumped into her chest? My number one teenage crush, Diana Rigg, didn't need either in order to be wholly convincing as kick-ass secret agent Emma Peel in the TV series *The Avengers.* Paired with a dapper male partner, John Steed (played by Patrick Macnee), Mrs. Peel was not only fully empowered but was also by far the more physically active of the two. In her mod pantsuits and go-go boots, she did most of the actual fighting in the kung fu-ish battles that climaxed virtually every episode, while Steed, perhaps mindful of potential damage to his impeccably cut Pierre Cardin suits, generally limited his martial activity to an occasional deft thrust with the umbrella.

7   Maybe if I'd come of age with visions of Madonna dancing in my head, I might find GI Demi devastatingly sexy rather than grotesque, but, objectively, I think the idea that women's power depends on either sculpted muscles or gigantic, orblike

breasts (much less both) smacks of desperation. Mrs. Peel wielded her power so coolly, so confidently, and clearly never felt the need to enhance it by strenuous training or expensive medical procedures. Comfort in one's own skin is always appealing, which is probably why, in this sweating, striving, aggressively self-improving era, I find bodies as diverse as Kate Moss's and Kate Winslet's mighty attractive. It's not the body type per se—neither the frail Kate nor the ampler one precisely conforms to my Riggian ideal—but a woman's attitude toward her body that makes her sexy.

Kate Winslet from *Titanic* days

8 What's unnerving about today's popculture images of women is how extreme they are—and how much emphasis they place on the *effort* required to correct nature, to retard the aging process, to be all that you can be (and not, God forbid, simply what you are). The ethic of progress through hard work and technology is deeply ingrained in our society, as is the democratic notion that everyone should be whatever he or she wants to be— a noble idea that gets a tad problematic when what everyone wants to be is a star. And every star wants to be a bigger star. As a result, we're seeing, in the movies and on television and in the pages of fashion magazines, increasingly bizarre manifestations of our paradoxical collective need to feel unique and, more, admired. Being really fat, for example, can confer on a person a certain distinction, but not the kind most of us yearn for. (In the old days, for men, a degree of heft often indicated prosperity; the movies embodied their image of financial success in portly figures such as Eugene Pallette and Edward Arnold. No more.) To stand out on the runway these days, a model has to be significantly gaunter—and younger—than even the FEED ME–era Moss. And to make her mark on the screen, an actress has several equally grueling options: starve herself skeletal, go to the gym and get muscular, or—sometimes in perverse combination with one of the previous—have her breasts inflated surgically. In each case, the result is a wild exaggeration of what would be, in moderation, a desirable quality: slimness, fitness or voluptuousness. When I look at women in the movies now, I often feel as if I were gazing not at real people but at cartoon characters—Olive Oyl, Popeye (in drag) and Jessica Rabbit.

9 Of course, there are exceptions: the spectacular Winslet; the cherubic and blissfully unself-conscious Drew Barrymore; the graceful, athletic Asian stars Michelle Yeoh and Maggie Cheung; and (no epithet necessary) Julia Roberts. But too many of the screen's great beauties have been developing a lean and hungry look in recent years. They've felt the burn, and something more than body fat appears to have been eliminated—a certain amount of joy seems to have melted away at the same time. Clearly, we live in extraordinarily ruthless and competitive times; and popular culture is bound

to reflect that condition, but I can't think of another age in which the competitive anxieties of the performers themselves were so mercilessly exposed to the public's view. When tough, chunky guys like Cagney squared off against one another in a boxing ring or on the mean streets of New York or Chicago, you sensed that the survival of an entire community of immigrants was at stake; you could see it in every movement of their squat brawler's bodies. And when the Depression was over, those fierce small men just about vanished from the movies, giving way to their larger, better-nourished children, who left the field, in turn, to generations who would be conscious of their bodies without having nearly as much use for them as their ancestors had had. What's at stake for today's action heroes and heroines, all pumped up with no place to go except to the "explosive" climax of a fanciful plot? The steroidal action pictures of the '80s and '90s created a race of pointless Supermen. Everyone in the audience was in on the joke: Bruce Willis and Tom Cruise and Nicolas Cage and Keanu Reeves didn't bulk up to save the world or any recognizable part of it; they did it because starring in an action franchise was, and remains, a surefire means of moving up the Hollywood ladder.

10   As the historian Lynne Luciano points out in her useful new book, *Looking Good: Male Body Image in America,* in a white-collar, service economy all most of us do with our bodies is compare them with everybody else's. We look, we admire, we envy, we check the mirror, we get dissatisfied, we go back to the old drawing board (the gym, the plastic surgeon, Jenny Craig, whatever). And this strikes many as perfectly reasonable and natural: You have to keep an edge, and you have to *work* on it. Constant vigilance is required for both men and women, and folks are starting to look a little haggard. This applies even to the beautiful people of the silver screen. We can see the strain as they try to hang on to their precarious positions, like Tom Cruise at the beginning of *M.I.2.* And who, aside from the stars themselves, their families and their agents, could possibly care?

11   I haven't used the word *narcissism* yet, and it's long overdue. The unseemly vanity once ascribed to poor Steve Reeves has become the norm in Hollywood, which, kind of hilariously, apparently believes that we're so vain we probably think their movies are about us. I can't come up with another explanation for berserk pictures like David Fincher's *Fight Club* (1999), in which Edward Norton, as a harried white collar Everyman, takes as his guru and alter ego an alarmingly buff *Übermensch* played by Brad Pitt. If the weak box-office returns are any indication, *Fight Club* did not strike the deep chord in the hearts of American men that its makers evidently thought it would, and, to add insult to injury, the picture didn't even provoke the "controversy" that might have validated the artists' sense of their own fearlessness and edginess. The whole spectacle was simply self-important and silly—as silly as *Hercules* and, because no one involved seemed to recognize it, then some.

12   It's time to stop the madness. Sure, we viewers are stressed-out and perhaps slightly self-absorbed, but more of us than Hollywood thinks have some perspective on the absurdities of our lives and the inanities of our culture. Fewer of us than the studios imagine actually believe that a diet or a set of weights or silicone implants will change our lives, even if every movie star worth his or her (pardon the expression) salt apparently does believe it. That's their business, and, as we know—though Hollywood has obviously forgotten— there's *no* business like show business. The feral, predatory creatures prowling across the screen for our amusement are in a world of their own. And although they carry themselves as if they

were wolves, magnificent in their power, they're really just coyotes, roaming the hills restlessly for scraps and deluding themselves even more doggedly than Chuck Jones's indefatigable Wile E. At least he knew what he was.

13   In a sense, body image represents the final frontier of postmodernism, the only area as yet untouched by our culture's pervasive irony. It would be useful, I think, for moviemakers to drop the pretense that entertainment is a life-and-death struggle, which only the strong survive. The stars of earlier eras, with their variety of unapologetically eccentric physiques, understood it was all a lovely con, a game played for pleasure: That's what those discreet little layers of flesh ultimately meant. But what would it take, I wonder, to make today's hardbodies lighten up and laugh at their own desperate exertions or, failing that, merely stop gazing out at us cowed viewers as if they were dying to beat the crap out of us? I don't know, but I suspect that cranky magazine columns won't do the job. A higher power will have to be invoked. Mrs. Peel, you're needed.

Rebecca Traister

"Real Beauty"—Or Really Smart Marketing?

Traister is staff writer for the "Life" section of Salon, the online news and culture journal which carried the following article in 2005. Her work typically considers issues related to women, gender, and power and has been published in a variety of publications, including *ELLE*, the *New York Times*, *Vogue*, and *The Nation*.

The words appear slowly, against the familiar powder-blue shape of the bird in flight—the Dove soap symbol—like soothing, watery poetry:

> *For too long*
> *beauty has been defined by narrow, stifling sterotypes [sic].*
> *You've told us it's time to change all that. We agree.*
> *Because we believe real beauty comes*
> *In many shapes, sizes and ages.*
> *It is why we started the Campaign for Real Beauty.*
> *And why we hope you'll take part.*

2   This is the lilting intro to the Web site that Dove has dedicated to its "Real Beauty" advertising campaign, for which it has picked six women who are not professional models—each beautiful, but

broader than Bundchen, heftier than an Olsen twin—to model in bras and panties.

3   The campaign is massive; these six broads are currently featured in national television and magazine ads, as well as on billboards and the sides of buses in urban markets like Boston, Chicago, Washington, Dallas, Los Angeles, Miami, New York, and San Francisco. And they've made quite an impact. Apparently, this public display of non-liposuctioned thighs is so jaw-droppingly revelatory that recent weeks have seen the Real Beauty models booked on everything from "The Today Show" to "The View" to CNN.

4   All the hoopla is precisely what Dove expected. According to a press release, Dove wants "to make women feel more beautiful every day by challenging today's stereotypical view of beauty and inspiring women to take great care of themselves." The use of "real women" (don't think too hard about the Kate Mosses of the world losing their status as biological females here) "of various ages, shapes and sizes" is designed "to provoke discussion and debate about today's typecast beauty images."

5   It's a great idea—a worthy follow-up to Dove's 2004 campaign, which featured women with lined faces, silver hair and heavy freckles, and asked questions like, "Wrinkled? Or Wonderful?" and also got a lot of attention, including a shout-out on the "Ellen DeGeneres Show."

6   As Stacy Nadeau, one of the Real Beauty models and a full-time student from Ann Arbor, Mich., says on the campaign Web site, "I have always been a curvier girl and always will be. I am proud of my body and think all women should be proud of theirs too. This is my time to encourage and help women feel great about themselves, no matter what they weigh or look like. Women have surrendered to diets and insane eating habits to live up to social stereotypes for too long. It's time that all women felt beautiful in their own skin."

7   But let's hope that skin doesn't have any cellulite. Because no one wants to look at a cottage-cheesy ass.

8   That's right. The one little wrinkle—so to speak—in this you-go-grrl stick-it-to-the-media-man empowerment campaign is that the set of Dove products that these real women are shilling for is *cellulite firming cream*. Specifically, Dove's new "Intensive Firming Cream," described as "a highly effective blend of glycerin, plus seaweed extract and elastin peptides known for their skin-firming properties." It's supposed "to work on problem areas to help skin feel firmer and reduce the appearance of cellulite in two weeks." There are also the Intensive Firming Lotion and the Firming Moisturizing Body Wash, which do pretty much the same thing.

9 The ad copy on the posters—in which the women stand alone, often looking over their rounded backsides—is composed of sing-it-sister lines like "Let's face it, firming the thighs of a size 2 supermodel is no challenge" and "New Dove Firming. As tested on real curves."

10 Meanwhile, on its Web site, Dove encourages us to get behind something called "The Dove Self-Esteem Fund," which involves a partnership with the Girl Scouts (and a program called *uniquely ME!*). It is supposed to help "girls to overcome life damaging hang-ups by putting beauty into perspective." Yes, when I think of putting beauty in perspective for girls, mostly I think of suggesting that they shell out for three separately sold products that will temporarily make it appear that they have less cellulite.

11 It's not that I have anything against firming cream. By all means, sell firming cream! Go ahead! I'm even prepared to believe that it may be a useful tool for women who truly are plagued by their cellulite and are thankful to have a product that can help them combat it. I also understand that companies sell stuff. They advertise, they flog product; thus is life and business.

12 But as long as you're patting yourself on the back for hiring real-life models with imperfect bodies, thereby "challenging today's stereotypical view of beauty and inspiring women to take great care of themselves," why ask those models to flog a cream that has zero health value and is just an expensive and temporary Band-Aid for a "problem" that the media has told us we have with our bodies. Incidentally, cellulite isn't even a result of being overweight! It's the result of cellular changes in the skin. Skinny people have cellulite. Old people have cellulite. Young people have cellulite. Gwyneth Paltrow has cellulite. All God's children have cellulite.

13 Why not run an ad that proclaims, "Cellulite: Uniquely MINE!"

14 Or, more realistically, why aren't these women selling shampoo? Or soap? Or moisturizer?

15 Stacie Bright, a spokeswoman for Unilever, Dove's parent company, emphasized that this campaign "is for women of all shapes and sizes, and a lot of women want firming products. It's about feeling good about yourself. And that's about bringing products that matter to women." Pressed on the inconsistency of having women who feel good about themselves sell a product that makes a lot of us feel bad about ourselves, Bright replied, "Let's face it, if you had a firming product, and you had a size 2 woman selling it, that would really be the contradiction."

16 Clearly the idea behind the campaign is a smart, worthwhile and rational one. It does feel refreshingly non-self-loathing to log

on to the Dove site and hear the models saying things like "I love these big ol' hips" and "I don't think about being slim." It's a little ray of sanity in this anorexic world. But it's also a business proposition and an advertising campaign. And doing something radically different—like presenting female consumers with models who actually resemble human beings they've met—is getting these products a lot of coveted attention. In fact, Dove may have tapped a zeitgeist vein, since the sport of lashing out at manipulated images of female beauty seems to be enjoying a bit of a vogue right now.

17   This spring, Oscar-winning actress Cate Blanchett spoke in interviews about her horror at the Botox craze. "I look at people sort of entombing themselves and all you see is their little pinholes of terror," said the actress. "And you think, Just live your life—death is not going to be any easier just because your face can't move." Blanchett also said that she thinks "that women and their vulnerabilities are played on in the cosmetic industry. . . . Women are encouraged to be terrified of aging." In this month's *Vogue*, Kate Winslet says of her battle with the press over her normal weight, "I'm relatively slim, I eat healthily, I keep fit. . . . I couldn't be 105 pounds even if I tried, and I really don't want to be 105 pounds."

18   And in just over a week, Bath and Body Works in association with American Girl dolls, will launch a line of "Real Beauty Inside and Out" personal care products "designed to help girls ages 8 to 12 feel—and be—their best." The line will include body lotions, splashes, soaps and lip balms, all dressed up in girl-friendly "hues of berry" and each arriving with an inspirational message like "Real beauty means no one's smile shines exactly like yours," "Real beauty is helping a friend," or "Real beauty is trusting in yourself."

19   It's a great gimmick—one that few of us can take issue with. But just like Dove's "love your ass but not the fat on it" campaign, much of this stuff prompts grim questions about whether it's even possible to break the feel-bad cycle of the beauty industry. Blanchett, after all, recently signed on as spokeswoman for SK-II line of cosmetics. And while it's all well and good to tell 8-year-old girls that real beauty is about trust, it's sort of funny to think about doing it while selling them minty lip shine or fruit-scented "My Way Styling Gel" for eight bucks a pop.

20   Let them be. After all, they have decades ahead of them in which to worry about eradicating the cellulite from their really beautiful curves.

The two visual arguments on this page, produced by an organization called Consumer Freedom, ridicule the idea that American corporations might be responsible for obesity.

David
Edelstein

Up in Smoke: Give Movies with Tobacco an Automatic 'R'

David Edelstein, an occasional playwright, is a film critic for *New York magazine* and National Public Radio's *Fresh Air*, as well as an occasional commentator on *CBS Sunday Morning*. His work has also appeared in the *Village Voice, Rolling Stone, Slate*, and the *New York Times*. The following blog post appeared on *New York magazine's* Web site in January 2010 as a response to a January 5 *New York Times* article by A. O. Scott called "Movies and Vice" that concluded, "Tobacco use is part of history—of movie history in particular. And in the course of that history lighting up has acquired connotations of individualism, rebellion, sophistication and sex that will be hard to eradicate even as they become increasingly shrouded in nostalgia."

A. O. Scott's meditation on tobacco in movies is a savvy piece of hipsterism: admit that smoking is bad but argue that anti-vice cultural crusaders are worse, and end with the hope that cigarettes will someday be akin to "time travel, or slapstick, or a mad drive to the airport to stop the one you love from getting on that plane—something that only happens in the movies." Those comparisons are facetious, of course. It's unlikely we'll see time travel in our lifetime; pratfalls in the real world are involuntary; and no one has to race to the airport in an era when anti-terrorist screenings hold passengers up for hours. Smoking, on the other hand, is a choice, and one that's deeply responsive to social cues. That's why tobacco companies pay millions to studios to have glamorous actors light up and strike sultry poses. In Scott's nicotine-fueled brain he knows this, but he doesn't want to sound like a bluestocking.

2   Over the years, I've gotten a lot of e-mails from anti-smoking groups demanding either a ban on cigarettes in movies or an automatic "R" rating when a character uses tobacco. My first response is indignation at the "nanny state." I remember how, more than two decades ago, I was forbidden from mentioning smoking in a profile I did in the late *Mirabella* on Jan Hooks, who chain-smoked through our two interviews. I loved her—but I also could see by how she smoked that she was very, very high-strung. It was an important detail, except that editor Grace Mirabella's husband, Dr. William Cahan, was an anti-tobacco crusader, and no mention of cigarettes was allowed in the magazine, ever. I fought and fought and finally, *finally* Mirabella yielded—but only if I wrote something like, "Her yellow-stained fingers

trembling, she nervously inserted another death stick between her brown, misshapen teeth." I was furious. I still am.

3   On the other hand, editors at a well-known music publication that same year told me that no anti-smoking references would ever appear in their magazine: Tobacco companies paid big bucks for ads on the back cover and to sponsor the regular live-performance centerpiece. Against such vast financial resources, anti-smoking crusaders had no leverage. In the end, it was only the dread "nanny state" that could keep tobacco ads away from the young and impressionable.

4   These days, I don't believe that the anti-smoking crusaders are so out of line, at least in their demand that movies with cigarettes get an automatic "R" rating. No, that doesn't mean we expunge smoking from movies already made. We just make it tougher for new films with cigarette use to influence kids. Just as important, when tobacco companies pay to put their wares in a film, that information needs to appear in the credits— *prominently*. It's one thing when everyone lights up in *Good Night and Good Luck*, in which the ubiquitous tobacco smoke evokes the era better than anything onscreen. (Too bad there was no list at the end of all the characters' real-life counterparts who died of lung cancer or associated heart disease.) It's another when cigarettes are a product placement akin to Cheerios or Apple computers.

5   This isn't an easy call. I treasure the image of William Powell and Myrna Loy attempting to out-drink one another in *The Thin Man*—I think of it often as I order my fourth or fifth whiskey. Somewhere, I still have a poster of Cheech and Chong in *Up in Smoke*, which probably retains the aroma of the bong that sat proudly beneath it in my dorm room. And damn if Bogie and Belmondo aren't still the apogee of cool. Scott is dead right in arguing that vice in movies can be very entertaining. But for our kids' sake, let's treat the addiction to deadly chemicals *as* a vice and not as a normal, healthy part of everyday life.

6   *Update*: Some people have written to accuse me of having a double standard, and to say that, if one follows my logic, kids should no longer be exposed to drinking, overeating, brutally killing people, or anything that might corrupt our little angels. And then, of course, as one correspondent put it, "Our movies would be a little less true." I happen to believe that glamorizing the act of sucking tar and nicotine into one's lungs results in images a lot less true than, say, skeletal lung-cancer patients dissolving from the inside out in an Intensive Care Unit. But let's leave that aside. I'm not arguing that smoking should be banned from movies or *always* associated onscreen with delinquency or death. I enjoy movies about people doing things that might not be good for them, whether it's lighting up or shooting up or crashing cars or screwing

sheep. Let's have a cinema for grown-ups that depicts anything and everything, healthy and unhealthy. But let's also keep tobacco companies and the greedheads who take their money from bombarding kids with the message that smoking is what cool people do.

Tony Newman

Criminalizing Smoking Is Not the Answer: Bans on Cloves and Outdoor Smoking Will Backfire!

Tony Newman is the director of media relations at the Drug Policy Alliance Network, which promotes policy alternatives to the War on Drugs. Before joining the organization, he was media director for the human rights organization Global Exchange and cofounded the public relations firm Communication Works. The following article appeared in September 2009 on *Huffington Post*, an Internet newspaper known for a slightly left-of-center political stance.

The war on cigarettes is heating up. This week a new federal ban went into effect making flavored cigarettes and cloves illegal. The new regulation halted the sale of vanilla and chocolate cigarettes that anti-smoking advocates claim lure young people into smoking. This ban is the first major crackdown since Congress passed a law in June giving the Food and Drug Administration the authority to regulate tobacco. There is already talk of banning Menthol cigarettes next.

2   Meanwhile, another major initiative to limit smoking wafted out of New York City last week. A report to Mayor Michael Bloomberg from the city's Health Commissioner called for a smoking ban at city parks and beaches to help protect citizens from the harms of second hand smoke. To his credit, Bloomberg rejected this measure citing concern over stretched city and police resources.

3   While I support many restrictions on public smoking, such as at restaurants and workplaces, and I appreciate public education campaigns and efforts aimed at discouraging young people from smoking, I believe the outdoor smoking ban and prohibition of cloves and possibly Menthols will lead to harmful and unintended consequences. All we have to do is look at the criminalization of other drugs, such as marijuana, to see some of the potential pitfalls and tragedies.

4   Cities across the country—from New York to Santa Cruz, California—are considering or have already banned smoking at parks and beaches. I am afraid that issuing tickets to people for smoking outdoors could easily be abused by overzealous law enforcement.

5   Let's look at how New York handles another "decriminalized" drug in our state, marijuana. Despite decriminalizing marijuana more than 30 years ago, New York is the marijuana arrest capital of the world. If possession of marijuana is supposed to be decriminalized in New York, how does this happen? Often it's because, in the course of interacting with the police, individuals are asked to empty their pockets, which results in the pot being "open to public view"—which is, technically, a crime.

6   More than 40,000 people were arrested in New York City last year for marijuana possession, and 87 percent of those arrested were black or Latino, despite equal rates of marijuana use among whites. The fact is that blacks and Latinos are arrested for pot at much higher rates in part because officers make stop-and-frisk searches disproportionately in black, Latino and low-income neighborhoods.

7   Unfortunately, when we make laws and place restrictions on both legal and illegal drugs, people of color are usually the ones busted. Drug use may not discriminate, but our drug policies and enforcement do.

8   Now let's look at the prohibition of cloves and other flavored cigarettes. When we prohibit certain drugs, it doesn't mean that the drugs go away and people don't use them; it just means that people get their drugs from the black market instead of a store or deli. We've been waging a war on marijuana and other drugs for decades, but you can still find marijuana and your drug of choice in most neighborhoods and cities in this country.

9   For many people, cloves or Menthols are their smoke of choice. I have no doubt that someone is going to step in to meet this demand. What do we propose doing to the people who are caught selling illegal cigarettes on the street? Are cops going to have to expend limited resources to enforce this ban? Are we going to arrest and lock up people who are selling the illegal cigarettes? Prisons are already bursting at the seams (thanks to the drug laws) in states across the country. Are we going to waste more taxpayer money on incarceration?

10   The prohibition of flavored cigarettes also moves us another step closer to total cigarette prohibition. But with all the good intentions in the world, outlawing cigarettes would be just as disastrous as the prohibition of other drugs. After all, people would still smoke, just as they still use other drugs that are prohibited, from marijuana to cocaine. But now, in addition to the harm of smoking,

we would find a whole range of "collateral consequences," such as black market-related violence, that crop up with prohibition.

11   Although we should celebrate our success curbing cigarette smoking and continue to encourage people to cut back or give up cigarettes, let's not get carried away and think that criminalizing smoking is the answer.

12   We need to realize that drugs, from cigarettes to marijuana to alcohol, will always be consumed, whether they are legal or illegal. Although drugs have health consequences and dangers, making them illegal—and keeping them illegal—will only bring additional death and suffering.

The American Legacy Foundation, based in Washington, D.C., is dedicated to "building a world where young people reject tobacco and where anyone can quit," according to its Web site (www.americanlegacy.org). Among other things, the foundation places antismoking ads in the mass media. The one published here appeared In *The New Yorker* in September 2002.

Garry Trudeau (1948-) won the Pulitzer Prize in 1975 for his comic strip *Doonesbury*. The strip published here appeared in January 2002.

PIPPA **WYSONG**

Modified

Pippa Wysong is a Canadian journalist who specializes in medical and science writing, especially for children. Her "Ask Pippa" column, which has run in the *Toronto Star* since 1988, answers kids' questions about scientific and medical matters. In "Modified," Wysong presents the potential dangers of piercings and tattoos and offers medical advice for those who simply cannot resist these increasingly popular forms of physical expression. Published in the March 2006 edition of *Current Health 2*, "Modified" comprises part of the *Weekly Reader* series of magazines for middle and high school classrooms.

Alexis Valentine was only 18 months old when her ears were first pierced, a common practice in her Italian family. Now the 16-year-old from West Chester, Pa., has three earrings in each ear plus a belly button ring, and she is likely to have more piercings in her future. Maybe even a tattoo or two.

2   These days, piercings often go well beyond earlobes. Belly buttons, tongues, ear cartilage, eyebrows, nipples, lips, and even genitals are targets for metallic barbells, delicate chains, and stud jewelry. Tattoos run the gamut of images, from a discreet star to Celtic-inspired bracelets around an arm to huge artistic undertakings with the body as a canvas.

3   Body art (also called body modification) used to be just for Goths, bikers, and certain cultures both ancient and modern. Today, piercings and tattoos (including decals, henna, or permanent ink) are common. An estimated 23 percent of teens have piercings, about 8 percent have tattoos, and another 21 percent want tattoos. It's all part of the effort to be cool or to do something that looks a little different.

Teens Tell All

4   At age 12, Alexis opted for second holes in her ear lobes, and at 13 she had the third ones put in. When she turned 15, she got her belly button pierced. Does she want more? You bet. "I want to get my tongue pierced," she says. But her mom put a hold on that, as well as the flower tattoo Alexis would like on her back. In most states, minors need a parent's permission to get a tattoo or a piercing. In some states, it is illegal for minors to get these procedures at all. (The Association of Professional Piercers notes that many regulations exclude piercing done with piercing guns, frequently used at mall kiosks to insert earlobe earrings.) Alexis's classmate Jessica Adamiak, 15, has pierced ears but is waiting for her parents' OK to get her nose pierced. "My dad keeps saying he wants me to wait until I'm 30. Can you believe that?" she asks.

Problems with Piercings

5   Though they may seem a cool means of self-expression, piercings also come with potential dangers, cautions Dr. Lynn McKinley-Grant, a dermatologist from Chevy Chase, Md. Some problems include
• chipped or cracked teeth caused by chomping on a tongue stud;
• allergic reactions to metals used in jewelry—a severe allergy can even lead to death;
• choking if a tongue ring becomes loose;
• infection, which can cause swelling, pain, and oozing pus, and require a trip to the hospital.

6   Tongue infections are among the worst to treat, especially when the tongue is so swollen that the stud has to be surgically removed, McKinley-Grant says. The biggest risks for infections are new piercings or trauma to the newly pierced area, such as scratches or bruises. Infections can happen if piercing equipment is not properly sterilized or if a piercing is not cared for properly before it has healed.

7   Alexis is familiar with the risks after seeing what her older sister Amanda went through. Amanda, 20, has piercings in her earlobe, ear cartilage, nose, and lip. She also has a tattoo she designed herself. Amanda's first problem was a keloid, a big reddish-brown bump that grew at a piercing site on her ear cartilage. Keloids happen when too much scar tissue forms, and they can be quite unsightly. Amanda had to have plastic surgery to remove it.

8   Problems are common in cartilage, according to McKinley-Grant. "It has little blood flow and does not heal as easily as the earlobes," she says. Other big risks from piercings include infection with human immunodeficiency virus (HIV) or hepatitis from reused or unsterilized needles.

9   Amanda also had problems with a piercing in the flesh between her thumb and forefinger. A severe infection landed her in the emergency room to have the stud removed. But Amanda's problems don't faze Alexis, who plans to get more piercings. Alexis's mom, though cool with the idea of piercing (she has two earrings in each ear herself), is keeping a watchful eye.

Thinking Before Inking

10   Then there is the allure of tattoos. Although many teens go for temporary ones from decals or henna, others pick the permanent type. It's important to remember that ink tattoos don't go away, says Barbara Freyenberger, a nurse-practitioner at the Children's Hospital of Iowa. In fact, it's tough to get rid of tattoos if you don't like the pattern anymore or the artwork isn't what you expected. One study showed that close to 4 percent of college students with tattoos had them removed. As people age, tattoo removal is more common.

Eric Lewis's cartoon, published in the October 30, 2000, issue of *The New Yorker*, pokes fun at tattooing.

11   Over several visits, a dermatologist zaps unwanted tattoos with special medical lasers—a different laser for each color, and each color requires a separate trip. Tattoo removal generally means about $500 to $1,000 per treatment. (And health insurance usually doesn't cover it!) Removal can leave a slight scar and some skin discoloration. "It can take a minimum of eight treatments to completely remove a tattoo," says McKinley-Grant. Some parts of the body scar more than others from the procedure, the worst being the back, chest, and upper arms.

12   Another hidden danger of tattoos is a lack of regulation in the pigments used in ink. They can vary in quality, and some colors might contain lead, which can cause brain and nerve damage. Some people have allergic reactions to hennas or ink ingredients and can develop a rash or other health problems from the chemicals. In addition, tattoo needles—like piercing instruments—can pass on infections from other clients.

13   If you decide to get a tattoo, take your time thinking about it, Freyenberger advises. Get it done by a professional in a clean, sanitary environment. Make sure the tattoo artist uses new needles fresh out of the package and that the needles are dipped in fresh (not used) ink pots.

Before Seeking the Needle

14   Though tattoos and piercings may look cool, you should seriously mull over the health risks. And consider whether you'll still want the tattoo or piercing when you're in your 20s or 30s—or older. If you decide to go ahead, check the age-limit laws in your state, get your parents' permission, research the medical implications, and find a safe, clean site.

15   Safety Tips for Piercings and Tattoos
- Go only to a professional, licensed piercer or tattooist.
- Ask about cleanliness and infection control; if you don't feel safe or get satisfactory answers, leave.
- Only patronize shops that use an autoclave, a device that sterilizes equipment between customers.
- Make sure the tattooist or piercer uses new needles out of fresh, new packages, and that he or she disposes of needles in a special biohazard container after use.
- Only use a tattooist who throws out leftover ink, instead of pouring it back into the bottle.
- For new piercings, wear only noncorrosive metals (stainless steel, 14-karat gold) until the wound has healed.
- Keep the tattoo or piercing clean: don't mess with it until the wounds are healed.
- Remember: Waiting is always an option. If you do decide to get a body piercing or tattoo, consider selecting a discreet place for it on your body. You may not like it later—and if you have it removed, there will be scarring.

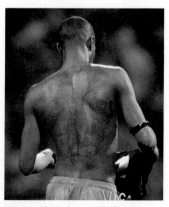

Can you imagine removing a tattoo as large as this one?

ISSUE IN FOCUS

Drinking on College Campuses

You know what The Problem is: On college campuses across the United States, excessive alcohol consumption is causing all kinds of trouble—deaths and serious illnesses related to alcohol poisoning (the result of "binge drinking"); property damage, personal violence, and other crimes; unwanted pregnancies and sexual assaults; academic failures and family breakups and long-term career setbacks. Some statistics dramatize the extent of the damage: A 2009 study conducted by the National Institute on Alcohol Abuse and Alcoholism (NIAAA) found that at least 1,825 drinking-related accidental deaths had occurred among 18- to 24-year-old students in 2005, up from 1,440 in 1998. The proportion of students who report that they had engaged in a recent episode of binge drinking is now at 45 percent. Almost 30 percent of students are saying that they have driven while under the influence of alcohol at least once in the past year. The Harvard School of Public Health estimates that 44 percent of college students are heavy drinkers, and it appears that alcohol abuse is responsible for over half a million injuries each year—not to mention any number of suicides or attempted suicides. NIAAA estimates that 696,000 students between the ages of 18 and 24 are assaulted by another student who has been drinking, and 97,000 students are victims of alcohol-related sexual assault or date rape. (For further details, see http://www.collegedrinkingprevention.gov/1College_Bulletin-508_361C4E.pdf.)

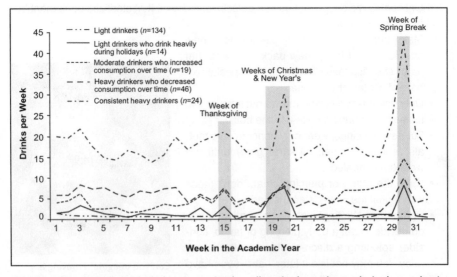

This chart shows trends in alcohol consumption by college freshmen by weeks in the academic year.

2   But what to do about it? That's not so easy to discern. Over the years, universities and partner organizations have developed a wide variety of programs aimed at decreasing the rates of dangerous drinking on college campuses. You have experienced most of them firsthand. Some focus on individuals—such as emphasizing personal responsibility and counseling students with identified drinking problems through Alcohol Awareness Weeks, programs during freshman orientation, or required coursework. Other solutions are centered on creating a safer community through the involvement of campus life personnel, residence hall programs, local law enforcement, and neighboring residents: some campuses ban alcohol in dormitories or offer alcohol-free entertainment options; others have tried vigorous enforcement of alcohol sales and consumption laws; and many others are cracking down on drinking in fraternities.

3   But nothing seems to be working very well. In 1984 President Ronald Reagan signed into law the Uniform Drinking Age Act, which penalized states that did not raise their legal drinking age to 21. By 1988, therefore, all fifty states had modified their laws to reflect this federal legislation. Because of this legislation and because of persistent public advocacy by Mothers against Drunk Driving (MADD) and other organizations, alcohol-related traffic accidents and arrests for underage drinking have deceased substantially in the general population.

4   Nevertheless, is it wise to criminalize alcohol consumption by those under the age of 21? Are healthy long-term drinking habits promoted when the age limit is 21? Is zero tolerance the best approach? Is the experience of other nations, most of whom have lower legal drinking ages, relevant here? When the legal drinking age was set at 21, many say, colleges became the enforcers of the law. That enforcement subsequently drove drinking out of quads, dorms, and fraternities and into off-campus hiding places where students get smashed before going out on the town or to tailgates or to other places where drinking is policed. In 2009 a group of college presidents began a campaign to reexamine the drinking age. Dubbed "The Amethyst Initiative," after a gemstone that is said to ward off intoxication, the initiative by the presidents has been vigorously supported (e.g., by presidents at Duke, Ohio State, Dartmouth, Johns Hopkins) and loudly opposed (e.g., by MADD, by many other college presidents, and by the International Association of Chiefs of Police).

5   In the Issue in Focus selections that follow, John M. McCardell presents the case for experimenting with a lower drinking age; he is the former president of Middlebury College as well as the founder and president of Choose Responsibility, a nonprofit organization that seeks to engage the public in the debate over the appropriate drinking age. Published on CNN.com in September 2009, McCardell's essay is supported by the next argument in *Good Reasons*, by physician Morris Chafetz, who founded the National Institute for Alcoholism and Alcohol Abuse in 1970 and who argued in *The Huffington Post* in August 2009 that laws setting the minimum drinking age of 21 are ineffective and should be repealed. Chafetz first gained national recognition at the 1984 White House Conference for a Drug-Free America, at which the Uniform Drinking Age Act was signed into law.

ACCOMPLISHMENTS AS...

A CHILD

MOMMY, DADDY!
I LEARNED HOW
TO RIDE A BIKE!

AN ADULT

GOOD NEWS,
HONEY. I MADE
PARTNER!

A COLLEGE STUDENT

I CAN'T BELIEVE
YOU DID 25 SHOTS
LAST NIGHT.

AWESOME.

DUDE, I WAS
SOOO DRUNK!

Many college campuses have a culture of binge drinking. What factors explain the pattern of drinking that prevails at your school?

6   Then we offer an argument in support of the 21-year-old drinking age. In a commentary published on CNN.com in September 2009, several distinguished health professionals (led by Toben F. Nelson and Traci Toomey) contend that placing the minimum drinking age at 21 has played a pivotal role in reducing alcohol-related deaths. Finally, we conclude this Issue in Focus with a piece by writer James Hibberd, who critiques how large beer manufacturers swell sales by enlisting a corps "campus representatives." Entitled "Barhopping with the Bud Girls," Hibbard's piece appeared on Salon.com in February 1999. It invites you to go beyond the debate about the legal drinking age to ponder how mixed messages about alcohol permeate college environments, and how you yourself feel about drinking on campus. What is the situation at your college or university? What is being done about it, and what might be done?

John McCardell

A Drinking Age of 21 Doesn't Work

In 2008, a group of college and university presidents and chancellors, eventually totaling 135, issued a statement that garnered national attention.

2   The "Amethyst Initiative" put a debate proposition before the public—"Resolved: That the 21-year-old drinking age is not working." It offered, in much the way that a grand jury performs its du-

ties, sufficient evidence for putting the proposition to the test. It invited informed and dispassionate public debate, and committed the signatory institutions to encouraging that debate. And it called on elected officials not to continue assuming that, after 25 years, the status quo could not be challenged or even improved.

3   One year later, the drinking age debate continues, and new research reinforces the presidential impulse. Just this summer a study published in *the Journal of the American Academy of Child and Adolescent Psychiatry* revealed that, among college-age males, binge drinking is unchanged from its levels of 1979; that among non-college women it has increased by 20 percent; and that among college women it has increased by 40 percent.

4   Remarkably, the counterintuitive conclusion drawn by the investigators, and accepted uncritically by the media, including editorials in *The New York Times* and *The Washington Post*, is that the study proves that raising the drinking age to 21 has been a success.

5   More recently, a study of binge drinking published in the *Journal of the American Medical Association* announced that "despite efforts at prevention, the prevalence of binge drinking among college students is continuing to rise, and so are the harms associated with it." Worse still, a related study has shown that habits formed at 18 die hard: "For each year studied, a greater percentage of 21- to 24-year-olds [those who were of course once 18, 19 and 20] engaged in binge drinking and driving under the influence of alcohol."

6   Yet in the face of mounting evidence that those young adults (age 18 to 20 toward whom the drinking age law has been directed) are routinely—indeed in life- and health-threatening ways—violating it, there remains a belief in the land that a minimum drinking age of 21 has been a "success." And elected officials are periodically reminded of a provision in the 1984 law that continues to stifle any serious public debate in our country's state legislative chambers: Any state that sets its drinking age lower than 21 forfeits 10 percent of its annual federal highway appropriation.

7   But it's not 1984 anymore.

8   This statement may seem obvious, but not necessarily. In 1984 Congress passed and the president signed the National Minimum Drinking Age Act. The Act, which raised the drinking age to 21 under threat of highway fund withholding, sought to address the problem of drunken driving fatalities. And indeed, that problem was serious. States that lowered their ages during the

1970s and did nothing else to prepare young adults to make responsible decisions about alcohol witnessed an alarming increase in alcohol-related traffic fatalities. It was as though the driving age were lowered but no driver's education was provided. The results were predictable.

9   Now, 25 years later, we are in a much different, and better, place. Thanks to the effective public advocacy of organizations like Mothers Against Drunk Driving, we are far more aware of the risks of drinking and driving. Automobiles are much safer. Seatbelts and airbags are mandatory. The "designated driver" is now a part of our vocabulary. And more and more states are mandating ignition interlocks for first-time DUI offenders, perhaps the most effective way to get drunken drivers off the road.

10   And the statistics are encouraging. Alcohol-related fatalities have declined over the last 25 years. Better still, they have declined in all age groups, though the greatest number of deaths still occurs at age 21, followed by 22 and 23. We are well on the way to solving a problem that vexed us 25 years ago.

11   The problem today is different. The problem today is reckless, goal-oriented alcohol consumption that all too often takes place in clandestine locations, where enforcement has proven frustratingly difficult. Alcohol consumption among young adults is not taking place in public places or public view or in the presence of other adults who might help model responsible behavior. But we know it is taking place.

12   If not in public, then where? The college presidents who signed the Amethyst Initiative know where. It happens in "pre-game" sessions in locked dorm rooms where students take multiple shots of hard alcohol in rapid succession, before going to a social event where alcohol is not served. It happens in off-campus apartments beyond college boundaries and thus beyond the presidents' authority; and it happens in remote fields to which young adults must drive.

13   And the Amethyst presidents know the deadly result: Of the 5,000 lives lost to alcohol each year by those under 21, more than 60 percent are lost *off* the roadways, according to the National Institute of Alcoholism and Alcohol Abuse. The principal problem of 2009 is not drunken driving. The principal problem of 2009 is clandestine binge drinking.

14   That is why the Amethyst presidents believe a public debate is so urgent. The law does not say drink responsibly or drink in moderation. It says don't drink. To those affected by it, those who

in the eyes of the law are in every other respect legal adults, it is Prohibition. And it is incomprehensible.

15   The principal impediment to public debate is the 10 percent highway penalty. That penalty should be waived for those states that choose to try something different, which may turn out to be something better. But merely adjusting the age—up or down—is not really the way to make a change.

16   We should prepare young adults to make responsible decisions about alcohol in the same way we prepare them to operate a motor vehicle: by first educating and then licensing, and permitting them to exercise the full privileges of adulthood so long as they demonstrate their ability to observe the law. Licensing would work like driver's education—it would involve a permit, perhaps graduated, allowing the holder the privilege of purchasing, possessing, and consuming alcohol, as each state determined, so long as the holder had passed an alcohol education course and observed the alcohol laws of the issuing state.

17   Most of the rest of the world has come out in a different place on the drinking age. The United States is one of only four countries—the others are Indonesia, Mongolia and Palau—with an age as high as 21. All others either have no minimum age or have a lower age, generally 18, with some at 16. Young adults know that. And, in their heart of hearts, they also know that a law perceived as unjust, a law routinely violated, can over time breed disrespect for law in general.

18   Slowly but surely we may be seeing a change in attitude. This summer, Dr. Morris Chafetz, a distinguished psychiatrist, a member of the presidential commission that recommended raising the drinking age, and the founder of the National Institute for Alcoholism and Alcohol Abuse, admitted that supporting the higher drinking age is "the most regrettable decision of my entire professional career." This remarkable statement did not receive the attention it merited.

19   Alcohol is a reality in the lives of young adults. We can either try to change the reality—which has been our principal focus since 1984, by imposing Prohibition on young adults 18 to 20—or we can create the safest possible environment for the reality.

20   A drinking age minimum of 21 has not changed the reality. It's time to try something different.

21   It's not 1984 anymore.

Morris E. Chafetz

The 21-Year-Old Drinking Age: I Voted for It; It Doesn't Work

In 1982 I accepted appointment to the Presidential Commission on Drunk Driving and agreed to chair its Education and Prevention Committee. The Commission met over the next 18 months and ultimately advanced 39 recommendations to President Reagan, in December 1983. All 39 received unanimous Commission approval.

2   The most conspicuous of those recommendations, and arguably the most controversial, called for raising the minimum legal drinking age to 21 nationwide. I will admit to having had serious reservations about this particular proposal. But in the interest of maintaining unanimity, I reluctantly voted yes. It is the single most regrettable decision of my entire professional career.

3   Legal Age 21 has not worked. To be sure, drunk driving fatalities are lower now than they were in 1982. But they are lower in all age groups. And they have declined just as much in Canada, where the age is 18 or 19, as they have in the United States.

4   It has been argued that "science" convincingly shows a cause-and-effect relationship between the law and the reduction in fatalities. Complicated mathematical formulas, which include subjective estimations (called "imputation") have been devised to demonstrate "proof." But correlation is not cause. We must neither confuse numbers with science nor interpret a lack of numbers as implying an absence of science.

5   But even if we concede that the law has had some effect on our highways, we cannot overlook its collateral, off-road damage. The National Institute for Alcoholism and Alcohol Abuse, which I founded in 1970, estimates that 5,000 lives are lost to alcohol each year by those under 21. More than 3,000 of those fatalities occur off our roadways. If we are seriously to measure the effects of this law, we cannot limit our focus.

6   And if we broaden our look, we see a serious problem of reckless, goal-oriented, drinking to get drunk. Those at whom the law is directed disobey it routinely. Enforcement is frustratingly difficult and usually forces the behavior deeper underground, into places where life and health are put at ever greater risk. The 600,000 assaults reported annually, the date rapes, the property damage, the emergency room calls do not in general occur in

places visible to the public. They are the inevitable result of what happens when laws do not reflect social or cultural reality.

7   The reality is that at age 18 in this country, one is a legal adult. Young people view 21 as utterly arbitrary—which it is. And because the explanation given them is so condescending—that they lack maturity and judgment, these same people who can serve on juries and sign contracts and who turned out in overwhelming numbers to elect our first black president—well, they don't buy it.

8   And neither do I. And neither should the American public.

9   Whether we like it or not, alcohol is woven into the fabric of our world, most of which has determined that the legal drinking age should be 18—or lower. And so far as I can tell, there is no evidence of massive brain impairment, alcohol dependency, or underage alcohol abuse, which the "experts" tell us will be the inevitable result of lowering the age in the United States. It is time to liberate ourselves from the tyranny of "experts," who invoke "science" in order to advance a prohibitionist agenda. Prohibition does not work. It has never worked. It is not working among 18-20 year-olds now.

10   The cult of expertise has made parents feel incapable of raising their children. In many states parents are disenfranchised from helping their sons or daughters learn about responsible alcohol consumption. But as a parent and psychiatrist I trust the instinct of parents more than I do the hubris of "experts."

11   Despite what these latter-day prohibitionists may think, the problem is not the drink—it is the drinker. There should be more emphasis on the person and the surroundings in which alcohol is consumed and less emphasis on alcohol itself. Personal and social responsibility, not the substance, is the real issue. But so long as the age remains a one-size-fits-all, federally-mandated 21, and so long as any state that may want to try something different, in hopes of reversing the dismal trend of binge-drinking that (maybe or maybe not coincidentally) has become more serious in the years since the drinking age was raised, forfeits 10% of its federal highway funds, nothing is likely to change for the better.

12   I do not believe that any state should be forced to adjust its drinking age. But I do believe that the genius of federalism should be allowed to work its will unimpeded, and from that genius, not only better practices, but also safer environments and more responsible consumption, are likely to emerge.

Toben F. Nelson, Traci L. Toomey, and co-authors

The Drinking Age of 21 Saves Lives

The national policy that set a minimum legal drinking age of 21 is being questioned by a group of 135 college and university presidents through an effort called the Amethyst Initiative. In a September 16 commentary on CNN.com, Amethyst Initiative leader John McCardell, a former president of Middlebury College, proposes lowering the drinking age, which he suggests will lead to less drinking and related problems among college students.

2   But history and a comprehensive review of the research tell a much different story. The evidence is clear, consistent, and compelling: A drinking age of 21 has led to less drinking, fewer injuries, and fewer deaths.

3   In the 1970s when many states reduced their drinking ages, drinking-related deaths among young people increased. When the drinking age of 21 was restored, deaths declined. This effect is not simply a historical artifact explained by advances in safety technology and other policies.

4   New Zealand recently lowered the drinking age based on many of the same arguments advanced by the Amethyst Initiative. The result was more alcohol-involved traffic crashes and emergency room visits among 15- to 19-year-olds. New Zealand is now considering raising its drinking age. The National Highway Traffic Safety Administration estimates that setting the drinking age at 21 saves the lives of 900 young people each year and has saved more than 25,000 lives since 1975.

5   It was on the basis of compelling research evidence about its lifesaving benefits that a bipartisan effort created Public Law 98-363, "The National Minimum Legal Drinking Age Act," in the first place. Subsequent research has strengthened the evidence. College students who are underage, for example, binge drink less than students aged 21-23. Underage students who attend colleges that rigorously enforce the drinking age, and who reside in states that have more laws restricting access to alcohol for those under the legal age, are less likely to binge drink.

6   Another myth promulgated by the Amethyst Initiative is that European young people are taught by families to drink responsibly because of the typically lower legal drinking ages there. The reverse is the case. Surveys of youth in multiple European countries show that rates of frequent binge drinking among adolescents are higher in Europe than in the United States. Panels of experts, convened separately by the National Institute on Alcohol Abuse and Alcoholism, the Substance Abuse and Mental Health Services Administration, the National Academy of Sciences Institute of Medicine and the Centers for Disease

Control and Prevention have studied the evidence on the age-21 law and concluded that it is effective public policy. Rather than lowering the drinking age, they recommended bolstering the law by closing loopholes in state law and strengthening enforcement.

7   There is a silver lining to the call for reopening discussion on the minimum legal drinking age. While some college presidents have signed on to the Amethyst Initiative, most have not. College presidents acknowledge that a serious problem exists on their campuses and that something needs to be done. Working effectively with their communities and states to address student drinking is the place to start, not with a discussion about lowering the drinking age.

8   College presidents must show leadership by promoting solutions recommended by a report from the National Institute on Alcohol Abuse and Alcoholism College Drinking Task Force released in 2002. These recommendations for college and community leaders included creating systems for reaching individual students with effective interventions; implementing, publicizing and enforcing laws to prevent alcohol-impaired driving and underage drinking; placing restrictions on alcohol retail outlets; increasing prices and excise taxes on alcoholic beverages; and insisting on responsible beverage service policies at on- and off-campus venues. Few colleges and their communities have even begun the steps needed to enact these efforts.

9   These recommendations will be difficult to implement and significant barriers exist, including resistance from the industries that profit from selling alcohol. College presidents cannot accomplish this alone. They need the support of students, regents, parents, alumni and their communities. State and local legislators need to pass tougher restrictions and provide resources for enforcement. Lobbying legislators to dismantle the effective drinking age law is a step in the wrong direction.

10   So rather than try the approaches advocated by the Amethyst Initiative that have no foundation in research, let's be clear about the issues. College student drinking is a serious problem. Each year more young people are injured, sexually assaulted, and die as the result of drinking. These statistics would be even worse without the age-21 law.

11   Lowering the drinking age will not save lives or make our campuses and communities better places to live. It will increase heavy drinking and the problems that accompany it in college communities and push the problem back into high schools. Real prevention requires constant vigilance, dedication, and the courage to implement difficult solutions

JAMES **HIBBERD**

Barhopping with the Bud Girls

I If you owned a beer company, what would be your ultimate marketing dream?

2   How about placing a beer commercial in every college bar and fraternity organization? There, luscious, tan-line-free women and confident, upper-social-strata jocks would aggressively promote your brands with all the slick enthusiasm of a Madison Avenue production. Imagine these commercials playing in continuous motion throughout the evening without ever resorting to the obvious loops of promotional films. Because this commercial would be live. That's right, real people targeting real college beer drinkers at that crucial moment in their lives when they establish brand loyalty, using no other sales technique than old-fashioned peer pressure.

3   For Anheuser-Busch, the parent company of Budweiser, the dream of student recruitment is real. It wasn't easy or cheap. Or, some argue, anywhere close to ethical. Parenting groups have recently attacked Anheuser-Busch for their animated frog 'n' lizard advertising campaign, but a CNN.com investigation has found that the brewer does more than create cute cartoon characters to court underage drinkers. By hiring popular fraternity members and attractive female students as representatives, Anheuser-Busch distributors directly target the largely underage college market.

4   Considering Harvard's well-publicized 1993 study declaring that 44 percent of American college students and 86 percent of fraternity members qualify as binge drinkers, such a marketing program seems ridiculously ill-advised. Isn't hiring college students a potential PR nightmare? After all, 90 percent of all rapes and most violent crimes on campus are alcohol-related.

5   Such statistics may not have deterred Anheuser-Busch, but they do explain why its college recruiting efforts are managed discreetly. Even the beer industry's most prominent critic, Mothers Against Drunk Driving, was unaware that college reps existed. "Hiring fraternity members as beer distributor reps on university campuses where the majority of students are under the legal drinking age of 21 is frightening and unbelievably irresponsible," said MADD's national president, Karolyn V. Nunnallee, upon hearing the news. "We urge the U.S. beer industry to re-examine its marketing efforts."

6   Last November, midlevel supervisors for Anheuser-Busch wholesaler Brown Distributing allowed me to join their college representatives working a Budweiser parade leading to a University of Texas football game and a night of "bar calls" in Austin. While many alcohol companies hire attractive women to push products in bars and sporting events across the country, these Bud representatives seemed to be recruited predominantly from the college population and assigned to a college beat: They frequent popular college watering holes, sporting events, and other events such as parties at the U.T. alumni center. Of more concern are the existence of fraternity members who work unsupervised in the promotion of their product for college parties. The access was unusual, and the vice president for Brown Distributing later expressed some irritation, commenting that any media inquiries normally require approval from a high-ranking executive.

7   In other words: oops.

8   "When we walk into a bar, all we have is ourselves," says 24-year-old Bud Girl Rachel Moore, a recent college graduate. "We may be passing out a key chain or something, but we make the promotion." Brown Distributing Bud Girls (we'll get to the male representatives later) are held to strict standards. A Bud Girl doesn't smoke, swear, use drugs, or have tattoos, non-ear piercings, or a criminal record. Her only permissible vice is drinking Budweiser, and that, of course, is mandatory. If a potential Bud Girl passes the interviews, background checks and drug testing, she's awarded a $15-an-hour part-time position and a Bud Girl wardrobe.

9   Bud Girl clothing isn't simply halter tops and spandex dresses. The wardrobe is Technicolor dream-wear that transforms attractive yet otherwise ordinary girls into a sort of beer-touting Justice League. Once in costume, the Bud Girls are superheroes whose sexual power turns any bar into one of those 1980s beer commercials, where the swimsuit model reduces men to puddles of gratitude and adoration. "I wonder who they think we actually are," says 28-year-old Bud Girl Griselda Mendoza. "[The clothes] change everything. They could see me at a supermarket and I won't get paid much attention. But put on a little Bud vest and all of a sudden guys want everything signed."

10   At one bar promotion I attended, the Bud Girls were asked to sign a promotional banner. They wrote: "This Bud's For You, We Love You." And, in their own way, they do. And men, in their own way, believe it. Bud Girls seem to enjoy their part-time work as hops goddesses as much as men enjoy begging at their feet for key chains and cozies. But just how widespread are these lust-driven promotions?

11   All of the Big Three American labels (Budweiser, Miller and Coors, which constitute nearly 80 percent of the U.S. beer market) practice some college recruiting. But Anheuser-Busch, with nearly 50 percent of the market, has the most extensive program. Miller marketing representative Ann Espey said her company has recently "shied away" from hiring on campus, and agreed that hiring male fraternity representatives is irresponsible. Similarly, Coors spokesman Dave Taylor says his company has "moved away" from such practices. Although "shied away" and "moved away" suggest that Coors and Miller have made significant policy changes, neither representative will say the practice is extinct.

12   "You need to understand the primary consumer target for beer companies is young adult males," Taylor says. "Historically, college programs were very common in the industry when the drinking age was 18. Now at the local level, with 600 independent distributors, does hiring models still occur? Probably, yes."

13   "At the local level" is another key phrase. Because beer girls and college programs are run by independent distributors, parent companies often feign ignorance of the practice. Likewise, while some distributors have never even heard of student recruiting ("College representatives?" asked a shocked receptionist at the Ann Arbor, Michigan, Anheuser-Busch wholesaler. "This is a *beer* distributor, sir"), wholesalers in cities like Tucson, Los Angeles, and Denver have programs in place.

14   To set the stage for the Bud Girls, these distributors pre-pack college bars with streamers, table tents, coasters, inflatable footballs, pool-table lamps, posters, and, of course, neon signs. Add the Bud Girls and the stage is set. The live commercial begins.

15   Two local students, Christi Voigt, 21, and Jaime Franks, 22, enter the Austin BW-3 chicken wing franchise during a Dallas Cowboys football game. They're wearing blue Bud Light halter tops and denim shorts. Bud Girls say they prefer the shorts-and-halter-top ensemble to the classic beer-can-print spandex dress, but noted that the distribution company prefers the tight dress because "It's more visible." (As Mendoza wryly

noted, "A lot of guys have a misconception that if a girl is wearing a dress that looks like a beer can, they can pick us up.")

16 Although Voigt and Franks give away some free key chains and beers to the rowdy crowd, they mostly distribute charm. Bud Girls have charm on the fly. Once in gear, the beer drinker is the center of attention. The beer drinker is witty and attractive. But if said beer drinker refuses to change brands or asks the nauseatingly common "Can I have you with that beer?" query, the Bud Girl downshifts: The beer drinker is a gnat, an impotent man unworthy of a Bud Girl's slightest concern. They remain professional—the smile never wavers—but the charm is gone and patrons can read "get lost" right through their Colgate teeth.

17 In other words, Bud Girls can really mess with a beer drinker's self-esteem.

18 Franks walks up to a table of four students. She makes eye contact with the tallest male in the group, tilts her head, and slowly asks, "What kind of beer are you drinking?"

19 He guiltily stammers something about Dos Equis.

20 She purposefully lays down a key chain bottle opener in front of him, never breaking eye contact.

21 "What will you drink now?"

22 "Uh, Buh-Bud."

23 She smiles: Good boy.

24 The display is impressive, but Voigt and Franks are rookies. Bud Girl supervisor Eric Bradford sips his Budweiser and wistfully recalls veterans who'd brazenly grab a customers' non-Bud beer and dump it out. Whether sweet or savage, all Bud Girls operate on the same basic principle: their well-endowed bodies become the curvy slates upon which beer slogans and men's horny dreams are projected.

25 The male of the Bud species functions a bit differently. He doesn't wear a spandex dress. He doesn't even need to wear his Budweiser polo shirt. His body is not a billboard for Budweiser. It's a double standard straight out of traditional beer commercials, where sexily dressed women wear the product and the cool guys just look like . . . cool guys. Whenever the male rep wishes, he goes unescorted to campus-area bars and buys Bud products for students with his expense account.

26 Corby Ferrell is one of the seven U.T. college reps (or "contemporary marketing representatives," as Budweiser calls them), all of whom are in separate fraternities. Together, the reps keep Budweiser products flowing from local sellers to the frat houses and campus-area parties. Ferrell is the 21-year-old former chairman of Phi Gamma Delta and has blond, anchorman-quality hair. Two or three times a week, Ferrell will go into Cain & Abel's bar located in the heart of Greek territory and approach attractive women drinking Miller or Coors.

27 "Hey, what do you think about switching to Bud Light for the night?" he'll ask. "The first one is on me, and I'll buy you another before I leave." Ferrell admits he has "an awesome job."

28 The second responsibility of male representatives is to arrange beer sales through local vendors. To dispel any confusion about the ethical or legal implications of this practice, Ferrell explains that technically the fraternity organizations do not pay for the beer: "Members who are at least 21 years old pool their cash to buy beer for parties." When his work with college fraternity members and local vendors leads to a volume sale (five cases of beer, for example), Ferrell is given a commission by Brown Distributing.

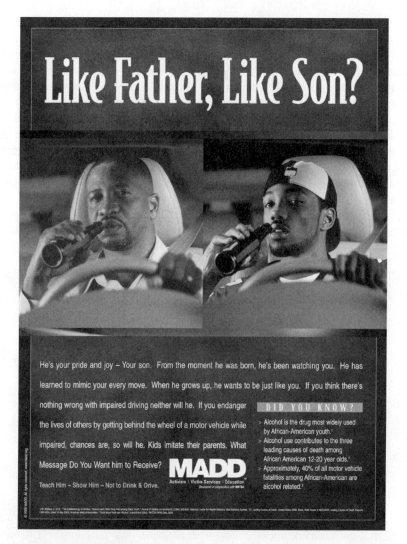

MADD—Mothers Against Drunk Driving—is one of the most respected nonprofit organizations in the United States. For the past 25 years MADD has championed the rights of victims of drunk driving and has promoted public awareness of the consequences of drunk driving. The ad on this page is one of many that were displayed on the MADD Web site (www.madd.org) in the summer of 2005.

29   One sales tactic is for the college rep to establish a relationship with campus-area sellers, then ask who's buying large quantities of competing brands. "Then I'll call the buyer and say, "I can get you 100 cases of [Anheuser-Busch product] Natural Light for at least as cheap as what you're paying for Keystone Light,'" Ferrell says. On average, Ferrell moves 300 cases per week to college buyers. "Fraternities drink the cheapest beer they can find," Bradford, the Bud Girl supervisor, explains. "And his job is to make sure they drink our cheap beer."

30   Neither Ferrell nor Bradford seem reckless or irresponsible, but still—having a Budweiser representative as fraternity chairman is like having Joe Camel as a high school football quarterback. Both popular figureheads not only have a vested interest in which brands are consumed, but the quantity as well. "I think it's better that we do have them out there because of the message that we're bringing," says Laurie Watson, vice president of Brown Distributing. "We're constantly preaching responsibility."

31   Watson was the only senior-level Anheuser-Busch representative willing to comment for this story. A marketing representative for the Anheuser-Busch corporate office at first denied any knowledge of the college program, then agreed only to confirm some facts and produce a copy of the Anheuser-Busch College Marketing Code. The code touts Anheuser-Busch's support of alcohol awareness education and stresses that distributors must limit event sponsorship to venues that check I.D.

32   Bartenders and doormen do check I.D.s, of course. But the Bud Girl handing out free beers doesn't know how much alcohol a patron has consumed. Likewise, frat

Some Signs that Substance Use Is a Problem

- Being uncomfortable at occasions when alcohol and/or drugs are not available
- When you are not using, regretting things you said or did when you were using
- Arguments with friends or family related to your use
- Being able to handle larger and larger amounts of alcohol and/or drugs over time
- Increased work, family, school, and social problems
- Feeling angry or depressed while using or the next day
- Lying about substance use to friends and loved ones
- Neglecting people and events that don't involve substance use
- "Blackouts" or not remembering what happened when under the influence
- Uncomfortable withdrawal symptoms when not using (e.g., shakiness, fatigue, insomnia, irritability)
- Needing substances to cope with strong feelings, stress, and/or sleeplessness
- Wanting to cut back on use, but not being able to
- Driving a car while under the influence
- Getting in trouble at work or school for using (e.g., showing up late, calling in sick, getting fired)

representatives only card the one individual buying beer for a party. "[Students are] going to have a beer," Watson says. "We just want them to be responsible about it. The representatives always talk to them about responsible drinking." "At least," she adds, "I hope they do. They're supposed to."

33   Imagine a 21-year-old Bud rep arranging a sale of 100 cases of Natural Light, then lecturing to the buyer about responsible drinking. It doesn't click, it doesn't work. The people at Bud must be dreaming. And maybe they are dreaming . . . still. Dreaming of college market saturation, dreaming of young male demographics and dreaming of decades of brand loyalty to come.

34   One week after my Bud barhopping tour, University of Texas junior and Phi Kappa Sigma fraternity member Jack Ivey consumed about 20 drinks, then fell asleep on his apartment couch. He was pronounced dead the next morning of alcohol poisoning, just the latest binge-drinking fatality. Whether Ivey is in the dreams of any beer marketers, no one can say.

Tips for Safer Drinking

- Drink slowly, don't gulp your drinks, avoid drinking games
- Avoid using alcohol along with other drugs
- Set a limit on how many drinks you are going to have and stick to it
- Eat before you drink, keep in mind that high protein foods help slow alcohol absorption into the bloodstream
- Alternate alcoholic with nonalcoholic drinks
- Don't give in if friends encourage you to drink more than you want to
- Avoid putting your drink down out of sight or accepting drinks from strangers
- Plan ahead! Designate a sober driver in advance, provide transportation at social gatherings where drinking is involved, or use public transportation
- Plan activities that don't involve drinking or drugs

Although these moderation tips are written to apply to the use of alcohol, you can easily adapt these ideas for drug use as well.
In addition, you can also always contact the Counseling Center if you or someone you care about has a problem with drugs and/or alcohol.

Paul Mikowski, PsyD
Postdoctoral Fellow, Counseling and Personal Development Center, Westchester Campus, Pace University

FROM READING TO WRITING

1. Analyze and compare any two arguments made in this chapter. How is each argument a product of its audience and purpose? What sources of argument are used—ethical appeals, logical appeals, emotional appeals—and what string of "good reasons" are proposed in order to make a case? Why do the composers of those arguments make those particular appeals? (For more on rhetorical analysis, see Chapter 5.)

2. Examine and compare the various visual arguments that appear in this chapter—the photos, ads, and cartoons. What argument, exactly, is being made in each case? How is that argument supported? (See Chapter 6 for information on analyzing visuals.)

3. Write an argument that makes its point by defining a key term related to the regulation of substances like tobacco, high-calory food, marijuana, alcohol, and so on. You might seek to change people's attitudes by redefining freedom or government regulation or advertising in such a way that your definition supports your views on regulating substances. (See Chapter 8 for more on writing definition arguments.)

4. Propose a particular policy related to the regulation of substances that is important in your community. For example, if binge drinking is an issue at your college or university, you might propose a single measure that might help to ameliorate the situation. Should your institution permit fans to purchase beer at sporting events? What should be the policy of major league baseball toward performance-enhancing drugs? (See Chapter 13 for advice on proposal arguments.)

5. Write a rebuttal of an argument in this chapter concerning the regulation of alcohol, tobacco, steroids, or other substances. (See Chapter 12.) Consider whether you want to show the weaknesses in the argument, or whether you wish to counterargue, or to do both.

6. Write an essay that recounts a personal experience of yours that makes an argument related to the regulation of a particular substance. What exactly does your personal experience lead you to conclude? See Chapter 11 for advice on narrative arguments. Alternatively, consider making your argument based on your observation of another person's experience.

28 | New Media

Personal Space in Cyberspace

Twenty-five years ago, everything seemed so simple and stable. There were a few cable TV stations, but the major networks—NBC, CBS, ABC—still ruled. Radio was delivering comfortable and predictable news, weather, and music to their listeners: Top 40 on one channel, country on another, oldies on a third; talk radio was a late-night-only phenomenon, and sports on the radio was built around familiar voices who were associated with particular teams over many years. The daily local newspaper arrived in the morning or afternoon or both. Every house and office had a central phone line, usually with a few extensions and usually serviced by AT&T.

Is this the future of media? In this publicity still from *Avatar*, all eyes are on the display. What are the consequences of the shift from old to new media?

Then everything changed. Cable television stations multiplied so that the established networks lost market share as well as their monopoly on evening entertainment and news coverage. Even sports coverage changed fundamentally when ESPN began offering its hour-long *SportsCenter* show, and network news gave up market share to the host of news and quasi-news shows that compete so vigorously for an audience today. When Rush Limbaugh created a large audience for his conservative political commentary, many radio stations created or expanded their talk-radio formats. And all that became jumbled still further with the advent of the Internet, which seems to be causing the slow demise of print journalism even as it encourages new, more participatory forms of media in cyberspace. Finally, social networking media and cell phone technologies in the past decade have put a sophisticated communications tool into the pockets and purses of just about everyone.

With these changes have come many concerns and controversies. The effects of new media on our political processes have been particularly criticized. On October 15, 2004, for example, less than three weeks before the presidential elections, popular Comedy Central comedian Jon Stewart, a guest on CNN's political talk show *Crossfire*, got into a celebrated donnybrook with news commentator Tucker Carlson. Stewart, whose hilarious political satire in the form of a mock TV news show sends many Americans to bed with smiles on their faces, took the opportunity of his appearance on *Crossfire* to challenge Carlson about the abysmal level of political commentary in the nation's media. At one point Stewart charged that *Crossfire* and shows like it—he was no doubt thinking of Bill O'Reilly and Rush Limbaugh and Keith Olbermann—are "bad, very bad," for America because they oversimplify and polarize discussion. "It's hurting America," said Stewart. "Stop, stop, stop, stop, stop hurting America." When Carlson protested that *Crossfire* presents intelligent debate from the political left and right, Stewart was outraged: "[Saying *Crossfire* is a debate show is] like saying pro wrestling is a show about athletic competition. You're doing theater when you should be doing debate. . . . What you do is not honest. What you do is partisan hackery . . . just knee-jerk reactionary talk."

While Stewart and his fans were taking their frustrations out on *Crossfire*, they were surely also thinking of much more. In the past decade many Americans have been increasingly concerned about certain trends in the popular media, especially in new media, including Internet news sites, podcasts, and blogs: the development of partisan (rather than "fair and balanced") news coverage; the concentration of news outlets and newspapers into the hands of a few powerful corporations; the impact of sensationalistic and one-sided talk radio and talk TV shows; the effects of the Internet on the political and cultural process; the dubious morality depicted on "reality TV"; attack coverage of events by bloggers and podcasters; and the effects of persistent advertising, violence, graphic sexuality, and cultural stereotyping that are associated now with films, magazines, and television programs. No wonder so many people cringe when they recall the nonstop, no-holds-barred, months-long tabloidization of Tiger Woods's marital infidelities.

Developments in new media—like Wikipedia, avatars, blogs, and Internet social networking sites—are making information and recreation more widely available, but the simplicity of posting anything on the Internet results in an overwhelming volume of material, a good deal of which is dubious in content. Between the partisanship (both obvious and subtle) of more traditional media and the questionable credibility of new media, many Americans are left wondering where to turn for reliable news and information, and for safe sources of family entertainment. Many, in fact, turn to relentless self-expression via blogs, twitter, Facebook, and the like—to the personal spaces in cyberspace that may or may not reflect reality. The writers of the selections in this chapter tease out the tensions between freedom and censorship, public and private, in both old and new media; and they ponder the implications of the various new media.

Contemporary Arguments

This chapter opens with four pieces that explore the delicate balance between freedom and restriction on the Internet, as well as the potential consequences of swinging too far in one direction. In "Is Google's Data Grinder Dangerous?" Andrew Keen accuses Google of nefariously plotting for world domination and suggests that the Internet is not (and never will be) the utopian, free intellectual space that John Perry Barlow describes in "A Declaration of the Independence of Cyberspace." Similarly, John Seigenthaler describes a less-than-utopian experience of being the subject of a false Wikipedia biography and the obstacles to finding the identity of the writer. Walt Handelsman's "Information Superhighway" cartoon follows the Internet thread as well; his humorous roadway image shows a strikingly real portrait of priorities on the Internet. All these pieces come together under the broad topic of media and its uses. What is the Internet's purpose? Who should control it? Whose opinions should it publish and validate? And, finally, what are the hidden effects, sacrifices, and benefits when people (and small nonprofit organizations) develop a significant Internet presence?

For many people worldwide, such questions take a backseat to the daily influence of the media in their lives. The balance of the selections in this chapter take up the issue of the Internet, identities, and the burgeoning trend of developing alter egos—and richly detailed alternative worlds—online. In "Where the Avatars Roam," Michael Gerson looks at cyberspace role-playing from a moral perspective: What happens to morality and freedom when we spend so much time in alternative realities where any choice is possible—even criminal or socially undesirable choices? Daniel Okrent follows with a 1999 speech on the future of print media; you will find it highly relevant in the light of what is happening these days to print newspapers, magazine circulation, and new e-book technologies such as Kindle and the iPad. (What do you make of the statement by J. K. Rowling, author of the Harry Potter books, that no books about Harry will appear in electronic form?) Then David Carr offers an endorsement of Twitter. Together, these articles tackle the tricky terrain of the private and the public in cyberspace. What kinds of personal expression are meant for public consumption? Should we differentiate between amateur and professional participation online, particularly if amateur expression is so common and so popular? Finally, just what is (and what should be) the purpose of new media—dissemination of information, recreation, commerce, or something else? Are we creating new media, or is it creating us?

The chapter concludes with an Issue in Focus: electronic games. As Chris Kohler indicates in his account of a new fitness game, Nintendo's Wii system actually can provide some exercise for participants, and so he counters concerns that rampant child obesity is the result of all video games. Can other new technologies encourage people to be more active? And what about the other charges against video games—that they undermine learning, encourage teen violence, isolate children socially, and reinforce harmful gender stereotypes? The Issue in Focus, takes up all these matters and more. More broadly speaking, to what purposes can we put new media, and how will these technological shifts influence our lives and cultures?

ANDREW **KEEN**

Is Google's Data Grinder Dangerous?

In *The Cult of the Amateur: How Today's Internet Is Killing Our Culture* (2007), Andrew Keen argues that the slew of amateur writing on the Internet—by anyone, about anything—doesn't contribute to knowledge or information, but rather bogs us down with uninformed opinions. Keen's view of the Internet is also evident in the article printed below. First published on July 12, 2007, in the *Los Angeles Times*, "Is Google's Data Grinder Dangerous?" puts a nefarious spin on the most popular Internet search engine—and its seeming quest to know all our private information so it can dominate the world (or at least make billions in advertising).

What does Google want? Having successfully become our personal librarian, Google now wants to be our personal oracle. It wants to learn all about us, know us better than we know ourselves, to transform itself from a search engine into a psychoanalyst's couch or a priest's confessional. Google's search engine is the best place to learn what Google wants. Type "Eric Schmidt London May 22" into Google, and you can read about a May interview the Google chief executive gave to journalists in London. Here is how he described what he hoped the search engine would look like in five years: "The goal is to enable Google users to be able to ask the question such as 'What shall I do tomorrow?' And 'What job shall I take?'"

2   Schmidt's goal is not inconsiderable: By 2012, he wants Google to be able to tell all of us what we want. This technology, what Google co-founder Larry Page calls the "perfect search engine," might not only replace our shrinks but also all those marketing professionals whose livelihoods are based on predicting—or guessing—consumer desires. Schmidt acknowledges that Google is still far from this goal. As he told the

London journalists: "We cannot even answer the most basic questions because we don't know enough about you. That is the most important aspect of Google's expansion."

3   So where is Google expanding? How is it planning to know more about us? Many—if not most—users don't read the user agreement and thus aren't aware that Google already stores every query we type in. The next stage is a personalized Web service called iGoogle. Schmidt, who perhaps not coincidentally sits on the board of Apple, regards its success as the key to knowing us better than we know ourselves.

4   iGoogle is growing into a tightly-knit suite of services—personalized homepage, search engine, blog, e-mail system, mini-program gadgets, Web-browsing history, etc.—that together will create the world's most intimate information database. On iGoogle, we all get to aggregate our lives, consciously or not, so artificially intelligent software can sort out our desires. It will piece together our recent blog posts, where we've been online, our e-commerce history and cultural interests. It will amass so much information about each of us that eventually it will be able to logically determine what we want to do tomorrow and what job we want.

5   The real question, of course, is whether what Google wants is what we want too. Do we really want Google digesting so much intimate data about us? Could iGoogle actually be a remix of "1984's" Room 101—that Orwellian dystopia in which our most secret desires and most repressed fears are revealed? Any comparison with 20th century, top-down totalitarianism is, perhaps, a little fanciful. After all, nobody can force us to use iGoogle. And—in contrast to Yahoo and Microsoft (which have no limits on how long they hang on to our personal data)—Google has committed to retaining data for only 18 months. Still, if iGoogle turns out to be half as wise about each of us as Schmidt predicts, then this artificial intelligence will challenge traditional privacy rights as well as provide us with an excuse to deny responsibility for our own actions. What happens, for example, when the government demands access to our iGoogle records? And will we be able to sue iGoogle if it advises us to make an unwise career decision?

6   Schmidt, I suspect, would like us to imagine Google as a public service, thereby affirming the company's "do no evil" credo. But Google is not our friend. Schmidt's iGoogle vision of the future is not altruistic, and his company is not a nonprofit group dedicated to the realization of human self-understanding. Worth more than $150 billion on the public market, Google is by far the dominant Internet advertising outlet—according to Nielsen ratings, it reaches about 70% of the global Internet audience. Just in the first quarter of 2007, Google's revenue from its online properties was up 76% from the previous year. Personal data are Google's most valuable currency, its crown jewels. The more Google knows our desires, the more targeted advertising it can serve up to us and the more revenue it can extract from these advertisers.

7   What does Google really want? Google wants to dominate. Its proposed $3.1-billion acquisition of DoubleClick threatens to make the company utterly dominant in the online advertising business. The $1.65-billion acquisition of YouTube last year made it by far the dominant player in the online video market. And, with a personalized service like iGoogle, the company is seeking to become the algorithmic monopolist of our online behavior. So when Eric Schmidt says Google wants to know us better than we know ourselves, he is talking to his shareholders rather than us. As a Silicon Valley old-timer, trust me on this one. I know Google better than it knows itself.

John Perry Barlow

A Declaration of the Independence of Cyberspace

After seventeen years as a Wyoming rancher who, on the side, wrote songs for the Grateful Dead, John Perry Barlow (born 1947) in the late 1980s began writing about computer-mediated communications. He served on the board of directors of WELL (the Whole Earth Lectronic Link), posts regularly on the WELL Web site, and is a cofounder of the Electronic Frontier Foundation, which advocates keeping government regulations out of the Internet. Since May 1998, he has been a fellow at Harvard Law School's Berkman Center for Internet and Society.

Governments of the Industrial World, you weary giants of flesh and steel, I come from Cyberspace, the new home of Mind. On behalf of the future, I ask you of the past to leave us alone. You are not welcome among us. You have no sovereignty where we gather.

2   We have no elected government, nor are we likely to have one, so I address you with no greater authority than that with which liberty itself always speaks. I declare the global social space we are building to be naturally independent of the tyrannies you seek to impose on us. You have no moral right to rule us nor do you possess any methods of enforcement we have true reason to fear.

3   Governments derive their just powers from the consent of the governed. You have neither solicited nor received ours. We did not invite you. You do not know us, nor do you know our world. Cyberspace does not lie within your borders. Do not think that you can build it, as though it were a public construction project. You cannot. It is an act of nature and it grows itself through our collective actions.

4   You have not engaged in our great and gathering conversation, nor did you create the wealth of our marketplaces. You do not know our culture, our ethics, or the unwritten codes that already provide our society more order than could be obtained by any of your impositions.

5   You claim there are problems among us that you need to solve. You use this claim as an excuse to invade our precincts. Many of these problems don't exist. Where there are real conflicts, where there are wrongs, we will identify them and address them by our means. We are forming our own Social Contract. This governance will arise according to the conditions of our world, not yours. Our world is different.

6   Cyberspace consists of transactions, relationships, and thought itself, arrayed like a standing wave in the web of our communications. Ours is a world that is both everywhere and nowhere, but it is not where bodies live.

7   We are creating a world that all may enter without privilege or prejudice accorded by race, economic power, military force, or station of birth.

8   We are creating a world where anyone, anywhere may express his or her beliefs, no matter how singular, without fear of being coerced into silence or conformity.

9   Your legal concepts of property, expression, identity, movement, and context do not apply to us. They are based on matter. There is no matter here.

10   Our identities have no bodies, so, unlike you, we cannot obtain order by physical coercion. We believe that, from ethics, enlightened self-interest, and the commonweal, our governance will emerge. Our identities may be distributed across many of your jurisdictions. The only law that all our constituent cultures would generally recognize is the Golden Rule. We hope we will be able to build our particular solutions on that basis. But we cannot accept the solutions you are attempting to impose.

11   In the United States, you have today created a law, the Telecommunications Reform Act, which repudiates your own Constitution and insults the dreams of Jefferson, Washington, Mill, Madison, deToqueville, and Brandeis. These dreams must now be born anew in us.

12   You are terrified of your own children, since they are natives in a world where you will always be immigrants. Because you fear them, you entrust your bureaucracies with the parental responsibilities you are too cowardly to confront yourselves. In our world, all the sentiments and expressions of humanity, from the debasing to the angelic, are parts of a seamless whole, the global conversation of bits. We cannot separate the air that chokes from the air upon which wings beat.

13   In China, Germany, France, Russia, Singapore, Italy, and the United States, you are trying to ward off the virus of liberty by erecting guard posts at the frontiers of Cyberspace. These may keep out the contagion for a small time, but they will not work in a world that will soon be blanketed in bit-bearing media.

14   Your increasingly obsolete information industries would perpetuate themselves by proposing laws, in America and elsewhere, that claim to own speech itself throughout the world. These laws would declare ideas to be another industrial product, no more noble than pig iron. In our world, whatever the human mind may create can be reproduced and distributed infinitely at no cost. The global conveyance of thought no longer requires your factories to accomplish.

15   These increasingly hostile and colonial measures place us in the same position as those previous lovers of freedom and self-determination who had to reject the authorities of distant, uninformed powers. We must declare our virtual selves immune to your sovereignty, even as we continue to consent to your rule over our bodies. We will spread ourselves across the Planet so that no one can arrest our thoughts.

16   We will create a civilization of the Mind in Cyberspace. May it be more humane and fair than the world your governments have made before. ▪

JOHN **SEIGENTHALER**

A False Wikipedia "Biography"

John Seigenthaler, now retired, is a distinguished journalist who founded the Freedom Forum First Amendment Center at Vanderbilt University—so he is anything but a censor at heart. Nevertheless, in the following essay (published in November 2005 in *USA Today*, a newspaper he helped launch) he expresses grave reservations about Wikipedia as he recounts a personal experience. The article printed below generated serious discussion about the reliability, credibility, and ethics of Wikipedia, which changed some of its policies subsequently. You can read more about the episode by going to en.wikipedia.org/wiki/ Seigenthaler_controversy. For a writing activity on Wikipedia, see page 599.

> John Seigenthaler Sr. was the assistant to Attorney General Robert Kennedy in the early 1960's. For a brief time, he was thought to have been directly involved in the Kennedy assassinations of both John and his brother Bobby. Nothing was ever proven.
>
> —*Wikipedia*

This is a highly personal story about Internet character assassination. It could be your story. I have no idea whose sick mind conceived the false, malicious "biography" that appeared under my name for 132 days on Wikipedia, the popular, online, free encyclopedia whose authors are unknown and virtually untraceable. There was more:

2 "John Seigenthaler moved to the Soviet Union in 1971, and returned to the United States in 1984," Wikipedia said. "He started one of the country's largest public relations firms shortly thereafter."

3 At age 78, I thought I was beyond surprise or hurt at anything negative said about me. I was wrong. One sentence in the biography was true. I was Robert Kennedy's administrative assistant in the early 1960s. I also was his pallbearer. It was mind-boggling when my son, John Seigenthaler, journalist with NBC News, phoned later to say he found the same scurrilous text on Reference.com and Answers.com.

4 I had heard for weeks from teachers, journalists and historians about "the wonderful world of Wikipedia," where millions of people worldwide visit daily for quick reference "facts," composed and posted by people with no special expertise or knowledge—and sometimes by people with malice.

5 At my request, executives of the three websites now have removed the false content about me. But they don't know, and can't find out, who wrote the toxic sentences.

Anonymous Author

6 I phoned Jimmy Wales, Wikipedia's founder and asked, "Do you . . . have any way to know who wrote that?"

7 "No, we don't," he said. Representatives of the other two websites said their computers are programmed to copy data verbatim from Wikipedia, never checking whether it is false or factual. Naturally, I want to unmask my "biographer." And, I am interested in letting many people know that Wikipedia is a flawed and irresponsible research tool.

8   But searching cyberspace for the identity of people who post spurious information can be frustrating. I found on Wikipedia the registered IP (Internet Protocol) number of my "biographer"—65-81-97-208. I traced it to a customer of BellSouth Internet. That company advertises a phone number to report "Abuse Issues." An electronic voice said all complaints must be e-mailed. My two e-mails were answered by identical form letters, advising me that the company would conduct an investigation but might not tell me the results. It was signed "Abuse Team."

9   Wales, Wikipedia's founder, told me that BellSouth would not be helpful. "We have trouble with people posting abusive things over and over and over," he said. "We block their IP numbers, and they sneak in another way. So we contact the service providers, and they are not very responsive."

10   After three weeks, hearing nothing further about the Abuse Team investigation, I phoned BellSouth's Atlanta corporate headquarters, which led to conversations between my lawyer and BellSouth's counsel. My only remote chance of getting the name, I learned, was to file a "John or Jane Doe" lawsuit against my "biographer." Major communications Internet companies are bound by federal privacy laws that protect the identity of their customers, even those who defame online. Only if a lawsuit resulted in a court subpoena would BellSouth give up the name.

Little Legal Recourse

11   Federal law also protects online corporations—BellSouth, AOL, MCI, Wikipedia, etc.—from libel lawsuits. Section 230 of the Communications Decency Act, passed in 1996, specifically states that "no provider or user of an interactive computer service shall be treated as the publisher or speaker." That legalese means that, unlike print and broadcast companies, online service providers cannot be sued for disseminating defamatory attacks on citizens posted by others. Recent low-profile court decisions document that Congress effectively has barred defamation in cyberspace. Wikipedia's website acknowledges that it is not responsible for inaccurate information, but Wales, in a recent C-Span interview with Brian Lamb, insisted that his website is accountable and that his community of thousands of volunteer editors (he said he has only one paid employee) corrects mistakes within minutes.

12   My experience refutes that. My "biography" was posted May 26. On May 29, one of Wales' volunteers "edited" it only by correcting the misspelling of the word "early." For four months, Wikipedia depicted me as a suspected assassin before Wales erased it from his website's history Oct. 5. The falsehoods remained on Answers.com and Reference.com for three more weeks. In the C-Span interview, Wales said Wikipedia has "millions" of daily global visitors and is one of the world's busiest websites. His volunteer community runs the Wikipedia operation, he said. He funds his website through a non-profit foundation and estimated a 2006 budget of "about a million dollars."

13   And so we live in a universe of new media with phenomenal opportunities for worldwide communications and research—but populated by volunteer vandals with poison-pen intellects. Congress has enabled them and protects them.

14   When I was a child, my mother lectured me on the evils of "gossip." She held a feather pillow and said, "If I tear this open, the feathers will fly to the four winds, and I could never get them back in the pillow. That's how it is when you spread mean things about people." For me, that pillow is a metaphor for Wikipedia.

Michael Gerson

Where the Avatars Roam

Michael Gerson, who once worked as a policy analyst and speechwriter under President George W. Bush, is columnist for the *Washington Post* and contributes to PostPartisan. His book about the future of conservative politics, *Heroic Conservatism*, was published in 2007. His areas of expertise span democracy and human rights, health and diseases, and religion and politics. Gerson is senior research fellow at the Institute for Global Engagement's Center on Faith and International Affairs. In "Where the Avatars Roam," published in the *Washington Post* July 6, 2007, Gerson asks, what happens to human freedom and human choices in alternative realities constructed online?

I am not usually found at bars during the day, though the state of the Republican Party would justify it. But here I was at a bar talking to this fox—I mean an actual fox, with fluffy tail and whiskers. It turns out that, in the online world of Second Life, many people prefer to take the shape of anthropomorphic animals called "furries," and

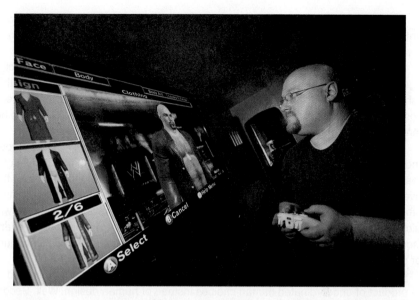

If you were to create an avatar, would you want to look like yourself or someone or something else? Why?

this one is in a virtual bar talking about her frustrating job at a New York publishing house. But for all I know, she could be a man in outback Montana with a computer, a satellite dish and a vivid imagination.

2   For a columnist, this is called "research." For millions of Americans, it is an addictive form of entertainment called MMORPGs—massively multiplayer online role-playing games. In this entirely new form of social interaction, people create computer-generated bodies called avatars and mingle with other players in 3-D fantasy worlds.

3   Some of these worlds parallel a form of literature that J.R.R. Tolkien called "sub-creation"—the Godlike construction of a complex, alternative reality, sometimes with its own mythology and languages. I subscribe along with my two sons (an elf and a dwarf) to The Lord of the Rings Online, based on Tolkien's epic novels, which sends its participants on a series of heroic quests. I'm told that World of Warcraft, which has more than 8 million subscribers, takes a similar approach. Some of the appeal of these games is the controlled release of aggression—cheerful orc killing. But they also represent a conservative longing for medieval ideals of chivalry—for a recovery of honor and adventure in an age dominated by choice and consumption.

4   Second Life, however, is a different animal. Instead of showing the guiding hand of an author, this universe is created by the choices of its participants, or "residents." They can build, buy, trade and talk in a world entirely without rules or laws; a pure market where choice and consumption are the highest values. Online entrepreneurs make real money selling virtual clothing, cars and "skins"—the photorealistic faces and bodies of avatars. Companies such as Dell, IBM and Toyota market aggressively within Second Life.

5   The site has gotten some recent attention for its moral lapses. A few of its residents have a disturbing preference for "age play"—fantasy sex with underage avatars—which has attracted the attention of prosecutors in several countries.

6   But Second Life is more consequential than its moral failures. It is, in fact, a large-scale experiment in libertarianism. Its residents can do and be anything they wish. There are no binding forms of community, no responsibilities that aren't freely chosen and no lasting consequences of human actions. In Second Life, there is no human nature at all, just human choices.

7   And what do people choose? Well, there is some good live music, philanthropic fundraising, even a few virtual churches and synagogues. But the main result is the breakdown of inhibition. Second Life, as you'd expect, is highly sexualized in ways that have little to do with respect or romance. There are frequent outbreaks of terrorism, committed by online anarchists who interrupt events, assassinate speakers (who quickly reboot from the dead) and vandalize buildings. There are strip malls everywhere, pushing a relentless consumerism. And there seems to be an inordinate number of vampires, generally not a sign of community health.

8   Libertarians hold to a theory of "spontaneous order"—that society should be the product of uncoordinated human choices instead of human design. Well, Second Life has plenty of spontaneity, and not much genuine order. This experiment suggests that a world that is only a market is not a utopia. It more closely resembles a seedy, derelict carnival—the triumph of amusement and distraction over meaning and purpose.

9   Columnists, like frontier trackers, are expected to determine cultural directions from faint scents in the wind. So maybe there is a reason that *The Lord of the Rings* is ultimately more interesting than Second Life. Only in a created world, filled with moral rules, social obligations and heroic quests, do our free choices seem to matter. And even fictional honor fills a need deeper than consumption.

10   G.K. Chesterton wrote that when people are "really wild with freedom and invention" they create institutions, such as marriages and constitutions; but "when men are weary they fall into anarchy." In that anarchy, life tends to be nasty, brutish, short—and furry. ■

Daniel Okrent

The Death of Print?

Daniel Okrent (born 1948) has spent his career in the publishing industry, as the writer of articles and books (his latest book, published in 2010, is on the Prohibition Era in the United States), as an editor for *Time* and *Life* and the *New York Times*, and in other roles. (He is also credited with inventing fantasy sports games in 1980.) The following was delivered as a lecture at Columbia University's School of Journalism on December 14, 1999, and archived by *The Digital Journalist* in February 2000.

Looking out at an audience of so many people who would forgo tonight's episode of "Dharma and Greg" or "Rivera Live" to come hear me talk, I feel highly responsible to provide you with entertainment or elucidation sufficient to justify your sacrifice. I also feel the burden to live up to the provocative title that the J-school's lecture producers and I have cooked up to get you out of your apartments and into this hall: "The Death of Print?" has both a nice, millenarian finality to it, and a perfect op-ed page sort of cop-out attached to it, namely that temporizing question mark.

2   "The Death of Print" also makes it pretty clear that I'm not going to be talking about the shrinking news staffs at the major networks, or the increasing tendency of local television news shows to devote their time to either highway mayhem or idiotic, grinning man-or-woman on the street interviews with people whose only qualification for demanding our attention is that they are, in fact, on the street.

3   If you sense a certain antipathy to television journalism in my tone, you're right. This is one way that I hope to establish my credentials with you as a paragon of print, an ink-stained wretch, someone with printer's ink coursing through his veins—pick your print media clichO, and it applies to me. I even spent some time looking through George Will's entire library of quotation dictionaries trying to find some apposite quote about the importance of print journalism, to show how widely read—in Quotation Dictionaries—I am. But all I could find was a sequence of pomposities and self-evidencies uttered decades ago by Walter Lippmann, our profession's most predicable Capital G Capital M Great Man. That's the problem with talking about the future of media or journalism, the tendency to float away on the helium of one's own pretentiousness.

4   So here goes. I am going to take a portion of my time this evening to sing a hymn of praise to print, to its irreplaceable role in our lives.

5   Newspapers, magazines, books—all those other wonderful creatures made possible by Gutenberg five centuries ago are, I'm sure you'll agree, the media that matter. I've spent my entire career engaged by them—going back to working on a daily newspaper when I was in college, then nine years in the book business, several more as a writer of books, and finally, until 1996, 14 years as a magazine editor. Forgive me the three years I spent on the web, navigating a turbulent sea of bits and bytes as Time Inc.'s editor of new media. I touched land several months ago, and now I'm writing and editing again. It's nice to be back.

6   Newspapers, magazines, books: A newspaper gives you timeliness, a magazine perspective, a book lasting value. Each is a firm, palpable entity, a presence in our lives, a companion to our days. I remember what it was like when I was a child, and my father brought home the newspaper after work. My mother would take what we called in those distant, benighted days the women's section—recipes, fashion news, the advice columns. My older brother, who was readying himself for a business career—he took the stock market pages. I reached for sports, the news of the athletic wonders committed daily by my heroes. My father had the general news section, and we'd each disappear into our own engagements with the wider world, regrouping in time for dinner and a shared conversation about what we had encountered in the daily paper. What could possibly replace something so comfortable, so safe, so adaptable as a daily newspaper?

7   As for magazines—well, I work for the world's largest magazine company, so it shouldn't be hard for me to make a case for the magazine. There are nearly 10,000 different magazines available in the U.S. today. Great, giant, mass circulation magazines like those Time Inc. publishes—*Time, Life, People, Fortune,* and so on—and tiny, narrowly focused magazines to cater to the reader's most special interest. I'm a scuba diver. I subscribe to two different scuba diving magazines, and if I wanted to I could subscribe to a dozen more. Interested in orchids? There are magazines for you. Guitars? I have a 19-year-old friend who subscribes to three guitar magazines. Magazines of every stripe and substance are there to build connections among those of us of a particular interest, or to set the terms of the national conversation on subjects of importance to all of us. Through the pages of *Ocean Realm* magazine I share a set of knowledge on our common passion with a scuba diver who lives 3,000 miles away from me. Through the pages of *Time*, I participate in a dialogue with him on matters of national concern—and with all of his neighbors, as well. Magazines bring us together into real communities, coming into our house as regular, periodic welcome visitors, requiring us to do nothing more than make a once-a-year request to the publisher to keep them coming. What could be easier than that?

8   Books? Every one of us in this room could write an anthem to the book. The feel of a fine binding, the smell of newly opened pages, the satisfying heft of a book in your hands—can anything top it? When I get home at night, before dinner I sit with a drink in my hand in a room full of books, each one of them an old friend who has accompanied me on part of my life voyage. The book of poems I loved in college, the biography that first introduced me to a great historical figure twenty years ago, the novel that entertained me on a vacation, or maybe the one that explained a piece of the world to me. As I was thinking about this talk, I happened to notice on my bookshelf a copy of the best novel about journalism ever written, Evelyn Waugh's *Scoop*, a book which I re-read every ten years or so to make certain that, if I stay in this business, I need to remain very, very careful.

9   As you can see, I can get sentimental about these things we call, by inference, the old media. They mean a lot to me, emotionally as well as economically—and I suspect they do to all of you, too. I believe they are, after food, clothing, and shelter, and after our family relations and our friendships, the most important things in our lives.

10   And I believe one more thing: I believe they, and all forms of print, are dead. Finished. Over. Perhaps not in my professional lifetime, but certainly in that of the youngest people in this room. Remove the question mark from the title of this talk. The Death of Print, full stop.

11   Twenty, thirty, at the outside forty years from now, we will look back on the print media the way we look back on travel by horse and carriage, or by wind-powered ship. In fact, that carriage, and that ship, will have their own print counterparts, which I will get to later. But first I would like to tell you why I am so convinced that those media to which I have devoted my 30 years of professional life are as relevant to our future as the carrier pigeon.

12   And please understand: I did not come to this conclusion as a zealot. Until I moved into my job as editor of new media for Time Inc., the Internet was merely a place for me to get late stock market news, or the baseball box scores. I didn't move into my

current job out of passion, or conviction, or technological facility, or even a particular interest in the subject. When I asked Don Logan, Time Inc.'s CEO, why he and Norman Pearlstine, our editor-in-chief, thought I was right for this job, Don said, "Because we need a little gray hair in that organization." In other words, I qualified because I was old.

13 So, to the point: why is print dead? It's a two-part argument, the first part fairly simple but worth some elaboration, the second part as obvious as the morning sun.

14 Part one, in a phrase, is that we have, I believe, finally learned not to underestimate the march of technological progress. A little over thirty years ago, I saw my first electronic calculator. It was about the shape of a laptop computer, maybe three inches deep, it weighed eight or nine pounds, and it cost my father's law firm $500 in 1967 dollars. Today, you can buy calculators the size and heft of a credit card in a convenience store for two dollars. I purchased my first computer, an Apple 2E, in 1980. What a wonder it was! White type—capital letters only—dropped out of a black screen; it processed words at a speed less than 1% as fast as the three-pound laptop that has become the locus, the library, and the lever of my entire professional life. Its built-in memory couldn't accommodate a long magazine article. And my friends and neighbors—sophisticated, educated people—would come over evenings to watch me move blocks of text from HERE to THERE on it. It was that new, that extraordinary. I don't need to tell you what the average computer can do today, nor do I need to tell you similar stories about telephones, or audio equipment, or any other piece of new technology. If we imagine it, they will build it.

15 So imagine this (and if you find it hard to imagine, trust me: I've seen it already, in the development office of a well-established Japanese computer electronics company): Imagine a tablet, maybe half an inch thick, shaped when held one way like an open book or magazine, when turned sideways much like a single page of a newspaper. It weighs six ounces. It's somewhat flexible, which makes it easy to transport. (The truly flexible one, which you'll be able to roll up and put in your pocket, is still a couple of years away, so this one will have to do). Its screen, utterly glare-free, neither flickers nor fades nor grows dull. To move beyond the first screen in whatever it is that you're reading, you run your finger across the top of the tablet LIKE THIS—a physical metaphor for the turning of the page. You are sitting on a beach on a Saturday afternoon with this little wonder, and you're reading this week's *Time* magazine. Then you decide you'd like something a little more, oh, entertaining. You press a series of buttons HERE, and a cellular hookup to a satellite-connected database instantaneously delivers you—well, Evelyn Waugh's *Scoop*. And when you've had enough of that—click, click—you move on, to the football news, or the office memoranda you didn't finish reading on Friday afternoon, or whatever it is that you want. Click, click again: each download, coming to you at dazzling speeds, and a central rights-clearance computer charges your account, much like a telephone account, for what you've read or listened to. The satellite operator keeps a small portion of the income, and the rest goes to the "publisher"—that is, to the agency that either created the material you are reading, or that represents the interests of those who created it.

16 Or imagine this: another message comes to you, from—let's say Coca Cola. It's an advertising message, and you have been paid to read it. You have been targeted by

Coca Cola, the marketers from that company have found you on the beach, and for the privilege of getting their message in front of you they have paid the satellite operator a carriage fee. The satellite operator, wanting to guarantee the advertising agency that the impression has been made, credits your master account a few cents. For reading the one-minute message from Coca Cola, you get the first five minutes of tomorrow's electronic newspaper for free. Everyone's happy.

17   As I said, this technology already exists. It's far too expensive today, and the critical elements of payment systems and copyright protection and royalty accounting have not yet been created. But, I guarantee you that such systems are either in development today or soon will be.

18   But, you say, who wants to read a good novel on a computer screen, no matter how clear and snappy and portable it is? Who wants to forgo the tactile engagement with a newspaper or magazine, or even moreso the deeper, more gratifying physical connection with a book, and replace it with this potentially alienating form of modern technology?

19   Well, that brings me to part two of my argument, the part I promised was as obvious as the morning sun. And that is this: last year, Time Inc., spent $1 billion dollars on paper and postage.

20   End of argument.

21   Or, if you'd like, let me put it this way: you may prefer to ride across town in horse-and-carriage, or across a lake in a wind-powered yacht, but no one makes that carriage or that yacht for you anymore, at least not at a reasonable price. So too with the book: in the future that I am imagining with you tonight, the book becomes an elite item for the very few, an *objet,* a collectible—valuable not for the words on the page but for the vessel that contains those words. Will it matter to the book-loving *littera-teurs* who stalk Morningside Heights? Probably so, though I can't imagine why. Will it matter to the millions who buy a John Grisham paperback and toss it when it's done? Not a chance.

22   Nor should it. For we—we who work today by accident in paper and ink; who demand, however sheepishly, that vast forests be cut down to make our paper, for vast sums to be invested in hypermodern printing presses and bindery machines that consume megawatts of environment-befouling energy—we should be happy. For we know—we *must* know—that the words and pictures and ideas and images and notions and substance that we produce is what matters—and *not* the vessel that they arrive in.

23   I want to step back for a few moments here to elaborate on business models, consumer prejudices, and what I hope is a somewhat sober-sided consideration of a few of the risks this new world will pose.

24   First, business models. To date, we have seen very few media institutions find a way to charge for their digitally-delivered content: the *Wall Street Journal*, which is as close as one gets in American journalism to being both unique and essential, has been the leader to date. I admire the *Journal* hugely, both in print and online, but I do want to share with you the real reason for its success, the thing that makes it essential. This was explained to by my boss, Norm Pearlstine, several years ago when he was the

Journal's editor: the paper's indispensability, he said, is predicated on the mortal fear, shared by every middle manager in American business, that the boss will say to him or her, "Did you see the piece in the *Journal* this morning about X?"

25   Well, that works online, too, and several hundred thousand people are now paying Dow-Jones for the online paper. But note that they are paying $59 for an annual subscription to the online edition, while the print edition costs $175. That's partly because the physical costs—the nearly $1 billion a year, in our case, that Time Inc. spends on manufacturing and distribution—have evaporated. In other words, savings have been passed on to the reader, and everybody wins. Except, of course, the paper manufacturers, the delivery services, and the US Post Office—so all of you who have been planning careers at International Paper or with the Postal Service, forget it.

26   But the real power of the business model resides in the potential of digital advertising. Except for direct mail, until the Internet came along no advertising medium existed in which the advertiser could be sure his message was received by his targeted audience. We go to the bathroom during commercials, we flip the pages past magazine and newspaper ads, radio and billboards are white noise. But with a truly interactive medium—with say, a question about the advertisement asked next to the button that gives you your thirty cent credit against the cost of reading your *Wall Street Journal*—the effectiveness of media advertising changes radically. And if you don't think advertisers influence the direction of American mass media, you ought to talk to Tom Goldstein about the curriculum here at the J-school.

27   Second digression: consumer prejudices. Inevitably, whenever and wherever I talk about the Death of Print, someone jumps up and says, "But I hate reading on a computer." This is after I have already explained that the technology will change, that economic incentive will create consumer-friendly reading devices, that my father once paid as much for a four-function telephone book-sized calculator as he did for a low-end used car. Or that Oscar Dystel, the former chairman of Bantam Books and one of the founders of the American paperback book industry in the 1940s, once said, "In due course, the word 'paperback' will lose its taint of unpleasantness." And he said that in 1984.

28   No, you won't be reading on a cathode ray tube sitting on your desk. No, the screen won't flicker, and the type won't have visible ragged edges. It won't feel anything like a computer. It won't even feel like those early avatars of the form, the Rocket eBook and the SoftBook Reader, that are already showing up in Christmas catalogs and in consumer electronics stores—not any more than a Model T feels or looks or drives like a 1999 BMW Z3. There's even a guy at MIT, an engineering genius named Jacobson, who's devised something called electronic ink, a palette of digitally changeable molecules that sit on a surface very much like a sheet of paper, and rearrange themselves sequentially into actual sentences and paragraphs.

29   Ah, but you say, who will be able to afford such wonderful devices? In fact, nearly everyone. Because we—the big media companies like Time Warner, the eight or ten major copyright oligarchs, as I like to call them, who control so much of the nation's supply of worthwhile content—we will give them away, for all practical purposes, on the

cell phone model. Agree to subscribe to *Time* and *Sports Illustrated* for two years, as well as to listen to a certain amount of, say, Warner Brothers Music, and we'll give you the device. We aren't interested in making money off of hardware; we make money off of what you read and watch and listen to.

30   Last digression: risk. Yes, there are risks. Disaggregated content has already been somewhat socially injurious, and it's only going to get worse, at least insofar as we like to imagine a citizenry that is not only informed, but informed across a range of subjects. The ability to be your own editor—to pick just what news on what topics you wish to read—destroys the potential for serendipity, and the ease with which we achieve balance. I don't know how we'll solve this one, but we must.

31   Similarly, there's a risk in the mutability of digital content. The good news is that if you libel someone at 9 A.M., you can correct it at 9:10 or at noon or whenever it is that you learn of your mistake; it's not like sending out a fleet of trucks with a million copies of the *Times* and then realizing what you did wrong. But by the same token, if the words are never written in stone, or at least in ink, what happens to the notion of historical record?

32   But, of course, that cat is already out of the bag. If great writers are producing their works on computer, as most now do, first drafts no longer exist for the study of future scholars—just as the hurried prose of a daily newspaper, "the first rough draft of history," as it has been called, may disappear to the corrections of lawyers.

33   Yet I think we can live with these things, largely because we must.

34   I will assert once again that The Death of Print is going to happen, far sooner than many of you may think. The word "Internet" was all but unknown in the U.S. six years ago, and Time Inc., which had not yet even imagined its potential impact, had no one working in the Internet arena. Today, the Internet is inescapable; through the advent of email, it is ubiquitous. In the financial markets, it as essential as dollars. Throughout Time Warner, more than 1,000 people are developing copyrighted internet product, or marketing it to consumers. Someday, we may even make money at it.

35   For now, though, all of this is destabilizing, particularly for those of us who are investing substantially in a future so tantalizingly clear in the ultimate goal, but the path to which is so tangled in thickets of doubt, uncertainty, and confusion. Yet I, for one, take a strange kind of solace in this. What I know to be true is that the human species is hungry for information; that the quality, timeliness, and reliability of information is paramount; and that those of us who grew up in print, who look at the technological future through unconfident eyes, will be asked to do tomorrow exactly what we have done in the past, which is to reach people—intellectually, viscerally, any way we can—on matters they care about it. My colleagues and I did not grow up wanting to be in the ink and paper and staples business; we wanted to be in—we *are* in—the business of words and sentences and pictures and ideas. Don't worry about the future of newspapers or magazines or books any more than you would worry about corrugated boxes or shrink-wrap. They are containers; the substance resides elsewhere—for instance, in this room. So thank you for your attention; you may now throw tomatoes at me.

DAVID **CARR**

Why Twitter Will Endure

David Carr is the author of "Media Equation," a column in the business section of the *New York Times* that focuses on media issues. His work analyzes media as it intersects with business, culture, and government. His writing has also appeared in *The Atlantic Monthly* and *New York Magazine.* The following *Times* article was published on January 3, 2010.

I can remember when I first thought seriously about Twitter. Last March, I was at the SXSW conference, a conclave in Austin, Tex., where technology, media, and music are mashed up and re-imagined, and, not so coincidentally, where Twitter first rolled out in 2007. As someone who was oversubscribed on Facebook, overwhelmed by the computer-generated RSS feeds of news that came flying at me, and swamped by incoming e-mail messages, the last thing I wanted was one more Web-borne intrusion into my life.

2   And then there was the name. Twitter. In the pantheon of digital nomenclature—brands within a sector of the economy that grew so fast that all the sensible names were quickly taken—it would be hard to come up with a noun more trite than Twitter. It impugns itself, promising something slight and inconsequential, yet another way to make hours disappear and have nothing to show for it. And just in case the noun is not sufficiently indicting, the verb, "to tweet" is even more embarrassing.

3   Beyond the dippy lingo, the idea that something intelligent, something worthy of mindshare, might occur in the space of 140 characters—Twitter's parameters were set by what would fit in a text message on a phone—seems unlikely.

4   But it was clear that at the conference, the primary news platform was Twitter, with real-time annotation of the panels on stage and critical updates about what was happening elsewhere at a very hectic convention. At 52, I succumbed, partly out of professional necessity.

5   And now, nearly a year later, has Twitter turned my brain to mush? No, I'm in narrative on more things in a given moment than I ever thought possible, and instead of spending a half-hour surfing in search of illumination, I get a sense of the day's news and how people are reacting to it in the time that it takes to wait for coffee at Starbucks. Yes, I worry about my ability to think long thoughts—where was I, anyway?—but the tradeoff has been worth it.

6   Some time soon, the company won't say when, the 100-millionth person will have signed on to Twitter to follow and be followed by friends and strangers. That may sound like a MySpace waiting to happen—remember MySpace?—but I'm convinced Twitter is here to stay.

7   And I'm not alone. "The history of the Internet suggests that there have been cool Web sites that go in and out of fashion and then there have been open standards that become plumbing," said Steven Johnson, the author and technology observer who wrote a seminal piece about Twitter for Time last June. "Twitter is looking more and more like plumbing, and plumbing is eternal."

8   Really? What could anyone possibly find useful in this cacophony of short-burst communication? Well, that depends on whom you ask, but more importantly whom you

follow. On Twitter, anyone may follow anyone, but there is very little expectation of reciprocity. By carefully curating the people you follow, Twitter becomes an always-on data stream from really bright people in their respective fields, whose tweets are often full of links to incredibly vital, timely information.

9 The most frequent objection to Twitter is a predictable one: "I don't need to know someone is eating a donut right now." But if that someone is a serious user of Twitter, she or he might actually be eating the curmudgeon's lunch, racing ahead with a clear, up-to-the-second picture of an increasingly connected, busy world. The service has obvious utility for a journalist, but no matter what business you are in, imagine knowing what the thought leaders in your industry were reading and considering. And beyond following specific individuals, Twitter hash tags allow you to go deep into interests and obsession: #rollerderby, #physics, #puppets and #Avatar, to name just a few of many thousands.

10 The act of publishing on Twitter is so friction-free—a few keystrokes and hit send—that you can forget that others are out there listening. I was on a Virgin America cross-country flight, and used its wireless connection to tweet about the fact that the guy next to me seemed to be the leader of a cult involving Axe body spray. A half-hour later, a steward approached me and said he wondered if I would be more comfortable with a seat in the bulkhead. (He turned out to be a great guy, but I was doing a story involving another part of the company, so I had to decline the offer. @VirginAmerica, its corporate Twitter account, sent me a message afterward saying perhaps it should develop a screening process for Axe. It was creepy and comforting all at once.)

11 Like many newbies on Twitter, I vastly overestimated the importance of broadcasting on Twitter; and after a while, I realized that I was not Moses and neither Twitter nor its users were wondering what I thought. Nearly a year in, I've come to understand that the real value of the service is listening to a wired collective voice.

12 Not that long ago, I was at a conference at Yale and looked at the sea of open laptops in the seats in front of me. So why wasn't my laptop open? Because I follow people on Twitter who serve as my Web-crawling proxies, each of them tweeting links that I could examine and read on a Blackberry. Regardless of where I am, I surf far less than I used to.

13 At first, Twitter can be overwhelming, but think of it as a river of data rushing past that I dip a cup into every once in a while. Much of what I need to know is in that cup: if it looks like Apple is going to demo its new tablet, or Amazon sold more Kindles than actual books at Christmas, or the final vote in the Senate gets locked in on health care, I almost always learn about it first on Twitter.

14 The expressive limits of a kind of narrative developed from text messages, with less space to digress or explain than this sentence, has significant upsides. The best people on Twitter communicate with economy and precision, with each element—links, hash tags and comments—freighted with meaning. Professional acquaintances whom I find insufferable on every other platform suddenly become interesting within the confines of Twitter.

15 Twitter is incredibly customizable, with little of the social expectations that go with Facebook. Depending on whom you follow, Twitter can reveal a nation riveted by the

last episode of "Jersey Shore" or a short-form conclave of brilliance. There is plenty of nonsense—#Tiger had quite a run—but there are rich threads on the day's news and bravura solo performances from learned autodidacts. And the ethos of Twitter, which is based on self-defining groups, is far more well-mannered than many parts of the Web—more Toastmasters than mosh pit. On Twitter, you are your avatar and your avatar is you, so best not to act like a lout and when people want to flame you for something you said, they are responding to their own followers, not yours, so trolls quickly lose interest.

16   "Anything that is useful to both dissidents in Iran and Martha Stewart has a lot going for it; Twitter has more raw capability for users than anything since e-mail," said Clay Shirky, who wrote "Here Comes Everybody," a book about social media. "It will be hard to wait out Twitter because it is lightweight, endlessly useful and gets better as more people use it. Brands are using it, institutions are using it, and it is becoming a place where a lot of important conversations are being held." Twitter helps define what is important by what Mr. Shirky has called "algorithmic authority," meaning that if all kinds of people are pointing at the same thing at the same instant, it must be a pretty big deal.

17   Beyond the throbbing networked intelligence, there is the possibility of practical magic. Twitter can tell you what kind of netbook you should buy for your wife for Christmas—thanks Twitter!—or call you out when you complain about the long lines it took to buy it, as a tweeter on behalf of the electronics store B & H did when I shared the experience on my Blackberry while in line. I have found transcendent tacos at a car wash in San Antonio, rediscovered a brand of reporter's notepad I adore, uncovered sources for stories, all just by typing a query into Twitter.

18   All those riches do not come at zero cost: If you think e-mail and surfing can make time disappear, wait until you get ahold of Twitter, or more likely, it gets ahold of you. There is always something more interesting on Twitter than whatever you happen to be working on.

19   But in the right circumstance, Twitter can flex some big muscles. Think of last weekend, a heavy travel period marked by a terrorist incident on Friday. As news outlets were scrambling to understand the implications for travelers on Saturday morning, Twitter began lighting up with reports of new security initiatives, including one from @CharleneLi, a consultant who tweeted from the Montreal airport at about 7:30 A.M.: "New security rules for int'l flights into US. 1 bag, no electronics the ENTIRE flight, no getting up last hour of flight." It was far from the whole story and getting ahead of the news by some hours would seem like no big deal, but imagine you or someone you loved was flying later that same day: Twitter might seem very useful.

20   Twitter's growing informational hegemony is not assured. There have been serious outages in recent weeks, leading many business and government users to wonder about the stability of the platform. And this being the Web, many smart folks are plotting ways to turn Twitter into so much pixilated mist. But I don't think so. I can go anywhere I want on the Web, but there is no guarantee that my Twitter gang will come with me. I may have quite a few followers, but that doesn't make me Moses.

Are Video Games Good for You?

The video game *Tomb Raider,* featuring Lara Croft as its British-archeologist hero-ine, was released in 1996 and soon developed into a pop culture phenomenon. In addition to becoming the most popular video game in history, *Tomb Raider* be-came a movie, and then a second movie (with Angelina Jolie in the starring

Angelina Jolie as Lara Croft in *Lara Croft Tomb Raider: The Cradle of Life* (2003), a film based on a series of bestselling video games.

role)—and then a comic book, a novel, and even a theme park ride. Lara Croft's fans regard her as an ideal female icon—as brave as she is beautiful, strong and daring and smart, resourceful and fiercely independent.

2   But Lara Croft has not been without her critics. Skeptics, noting how Lara Croft's breast size seemed to increase along with her popularity, have contended that she is simply reinforcing traditional stereotypes, that her popularity derives from her starring role in the sexual fantasies of the predominantly male audience that enjoys "playing with her." Almost all teenage boys play video games, but only about half of girls do so, and so no wonder parents worry about the effect of video games on their consumers' sex and gender attitudes. For *Tomb Raider* is hardly the only game that depicts women and men in traditional roles, the men as active adventurers, the women as passive victims or sex objects.

3   Critics of video games wonder about other issues as well, just as an earlier generation worried about the effects of television. While many video games depend on social interactions, requiring or permitting multiple players to interact via networked systems and thus bringing people together, many other games can be played individually. Do video games lead to social isolation? Is there an addictive element to gaming that makes their consumers socially inept?

4   And what about the stylized violence that lies at the heart of many video games? If games ask players to abuse women and shoot policemen, is it any wonder that those activities persist in real life? When those who carry out school shootings are shown to be devotees of video games, shouldn't we worry about the effects of prolonged exposure to gaming? True, the games are age-rated, like movies are, but it is easy to evade the rules and obtain adult-rated games illegally. And it is worrisome that adult males are especially eager players of violent video games, particularly when the violence in the games is directed at women. Even though juvenile crime rates actually seem to be down, suggesting that people can usually distinguish the difference between game life and real life, it seems natural to expect that video games are affecting people's values—and actions—negatively. Are video games a kind of propaganda—do the games sensationalize drugs and alcohol and illicit sex, in effect "advertising" a way of life that is socially destructive? Or is it all in good fun?

5   Indeed, people criticize video games irrespective of their content. They contend that video games make people not just socially inept but also sedentary. Is the national obesity epidemic related to the popularity of video gaming? Do games, like television, encourage people to avoid real physical activity in order to perform fantasy deeds in front of a screen? And are children playing video games instead of reading or doing homework? In other words, are video games compromising our educational aspirations? Or do they actually help their users, not only by honing hand-eye coordination and visual perception skills but by improving the analytical and problem-solving abilities of users as well as their creativity and ability to concentrate. It has even been suggested that video games can assist in the treatment of autism and certain other mental health conditions.

6   The selections in this Issue in Focus propose answers to those questions. John Beck and Mitchell Wade blame video games for giving people an unreal sense of reality, while James Paul Gee defends video games for their educational value. Kevin Moss, with a substantial sense of irony, makes a strong case that video games set women back. Finally, Clay Shirky concludes the segment, and the chapter, with a fascinating defense of new media that is based on their ability to bring us together and shake us into becoming our most creative selves. (You should also consult the essay on this topic by student Armadi Tansal in Chapter 9.)

John C. Beck and Mitchell Wade

How the Gamer Revolution Is Reshaping Business Forever

DEFINITELY NOT IN KANSAS ANYMORE

Games are a technology that has been universally adopted by a large, young cohort and ignored by their elders. That's powerful enough to start with. But when you look at the experience that technology delivers—the content and the nature of the gamers' world—things really get interesting. Universally, and almost subliminally, games deliver a "reality" where the rules are quite different from any found out here in the rest of the world. Take a look at this quick overview of the lessons games teach:

The Individual's Role

2
- *You're the star.* You are the center of attention of every game unlike, say, Little League, where most kids will *never* be the star.
- *You're the boss.* The world is very responsive to you. You can choose things about reality, or switch to different experiences, in a way that is literally impossible in real life.
- *You're the customer, and the customer is always right.* Like shopping, the whole experience is designed for your satisfaction and entertainment; the opponents are tough, but never *too* tough.
- *You're an expert.* You have the experience of getting really, really good—especially compared to others who actually see you perform—early and often.
- *You're a tough guy.* You can experience all sorts of crashes, suffering, and death—and it doesn't hurt.

How the World Works

3
- *There's always an answer.* You might be frustrated for a while, you might even never find it, but you know it's there.
- *Everything is possible.* You see yourself or other players consistently do amazing things: defeat hundreds of bad guys singlehandedly, say, or beat the best N.B.A. team ever.
- *The world is a logical, human-friendly place.* Games are basically fair. Events may be random but not inexplicable, and there is not much mystery.
- *Trial-and-error is almost always the best plan.* It's the only way to advance in most games, even if you ultimately break down and buy a strategy guide or copy others on the really hard parts.
- *Things are (unrealistically) simple.* Games are driven by models. Even complex models are a lot simpler than reality. *You can figure a game out, completely.* Try that with real life.

How People Relate

4
- *It's all about competition.* You're always competing; even if you collaborate with other human players, you are competing against some character or score.
- *Relationships are structured.* To make the game work, there are only a few pigeonholes people (real or virtual) can fit into, such as competitor/ally and boss/subordinate.
- *We are all alone.* The gaming experience is basically solitary, even if played in groups. And you don't experience all of the activity, for any sustained time, as part of a group.
- *Young people rule.* Young people dominate gaming. Paying your dues takes a short time, youth actually helps, and there is no attention paid to elders.
- *People are simple.* Most in games are cartoon characters. Their skills may be complex, multidimensional, and user-configurable, but their personality types and behaviors are simple. There's big and strong, wild and crazy, beautiful and sexy, and a few other caricatures. That's it.

What You Should Do

5
- *Rebel.* Edginess and attitude are dominant elements of the culture.
- *Be a hero.* You always get the star's role; that is the only way to succeed or get satisfaction.
- *Bond with people who share your game experience, not your national or cultural background.* It's a very global world, in design, consumption, and characters, and in the phenomenon of the game generation.
- *Make your own way in the world.* Leaders are irrelevant and often evil; ignore them.
- *Tune out and have fun.* The whole experience of gaming is escapist. When reality is boring, you hop into game world. When a game gets boring, you switch to one that isn't.

6
    Not exactly like "real life," is it? And remember, this other-worldly experience has been exclusive to gamers. ■

JAMES PAUL **GEE**

Games, Not Schools, Are Teaching Kids to Think

The US spends almost $50 billion each year on education, so why aren't kids learning? Forty percent of students lack basic reading skills, and their academic performance is dismal compared with that of their foreign counterparts. In response to this crisis, schools are skilling-and-drilling their way "back to basics," moving toward mechanical instruction methods that rely on line-by-line scripting for teachers and endless multiple-choice testing. Consequently, kids aren't learning how to think anymore—they're learning how to memorize. This might be an ideal recipe for the future Babbitts of the world, but it won't produce the kind of agile, analytical minds that will lead the high tech global age. Fortunately, we've got *Grand Theft Auto: Vice City* and *Deus X* for that.

2   After school, kids are devouring new information, concepts, and skills every day, and, like it or not, they're doing it controller in hand, plastered to the TV. The fact is, when kids play videogames they can experience a much more powerful form of learning than when they're in the classroom. Learning isn't about memorizing isolated facts. It's about connecting and manipulating them. Doubt it? Just ask anyone who's beaten *Legend of Zelda* or solved *Morrowind*.

3   The phenomenon of the videogame as an agent of mental training is largely unstudied; more often, games are denigrated for being violent or they're just plain ignored. They shouldn't be. Young gamers today aren't training to be gun-toting carjackers. They're learning how to learn. In *Pikmin*, children manage an army of plant-like aliens and strategize to solve problems. In *Metal Gear Solid 2*, players move stealthily through virtual environments and carry out intricate missions. Even in the notorious *Vice City*, players craft a persona, build a history, and shape a virtual world. In strategy games like *WarCraft III* and *Age of Mythology*, they learn to micromanage an array of elements while simultaneously balancing short- and long-term goals. That sounds like something for their resumes.

4   The secret of a videogame as a teaching machine isn't its immersive 3-D graphics but its underlying architecture. Each level dances around the outer limits of the player's abilities, seeking at every point to be hard enough to be just doable. In cognitive science, this is referred to as the "regime of competence principle," which results in a feeling of simultaneous pleasure and frustration—a sensation as familiar to gamers as sore thumbs. Cognitive scientist Andy diSessa has argued that the best instruction hovers at the boundary of a student's competence. Most schools, however, seek to avoid invoking feelings of both pleasure and frustration, blind to the fact that these emotions can be extremely useful when it comes to teaching kids.

5   Also, good videogames incorporate the principle of expertise. They tend to encourage players to achieve total mastery of one level, only to challenge and undo that mastery in the next, forcing kids to adapt and evolve. This carefully choreographed dialectic has been identified by learning theorists as the best way to achieve expertise in any field. This doesn't happen much in our routine-driven schools, where "good" students are often just good at "doing school."

6   How did videogames become such successful models of effective learning? Game coders aren't trained as cognitive scientists. It's a simple case of free-market economics: If a title doesn't teach players how to play it well, it won't sell well. Game companies don't rake in $6.9 billion a year by dumbing down the material—aficionados condemn short and easy games like *Half Life: Blue Shift* and *Devil May Cry 2*. Designers respond by making harder and more complex games that require mastery of sophisticated worlds and as many as 50 to 100 hours to complete. Schools, meanwhile, respond with more tests, more drills, and more rigidity. They're in the cognitive-science dark ages.

7   We don't often think about videogames as relevant to education reform, but maybe we should. Game designers don't often think of themselves as learning theorists. Maybe they should. Kids often say it doesn't feel like learning when they're gaming—they're much too focused on playing. If kids were to say that about a science lesson, our country's education problems would be solved.

Kevin Moss

Blog Entry: The Enemy of My Irony Is My Friend

I thought I could keep myself away from this kind of thing. Remember when "blogging" used to be called "keeping an online diary"? Yeah, me too. This was one of the most fun things I used to do, back when sites like Diaryland and Xanga ruled the roost. Those were the days. . . . But here we are again, back to those times of endless amounts of typing about nothing of any particular importance. I'm definitely not promising any kind of commitment to this, I just got an itching for typing crazy things again, and I'm willing to indulge myself (with the added justification that I was doing this kind of thing before the blogosphere had reached it's Seventh Day).

2   In any event, what might be appropriate for the first of several Zebra Tales is a rant on a very particular new gaming vehicle that I just became aware of. While on the website I use for all my news, I learned about "GameCrush," a system that sets women back at least 200 years. Now we all know that a lot of the people who game are lonely boys, either very fat or very skinny, who sit in their domestic caves and glue their greasy little eyes to a screen to live out a life where they actually matter. By the light of day these boys are worthless, shunned by almost every caste, from Bro to Awkward-Plain Girl Who Could Be Pretty With Some Make-Up Maybe to Over-Acheiver Kid to Slutty Slut Slut McGee. But when the lights go down and school/work ends, these bepimpled boys can transform into muscle-bound demi gods or elite covert operatives or (in the really creepy department) even hot

slutty girls whose every purpose in-game is to look sexy with the right video card. And so perhaps it was only a matter of time before some idiots like the guys at GameCrush decided to capitalize on the pathetic state of your average gamer boy—and crap all over women in the process.

3   GameCrush is a website that ostensibly encourages boy-girl interactions via games. Boys sign on as "Players" and girls sign on as "PlayDates" (yeah, I'll let you draw your own conclusions). These girls set up a MySpace-like homepage that shows a picture, what games she'd like to pay (currently it allows for Xbox Live support) and several other *vital* statistics. One of these is a Facebook status-like idea which lets the girl set her inclination to either "Flirty" or "Dirty" (and here I thought women were complex). She can include pictures of herself, videos, and an About Me section for showing, I guess, how chaste she is. Now Players (the aforementioned nerdy nerds) select a PlayDate they want to . . . um . . . play with and send her an invite. Now the invite can include anything, from chatting with her to webcamming to actually playing a game with her. But here's the catch: the Players must purchase credits to spend *any* time gaming with the PlayDates in the first place. A certain number of credits get you a certain number of minutes to spend with the girl. The game economics are structured so that you will invariably have credits left over so that, when your session is over, the Players are prompted to spend their remaining credits as a *tip* for the PlayDate.

4   Now whether you tip your PlayDate is open to the Player's discretion, but I have a funny feeling it'll have *something* to do with how flirty or dirty she's been with the Player during their 10 minute rendezvous. . . . But that's just me. Oh, and guess what these lovely ladies can do with these tips? Well they can EXCHANGE THEM FOR CASH. Yes, that's right, cash monies. GameCrush lets their women keep 60% of the money they get from their Johns, I mean Players. And the company keeps the other 40% because, well, Daddy has bills to pay.

5   Then, if this weren't bad enough, the girls are then rated by the Players they interact with on things like hotness and flirtiness. The girls with the highest ratings will not only attract more attention and so make more money for Daddy and themselves but the company behind GameCrush will actually promote their top PlayDates on another website called JaneCrush where these PlayDates will effectively be turned into mini-celebrities. Whether you're looking at this from a Darwinistic view, a Capitalistic view, or a just plain friggin' common sense view, it's clear that the girls who are sluttier on this website will get paid more. Indeed, the girls who are just normal human beings who just want to play a game (god forbid) will be relegated to the unsightly realm of unpopular shunned frag hags. Hey, I like that one, maybe it'll catch on.

6   Now, in some sort of weak preliminary defense for the kind of outcry from certain circles that this company is sure to receive, they claimed in their press release for GameCrush that the game economics are based on the concept and the cost of buying a girl a drink in a bar which, they argue, is not for the purpose of getting to know a new person but really for an ulterior motive. Let me explain to the idiots who made up that ridiculous explanation why the two are *completely* different. When you walk into a bar and see a girl you think is hot, you don't *have* to spend money on her to get her to pay attention to you (maybe you should, but spending money on strange women isn't *built in* to the mechanics of life). You can talk with her, dance with her, even go home with her without being required by the bar owners to liquor her up on your own dime. Now often, a girl *will* broadcast something about her sluttiness in just what she wears so maybe this could be akin to some sort of typed status about how horny she is that everyone can see. Kinda. Oh, and before everyone starts yelling about how sexist it is to even *suggest* that you can infer *anything* from a girl's clothing choice, let me just say that I've known plenty of complete hookers who rarely go out to a social setting looking anything other than complete hookers, and I've known plenty of sweet reserved girls who rarely go out looking like complete hookers. I don't think I've ever seen the innocent, just kisses on the first date, girl next door go out in a microskirt and orange tan.

7   And, as for guys, there's a reason I go to bars in a nice polo and jeans and not a wifebeater, gold necklace, sideways baseball cap, and slicked back hair. Just sayin. But what most bars definitely do *not* have is a system whereby male patrons get to rate these girls on the basis of their flirtiness and hotness. Can you imagine talking to a girl for a little while and then saying, "well I haven't really enjoyed talking to you, bitch, you get a 3 on flirtiness and definitely a 2 on hotness, and forget the tip sweetheart, next time go for the tube top." Damn.

8   Oh yeah, guys tip the *bartender* not the girl they're talking to. Jesus. Should there also be a big bulletin board on the outside of bars that has pictures of all the girls inside with ratings from all the guys they've talked to based on their hotness? Now *that* would be something. Funny how the more you put the GameCrush system in terms of real life it becomes clear that this would be almost completely unacceptable. But for some reason, when it comes to the Internet, here we are.

9   And how did GameCrush get its first batch of PlayDates? Well they opened up an ad on Craigslist. Yeah, no joke. Craigslist. When I think completely consensual and not creepy in any way I think Craigslist. I was reading an article on IGN about it and they actually posted a sample of what one of the PlayDates has on

her page, complete with her picture. Just scroll down to the middle until you see the pic of the sexy blonde. Mmm, must sign up. Damnit GameCrush! The guy who wrote the article actually seems the think GameCrush might be a *good* idea, but I guess when you work with Jessica Chobot you get a slightly warped idea of what the average gamer girl is like.

10   But the worst impact of GameCrush may be its role in further marginalizing women in an everyday environment. Time was, girls were *extremely* rare in online games. As someone who's been gaming online since StarCraft I remember that if ever there was the rarity of seeing a girl in-game it was like throwing a gallon of blood in a kiddie pool filled with vampire sharks. Comments ranged from the more "mild" forms of sexual harassment (are you hot, how old are you, are you single, etc.) to the real depraved and disgusting stuff that most guys would only feel comfortable saying behind the safety of their computer screens. But these days more and more and more girls are taking part in online games, partly because back in the day almost all of the games that had online support were wargames and shooters while today you can play almost any- thing with friends and also because as games become mainstream acceptable (with things like Wii Fit and RockBand bringing in all sorts) they are becoming more attractive to more than just the super nerds who live off them.

11   Now that we're not only encouraging the vampire sharks but providing the kiddie pool and blood for a small fee, we're saying to girls "sure, you can do what you'd normally do in the privacy of your own home for fun, but you're going to have be slutty and sexy and be ready to pay attention to any asshole who talks to you in the process." I told Dana about this and she raised a good point: why is it necessary to sexualize everything women do? Why can't they just do shit and that's it? Why do I have to pay a girl to play a game with me when I could just go out and friggin ASK one of the tens of thousands to just play?

12   Interestingly enough, I think I actually pissed off one of my feminst-inclined Oberlin friends when I posted something about this as my fb status. Because the system is outlined by gender roles (as far as I can tell, guys can't be PlayDates), I suggested that the sexist part about this system is the fact that GameCrush discriminates against *men* because they can't play both parts and get paid. It should be obvious why this is *not* the main problem with GameCrush, but ironically it seems as though I pissed off one of the many people I was trying to speak up for.

13   But then there's just something deliciously funny about that.

Clay Shirky

Gin, Television, and Social Surplus: A Speech—April 26, 2008

I was recently reminded of some reading I did in college, way back in the last century, by a British historian arguing that the critical technology, for the early phase of the industrial revolution, was gin. The transformation from rural to urban life was so sudden, and so wrenching, that the only thing society could do to manage was to drink itself into a stupor for a generation. The stories from that era are amazing—there were gin pushcarts working their way through the streets of London.

2 And it wasn't until society woke up from that collective bender that we actually started to get the institutional structures that we associate with the industrial revolution today. Things like public libraries and museums, increasingly broad education for children, elected leaders—a lot of things we like—didn't happen until having all of those people together stopped seeming like a crisis and started seeming like an asset. It wasn't until people started thinking of this as a vast civic surplus, one they could design for rather than just dissipate, that we started to get what we think of now as an industrial society.

3 If I had to pick the critical technology for the 20th century, the bit of social lubricant without which the wheels would've come off the whole enterprise, I'd say it was the sitcom. Starting with the Second World War a whole series of things happened—rising GDP per capita, rising educational attainment, rising life expectancy and, critically, a rising number of people who were working five-day work weeks. For the first time, society forced onto an enormous number of its citizens the requirement to manage something they had never had to manage before—free time.

4 And what did we do with that free time? Well, mostly we spent it watching TV.

5 We did that for decades. We watched "I Love Lucy." We watched "Gilligan's Island." We watch "Malcolm in the Middle." We watch "Desperate Housewives." "Desperate Housewives" essentially functioned as a kind of cognitive heat sink, dissipating thinking that might otherwise have built up and caused society to overheat. And it's only now, as we're waking up from that collective bender, that we're starting to see the cognitive surplus as an asset rather than as a crisis. We're seeing things being designed to take advantage of that surplus, to deploy it in ways more engaging than just having a TV in everybody's basement.

6 This hit me in a conversation I had about two months ago. I've finished a book called *Here Comes Everybody*, which has recently come out, and this recognition came out of a conversation I had about the book. I was being interviewed by a TV producer to see whether I should be on their show, and she asked me, "What are you seeing out there that's interesting?" I started telling her about the Wikipedia article on Pluto. You may remember that Pluto got kicked out of the planet club a couple of years ago, so all of a sudden there was all of this activity on Wikipedia. The talk pages light up, people are editing the article like mad, and the whole community is in

an ruckus—"How should we characterize this change in Pluto's status?" And a little bit at a time they move the article—fighting offstage all the while—from, "Pluto is the ninth planet," to "Pluto is an odd-shaped rock with an odd-shaped orbit at the edge of the solar system."

7   So I tell her all this stuff, and I think, "Okay, we're going to have a conversation about authority or social construction or whatever." That wasn't her question. She heard this story and she shook her head and said, "Where do people find the time?" That was her question. And I just kind of snapped. And I said, "No one who works in TV gets to ask that question. You know where the time comes from. It comes from the cognitive surplus you've been masking for 50 years."

8   So how big is that surplus? If you take Wikipedia as a kind of unit, all of Wikipedia, the whole project—every page, every edit, every talk page, every line of code, in every language that Wikipedia exists in—that represents something like the cumulation of 100 million hours of human thought. I worked this out with Martin Wattenberg at IBM; it's a back-of-the-envelope calculation, but it's the right order of magnitude, about 100 million hours of thought.

9   And television watching? Two hundred billion hours, in the U.S. alone, every year. Put another way, now that we have a unit, that's 2,000 Wikipedia projects a year spent watching television. Or put still another way, in the U.S., we spend 100 million hours every weekend, just watching the ads. This is a pretty big surplus. People asking, "Where do they find the time?" when they're looking at things like Wikipedia don't understand how tiny that entire project is, as a carve-out of this asset that's finally being dragged into what Tim calls an architecture of participation.

10   Now, the interesting thing about a surplus like that is that society doesn't know what to do with it at first—hence the gin, hence the sitcoms. Because if people knew what to do with a surplus with reference to the existing social institutions, then it wouldn't be a surplus, would it? It's precisely when no one has any idea how to deploy something that people have to start experimenting with it, in order for the surplus to get integrated, and the course of that integration can transform society.

11   The early phase for taking advantage of this cognitive surplus, the phase I think we're still in, is all special cases. The physics of participation is much more like the physics of weather than it is like the physics of gravity. We know all the forces that combine to make these kinds of things work: there's an interesting community over here, there's an interesting sharing model over there, those people are collaborating on open source software. But despite knowing the inputs, we can't predict the outputs yet because there's so much complexity. The way you explore complex ecosystems is you just try lots and lots and lots of things, and you hope that everybody who fails fails informatively so that you can at least find a skull on a pikestaff near where you're going. That's the phase we're in now.

12   Just to pick one example, one I'm in love with, but it's tiny. A couple of weeks one of my students forwarded me a project started by a professor in Brazil, in Fortaleza, named Vasco Furtado. It's a Wiki Map for crime in Brazil. If there's an assault, if there's a burglary, if there's a mugging, a robbery, a rape, a murder, you can go and put a push-pin on a Google Map, and you can characterize the assault, and you start to see a map of where these crimes are occurring.

13   Now, this already exists as tacit information. Anybody who knows a town has some sense of, "Don't go there. That street corner is dangerous. Don't go in this neighborhood. Be careful there after dark." But it's something society knows without society really knowing it, which is to say there's no public source where you can take advantage of it. And the cops, if they have that information, they're certainly not sharing. In fact, one of the things Furtado says in starting the Wiki crime map was, "This information may or may not exist some place in society, but it's actually easier for me to try to rebuild it from scratch than to try and get it from the authorities who might have it now."

14   Maybe this will succeed or maybe it will fail. The normal case of social software is still failure; most of these experiments don't pan out. But the ones that do are quite incredible, and I hope that this one succeeds, obviously. But even if it doesn't, it's illustrated the point already, which is that someone working alone, with really cheap tools, has a reasonable hope of carving out enough of the cognitive surplus, enough of the desire to participate, enough of the collective goodwill of the citizens, to create a resource you couldn't have imagined existing even five years ago.

15   So that's the answer to the question, "Where do they find the time?" Or, rather, that's the numerical answer. But beneath that question was another thought, this one not a question but an observation. In this same conversation with the TV producer I was talking about World of Warcraft guilds, and as I was talking, I could sort of see what she was thinking: "Losers. Grown men sitting in their basement pretending to be elves."

16   At least they're doing something.

17   Did you ever see that episode of "Gilligan's Island" where they almost get off the island and then Gilligan messes up and then they don't? I saw that one. I saw that one a lot when I was growing up. And every half-hour that I watched that was a half an hour I wasn't posting at my blog or editing Wikipedia or contributing to a mailing list. Now I had an ironclad excuse for not doing those things, which is that none of those things existed then. I was forced into the channel of media the way it was because it was the only option. Now it's not, and that's the big surprise. However lousy it is to sit in your basement and pretend to be an elf, I can tell you from personal experience it's worse to sit in your basement and try to figure if Ginger or Mary Ann is cuter.

18   And I'm willing to raise that to a general principle. It's better to do something than to do nothing. Even lolcats, even cute pictures of kittens made even cuter with the addition of cute captions, hold out an invitation to participation. When you see a lolcat, one of the things it says to the viewer is, "If you have some sans-serif fonts on your computer, you can play this game, too." And that's message—I can do that, too—is a big change.

19   This is something that people in the media world don't understand. Media in the 20th century was run as a single race—consumption. How much can we produce? How much can you consume? Can we produce more and you'll consume more? And the answer to that question has generally been yes. But media is actually a triathlon, it's three different events. People like to consume, but they also like to produce, and they like to share. And what's astonished people who were committed to the structure of the previous society, prior to trying to take this surplus and do something interesting, is that they're discovering that when you offer people the opportunity to produce and to share, they'll take you up on that offer. It doesn't mean that we'll never sit around mindlessly watching "Scrubs" on the couch. It just means we'll do it less.

20   And this is the other thing about the size of the cognitive surplus we're talking about. It's so large that even a small change could have huge ramifications. Let's say that everything stays 99 percent the same, that people watch 99 percent as much television as they used to, but 1 percent of that is carved out for producing and for sharing. The Internet-connected population watches roughly a *trillion* hours of TV a year. That's about five times the size of the annual U.S. consumption. One per cent of that is 100 Wikipedia projects per year worth of participation.

21   I think that's going to be a big deal. Don't you?

22   Well, the TV producer did not think this was going to be a big deal; she was not digging this line of thought. And her final question to me was essentially, "Isn't this all just a fad?" You know, sort of the flagpole-sitting of the early early 21st century? It's fun to go out and produce and share a little bit, but then people are going to eventually realize, "This isn't as good as doing what I was doing before, and settle down. And I made a spirited argument that no, this wasn't the case, that this was in fact a big one-time shift, more analogous to the industrial revolution than to flagpole-sitting. I was arguing that this isn't the sort of thing society grows out of. It's the sort of thing that society grows into. But I'm not sure she believed me, in part because she didn't want to believe me, but also in part because I didn't have the right story yet. And now I do.

23   I was having dinner with a group of friends about a month ago, and one of them was talking about sitting with his four-year-old daughter watching a DVD. And in the middle of the movie, apropos nothing, she jumps up off the couch and runs around behind the screen. That seems like a cute moment. Maybe she's going back there to see if Dora is really back there or whatever. But that wasn't what she was doing. She started rooting around in the cables. And her dad said, "What you doing?" And she stuck her head out from behind the screen and said, "Looking for the mouse."

24   Here's something four-year-olds know: A screen that ships without a mouse ships broken. Here's something four-year-olds know: Media that's targeted at you but doesn't include you may not be worth sitting still for. Those are things that make me believe that this is a one-way change. Because four-year-olds, the people who are soaking most deeply in the current environment, who won't have to go through the trauma that I have to go through of trying to unlearn a childhood spent watching "Gilligan's Island," they just assume that media includes consuming, producing and sharing.

25   It's also become my motto, when people ask me what we're doing—and when I say "we" I mean the larger society trying to figure out how to deploy this cognitive surplus, but I also mean we, especially, the people who are working hammer and tongs at figuring out the next good idea. From now on, that's what I'm going to tell them: We're looking for the mouse. We're going to look at every place that a reader or a listener or a viewer or a user has been locked out, has been served up passive or a fixed or a canned experience, and ask ourselves, "If we carve out a little bit of the cognitive surplus and deploy it here, could we make a good thing happen?" And I'm betting the answer is yes.

26   Thank you very much.

FROM READING TO WRITING

1. Analyze the arguments by Michael Gerson and Daniel Okrent: How is each argument the product of its audience and purpose? What sources of argument (ethical appeals, emotional appeals, and logical appeals) does each author choose and why? (See Chapter 5 for more on rhetorical analysis.)

2. Write an argument that makes its point by defining a key term related to new media. You might choose to change someone's attitude toward a particular technology or concept in order to defend or challenge it, for instance, by defining it in a certain way. For example, you might start with the claim that "Facebook is just a marketing ploy based on the same principles that define high school yearbooks" or "Second Life is actually a blessing for people who are shy by nature." (See Chapter 8 for strategies for writing definition arguments.)

3. Write a humorous story about your own experience with a particular new media technology—but write your story in order to make a point. (See Chapter 11 for advice on writing narrative arguments.) For example, you could report on your unfortunate experience with a new cell phone or video game in order to convince people to avoid making the same mistake.

4. Propose a change in policy related to a technology issue in your community. Are there regulations that would improve the social impact of video games, for example, or Wikipedia? (See Chapter 13 for help with writing a proposal argument.)

5. Write a rebuttal of an article related to the new media in your local or school newspaper. Are there misperceptions that you want to correct? (See Chapter 12 for advice on rebuttals.) Consider whether you wish to show the weaknesses in the article, whether you wish to counterargue, or both.

6. Write an essay that argues for the existence of a particular social effect that has resulted from a new media technology. For example, you might argue that the success of a particular local charity derives from its ability to connect with people despite a small staff. Or you might write about the effects of new technology on your local library's internal architecture. Or you could argue that new technologies have actually created a range of new jobs at your university. (For more on cause and effect arguments, see Chapter 9.)

7. Many new media technologies permit people to participate anonymously. Wikipedians, for example, are notoriously anonymous, video games networked through the Internet permit people to play with anonymous others, and people are able to make anonymous comments in online chat rooms and in response to online news sources. Analyze the effects of this anonymity: reflect on the impact of anonymity on your own participation, or your own consumption, of online media.

Glossary

A

abstract A summary of an article or book

aesthetic criteria Evaluative criteria based on perceptions of beauty and good taste

analogy An extended comparison of one situation or item to another

APA American Psychological Association

APA documentation Documentation style commonly used in social-science and education disciplines

argument A claim supported by at least one reason

assumption An unstated belief or knowledge that connects a claim with evidence

audience Real or assumed individuals or groups to whom a verbal or written communication is directed

B

bandwagon appeal A fallacy of argument based on the assumption that something is true or correct because "everyone" believes it to be so

bar chart Visual depiction of data created by the use of horizontal or vertical bars that comparatively represent rates or frequencies

because clause A statement that begins with the word *because* and provides a supporting reason for a claim

begging the question A fallacy of argument that uses the claim as evidence for its own validity

bias A personal belief that may skew one's perspective or presentation of information

bibliography List of books and articles about a specific subject

blog A Web-based journal or diary featuring regular entries about a particular subject or daily experiences (also known as a Web log)

brainstorming A method of finding ideas by writing a list of questions or statements about a subject

C

causal argument An argument that seeks to identify the reasons behind a certain event or phenomenon

claim A declaration or assertion made about any given topic

claim of comparison A claim that argues something is like or not like something else

common factor method A method used by scientists to identify a recurring factor present in a given cause–effect relationship

consequence The cause–effect result of a given action

context The combination of author, subject, and audience and the broader social, cultural, and economic influences surrounding a text

contextual analysis A type of rhetorical analysis that focuses on the author, the audience, the time, and the circumstances of an argument

counterargument An argument offering an opposing point of view with the goal of demonstrating that it is the stronger of two or more arguments

criteria Standards used to establish a definition or an evaluation

critical reading A process of reading that surpasses an initial understanding or impression of basic content and proceeds with the goal of answering specific questions or examining particular elements

cropping In photography, the process of deleting unwanted parts of an image

cultural assumptions Widely held beliefs that are considered common sense in a particular culture

D

database Large collection of digital information organized for efficient search and retrieval

debate A contest or game in which two or more individuals attempt to use arguments to persuade others to support their opinion

definition argument An argument made by specifying that something does or does not possess certain criteria

diction The choice and use of words in writing and speech

E

either–or A fallacy of argument that presents only two choices in a complex situation

emotional appeal An argumentation strategy that attempts to persuade by stirring the emotions of the audience

empirical research Research that collects data from observation or experiment

ethos An appeal to the audience based on the character and trustworthiness of the speaker or writer

evaluation argument An argument that judges something based on ethical, aesthetic, and/or practical criteria

evaluation of sources The assessment of the relevance and reliability of sources used in supporting claims

evidence Data, examples, or statistics used to support a claim

experimental research Research based on obtaining data under controlled conditions, usually by isolating one variable while holding other variables constant

F

fallacy of argument Failure to provide adequate evidence to support a claim. See *bandwagon appeal, begging the question, false analogy, hasty generalization, name calling, non sequitur, oversimplification, po-*

larization, post hoc fallacy, rationalization, slippery slope, straw man

false analogy A fallacy of argument that compares two unlike things as if they were similar

feasibility The ability of a proposed solution to be implemented

figurative language The symbolic transference of meaning from one word or phrase to another, such as with the use of metaphor, synecdoche, and metonymy

firsthand evidence Evidence such as interviews, observations, and surveys collected by the writer

font The specific size and weight of a typeface

freewriting A method of finding ideas by writing as fast as possible about a subject for a set length of time

G

generalization A conclusion drawn from knowledge based on past occurrences of the phenomenon in question

good reason A reason that an audience accepts as valid

H

hasty generalization A fallacy of argument resulting from making broad claims based on a few occurrences

I

idea map A brainstorming tool that visually depicts connections among different aspects of an issue

image editor Software that allows you to create and manipulate images

intellectual property Any property produced by the intellect, including copyrights for literary, musical, photographic, and cinematic works; patents for inventions and industrial processes; and trademarks

J

journal A general category of publications that includes popular, trade, and scholarly periodicals

K

keyword search A Web-based search that uses a robot and indexer to produce results based on a chosen word or words

L

line graph A visual presentation of data represented by a continuous line or lines plotted at specific intervals

logos An appeal to the audience based on reasoning and evidence

M

metaphor A figure of speech using a word or phrase that commonly designates one thing to represent another, thus making a comparison

metonymy A type of figurative language that uses one object to represent another that embodies its defining quality

MLA Modern Language Association

MLA documentation Documentation style commonly used in humanities and fine-arts disciplines

multimedia The use of multiple content forms including text, voice and music audio, video, still images, animation, and interactivity

N

name calling A fallacy of argument resulting from the use of undefined, and therefore meaningless, names

narrative arguments A form of argument based on telling stories that suggest the writer's position rather than explicitly making claims

non sequitur A fallacy of argument resulting from connecting two or more unrelated ideas

O

oversimplification A fallacy in argument caused by neglecting to account for the complexity of a subject

P

pathos An appeal based on the audience's emotions or deeply held values

periodical A journal, magazine, or newspaper published at standard intervals, usually daily, weekly, monthly, or quarterly

periodical index Paper or electronic resource that catalogs the contents of journals, magazines, and newspapers

pie chart A circular chart resembling a pie that illustrates percentages of the whole through the use of delineated wedge shapes

plagiarism The improper use of the unauthorized and unattributed words or ideas of another author

podcast Digital media files available on the Internet for playback on a portable media player, such as an iPod

polarization A fallacy of argument based on exaggerating the characteristics of opposing groups to highlight division and extremism

popular journal A magazine aimed at the general public; usually includes illustrations, short articles, and advertisements

position argument A general kind of argument in which a claim is made for an idea or way of thinking about a subject

post hoc fallacy A fallacy of argument based on the assumption that events that follow each other have a causal relationship

practical criteria Evaluative criteria based on usefulness or likely results

primary research Information collected directly by the writer through observations, interviews, surveys, and experiments

process of elimination method A means of finding a cause by systematically ruling out all other possible causes

proposal argument An argument that either advocates or opposes a specific course of action

R

rationalization A fallacy of argument based on using weak explanations to avoid dealing with the actual causes

reason In an argument, the justification for a claim

rebuttal argument An argument that challenges or rejects the claims of another argument

reference librarian Library staff member who is familiar with information resources and who can show you how to use them (you can find a reference librarian at the reference desk in your library)

refutation A rebuttal argument that points out the flaws in an opposing argument

rhetorical analysis Careful study of a written argument or other types of persuasion aimed at understanding how the components work or fail to work

rhetorical situation Factors present at the time of writing or speaking, including the writer or speaker, the audience, the purpose of communicating, and the context

S

sans serif type A style of type recognized by blunt ends and a consistency in thickness

scholarly journals Journals containing articles written by experts in a particular field; also called peer-reviewed or academic journals

secondary research Information obtained from existing knowledge, such as research in the library

secondhand evidence Evidence from the work of others found in the library, on the Web, and elsewhere

serif type A style of type developed to resemble the strokes of an ink pen and recognized by wedge-shaped ends on letter forms

single difference method A method of finding a cause for differing phenomena in very similar situations by identifying the one element that varies

slippery slope A fallacy of argument based on the assumption that if a first step is taken, additional steps will inevitably follow

straw man A fallacy of argument based on the use of the diversionary tactic of setting up the opposing position in such a manner that it can be easily rejected

sufficiency The adequacy of evidence supporting a claim

synecdoche A type of figurative language in which a part is used to represent the whole

T

textual analysis A type of rhetorical analysis that focuses exclusively on the text itself

thesis One or more sentences that state the main idea of an argument

typeface A style of type, such as serif, sans serif, or decorative

U

URL (Universal Resource Locator) An address on the Web

V

visual argument A type of persuasion using images, graphics, or objects

voice In writing, the distinctive style of a writer that provides a sense of the writer as a person

W

Web directory A subject guide to Web pages grouped by topic and subtopic

Web editors Programs that allow you to compose Web pages

wiki A Web-based application designed to let multiple authors write, edit, and review content, such as Wikipedia

working thesis A preliminary statement of the main claim of an argument, subject to revision

Credits

Photo Credits

Page 2: © MadV; 15: © Rebecca Roth; 22, 27: © Frank O'Connell/The New York Times/Redux; 76: © BP p.l.c.; 78 (both): © Dr. Michael Wesch; 83: © Courtesy Hofstra University; 96: © Popperfoto/Getty Images; 99: © jacksfilms; 113: © Sylvain Sonnet/Getty Images; 122: © Ruby Washington/The New York Times/Redux; 139 © Car Culture/Corbis; 143: © Transtock Images; 157 © Amanda Byrd/Alaska Stock; 169: © Phil Crawford/Greenpeace/Reuters/Landov; 175: FOXTROT © 2010 Bill Amend. Reprinted with permission of Universal Press Syndicate. All rights reserved.; 192: © David Bebber, Pool/AP Images; 294, 295: © The New York Times/Redux; 309: © Nigel Hicks/Dorling Kindersley; 313: © Danny Lehman/Corbis; 314: © Stocktreck Images/Alamy; 315 (top to bottom): © Borderlands/Alamy, © Michael Sewell/Photolibrary, © Biosphoto/ Labut Jean-Michel/Photolibrary, © AFP/Getty Images, © Jonathan Blair/Corbis, © Hervé Hughes/Hemis/Corbis; 316 (top to bottom): © Robyn Beck/AFP/Getty Images, © Kennan Ward/Corbis, © Art Wolfe/Photo Researchers; 317: © Lawrence Bender Prods./The Kobal Collection; 319: © The New York Times/Redux; 320: © 2009 Union of Concerned Scientists www.ucsusa.org.; 321 (both): © NASA; 330, 332 (top): © The New York Times /Redux; 332 (bottom): © Mike Stewart/Sygma/Corbis; 344: © Erik Jacobs/The New York Times/Redux; 350: © CBS/Landov; 359: © The New York Times/Redux; 365: © Pete Mariner/Retna UK /Landov; 366: © Liz Margelsdorf/San Francisco Chronicle; 367: © Deanne Fitzmaurice/San Francisco Chronicle; 368: © Tribune Media Services, Inc. All Rights Reserved. Reprinted with permission; 379: © Dave Bartruff/Danita Delimont Photography; 380: © Alyssa Banta/Redux/Redux; 382: © Aislin, The Gazette, Cartoon Arts International, Inc.; 397, 399: © FILM 4/Celador Films/Pathe International/The Kobal Collection; 400: © The New York Times/Redux; 401: © Royalty-Free/Masterfile; 403: © The New York Times/Redux; 409: Henry Payne: © Detroit News. Reprinted with permission of United Feature Syndicate. All rights reserved.; 414: © NON SEQUITUR © 2010 Wiley Miller. Reprinted with permission of Universal Press Syndicate. All rights reserved.; 415: © The New York Times/Redux; 416: © Warner Bros/The Kobal Collection; 419: © Archive Photos/Getty Images; 422: © The New York Times/Redux; 424: © Doug Savage; 430: © 20th Century Fox/The Kobal Collection; 436: © Geoff Brightling/Getty Images; 444: © James Leynse/Corbis; 448: © Ben Edwards/Getty Images; 456: © The New York Times/Redux; 459: www.CartoonStock.com; 461: © Peter Newcomb/Reuters/Corbis; 476: © The New York Times/Redux; 477: © Dennis MacDonald/PhotoEdit; 478: © The New York Times/Redux; 480: © Kyodo/Newscom; 486: CLOSE TO HOME © 2010 John McPherson. Reprinted with permission of Universal Press Syndicate. All rights reserved.; 487: © Paul Sakuma/AP Images; 494: © Stockbyte/Getty Images; 498: © 20th Century Fox/Dreamworks/The Kobal Collection; 511: Courtesy of Fujitsu; 513: © The New York Times/Redux; 515 (top): © Kansas State Historical Society; 515 (bottom): © Advertising Archive; 516: © The New York Times/Redux; 528: © Mark Wilson/Getty Images; 530: © Lilly Lane/Corbis; 532: © Los Angeles Daily News/Corbis; 538 (both): Courtesy of the Center for Consumer Freedom; 543: © Richard Avedon/Courtesy of the American Legacy Foundation; 544: DOONESBURY © 2010 G. B. Trudeau. Reprinted with permission of Universal Press Syndicate. All rights reserved.; 546: © Eric Lewis's cartoon, published in the October 30, 2000, issue of the New Yorker/thecartoonbank.com; 547: © AFP/Getty Images; 550: © Jeff Keacher/zoitz.com; 561: Courtesy of Mothers Against Drunk Driving (MADD); 565: © Mark Hellman/Newscom; 574: © Tribune Media Services, Inc. All rights reserved. Reprinted with permission; 586: © Paramount/courtesy Everett Collection. All other photos provided by the author.

Text Credits

Mark Anslow, "Ten Reasons Why GM Won't Feed the World." This article first appeared in March 2008 issue of The Ecologist. Reprinted with permission.

Leo Benedictus, "Bye, Bye, Pandas?" debate Chris Packham, *The Guardian*, 23 September 2009. Copyright © 2009 Guardian News & Media Ltd. Used with permission.

Ben Burkett, "Green Revolution: A Failure in Africa." Copyright © Ben Burkett. www.mississippiassociation .coop.

Warren J. Blumenfeld, "Homophobia" by Warren J. Blumenfeld. Copyright © 1992 by Warren J. Blumenfeld. Reprinted by permission of Beacon Press, Boston.

Patrick J. Buchanan, "To Reunite A Nation" speech given at Nixon Library in Yerba Linda, CA, 1/10/00. Copyright © 2000 Patrick J. Buchanan. www.buchanan.org.

Rachel Carson, "A Fable for Tomorrow" and "The Obligation to Endure" from *Silent Spring* by Rachel Carson. Copyright © 1962 by Rachel L. Carson. Renewed 1990 by Roger Christie. Reprinted by permission

Index